Christian Platonism

Platonism has played a central role in Christianity and is essential to a deep understanding of the Christian theological tradition. At times, Platonism has constituted an essential philosophical and theological resource, furnishing Christianity with an intellectual framework that has played a key role in its early development, and in subsequent periods of renewal. Alternatively, it has been considered a compromising influence, conflicting with the faith's revelatory foundations and distorting its inherent message. In both cases the fundamental importance of Platonism, as a force which Christianity defined itself by and against, is clear. Written by an international team of scholars, this landmark volume examines the history of Christian Platonism from antiquity to the present day, covers key concepts, and engages issues such as the environment, natural science and materialism.

Alexander J. B. Hampton is Assistant Professor of Religion at the University of Toronto, specialising in metaphysics, poetics and nature. He is the author of *Romanticism and the Re-Invention of Modern Religion* (Cambridge 2019). He is currently writing a study of nature and metaphysics, and editing the forthcoming *Cambridge Companion of Religion, Nature and the Environment in the West*.

John Peter Kenney is Professor Emeritus of Religious Studies at Saint Michael's College. He is the author of *Mystical Monotheism: A Study in Ancient Platonic Theology*, *The Mysticism of Saint Augustine: Rereading the* Confessions, *Contemplation and Classical Christianity: A Study in Augustine* and *On God, the Soul, Evil, and the Rise of Christianity*.

Christian Platonism

A History

Edited by

ALEXANDER J. B. HAMPTON
University of Toronto

JOHN PETER KENNEY
Saint Michael's College

CAMBRIDGE
UNIVERSITY PRESS

Shaftesbury Road, Cambridge CB2 8EA, United Kingdom

One Liberty Plaza, 20th Floor, New York, NY 10006, USA

477 Williamstown Road, Port Melbourne, VIC 3207, Australia

314–321, 3rd Floor, Plot 3, Splendor Forum, Jasola District Centre, New Delhi – 110025, India

103 Penang Road, #05–06/07, Visioncrest Commercial, Singapore 238467

Cambridge University Press is part of Cambridge University Press & Assessment, a department of the University of Cambridge.

We share the University's mission to contribute to society through the pursuit of education, learning and research at the highest international levels of excellence.

www.cambridge.org
Information on this title: www.cambridge.org/9781108741408

DOI: 10.1017/9781108590341

First published 2021
First paperback edition 2023

A catalogue record for this publication is available from the British Library

Library of Congress Cataloging-in-Publication data
NAMES: Hampton, Alexander J. B., editor. | Kenney, John Peter, editor.
TITLE: Christian Platonism : a history / edited by Alexander J.B. Hampton, John Peter Kenney.
DESCRIPTION: Cambridge, United Kingdom ; New York, NY : Cambridge University Press, 2021. | Includes bibliographical references and index.
IDENTIFIERS: LCCN 2020026276 (print) | LCCN 2020026277 (ebook) | ISBN 9781108491983 (hardback) | ISBN 9781108590341 (ebook)
SUBJECTS: LCSH: Christian philosophy – History. | Platonists. | Philosophy and religion.
CLASSIFICATION: LCC BR100 .C534 2021 (print) | LCC BR100 (ebook) | DDC230.01–dc23
LC record available at https://lccn.loc.gov/2020026276
LC ebook record available at https://lccn.loc.gov/2020026277

ISBN   978-1-108-49198-3   Hardback
ISBN   978-1-108-74140-8   Paperback

For Mark A. McIntosh, who had the divine idea for this volume.

Contents

Contents

Figures

Contributors

Olivier Boulnois (École Pratique des Hautes Études) specializes in medieval philosophy and has written extensively on Platonic and Aristotelian influences on Christian moral and metaphysical philosophy, especially in the thought of Duns Scotus. His most recent book is *Lire le Principe d'individuation de Duns Scot* (Vrin, 2014).

Stephen R. L. Clark (University of Liverpool) is Professor Emeritus of Philosophy. His research specializes in the philosophy of religion, moral philosophy, the Platonic tradition and animal rights. He has contributed to or edited 120 books and is the author of nineteen monographs, the latest being *Plotinus: Myth, Metaphor and Philosophical Practice* (University of Chicago Press, 2016).

Kevin Corrigan (Emory University) is Samuel Candler Dobbs Professor of Interdisciplinary Humanities. His many books include, most recently, *Mind, Soul and Body in the 4th Century: Evagrius of Pontus and Gregory of Nyssa* (Ashgate Press, 2009), *Reason, Faith and Otherness in Neoplatonic and Early Christian Thought* (Ashgate Press, 2013) and *Love, Friendship, Beauty, and the Good: Plato, Aristotle, and the Later Tradition* (Wipf and Stock, 2018).

Andrew Davison (University of Cambridge) is Starbridge Lecturer in Theology and Natural Sciences at the University of Cambridge and Fellow in Theology and Dean of Chapel at Corpus Christi College, Cambridge. He is trained in theology, chemistry and biochemistry. His books include *Participation in God: A Study in Christian Doctrine and Metaphysics* (Cambridge University Press, 2019). He is a regular contributor to *Church Times* and the *Times Literary Supplement*, and is a priest of the Church of England.

John Dillon (Trinity College Dublin) is Regius Professor of Greek Emeritus. His chief publications are *The Middle Platonists* (Cornell University Press, 1977, 2nd ed. 1996), *Iamblichus, De Anima* (with John Finamore, Society of Biblical Literature, 2000), *Alcinous: The Handbook of Platonism* (Oxford University Press, 1993), *The Heirs of Plato* (Oxford University Press, 2003) and *The Roots of Platonism* (Cambridge University Press, 2019).

Mark Edwards (Oxford University) is Professor of Early Christian Studies. Among his books are *Origen against Plato* (Ashgate, 2002), *Words and Images in Late Antique Talk of God* (Ashgate, 2012), *Image, Word and God in the Early Christian Centuries* (Ashgate, 2013), *Religions of the Constantinian Empire* (Oxford University Press, 2015) and *Aristotle and Early Christian Thought* (Routledge, 2019).

Joshua Levi Ian Gentzke (Michigan State University) is Assistant Professor in the Department of Religious Studies. Positioned at the intersection of the history of religions and cultural studies, his research explores western religious thought, the ecological imagination and comparative mysticism, with a focus on marginalized alternative currents. Gentzke is working on a monograph on Böhme as well as a book project on the ethical and existential issues linked to the valuation of natural phenomena.

Stephen Gersh (University of Notre Dame) is Emeritus Professor of Medieval Studies and Philosophy. He has published many books on authors from Cicero to Derrida, including *From Iamblichus to Eriugena* (Brill, 1978), *Middle Platonism and Neoplatonism, The Latin Tradition*, 2 vols. (University of Notre Dame Press, 1986) and *Platonism in Late Antiquity* (University of Notre Dame Press, 1992). He is currently editing and translating the *Commentary on Plotinus* by Marsilio Ficino for Harvard University Press.

Lloyd P. Gerson (University of Toronto) is Professor of Philosophy. He is the editor of *The Cambridge History of Philosophy in Late Antiquity* (Cambridge University Press, 2010) and the author of many books, including most recently *Aristotle and Other Platonists* (Cornell University Press, 2005), *From Plato to Platonism* (Cornell University Press, 2013) and *Platonism and Naturalism: The Possibility of Philosophy* (Cornell University Press, 2020).

Alexander J. B. Hampton (University of Toronto) is Assistant Professor specialising in metaphysics, poetics and nature at the Department for the Study of Religion. He is the author of *Romanticism and the Re-Invention of Modern Religion* (Cambridge 2019). He is currently writing a study of nature and metaphysics, and editing the forthcoming *Cambridge Companion of Religion, Nature and the Environment in the West*.

Douglas Hedley (University of Cambridge) is Professor of the Philosophy of Religion in the Faculty of Divinity. His books include *Coleridge, Philosophy and Religion: Aids to Reflection and the Mirror of the Spirit* (Cambridge University Press, 2000), *Living Forms of the Imagination* (T&T Clark, 2008), *Sacrifice Imagined: Violence, Atonement and the Sacred* (Continuum, 2011) and *The Iconic Imagination* (Bloomsbury, 2016).

John Peter Kenney (Saint Michael's College) is Professor Emeritus of Religious Studies. He is the author of *Mystical Monotheism: A Study in Ancient Platonic Theology* (Brown University Press, 1991), *The Mysticism of Saint Augustine: Rereading the* Confessions (Routledge, 2005), *Contemplation and Classical Christianity: A Study in Augustine* (Oxford University Press, 2013) and *On God, the Soul, Evil, and the Rise of Christianity* (Bloomsbury, 2019).

Mario Meliadò (University of Siegen) is Junior Professor of the History of Philosophy. His research focuses on the philosophy of the late Middle Ages and the Renaissance, as well as on their reconstruction and appropriation in modern philosophical historiography. He has published the book *Sapienza peripatetica. Eimerico di Campo e i percorsi del tardo albertismo* (Aschendorff, 2018) on the history of fifteenth-century Albertism.

Derek A. Michaud (University of Maine) is Lecturer in Philosophy and Coordinator of the Religious and Judaic Studies programmes. His research treats the Cambridge Platonist John Smith, Plotinus, Origen, Bonaventure and Nicholas of Cusa. His book *Reason Turned into Sense: John Smith on Spiritual Sensation* was published by Peeters in 2017.

Cecilia Muratori (Queen Mary University of London) is Research Fellow in the Centre for Anglo-German Cultural Relations, and a tutor at the Institute of Continuing Education, University of Cambridge. She is the author of *'The First German Philosopher': The Mysticism of Jakob Böhme as Interpreted by Hegel* (Springer, 2016) and *Renaissance*

Vegetarianism: The Philosophical Afterlives of Porphyry's On Abstinence (Legenda, 2020). She is interested in the mediation of philosophical concepts through the visual arts, and is co-curator of a series of exhibitions on Jacob Böhme for the Staatliche Kunstsammlungen in Dresden.

Catherine Pickstock (University of Cambridge) is the Norris-Hulse Professor of Divinity in the Faculty of Divinity. Her research focuses on the reinterpretation of pre-modern theology and metaphysics and the reconsideration of the Platonic tradition in interaction with biblically based faiths, in particular the question of theurgy and understandings of the soul. She is currently completing two monographs, *Aspects of Truth* (Oxford University Press) and *Platonic Poetics* (Ad Solem Press, Paris).

Andrew Radde-Gallwitz (University of Notre Dame) is Associate Professor of Liberal Studies. Among his works are *Basil of Caesarea, Gregory of Nyssa, and the Transformation of Divine Simplicity* (Oxford University Press, 2009), *Basil of Caesarea* (Wipf and Stock, 2012) and *Gregory of Nyssa's Doctrinal Works: A Literary Study* (Oxford University Press, 2018).

Lydia Schumacher (King's College, London) is Reader in Historical and Philosophical Theology. She is the author of *Divine Illumination: The History and Future of Augustine's Theory of Knowledge* (Wiley-Blackwell, 2011), *Rationality as Virtue* (Ashgate, 2015), *Theological Philosophy* (Ashgate, 2015) and *Early Franciscan Theology: Between Authority and Innovation* (Cambridge University Press, 2019).

Jacob Holsinger Sherman (California Institute of Integral Studies) is Professor of Philosophy and Religion. He taught previously at King's College, London and the University of Cambridge. Among his publications is *Partakers of the Divine: Contemplation and the Practice of Philosophy* (Fortress Press, 2014).

Charles Taliaferro (St Olaf College) is the Oscar and Gertrude Overby Distinguished Chair and Professor of Philosophy. He is the author or co-author of 100 articles and book chapters, the co-author or editor of over thirty books and the Editor-in-Chief of Open Theology.

Rudi A. te Velde (Tilburg University) is lecturer in philosophy and professor by special appointment in the philosophy of Thomas Aquinas in relation to contemporary thought at the School of Catholic Theology.

His many publications about the philosophical thought of Aquinas include *Participation and Substantiality in Thomas Aquinas* (Brill, 1995).

Torstein Theodor Tollefsen (University of Oslo) is Professor of Philosophy. His books include *The Christocentric Cosmology of St Maximus the Confessor* (Oxford University Press, 2008), *Activity and Participation in Late Antique and Early Christian Thought* (Oxford University Press, 2012) and *St Theodore the Studite's Defence of the Icons, Theology and Philosophy in Nineth-Century Byzantium* (Oxford University Press, 2018).

Daniel J. Tolan (University of Cambridge) is a Fellow of Clare College, Cambridge and Secretary of the Cambridge Centre for the Study of Platonism. He is the author of 'The Impact of the Ὁμοούσιον on the divine ideas', in P. G. Pavlos, L. F. Janby, E. K. Emilsson and T. T. Tollefsen (eds.), *Platonism and Christian Thought in Late Antiquity* (Routledge, 2019).

Richard Viladesau (Fordham University) is an emeritus professor in the Department of Theology. A priest of the Diocese of Rockville Centre, New York, he obtained his doctoral degree at the Pontifical Gregorian University in Rome. His work concentrates on philosophical questions in theology, including the relation of aesthetic modes of thinking to empirical and conceptual thought.

Acknowledgements

This volume had its beginnings in the kindred conversations that were had at the many meetings of the Platonism and Neoplatonism Group of the American Academy of Religion. Despite its annual American location, this meeting always draws an international group of scholars with a shared interest in the interactions of Platonic and Christian thought from antiquity to the present. Many of those conversations find their expression here.

The very idea of the volume too had its origin there, with a suggestion made by Mark Allan McIntosh (Loyola University, Chicago). His was the divine idea that is instantiated in these pages. Indeed, it is his kindness and collegiality that attracted many of us to the project.

At Cambridge University Press, Beatrice Rehl has been a strong supporter of the project since its inception. She and Eilidh Burrett have thoughtfully and patiently shepherded the volume to publication. Katarina Pejovic worked swiftly and diligently, assisting with the notes and index. We also wish to express our gratitude to Kathleen Fearn for her meticulous care with the copy-editing of the manuscript.

Elements of the research and editing of this text have been supported by the Social Sciences and Humanities Research Council of Canada.

Richard Viladesau is to be thanked for his assistance with the images, and for his own reproductions.

Others have been kind in their support of the project, including Nicole Percifield and Ann Jason Kenney.

INTRODUCTION

Christianity and Platonism

Alexander J. B. Hampton and John Peter Kenney

Anyone wishing to understand the Christian tradition deeply must consider the central, formative role of Platonism. At various times Platonism has constituted an essential philosophical and theological resource, furnishing Christianity with a fundamental intellectual framework that has played a key role in its early development, and in subsequent periods of renewal. Alternately, at other times, it has been considered a compromising influence, conflicting with the faith's revelatory foundations and distorting its inherent message. In both the positive and negative cases, the central importance of Platonism, as a force which Christianity defined itself by and against, is clear. Equally, this process of influence is not unidirectional. Whereas Platonism played a key role in the development of Christianity, the further development of Platonism beyond antiquity was dependent to a large degree upon Christian thinkers. The importance of this dialogue provides an answer to Tertullian's celebrated question: 'Quid ergo athenis et hierosolymis?', usually rendered, 'What has Athens to do with Jerusalem?'[1] The emphatic answer, detailed in the chapters of this volume, and at odds with Tertullian's own, is everything.

In using the term 'Christian Platonism', this volume intends to draw attention to the complex relationship of Christian thought to Platonism and to underscore the varieties of that association historically. As the chapters that compose this volume make manifest, the conjunction of Platonism and Christianity shifted diachronically, with distinctive themes

---

[1] Tertullian, *De praescriptione haereticorum*, 7. *Library of Latin Texts. Series A.* (Turnhout: Brepols, 2000). http://clt.brepolis.net/LLTA/pages/TextSearch.aspx?key=PTERT0005.

coming to the fore in different historical periods. 'Christian Platonism' thus took on a conceptual shape conditioned by the philosophical and theological issues exigent at various times. But having said that, there was one element that has remained constant and fundamental. That is Platonism's commitment to transcendence, its adherence to an ontology countenancing the existence of a higher level of reality beyond the manifest image of the physical world. In this regard Platonism has been, and remains, the most powerful tradition of realism and anti-materialism in Western thought. That has been the source of Platonism's appeal to Christians since antiquity, since it offered a conceptual language by which to articulate the deeper reality of God, Christ, and the human person more systematically than could be found in the sacred scriptures. The exact character of this transcendentalism and its epistemic foundations have been matters of ongoing debate, among both pagan and Christian Platonists alike. That discussion is a major thread running through the essays in this volume.

This powerful assertion of ontological transcendence by Platonists entailed the sovereignty of the Good – to adapt a phrase from Iris Murdoch.[2] Platonism, both in antiquity and in its subsequent reception into the Abrahamic traditions, has been committed to an ultimate first principle, one that is absolutely good and the foundation of all reality. Platonism did not just assert the existence of a level of being higher than the earthly realm, it recognized that this transcendent existence must be grounded in Goodness itself, the perfect source of all subsequent reality. That divine absolute – whether described as the One, the Good, the Beautiful, or God – came to be understood by Platonists not just as a theoretical construct postulated at a distance, but as infinite reality itself in which human souls participate by the fact of their existence. The infinite Good transcended finite description or conscious appraisal, and was perceived in a fashion that exceeded knowledge. The Good could only be discerned through interior contemplation, in the certainty of its deep presence to the soul. As the soul sheds the contingency of materiality and intensifies its inner consciousness of the Good, it participates in the immutable, the eternal, the transcendent. Platonism thus initiated and sustained a philosophical and theological culture of transcendentalism, centred on the Good or the One. It was this transcendentalism that served as a powerful resource for Jewish, Christian, and Islamic thinkers, generating a distinctive trajectory of thought through its reception into the

---

[2] Iris Murdoch, *The Sovereignty of Good* (New York: Schocken Books, 1971).

Abrahamic traditions. Rather than a strictly essentialist philosophical-theological concept, therefore Christian Platonism can be seen as one branch of a larger culture of transcendentalism, coming into prominence in different historical periods whenever Christians sought to emphasize or restore that dimension to their theological tradition.

Augustine of Hippo, perhaps the single most influential voice in the Christian Platonist tradition, affirmed this transcendentalist perspective in crucially important teachings – often adumbrating many of the most ingenious ways in which Christian thinkers would discover not only the fulfilment but also the conversion of reason's greatest aspirations in the mystery of the Word made flesh. In the Word, said Augustine (and countless other Christian Platonists in every period), dwell the real and imperishable archetypes of all that is. For the Christian Platonist tradition, this signal fulfilment and transformation of Plato's ideas became the motive force behind a seemingly inexhaustible theological creativity across the ages. It is manifest in those works that rejoice at the luminous goodness and compelling beauty of the creation, echoing with its eternal significance in God. Equally, it is present in the probing critiques of human injustice and local xenophobic evasions of true and more universal justice. Furthermore, it can be observed in the boundary-breaking assertions of the authentic role of desire and love in epistemic success. In many ways one can only fully perceive the inner conceptual beauty and meaning of Christianity's most significant theological achievements by uncovering the Christian Platonist dimensions at their core. Whether this leads primarily to deeper understanding or also to critique and amendment, neither would be possible without a grasp of the Christian Platonist role in the history of Christian thought.

This volume offers a systematic overview of Christian Platonism. One can easily identify reasons for the hesitancy to recognize and engage constructively with the Platonic tradition within Christianity. From the time of the Reformation, Protestant scholarship had sought to disentangle what it conceived as authentic biblical Christianity from what it saw as the distortions of philosophical traditions (even if a number of Protestant thinkers continued to embrace and develop Christian Platonist perspectives; though these sometimes flourished most recognizably in more marginal, often esoteric, schools of thought, coming to be regarded uneasily in both academy and church). This tendency to devalue the significance of Platonist elements in Christianity gained a powerful new impetus with the scholarly influence of Adolf von Harnack and the quest for a putatively pure and simple essence of Christianity, free from Hellenistic influences.

Moreover, more particularly philosophical reasons for the paucity of scholarship on Christian Platonism may be located in its twentieth-century critique. In the nineteenth century, Kierkegaard attacked the highly Platonized German Romantics, whilst Nietzsche launched an attack on Platonic metaphysics. Under the influence of both, Heidegger developed his significant accusation of ontotheology against the meta-physical enterprise. The consequent postmodern attack on metaphysics, led by Derrida, took singular aim at Platonism. Equally, twentieth-century positivism offered its own demolition of metaphysics and the possibility of transcendent knowledge.

In the present day, the influence of these powerful critiques may be in decline. The social, cultural, and ecological crises towards the end of the last century, and in the initial decades of the current one, has led to the questioning of twentieth-century assumptions, most powerfully in the case of secularization. Concepts such as post-secularism and re-enchantment have opened possibilities for the renewal of metaphysics in general, and Platonism in particular, both within and without the Christian tradition. In Charles Taylor's phrase, the 'immanent frame' of modern thought (obscuring any basis for reference to a transcendent reality) has now, itself, become an object of critical awareness and questioning.[3] The present intellectual landscape suggests the very real timeliness of a comprehensive guide to one of the single most transcendent-oriented dimensions of religious thought.

The systematic consideration of Christian Platonism presented in this volume aims to provide its reader with crucial insights regarding a key dimension in Christianity's long engagement with Western thought. To achieve this, it is divided into three sections. The first, titled 'Concepts', offers an analytical and synthetic investigation of Platonic themes across a range of writers and periods. In doing so it introduces readers to the conceptual patterns of Christian Platonism. The second section, called 'Histories', takes up the history of Christian Platonism from antiquity to the present day, overcoming the overwhelming focus on its early mani-festations to the neglect of its later development. 'Engagements', the final section, turns to a constructive set of conversations with the tradition, with the aim of illustrating the continued importance, validity, and possi-bilities of the tradition.

---

[3] Charles Taylor, *A Secular Age* (Cambridge, MA: Belknap Press of Harvard University Press, 2007).

FIGURE 1. Leopold von Klenze, *Der Camposanto in Pisa*. Photo by Fine Art Images/Heritage Images/Getty Images.

Der Camposanto in Pisa (1858) (see Figure 1), by the architect and artist Leo von Klenze, provides an illustrative opportunity to consider the multi-layered influence of the Christian Platonic tradition, both conceptually and throughout time.[4] In nuce it offers what the many pages of this volume aim to explicate. The Camposanto Monumentale, at the northern edge of the Piazza dei Miracoli in Pisa, is itself built around the holy field for which it is named. The field is said to be composed of the sacred soil of Calvary, borne back to Pisa in the holds of archbishop Ubaldo Lanfranchi's sixty-three galleys returning from the third crusade.[5] Lanfranchi's logic reflects the metaphysics of methexis that was adopted so vigorously into the Christian tradition. It held that created reality shared in divine reality, and indeed that some parts of creation concentrated the divine presence. In turn, beginning in 1278, the holy field was

[4] *Neue Pinakothek: Katalog der Gemäkde Skupturen*, ed. Bayerischen Staatgemä ldesammlungen (Cologne: Pinakothek-DuMont, 2003), 189.
[5] 'Pisa', in *The Grove Encyclopedia of Medieval Art and Architecture*, ed. Colum P. Hourihane, 6 vols. (New York: Oxford University Press, 2012), 5, 29–38.

compassed with the cloister-like Camposanto building, with its four covered colonnades, as depicted on the right of the canvas. The elegant tracery of the quatrefoils that enclose the cloister enact the heavenward striving of creation back to its divine source. The Camposanto, along with abbot Abbé Suger's rebuilding of the abbey church of Saint Denis a century and a half earlier, represents the development of the gothic form that embodies this heavenward striving.

In the middle ground of von Klenze's canvas, drawing the eye slightly to the right, is a depiction of the fresco known as the *Cosmographia Teologia*, thought to be painted by Piero di Puccio around 1390. According to Vasari, it depicts 'God who with his arms holds the heavens and the elements, or rather the whole machine [*machina*] of the universe'.[6] These are represented in terms of a hierarchical structure, with the heavens, the angels, the zodiac, and then the elements of fire, air, and finally earth at the centre. Underneath these successive emanations of God, as if supporting the depiction from below, and translating divine reason to human understanding, are two of the great contributors to the story of Christian Platonism, Saints Augustine and Aquinas.[7]

Finally, with the two characters depicted in the right of the middle foreground we are drawn to the perspective and presence of von Klenze himself, who in living the turn from the eighteenth to the nineteenth century, witnessed the philhellenism of Neoclassicism, and the Romantic revival of Platonism.[8] As court architect, and then director of building for Ludwig I of Bavaria, von Klenze endeavoured to find a conciliatory passage between the rationalism of the French enlightenment and the idealism of Hellenistic classicism. In his writing, such as in *Anweisung zur Architectur des christlichen Cultus* (*Instruction on the Architecture of the Christian Worship*, 1822), his design, such as in the Alte Pinakothek in Munich, and here in his painting, von Klenze drew inspiration from the Christian Platonic tradition he observed in his frequent trips to Italy. The detail of the mother and the child act to both contrast and consummate the image. Their presence manifestly contrasts the contemplative and

---

[6] Giorgio Vasari, *Le vite de' più eccellenti pittori, scultori e architettori*, ed. Gaetano Milanesi, 9 vols. (Florence: G.C. Sansoni, 1876–81), 1, 513. Vasari incorrectly attributed the fresco to Buonamico Buffalmacco.

[7] Giovanni Lodovico Bertolini, 'La Cosmographia Teologia del Camposanto di Pisa', *Nova antologia* 147 (1910), 720–72.

[8] Alexander J. B. Hampton, *Romanticism and the Re-Invention of Modern Religion: The Reconciliation of German Idealism and Platonic Realism* (Cambridge: Cambridge University Press, 2019), 1–12, 125–32.

structural atmosphere of the painting, and the historical and intellectual layers of Christian Platonic meaning it depicts. Yet they consummate the central message of Christian Platonism, which is not an intellectualizing and abstract tendency, but rather a focus on the incarnational, participatory, and sacramental character of being, which calls us back to its motive force in love.

Bibliography

Bertolini, Giovanni Lodovico. 'La Cosmographia Teologia del Camposanto di Pisa', *Nova Antologia* 147 (1910): 720–72.

Hampton, Alexander J. B., *Romanticism and the Re-Invention of Modern Religion: The Reconciliation of German Idealism and Platonic Realism.* Cambridge: Cambridge University Press, 2019.

Murdoch, Iris. *The Sovereignty of Good.* New York: Schocken Books, 1971.

Neue Pinakothek: Katalog der Gemäkde Skupturen. Edited by Bayerischen Staatgemäldesammlungen. Cologne: Pinakothek-DuMont, 2003.

'Pisa', *The Grove Encyclopedia of Medieval Art and Architecture.* Edited by Colum P. Hourihane, 6 vols. New York: Oxford University Press, 2012: 5, 29–38.

Taylor, Charles, *A Secular Age.* Cambridge, MA: Belknap Press of Harvard University Press, 2007.

Tertullian. *De praescriptione haereticorum.* Library of Latin Texts. Series A. Turnhout: Brepols, 2000. http://clt.brepolis.net/LLTA/pages/TextSearch .aspx?key=PTERT0005_.

Vasari, Giorgio. *Le vite de' più eccellenti pittori, scultori e architettori.* Edited by Gaetano Milanesi, 9 vols. Florence: G. C. Sansoni, 1876–81.

I

CONCEPTS

The Perennial Value of Platonism

Lloyd P. Gerson

By the time of the Council of Nicea in 325 CE, self-declared Christians who wanted to reflect philosophically on their religion did so almost exclusively within a Platonic context. This is because, from among all the philosophical schools that continued to flourish and vie for adherents more or less into the Hellenistic period, Platonism emerged clearly victorious. In fact, we know of almost no Peripatetics, Epicureans, or Stoics after the beginning of the third century. The closure of the Academy by Justinian in 529 – just to pick a convenient terminus – meant the virtual end of the public teaching of any pagan philosophy. At about the same time, the extent to which Christian theologians had appropriated Platonism and incorporated elements of it into their thinking was most dramatically evident in the works of Pseudo-Dionysius, a student of the aggressively pagan Platonist Proclus. In this chapter, I aim first to provide a relatively concise account of Plato's Platonism. I will then focus on those features of Platonism that emerged in the Hellenistic period and after as most apt for theological criticism and appropriation. Among these are the personhood of the first principle of all, the meaning of creation, and the eternity of the world.

PLATO'S PLATONISM

The most distinctive features of Plato's philosophical system are (1) his rejection of the naturalistic scientific and philosophical approaches of his predecessors in favor of a radically different mode of explanation, and (2) his positing of an absolutely simple first principle of all. It is the latter point that provides the justification for speaking of Plato's philosophy as a system.[1] That is, the first principle of all is the ultimate *explanans* upon which all investigations converge, those in metaphysics and epistemology as well as in ethics and moral psychology. What makes Platonism a system is just this unitary explanatory framework. Needless to say, this feature of Plato's philosophy was extremely attractive to Christian theologians aiming to transpose the historical accounts of scripture into a universal theoretical framework.

Plato's programmatic announcement of his rejection of most pre-Socratic accounts of nature is found in Socrates' "autobiography" in his *Phaedo*.[2] The upshot of this all-important passage is that the putative scientific explanations offered by Anaxagoras in particular or by anyone proceeding in a similar manner are in principle capable of being no more than necessary conditions as opposed to real explanations.[3] It is crucial to Socrates' argument that such naturalistic pseudoexplanations are not merely incomplete, but rather radically different from what a real explanation should do. If, for example, one seeks an explanation for some natural event or process or state of affairs, and if one does so employing natural elements of whatever sorts, none of these can ever provide the real explanation because the very same elements are capable of belonging to an explanation for a different or contrary result. So, a composition of some material does not make something large because the same material can make it small and the shape and colors of Helen do not explain her beauty because the same shapes and colors are part of an account of her being the opposite. But even if we focus on a particular case – the property that something has here and now – and even if we provide all the conditions that taken together can be said to be necessary and sufficient, we still do not have a true explanation. The reason for this is as follows. Let "X is f"

---

[1] I shall assume here without argument that Plato's philosophy is not simply identical to what we find in the dialogues. Rather, his oral teaching as recounted by Aristotle and the indirect tradition is an essential supplement to what we do find in the dialogues. Even if one were to reject the accuracy of Aristotle's testimony, there is no doubt that later self-declared Platonists like Plotinus took it seriously. The Platonism that was in 529 left on the table, so to speak, was significantly shaped by it. See D. Nikulin, *The Other Plato. The Tübingen School of Plato's Inner-Academic Teaching* (Albany, NY: SUNY Press, 2012) for a brief introduction to the evidence relating to Plato's unwritten teachings.

[2] *Phd.* 95A4–102A9. That this "autobiography" is in fact in all likelihood that of Plato himself and not Socrates has been well argued by David Sedley, "The Dramatis Personae of Plato's Phaedo," *Proceedings of the British Academy* 85 (1995): 3–26.

[3] The word being translated by "explanation" is αἰτία, which may also be rendered "reason" or "cause."

represent the *explanandum*. The predicate "is f" gives us more information than does "X." But it also gives us a different kind of information
from that of the name "X." That is, "X is f" indicates something different
from "X + f." The "is f" expresses, shall we say, a "part" of the identity of
X. But how can this be so? Isn't the identity of X *entirely* indicated by
"X?" Plato does not take seriously the claim that the only thing we can say
about X is that it is X.[4] If he is right not to do so, then an explanation for
the truth of "X is f" cannot be provided by Anaxagoras or any other
naturalist. For predicative identity cannot be reduced to formal identity.
That is, if the supposed naturalistic explanation provides necessary and
sufficient conditions for the truth of "X is f," it does this only by producing
a formally identical result. Thus, the necessary and sufficient conditions
for X are just the components of X, what X's formal identity is. If one
objects that the formally identical result *includes* the predicative identity
as well, then the latter would be reduced to the former. Predicative identity
is only distinct and irreducible to formal identity if the source of the
former is distinct from and irreducible to the source of the latter. So,
Helen is beautiful because she partakes of Beauty and the group of items
is odd because it partakes of Oddness, and so on. The explanation for
Helen's beauty is not reducible to the necessary and sufficient conditions
for her being beautiful.

The intelligible world, including the *explanantia* for predicates here
below as well as a superordinate first principle of all and immaterial souls
or intellects is, as Plato says in *Republic*, the subject matter of philosophy.[5]
The core claim of Platonism is that there is a distinct subject matter for
philosophy, that the intelligible world is that subject matter, and that it
has an explanatory primacy.[6] Christian Platonism will obviously have no
difficulty in appropriating a metaphysical claim for the primacy of the
intelligible over the sensible or the immaterial over the material. In addition, it will enthusiastically embrace the hierarchical ordering of the

---

[4] See *Tht.* 201D–E; *Soph.* 251Dff.

[5] *Rep.* 476A9–D6. At 484B4–7, Socrates clearly distinguishes between philosophers and
nonphilosophers by the subject matter with which they are concerned, namely, the intelligible and the sensible worlds. Cf. 485A10–B3; *Phd.* 79A6–7; *Tim.* 27D6–7, where a sharp
distinction between the sensible and the intelligible is made along with the mode of
cognition appropriate to each. Also, 51D3–E6.

[6] I use the term "world" advisedly, realizing that many contemporary Plato scholars have
expressed their disdain for an interpretation of Plato that rests upon a "two-world"
metaphysics. But the word "world" has a perfectly ordinary English use in such phrases
as "the business world," "the world of dance," and "the fashion world." I use it in this
sense.

intelligible and the sensible, for many reasons, but especially based upon the explanatory priority of the former.

But this is only part of the story, and arguably not the most important part. For the intelligible world – without which there could be no such thing as intelligible discourse – is anything but a disorganized array of "monadic" Forms, each a little island of intelligibility. As Plato says explicitly in *Republic*, at the apex of the intelligible world is the super-ordinate Idea of the Good, the unhypothetical first principle of all.[7] It is this principle that provides the explanation for the existence and essence of the Forms and, indirectly, for everything else.[8] As mentioned above, what justifies us in calling Platonism a "system" is the ordered array of intelligible entities at the apex of which is an absolutely simple principle which must be adduced for explanatory adequacy. At the most basic level, "Platonism" is just a label for the view that there is a distinct, hierarchic-ally arrayed subject matter irreducible to the material or physical world. But beyond or beneath this elementary level, a host of problems naturally arise, among which is the portentous issue of how the immutable and eternal intelligible world is supposed to be related to the sensible world. Stated otherwise, and with a view to later Christian interventions, the problem is how the necessary is related to the contingent.

Before addressing this issue, however, a word should be said about Plato's reasons for the bold positing of a first principle that is "beyond essence or *ousia*." I think it is safe to assume that Plato is sufficiently in line with his philosophical and scientific predecessors to simply assume that inquiry is essentially reductive. That is, in seeking for scientific or philo-sophical explanations, we seek to explain the complex by the simple and not the other way around. This assumption is evident right from the beginning of philosophy in the search for the element or elements that underlie all of nature and therefore are suitable for explaining the way things are. For all that, it is just as evident today in the search for the ultimate constituents or principles of reality, especially in the idea that underlying the four "fundamental" forces in nature is one unifying prin-ciple or equation.

This reductive tendency, carried to its logical conclusion, led Plato to reject any putative first principle of all that was composite in any way. So, even a Form, and even apart from whatever compositeness it has owing to what its "content" is, is composed of its essence and existence, that is,

---

[7] *Rep.* 510B6–7; 511B5–6; 533A8–9, C7–D4.
[8] *Rep.* 509B9–10; 516B8–C2; 517B7–C4.

what it is and the fact that it is. If this is so, the first principle of all must be absolutely simple in the sense that there is *no* composition of essence and existence in it. Hence, the Idea of the Good is posited to be "above essence," although it is not above existence altogether; it is only above the sort of existence that implies the possession of an essence and hence complexity.[9] Yet the more the absolute simplicity of the first principle of all is stressed, the more difficult it is to see how it can have any sort of explanatory role.

Plato tells us without elaboration that the Good is "overflowing" (*epirutton*).[10] The only hint we get is that in this respect the Good is analogous to the sun from which light flows, illuminating everything. Setting aside for the moment what the metaphysical analogue of light is, what is the reasoning behind the claim that the Good "overflows" at all? Again, this is a question that Plato does not address directly, and it is left to later Platonists to reflect on the nature of the Good in order to determine its unique causal power. What we can glean from Plato is the following. Everyone and everything desires its own good, which is nothing else but a manifestation of the one Good.[11] The idea here is that there would not be one Good at which all things aim unless that Good were the source from which all things come. Why should we suppose this to be so? Why, in other words, should we suppose that the dynamic metaphysical structure of the universe is, so to speak, circular rather than linear? Why not suppose that the ultimate end of each thing is diametrically opposed to its source?[12] What, in other words, is the commensurating link between source and end?

For an answer to this question we need to recur to Aristotle's testimony about Plato's philosophy. The core bit of testimony most relevant here is that Plato identified the Idea of the Good with the

---

[9] See M. Baltes, "Is the Idea of the Good in Plato's *Republic* beyond Being?" in *Studies in Plato and the Platonic Tradition*, ed. M. Joyal (London: Ashgate, 1997), 1–23, who shows with an abundance of evidence that the transcendence of the Good does not mean that the Good does not exist or is beyond being altogether. Baltes's positive interpretation, however, according to which the Good is being itself or the sum of all beings is based on no evidence.

[10] *Rep.* 508B6–7. This text is the origin of the principle *bonum est diffusivum sui*. See K. Kremer, "Bonum est diffusivum sui: Ein Beitrag zum Verhältnis von Neuplatonismus und Christentum," in *Aufstieg und Niedergang der Römischen Welt* 36/2, ed. W. Hasse and H. Temporini (Berlin: Walter de Gruyter, 1987), 994–1032.

[11] *Rep.* 505D5–9.

[12] Speusippus, Plato's nephew and successor as head of the Academy, did exactly that, concluding that the first principle of all, since as source, it is other than an end, must not be the Good.

One.[13] I shall not here attempt to defend the accuracy of this testimony.[14] What is undeniable is that the later tradition is united in taking it as an authentic expression of Platonic doctrine. My concern here is to try to indicate the rationale for this identification and the profound effect it had on the course of Platonism.

"One" may indicate a unit of measurement and it may indicate incompositeness.[15] Aristotle thinks that the former is prior to the latter.[16] By contrast, Plato thinks that since the first principle of all must be unqualifiedly simple or incomposite, that the latter is prior to the former. Hence, it is also the principle of the former. So, the One is the ultimate explanation for everything but also, along with the Indefinite Dyad, the principle of measure. Returning to the question of that which links source and end, the One is the principle of the being of everything. But it is so via the intermediaries that are the Forms. The good for each thing is to achieve the fulfillment of its nature. This is the achievement of an integrative unity of parts. Since the One is the principle of being, it is also the principle as a goal. Things achieve their good by achieving unity as far as is possible for them. As we shall see, this structural dynamic is one of the main features of Platonism elaborated on by later Platonists both pagan and Christian.[17]

Within this dynamic, the entirety of Plato's moral philosophy can be articulated. We can conceive of life as a line drawn from the One to its opposite, the unlimited or undefined or unintegrated or, as Plotinus will add, unintelligible, matter. Along this line, human beings (and everything else in the universe) are found. Moral improvement requires advancement toward the terminus that is the Good; moral decay is motion in the opposite direction.[18] Virtue is a practice that promotes integrative unity

---

[13] See *Meta.* A 6, 987b18–25; 988a8–14; N 4, 1091b13–15. Cf. also *EE* A 8, 1218a15–32, which refers to those who hold that τὸ ἕν is αὐτὸ τἀγαθόν. In the passage in book N, it is clear that the One is prior to the Good since it is the οὐσία of it. This is a crucial hint as to how Plato developed. That is, the One, the absolutely simple first principle of all must be the Good because the goal of all things must be their source, not the other way around. Cf. Proclus, *Platonic Theology* II 6, 40.25–27.

[14] See Lloyd Gerson, *Platonism and Naturalism: The Possibility of Philosophy* (Ithaca, NY: Cornell University Press, 2019), ch. 5.

[15] See Aristotle, *Meta.* I 1.   [16] I 1, 1052b15–19.

[17] See A. C. Lloyd, *The Anatomy of Platonism* (Oxford: Oxford University Press, 1990), ch. 5; F. O'Rourke, *Pseudo-Dionysius and the Metaphysics of Aquinas* (South Bend, IN: Notre Dame University Press, 2005).

[18] See *Phd.* 99C5–6 on the Good as the principle of integrative unity. Also, *Rep.* 443E1–2 on virtue as an achievement of integrative unity. Cf. 554E4–6 and *Phd.* 83A7–B2 on the role of philosophy persuading the soul "to gather oneself into oneself."

and so increase proximity to the Good; vice is the opposite. Because we all desire the real good, every act in the direction of the Good is freely undertaken, that is, it is according to one's desire. Every act that draws us in the opposite direction is constrained or unfree just because it is the opposite of what we desire. So, Plato's frequently repeated claim that no one does wrong willingly is given a metaphysical foundation.[19] Here, "wrong" is understood as indicating any action drawing one away from the Good and in the direction of oblivion. No one willingly does that. And yet, Plato unequivocally supports the idea of moral responsibility.[20] How can one be responsible for that which he does not will? The easy answer to this question is that it is owing to ignorance that one (unwillingly) does wrong. But can one be held responsible for one's ignorance? Plato clearly wants to say yes, but how this is possible is not so easy to discern.

I believe the core of the answer is this. We are rational souls. That is our endowment. As embodied rational souls, we are not just capable of thinking but also of acting. We cannot but act as rational souls. Even when we, so to speak *follow* appetite, it is we the rational souls who do so. We cede temporary authority to the subject of the appetite, a rational subject to be sure, but one which employs that rationality purely instrumentally in the service of the appetite. Even in such a state, it is we, the rational soul, who endorse this ceding of authority. We do so because we are employing our reason universally, in this case to endorse a universal rule of action. And it is we who desire the real Good who do so. So, we believe we are achieving our own good by, say, doing something bad. But that is not possible any more than it is possible to make the sum of two numbers come out to be different from what they in fact are. Thinking universally, we act irrationally if we take our own appetites as exempt from the reach of the Good. That is, it is not possible to achieve one's own good by means of instantiating what is the opposite of good for anyone else. We cannot rationally both endorse a universal rule of action and reject it by subordinating reason to appetite at the same time. So, wrongdoing is irrational; it is a defect in rationality, but it is one whose presence is available to us for observation regardless of the personal impediments that have been thrown up as obstacles to our virtuous behavior. The blameworthiness of wrongdoing, on this account, admits of degrees, the

---

[19] *Me.* 77C1–2; *Ap.* 37A5; *Gorg.* 488A3; *Protag.* 345D8, 358C7; *Rep.* 589C6; *Tim.* 86D7–C1; *Lg.* 731C–D.
[20] See *Rep.* 617D2–E6; cf. 379C3–7; *Tim.* 41E1–4.

termini of which are complete absence of impediments to perfectly rational behavior and insuperable impediments to that.[21]

It is the identity of the Idea of the Good with the absolutely simple One that actually gives content to morality. For integrated unity is concretely indexed to kind.[22] The *technē* of ruling – the state and oneself – is the ability to apply the knowledge of what integrated unity for each is and what contributes and what does not contribute to it. The principle of the *technē* is the necessity that the Good, hence, unity, is never achieved by instantiating its opposite. In other words, my good is never achievable by doing something that adhibits the opposite of good for anyone or anything else. This is, for the most part, not so difficult to discern both in public and in private life, as tempting as it might be to countenance exceptions.

The picture of Platonism as received by later philosophers and theologians would be incomplete without the inclusion of the Demiurge or divine νοῦς who is responsible for imposing order on the disordered precosmic soup.[23] It is essential for the appreciation of the Platonic system that the Demiurge be understood in its relation to the Good, to the Forms, and to the sensible cosmos, especially the soul of the universe, and to creatures like us who are able to participate in *nous*. In relation to the Good, the unhypothetical first principle of all, it seems clear that the Demiurge is not to be identified with that.[24] As we shall see, later Platonists will be irresistibly attracted to the idea of conflating the Demiurge with the Good thereby investing the latter with the personal attributes of the former, including and especially being good and therefore being ungrudging.[25] But if the Demiurge is subordinate to the Good,

---

[21] It might be noted in passing that the above solution pertains to the travails of embodiment. Within a Christian context, a somewhat different account, with the rebellion of Satan as paradigm, must be given.

[22] See *Rep.* 422E–423B, 462A–B, where it is clear that the difference between a successful or good state and a bad one is in the presence or absence of integrative unity. Also, cf. *Symp.* 192C–D on love as integrative unity. See Aristotle, *EE* A 8, 1218a19, discussing the Good, on justice and health as τάξεις. Cf. Plotinus, II 1 [33], 1.1–12; V 8 [31], 13.20; VI 6 [34] 1, 10–14; VI 9 [9], 9.11–13. Also, see *Rep.* 422E–423B on the geographical requirements for the unity of the ideal city and *Lg.* 739D on the unity of the state as a desideratum.

[23] See esp. *Tim.* 2828C3ff; *Phil.* 26E6ff; *Sts.* 273B1ff; *Lg.* 867B5–6.

[24] See *Tim.* 48C2–6 with 53D4–7 where Timaeus specifically declines to discuss "the principle or principles" (ἀρχὴν εἴτε ἀρχὰς) of all. This implies that the Demiurge is not one of those principles since it is extensively discussed in this dialogue.

[25] *Tim.* 29A2, E1–2.

explicating the relation between them remains the highest priority for those intent on a Platonic philosophical basis for a religion.

In relation to the Forms, the preponderance of evidence suggests that the Forms are not concepts or ideas in the mind that the Demiurge is, but that the Demiurge is cognitively identical with Forms.[26] It is clear enough that Forms are not themselves concepts, but if what the Demiurge possesses are concepts of Forms, then the Forms themselves remain unconnected among themselves apart from their all having the identical source, the Good. Among other problems, this would make it impossible to explain the necessary connectedness of Forms that explains the eternal truths of mathematics. The Demiurge itself is said to be the "the best among things intelligible and eternal" and it seems reasonable to suppose that this means that in some sense it is identical with the fundamentally intelligible Living Being, which includes Forms of all living things.[27]

Finally, in relation to the sensible world generally and souls in particular, the Demiurge has an undeniable creative role to play, even if we insist that this role be demythologized. By this I mean, that we do not need to suppose that the Demiurge acts like temporal beings with intellects; rather, that it acts eternally and that the effects of its acting depend upon the suitability and preparedness of things in the receptacle for receiving those acts. Thus, the Demiurge serves both as the explanation for the intelligibility of the sensible world and also for the necessary truths upon which this intelligibility rests. And its acts, echoing *Phaedo*, are all done in order that the world be as good as possible.[28]

Platonism is a system in the sense that it has a fundamental structural dynamic according to which the absolutely simple first principle of all, the One, is also the good for each thing. Without eternal Forms and an eternal Demiurge, however, there could not be a variegated universe consisting of a multiplicity of things. The dynamic provides the framework for practical as well as for theoretical science.[29] This dynamic is hierarchical in nature where everything can be located and judged along the axis of proximity to the apex of the hierarchy. Thus, normativity and metaphysics are inseparable. The dynamic is also the mold within which Christian scriptural content was to be poured. In the following section, I would like to fill out this sketch of Platonism by briefly mentioning some of the salient

---

[26] See *Tim.* 29E1–3, 30C2–D1, 39E3–7.   [27] *Tim.* 37A1.   [28] *Tim.* 29D7–30A6.
[29] Socrates' "autobiography" in *Phaedo* neatly unites these two by conflating the normative with the descriptive.

contributions of later Platonists to the basic account of the structural dynamic.

PLATONISTS AFTER PLATO

I take Platonism to have been a collaborative project, with Plato himself as the guiding light but with scores of philosophers – most of whose work is not extant – making contributions to the project in at least two specific ways.[30] First, there are defenses of Platonism against its opponents, including Peripatetics, Stoics, Epicureans, and eventually Christians. In these defenses new features of the dynamic are discovered and deployed. Second, there are disputes among Platonists regarding the correct articulation of the details of the system. Thinking about the difficult and often obscure claims that Plato made, later Platonists disputed the implications of these claims and their precise meaning. It is the Platonism so reformulated and expanded that Christian philosophers later encountered and sought to appropriate.

According to the above sketch of Platonism, it no longer seems to me to be even controversial to call Aristotle a Platonist. This is so despite his obvious objections to features of Platonism. The central claim against which Aristotle does not object is that there must be an absolutely simple first principle of all.[31] Aristotle provides an argument *ex motu* in Book Lambda of his *Metaphysics* for the existence of an Unmoved Mover. In chapter eight, he argues that the Unmoved Mover is unique and simple.[32] Aristotle's further reasoning about the nature of this principle is remarkable. He says that since the Unmoved Mover is simple, it must be pure activity (*energeia*), since if it were a composite of act and potency, it would be complex.[33] Aristotle assumes, though doesn't argue, that what pure activity must

---

[30] See M.-L. Lakmann, *Platonici Minores* (Leiden: Brill, 2017); G. R. Boys-Stones, *Platonist Philosophy, 80 bc to ad 250* (Cambridge: Cambridge University Press, 2018); C. Riedweg, C. Horn, and D. Wyrwa, *Philosophie der Kaiserzeit und Spätantike*, vol. 5/2 (Basel: Schwabe, 2018) for the vast variety of work that belongs under the heading "Platonism" in the period, roughly, 80 BCE to 250 CE.

[31] See *Meta.* Λ 6, 1071b3ff.

[32] At Λ 8, 1074a31–37, he concludes from the unicity of the cosmos that its ultimate cause is one both in number and in λόγος. That is, there is no real distinction within it that would answer to more than one account. Hence, the Unmoved Mover is absolutely simple. Cf. 7, 1072a32–34.

[33] See Λ 7, 1072b15–30.

be is thinking. If this is so, then the Unmoved Mover has or, more accurately, is a life, since life is the activity of thinking.[34]

Later Platonists found no difficulty in concluding that the Unmoved Mover was Aristotle's "version" of the Demiurge. But as we have seen, for Plato the Demiurge is not the absolutely simple first principle of all; the Good or One is. And this principle is not a life nor is it thinking. So, the dilemma for Platonists, especially those who were happy to mine Aristotle for contributions to the Platonic project, was how to combine the exigency of metaphysics with theology. That is, how can there be a first principle that is absolutely simple and also be capable of, for example, providential activity. If it is simple, then we must remove from it any complexity, including the epistemological complexity that would seem to be necessary for planning or, in other words, matching up means and ends, which is the essence of providence.

One way of addressing this dilemma is by embracing both horns. This is what Alcinous does in his valuable *Didaskalikos* or "Handbook" of Platonism, perhaps a product of a second-century-CE Platonist or, less helpfully, "Middle Platonist."[35] In the famous chapter ten of this work, Alcinous quite consciously conflates the Demiurge with the Unmoved Move *and* with the Idea of the Good of *Republic*. He does this, it seems, by relaxing the requirement of absolute simplicity. Thus, the Good-Demiurge-Unmoved Mover thinks all the Forms, but this does not compromise its simplicity since all the Forms are in fact the ἰδέα that the Good is. As he goes on to argue, we may assume that the distinctions among the Forms are merely conceptual distinctions, not real distinctions. So, too, are the truth, beauty, and commensurabilty that this first principle possesses or, rather, is.[36] Combined with the diffusive activity of the Good as expressed in *Republic*, Alcinous can plausibly attribute providence to this

---

[34] Λ 7, 1072b26–27. The word ἐνέργεια can be translated both as "activity" and as "actuality." The latter translation implies the potency of which the actuality is a correlate. But the Unmoved Mover has no potency, so it is less misleading to translate the word as "activity" in this case.

[35] See J. Dillon, *Alcinous. The Handbook of Platonism* (Oxford: Oxford University Press, 1993), introduction, for the relevant best guesses about the provenance, date, and authorship of this work. For our purposes, what is most important is that, as a "handbook," it probably represents the opinions of many of the scores of Platonists working in the period roughly bounded by the first century BCE and the third century CE and typically dubbed "Middle Platonic."

[36] See *Didask.* 10, 164.27–165.4 Whittaker. Alcinous is here alluding to Plato's *Philebus* 65A–B.

principle.[37] That is, god is goodness itself, and eternally thinking about the transmission of this goodness to creation.

Numenius, who flourished around the middle of the second century CE, and whose link to later Platonism is forged especially by the accusation, reported by Porphyry, that Plotinus plagiarized from him, provides an alternative to Alcinous' simple conflation of the Good and the Demiurge. In his work, *On the Good*, which exists now only in fragments, Numenius argues that the first god, the Idea of the Good, must be distinct from the Demiurge precisely because the former is absolutely simple, whereas the latter is not.[38] Nevertheless, because the second god, the Demiurge, is intellect, intellect must itself be derived from the first. That is, the first must be intellect, too.[39] Recurring to the "overflowing" of the Good in *Republic*, Numenius reasons that the first intellect must have some sort of "innate motion" (*kinēsin sumphuton*) owing to which it is able to have some effects, in particular, that it can be accounted providential.[40] By identifying the Good as intellect, which is also the way that the Demiurge is identified, Numenius provides a somewhat tenuous ground for the assimilation of the one to the other while keeping them distinct.[41] Nevertheless, he seems to rely solely on Aristotle in maintaining that an intellect can be unqualifiedly simple. It is not so much the simplicity of the first that Numenius cannot accommodate as it is the idea that an intellect can act. For he insists that the first cannot "produce" (*dēmiourgein*) anything given its contemplative nature.[42] Rather, it entrusts creation to the second god, while it itself is inactive. This is so even though the second god is an intellect as well.

Plotinus will reject all of the attempts of Middle Platonists to conflate the Good or One and the Demiurge or Unmoved Mover. He argues for an irreducible hierarchy of distinct principles, Good, Intellect, and Soul.[43] The Platonic provenance of these principles or *hypostases* is clear. The first principle of all is the Idea of the Good as postulated in *Republic*, identified with the One, according to Aristotle's testimony.[44] The second

---

[37] *Didask.* 10, 167.13 Whittaker.   [38] See Numenius, fr. 11.12 Des Places.

[39] Fr. 20.7–12 Des Places. Cf. frs. 16.1–3, 17.2, 19.4–5.

[40] See fr. 15, where the providence is called the world's "preservation" (σωτηρία).

[41] See fr. 16.14 Des Places. It is clear enough that the Demiurge, the second god, is inferior to the first, since it is its imitator (μίμητης).

[42] Fr. 15.1 Des Places.

[43] See Enn. esp. V 1 [10]. See E. Perl, *Ennead V 1. On the Three Primary Levels of Reality* (Las Vegas, NV: Parmenides Press, 2015) for an historically and philosophically astute commentary on this crucial treatise.

[44] Aristotle's testimony is that Plato posited the Indefinite Dyad along with the One as first principles, suggesting the obvious problem that if these are coordinate principles, there is

principle of all, Intellect, is the Demiurge of *Timaeus*. The third principle is Soul, whose primary manifestations are the soul of the universe and the souls of each individual living thing. We should add, for the sake of completeness, that Nature is what Plotinus calls the "lowest part of soul," the active principle in living things, inseparable from bodies. It is not a separate *hypostasis*. Nature is, roughly, the organic structure of all living things which, among other things, determines the sorts of bodies that living things possess.

Plotinus' philosophy may be characterized generally as his attempt to provide comprehensive answers to the entire budget of philosophical problems current in the middle of the third century CE. This means that Plotinus repeatedly draws upon the fundamental principles both to respond to opponents of Platonism and to solve problems unknown to Plato himself. Plotinus' originality is found in how he performs both tasks. He himself rejected any claim to originality, maintaining that the principles – the basic architecture of the system – were Plato's.

One of Plotinus' major contributions to the Platonic project is in his use of Aristotelian insights to articulate and defend the Platonic system. Aristotle, as we have seen, reasons that the first principle of all must be *energeia*, activity without imperfection or incompleteness. Plotinus agrees that this is how the first principle must be characterized if it is to be absolutely simple and perfect. But he denies that Intellect or the Unmoved Mover can be this principle, since the Unmoved Mover is irreducibly complex. Its complexity lay in the distinction between thinking and the object of thought and also in the multiplicity of intelligible objects.[45] Hence, the absolutely simple first principle of all must be "beyond" Intellect or the Unmoved Mover. Its simplicity and perfection suggests to Plotinus, among other things, that it is self-caused.[46] This claim, I take it, is equivalent to the claim that the first principle of all must be uncaused, that is, uncaused by anything else. The self-caused absolutely incomposite first principle of all must be eternally active. Plotinus explains this eternal activity according to the Aristotelian analysis of *energeia*.[47] But unlike the *energeia* of the Unmoved Mover,

---

not one first principle and therefore Plato is in some sense a dualist. Plotinus, along with all later Platonists denied this. Plotinus identifies the Indefinite Dyad with the first (logical) "phase" of Intellect's generation from the One. It becomes Intellect when it turns toward the One and thinks all that the One is virtually, that is, all intelligibles. See V 1 [10], 5.6–14.

[45] See V 6 [24]. [46] VI 8 [39], 14.41. Cf. VI 9 [9], 4.44–45.
[47] See V 4 [7], 2.28–39; VI 8 [39], 16.16–17, 20.9–15.

characterized by Aristotle as being exclusively engaged in self-directed thinking, Plotinus draws on Plato's characterization of the Idea of the Good as overflowing.[48] Since the Good or One is incomposite and self-caused, there is nothing either to limit its activity or to diminish it. So, we are led to distinguish its "internal" activity and its "external" activity.[49] The external activity of the One just is Intellect and Intellect's external activity just is Soul, thus generating a hierarchy of principles, with Intellect and Soul being at once principles and instruments of the first principle of all.

The external activity of the Good produces, with the instrumental causality of Intellect and then Soul, all being. The procession of everything that is possible ends in matter.[50] Without matter, there could be no embodied thing; but we know these are possible from their actuality. Matter is, on the one hand, the condition for the possibility of anything that is composite, and on the other hand, the terminus of the outpouring of the Good. So, matter is the principle of the opposite of the Good, namely, evil, but only in the sense of a terminus, that is, a terminus of a trajectory away from the Good. As the mere principle of the possibility of complex being, matter is neither good nor evil.[51]

Although Plotinus rejects the Aristotelian claim that the first principle of all is thinking, he nevertheless attributes to it "superthinking" (*huper-noēsis*) and "grasping" (*katanoēsis*).[52] Indeed, he adds that it has a "will" (*boulēsis*) and that it is "love" (*erōs*).[53] It remains a puzzle for later Platonists, both Christian and non-Christian, to decide how or to what extent these "attributes" of the One are sufficient to make it a person. One indication of the divide between the non-Christian and Christian reflections on this puzzle is that the former do not think that petitionary prayer makes any sense in relation to the One, whereas the Christians do.[54]

---

[48] Plotinus adds that the One is "spring" (πηγή) from which all things flow. See, for example, I 6 [1], 9.41; III 8 [30], 10.27; VI 7 [38], 23.21.

[49] This is expressed as ἐνέργεια τῆς οὐσίας and ἐνέργεια ἐκ τῆς οὐσίας. See V 1 [10], 3.10–12; V 4 [7], 2.27–36, etc.

[50] On matter, see esp. II 4 [12].

[51] Matter underlies all complex being, including complex being in the intelligible world. There it is intelligible matter.

[52] See VI 8 [39], 16.32; V 4 [7], 2.17.

[53] See on the will of the One VI 8 [39], 6; on the One as ἔρως see VI 8 [39], 15.

[54] It should be added that Plotinus does in fact mention prayer in relation to the One. See V 1 [10], 6.11–12; IV 9 [8], 4.6–7; V 5 [32], 3.12–13. But it's unclear in what sense this can be called petitionary prayer.

This puzzle recedes into the background within a polytheistic framework. That is precisely what we find in Proclus (412–485). Proclus, like all Platonists after Plotinus, accepts the basic three architectural principles articulated by him. In addition, Proclus gives us the most extensive expression of the dynamics of this system, namely, the "moments" of "remaining" (*monē*), "procession" (*proodos*), and "reversion" (*epistrophē*).[55] Procession and reversion are grounded in the overflowing of the Good and the desire of all things for the Good, that from which they originate. Remaining is based on the text in *Timaeus* in which it is said that the Demiurge "remained in himself in his accustomed manner" while ordering the cosmos.[56] The structure is dynamic owing to the essential activity of the first principle of all. The dynamism does not result ultimately in dissolution because reversion is guaranteed by the remaining and the procession. It is so guaranteed because the procession is from the self-loving first principle. If its self-loving were a property of it, that is, if it were distinct from its self-loving, then procession from it would not produce eros in everything else. Procession, if it is to be part of a system, must be from the essence of that which proceeds.

This dynamic structure is primarily eternal. In the eternal realm, procession and reversion are no less eternal than the remaining of the Good. Because the temporalized cosmos is an image of this eternal dynamic structure, it represents it imperfectly. Thus, in all erotic activity the relation between eternal intellect and the Good is recapitulated in a diminished way. That is, the lover satisfies his desire for the Good by achieving the fulfillment of his own nature as intellect. Beauty is the Good as attractive. But the intellects of embodied human beings are the intellects of temporalized souls. So, the desires of embodied souls are themselves images of intellectual desire. The reversion of all embodied souls to the Good is, in one sense, a quest for the unknown. But no one seeks for that which is completely unknown, a point made in a limited and focused manner in Meno's paradox. The quest for the unknown is a reversion because it is a quest to return to the source of one's own being. The soul that reverts is engaged in an attempt to recover itself as it is found in its cause.

[55] See esp. *Elements of Theology* (*ET*), Props. 25–39.
[56] See *Tim.* 42E5–6. Cf. Plotinus, III 8 [30], 10.5–10, where remaining is paradigmatically in the One or Good. Cf. IV 8 [6], 6.1–18; V 1 [10], 3.11–15, 6.27–30; V 2 [11], 1.7–21; V 5 [32], 12.40–49. Also, Proclus, *Commentary on Timaeus* (*In Tim.*) 1.282, 26–31.

Proclus actually begins the *Elements of Theology* with the sentence: "Every plurality participates in that which is one in some way."[57] It is the small word *pē* ("in some way") that conceals the problem. Proclus specifically denies that the One is *energeia*.[58] Nevertheless, he insists that the One is the cause of everything, that which preserves (*sōzesthai*) all things in existence.[59] How can it do this without being participated in? How does participating "in some way" solve the problem?

Proclus reasons that, given the absolute simplicity of the first principle of all, the One, it is not possible to derive directly the multiplicity of intelligibles. Therefore, there needs to be posited Henads, participatable Ones, one each for every intelligible.[60] The first principle, generally unparticipatable, is participatable "in some way" by participation in the Henads.[61] That is, while each Form is a one, its own unity is participated, and that unity cannot be the first principle. Hence, there must be an intermediary more unified than each Form but less unified that the One itself.[62]

The Henads are derived from or produced by the One not by any means that implies that these Henads participate in the One.[63] Since procession from the One implies absence of identity, but since there can be no participation in the One as a result of procession, the Henads are said to proceed by way of unity.[64] Whereas Plotinus argued that the uniqueness

---

[57] See *ET* Prop. 1, 2.1: Πᾶν πλῆθος μετέχειν πῃ τοῦ ἑνός. Cf. *Platonic Theology* (*PT*) II 4, 34.24–35.9; Plotinus, VI 9 [9], 1.1.

[58] See *Commentary on Parmenides* (*In Parm.*) VII 1172.18–19, πρὸ ἐνεργείας ἐστὶ πάσης τὸ ἕν. Also, VI 1106.5–6, where Proclus rejects the view of those who place ἐνέργεια prior to οὐσία. Cf. *PT* II 7, 50.14: μήτε ἐνεργοῦντος; III 1, 6.1: καὶ πάσης ἐνεργείας κεχωρισμένην [the primary cause, that is, the One].

[59] See *In Parm.* VII 1150.13–17; *ET* Prop. 57, 56.14–16; *PT* II 1, 3.6–8, πρωτίστην αἰτίαν.

[60] See *In Tim.* IV 12.22–30. Cf. *In Parm.* I 702.29–34, V 1032.20–24, VI 1043.9–29; *PT* III 3, 13.6–14.3.

[61] See *PT* III 4, 14.11–15.15. See C. D'Ancona Costa, "Enadi e archai nell'ordine sovrasensibile," *Rivista di storia della filosofia* 2 (1992): 265–294; E. Butler, *Essays on the Metaphysics of Polytheism in Proclus* (New York: Phaidra Editions, 2014) for philosophical treatments of the Henads in Proclus.

[62] See *PT* III 6, 28.18–19; 12, 45.13–46.22; 14, 51.6–7; 24, 86.7–9, passages which perhaps contain the solution: there is a hierarchy of Henads, at the apex of which are the Henads identified with the principles of Limit and Unlimited. See G. Van Riel, "The One, the Henads, and the Principles," in *All from One: A Guide to Proclus*, ed. P. D'Hoine and M. Martijn (Oxford: Oxford University Press, 2017), 73–97 at pp. 89–94.

[63] See *In Parm.* VII 1190.4–1191.7. Here, the Henads are said to be ἄλλα ("other") than the One but not ἕτερα ("different from") it. Cf. *In Tim.* I 363.26–364.11. Even the Demiurge does not participate in the One.

[64] *In Parm.* II 745.14–747.14. Cf. *PT* III 3, 12.10–14.

of the absolutely simple entails that whatever proceeds from the One is different from it, Proclus attempts to infer a sense of "otherness" that is not "difference." If the Henads, as superessential Ones, are not different from each other by essence, their difference from each other may be contrasted with their otherness in relation to the One. If this is the case, then each Henad can provide the unity that participating in an intelligible nature requires without thereby implicating the One itself.

Proclus explicitly justifies this move as necessary to explain his polytheism.[65] Indeed, it is clear that his polytheism is the driving force in the system. For, as he says in the *Parmenides Commentary*, "each of the gods is nothing other than the One as participated."[66] Leaving aside Proclus' religious motivation, the problem remains the same whether there are multiple gods or one god, identified or not identified unqualifiedly with the first principle of all. Insofar as this god must be absolutely simple, it cannot it seems be participated in; but if it cannot be participated in, its causal role seems to be exiguous along with its ability to interact with rational creatures.

Proclus adds another reason for the positing of Henads either in addition to or instead of the absolutely simple One. Since the One is the Good and the Good is self-diffusive, it cannot proceed by way of a weakening or diminution of itself.[67] But any plurality would *ipso facto* represent such a diminution. By contrast, Plotinus insists on the logical point that any procession from the One will be inferior to it but this does not indicate a diminution of the Good itself.

The problem that was perhaps first identified by Iamblichus and later addressed by Proclus with the postulation of Henads comes to the fore again with the remarkable writings of the last "head" of Plato's Academy, Damascius (*c.* 460–*c.* 540). Despite the fact that Damascius' works were for centuries ignored and even misattributed, his analysis and aporetic conclusion regarding a first principle of all indirectly cast a shadow over philosophical theology ever after.[68] Damascius reasoned as follows. If

---

[65] See *ET* Prop. 113.

[66] See *In Parm.* VI 1069.5–6: καὶ οὐδὲν ἄλλο ἐστὶν ἕκαστος τῶν θεῶν ἢ τὸ μετεχόμενον ἕν.

[67] See *PT* II 7, 50.12–51.19.

[68] See D. Cürsgen, *Henologie und Ontologie: Die metaphysische Prinzipienlehre des späten Neuplatonismus* (Würzburg: Königshausen und Neumann, 2007); Van Riel, "The One, the Henads, and the Principles"; S. Rappe, *Reading Neoplatonism* (Cambridge: Cambridge University Press, 2010); C. Metry-Tresson, *L'aporie ou l'expérience des limites de la pensée dans le Péri Archônde Damaskios* (Leiden: E. J. Brill, 2012) for the most recent discussions of the thought of Damascius.

there is to be a first principle of all, then either this principle transcends the all or it does not. But if it transcends the all, then the supposed all is not in fact that because it excludes the first. But if the first principle is a "part" of the all, then the all has no explanatory first principle.[69] Nevertheless, there must be some explanatorily first principle. In the face of this dilemma, Damascius concludes that the first is so remote that even calling it "ineffable" is misleading.[70] There is no space here to explore how Damascius goes on to reappropriate the Neoplatonic One, Intellect, and Soul. What is most important for my purposes here is that Damascius' arguments pose a severe problem for metaphysics whether or not it is allied to Christian theology. For the underlying assumption of Platonism and ancient Greek philosophy generally was that the world – both the sensible world and the intelligible world – is accessible to reason and hence to explanation. Apart from little pockets of unintelligibility, including chance and matter, explanation was available to reason. And explanation meant ultimately ascending to a first principle of all. But if that is not available to us, then all explanation will be wrong or at best incomplete, just as Plato thought was the case for Anaxagoras. Having rejected the solution of Proclus, the problem that Damascius revealed appeared to indicate a plausible need for Christian revelation at least for that which was unavailable to reason. But as Porphyry showed, that revelation in scripture chafed against the purely metaphysical framework of Platonism.

PLATONISM ENCOUNTERS CHRISTIANITY

It should be obvious to the reader that the problem Proclus met with the postulation of Henads is anticipated in prior and contemporary Christian reflections on the transcendence of God and the mediating role of the second person of the Trinity. As a theological issue, this is far outside the scope of this chapter. As a philosophical issue, it has its roots in the Platonic postulation of an unhypothetical first principle of all that must also be the Good for all things. As Proclus saw, even the subordination of Intellect to the One does not completely solve the problem of how the absolutely simple can be participated in.

Platonism encountered Christianity in a particularly dramatic fashion during the persecution of Christians by the pagan Emperors Diocletian, Maximius, Galerius, and Constantius in the period beginning explicitly in 303 CE and ending with the conversion to Christianity of Constantine in

---

[69] See *De prin.* 1.1.4.2–20.   [70] *De prin.* 1.4.13–5.17.

312 and the Edict of Milan in 313. I am not here concerned with the political and social aspects of this period but with the philosophical points of contention.

What is it, we may ask, that makes Christianity something other than just a version of Platonism, one among numerous others? I would suggest that the fundamental difference is that Christian philosophy is required to represent itself as a mixed science, that is, a mixture of philosophical theory and history. What differentiates pagan Platonism from Christian Platonism is that Platonists, qua Platonists, are in principle indifferent to history, whereas Christians are essentially dependent on historical claims. To these claims, they add a theoretical framework. The dynamic of the Platonic system, as articulated by Proclus, and adopted by Pseudo-Dionysius, is self-evidently a powerful theory for representing the relation between the intelligible and the sensible *and*, of course, conversely, in the *epistrophē* of all things to their source. The actual particularity of history is merely background to this theory. Christian Platonism, by contrast, must start from an utterly unique manifestation of the intelligible in the sensible in the Incarnation. And it must also start from an utterly unique manifestation of the return of the sensible to the intelligible in the Resurrection.

The mixture, as I would put it, of history and theory, inevitably impacts theory. So, for example, the personhood of the historically incarnated God becomes relevant to theory. In addition, since the incarnate God is a paradigm of personhood, the philosophical analysis of the human person is led to see the ideal person as a resurrected person, something that Platonists find absurd. Accordingly, the Platonic philosophical analysis of moral improvement and even conversion as a process of disengagement with the body is in tension with the idea of a resurrected body–soul composite as the ideal sought.

Platonist antipathy to Christianity owing to the latter's essential connection with history is evident in Porphyry's *Contra Christianos*. The criticism of Christianity in this work is almost entirely historical, pointing out inconsistencies in scriptural accounts of Jesus and his life. Yet at the same time, Iamblichus, perhaps Porphyry's pupil, recognizes the emotional appeal of historical as opposed to theoretical claims, elaborating a sort of pagan sacramentalism as a prophylactic against the apparently unstoppable Christian versions. The tension between theory and history actually explains I think the marginalizing of history in the Christian works of Pseudo-Dionysius. But the inseparability of history from Christianity is also indicated by the author's apparent self-identification with an historical scriptural figure, in a way implicitly privileging history over theory. Many influential Christian Platonists before and after Pseudo-Dionysius sought to bring together scriptural exegesis and some version of Platonic metaphysics, including those of the so-called Middle Platonists and Neoplatonists. This historical development – the subject-matter of this book – reaches a high-point in the attempt of Thomas Aquinas to reinvigorate the metaphysics ultimately found in Plato himself.

Bibliography

Baltes, M. "Is the Idea of the Good in Plato's Republic beyond Being?" in *Studies in Plato and the Platonic Tradition*, ed. M. Joyal. London: Ashgate, 1997: 1–23.

Boys-Stones, G. R. *Platonist Philosophy, 80 BC to AD 250*. Cambridge: Cambridge University Press, 2018.

Butler, Edward. *Essays on the Metaphysics of Polytheism in Proclus*. New York: Phaidra Editions, 2014.

Cürsgen, D. *Henologie und Ontologie: Die metaphysische Prinzipienlehre des späten Neuplatonismus*. Würzburg: Königshausen & Neumann, 2007.

D'Ancona Costa, C. "Enadi e archai nell'ordine sovrasensibile," *Rivista di storia della filosofia* 2 (1992): 265–294.

Dillon, J. *Alcinous: The Handbook of Platonism*. Oxford: Oxford University Press, 1993.

Gerson, L. *Platonism and Naturalism: The Possibility of Philosophy*. Ithaca, NY: Cornell University Press, 2019.

Kremer, K. "Bonum est diffusivum sui: Ein Beitrag zum Verhältnis von Neuplatonismus und Christentum," in *Aufstieg und Niedergang der Römischen Welt*, vol. 36/2, ed. W. Hasse and H. Temporini. Berlin: Walter de Gruyter, 1987: 994–1032.

Lakmann, M.-L. *Platonici Minores*. Leiden: Brill, 2017.

Lloyd, A. C. *The Anatomy of Platonism*. Oxford: Oxford University Press, 1990.

Metry-Tresson, C. *L'aporie ou l'expérience des limites de la pensée dans le Péri Archôn de Damaskios*. Leiden: E. J. Brill, 2012.

Nikulin, D. *The Other Plato. The Tübingen School of Plato's Inner-Academic Teaching*. Albany, NY: SUNY Press, 2012.

O'Rourke, F. *Pseudo-Dionysius and the Metaphysics of Aquinas*. South Bend, IN: Notre Dame University Press, 2005.

Perl, E. *Ennead V 1. On the Three Primary Levels of Reality*. Las Vegas, NV: Parmenides Press, 2015.

Rappe, S. *Reading Neoplatonism*. Cambridge: Cambridge University Press, 2010.

Riedweg, C., Horn, C., and Wyrwa, D. *Philosophie der Kaiserzeit und Spätantike*, vol. 5/2. Basel: Schwabe, 2018.

Sedley, D. "The Dramatis Personae of Plato's *Phaedo*," *Proceedings of the British Academy* 85 (1995): 3–26.

Van Riel, G. "Damascius," in *The Cambridge History of Philosophy in Late Antiquity*, vol. 2, ed. Lloyd P. Gerson. Cambridge: Cambridge University Press, 2010: 667–696.

Van Riel, G. "The One, the Henads, and the Principles," in *All from One: A Guide to Proclus*, ed. P. D'Hoine and M. Martijn. Oxford: Oxford University Press, 2017: 73–97.

The Ideas as Thoughts of God

John Dillon and Daniel J. Tolan

THE OLD ACADEMY

The precise origin of the concept of the Platonic Forms, or Ideas, as thoughts of God is a long-standing puzzle in the history of Platonism, which I am on record as dismissing somewhat brusquely in various works.[1] I propose to begin my consideration of it on this occasion by returning to the seminal article of Audrey Rich, published in *Mnemosyne* back in 1954.[2] Rich's thesis in that article was that the concept arose, whenever it arose – sometime in the early Hellenistic age, was her guess – as a reaction to Aristotle's concept of the Unmoved Mover of *Met.* Lambda as an intellect thinking itself, and 'a desire to reconcile the Theory of Ideas with the Aristotelian doctrine of immanent form' (p. 132).

It seems to me that Rich was broadly correct in this conjecture, but that she was simply too cautious in her attribution of the origin of the theory. I would argue – and have indeed argued on a number of occasions before this – that really all that is required for the development of such a theory (though no doubt stimulated by both the theorizing and the gibes of Aristotle) is the postulation that the account of the nature and activities of the Demiurge in Plato's *Timaeus* is not to be taken literally; and we know this position to have been maintained, among his immediate

---

[*] This chapter is an expanded version of chapter 3 in John Dillon's *The Roots of Platonism* (Cambridge: Cambridge University Press, 2019), with additional sections by Daniel Tolan.

[1] For example, John Dillon, *The Middle Platonists* (London/Ithaca, 1977), p. 95; *The Heirs of Plato* (Oxford, 2003), pp. 107–11.

[2] 'The Platonic Ideas as the Thoughts of God', *Mnemosyne* ser. 4, vol. 7 (1954), pp. 123–33.

successors, by both Speusippus and Xenocrates.[3] After all, once it has been agreed that the Demiurge and his temporal creative activities, involving his contemplating of a Paradigm distinct from, and logically superior to himself, is a myth, the alternative more or less imposes itself of a divine intellect eternally engaged in creative activity, modelling the physical universe which it creates upon a system of formal principles which constitute the contents of its intellect. How this would have worked for Speusippus is less perspicuous, I think, than how it would have worked for Xenocrates,[4] so it is to Xenocrates that I prefer to turn.

First of all, it seems best to distinguish what we know, or think we know, about Xenocrates' theology, before we turn to the airing of conjectures, however plausible. From the doxographic notice of Aetius (*Placita* I 7, 30, p. 304 Diels[5] = Fr. 15 Heinze/213 Isnardi Parente), we may gather that, for Xenocrates, the supreme principle was, among other things, an Intellect. The relevant part of the passage runs as follows:

Xenocrates, son of Agathenor, of Chalcedon, <holds> as gods the Monad and the Dyad, the former as male, having the role of Father, reigning in the heavens (*en ouranōi basileuousan*), which he terms 'Zeus' and 'odd' (*perittos*) and 'intellect' (*nous*), which is for him the primary God.

We have, then, a primary God (*prōtos theos*), who is both unitary and an intellect (no contradiction between these two characterizations, it seems, being discerned by philosophers before Plotinus). The Monad is also identified by Xenocrates, as we learn from Plutarch (*Proc. An.* 1012E), as 'the undivided and unchanging' element in the formation of the World Soul by the Demiurge at *Timaeus* 35A. This latter piece of information might seem to pose a problem, but it really ceases to be such, if we bear in mind the other fact that we think we know about Xenocrates, mentioned above: to wit, that he did not take the creation account in the *Timaeus* literally. This would make it more or less inevitable that the Demiurge be identified with Xenocrates' Nous-Monad, and that it is the blending of this entity with his second principle, the Indefinite Dyad (represented by 'that substance which is divided about bodies'), that produces Soul.

---

[3] Scholiast on Ar. *De Caelo* 279b32ff. = Speusippus, Fr. 61 Tarán.

[4] For Speusippus, after all, the supreme principles are a (supra-essential) One and an Indefinite Dyad, or (principle of) Multiplicity (*plēthos*), so that demiurgic activity proper, together with the generation of Forms (and their projection on the material substratum to form the physical world) becomes the role rather of the World Soul.

[5] Originally derived from Stobaeus, *Anth.* I 36 Wachs.

If the above be accepted as data that we can rely on, then all that calls for conjecture, it seems to me, is the contents of this divine intellect. Here, although explicit evidence fails us, we are left with some pointers. We know a certain amount about Xenocrates' theory of Forms, after all, albeit mainly from the hostile reports of Aristotle. Aristotle reports indignantly (or derisively)[6] that Xenocrates identified the Forms with numbers, but he nowhere specifies where Xenocrates wished to situate them. From certain remarks of Theophrastus, in his little aporetic volume entitled *Metaphysics* (2. 10, 5b26 ff.), however, we might conclude that some Platonist (presumably Xenocrates), had a concept of the first princple that combined Aristotle's Unmoved Mover (about which Theophrastus has just been raising some problems), with something rather more positive, derived from a demythologized interpretation of the *Timaeus*. The problem that Theophrastus is raising here is why, if the first principle wishes the best for all its products, they are not all equally good:[7]

And if from the best comes the best, the heavenly bodies should derive something finer than their rotation from the first principle, unless indeed they were prevented by not being able to receive anything better; *for surely that which is first and most divine is something that wishes for everything what is best.* But perhaps this is something immoderate and not to be sought for; for he who says this is demanding that all things should be alike and in the best of all states, exhibiting little or no difference between them.

Now this may or may not be a very effective line of criticism. The important thing for our purposes, though, is what it is a criticism *of.* Not, surely, any longer Aristotle's Prime Mover, for that wishes nothing for anything. This entity seems rather to be a combination of the Aristotelian Prime Mover with something like a demythologized Timaean Demiurge, who does 'wish all things to be as good as possible' (*Tim.* 29E); and that, I suggest, is the sort of entity that Xenocrates wished to postulate his Nous-Monad as being. What we seem to have here, then, is a Prime Mover with some form of outward-directed intentionality; and it can hardly wish the best for all things without having some conception, first of all, of the things concerned, and secondly, what would be their best state. We have here, then, a God with Thoughts, thoughts which are formative of physical reality.

---

[6] For example, *Met.* H 1028b24ff.; M 1076a20ff.; N 1085 6a5ff.

[7] I have discussed this passage already in John Dillon, 'Theophrastus' Critique of the Old Academy in the *Metaphysics*', in W. W. Fortenbaugh and G. Wöhrle (eds.), *On the Opuscula of Theophrastus* (Stuttgart, 2002), pp. 175–87.

To support this, there is also the contemporary, if rather dim-witted, attestation of the Sicilian Alcimus,[8] reported by Diogenes Laertius (III 13), that 'each one of the Forms is eternal, a thought (*noēma*), and moreover impervious to change'. Alcimus does not specify who is thinking the thought that each Form is, but in the context it really cannot be an individual human mind; the Forms must be the thoughts of an eternal Thinker. Such a report need not be dismissed out of hand as a misunderstanding of Plato's own doctrine;[9] it may well reflect the accepted position of the Academy under Xenocrates.

Lastly, the Xenocratean definition of the soul – also satirized by Aristotle[10] – as 'number moving itself' (*arithmos heauton kinōn*) would seem to indicate that, since Forms are held by Xenocrates to be numbers, what Soul does is to set in motion, and project further, the Forms that are imprinted on it by Intellect. What Soul adds to what it receives from Intellect is motion, in the sense of both mobility and motivity.

ANTIOCHUS OF ASCALON

The evidence, then, for the doctrine of Forms as thoughts of God in the Old Academy, at least from Xenocrates on, while no more than circumstantial, is, I think, reasonably plausible.[11] We must now examine the further stages of its development, where the evidence is firmer.

First we must turn to Antiochus of Ascalon. It happens that I have just been reading through a distinguished collection of essays on Antiochus, products of a conference held in Cambridge in July 2007 (in which I was not involved), shortly to be published by Cambridge University Press, and I have been interested by the attitudes of the participants to the possibility that Antiochus had a Theory of Forms of any kind. There is an 'austere' view of the evidence, propagated by Jonathan Barnes in an influential paper,[12] which basically denies that we can attribute to Antiochus anything like

---

[8] Alcimus' purpose in writing his book was to prove that Plato had borrowed all his best ideas from Epicharmus – a piece of Sicilian chauvinism over which we will draw a veil.

[9] After all, the argument presented in the *Parmenides* (132Bff.) against the Forms being thoughts need not be relevant here. That is an argument against subjectivity: the Forms being merely constructs of the human mind.

[10] *De An.* I 2, 404b27–8, etc. (= Fr. 60 H/165–87 IP).

[11] While recognizing that we have no explicit evidence of Polemon's views on the Forms or their proper place, there is no reason to suppose that he would have dissented from the position of Xenocrates in this matter.

[12] 'Antiochus of Ascalon', in J. Barnes and M. Griffin (eds.), *Philosophia Togata: Essays on Philosophy and Roman Society* (Oxford, 1989), pp. 51–96 (see esp. appendix E).

a Platonic Theory of Forms, and this line is broadly followed by, for instance, Charles Brittain, while Mauro Bonazzi, and, I am glad to say, David Sedley, adopt a more 'generous' interpretation of the evidence, with which I would concur. Neither, however, seems to me to accord proper attention to the evidence of Antiochus' faithful follower M. Terentius Varro, to which I would accord considerable weight (see below, 40).

It was the view of Willy Theiler,[13] enunciated back in 1930, that the theory of the Forms as thoughts of God was in fact an innovation of Antiochus himself. As will be clear from what has preceded, I do not see this theory as Antiochus' invention, but I do agree that Antiochus contributes a new twist to it. This 'twist' comes, in my view, from Antiochus' thoroughgoing adoption of Stoic metaphysics. This in turn results from Antiochus' judgement that the Stoic doctrine of God and his relation to the world may be viewed as merely a formalization of Plato's doctrine in the *Timaeus*, as this was rationalized in the later Academy by Xenocrates and Polemon. This rationalization involves, first, demythologizing the account of the creation of the soul and the world by the Demiurge, so that the Demurge becomes a divine intellect, whose action upon the universe is eternal rather than initiated at a point in time, and who is employing for this action, not any kind of 'paradigm' external to himself, but rather the contents of his own intellect. If Polemon contributed anything further to this scenario, it would in my view be the specification that this divine intellect is not transcendent over, but immanent within the cosmos – if we may derive that conclusion from the admittedly very bald doxographic report by Aetius[14] that 'Polemon declared that the cosmos was God'.

This in turn brings us very near to the Stoic position, as enunciated by Polemon's erstwhile pupil Zeno. The only question that remains uncertain is whether Polemon still retained a belief in immaterial essence, as being proper to God – and indeed to Forms and Soul – or whether he had been prepared to entertain the theory that was going the rounds in some quarters in the later Academy (such as Heraclides of Pontus, for example)[15] that soul, at least, and possibly also the supreme divinity, was composed instead of a very special kind of fire (comparable to Aristotelian aether), of which the stars also are composed.

---

[13] In *Die Vorbereitung des Neuplatonismus* (Berlin, 1930).

[14] Reported in Stobaeus, *Anth.* I 36, 5 W.-H., just before his doxographic report of Xenocrates' views, discussed above, 35–37. It is not in fact entirely clear to me whether Xenocrates in his turn regarded this supreme Nous-Monad as transcending the cosmos, as he presents it as 'ruling in the heavens'. But that cannot be pressed too far, I suppose.

[15] Cf. Frs. 98–9 Wehrli.

I put forward this possibility only very tentatively, and it is by no means crucial to my overall position. There is no need to deny Zeno and his followers a certain measure of originality, and the development of a doctrine of 'craftsmanly fire' (*pyr tekhnikon*) as a suitable material for the Active Principle of the universe to be composed of can be seen as a reasonable solution to certain worries about the mode of interaction between immaterial and material essence that seem to have been besetting the Academy in the decades before Zeno appeared on the scene. After all, a key dictum on this topic can be derived (and seems to have been so derived by Zeno, among others – including Antiochus later) from Plato's *Sophist* 248C: 'We proposed as a sufficient mark of real things the presence in a thing of the power of being acted upon or of acting in relation to however insignificant a thing.' The conclusion is ready to hand that things cannot act upon one another, or be acted upon, unless they have some quality or substance in common, and that would be some degree of materiality.

However, I am in danger of wandering from the main point. This is all by way of background to what I wish to maintain, to wit, that Antiochus need not have felt that accepting the Stoic doctrine of *pyr tekhnikon* or *pyr noeron* was in conflict with his position as a champion of the Old Academy – an institution about whose views, as we must continually remind ourselves, he knew a great deal more than we do. Once that is accepted, it seems to me that Antiochus can both employ very Platonic-sounding terminology to describe the Forms, as he (or at least his spokesman, 'Varro') does at *Acad.* I 30–2: 'that which is eternally simple and uniform and identical with itself' – a formulation borrowed pretty closely from *Phaedo* 78D – and yet view these Forms, or this system of Forms, as none other than the system of *logoi spermatikoi* constituting the contents of the cosmic Logos, this Logos in turn being for him nothing other than an updating and rationalization of the Demiurge and World Soul of the *Timaeus*. And of course, in the Stoic system, which Antiochus could quite happily adopt, the contents of the cosmic Logos are reflected in the contents of our individual minds, since our minds are mere sparks, so to speak, emanating from the cosmic Logos. In this way, the Forms can be also seen as concepts (*ennoiai* or *prolēpseis*) in our minds. This does not, however, make them purely subjective entities, as they are only reflections of the *logoi spermatikoi* in the Logos.

Now all this seems to me quite a logical development, and it seems to me perfectly reasonable also that Antiochus should express himself, in describing his Theory of Forms, with what must appear to us a certain degree of systematic ambiguity, but I have to recognize that, to a certain type of scholarly mind of the Barnesian persuasion, all this appears quite fantastic.

To quote Barnes himself, in the paper above-mentioned: 'Any attempt to reconstruct Antiochus' thought requires fantasy and imagination. But fantasy must be responsible to the evidence, and imagination must acknowledge one sobering fact: we do not know very much about Antiochus.' My reply to that is that, if one is not prepared to make (judicious) use of fantasy and imagination, not only in respect of Antiochus, but also in respect of the Old Academy and of Middle Platonism in general, one had better steer clear of the area altogether. It all depends, after all, what one regards as 'evidence'; the attitude of a forensic defence lawyer, favoured by Barnes and others, such as Charles Brittain, is not going to get us very far at all.

After getting that off my chest, I turn to what I regard as a decisive piece of evidence as to Antiochus' theory of the Forms as thoughts of God, and that is a passage from the works of his follower Varro, preserved in Augustine's *De Civitate Dei* (VII 28).[16] The context is slightly odd, but compelling enough for all that. I will quote it at some length, as it gives a useful insight into Varro's Antiochian theology in general:[17]

What success attends the effort of Varro, that shrewdest of scholars, to reduce those gods, by would-be subtle arguments, to the sky and the earth, and give that reference to them all? The attempt is impossible. The gods wriggle out of his clutches; they jump from his hands, slip away, and tumble to the ground. Before speaking of the females, the goddesses that is, he says:
    '*As I have already said in the first book about places,*[18] *there are two recognised sources of origin for the gods, the sky and the earth. Hence some gods are called celestial, others terrestrial. I started, earlier on, with the sky, speaking about Janus, whom some have identified with the sky, others with the world. So now I will begin to treat of feminine deities by speaking about Tellus.*'
    I understand the difficulty experienced by an intelligence of such range and quality. A plausible line of argument leads him to see the sky as an active principle, the earth as passive. And so he attributes masculine energy to the former, feminine to the latter; and he fails to realise that the activity in both spheres is the activity of

---

[16] The suggestion, put forward by Barnesians (such as David Blank in the collection of essays above-mentioned), that it is rash to assume that Varro is simply representing the position of Antiochus on philosophical questions, is surely quite absurd. Varro was indeed a very learned man in many areas, but in philosophy he is attested, by both Cicero and Augustine, on the basis of evidence available to them, to be a thoroughgoing disciple of Antiochus, and there is no reason to doubt this.

[17] Augustine is quoting here from the final book of Varro's vast compilation *Antiquitates rerum humanarum et divinarum*, in forty-one books, the last fifteen of which concerned divine matters. In this final book, he discussed 'select gods', that is, the central deities of the Greco-Roman pantheon. I employ here the Penguin translation of Henry Bettenson.

[18] That, it would seem from *CD* VI 3, means the fourth book of the second part of the *Antiquitates*, and the twenty-ninth of the whole work.

him who created both.[19] Varro uses the same line of interpretation in his previous book,[20] in dealing with the celebrated mysteries of Samothrace.

He starts by making a solemn undertaking (adopting a kind of religious tone of voice) that he will explain those teachings in writing and convey their meaning to the Samothracians themselves, who do not understand their purport. He says, in fact, that a study of the evidence in Samothrace leads to the conclusion that one of their images represented the sky, another the earth, another the archetypes which Plato called 'forms'. He urges that Jupiter should be understood as the sky, Juno as the earth, Minerva as the forms; the sky being maker, the earth material, the forms providing the patterns for creation. I pass over the fact that Plato ascribes such importance to his 'forms' that, according to him, the sky does not create anything, using them as patterns ; in fact it is itself so created.

Augustine tries here to confute Varro by appealing to a literal interpretation of Plato's *Timaeus,* in accordance with which the heavens are created with the rest of the world (*Tim.* 37D), but this just serves to point up the fact that Varro/Antiochus is basing himself on a demythologized, Stoicized interpretation of the same dialogue, according to which the Demiurge becomes the Stoic active principle (*to poioun*), while the Receptacle becomes the passive principle, and the Paradigm the active principle's creative reason-principles, or *logoi*.

What we may note in particular about this piece of allegorization by Varro is the natural and uncontroversial way in which he introduces the conception that Minerva (Athena), springing as she does from the head of Zeus, may represent the totality of Forms as thoughts of God. Varro is not trying to introduce his readers to this concept as something innovative; rather, he is making use of it, as something he expects to be well recognized, as a basis for delivering an allegorization of the Great Gods of Samothrace. This should surely tell us something about the degree of acceptability of the concept of the Forms as thoughts of God in the intellectual circle which Varro is addressing.

---

[19] Here Augustine slips in a bit of propaganda for his own (Christian) position. In fact, we see here Varro adopting, as did Antiochus, the basic Stoic distinction between an active and passive principle in the universe, symbolizing the first by the sky and masculine divinities, the latter by the earth and feminine divinities. There is no question of postulating a further, higher divinity, 'who created both'.

[20] That is to say, Book 40, in which he discussed 'uncertain gods', that is, divinities which it is difficult to identify with certainty. The identity of the Kabeiroi, the Great Gods of Samothrace was quite uncertain, since they were pre-Indo-European entities, but conjecture linked them with the Dioscuri, who had a heavenly and a chthonic aspect.

PHILO OF ALEXANDRIA

So then, I would maintain, a Stoicized version of the doctrine of the Forms as thoughts of God is a feature of the Platonism propounded by Antiochus of Ascalon. Let us move on from this, then, to observe its next manifestation.

This occurs in the works of the Platonizing Alexandrian Jewish philosopher Philo, a half-century after Antiochus. Philo is actually the first author unequivocally to present the formulation of Forms as thoughts of God, and this circumstance has unfortunately seduced some Philo scholars, such as Roberto Radice of Milan, in his study *Platonismo e creazionismo in Filone di Alessandria* (Milan, 1989), to claim him as the inventor of it. While this notion is plainly quite untenable, there is yet a certain amount for which Philo may perhaps be given credit. Philo inherits a Platonism which seems to have evolved somewhat from the solidly Stoicized metaphysics propounded by Antiochus towards a renewed concept of the transcendence and immateriality of God, helped on its way, it would seem, by the revival, in the mid-first century BC, of the Pythagorean tradition, which may be associated with the figure of Eudorus of Alexandria, an older contemporary of Philo's, with whom he may have been personally acquainted. At any rate, we find in Philo, particularly in such a work as the *De Opificio Mundi,* a system involving a transcendent supreme God, an intelligible world (*kosmos noetos*), presented as the 'internal reason' (*logos endiathetos*) of God, and a Logos that goes forth and creates the physical cosmos (*logos prophorikos*), and thereafter holds it together. At *Opif.* 16, for instance, we find the following description of God's creative activity:

For God, because he is God, understood in advance that a beautiful copy (*mimēma*) would not come into existence apart from a beautiful model (*paradeigma*), and that none of the objects of sense-perception would be without fault, unless it was modeled on the archetypal and intelligible Idea. Having resolved to create this visible world of ours, He fashioned first the intelligible world, in order that in fashioning the physical world he might be able to use an immaterial and most godlike model, producing from this older model a younger copy which would contain within itself as many sensible classes of being as there were intelligible ones in the original.[21]

This plainly owes much to the *Timaeus* (28AB, 48E, etc.), but with the significant difference that now the paradigm is nothing other than the

---

[21] Philo, *On the Creation (De Opificio Mundi),* I. v. I, trans. F. H. Colson and G. H. Whitaker.

contents of the divine intellect. Philo goes on (17–18) to present us with the vivid image of an architect being commissioned to build a fine city, with all its accoutrements (he probably has the original planning of Alexandria in mind!), and carrying round the whole plan of the city in his head as a model in accordance to which he can refer when laying out the physical city. Such is God's situation with regard to the physical universe. Now, the elaboration of this exemplum is no doubt Philo's own work, but the exemplum itself may not be original to him. It bears a certain similarity to the exemplum used by Cicero in *Orator* s.8, which adduces Pheidias and his statues of Zeus and Athena, and which may well derive from Antiochus (though the 'austere' school of thought would demur on this, since Antiochus is not referred to); but there is also the significant difference that Pheidias is presumed to be contemplating something like a 'Platonic' Form of the divinity concerned, whereas the architect is simply drawing on his own expertise. However, as we shall see in a moment, both images seem to be combined in the reference to the artist adduced by Alcinous, in ch. 9 of his *Didaskalikos,* to which we may now turn.

ALCINOUS AND MIDDLE PLATONISM

There is much more evidence, of course, to be derived from Philo, but I take it that on this occasion I am not so much delivering a general survey of the concept of the Forms as thoughts of God in the later Platonist tradition as trying to establish its provenance, so we may spare ourselves a full investigation of Philo's employment of the concept. On the face of it, his main contribution (though I do not believe that it is original to himself)[22] is the concept of the *kosmos noetos* – although even this is not much more than a demythologization of the 'intelligible living being' (*noēton zōion*) of *Tim.* 30C–31B.

Let us turn instead to a consideration of Alcinous. Alcinous (now that we are no longer allowed to identify him with Albinus) is a slightly mysterious figure, but he may reasonably be situated in the mid-second century AD, and his *Didaskalikos,* or 'Handbook of Platonism', does not aspire to be a work of any originality – indeed, there is some evidence

---

[22] We may note that Timaeus Locrus uses the phrase *idanikos kosmos* (§30), and he is hardly likely to be dependent on Philo, even if he post-dates him. The influence is more likely to be the other way about (Philo does at least know of pseudo-Pythagoric writings, such as that of Ocellus Lucanus (*Aet.* 12)).

(including one more or less verbatim passage in ch. 12) that his work is essentially an 'update' of a similar work by Arius Didymus, back in the late first century BC.[23] At any rate, there can be little chance that he is in any way influenced by Philo.

What he presents us with, in ch. 9, is a fairly bald summary of Platonist doctrine on the Forms. It is worth quoting this at some length:[24]

Matter constitutes one principle,[25] but Plato postulates others also, to wit, the paradigmatic, that is the Forms, and that constituted by God, the father and cause of all things. Form (*idea*) is considered, in relation to God, his thinking (*noēsis*); in relation to us, the primary object of thought (*prōton noēton*); in relation to matter, measure (*metron*); in relation to the sensible world, its paradigm; and in relation to itself, essence. For in general everything that we can conceptualize must come to be in reference to something of which the model (*paradeigma*) must pre-exist, just as if one thing were to be derived from another, in the way that my image derives from me; and even if the model does not always subsist eternally, in any event every artist, having the model within himself, applies the structure of it to matter.

He goes on to say, just below, in connection with the question 'Of what things are there Forms?', that 'the Forms are the eternal and perfect thoughts of God'. And just below that again, in relation to the question 'Are there such things as Forms?', he argues: 'Whether God is an intellect or possessed of an intellect, he has thoughts, and these are eternal and unchanging; and if this is the case, Forms exist.'

We see here the theory of Forms as thoughts of God in what one might term its 'classical' or fully fledged form, presented by Alcinous as basic Platonic doctrine. Indeed, the proposition that, since God is either an intellect or at least possessed of an intellect, he must necessarily have thoughts, is used as the premiss for a further conclusion, that there are such things as Forms at all. We may note also the passing allusion to the exemplum of the artist having a conception in his mind, which he then transfers to canvas, or embodies in stone or bronze. This seems to form a bridge between Cicero's Pheidias example and Philo's architect, and indicates that the image was by Alcinous' time a fairly well-worn one, in support of the argument for the Forms being divine thoughts.

In Plutarch also, somewhat earlier than Alcinous, the premiss that the Forms are divine thoughts or *logoi* turns up at a number of points in the

---

[23] *Pace* Tryggve Göransson, *Albinus, Alcinous, Arius Didymus* (Gothenburg, 1995), who produces some good negative arguments, but does not ultimately convince me.

[24] The translation is my own, from John Dillon, *Alcinous, The Handbook of Platonism* (Oxford, 1993).

[25] He has dealt with this in the previous chapter.

corpus, though never (in the surviving works) quite as directly as we find in Alcinous. In the *De sera numinis vindicta,* for example (550D), we find a description of God setting himself up as a paradigm for all moral goodness, and thus establishing that the pursuit of virtue is nothing else than 'assimilation to God' (*homoiosis theōi*). This is not as clear as one might wish as a statement of the theory, but we may combine this with a striking passage from the *De Iside et Osiride* (373AB), where Osiris is presented allegorically as the Logos of God, filled with *logoi* which impress themselves on matter 'like figures stamped on wax' (a reference to *Theaet.* 191Cff.). Further, we find a distinction made between the 'soul' and the 'body' of Osiris, the former being the Logos as residing within the mind of God, the latter the Logos in its emanatory mode, infusing the physical world with its contents – a scenario, indeed, very like that which we found in Philo a few generations earlier.

One finds a somewhat clearer exposition of the doctrine, in fact, in the works of the later Athenian Platonist Atticus, in the second half of the second century. In the course of a polemical treatise entitled *Against Those who Claim to Interpret Plato through Aristotle,*[26] extensive passages of which have been preserved for us by the ecclesiastical writer Eusebius of Caesarea, he has occasion to commend Plato's Theory of Forms (Fr. 7 Baudry):

> It is just in this respect that Plato surpasses all others. Discerning, in relation to the Forms, that God is Father and Creator and lord and guardian of all things, and recognizing, on the analogy of material creations, that the craftsman (*demiourgos*) first forms a conception (*noêsai*) of that which he is proposing to create, and then, once he has formed his conception, applies this likeness to the material, he concludes by analogy that the thoughts (*noêmata*) of God are anterior to material objects, models (*paradeigmata*) of the things that come to be, immaterial and intelligible, always remaining identically the same.

This seems to touch all the right bases, alluding both to the *Timaeus* (God as Father and Maker, *demiourgos, paradeigmata*) and to the *Phaedo* ('always remaining identically the same'), while adducing the process of artistic or craftsmanly creation.

This is not quite the end of the story, however. There is a troubling report, emanating from Proclus (*In Tim.* I 394, 6ff.), via Porphyry, who should have known, criticizing Atticus for situating the Paradigm, as

---

[26] Probably directed against his contemporary, the Peripatetic Aristocles, the teacher of Alexander of Aphrodisias, who had had the audacity to compose a work (also quoted by Eusebius) commending Plato as a promising predecessor of Aristotle.

repository of the Forms, as distinct from, though inferior to, the Demiurge, whom he takes to be the supreme God. One does not know quite what to make of that, but it may be that Atticus, in wishing to preserve the objective reality of the Forms, saw no problem in postulating them as distinct from, though ontologically inferior to, his supreme deity, while also being intelligized by him.[27] At any rate, the problem of their exact status continued into the next century with Longinus, who was head of the Academy in Athens, and Porphyry's teacher before he came to Plotinus in Rome, and in ch. 18 of his *Life of Plotinus,* Porphyry tells against himself the story of his producing this doctrine in Plotinus' seminar, and, after a long debate, being converted to the Plotinian view that the Forms are in fact in the mind of the Demiurge – the only catch being, of course, that now the Demiurge is no longer the supreme principle, but a secondary one, Intellect, the One being superior to the Forms!

ORIGEN AND ANCIENT CHRISTIAN PLATONISM

This is an issue that certainly exercised Plotinus, who would champion the position that the 'intelligibles are not external to the intellect' (V.5). This position, it should be noted, was anticipated by the great Christian theologian Origen. Counterintuitively, however, one finds the grounds for this in Origen's rejection of the '*ideai*' at II.3.6 of *De Principiis*; Origen writes,

It is difficult for us to explain this other world, lest, by chance, it allowed some to think us to affirm certain 'ideas' which the Greeks call ἰδέας. For assuredly it is foreign to us to speak of an incorporeal world, which consists solely of the phantasy of mind or the slippery realm of thoughts.[28]

---

[27] Atticus is also criticized, we may note (along with Plutarch and Democritus the Platonist), by Syrianus, in his *Commentary on the Metaphysics* (p. 105, 35ff.), for holding 'that the Forms are universal reason-principles (*logoi*) subsisting eternally in the substance of the Soul; for even if they distinguish them from the commonalities (*koinotêtes*) present in sensible objects, nevertheless one should not confuse together the reason-principles in the soul and the so-called "enmattered intellect" (*enulos nous*) with the paradigmatic and immaterial Forms and demiurgic intellections.' This complicates the situation even further! See on all this the most judicious analysis of Alexandra Michalewski, *La causalité des formes intelligibles dans la philosophie de Plotin* (Paris, 2008), pp. 71–91.

[28] Origen, *De Prin.* II.3.6; PG 11:195ab: 'Cujus mundi difficilem nobis esse expositionem idcirco praediximus, ne forte praebeatur aliquibus occasio illius intelligentiae, qua putent nos imagines quasdam quas Graeci ἰδέας nominant, affirmare: quod utique a nostris alienum est, mundum incorporeum dicere, in sola mentis phantasia vel cogitationum lubrico consistentem.' Translation by Daniel J. Tolan, in 'The Impact of the Ὁμοούσιον on the Divine Ideas', in P. G. Pavlos, L. F. Janby, E. K. Emilsson, and T. T. Tollefsen (eds.), *Platonism and Christian Thought in Late Antiquity* (London, 2019), p. 135.

While this appears to be an abjuration of Platonic metaphysics, Origen should actually be understood as denying the Athenian reading of the *Timaeus*, which takes the 'living being' as standing apart from the Demiurge.[29] This is to say that Origen is rejecting the proposition that the *ideai* stand apart from the divine mind,[30] not exemplarism. The fact that this is the case is reinforced by the omnipresence of exemplarism throughout Origen's corpus.

Moreover, immediately before his 'rejection' of the *ideai*, Origen is found propounding a specific understanding of exemplarism. One of the central metaphysical moves that Origen wishes to make is to align John's Λόγος with σοφία, as presented in Prov. 8:22. To this end, Origen writes:

> Now, in the same way in which we have understood that Wisdom was the beginning of the ways of God, and is said to be created, prefiguring (*praeformans*) and containing within herself the forms (*species*; *eidē*) and reason-principles (*rationes*; *logoi*) of all creatures, must we understand her to be the Word of God, because of her disclosing to all other beings, i.e., to universal creation, the nature of the mysteries and secrets which are contained within the divine wisdom; and on this account she is called the Word, because she is, as it were, the interpreter of the secrets of the intellect (*arcanorum mentis interpres*).[31]

This passage witnesses to the relationship between the *Logos* and *sophia* by demonstrating that *sophia* is the intelligible world *in se*, while the *Logos* is the intelligibles turned towards creation.[32] Elsewhere, Origen informs us that the emergence of the *theōrēmata* in the *Logos* allows the *Logos* to be understood as the 'image of the invisible', namely the Father; Origen likens this shift from the beyond-intelligible to the intelligible unto a belch which makes hidden wind manifest.[33]

Origen further details the emergence of the intelligible when he discusses God's creation *in sophia* in his *Commentary on John*. Origen deploys imagery familiar from Philo in order to demonstrate the way in which the ideas for creation pre-exist;[34] he writes,

---

[29] For an outline of Alcinous' reading and the Athenian reading of the *Timaeus*, see John P. Kenney, *Mystical Monotheism: A Study in Ancient Platonic Theology*, 2nd ed. (Eugene, 2010), pp. 74–88.

[30] Henri Crouzel and Manlio Simonetti, *Origène, Traité des Principes*, vol. 2 (Paris, 1978), p. 150.

[31] Origen, *De Prin.* II.2.3. Translation is taken in a modified form from Alexander Roberts and James Donaldson (eds.), *Ante-Nicene Fathers, Volume 4: Tertullian, Part Fourth; Minucius Felix; Commodian; Origen, Part First and Second* (New York: Christian Literature Publishing Co., 1885).

[32] Cécile Blanc, *Origène, Commentaire Sur Saint Jean* (Paris, 1966), 120 N2.

[33] Origen, *CommJn.* I.38.283. [34] Philo, *De Opif.* 20.

For I think, just as a house and a ship are built or framed according to architects' plans, the *arche* of the house and of the ship having their respective plans (*tupous*) and reasons (*logous*) in the craftsman; thusly, all things come about according to the reasons (*logous*) made clear in advance by God in wisdom (*sophia*), 'for He made all things in wisdom.' And it must be said, if I might say it thusly, that God made ensouled wisdom, He entrusted to her the moulding (*plasin*) and the forms (*eidē*) for existence (*ousia*) and matter (*hylē*) from the plans (*tupōn*) which exist in her, but I stop short of saying if this is also their essences (*ousias*). Thus, therefore, it is not difficult to say that, roughly, the *arche* of beings (*ontōn*) is the Son of God, as it says, 'I am the *arche* and the *telos*, the A and the Ω, the first and the last.' But, it is necessary to know that He Himself is not called the *arche* according to all that He is called.[35]

Here, one finds the image of the craftsman's thought of his creation discussed at the level of *Sophia-Logos*, not God the Father, for God has entrusted to her the moulding and forms for being. While this distinction might amount to much the same thing in the context of creation,[36] it is of no small significance to Origen's understanding of the relationship between the Father and the Son.[37] All the same, it remains that both the *eidē* and the *logoi* are proper to *sophia*, strengthening our earlier suggestion that the Greek terms *eidē* and *logoi* underlie Rufinus' use of *species* and *rationes*.

It is clear that Origen is presenting an informed response to currents in the Platonism of his day by placing the ideas in the divine mind, which, at times, bears a striking resemblance to Plotinus' second hypostasis. Nevertheless, one must not forget that Origen is likely also indebted to Judeo-Christian figures in Alexandria, such as Philo and Clement. In this regard, one may observe a similarity with Philo when considering the way in which Origen has brought σοφία and the Λόγος together, while retaining their difference.[38] Clement, moreover, provides Origen with Christian

---

[35] Origen, *CommJn.* I.19.114–16 (trans. Daniel J. Tolan, 'The Impact of the Ὁμοούσιον on the Divine Ideas', p. 135.

[36] Hal Koch, *Pronoia Und Paideusis: Studien Über Origenes Und Sein Verhältnis Zum Platonismus* (Berlin, 1932), p. 255.

[37] Origen, *CommJn.* II.2.18.1–7 (trans. Daniel J. Tolan, 'Origen's Refutation of the Divine Ideas in Περὶ Ἀρχῶν II.2.6 as the Emergence of "Neoplatonism"', in *Studia Patristica*, forthcoming):

Therefore the God is true God. And the gods are formed according to him as icons of the prototype; but again the archetypal icon of the many icons is the λόγος who is with the God, who was 'in the beginning', by virtue of being 'with the God', always remaining 'God', and he would not possess this if he were not with God; yet, he would not remain God, if he did not remain in unbroken contemplation of the paternal depth.

[38] Philo distinguishes Sophia from the Logos by presenting the former as the 'mother' of the latter (e.g. *Fug.* 109; *Det.* 115–16).

precedent for considering God as the divine mind, or place of the ideas.[39] Or, put in other terms, for Clement an *idea* is a thought (*ennoēma*) of God.[40] Where Origen differs significantly from Clement is the way in which the intelligibles emerge. Clement makes clear that the *Logos*, as the intelligible realm, comes out of the divine mind.[41] This is very much in the middle Platonic tradition of 'two minds'.[42] Origen, on the other hand, appears to be arriving at Neoplatonism by placing the Father *beyond* the Son, with the ideas emerging at the level of the Son;[43] one such instance of this is when Origen notes that the Father, being the father of truth, wisdom, and light, is beyond truth, wisdom, and light because he is their source.[44]

While the position of the ideas in Origen's thought appears to reflect the transition from Middle Platonism to Neoplatonism, it remains a witness to the way in which Christians baptized this tradition by fitting it to the exigencies of their own tradition and scriptural authorities.[45] Moreover, by the time one reaches Augustine, this doctrine has been fully embraced. Augustine notes the centrality of the ideas to creation when he notes,

the ideas are certain original and principal forms of things, i.e., reasons, fixed and unchangeable, which are not themselves formed and, being thus eternal and existing always in the same state, are contained in the Divine Intelligence. And though they themselves neither come into being nor pass away, nevertheless, everything which can come into being and pass away and everything which does come into being and pass away is said to be formed in accord with these ideas.[46]

Thus, the divine ideas are seen as the unchanging and stable basis of creation. Augustine reiterates that the ideas are squarely in the mind of God when he notes,

---

[39] Clement, *Strom.* IV.155.2, V.73.2.   [40] Clement, *Strom.* V.16.3.

[41] Clement, *Strom.* V.16.5.

[42] Numenius may be taken as a representative of this sort of theology. He presents the 'first God' at rest and devoted to the contemplation of the *noēta*, while the 'second god' is in motion and concerned with both the *noetic* and the sensible (Fr. 15); cf. John Dillon, *The Middle Platonists*, 2nd ed. (Ithaca and London, 1996), 367; Kenney *Mystical Monotheism*, p. 73; Eric F. Osborn, *Clement of Alexandria* (Cambridge, 2005), pp. 116–22. Alcinous also posits an intellect that transcends the divine intellect, which contemplates the ideas (*Didaskalikos* 10.2).

[43] Henri Crouzel, *Origène Et Plotin: Comparaisons Doctrinales* (Paris, 1991), pp. 39–40; 79–80.

[44] Origen, *CommJn.* II.23.151; cf. *CommJn.* I.10.119.

[45] Clement explicitly notes the parallel with Plato (*Strom.* V.73.3).

[46] David L. Mosher (trans.), *Augustine, Eighty-Three Different Questions* (Washington, D.C., 1982), 46.2.

As for these reasons, they must be thought to exist nowhere but in the very mind of the Creator. For it would be sacrilegious to suppose that he was looking at something placed outside himself when he created in accord with it what he did create.[47]

Accordingly, one can see the migration of the ideas into the mind of God gaining demonstrable traction in Christian metaphysics.

The divine ideas receive one further twist in the thought of Maximus the Confessor, who wishes to associate the ideas more closely with the divine will. While Maximus holds traditional positions, such as the Logos containing in Himself the pre-existing *logoi* and that the belief that the pre-existing *logoi* are the basis of creation,[48] he also introduces the element of God's will through his exegesis of Dionysius the Areopagite.[49] Although one might not be able to separate divine thinking from divine willing neatly,[50] it is clear that Maximus wishes to emphasize the existence of the ideas in God's will in order to maintain God's transcendence. This much is clear when Maximus writes, 'For it is not possible . . . that He who is beyond all beings should know beings in a manner derived from beings, but we say that He knows beings as His own wills'.[51] Thus, while Maximus asserts that God foreknows all that is to come about,[52] he also wishes to maintain that God is beyond the intelligence of any creature. Nevertheless, Maximus wishes to retain the position that God is actively planning out and being attentive to creation. Thus, Maximus leans on God's will in order to explain how God is beyond creaturely cognition while simultaneously being mindful of creatures themselves.

CONCLUSION

While the precise emergence of the divine idea tradition may be contestable, what is not contestable is that it came to be an enduring means by which to consider God's relationship to the world. Moreover, this understanding of creation has proven economical enough to be valued in Platonic, Jewish, and Christian thought, as is demonstrated by the figures touched upon in the preceding. With this doctrine alone one is able to answer the Platonic question of the one and the many and metaphysical

---

[47] Mosher, *Augustine, Eighty-Three Different Questions*, 46.2.

[48] Maximus, *Amb Io.* 7.16; cf. 7.19.

[49] *Amb Io.* 7.24.1–2: Τούτους δὲ οὓς ἔφην τοὺς λόγους ὁ μὲν Ἀρεοπαγίτης ἅγιος Διονύσιος "προορισμοὺς" καὶ "θεῖα θελήματα".

[50] Consider the way in which Plotinus brings both of these together in *Enneads* VI.8.6.36.

[51] Maximus, *Amb. Io.* 7.24.11–14.   [52] Maximus, *Amb Io.* 7.19.

inquiries that are both epistemological and axiological. Thus, the above establishes the provenance of the divine ideas by detailing not only the emergence of the tradition, but also by drawing attention to some of the important commitments that developed as the doctrine was further articulated.

Bibliography

Augustine, *Concerning the City of God against the Pagans*, trans. Henry Bettenson. London: Penguin Books, 2003.

Barnes, J. 'Antiochus of Ascalon', in J. Barnes and M. Griffin (eds.), *Philosophia Togata: Essays on Philosophy and Roman Society*. Oxford: Oxford University Press, 1989, 51–96.

Blanc, Cécile. *Origène, Commentaire Sur Saint Jean*. Paris: Éditions du Cerf, 1966.

Colson, F. H. and G. H. Whitaker, trans. *Philo*, vol. 1. Loeb Classical Library. Cambridge, MA: Harvard University Press, 1971.

Constas, Nicholas. *Maximus the Confessor, On Difficulties in the Church Fathers: the Ambigua*, vol. 1. Cambridge, MA: Harvard University Press, 2014.

Crouzel, Henri. *Origène et Plotin: Comparaisons Doctrinales*. Paris: Téqui, 1991.

Crouzel, Henri and Manlio Simonetti. *Origène, Traité Des Principes*, vol. 2. Paris: Éditions du Cerf, 1978.

Des Places, Édouard. *Numénius, Fragments*. Paris: Les Belles Lettres, 1973.

Dillon, J. *Alcinous, The Handbook of Platonism*. Oxford: Oxford University Press, 1993.

The Heirs of Plato. Oxford: Oxford University Press, 2003.

The Middle Platonists. London/Ithaca: Cornell University Press, 1977 (2nd ed. 1996).

'Theophrastus' Critique of the Old Academy in the *Metaphysics*', in W. W. Fortenbaugh and G. Wöhrle (eds.), *On the Opuscula of Theophrastus*. Stuttgart: Franz Steiner Verlag, 2002, 175–87.

Ferrari, F. *Dio, idee e materia: la struttura del cosmo in Plutarco di Cheronea*. Naples: D'Auria, 1995.

Göransson, Tryggve. *Albinus, Alcinous, Arius Didymus*. Gothenburg: Acta Universitatis Gothoburgensis, 1995.

Kenney, John P. *Mystical Monotheism: A Study in Ancient Platonic Theology*. Hanover: Brown University Press, 1991. 2nd ed. Eugene, Oregon: Wipf and Stock, 2010.

Koch, Hal. *Pronoia und Paideusis: Studien über Origenes und sein Verhältnis zum Platonismus*. Berlin: De Gruyter, 1932.

Michalewski, A. *La causalité des Formes intelligibles dans la philosophie de Plotin*. Paris: Leuven University Press, 2008.

Mosher, David L., trans. *Augustine, Eighty-Three Different Questions*. Washington, D.C.: Catholic University of America Press, 1982.

Osborn, Eric F. *Clement of Alexandria*. Cambridge: Cambridge University Press, 2005.

Radice, R. *Platonismo e creazionismo in Filone di Alessandria*. Milan: Pubblicazioni del Centro di richerche di metafisica, 1989.

Rich, A. 'The Platonic Ideas as the Thoughts of God', *Mnemosyne* ser. 4, vol. 7 (1954): 123–33.

Roberts, Alexander and James Donaldson, eds. *Ante-Nicene Fathers, Volume 4: Tertullian, Part Fourth; Minucius Felix; Commodian; Origen, Part First and Second*. New York: Christian Literature Publishing Co., 1885.

Theiler, W. *Die Vorbereitung des Neuplatonismus*. Berlin: Weidmann, 2001.

Tolan, Daniel J. 'The Impact of the Ὁμοούσιον on the Divine Ideas', in P. G. Pavlos, L. F. Janby, E. K. Emilsson, and T. T. Tollefsen (eds.), *Platonism and Christian Thought in Late Antiquity*. London: Routledge, 2019.

'Origen's Refutation of the Divine Ideas in Περὶ Ἀρχῶν II.2.6 as the Emergence of "Neoplatonism"', *Studia Patristica*, forthcoming.

1.3

The One and the Trinity

Andrew Radde-Gallwitz

But [Plato] also says that there is a "Father of the Cause."[1]

The confession of Christian faith that emerged from late antiquity with
imperial and ecclesiastical sanction was novel. The church professed belief
in a creator God, a metaphysical first principle, who is not merely undifferentiated, simple unity, but "one God in Trinity and Trinity in unity."[2]
Triads there had been, but to proclaim the first principle as triadic unity
was new. Platonists had articulated a triad of three moments – being, life,
and intellect – in the hypostasis of *nous*, but for them *nous* was not
metaphysically first or ultimate; the absolutely first principle was the
utterly simple One or the Good.[3] Trinitarian faith, by contrast, contained
two essential elements: a distinction of three hypostases and an identity of
the three in substance, power, and glory, with no priority residing in either
the unity or the trinity. Yet the uniqueness of this creed does not mean that
its defenders relied solely on natively Christian premises. To the contrary,
the principal Greek and Latin pro-Nicene theologians from the late fourth
century drew extensively on non-Christian philosophical resources, and
Platonism in particular, in their Trinitarian theologies.

---

[1] Plotinus, *Enn.* 5.1.8.4, quoting Plato, *ep.* 6, 323d4.   [2] *Quicumque vult* (4 Burn).
[3] See John Dillon, "Logos and Trinity: Patterns of Platonist Influence on Early Christianity,"
in Godfrey Vesey, ed., *The Philosophy in Christianity* (Cambridge: Cambridge University
Press, 1989), 1–13; John D. Turner, "The Platonizing Sethian Treatises, Marius
Victorinus's Philosophical Sources, and Pre-Plotinian *Parmenides* Commentaries," in
John D. Turner and Kevin Corrigan, eds., *Plato's Parmenides and its Heritage*, vol. 1:
History and Interpretation from the Old Academy to Later Platonism and Gnosticism
(Atlanta: Society of Biblical Literature Publications, 2010), 131–172; cf. Augustine,
Confessions XIII.xi.12.

In fact, several Christian theologians presented the Christian Trinity as not wholly unique within ancient thought. A tradition going back to the second century sought to underscore the fundamental harmony between Christian and Platonist conceptions of the first principle. In his apologetic *Legatio* (*c.* AD 170–180), Athenagoras summarizes Plato's theological views. He says, with reference to *Timaeus* 28c, "Here [Plato] understands the unoriginated and eternal (ἀγένητον καὶ ἀίδιον) God to be one."[4] When Athenagoras turns to Christian belief, he picks up directly from his characterization of Plato: according to Christians, God is "unoriginated, eternal (ἀγένητον καὶ ἀίδιον), invisible, impassible, incomprehensible, and uncontained, apprehensible by mind and reason alone (νῷ μόνῳ καὶ λόγῳ καταλαμβανόμενον)."[5] The epithets echo not only Athenagoras' own description of Plato, but also contemporary presentations of Platonist doctrine such as Alcinous' *Didaskalikon*, likely a rough contemporary to Athenagoras who says the "eternal" (ἀίδιος) God "is ineffable and apprehensible by mind alone" (Ἄρρητος δ' ἐστὶ καὶ νῷ μόνῳ ληπτός).[6] Athenagoras adds that Christians also believe in a Son of God, though not one like the poets write about in their myths. Rather, the Son is "Word of the Father in form and in act" (λόγος τοῦ πατρὸς ἐν ἰδέᾳ καὶ ἐνεργείᾳ) and the one "from whom and through whom all things come to be" (πρὸς αὐτοῦ καὶ δι' αὐτοῦ πάντα ἐγένετο).[7] He is the "mind and reason (νοῦς καὶ λόγος) of the Father," who is himself "eternal mind" (νοῦς ἀίδιος); again, this language has parallels in Alcinous. For Athenagoras, the Father's mind is called Son because he "came forth in order to be form and act (ἰδέα καὶ ἐνέργεια) for all material things."[8] The generally Platonizing drift of these terse labels is clear. Athenagoras thinks of the Son in the language of paradigmatic causality.

Around 180, Theophilus of Antioch ascribes two contradictory views to "Plato and those of his school": first, "that God is unoriginated (ἀγενήτον) and the father and maker of the universe" and, second, "that matter as well as God is unoriginated (ἀγενήτον)."[9] God cannot be maker of all if there is another unmade principle. In a move that would become

---

[4] Athenagoras, *Leg.* 6.2 (12 Schoedel). Athenagoras does not directly ascribe any position on matter to Plato, but when he summarizes his own Christian position on it, his phrase "unqualified nature" (ἀποίου φύσεως) corresponds to Alcinous, who calls matter ἄποιον: *Leg.* 10.3 (22 Schoedel); Alcinous, *Didaskalikon* 8, 162.36 (19 Whittaker).
[5] Athenagoras, *Leg.* 10.1 (20 Schoedel).
[6] Alcinous, *Didaskalikon* 10, 165.5 (23 Whittaker).
[7] Athenagoras, *Leg.* 10.2 (20 Schoedel).   [8] Athenagoras, *Leg.* 10.3 (22 Schoedel).
[9] Theophilus, *Ad Autolycum* 2.4 (26 Grant).

customary for Christians, Theophilus sides with the Platonists on the nature of God but against them on matter.[10] While Theophilus does not connect this account of God's nature with any proto-Trinitarian concerns, the reader cannot miss the partial overlap between Platonist and Christian theology of the first principle, as he presents them.

In his *Stromateis* (c. 200–215), Clement of Alexandria promotes a harmony of the Christian Trinity with Plato's theology. Note the following passage from *Stromateis* 5, in which Clement is discussing *Timaeus* 41a, where Plato calls the demiurge "Father."[11] He links this text with both the *Second Epistle* of Plato and the New Testament:

As a result, when [Plato] says "all things are around the king of all, and all things exist for it, and it is the cause of all beautiful things; and second around the secondary things, and third around the tertiary things" (*ep.* 2, 312e1–4), I for my part cannot understand these words in any other way than as revealing the Holy Trinity: third is the Holy Spirit and the Son is second, "through whom all things came to be" (John 1:3) according to the will of the Father.[12]

While some in the mainstream Platonist tradition might have balked at Clement's connection of Plato with John's Gospel, his "Trinitarian" reading of the *Second Epistle* was not strange.[13] Plotinus uses the same Platonic text to a similar end:

And it is also because of this that we get Plato's threefold division: the things "around the king of all" – he says this, meaning the primary things – "second around the secondary things," and "third around the tertiary things." And he says there is a "father of the cause," meaning by "cause" (*aition*) Intellect. For the Intellect is his Demiurge. And he says that the Demiurge makes the Soul in that "mixing-bowl." And since the Intellect is cause, he means by "father" the Good, or that which transcends Intellect and "transcends Substantiality."[14]

The *Ennead* from which this quote is taken (5.1) became a favorite for Christians beginning with Eusebius of Caesarea, who cited it in his *Preparation for the Gospel* as a parallel with the Christian Trinity.[15]

---

[10] See Theophilus, *Ad Autolycum* 1.4 (6 Grant), where Theophilus in his own voice speaks of God as unoriginated (ἀγενήτον), father, and maker of the universe.

[11] See Salvatore R. C. Lilla, "The Neoplatonic Hypostases and the Christian Trinity," in Mark Joyal, ed., *Studies in Plato and the Platonic Tradition. Essays Presented to John Whittaker* (Aldershot: Ashgate, 1997), 127–189, at 129.

[12] *Strom.* V.103.1 (395, 12–17). See also Origen, *Against Celsus* 6.18 (222–224 Borret).

[13] For evidence of non-Christian Platonist citations of John 1, see Amelius apud Eusebius, *Preparation* XI.19.

[14] Plotinus, *Enn.* 5.1.8.1–8 (trans. Gerson et al., 543, altered slightly); cf. Lilla, "Neoplatonic Hypostases," 130.

[15] Eusebius, *Preparation for the Gospel*, XI.17–21.

Within the Latin tradition, the harmonization effort in a sense begins with Marius Victorinus' Trinitarian works (359–362). On one hand, especially in *Against Arius*, Victorinus speaks of the Trinity in highly Platonic language; on the other hand, he does not mention any non-Christian author or directly quote any text. Scholarly discussion has focused on the question of what was Victorinus' source, but the sheer fact that he left the source unnamed is noteworthy for present purposes, since his silence differs from other Christian texts that name their non-Christian interlocutors.[16] In addition to his Trinitarian works, we know that Victorinus translated into Latin "certain books of the Platonists," likely works of Plotinus and perhaps Porphyry too, which Augustine read in Milan in 385 shortly before his conversion.[17] In a famous harmonization passage in *Confessions* VII, Augustine recounts what he had found, over a decade earlier, when he first encountered these books:

There I read, not of course in these words, but with entire the same sense and supported by numerous and varied reasons, "In the beginning was the Word and the Word was with God and the Word was God. He was in the beginning with God. All things were made by him, and without him nothing was made. What was made is life in him; and the life was the light of men. And the light shone in the darkness, and the darkness did not comprehend it." (John 1:1–3)[18]

Augustine's harmonization is not merely a product of the argument of *Confessions* VII. In *City of God* X, he characterizes Porphyry's of first principles similarly: "he here refers to God the Father and God the Son, Whom he calls in Greek the intellect or mind of the Father."[19] In both works, Augustine presumes that the two traditions refer to the same subjects, despite differences of nomenclature.

We can mention two similar instances from fifth-century Greek Christianity. Theodoret of Cyrrhus cites various Platonists in his apologetic *Cure of Greek Maladies* (unknown date, prior to 449). Theodoret groups Plotinus together with Numenius, probably following Eusebius.

[16] See Volker Henning Drecoll, "Is Porphyry the Source Used by Marius Victorinus?," in John D. Turner and Kevin Corrigan, eds., *Plato's Parmenides and its Heritage*, vol. 2: *Reception in Patristics, Gnostic, and Christian Neoplatonic Texts* (Atlanta: Society of Biblical Literature Publications, 2010), 65–80.

[17] *Conf.* VII.ix.13 (101 Verheijen), VIII.ii.3 (114 Verheijen); see Pier F. Beatrice, "Quosdam Platonicorum Libros: The Platonic Readings of Augustine in Milan," *Vigiliae Christianae* 43 (1989), 248–281.

[18] Augustine, *Confessions* VII.ix.13 (101 Verheijen; trans. Chadwick, 121).

[19] *Civ.* X.23 (296–97 CCSL; trans. Dyson, 425).

After citing *Ennead* 5.1, Theodoret harmonizes these two Platonists' triad with Christian teaching:

> Plotinus and Numenius claimed that [Plato] said there are three beyond time and eternal – the Good, Intellect, and the All-Soul – giving the name "the Good" to the one we call Father; and "Intellect" to the one we entitle "Son" and "Word"; and calling "Soul" the power that gives life to and animates all things, which the divine books entitle "Holy Spirit."[20]

Theodoret's rival Cyril of Alexandria, in Book VIII of *Against Julian*, correlates Plotinus' three hypostases with the Christian Trinity in precisely the way we have seen in Augustine and Theodoret. The presumption is that Plotinus merely gave different names for the Father, Son, and Holy Spirit. For instance, after citing *Ennead* 5.1.2 on the World Soul, Cyril asks rhetorically: "Does he then not clearly and in the plainest terms describe the creative and life-giving operation of the Holy Spirit among us ourselves?"[21] Cyril's emphasis on the harmony between Plotinus and Christianity serves his agenda, as he debunks Julian's anti-Trinitarian arguments through appeals to Christian scripture and to Julian's own Hellenic tradition. Differently from Augustine and Theodoret, however, Cyril also points out the differences in theology, noting that Plotinus lacks the confession of consubstantiality and posits a diversity of natures among his three hypostases, a point to which we will return.

The instances cited thus far contain overt references to or citations of Plato and Platonists. There were subtler ways of harmonizing the Platonist hypostases with Trinitarian theology, which we can bypass.[22] The evidence cited here is not meant to suggest that Christian and Platonist Trinities were identical, or that the very idea of a Trinity was originally Platonist. The goal is merely to indicate the extent to which Christians were eager to harmonize their ideas with those of the Platonic tradition. Without taking the two traditions as identical, one can still hold that the similarities were more than superficial. They were more than purely apologetic or conciliatory olive

---

[20] Theodoret, *cur.* 2.85 (161–62 Canivet).

[21] Cyril, *Against Julian* 8.33 (577 Kinzig and Brüggemann; trans. Crawford, forthcoming); cf. 1.47–49 (79–81 Riedwig). I am grateful to Matthew R. Crawford for sharing his draft translation, which he is preparing in collaboration with Aaron P. Johnson, in advance of its publication with Cambridge University Press.

[22] See, for example, Basil of Caesarea, *On the Holy Spirit* 9.22–23, cited below, 000, which bears the imprint of Plotinus without any mention of him; Pseudo-Dionysius, *Divine Names* 2.7 – in Dodds' words, a "grotesque" transfer to the Son and Spirit of "the epithets with which Proclus had adorned his henads": *Proclus: The Elements of Theology*, ed. and trans. E. R. Dodds, 2nd ed. (Oxford: Clarendon Press, 1963), xxviii.

branches that did not touch the core of Christian teaching. However, the view that Christian Trinitarianism was only incidentally related to Platonism is not uncommon within Christian theology today. To explain the foundations of this prevalent theological opinion, we must examine two scholarly tropes that have contributed to its dissemination. Once we have identified these tropes, which often function as hidden and unstated assumptions in contemporary theology, we will better positioned to offer a sympathetic picture of late ancient pro-Nicene Trinitarianism as integrally related to Christian Platonism. As we will see, the influence goes deeper than the attempts noted above at harmonization.

ARIANISM AS PLATONISM?

One major obstacle to a sympathetic portrait of Platonism within Trinitarian theology is the common assumption that only ante- and anti-Nicene theologies were inspired by Platonism, or at least that *especially* those theologies were so inspired. This is the Arianism-as-Platonism trope; with it, we can mention the concomitant idea that anti-Arianism was necessarily also anti-Platonism. Witness this example from Hans Urs von Balthasar's influential monograph on Gregory of Nyssa:

What distinguishes Gregory at once from Philo and Plotinus is the radical opposition between the triune God and the creature, an opposition that is not mitigated by any kind of intermediary zone. In Origen's Trinity, the Son and the Spirit, even though they were formally affirmed as being God, served as ontological mediators between the Father and the world. After Arius, something like this is no longer conceivable.[23]

If Balthasar's intent is merely to observe a difference between, on the one hand, Philo, Origen, Plotinus, and Arius and, on the other hand, Gregory, then the claim could in principle be assessed by a look at the relevant evidence. However, Balthasar seems to have something bigger and more nebulous in mind, namely, that Gregory's *purpose* when writing against Eunomius was not principally to refute Eunomius but rather to rebut Origen and Plotinus by proxy, despite the lack of references to Origen and Plotinus in the work.[24] Balthasar treats Gregory's text as if it were

---

[23] Hans Urs von Balthasar, *Presence and Thought: An Essay on the Religious Philosophy of Gregory of Nyssa*, trans. Mark Sebanc (San Francisco: Ignatius, 1995; orig. pub. 1942 as *Présence et pensée: Essai sur la philosophie religieuse de Grégoire de Nysse*), 18–19.

[24] See Michel René Barnes, *The Power of God: Δύναμις in Gregory of Nyssa's Trinitarian Theology* (Washington, D.C.: The Catholic University of America Press, 2000), 221–222.

principally a rebuke of Platonism. In a footnote Balthasar characterizes the theme of *Contra Eunomium* as the "victory of Christian thought over Greek thought" rather than intra-Christian controversy.[25]

Of course, Balthasar did not invent the assumptions he brought to his reading. The conflation of Origen, Arius, and Eunomius on one hand with Plotinus and the Neoplatonists on the other had become by his time an ecumenical commonplace. In his *Commentary on Boethius'* De Trinitate, Thomas Aquinas argues that Arianism was influenced, through the mediation of Origen, by Platonism's three hypostases. To justify the narrative, Aquinas combines the account of the Neoplatonist hypostases in *City of God* X and Macrobius with Epiphanius' argument that Origen was Arius' inspiration.[26] Various theologians, both well-known and forgotten, have followed suit.[27] In 1827, the Pietist theologian Georg Christian Knapp, in an influential set of lectures, stated the equivalence unequivocally: "the belief in the subordination of the Son to the Father for which Arianism is the later name, flowing as it did directly from Platonic principles, was commonly accepted by most of these fathers [namely, Theophilus, Clement, and Origen] of the second and third centuries."[28] Thus, "subordinationism" – incidentally, it was perhaps from Leonard Woods' translation of Knapp's lectures that this term entered the English language[29] – and "Arianism" are treated as interchangeable labels for a doctrine that is fundamentally Platonist in its roots. The rejection of such Platonism, a rejection which Knapp regarded as providential, was the accomplishment of the Nicene fathers.

One can understand why the Trinity's modern defenders would have been motivated to embrace this construal of orthodoxy as surpassing Platonism. Scores of anti-Trinitarians, beginning with Michael Servetus

---

[25] Balthasar, *Presence and Thought*, 19, n. 16. Balthasar drew on Endre von Ivanka, "Vom Platonismus zur Theorie der Mystik. Zur Erkenntnislehre Gregors von Nyssa," *Scholastik* 11 (1936), 163–195.

[26] Thomas Aquinas, *Super Boetium de trinitate*, q. 3, art. 4, co. 1–2. For the claim that Origen influenced Arius, Aquinas cites Epiphanius.

[27] For example, Denis Petau, *Dogmata theologica*, vol. 2: *primum de praedestione, postea de Trinitate* (Paris: Le Vivès, 1865–1867 [orig. pub. 1643]), *De Trinitate* I.i.iv (p. 284); I.vi.i (p. 319). In addition to Aquinas' sources, Petavius cites Eusebius of Caesarea's *Preparation* and Cyril's *Against Julian* 1.

[28] Georg Christian Knapp, *Lectures on Christian Theology*, vol. 1, trans. Leonard Woods, 1st ed. (New York: G. & C. & H. Carvill, 1831 [orig. pub. (posthumously) as *Dr. Georg Christian Knapp's Vorlesungen über die Christliche Glaubenslehre nach dem Lehrbegriff der evangelische Kirche*, ed. Johann Karl Thilo (Halle: Buchhandlung des Waisenhauses, 1827)]), 299.

[29] See Knapp, *Lectures*, vol. 1, 321.

in the sixteenth century, had presented the traditional doctrine as damning evidence of a Platonized, and thus corrupted, version of Christianity.[30] Perhaps the most famous version of the story was told by the liberal Protestant historian Adolf von Harnack under the influence of Albrecht Ritschl's theology.[31] According to Harnack, Arius subscribed to Platonic cosmology mixed with Aristotelian rationalism. In opposition, Athanasius emphasized redemption rather than cosmology, thus marking himself as authentically, though imperfectly Christian – imperfect, on Harnack's reading, because of his inattention to the historical Jesus. However, for Harnack, later in the fourth century we see the revival of Aristotelian rationalism and Platonist cosmology, but now split between two parties: the Eunomian rationalists on one side and the Cappadocian Neoplatonists on the other. Hence the victory engineered by Athanasius of authentic Christianity over Platonist cosmological speculation was a pyrrhic one.[32] According to Harnack, the Cappadocians reenshrined the Platonism originally defeated at Nicaea. It was this sort of critical narrative that modern supporters of traditional doctrine – the doctrine of the Cappadocians and Augustine – sought to overturn. The apologetic counter-narrative of orthodoxy as breaking with Platonism enabled modern orthodox Protestant and Catholic theologians to place Platonist metaphysical and cosmological speculation squarely in the church's *past*, as part of a youthful, unconsummated flirtation of the church with Greek thought. According to the counter-narrative, when fourth-century pro-Nicenes denied that the Son and Spirit were created and thus part of the cosmos, they definitively severed Trinitarian theology from Platonist cosmology.[33]

---

[30] Catalogued in Jonathan Z. Smith, "On the Origin of Origins," in *Drudgery Divine: On the Comparison of Early Christianities and the Religions of Late Antiquity* (Chicago: University of Chicago Press, 1990), 1–26.

[31] See Wolfhart Pannenberg, "The Appropriation of the Philosophical Concept of God as a Dogmatic Problem of Early Christian Theology," in *Basic Questions in Theology: Collected Essays*, vol. 2, trans. George H. Kehm (Philadelphia: Fortress, 1971), 119–183. Orig. pub. in German in *Zeitschrift für Kirchengeschichte* 70 (1959), 1–45.

[32] See Adolf von Harnack, *History of Dogma*, vols. 4 and 5, trans. Neil Buchanan (New York: Dover, 1961 [translated from the 3rd German edition of 1900]), 26–48, 88–89.

[33] See Friedo Ricken, "Das Homoousios von Nikaia als Krisis des altchristlichen Platonismus," in Bernhard Welte, ed., *Zur Frühgeschichte der Christologie: Ihre biblischen Anfänge und die Lehrformel von Nikaia*, Quaestiones Disputatae 51 (Freiburg, Basel, Vienna: Herder, 1971), 74–99 (orig. pub. in *Theologie und Philosophie* 44 (1969), 321–341).

The Arianism-as-Platonism trope appears throughout the twentieth century in influential books on the history of doctrine. J. N. D. Kelly, for instance, writes that "the impact of Platonism reveals itself in the thoroughgoing subordinationism which is integral to Origen's Trinitarian scheme."[34] Likewise, Kelly portrays Aetius and Eunomius as "presenting a restatement of fundamental Christian dogma in terms of a Neo-Platonic metaphysic of three hierarchically ordered, mutually exclusive οὐσίαι."[35] More recently, David Bentley Hart identifies an Alexandrian tendency to subordinationism that was common among Platonists and Jews like Philo, as well as ante-Nicene and Arian Christians.[36] He elegantly contrasts the God of Nicaea and Constantinople with that system: "He was not the Most High God of Arius, immune to all contact with the finite, for the Logos in which he revealed himself as creator and redeemer was his own, interior Logos, his own perfect image, his own self-knowledge and disclosure; nor certainly was his anything like the paradoxical transcendence of the One of Plotinus, 'revealed' only as a kind of infinite contrariety."[37]

It would be foolish to dismiss this sort of reading out of hand. Neither Eunomius nor Plotinus could countenance the idea that the divine hypostases are entirely coordinate. However, the connection between Eunomian and Platonist "subordinationism" is rarely, if ever, made in the late ancient sources, and where it is, the point is different from the Arianism-as-Platonism narrative we have encountered thus far. For instance, in one passage from *Against Eunomius*, Gregory of Nyssa notes that "some of [the Greeks] think that there is a great God supreme above the others and they confess certain inferior powers differing from one another as greater and lesser by some ordering and sequence but all equally subject to the superior one."[38] A parallel passage in Gregory's *Refutation of Eunomius' Confession* reveals that Gregory's point is slightly different than one might expect. In the *Refutation*, Gregory accuses Eunomius of following either Judaism or Plato's *Timaeus* in his understanding of the biblical title "Father."[39] To be sure, this parallel

---

[34] J. N. D. Kelly, *Early Christian Doctrines*, rev. ed. (New York: Harper, 1978), 131.

[35] Kelly, *Early Christian Doctrines*, 249; for a survey of the literature up to 1988, see R. P. C. Hanson, *The Search for a Christian Doctrine of God: The Arian Controversy, 318–381* (Grand Rapids, MI: Baker Academic, 1988), 85–89.

[36] David Bentley Hart, *The Hidden and the Manifest: Essays in Theology and Metaphysics* (Grand Rapids, MI: Eerdmans, 2017), 143.

[37] Hart, *The Hidden and the Manifest*, 149–150.   [38] *Eun.* 3.9.59 (286.21–26 Jaeger).

[39] See the parallel at *Refutation of Eunomius' Confession* 48 (332.4–14 Jaeger), where Gregory accuses Eunomius of following either Judaism or Plato's *Timaeus*.

confirms that "the Greeks" whom Gregory has in mind in *Against Eunomius* are indeed Plato and his school. Thus Gregory was capable on at least one occasion of accusing Eunomius of possibly following Plato. However, the divinities in question are not the One, *Nous*, and Soul, but rather the Demiurge and the subordinate gods of *Timaeus* 39a–41d. Thus the equation between the Neoplatonist hypostases and the Arian or Eunomian Trinity is not one that Gregory ever draws. Gregory is more perceptive here than his modern defenders, since Eunomius' theology, with its emphasis on the Father's commands and the Son's obedience, is much more akin to the relation of the Demiurge to his subordinates in the *Timaeus* story than it is to the three principal hypostases of Neoplatonism.

The familiar trope likewise is absent from Augustine. Neither in *Confessions* nor in *City of God* does Augustine raise any concern about "subordinationism" (under whatever name) in Platonism. The *City of God* passage cited above is more hostile to Platonism than is *Confessions* VII, but the two objections Augustine articulates there about Porphyry are not that his second principle was ranked below the first, but rather that he spoke in the plural of principles capable of purifying humanity, instead of maintaining a single principle of purification, and that he denied the incarnation. Of course, these are major differences, but the objections have nothing to do with subordination, and they should not lead us to neglect Augustine's almost seamless harmonization of Christian and Neoplatonic language in naming the first and second persons of the Trinity.

The more interesting case is Cyril of Alexandria, who does accuse Plotinus and the Neoplatonists of positing a "dissimilarity of natures" among their three hypostases and of denying their consubstantiality.[40] This terminology is telling. For modern scholars, Platonism is the root of the subordinationism found in Arius, Eunomius, and the like. Cyril's formulation reverses this model. In his critique of Platonism, Cyril uses descriptions that derive from, and make the most sense within, pro-Nicene polemic against non-Nicene theology. Thus, Cyril's anti-Platonism is implicit anti-Arianism, but not because Arianism is Platonism but rather because, to him, Platonism resembles Arianism. In using this explanatory model, Cyril follows the opening chapters of Gregory of Nyssa's *Catechetical Oration*, where Gregory uses anti-"Arian" arguments against the polytheism of the Greeks, including

---

[40] Cyril, *Against Julian* 8.26 (567 Kinzig and Brüggemann; trans. Crawford, forthcoming); 8.30 (573 Kinzig and Brüggemann; trans. Crawford, forthcoming).

philosophical Greeks.[41] The Greeks, according to Gregory, err in positing a "more and a less" in the divinity – though again, this more likely refers to *Timaeus* than to the Neoplatonist hypostases. The key point here is that this is the same language Gregory uses to describe his opponents' theology in his (likely earlier) books against Eunomius and the Pneumatomachians. Gregory and Cyril by implication, though not explicitly, accuse their non-Christian rivals of Arianism; they do not accuse their Christian rivals of Platonism, or at least not of copying the Neoplatonist three hypostases. The genealogy envisioned in modern works, according to which a common doctrine of subordinationism originates among the Platonists and emanates thence to the Arians, could nonetheless be true; the point here is that it is not native to the sources. To the contrary, the pro-Nicene texts instead emphasize the continuity between Platonism and what they take as orthodox Trinitarianism. In Cyril's words: "the Greeks themselves also agree with the views of the Christians, since they set forth three primal *hypostases*, insist that the essence of God reaches as far as three *hypostases*, and sometimes even use the word 'Trinity'."[42] In fact, Cyril notes that other Plotinian passages cohere well with pro-Nicene doctrine. He cites 5.16, where Plotinus emphasizes what Cyril calls the "inseparability" of the hypostases; in Plotinus' terms, the three "are only separated by being different," which Cyril notes is impeccably orthodox.[43]

We know of no comparable harmonization effort by an anti-Nicene author. To be sure, Eusebius' theology does not correspond to later pro-Nicene orthodoxy. Still, the work in which Eusebius lays out his harmonization, the *Preparation for the Gospel*, was composed prior to the outbreak of the Nicene and post-Nicene conflicts (such as Eusebius' writings against Marcellus) and it bears no trace of those debates. Moreover, the *Preparation* was used liberally by later pro-Nicenes like Theodoret and Cyril, for whom its harmonizing argument was evidently not totally colored by an anti-Nicene agenda.

The purported similarity between "Arianism" and "Platonism" weakens further when we consider the importance of voluntarism to Arius and Eunomius. The strongly voluntarist character of non-Nicene theologies – as

---

[41] See Andrew Radde-Gallwitz, *Gregory of Nyssa's Doctrinal Works: A Literary Study* (Oxford: Oxford University Press, 2018), 247–56.

[42] Cyril, *Against Julian* 8.26 (567 Kinzig and Brüggemann; trans. Crawford, forthcoming).

[43] Plotinus, *Enn.* 5.1.6.53, cited at Cyril, *Against Julian* 8.31 (573 Kinzig and Brüggemann; trans. Crawford, forthcoming).

evident in the surviving works of Arius or Eunomius – clashes with main-stream Platonism.[44] Plotinus insists that Intellect's emergence from the One is not a result of any act of willing on the part of the One.[45] The production of Intelligence from the One is instead like light radiating from the sun, heating from fire, cool from snow, scent from perfume. Plotinus does not entirely deny the voluntariness of the One's activity, but for him it coincides with the necessity of its acts.[46] He finds vacuous any appeal to divine will to explain the everlasting existence of the cosmos.[47] By contrast, for Arius, God's will is the sole explanatory principle for creation. The Son himself was created "by the will" of God.[48] Arius explicitly rejects the comparison of the Son's generation to the lighting of one lamp from another. For Eunomius, the Son was begotten by the Father's will rather than from the Father's being.[49] The Son is obedient to the Father's command in his works, as the Spirit is to him.[50]

No pro-Nicene author represents the Trinity in such highly voluntarist terms.[51] Take Gregory of Nazianzus as an example. On the surface Nazianzen seems to exemplify the narrative of pro-Nicene rejection of Platonism, since he rejects an image used by "one of the Greek philosophers" in which the first principle's generation of the second hypostasis is likened to an "overflowing bowl."[52] The image apparently is taken both from Plotinus and the *Chaldean Oracles*.[53] For Gregory, the image implies that the eternal generation is involuntary, a notion he rejects. But Gregory rightly associates his non-Nicene opponents with the opposite view, namely, that the Son is generated from the Father's will. His response is not to embrace voluntarism or involuntarism but rather to deny that one can separate God's will from God's act of generating, an argument that

---

[44] Rowan Williams, *Arius: Heresy and Tradition*, rev. ed. (Grand Rapids, MI and Cambridge, UK: Eerdmans, 2002), 209.

[45] Plotinus, *Enn.* 5.1.6.25–27; 5.3.12.28–31.   [46] *Enn.* 6.8.21.

[47] *Enn.* 2.1.1.1–4; R. J. Hankinson, *Cause and Explanation in Ancient Greek Thought* (Oxford: Clarendon Press, 1998), 419.

[48] Arius, *Letter to Eusebius of Nicomedia* 4 (3 Opitz); *Letter to Alexander of Alexandria* 2 (13 Opitz).

[49] Eunomius, *Apol.* 14. (line) 16 (50 Vaggione), 15.9 (52 Vaggione), 23.15–24.4 (64 Vaggione), 28.12–14 (a Eunomian confession appended to the *Apol.* in manuscripts; 74 Vaggione).

[50] Eunomius, *Apol.* 17.12 (54 Vaggione), 20.20–21 (60 Vaggione), 26.22 (70 Vaggione), 27.2 (70 Vaggione), *Expositio fidei* 3.22–25, 35–36 (154 Vaggione).

[51] See, for example, Athanasius, *Orations Against the Arians* 3.59–67.

[52] Gregory of Nazianzus, *Oration* 29.2.19–22 (180 Gallay).

[53] Ruth Majercik, "A Reminiscence of the 'Chaldean Oracles' at Gregory of Nazianzus, *Or.* 29.2: ΟΙΟΝ ΚΡΑΤΗΡ ΤΙΣ ΥΠΕΡΕΡΡΥΗ," *Vigiliae Christianae* 52 (1998), 286–292.

seems rather like Plotinus' account of the will of the One.[54] Thus, Nazianzen, who on the surface distances himself from "the Greeks" on this issue, provides no evidence for any connection between anti-Arianism and anti-Platonism.

The criticism offered here of the Arianism-as-Platonism trope should not be taken too far. There is no sense in denying any and all influence of Platonism on figures like Arius or Eunomius. There has been some controversy of the precise nature of the Platonism of Arius in particular, but unquestionably some of his language echoes Platonist metaphysics.[55] The point of the present discussion is that it is not Arianism as such that was Platonist; Arius and those labelled "Arians" were no more especially Platonizing, and were in important respects less so, than their Nicene opponents. Nor was anti-Arianism implicit or covert anti-Platonism. In one or two cases, anti-Platonism was implicit or covert anti-Arianism, but generally the pro-Nicenes identified greater continuity between their own doctrine and that of their Platonist sources than between their opponents and the Platonists.

FROM PLATONISM TO TRINITARIANISM?

A second obstacle that a sympathetic account needs to overcome lies in the notion that the "authentically Christian" Creator–creature distinction competed with, and perhaps rendered redundant, the "Platonic" intelligible–sensible distinction. The kernel of truth in this view is that pro-Nicene theology, as it emerged in the later fourth century, depended heavily on an appeal to the absolute distinction between the uncreated and the created. This dichotomy appears especially in pro-Nicene works on the Holy Spirit, which was believed by some figures – labeled "Pneumatomachians" or "Spirit-fighters" by the pro-Nicenes – to occupy an ambiguous intermediary zone between God and creation, like the angelic spirits. Certainly, as figures like Gregory of Nyssa pointed out, the distinction of uncreated and created is different from the traditionally Platonic one between intelligible and sensible reality. However, the scholarship has pushed Gregory's parsing of the two distinctions to do more work than it can bear. The implication of the scholarship is that the two distinctions were mutually exclusive *and* that they were the site of a kind of culture war between authentic Christianity and Platonism. Naturally, such a reading is important for those

[54] Plotinus, *Enn.* 6.8.21.
[55] Williams, *Arius*, 181–232 and the articles by Christopher Stead cited there.

modern theologians who maintain that one can be dogmatically orthodox – espousing a Trinitarian theology and Christology in line with the first four councils – without espousing classical metaphysics.[56] Whatever one's perspective on that question, it is worthwhile to ask about the validity of the underlying historical narrative.[57]

If we return to Augustine's *Confessions* VII, we might recall that, in addition to identifying analogues to the persons of the Christian Trinity in the books of the Platonists, Augustine tells it was these books that first taught him to think of God as immaterial.[58] This point bears emphasis. As Augustine's own story makes plain, this Platonist tenet makes for a somewhat counterintuitive reading of the Christian scriptures, with their anthropomorphic imagery and their depictions of God as spirit and light. Some early Christians, most prominently Tertullian, endorsed the broadly Stoic principle that only what is corporeal has being, and thus held that God must be a refined sort of spiritual body.[59] It is reasonable to believe that this "Stoic" position was somewhat widely held, despite the relative lack of evidence for it; after all, it is the first misconception that Origen seeks to correct in *On First Principles*. But no matter how widespread Christian Stoicism might have been in Origen's time, it had little influence on the development of Trinitarian theology. In Origen and many others we see a notion of God as entirely unoriginated, incorporeal, immaterial, unchanging, and metaphysically simple. These Christians described God's nature, in the lingo of Platonism, as intelligible rather than as sense-perceptible. They read Exodus 3:14 ("I am the one who is") as revealing that God is Being itself, not becoming and flux and dependency.

While scholars widely acknowledge that privatives like immutability and ingeneracy were central to early Christian Trinitarian thought, their rootedness in Platonism is sometimes obscured in scholarship. Sometimes such ideas are presented as implicit in scripture or in ideas, such as *creatio ex nihilo*, which are derived from scripture and native to early Jewish and Christian thought in contradistinction from Platonism.[60] For instance,

---

[56] Perhaps most influentially, Pannenberg, "The Appropriation of the Philosophical Concept of God."

[57] For an account that stresses the centrality of the principles discussed here for pro-Nicene thought, see Lewis Ayres, *Nicaea and Its Legacy: An Approach to Fourth-Century Trinitarian Theology* (Oxford: Oxford University Press, 2004), 281.

[58] Augustine, *Confessions* VII.x.16ff.

[59] Tertullian, *On the Flesh of Christ* 11.2–4 (258 Mahé).

[60] For example, Stephen Duby, *Divine Simplicity: A Dogmatic Account* (London: Bloomsbury T & T Clark, 2016), 91; Jordan P. Barrett, *Divine Simplicity: A Biblical and Trinitarian Account* (Minneapolis: Fortress, 2017), 133–68.

Janet Soskice has claimed that Philo stands behind such philosophical theology, and she reads Philo as a highly independent thinker whose great originality vis-à-vis Greek philosophy stems from his Jewish commitments.[61] Such historical reconstruction makes Platonism unnecessary for explaining the attraction of early Christians to the idea of God as Being itself. An adequate response to such a genealogy would require a fuller study, but I see no reason why we should not follow Augustine – and we could cite other examples from the likes of Justin Martyr and Athenagoras – and credit Platonism for a salutary influence on Christian thinkers, as the latter joined the former in a twin battle against cruder interpretations of their respective religious traditions.

A related scholarly narrative states that although Platonist accounts of God as intelligible influenced ante-Nicene theology, as Trinitarian orthodoxy developed, Christians moved past the intelligible–sensible distinction. In William Moore and Henry Austin Wilson's prologue to the 1893 *Nicene and Post-Nicene Fathers* volume of Gregory of Nyssa's writings, the contest between this distinction and the Creature–creator distinction stands as microcosm of Christianity's relation to Platonism: "instead of the Platonic antithesis of the intelligible and sensible world, which Origen adopted ... [Gregory] brings forward the antithesis of God and the world."[62] This account, which would be echoed by numerous later scholars, is puzzling, since Gregory endorses both antitheses. In distinct parts of *Against Eunomius*, Gregory first calls the one and then the other "the highest division of all beings" (πάντων τῶν ὄντων ἡ ἀνωτάτω διαίρεσις).[63] Because the two distinctions do similar, but distinct work, Gregory continues to invoke both throughout his corpus for different purposes. From Moore and Wilson's account, one would assume that the God–world distinction had superseded the Platonic intelligible–sensible distinction, the presumption being that the two were held to be in competition.[64] The evidence, however, suggests

---

[61] Janet M. Soskice, "Athens and Jerusalem, Alexandria and Edessa: Is There a Metaphysics of Scripture?," *International Journal of Systematic Theology* 8 (2006), 149–162. Similar claims have been made about Thomas Aquinas: for example, Etienne Gilson, *Christian Philosophy: An Introduction*, trans. Armand Maurer (Toronto: Pontifical Institute of Medieval Studies, 1993 [orig. pub. in French, 1960]), 31.

[62] *Nicene and Post-Nicene Fathers*, second series, vol. 5: *Gregory of Nyssa: Dogmatic Treatises, etc.*, trans. William Moore and Henry Austin Wilson (Peabody, MA: Hendrickson, 1999, reprint [orig. pub. 1893]), 18.

[63] *Against Eunomius* 1.270 (105.19 Jaeger), 3.6.66 (209.19–26 Jaeger), cf. 3.3.3 (107.5–108.1 Jaeger).

[64] For example, David L. Balás, *Metousia Theou: Man's Participation in God's Perfections According to Saint Gregory of Nyssa*, Studia Anselmiana 55 (Rome: Herder & Herder,

a complementary rather than a competitive relationship between the two
distinctions. A developmental hypothesis is out of the question, since in
Gregory's late homilies *On the Song of Songs*, as in *Against Eunomius* 1,
Gregory invokes not only the uncreated–created distinction but also the
intelligible–sensible distinction, which he calls the highest dichotomy (τὴν
ἀνωτάτω διαίρεσιν) according to which "the nature of beings" (ἡ τῶν ὄντων
φύσις) is bifurcated.[65] It is logically though not ontologically prior to the
uncreated–created distinction, since without it one could not account for the
incorporeality of both God and created intelligibles, while any scheme that
conflates the two distinctions could not account for the endless dynamism of
created intelligible life.[66] Only an account that includes both distinctions can
capture both the relevant similarities and differences between God and
created intelligible substances such as the human soul. If Gregory is at all
representative in this regard, the task for scholars would be to narrate the
history of Christian doctrine in a way that reflects this complementarity,
rather than in a way that begs the question by presuming an irreconcilable
conflict between Platonism and Christianity.

The more consequential historical dividing point on this topic is not
that between ante- and pro-Nicene thought but that between Christians
prior to and after Pseudo-Dionysius. While Gregory was happy to speak
of the uncreated–created division as somehow fitting into a general division "of beings" (τῶν ὄντων), once we reach Pseudo-Dionysius a century
or so later, we encounter a thoroughgoing criticism of any attempt to
speak of God as being or a being. Drawing on Plotinus and Proclus,
Pseudo-Dionysius insists that God, as the cause of being, is beyond even
intelligible being. Of course, one should not overemphasize the gap
between Gregory and Pseudo-Dionysius, since Gregory's apophaticism
and his portrait of the divine darkness were touchstones of Dionysian
theology. Moreover, Pseudo-Dionysius continues to accept the intelligible–sensible distinction; he merely denies that God is either logically or
ontologically encompassed by it. He is not entirely discontinuous with
Gregory, but he does move beyond him in arguing that God transcends the
category of substance itself. Yet, the key point for the present chapter is

---

1966), 34–52; For the broader tradition, for example, Andrew Louth, *St John
Damascene: Tradition and Originality in Byzantine Theology* (Oxford: Oxford
University Press, 2002), 93.
[65] *Homilies on the Song of Songs* 3 (173.7–8 Langerbeck).
[66] *Homilies on the Song of Songs* 3 (173.7–174.20 Langerbeck).

that even this move evinces increased influence of contemporary Platonism on Christian thought rather than a break with it.

VARIETIES OF TRINITY AND PLATONISM: THE METAPHYSICS OF PARTICIPATION

If Christian Trinitarianism was integrally linked with but not reducible to Platonism, it is also true Platonist principles could be employed within quite distinct Trinitarian theologies. A sympathetic portrait of Christian-Platonist Trinitarianism ought to be sensitive to this variety. One Platonist principle that was adopted by several Christians had to do with the metaphysics of participation. Far from determining their thought, however, the principle was fitted into various Trinitarian schemes. This section will outline the use of participation in four distinct stages of Trinitarian theology: in Origen, in a trio of early pro-Nicene authors, in Gregory of Nyssa, and in Pseudo-Dionysius.

First, then, a brief remark on Origen. Origen's use of the language of participation within his Trinitarian theology raises certain questions we cannot address here.[67] It will satisfy our purposes to glance at a section of his *Commentary on John* which comments on John 1:1: "In the beginning was *the* Word (ὁ λόγος) and the Word (ὁ λόγος) was with *the* God (πρὸς τὸν θεόν), and the Word (ὁ λόγος) was God (θεός)." A question arises over the presence or absence of the article before Logos and God. Origen assumes that the shift from *the* God to God is deliberate and significant. His explanation involves participatory metaphysics: "For as the God who is over all is '*the* God' and not simply 'God', so the source of reason (λόγου), in each rational being is '*the* Word'."[68] The definite article tells the reader that we are dealing with whatever it is that causes the perfection in question, without itself receiving it from a higher source: "Everything besides the very God (τὸ αὐτόθεος), which is made God by participation in his divinity (θεότητος), would more properly not be said to be '*the* God', but 'God'."[69] The two perfections, divinity and reason, are analogous, and their explanation requires two principles: "The reason which is in each rational being has the same position in relation to the Word which is

---

[67] See John Dillon, "Origen's Doctrine of the Trinity and Some Later Neoplatonic Theories," in Dominic O'Meara, ed., *Neoplatonism and Christian Thought* (Albany: SUNY Press, 1982), 19–23; Mark J. Edwards, "Origen's Platonism: Questions and Caveats," *Zeitschrift für Antikes Christentum* 12 (2008), 20–38, at 29–30.

[68] Origen, *Commentary on John* 2.15 (54 Preuschen; trans. Heine, 98).

[69] Origen, *Commentary on John* 2.17 (54–55 Preuschen; trans. Heine, 98–99).

in the beginning with God, which is God the Word, which God the Word
has with God . . . For both hold the place of a source; the Father, that of
divinity, the Son, that of reason."[70] Thus there is a relationship of participation between the Word and God and not merely between the two, on
the one hand, and the created world, on the other. Somewhat similarly, in
a famous passage from *On First Principles*, Origen states that any creature
that is holy is so by participation in the Holy Spirit; any creature that is
rational is so by partaking in the Logos; and any creatures that has being
does so by participating in the Father.[71] Similar to the *Commentary on
John*, Origen here envisions distinct relations of participation with the
three hypostases. Differently from the *Commentary*, he does not speak of
the Son or Spirit participating in the Father's divinity, or at least not in the
version we have from Rufinus.

Origen's idea of "intra-Trinitarian" participation would drop out in
our second stage. Yet we still see a common argument regarding participation emerging in the texts of various supporters of Nicaea from
around 360 through the mid-370s; here we can cite Athanasius,
Didymus, and Basil. For these pro-Nicenes, a corollary of thinking of
the Son or Spirit as divine is denying that either participates in any
superordinate principle. We can begin with Athanasius' *De synodis*,
written around 359:

And moreover, if, as we said, the Son does not exist by participation (ἐκ
μετουσίας) – rather, while all generated things have grace from God by participation, he is the Wisdom and Word of the Father in whom all things partake – then
clearly he is the deifying and illuminating power (τὸ θεοποιὸν καὶ φωτιστικόν) of the
Father, in which all things are deified and given life, he is not foreign-in-substance
(ἀλλοτριοούσιος) to the Father but same-in-substance (ὁμοούσιος).[72]

While it would be a mistake to say that Athanasius came to accept the
homoousion because of the principle that the Son is participated but does
not participate, the sentence just quoted does present the creedal

---

[70] Origen, *Commentary on John* 2.20 (55 Preuschen; trans. Heine, 99–100).

[71] Origen, *On First Principles* 1.3.8: "God the Father bestows existence on all things, but
participation in Christ, in accordance with his being the Word (or Reason), makes them
rational . . . [T]he grace of the Holy Spirit is present – so that those who are not holy in
their substance may become holy through participation in it." Paul Koetschau, ed.,
Origenes Werke, Fuenfter Band: De Principiis, GCS (Leipzig: Hinrisch'sche
Buchhandlung, 1913), 60–61; trans. Brad Storin in Radde-Gallwitz, ed., *Cambridge
Edition of Early Christian Writings, Volume One*, 104.

[72] Athanasius, *On the Synods* 51 (348 Martin and Morales; trans. Radde-Gallwitz,
209–10).

confession as following from that principle. In his roughly contemporaneous *Letters to Serapion*, Athanasius applies the same logic to the Holy Spirit. After affirming that creatures are "given life" in the Spirit, Athanasius specifies that the Spirit "does not participate in life, but is himself participated in" and is thus ontologically distinct from creatures.[73]

Didymus the Blind likewise appeals to the premise to show the Spirit's full divinity in *On the Holy Spirit* (360–365), a work that survives only in Jerome's Latin translation.

[E]verything which is capable of participating in the good of another is separated from this substance [of God]. All such realities are creatures. Now because he is good, God is the source and principle of all goods. Therefore he makes good those to whom he imparts himself; he is not made good by another, but is good. Hence it is possible to participate in him but not for him to participate. Furthermore, his only-begotten Son is Wisdom (1 Cor 1:24) and sanctification; he does not become wise but makes wise, and he is not sanctified but sanctifies. For this reason too it is possible to participate in him but not for him to participate ... Let us once more consider the Holy Spirit: if he too is actually holy through participation in another's sanctity, then he should be classed with the rest of creatures. But if he sanctifies those who are capable of participating in him, then he should be placed with the Father and the Son ... [T]he Holy Spirit can be participated in and cannot participate in others.[74]

Didymus stipulates that if something is capable of participating in another – that is, in a superordinate principle – it must be a creature, and if some subject is participated but does not participate in any superordinate principle, it must not be a creature. The Spirit is what makes holy without itself being made holy by participation; hence, it is ranked with the Father – called "God" in the passage – and the Son. Didymus thereby supplies content for understanding the uncreated–created distinction, as he identifies it with the relationship between holiness in the uncaused cause of holiness and in those who participate in it.

In his first major theological work, *Against Eunomius* (c. 364–365), Basil of Caesarea likewise applies an equivalent distinction to the Spirit: "the holy powers and the Holy Spirit differ in this regard: for the latter, holiness is nature, whereas for the former, being made holy comes from

---

[73] Athanasius, *Letters to Serapion* 1.23.3 (PG 26, 584C; trans. DelCogliano, Radde-Gallwitz, and Ayres, 89). Compare 1.24.1–4, 1.27.1–2.

[74] Didymus, *On the Holy Spirit* 16–17, 19 (156–60 Doutreleau; trans. DelCogliano, Radde-Gallwitz, and Ayres, 148–149, altered for consistency); cf. Athanasius, *ep. Serap.* 1.23.3, 1.27.2.

participation."[75] As in Didymus, Basil presents this distinction as equivalent to the opposition of divinity and creation. The same type of argument appears more expansively in his *On the Holy Spirit* (373–375), where he maintains that one who hears the name "Spirit" will think of the underlying nature as follows:

> one will necessarily think of an intellectual substance (νοερὰν οὐσίαν), infinite in power, unlimited in magnitude, not measured by times or ages, unsparing with the goods it possesses … perfecting others, but itself deficient in no respect … filling all things with its power, but partaken of (μεθεκτόν) only by those who are worthy, and participated (μετεχόμενον) not to a uniform degree but dividing its activity "in proportion to faith" (Romans 12:6); simple in substance but diverse in powers; wholly present to each and being everywhere as a whole. Impassibly divided and participated (μετεχόμενον) in its entirety, as, for illustration, with the sun's ray, whose charm is present to one who enjoys it as if to him alone, while it shines upon the earth and the sea and mingles with the air.[76]

We can bypass the debated scholarly question of whether Basil used Plotinus in this passage and its immediate sequel.[77] The key is that for Basil, as for Athanasius and Didymus, two dichotomies – either being participated or not being participated and either participating or not participating – structure the account of the relation between the creator and the universe. All three of these authors use this framework to explicate the divinity of the Son and the Spirit. It is notable that all three apply the logic to these hypostases individually, rather than to a shared divine nature.

In the polemical works of Gregory of Nyssa, which were written in the years following Basil's death, we see the extension of the framework to the divine nature as such. Gregory distinguishes the uncreated nature of the Trinity from created intelligible natures. While angels and rational souls are like God in their immaterial nature, unlike God they admit of degrees of goodness corresponding to their moral inclinations and choices.

> The uncreated nature is far removed from this sort of differentiation, since it does not possess the good as something acquired and does not admit the beautiful in itself by participation in any transcendent beauty (κατὰ μετοχὴν ὑπερκειμένου τινὸς

---

[75] Basil, *Against Eunomius* 3.2 (SC 305, 154; trans. DelCogliano and Radde-Gallwitz, 188).

[76] Basil, *On the Holy Spirit* 9.22 (324–326 Pruche), cf. 16.48.

[77] See John Rist, "Basil's 'Neoplatonism': Its Background and Nature," in Paul Jonathan Fedwick, ed., *Basil of Caesarea: Christian, Humanist, Ascetic*, vol. 1 (Toronto: PIMS, 1981), 137–220, at 201, 208. For Rist, the only firm conclusion is that in *On the Holy Spirit* 9.23, Basil uses *Enn.* 5.1.10.24–26.

καλοῦ). Rather, whatever it is by nature, it is and is understood to be good and the simple, uniform, and non-composite source of good, as is testified even by our opponents.[78]

Here the subject is not the Son's or the Spirit's nature, but the nature distinguished by the "uncreated" differentia. The extension of the principle to cover a universal divine nature rather than merely the natures of the persons has clear benefits for Gregory's Trinitarian argument. Yet it also removes one of the reasons that had motivated earlier Christians to apply the language of participation to the Trinity, namely, the appearance of homonymous terms as special names of the persons (for instance, *logos* for the Son and holiness for the Spirit) and as predicates of creatures. For Gregory, who here is following an insight in a few passages of his older brother, the relevant predicates are now viewed as common predicates of the divine nature. In the passage just quoted, Gregory's point is that distinctions among the Father, Son, and Spirit must be understood as somehow within and corresponding to this common divine nature. This nature is the ultimate explanatory principle for the perfections he names; it therefore cannot admit of degrees of perfection. Accordingly, the persons who belong to it cannot be spoken of as greater or lesser than one another, as Eunomius had done. Gregory does not build his case, as earlier pro-Nicenes had done, by addressing the hypostases one by one; rather, he applies the participated-not-participating premise to the divine nature as such. For him, creatures participate in the divine nature; they do not stand in distinct participation relations with the three hypostases. The doctrinal effect of Gregory's argument might be akin to that of his predecessors, but the underlying framework has changed.[79]

The ground shifts once again in the Corpus Dionysiacum. In *Divine Names* 2, Pseudo-Dionysius distinguishes those names which are said of the entire divinity from those which are said specifically of only one of the hypostases. The former are "united in keeping with the divine distinction."[80] That is, they are ascribed to the three persons in union, while respecting the distinctions among the three. The examples of such names link them with participation:

non-reciprocal gifts of participation (αἱ ἄσχετοι μεταδόσεις), creations of substance, life, and wisdom, and the other gifts of goodness of the cause of all,

---

[78] Gregory of Nyssa, *Against Eunomius* 1.276 (107.4–10 Jaeger).
[79] Cp. Gregory of Nyssa, *On the Holy Spirit Against the Macedonians* 3–4 (90.19–92.30 Mueller).
[80] Pseudo-Dionysius, *DN* 2.5 (128.17 Suchla)

according to which [gifts] those which are participated without participation (τὰ ἀμεθέκτως μετεχόμενα) are hymned by the participations and the partakers.[81]

In context, the plural τὰ ἀμεθέκτως μετεχόμενα refers to the three persons. His reference to union within distinction is a way of saying, not unlike Gregory of Nyssa, that creatures participate in the entire Trinity, rather than in any single hypostasis. At the same time, the phrase introduces a nuance we have not yet encountered. The point is not, as we saw in our fourth-century authors, that the Trinity does not participate in a superordinate perfection, but rather that it is in one sense participated and in another sense unparticipated. The Trinity gives substance, life, wisdom, and the like, which are the subjects of participants' praises, but it does not exemplify the perfections it causes. The non-reciprocal character of participation is such that it can in a sense be more adequately denied than affirmed; thus Pseudo-Dionysius speaks of "the non-participation (ἡ ... ἀμεθεξία) of the all-causing divinity."[82]

Pseudo-Dionysius' terms ἀμεθέκτως and ἀμεθεξία evoke Proclean doctrine. According to Proclus, prior to any intelligible item that is participated (τὸ μετεχομένον) lies that which is unparticipated (τὸ ἀμέθεκτον); there is an ontological hierarchy descending from unparticipated to participated to participant (τὸ μετέχον).[83] Pseudo-Dionysius alters Proclus' scheme by identifying the levels of unparticipated and participated, using "unparticipatedly" as an adverbial qualification of "participated." The move might seem to entail a contradiction, but the context suggests that he is merely saying that the participated source does not exemplify the state that it causes in the participant, just as fire burns other things but is not itself burned.[84] Pseudo-Dionysius *must* identify the participated and the unparticipated, since for him what is participated is the Trinity beyond which there is nothing. Thus the denial of a superordinate order is implicit in his seemingly puzzling language. The *entire* divinity – Father, Son, and Spirit – is participated in each instance of participation; he leaves no opening for distinct participations in the three hypostases, such that the Father might be unparticipated while the Son and Spirit are participated.

[81] Pseudo-Dionysius, *DN* 2.5 (128.17–129.3 Suchla). On the translation of ἄσχετος, see Andrew Radde-Gallwitz, "Pseudo-Dionysius, the *Parmenides*, and the Problem of Contradiction," in John D. Turner and Kevin Corrigan, eds., *Plato's Parmenides and its Heritage*, vol. 2: *Reception in Patristic, Gnostic, and Christian Neoplatonic Texts* (Atlanta: Society of Biblical Literature, 2010), 243–254, at 248–249.

[82] Pseudo-Dionysius, *DN* 2.4 (129.9–11 Suchla).

[83] Proclus, *Elements of Theology* 23–24 (26–29 Dodds).

[84] Pseudo-Dionysius, *DN* 2.8 (132.17–133.4).

What distinguishes Pseudo-Dionysius from his predecessors is his thorough application of the idea that the Trinity exists beyond being and intelligence, which leads him to avoid the language of divine nature and substance that had featured prominently in previous authors. We have, then, the language of participation in the Trinity placed within a more thoroughly Neoplatonic metaphysical framework. At the same time, Pseudo-Dionysius' Trinitarian commitments lead him to revise Proclus' use of the language of non-participation.

Each of these four stages represents a distinct model of Trinitarian theology worthy of reflection in its own right. As we look across the four, we can at the least conclude that the development of Trinitarian orthodoxy did not lead to any disengagement with Platonist metaphysics. The survival of participation metaphysics in these authors, and many after them, forces us to ask whether Christian theology can get by without it. While it is true that, after Origen, participation ceases to do the work of explaining relations among the Trinitarian hypostases, it would not be easy to find an alternative scheme that expresses exactly the point made by Athanasius or his successors. Simply invoking a dichotomy between "Creator" and "creature" (or "God" and "world") captures a difference but overlooks the concomitant likeness, and it fails to introduce the linguistic issue of homonymy that the doctrine of participation identifies. As we have seen, the patristic authors surveyed here are interested in cases where the same predicate is applied to both God and a creature: for instance, when one says "the Holy Spirit is holy" and "the angel Gabriel is holy." Our authors give interestingly different accounts of the first proposition: is it true in virtue of the Spirit's nature or the divine nature? Does the supersubstantial divinity transcend even holiness? Despite these differences, each account relies on the notion of divinity as that which is participated without itself participating.

CONCLUSION

This chapter has highlighted the formative role of Platonism in the making of Christian doctrine. Even if one grants this point, however, it remains obviously true that not every element essential to pro-Nicene Trinitarian thought stems from Platonism. The development of this doctrine was rooted in the exegesis of the Christian scriptures, it was inextricably tied to the practice of baptism in the triune name, and it was shepherded by the institution of the Christian episcopacy, which since Constantine worked under imperial patronage. Even on the conceptual level, we have seen differences between the idea of three metaphysically coordinate hypostases and the absolutely undifferentiated first principle of Neoplatonism.[85] Although a number of pro-Nicenes saw a harmony between the Father, Son, and Spirit and the One, *Nous*, and Soul, Platonism's greatest substantive influences on Christian Trinitarian theology lay in the area of participation metaphysics as well as in inspiring the more general theological dictum of divine immateriality and intelligibility. These ideas gave content to how Christians understood the relation between the triune Creator and the creation.

Bibliography

Athanasius and Didymus. *Works on the Spirit.* Translated by Mark DelCogliano, Andrew Radde-Gallwitz, and Lewis Ayres. Yonkers, NY: St. Vladimir's Seminary Press, 2011.

Ayres, Lewis. *Nicaea and its Legacy: An Approach to Fourth-Century Trinitarian Theology.* Oxford: Oxford University Press, 2004.

Balás, David L. *Metousia Theou: Man's Participation in God's Perfections According to Saint Gregory of Nyssa,* Studia Anselmiana 55. Rome: Herder & Herder, 1966.

Balthasar, Hans Urs von. *Presence and Thought: An Essay on the Religious Philosophy of Gregory of Nyssa.* Translated by Mark Sebanc. San Francisco: Ignatius, 1995.

Barnes, Michel René. *The Power of God: Δύναμις in Gregory of Nyssa's Trinitarian Theology.* Washington, D.C.: The Catholic University of America Press, 2000.

Barrett, Jordan P. *Divine Simplicity: A Biblical and Trinitarian Account.* Minneapolis: Fortress, 2017.

Beatrice, Pier F. "Quosdam Platonicorum Libros: The Platonic Readings of Augustine in Milan." *Vigiliae Christianae* 43 (1989): 248–281.

Dillon, John. "Logos and Trinity: Patterns of Platonist Influence on early Christianity." In *The Philosophy in Christianity,* edited by Godfrey Vesey, 1–13. Cambridge: Cambridge University Press, 1989.

"Origen's Doctrine of the Trinity and Some Later Neoplatonic Theories." In *Neoplatonism and Christian Thought,* Studies in Neoplatonism: Ancient and Modern 3, edited by Dominic O'Meara, 19-23. Albany: SUNY Press, 1982.

Drecoll, Volker Henning. "Is Porphyry the Source Used by Marius Victorinus?" In *Plato's Parmenides and its Heritage,* vol. 2: *Reception in Patristics, Gnostic, and Christian Neoplatonic Texts,* Writings from the Greco-Roman World Supplements 3, edited by John D. Turner and Kevin Corrigan, 65–80. Atlanta: Society of Biblical Literature Publications, 2010.

---

[85] On what appears to be an attempt at a compromise by Olympiodorus, see Jan Opsomer, "Olympiodorus," in Lloyd P. Gerson, ed., *The Cambridge History of Philosophy in Late Antiquity,* vol. 2 (Cambridge: Cambridge University Press, 2010), 697–710 at 702–704.

Duby, Stephen. *Divine Simplicity: A Dogmatic Account.* London: Bloomsbury T & T Clark, 2016.

Edwards, Mark J. "Origen's Platonism: Questions and Caveats." *Zeitschrift für Antikes Christentum* 12 (2008): 20–38.

Gilson, Etienne. *Christian Philosophy: An Introduction.* Translated by Armand Maurer. Toronto: Pontifical Institute of Medieval Studies, 1993.

Hankinson, R. J. *Cause and Explanation in Ancient Greek Thought.* Oxford: Clarendon Press, 1998.

Hanson, R. P. C. *The Search for a Christian Doctrine of God: The Arian Controversy, 318–381.* Grand Rapids, MI: Baker Academic, 1988.

Harnack, Adolf von. *History of Dogma,* vols. 4 and 5. Translated by Neil Buchanan. New York: Dover, 1961.

Hart, David Bentley. *The Hidden and the Manifest: Essays in Theology and Metaphysics.* Grand Rapids, MI: Eerdmans, 2017.

Ivanka, Endre von. "Vom Platonismus zur Theorie der Mystik: Zur Erkenntnislehre Gregors von Nyssa." *Scholastik* 11 (1936): 163–195.

Kelly, J. N. D. *Early Christian Doctrines.* Rev. ed. New York: Harper, 1978.

Knapp, Georg Christian. *Lectures on Christian Theology,* vol. 1. Translated by Leonard Woods, 1st ed. New York: G. & C. & H. Carvill, 1831.

Lilla, Salvatore R. C. "The Neoplatonic Hypostases and the Christian Trinity." In *Studies in Plato and the Platonic Tradition. Essays Presented to John Whittaker,* edited by Mark Joyal, 127–189. Aldershot: Ashgate, 1997.

Louth, Andrew. *St John Damascene: Tradition and Originality in Byzantine Theology.* Oxford: Oxford University Press, 2002.

Majercik, Ruth. "A Reminiscence of the 'Chaldean Oracles' at Gregory of Nazianzus, *Or.* 29,2: ΟΙΟΝ ΚΡΑΤΗΡ ΤΙΣ ΥΠΕΡΕΡΡΥΗ." *Vigiliae Christianae* 52 (1998): 286–292.

Moore, William and Henry Austin Wilson, trans. *Nicene and Post-Nicene Fathers,* second series, vol. 5: *Gregory of Nyssa: Dogmatic Treatises, etc.* Peabody, MA: Hendrickson, 1999.

Opsomer, Jan. "Olympiodorus." In *The Cambridge History of Philosophy in Late Antiquity,* vol. 2, edited by Lloyd P. Gerson, 697–710. Cambridge: Cambridge University Press, 2010.

Origen. *Commentary on the Gospels of John. Books 13–32.* Translated by Ronald E. Heine. Fathers of the Church Series, 89. Washington, D.C.: Catholic University Press, 1993.

Pannenberg, Wolfhart. "The Appropriation of the Philosophical Concept of God as a Dogmatic Problem of Early Christian Theology." In *Basic Questions in Theology: Collected Essays,* vol. 2, translated by George H. Kehm, 119–183. Philadelphia: Fortress, 1971.

Petau, Denis. *Dogmata theologica,* vol. 2: *primum de praedestione, postea de Trinitate.* Paris: Le Vivès, 1865–1867.

Plotinus. *The Enneads.* Edited and translated by Lloyd Gerson. Cambridge: Cambridge University Press, 2018.

Proclus. *The Elements of Theology.* Edited and translated by E. R. Dodds, 2nd ed. Oxford: Clarendon Press, 1963.

Radde-Gallwitz, Andrew. *Gregory of Nyssa's Doctrinal Works: A Literary Study.* Oxford: Oxford University Press, 2018.

"Pseudo-Dionysius, the *Parmenides*, and the Problem of Contradiction." In *Plato's Parmenides and its Heritage*, vol. 2: *Reception in Patristic, Gnostic, and Christian Neoplatonic Texts*, edited by John D. Turner and Kevin Corrigan, 243–254. Atlanta: Society of Biblical Literature, 2010.

Radde-Gallwitz, Andrew, ed. *The Cambridge Edition of Early Christian Writings, Volume One: God.* Cambridge: Cambridge University Press, 2017.

Ricken, Friedo. "Das Homoousios von Nikaia als Krisis des altchristlichen Platonismus." In *Zur Frühgeschichte der Christologie: Ihre biblischen Anfänge und die Lehrformel von Nikaia*, Quaestiones Disputatae 51, edited by Bernhard Welte, 74–99. Freiburg, Basel, Vienna: Herder, 1971.

Rist, John. "Basil's 'Neoplatonism': Its Background and Nature." In *Basil of Caesarea: Christian, Humanist, Ascetic*, vol. 1, edited by Paul Jonathan Fedwick, 137–220. Toronto: PIMS, 1981.

Saint Augustine. *The City of God against the Pagans.* Translated by R. W. Dyson. Cambridge: Cambridge University Press, 2005.

Confessions. Translated by Henry Chadwick. Oxford: Oxford University Press, 1991.

Saint Basil of Caesarea. *Against Eunomius.* Translated by Mark Delcogliano and Andrew Radde-Gallwitz. Fathers of the Church Series. Washington, D.C.: Catholic University of America Press, 2011.

Smith, Jonathan Z. *Drudgery Divine: On the Comparison of Early Christianities and the Religions of Late Antiquity.* Chicago: University of Chicago Press, 1990.

Soskice, Janet M. "Athens and Jerusalem, Alexandria and Edessa: Is There a Metaphysics of Scripture?" *International Journal of Systematic Theology* 8 (2006): 149–162.

Turner, John D. "The Platonizing Sethian Treatises, Marius Victorinus's Philosophical Sources, and Pre-Plotinian *Parmenides* Commentaries." In *Plato's Parmenides and its Heritage*, vol. 1: *History and Interpretation from the Old Academy to Later Platonism and Gnosticism*, edited by John D. Turner and Kevin Corrigan, 131–172. Atlanta: Society of Biblical Literature Publications, 2010.

Williams, Rowan. *Arius: Heresy and Tradition.* Rev. ed. Grand Rapids, MI and Cambridge, UK: Eerdmans, 2002.

I.4

Creation, Begetting, Desire, and Re-Creation

Kevin Corrigan

INTRODUCTION: A NOTE ON "CHRISTIAN PLATONISM"

"Christian Platonism" is a problematic phrase. It seems to imply that Christianity is adjectival, an attribute of some nebulous subject "Platonism." But if we reverse the terms as in "Platonizing Christianity," this suggests Harnack's thesis of "Hellenization" as a contaminating form of some pure Christianity or an overlying layer upon a Jewish-Semitic, nonphilosophical context for understanding the birth of Christianity. Yet while the figure of Jesus resists categorization (including Jesus as prototype for later Cynic philosophers), the early Church was born in the context of Hellenized Jews, namely, the first 3,000 converts present at Pentecost in Jerusalem in Acts 2:9–11; and Paul expressly meets with Stoic and Epicurean philosophers in Athens in Acts 17:18, which indicates that philosophy was already a rival, even if it taught foreign truths and possessed no divine authority. So Christian Platonism is a catch-all phrase. It recognizes that Plato and his successors, including the whole of ancient pagan thought, especially Aristotle as Christianity gradually came to define itself, formed part of the complex background to the emergence of a new religion. Not only Christian intellectuals such as Tatian, Tertullian, and Justin Martyr, but also ordinary people, literate and illiterate, remained hostile to pagan influences; and prominent pagan intellectuals like Porphyry were equally hostile. And yet, as I shall argue here, both pagans and Christians were mutually transformed by their prolonged encounter on many issues, but especially on the questions of creation, desire, and return. I shall start in an unfamiliar way with Judeo-Christian influence upon major features of the Platonic tradition before

79

articulating a hidden conversation that lies behind Christian thinking about the Trinity, the structure of reality, and the creation of the human being.

TERMS AND BACKGROUND

Let us first look at the principal terms and contrast "creation" with "craftsmanship." The creation tradition is, above all, Jewish. In Genesis and elsewhere, the verb to create is *bara* (בָּרָא); the verb to make or to do, *asah* (עָשָׂה). What is the difference between them?[1] Does God create out of nothing or does God simply make? The two verbs can be used interchangeably. Gen 1.1: God *created* the heavens and the earth; Gen 1.7: God *made* the expanse between the waters above and below. But Gen 2.3: God created *and* made all His works. God is usually the subject of the verb *bara*, while human beings make (*asah*), but God both creates (*bara*) *and* makes (*asah*).[2] In addition, we know from Genesis 2:7 that God formed (יָצַר, *yatsar*) Adam from the dust of the earth and in Genesis 2:22 that God fashioned (בָּנָה, *banah*) Eve from the rib of Adam. So within divine creating, making, doing, forming, and fashioning are included. In addition, God orders and reorders the "chaos" of primeval formlessness (Gen 1:2), the untamed forces of the world (Isa 51:9–10; Pss 74:12–17, 89:9–13, 93:3–4, 104:2b–9; Job 38:8–11, 41:1–34), and sin and idolatry (e.g. Ex 32: 9–10; Dt 8: 11–20; Hos 2: 8–9). Hence, creation and redemption are intertwined.[3]

There is a similar usage in the New Testament. In John 1:3, all things *came into being* (ἐγένετο) by the Word of God, who is Jesus Christ (John 1:14). In Colossians 1:16, all things were created or founded (ἐκτίσθη) by and for Christ. In Hebrews 1:2 Christ made (ἐποίησεν) the original creation by His Word (cf. Heb 11:3). "To come into being," "create," and "make" in these passages clearly refer to the same divine activities in Genesis 1 and 2. In the Vulgate, similarly, Gen 1.1: "In principio creavit Deus"; 1.3: "Fiat lux. Et lux facta est"; and Gen. 2.3 gives a similar meaning: "creavit Deus ut faceret" – God rested from all his work which God created and made.[4] Here, as in the Hebrew Bible, the notion

---

[1] See generally *JPS Hebrew–English Tanakh: The Traditional Hebrew Text and The New JPS Translation* (Philadelphia, PA: The Jewish Publication Society, 1999), 1–20.

[2] Two exceptions: in Joshua 17:15, 18 and 1 Samuel 2:29 man is the subject of *bara*.

[3] See P. M. Blowers, "Doctrine of Creation," in *Oxford Handbook of Early Christian Studies*, ed. Susan Ashbrook Harvey and David G. Hunter (Oxford: Oxford University Press, 2008), 906–922, at p. 906.

[4] For the later Christian tradition on God's creation of all things, including matter, see Hermas, *Mand.* 1; Justin Martyr, *The First Apology* 59; Tatian, *Address to the Greeks* 5;

of timeless *creatio ex nihilo* seems to be predominant, despite the Biblical description of "days" and despite the fact that Tertullian envisages a beginning *in time* (*Herm.* 19) or the Word is in between Creator and creation (Methodius, *Creat.* 9, 11); but what the "nothing" of creation may be is unclear: God's complete freedom (Tertullian, *Herm.* 6, and others); the formless matter of God's creation in need of God's care (Athanasius, *Inc.* 3–5), or pure (Neoplatonic) privation, "almost nothing" (Augustine, *Conf.* 12. 6. 6); or Christ as *archē* (Origen; cf. Colossians 1:16: "in him all things were created, in heaven and on earth" (*Comm. Gen.* 1b–2a); or God as nonbeing by human standards (Basilides); or God making nonexistent material existent by creation; or some intelligible matter in God as a kind of Neoplatonic emanation (Gregory of Nyssa; *DHO* 23–24).[5] In other words, creation from pure nothingness seems philosophically problematic if not altogether incoherent.[6]

The general distinction between creating and making, or doing, may well be what Philo has in mind in his work *On Dreams*, I.76: "And above all, as the sun when it rises makes visible objects which had been hidden, so God when He gave birth (γεννήσας) to all things, not only brought them into sight, but also made (ἐποίησεν) things which before were not, not just handling material as an artificer (δημιουργός), but being Himself its creator (κτίστης)." Here we have Philo's implicit criticism of Plato, despite the common impression that he follows Plato rather than Genesis. In the *Timaeus*, God is the craftsman (δημιουργός) who brings the world into order, *not the creator* or establisher (κτίστης) who made (ἐποίησεν) the world, or at least its contents, apparently from nothing (ἃ πρότερον οὐκ ἦν). Nonetheless, early Christianity used δημιουργός in the sense of creator.

FROM PLATO AND ARISTOTLE TO PLOTINUS

The Platonic-Aristotelian tradition presents a distinct contrast to the Judaic-Christian tradition to the point of being challenged by it to think through its own primary principles about creation. In Plato's *Timaeus* (and also in the myth of the *Statesman*), God, the Demiurge (together with the lesser gods), is represented as doing or making many things: the

---

12; Theophilus of Antioch, *To Autolycus* 2, 4; Athenagoras, *Plea for the Christians* 4; Irenaeus, *Against Heresies* 2.10.2–4; Tertullian, *Against Hermogenes* 34; 45; Clement, *Stromata* 6.16; Origen, *De Princ.* Preface 4; 3.5. etc.
5 Blowers, "Doctrine of Creation," 911–916.   6 Blowers, "Doctrine of Creation," 915.

Demiurge looks to the paradigm of the Eternal Living Creature, deliber-
ates, plans, desires, frames,[7] and so on, not unlike the God of the Bible.
This divine creative function is why Numenius later will describe Plato as
"Moses speaking Greek"[8] or why Eusebius will persistently see Plato as
borrowing from Moses.[9] At the same time, however, in looking to the
Paradigm, the Demiurge seems dependent upon something above and
beyond himself, on the one hand; and in managing the Receptacle or
Chora, there enters the possibility that the Demiurge and *Chora* may be
coeval principles, something anathema to Christianity.

Later the demiurgic or creative function gets divided (as in the
Chaldaean Oracles or Numenius)[10] between a contemplative aspect
and a doing or making aspect or even acquires an evil feature, like
the irrational World Soul in Atticus and Plutarch of Chaeronea,[11] or
is downgraded to become ignorant and blundering like the
Valentinian Demiurge.[12] Here there is no real creation as in early
Judaic-Christian thought. In Plato, the Demiurge makes, forms, and
moves the cosmos in a rather distant primordial, if anthropomorphic
way (though Plato expresses this differently elsewhere, more akin to
the Judeo-Christian tradition);[13] or in Gnostic texts the demiurge
becomes blinded and loses sight of the truth. For Christians, this is
not a God one might want to intervene in cosmic life. It is also not
a God – notwithstanding many elements in Plato's dialogues to the
contrary[14] – that one can imagine loving everyone or, perhaps,
anyone.

The situation seems worse in Aristotle. In Aristotle's *Metaphysics* and
elsewhere, God or *Nous* does not do or make anything, unlike Plato's
anthropomorphic Demiurge. God moves remotely, it would seem, by

---

[7] *Timaeus* 28a–37d; *Statesman* 271d–274e.

[8] Numenius, fr. 8, Des Places numbering, in Robert Petty, *The Fragments of Numenius of
Apamea* (London: The Prometheus Trust, 2012).

[9] *Preparatio Evangelica* XV *passim*.

[10] *Chaldean Oracles*, The First God thinks alone – frs. 37, 39, 40, and the Second God is
divided – frs. 5, 33, 35, 37 (Majercik); Numenius, fr. 16 (Petty).

[11] Proclus, *In Timaeum* I 381, 26 ff.

[12] See *Tripartite Tractate* 104, 25ff. For overview, J. D. Turner, *Sethian Gnosticism and the
Platonic Tradition* (Québec: Presses de l'Université Laval, 2001).

[13] See, for example, *Sophist* 265b–c: "every power is productive which causes things to
come into being which did not exist before … shall we say that *they came into being*
(*gignesthai*), *not having been before*, in any other way than through God's workman-
ship?" (trans. H. N. Fowler, Loeb).

[14] Cf. K. Corrigan, *Love, Friendship, Beauty, and the Good: Plato, Aristotle and the Later
Tradition* (Eugene, OR: Wipf & Stock, 2019), 84–85.

being unmoved, that is, as a final cause: "as being loved."[15] For Aristotle,
God's thought is the originative source of motion only as the object of
desire, real or apparent; and this divine "thinking of thinking" is activity
or energy in the purest sense,[16] that is, contemplation (θεωρία),[17] a life that
we sometimes participate in, but rarely and fleetingly (*Met.* 12, 7). Such
a principle as the Unmoved Mover, then, is hard to associate with direct
creativity, love, or even what we might call desire. The Unmoved Mover
expressly does not make or fashion anything in the cosmos, despite its
undoubted pervasive influence in other senses;[18] and on the other hand,
the contemplative life, which is the highest life for a human being, seems
solitary and hard to associate with the ideal of the practical life,[19] in which
the human being enjoys community intrinsically and needs good friends
for his or her best self-development.[20]

This is, of course, a caricature of Plato and Aristotle, but the outcome
still seems unpromising: quite apart from the heritage of Stoicism,
Epicureanism, and Skepticism, the Platonic Demiurge is not a God who
creates *out of nothing*, not a God who really *wills* creation (as in Genesis:
fiat lux), and not a God who *loves* necessarily (though we may be more or
less god-beloved in many Platonic dialogues, it is true); and the
Aristotelian Unmoved Mover neither *wills* nor *loves* anything, especially
not individuals, if on the Peripatetic view (of Alexander of Aphrodisias)
divine providence only extends as far as the movements of the heavenly
bodies and the maintenance of sublunary species, but not as far as *sublunary individuals*.[21] If so, God's sustaining activity does not meaningfully
reach our lives. As a consequence perhaps, even major Middle Platonic
thinkers, such as Numenius, seem to have no clear idea about what divine
activity might be. For instance, Numenius says in one fragment that the
"first God" is "idle of all works," while the demiurgic God rules "as he

---

[15] *Metaphysics* 12, 7, 1072b3; Cf. Alcinous, *Didaskalikos* 10, 2, 5–9.
[16] *Metaphysics* 12, 9, 1075b34.
[17] Cf. A. C. Lloyd, *The Anatomy of Neoplatonism* (Oxford: Oxford University Press, 1990),
    182–3.
[18] On this, see Corrigan, *Love, Friendship, Beauty*, 12–23.
[19] For assessment see H. H. Joachim, *Aristotle. The Nicomachean Ethics* (Oxford:
    Clarendon Press, 1970), 241–3, and compare 284–97; J. Lear, *Aristotle: The Desire to
    Understand* (Cambridge: Cambridge University Press, 1988), 309–20; T. Irwin,
    Aristotle's First Principles (Oxford: Clarendon Press, 1988), 347–72.
[20] See, especially, *EN* 8–9; Joachim, *Aristotle. The Nicomachean Ethics*, 241–61.
[21] In the Arabic *De Providentia* 1, 1–9, 2, translated by Ruland, in R. W. Sharples,
    "Alexander of Aphrodisias on Divine Providence: Two Problems," *Classical Quarterly*
    31, no. 1 (1982), 198–211.

goes through the heavens" (fr. 12, 12–14, Petty). The Demiurge "directs," "steers," and "takes judgment from contemplation [of the First], but is impelled by desire" (fr. 18, 10–14); and in another striking fragment, contemplation seems to alternate with demiurgic activity: "for the second [god], being double, self-makes his own idea and the cosmos, being demiurge, then is wholly contemplative" (fr. 16, 10–12, Petty). In other words, in one of the principal pre-Plotinian figures (whom Plotinus was accused of plagiarizing)[22] there is not only no coherent account of divine activity or agency, but divine making is really a derivative activity. God in the primary sense is proudly noncreative ("the First god is idle of any act whatsoever and king"). This is presumably Numenius' interpretation of Plato's *Second Letter* 312e and of the Good "beyond being" of *Republic* Book 6: the Highest God is unlike any Judeo-Christian Creator. He is utterly beyond creativity.[23]

If we put this into the context of Peripatetic thought (that appears to reject divine agency in the lives of individuals) and of Gnostic thought (that tends to present an externalized view of contemplation in privileged visions presented as interpretations of ancient texts [the Bible, Plato, Aristotle, and so on],[24] privileged because access is open only to the few by contrast with the oblivion of ordinary humans), then we see with some clarity the pressing issues of divine and human creative agency with which Plotinus came to wrestle in the *Enneads*.

Plotinus, of course, is the pagan thinker who is closest to "creation" and "return" as the fundamental structure of reality: procession from the One, self-constitution, and return or *epistrophē* through desire and love. Plotinus' universe is thoroughly generative:[25] the One "generates," "gives birth" to subsequent realities, just as Nous and Soul give birth in their own ways – and as Plato's "lovers" generate in the beautiful or give birth on the ladder of ascent to discourses, images, or, finally, true things.[26] Love in different forms is the force that makes all subsequent beings convert to their begetter, even matter as pure privation that is not independent of the One's creative power.[27] Here Plotinus not only unites and develops the

---

[22] Porphyry, *Life of Plotinus* 17, 1–7.

[23] As Petty, *Fragments of Numenius*, observes ad loc.

[24] On Sethian Gnostic thought generally see Turner, *Sethian Gnosticism and the Platonic Tradition*.

[25] See J. H. Sleeman and Gilbert Pollet, *Lexicon Plotinianum* (Leiden: Brill, 1980), *gennan, gennēma, gennesis*, 199–201.

[26] *Symposium* 210a–212a. *Republic* 6, 490a–b.

[27] For matter, see especially *Ennead* I. 8 [51] 14.

thought of Plato and Aristotle but transmits it to later ages to the point that the Neoplatonic triad "abiding–procession–return"[28] prefigures the overall structure of Aquinas' *Summa Theologica* and Plotinian-Proclan thought provides the Islamic tradition with the *Theology of Aristotle* and the *Liber de Causis* that will receive commentaries by Al Farabi, Ibn Sina, and others. That Plotinus has any notion of creation, however, has been vigorously denied.[29]

CREATION AND LOVE: PAGAN AND CHRISTIAN

Here I shall pick three examples of a hidden conversation in Plotinus, which show that Platonic "pagan" thought was decisively influenced and, indeed, transformed by "Christian" Platonism. The first is Plotinus' treatment of the free will of the Good and the second is his striking affirmation of creation out of nothing, in VI. 8 [39], where he builds into his treatment of freedom some features of Christian Gnostic thought, such as the characterization of the Good as self-love and its own self-production, as in the Valentinian *Tripartite Tractate* and earlier Platonism.[30]

In VI. 8, Plotinus is plainly responding to Jewish, Christian, Gnostic, and other pagan perspectives in which God wills creation and intervenes in the world. From treatise 30 to 38, Plotinus had developed two models of production or making, first, a model of creative contemplation in III. 8 [30], and second, a model of divine production in V. 8 [31], 5–7 and VI. 7 [38] 1–13.

---

[28] This triad is later than Plotinus; see R. T. Wallis, *Neoplatonism* (London: Duckworth/Hackett, 1995), 132–33, 145.

[29] Against "creation" in Plotinus, see D. O'Brien, "Plotinus on the Making of Matter: The Identity of Darkness, Part III," *International Journal of the Platonic Tradition* 6, no. 1 (2012), 72–6; in favor, B. Zimmerman, "Does Plotinus Present a Philosophical Account of Creation?" *Review of Metaphysics* 67 (2013), 55–105. Zimmerman rightly argues, following Aquinas and Islamic thought, that if the metaphysical idea of creation demarcates "the production of a thing into being according to its entire substance, such that the product is dependent on its cause for its continued existence," then Plotinus presents a philosophical account of creation.

[30] For example, the One as love (VI.8.16, 34; 19, 13; *Trip. Tract.* 55.22); self-production of the First principle – VI.8, chapter 13, 54; 21, 17; *Trip. Tract.* 56, 1–4 and for Gnostic and Hermetic self-generation see *Tripartite Tractate*, NH 1.5, 56, 1–6; *Gospel of the Egyptians*, NH IV 2, 79, 5–6; *Three Steles of Seth*, NH VII 5, 124, 25–29; 126, 1–7; *Zostrianos*, NH VIII 1, 20, 4–14; 74, 20–24; NH VII 1, 124, 17–19; *Allogenes*, NH XI 3, 56, 10–15; 65, 22–27; *Corpus Hermeticum*, IV 10, 17; *Eugnostos the Blessed*, NH III 3, 75, 2–8. See also Numenius, fr. 16; Alcinous, *Didaskalikos* 10, 3, 15–18: The good "by his own will ... has filled all things with himself, rousing up the soul of the world"; *Chaldean Oracles* 37, 2, 4; 81, 4; 107, 4.

According to the first model, contemplation or philosophic wisdom, far from being private or external to the world, as the Gnostics appeared to hold,[31] is the fundamental form of all natural making and, indeed, of all life. Everything – even plant life – is either contemplation (in the sense that it contains its intelligibility within itself, as does intellect)[32] or a product or consequence of contemplation (in the sense that if you unpacked the intelligibility in anything whatsoever, it would lead you to everything else in the universe or to a more comprehensive view of reality as a whole) or, finally, a substitute for contemplation (in the sense that action and production are ways of coming to see or understand a reality that is at first too densely compacted for us to grasp it altogether).[33] Contemplation or insight, therefore, is the primary *creative* force in both the spiritual and physical worlds.

Plotinus here develops a model for creative activity *inter alia* from Aristotle's *Nicomachean Ethics*. Contemplation is not *praxis* or *poesis*, that is, doing or making in the ordinary sense of acting or making things, but *energeia*, pure creative activity that makes doing and making possible and that ultimately expresses Divine creative energy. *Theoria* (III. 8, 5, 29–30) is without limit, like the Good itself,[34] and the final cause is the original mover of the desire to return "if" Nous is *both* origin and goal (III. 8 [30] 7, 1–15; cf. *EN* 1143b10).

This is one model, then, for understanding spiritual making or coming-to-be. Spiritual activities, like Nous or Soul, neither *make* nor *act* in an anthropomorphic way; nor do they *come-to-be* like physical things. Their making or coming-to-be (phrases Plotinus uses) are instantaneous activities complete in themselves like contemplation. In other words, Plotinus develops a pagan model for "creation" from Aristotle's ethics and theology that, because of Aristotle's criticism of Plato's Demiurge, had rejected anthropomorphic creative production in favor of an eternal cosmos. Like Plotinus, Origen – and the Cappadocians later – posits a double creation, that is, a noetic realm, created but eternal, containing rational beings, and, prior ontologically, though not temporally, to the physical world (*Princ.* 2.9.4).[35] Most important, as we shall see, Plotinus implicitly inscribes within contemplative creation a form of *intelligible coming-to-be* between hypostases, such as Intellect and Soul, and *within* single hypostases such as Intellect, thus providing an implicit paradigm of

---

[31] Cf. II. 9 [33] 18, 35–6.   [32] III. 8 [30] 7, 1 ff.; 8 passim; cf. VI. 7 [38] 1–7.
[33] III. 8 [30] 7, 1ff.   [34] Cf. VI. 7 [38] 23–35.
[35] *De Princ.* 2.9.4 (and *Genesis Homilies* 1.5 re Genesis 1:1).

"begetting" without "creation" of something different for later Christian thinkers.

According to a second model, developed in V. 8 [31] and VI. 7 [38], Plotinus argues that the production of the sensible world out of the Intelligible World involves no rationality or deliberation, since divine intelligible production as a function of the purest thought or contemplation must already be complete in itself so that it can be unfolded later in time and space. What is *enfolded* in the Demiurgic Intellect becomes *unfolded* in the Sensible Cosmos, but in such a way that we can see purpose and teleology after the fact, so to speak, in the Cosmos's unfolding without there ever having been rational, anthropomorphic purpose or design in Intellect itself.[36]

These sophisticated models of production lead to the need for Plotinus to write VI. 8, immediately after VI. 7. If contemplation is primarily creative (according to III. 8), and if demiurgic production involves no deliberation or even rationality (according to VI. 7), does the individual agent have a role in this and is spiritual production free? To answer these questions, Plotinus traces the reality of human free will back through the individual agent (VI. 8, chapters 1–6) through Intellect and up to the Good. But then one might ask: can the necessary spontaneous emanation of everything from the Good be described as *free*? In fact, can the Good actually create *out of nothing*? In VI. 8, Plotinus replies affirmatively, even if he acknowledges that he is not speaking properly: [the Good's] "something-like-substance *is together with it* and, so to speak, *comes to be eternally together* with its activity and *it makes itself from both, for itself* and *from nothing*" (7, 52–54: αὐτὸ αὑτὸ ποιεῖ, καὶ ἑαυτῷ καὶ οὐδενός). Strictly, of course, there can be no multiplicity whatsoever in the Good, but Plotinus' argument shows: first, that in the First God (in Numenius' language) there is no solitariness in the sense of privation; second, that there is no black hole of inactivity, but a supreme self-generative togetherness; and, third, that there is no preexistent matter upon which such a principle might depend; instead, the Good is *self-producing and its production is out of nothing*.[37]

But is creation here instrumentalist? The Good may create itself, but it makes everything else *by means of* Intellect and Soul. However, this is not

---

[36] See V. 8 [31] 5–7 and VI. 7 [38] 1–11.

[37] On this generally see K. Corrigan and J. D. Turner, *Plotinus, Ennead VI. 8: On the Voluntary and the Free Will of the One* (Las Vegas, Zurich, Athens: Parmenides Press, 2017), 227–29 (17–59).

the case. The Good itself makes everything *directly*, but also by means of intermediaries. One of Plotinus' most striking statements is found in VI. 7 [38] 22, 22–25. "What does the Good make now?" he asks, and he replies: "Now as well it is keeping those things in being and making the thinking things think (*noein*) and the living things live, inspiring thought (*noun*), inspiring life (*zōēn*) and, if something cannot live, existence (*einai*)." The Good is the direct cause of intellect, life, and being – just as in Proclus and Dionysius, the higher the principle the more *piercing* or *penetrating* is its influence.[38] Other things are instrumental; the Good creates directly.

Here then we have the strongest statement that the Good eternally creates itself [and everything else] out of nothing – even if we have to understand this with an "as it were." What does "of nothing" or "out of nothing" mean in this context? Here it means that God's creation is purely self-dependent, and if so, supreme self-dependence is the condition for the totality of the being of all subsequent creatures. This view of creation out of nothing seems to me to be philosophically coherent – and indeed, necessary, since pure self-dependence in the singularity of Divine Creation is also the model for all subsequent forms of self-dependence, including thought.[39] So while Plotinus' view of divine freedom is already implicit in earlier work – see, for example, III. 1 [3], nowhere before the thirty-ninth treatise does Plotinus invoke directly the Good's creation out of nothing. I suggest, then, that, like Origen, Plotinus believed in divine and human freedom from the beginning of his writing career, but that this formulation in VI. 8 and his striking insistence upon divine self-creation out of nothing emerged almost certainly from his own dialogue (either with himself or members of his school or both) between the pagan Platonic and the Judeo-Christian Platonic traditions.

The third feature is related to this, namely, the implicit connection between an intense love of the soul for the Good in VI. 7 [38] and the self-love of the Good itself in VI. 8 [39], a connection which shows that Plotinus is thinking about divine and human love in the context not only of the heritage of Plato and Aristotle but also of Jewish and Christian concerns as evidenced in Gnostic texts.[40] In VI. 7, soul's love is effectively infinite responding intimately to the infinity of the One.[41] As in III. 8 [30], soul or intellect is drawn incessantly by desire to the One, so much so that in mystical union it leaves intellect proper behind in its "mad"

---

[38] Proclus, *Elements of Theology*, prop. 57; cf. (re Iamblichus) Olympiodorus, *In Alc.* 110, 13ff., Creuz.
[39] See especially VI. 7 [38] 40, 4–20.   [40] See n. 24 above.   [41] VI. 7 [38] 23–35.

passion[42] and is "mingled" with the One.[43] Gregory of Nyssa's doctrine of *epektasis*,[44] or the notion that soul in its desire for return is bound up in the infinity of the Good, is a profoundly original meditation on part of this motif in III. 8 and VI. 7. We may compare *Ennead* III. 8 [30] 11, 22–24: intellect "is always desiring and always hitting upon the object of its desire" (καὶ ἐφιέμενος ἀεὶ καὶ ἀεὶ τυγχάνων); and a passage from the *Life of Moses*, which is more closely related to the soul or intellect-of-soul focus in *Ennead* VI. 7, chapters 30–35: since the only limitation of virtue is vice, Gregory writes, and since the divine nature excludes anything contrary to it, "then the divine nature is conceived without bound or limit. But the soul that pursues true virtue actually participates in God himself, because he is infinite virtue. Now since those who have come to know the highest good, desire completely to share in it, and since this good is limitless, it follows that their desire must necessarily be coextensive with the limitless, and therefore have no limit" (*Life of Moses*, PG 44, 301a–b; Daniélou, i, 6–7).[45] Here Gregory takes and transforms an idea in Plotinus.

But my central point[46] is that if the soul is mingled by love with the One in VI 7, and if in the very next work, VI 8, Plotinus argues that the Good loves itself, then at this highest level the Good *must* also love the soul; and God or the Good must *be* love. Nowhere does Plotinus actually say this; nowhere does he say that God's love *creates* the soul. Partly (but not really), this will be remedied by Iamblichus and Proclus in their notions of providential love from above and converting love from below[47] and, more fully, by Dionysius the Areopagite who will bring elements of pagan and Christian thought together in the daring notion that God's love for everything actually makes God transcendently vulnerable to God's own creation.[48] This is a striking feature of the hidden interweaving of two traditions. But what is noteworthy in the case of Plotinus is that in these two consecutive treatises there occurs a major development in his thought that must have been occasioned – at least in part – by a deeper

---

[42] VI. 7 [38] 35, 23–27   [43] VI. 7 [38] 35, 5–16.

[44] J. Daniélou, *Platonisme et théologie mystique* (Paris: Aubier, 1944), 309–26.

[45] Cf. *Commentary on the Canticles* 8, 940c–941c.

[46] Cf. J. M. Rist, *Eros and Psyche: Studies in Plato, Plotinus and Origen* (Toronto: University of Toronto Press, 1964), 82.

[47] Proclus, *In Alc.* 54–56, Westerink–O'Neill.

[48] On this see Corrigan, *Love, Friendship, Beauty*, 110–13 – a motif foreshadowed in Origen (*Homilies on Ezekiel* 6.1) and Evagrius, *Prayer* 63; 70.

philosophical conversation between the ancient pagan tradition and Christianity broadly conceived.

We have seen the interlacing of traditions and, specifically, the hidden dialogue with Judeo-Christianity that inhabits Plotinus' thought on creation, desire, and return. Let us now turn to some details of this complexity, starting with the so-called hypostases of Origen and Plotinus, in order to see how a dialogue with Plotinus and later Neoplatonism inhabits the 'Platonism' of the Cappadocians.

PLOTINUS AND ORIGEN: THE HYPOSTASES

If, as is generally assumed, Origen studied together with Plotinus under Ammonius Saccas (the Socrates of Neoplatonism),[49] then two strands of "Neoplatonism," Christian and pagan, were born together in Alexandria in the third century. For Origen, the triune God, who creates matter and thinks all the Forms, replaces the three *archai* of Middle Platonism, God, forms, and matter. Origen rejects the positing of only one hypostasis, the Father, as one *archē* instead of three (*Heracl.* 3.20–4.9). So the *archai* (which Rufinus in the preface to his translation of Books 1–2 translated as *principia* and *principatus*, "principles" and "powers") are primarily the Trinity's three hypostases, which open *De Principiis* and appear again as *archikē Trinitas* in 1.4.3. and as "three principal hypostases" in Eusebius and in Porphyry's titles of Plotinus' treatises. To explain the use of the definite article in John 1.1, Origen characterizes the Father (*ho theos*) as *autotheos*, very God, in contrast to the Son who is merely *theos* (*CommJohn* 2.7.16–18) – even "another god" (*Heracl.* 2) and a "second god" on two occasions in *Against Celsus* (5.39, 5.61). Nonetheless, if the Son is the wisdom and power of the Father (1 Corinthians 1:24) and the world was created through him (Hebrews 1:2), and if the Son is that divine helpmate whom the Lord is said (Proverbs 8:22) to have "created" in the beginning, as the mirror of his unspotted majesty (Wisdom 7:26), the verb "created" in this text (which Origen prefers to the alternative reading "possessed")[50] does not imply that the Son has a temporal beginning, but that, having no other substrate than the Father's will, he expresses that will more perfectly than the things that are "made" from matter (unlike

[49] M. Edwards, *Aristotle and Early Christian Thought* (London/New York: Routledge, 2019), 46.
[50] LXX ἔκτισέν ("created") versus *qā-nā-nî* ("possessed" or "acquired"). Athanasius (Or. 2, 44–56), Basil (*Adv. Eun.* 2.20), and Gregory Nazianzus read "created" (Or. 30, 2).

Arius' famous formula, "there was a time when he was not") (*De Princ.* 1.2, 1–2). So Origen is the first thinker to assert unequivocally that the "three hypostases" of the Trinity are eternal not only in nature, but also in their hypostatic character (*De Princ.* 1.2).[51]

There are also for Plotinus three primary *archai* or originative principles – the One or the Good, Intellect, and finally Soul. In *Ennead* V. 1 [10], chapter 10, Plotinus makes clear that they are the foundation of all reality and do not belong to us, but instead we to them. They are divine principles, derived from Plato's *Parmenides* (V. I [10] 8, 23–27), from *Republic* 6 on the Good, and from the famous three kings passage from Plato's *Second Letter*, together with testimony about the "unwritten teachings" of Plato (and perhaps Plato's final lecture on the Good as the One).[52]

One may reasonably ask: if these hypostases are three divine realities or "gods,"[53] how are they interrelated and should we "count" them up quantitatively? It is fairly clear that this cannot be the case, first, because the Good or the One is beyond substance and, therefore, beyond quantity and, second, because countable quantity is posterior to substance, and Intellect and Soul, for Plotinus, are clearly in some sense "substances"[54] and therefore prior to anything quantifiable. The same must be true of Origen's hypostases, but if so, how?

If Soul and Intellect are really distinct, how in practice can we distinguish the "substance" of each except by quantification? On the one hand, the logic of the hypostases surely requires that they cannot be *added together*; and the logic of Plato's two-world theory also supports this, for these cannot be two worlds in quantitative terms, since substance is prior to quantity.[55] On the other hand, how does one distinguish substances if one cannot count them? So any dialogue with Origen and Plotinus on this question has to tackle the problem of these three as nominally and functionally equivalent to three "gods." This becomes more urgent a little later since Iamblichus multiplies intelligible entities and approves of Pythagorean number theory as essential to our understanding of the many substances of the intelligible world: 'the substance of

[51] Throughout I follow M. Edwards, 'Origen', *Stanford Encyclopedia of Philosophy* (2018), https://plato.stanford.edu/archives/sum2018/entries/origen/.

[52] Plato, *Second Letter* 312e; on the unwritten teachings, Aristotle, *Metaphysics* 987a32–b14; 988a9–14; and on Plato's final lecture, Aristoxenus, *Elementa harmonica* II 30–31. See also *Enneads* II. 9 [33] 1, 12, 15–16; VI. 7 [38] 42, 1–6.

[53] Cf. V. 1 [10] 5, 1 and chapter 10 *passim*.

[54] Compare *Ennead* IV. 1 [2] and IV. 2 [1] with V. 2 [11].

[55] As the argument of Socrates at *Phaedo* (96a–101e) anticipates.

the gods is defined by number" (τὴν ἀριθμῷ ὡρισμένην οὐσίαν τῶν θεῶν).
So if number is fundamental to the possibility of divine science or theology, how can we avoid counting divine quantities?

HYPOSTASIS AND SUBSTANCE: PLOTINUS AND IAMBLICHUS, BASIL OF CAESAREA AND GREGORY OF NYSSA

This real polytheistic threat to Trinitarian thought Basil of Caesarea
confronts in his *De Sancto Spiritu* (*DSS*), where he distances his own
view from quantitative "originary hypostases." In *DSS* XVI, 38 he writes:
"And in the creation of reasonable natures think for me of the *pre-original
principal cause* of what comes into being, the Father; the *creative/demiur-
gic cause*, the Son; the *perfecting cause*, the Spirit ... And let no one think
that *I am speaking of three originary hypostases or saying that the activity
of the Son is incomplete* for the *arche* of beings is one creating through the
Son and perfecting in the Spirit."

Just as Plotinus affirms God's necessarily *complete* activity in *Ennead*
VI. 7 [38] 1, in accord with Plato's *Timaeus*,[56] so for Basil no activity of
God's causality can be incomplete. All is concretely present – common and
particular – from the beginning. So while number is a sign indicative for us
of the plurality of subjects (*DSS* XVII, 43), in the case of God, we must
worship "God from God, [and] confess *the proper character of the hypostases* [abiding] upon the monarchy, without scattering the theology into
a divided plurality"(*DSS* XVIII, 44, 404, 20–406, 8).[57] Basil emphasizes,
with Origen, but against Plotinus, that hypostases are properly designa-
tions of substance and, therefore, must apply *primarily* not to the different
hypostases of Intellect and Soul, but to God's substance; they cannot
therefore be quantities or derivative substances; instead, God's substance
is necessarily unitary yet triadic. Hence, creation must be holistic, not
derived through Intellect and Soul, but *immediate* through the Trinitarian
activity of God that is not a quantifiable movement but a single abiding
reality.

Here Christian thinkers had to rethink two principal models of substance from early and later Neoplatonism. On the one hand, Plotinus'
positive *homoousios* model linked everything back by focal equivocity to

---

[56] Plato, *Timaeus* 30c; also Aristotle, *Physics* 201b16–202a12.

[57] Compare Gregory Nazianzus on the eternal movement from unity that must stop at three
(*Oratio* 29, 2; cf. Plotinus, VI. 7 [38] 13, 13–21) and against a "Eunomian" counting of
substances, *Oratio* 31, 17–20.

a *unitary substance* of soul and intellect; on the other hand, Iamblichus rejected hypostases in favor of "ranks" or orders, insisting on the *differences* in substances and kinds – gods, archangels, angels, demons, heroes. For Iamblichus, there cannot be a *shared hypostasis* to blur the differences among kinds: "anything completely transcendent cannot become one with that which has gone forth from itself; nor can the soul produce *some one form of hypostasis* in communion with the divine inspiration" (*De Mysteriis (DM)* III 21, 150, 9–12: οὐδὲ ψυχὴ τοίνυν μετὰ τῆς θείας ἐπιπνοίας ἕν τι ποιε ὑποστάσεως ε δος); "what is this mixed form of hypostasis" *but* quantities? (*DM* III 21, 15, 10–12). So, on the one hand, with Iamblichus, there is a hierarchy of different substances that can be adapted later through Proclus and Dionysius to Christian perspectives; on the other hand, there is a multiplicity of gods – hypercosmic and cosmic – that does not fit Christian thinking at all.

Iamblichus' model, therefore, fits divine hierarchy but *not divine substance*, whereas Plotinus' broader view of substance elides the division between intelligible and sensible, radically undermining the necessary distinction between producer and produced, yet it also provides several powerful models for reframing *shared substance*, that is, *intrahypostatic* being. Therefore, the Cappadocians, following Origen and the earlier tradition, insist upon the fundamental distinction between the Uncreated and the Created; and recast the generative interhypostatic relations in Plotinus into the intrasubstantial hypostases of the single Divine substance that *begets* within itself without *creating* something different from itself, just as within Plotinus' thought not only does the One produce Intellect but *Intellect also makes itself*. For Christian thinkers, there is a begetting at the heart of creation that abides in itself – as is logically necessary also in Plotinus.

CREATION AND BEGETTING: TRINITARIAN MODELS CONTRA
EUNOMIUS AND IAMBLICHUS

Although Plotinus can describe the emergence and return of Intellect and Soul to the One in many different ways,[58] there are three major models in the *Enneads* that the Cappadocians evidently took into account in thinking about intra-Trinitarian making or begetting.

---

[58] See, for example, V. 4 [7] 1–2; V. 1 [10] 5–7; V. 2 [11] 1; II. 4 [12] 5, 32–35; VI. 6 [34] 9, 29–10, 4; VI. 7 [38] 16, 16–22; 17, 14–19; 35–36; V. 3 [49] 11.

First, not only is Intellect an image of its paradigm, the One, but it is also internally *an image of itself as paradigm* (VI. 8 [39] 18, 41–42), as is the soul both image and paradigm to itself (VI. 9 [9] 11, 39–46). Second, Intellect is caused by the One, but it is also cause of itself; it therefore has an internal relation of cause and caused (cf. V. I [10] 4: "The cause of thinking is something different, which is also cause of being. Of both therefore simultaneously there is a cause that is other [than themselves]. For they are *simultaneous* and *belong together*" (ἅμα μὲν γὰρ ἐκεῖνα καὶ συνυπάρχει). In other words, there is an internal causal relation in Intellect that Plotinus describes here (and in later works) as *synhyparxis/synhypostasis*.[59] Third, in the later chapters of VI. 8 [39], to intimate the dynamic reality of the Good's freedom as *causa sui*, Plotinus provides implicitly a Trinitarian model for thinking through what it means to say that the Good is self-caused.

Basil, therefore, in the *DSS* insists that, on Platonism's own terms, the archetype-image configuration should be understood as nonsubordinationist and nonaggregative in Divine Being, namely, Being that is the proper model for understanding Divinity. Basil implicitly uses elements from Plotinus logically against Neoplatonism (such as, in *DSS* XVIIff.), when he argues that the Christian "One" is truly one and neither composite nor a "one from many" (unlike Plotinus' Intellect)[60], nor again a formless unity, but a "one form/shape, as it were," through whose illuminative power "we fix our gaze upon the beauty of the image of the invisible God and are led to the vision beyond beauty of the archetype" (*DSS* 47, 1–3).[61]

We should compare the similar language of Basil's little brother:[62] "That is indeed why the one as cause of its (two) causeds, we say is one God; since indeed it co-exists (συνυπάρχει) with them" (*Adversus Graecos* 25, 6–8).[63] Here Gregory is reading Plotinus to combat the Eunomian-type view that

---

[59] VI. 7 [38] 2. 38ff: a *synhypostasis* of all things together, of things caused having their causes in themselves (ἐν αὐτοῖς ἂν ἔχοι τὰ αἰτιατὰ τὰς αἰτίας) – that is, of all intelligibles reaching down into *logoi* even in the sensible world (see also VI. 8 [39] 14, 21ff.), but primarily *synhypostasis* in Intellect, as in VI. 7, 40, 44–50.

[60] See, for example, V. 1 [10] 5, 1; 8, 26.

[61] For the vision beyond beauty, see Plotinus VI. 7 [38] 32, 26–39.

[62] Especially V. 1 [10] 4, 30–32: "the cause of thinking is something else, which is also cause of being; they both therefore have a cause other than themselves. For they are simultaneous and belong together and do not abandon one another" (τοῦ δὲ νοεῖν αἴτιον ἄλλο, ὃ καὶ τῷ ὄντι· ἀμφοτέρων οὖν ἅμα αἴτιον ἄλλο. ἅμα μὲν γὰρ ἐκεῖνα καὶ συνυπάρχει).

[63] Compare Basil, *DSS* XXVI, 63: true *synhyparxis* applies primarily to the Trinity.

there can be no *synhyparxis*; for Eunomius, the only legitimate name of God is not *causa sui*, but the Unbegotten.[64]

Against Eunomius, then, to be 'cause of itself' for Gregory must mean, in the case of God, that the Unbegotten, the Only-Begotten, and the Spirit form a community of nature, the logic of whose relations was anticipated, but misunderstood by Neoplatonism.[65] And so Gregory argues for the hidden logic of Plotinus' position, reshaped by Basil, against the Christian Bishop Eunomius and the pagan Iamblichus[66] who reject the *synhyparxis-causa sui* model of Divinity in favor of what for them is the only appropriate name: the Unbegotten. Christian Platonism, therefore, is often a sophisticated, critical, but sympathetic dialogue, that thinks through the logic of language in relation to God, while freely acknowledging our inability to know anything about God's nature. This is why Aristotle's *organon* assumes such importance for Theology – as it did naturally for the later pagan Neoplatonists.[67]

There is space here only for two further features of ancient Christian Platonism, one from the Greek tradition, Gregory of Nyssa's definition of man in *De Opificio Hominis* – the logical conclusion of the Cappadocian view of Divine substance, and the other from the Latin tradition, Augustine's intuition of creation through reading the *Libri Platonicorum*.

THE CREATION OF THE HUMAN BEING: GREGORY OF NYSSA

In the "double creation" in Gregory or Evagrius, we might think there is an illogical duplication of entities or a fatal distance between God and creation, but this is not so. When Plotinus develops the enfolding/unfolding model of the Demiurge's "complete activity" and goes on to define the human being in that light in VI 7, 1–5, he starts from the premise of Plato's *Timaeus* 30c, that "nothing that is a likeness of anything *incomplete* could ever turn out beautiful" and argues that "if every divine activity must not be *incomplete* (εἰ δεῖ ἑκάστην ἐνέργειαν μὴ ἀτελῆ[68] εἶναι), it is unlawful to

---

[64] Eunomius, *Liber Apologeticus*, 10, 10–15 (Vaggione).

[65] Compare Gregory Nazianzus, *Oratio* 31, 23 on the Unbegotten; for the distinction between creation and begetting, *Oratio* 30, 2.

[66] Iamblichus, *De Mysteriis*, III 19, 146, 12–14; III 21, 151, 7–152, 5 (Clarke, Dillon, Hershbell).

[67] See G. Bechtle, "Categories and Conversion," in *Religion and Philosophy in the Platonic and Neoplatonic Traditions*, ed. K. Corrigan and J. D. Turner (Sankt Augustin: Akademia, 2012), 107–20; Edwards, *Aristotle and Early Christian Thought*.

[68] See also Aristotle, *Physics* 201b16–202a12.

suppose that *anything of God is other than whole* ... everything must pre-exist in God as to become unfolded later in time" (VI. 7, 1, 45–48). He then develops a theory of whole-formation that allows for the priority of soul to body and concludes that the human being cannot be simply soul; "this human being here"[69] must be, he argues, "a productive *logos* indwelling, not separate"(4, 26–30) so that this human being is "a compound entity, soul in a specific forming principle [i.e., a bodily structure of a certain kind], the forming principle being a determinate activity which cannot exist without the active subject. For this is how the forming principles in seeds are; for they are neither without soul nor simply souls" (5, 2–6).

For Gregory later, Plotinus does not go far enough, since *on his own terms* body, and compound being, is a *logos*. Gregory writes in the *De Hominis Opificio* (*DHO*), chapter 29:

But since the human being is one, the being consisting of soul and body, we are to suppose that the origin of his structure is one and common (Ἀλλ' ἑνὸς ὄντος τοῦ ἀνθρώπου, τοῦ διὰ ψυχῆς τε καὶ σώματος συνεστηκότος, μίαν αὐτοῦ καὶ κοινὴν τῆς συστάσεως τὴν ἀρχὴν ὑποτίθεσθαι) so that he should not turn out to be older and younger than himself, the bodily taking the lead in him and the other turning up later. But we are to say that in the foreknowing power of God (τῇ μὲν προγνωστικῇ τοῦ Θεοῦ δυνάμει), according to the account adopted a little earlier, the entire fullness of humanity presubsisted.[70]

For Gregory, the preexistence of soul without the preexistence of body[71] contravenes fundamental principles of Platonic thought (that no work or activity of God can be *incomplete*)[72] and he proceeds in chapters 29 and 30, to work out the unfolding of *both body and soul together and immediately from God's prognostic power* as we actually experience this in seeds, the growth of limbs, and complementary development of organic structure and thought. This is a revolutionary development in the history of thought that deserves better recognition. From the principles of Plato's *Timaeus*, Aristotle's *Physics*, and Plotinus, Gregory argues for a new radical unity of soul and body in their origin and emergent synergy in their development.

---

[69] See VI. 7 [38] 4, 28–30: "What is it then to be a human being? And this is, what it is that has made *this man, indwelling, not separate?*"

[70] Compare Plotinus VI. 7 [38] 1, 45–49.

[71] Neither Plato nor Plotinus (nor Origen, Gregory, or Evagrius) believed in a literal, that is, temporal, preexistence of the soul; only a logical, nontemporal preexistence.

[72] On 'incomplete deity' see Gregory Nazianzus, *Oratio* 31, 4.

And so, in the culminating thesis of *DHO*, in chapter 30, Gregory concludes with an independent examination of the construction of the body from the medical viewpoint, thus indicating his approval of, and continuity with, a long tradition rooted in Genesis and in the *Timaeus'* account of the generation of the human body, on the one hand, and his radical departure from – or Christian completion of – that tradition, on the other, depending on one's point of view:

> For the project was to show that the seminal cause of our constitution is neither an incorporeal soul nor an unsouled body,[73] but that from animated and living bodies it is generated in the first constitution as a living, animate being, and that human nature, like a nurse, receives … it … ;[74] and it grows in both aspects and makes its growth manifest correspondingly in each part. For straightaway, by means of this … process of formation, it shows the power of soul interwoven[75] in it, appearing rather dimly at first, but subsequently shining more brilliantly with the perfection of the instrument.

Even in this final passage we can see decisive elements for understanding how Gregory receives a textual tradition and thinks critically through it. The phrase "neither an incorporeal soul nor an un-souled body" picks up the conclusion of Plotinus' striking definition of the human being in VI. 7 [38] 4–5. There Plotinus concludes that the human being cannot be simply soul; "this human being here"[76] must be, he argues, "a compound entity, soul in a specific forming principle [i.e., a bodily structure of a certain kind], the forming principle being a determinate activity which cannot exist without the active subject. For this is how the forming principles in seeds are; *for they are neither without soul nor simply souls*" (5, 2–6). Compare Gregory: "*our [seminal] constitution is neither an incorporeal soul nor an un-souled body*" (DHO 30, 253, 18–22).

While Plotinus in VI. 7, chapters 5–7, goes on to argue for the priority of soul over body, Gregory argues effectively that Plotinus' *own definition* of the concrete interrelated reality, that is, "this human being" is in fact contrary to any genetic or seminal priority of soul over body. Otherwise, demiurgic power would be refuted as incomplete. Whole formation requires, first, a radical equality of body and soul; second, not a World Soul from outside, as Plotinus had argued famously in the next chapters of VI. 7, 5–7,[77] but a concrete "human nature, like a nurse" that receives and

---

[73] Compare *Ennead* VI. 7 [38] 1–7, especially 5, 5–8.

[74] As opposed to VI. 7 [38] 7, 8–16; cf. IV. 3 [27] 9. That is, no World Soul, no Platonic *Chora*.

[75] Compare Plato, *Timaeus* 36e2, *diaplakeisa*; see also Plotinus, I. 1[53] 3.

[76] See n. 69 above.   [77] Especially VI. 7 [38] 7, 8–16.

complements human growth *with her own proper powers* for psycho-somatic development; and, third, this is, Gregory intimates, in accordance with a plausible philosophical interpretation of Plato's statement in the *Timaeus* that the soul is *interwoven right through* body (if from animated and living bodies our first constitution is established as "a living animate being)."[78] Even if soul is worthier than body, soul-body involves whole-formation genetically or creatively.

CREATION, RE-CREATION: AUGUSTINE'S CONFESSIONS AND CHRISTIAN PLATONISM

Augustine is perhaps the most startling example of Christianity's ability to navigate boundaries. In *Confessions* 7.10.16, Augustine describes how he came to the truth of creation for the first time through reading the *Libri Platonicorum* – how he thereby escaped materialism, astral determinism, and Manichean dualism in order to encounter God in truth. Augustine's conversion occurs narratively later in Book 8, but Book 7 remains a fulcrum for the *Confessions*, the midpoint of thirteen books and a hinge between Augustine's discovery of the distinction between God and the world in the first half and his deeper insight into the relation between God and the world in the second half.[79] In Augustine's account, the fundamental pivot of the first half leads organically into the conver-sion and deeper meditation of the second part – as if Platonism were, indeed, a porous membrane between the Bible and pagan thought by which re-creation, through divine grace, might be uniquely effected and yet made open to everyone. "*By the Platonic books* I was admonished *to return into myself* [cf. *Enn.* V. 1.1]. *With you as my guide*, I entered into my innermost citadel ... and saw [above my soul's eye] the immutable light beyond my mind ... It was superior because it *made me* ... Love knows it [cf. *Enn.* I. 6, 7, 2; VI. 9, 9, 46] ... you are my God. To you I sigh 'day and night' (Psalm 42.2)" (trans. H. Chadwick).

CONCLUSION

We have seen the mutual influence between Christianity and pagan thought. On the one hand, on the questions of creation, love, and free

---

[78] *Timaeus* 36e.

[79] See F. Crosson, "Structure and Meaning in Augustine's *Confessions*," in *The Augustinian Tradition*, ed. G. Matthews (Berkeley: University of California Press, 1999), 32–37.

will, Plotinus unequivocally states, in implicit dialogue with strands of Christian thought, that the Good makes itself "for itself and of nothing." Creation out of nothing, therefore, is conspicuously part of Plotinus' thought. In addition, love of and desire for the Good assume new significance in Plotinus' middle works and in later Neoplatonism, both pagan and Christian, a development that builds upon features latent in Plato and Aristotle's thought.[80] On the other hand, there is a kindred quality in the thought of Plotinus and Origen about the hypostases and about divine substance that leads to the distinction between "creating" and "begetting" within the Trinity, a distinction that utilizes models strikingly present in Plotinus but takes them to their logical (Christian) conclusions. Thus, for the Cappadocians there is a begetting inscribed at the heart of creation that remains self-dependent and yet simultaneously through creation draws all created beings back into the mystery of creation itself. In this, I suggest, we find one of the best features of Christian Platonism, namely, a confidence to think through major theological problems in implicit dialogue, however critical, with different forms of thought and even the confidence to embrace the other as a genuine means of discovering not only creation but also the re-creation thereby effected.

Bibliography

Bechtle, G. "Categories and Conversion." In *Religion and Philosophy in the Platonic and Neoplatonic Traditions*, ed. K. Corrigan and J. D. Turner, 107–120. Sankt Augustin:Akademia, 2012.

Blowers, P. M. "Doctrine of Creation." In *Oxford Handbook of Early Christian Studies*, ed. Susan Ashbrook Harvey and David G. Hunter, 906–922. Oxford: Oxford University Press, 2008.

Chadwick, Henry, trans. *Saint Augustine: Confessions*. Oxford: Oxford University Press, 1991.

Corrigan, K. *Love, Friendship, Beauty, and the Good: Plato, Aristotle and the Later Tradition*. Eugene, OR: Wipf & Stock, 2019.

Corrigan K. and J. D. Turner. *Plotinus, Ennead VI. 8: On the Voluntary and the Free Will of the One*. Las Vegas, Zurich, Athens: Parmenides Press, 2017.

Crosson, F. "Structure and Meaning in Augustine's *Confessions*." In *The Augustinian Tradition*, ed. G. Matthews, 32–37. Berkeley: University of California Press, 1999.

Daniélou, J. *Platonisme et théologie Mystique*. Paris: Aubier, 1944.

Edwards, M. *Aristotle and Early Christian Thought*. London/New York: Routledge, 2019.

---

[80] On this, see Corrigan, *Love, Friendship, Beauty*, 82–125.

'Origen', *Stanford Encyclopedia of Philosophy*. https://plato.stanford.edu/arch ives/sum2018/entries/origen/. 2018.

Fowler, Harold N., trans. *Plato VII: Theaetetus and Sophist*. Loeb Classical Library. Cambridge, MA: Harvard University Press, 1921.

Irwin, T. *Aristotle's First Principles*. Oxford: Clarendon Press, 1988.

Joachim, H. H. *Aristotle, The Nicomachean Ethics*. Oxford: Clarendon Press, 1970.

JPS Hebrew–English Tanakh: The Traditional Hebrew Text and The New JPS Translation. Philadelphia, PA: The Jewish Publication Society, 1999.

Lear, J. *Aristotle: The Desire to Understand*. Cambridge: Cambridge University Press, 1988.

Lloyd, A. C. *The Anatomy of Neoplatonism*. Oxford: Oxford University Press, 1990.

O'Brien, D. "Plotinus on the Making of Matter: The Identity of Darkness, Part III." *International Journal of the Platonic Tradition* 6, no. 1 (2012): 72–76.

Petty, Robert. *The Fragments of Numenius of Apamea*. London: The Prometheus Trust, 2012.

Rist, J. M. *Eros and Psyche: Studies in Plato, Plotinus and Origen*. Toronto: University of Toronto Press, 1964.

Sharples, R. W. "Alexander of Aphrodisias on Divine Providence: Two Problems." *Classical Quarterly* 31, no. 1 (1982): 198–211.

Sleeman, J. H. and Gilbert Pollet. *Lexicon Plotinianum*. Leiden: Brill, 1980.

Turner, J. D. *Sethian Gnosticism and the Platonic Tradition*. Québec: Presses de l'Université Laval, 2001.

Vaggione, R. P. *Eunomius of Cyzicus and the Nicene Revolution*. Oxford: Clarendon Press, 2001.

Wallis, R. T. *Neoplatonism*. London: Duckworth/Hackett, 1995.

Zimmerman, B. "Does Plotinus Present a Philosophical Account of Creation?" *Review of Metaphysics* 67 (2013): 55–105.

1.5

The Concept of Theology

Olivier Boulnois

One of the most remarkable contributions of the Middle Ages to Western thought is the invention of theology as a rational science of faith. But where does the concept of *theologia* come from? It appears in Greek in Plato, in order to designate mythology, that is, precisely what philosophy is supposed to go beyond.[1] In Aristotle's work, it is radically opposed to the scientific knowledge of the divine, known as a 'theological science' (*episteme theologikè*).[2] How could this concept overcome this opposition with science, merge with it, and become the pinnacle of philosophical speculation? How did it come to be used to designate a Christian discipline, the rational interpretation of faith?

A first step was taken by Neoplatonism, especially by Proclus, for whom 'the oracles, held to be divine, are included among the authorities of philosophy', and 'philosophical texts themselves, in the first place those of Plato, are raised up to the level of divine revelations'.[3] *Platonic Theology* therefore designates both human knowledge and divine inspiration. For Proclus, there are two main kinds of theology, according to whether they are allusive or explicit, which are subdivided into four subspecies: (A) Within the allusive discourse: (1) The symbolic mode, expressed by 'mythical' names; (2) The image mode (*apo tôn eikonôn*), using 'mathematical' names. (B) In the clear discourse: (3) The mode inspired (*entheastikôs*) by the gods, or names 'worthy of the

---

[1] Plato, *Republic* II, 379a. [2] Aristotle, *Metaphysics* E, 1, 1026a15–19.
[3] Henri-Dominique Saffrey, 'Theology as Science (3rd–6th Centuries)', *Studia Patristica* 29 (1997), 321–9 at p. 334; cf. Proclus, *Theologia Platonica* I, 3, 14.

sacred'; (4) The scientific mode (*kat' epistemen*), using 'dialectical' names.[4]

To understand the genesis of the concept of theology as we understand it today, we must analyse how Dionysius adapted Proclian theology to Christian mysteries, then how John Scotus Eriugena integrated the rational procedures of the arts of language into the interpretation of Scripture, and finally how, from Aristotelian and Boethian elements, a theory of *theologia* as science could be born.

DIONYSIUS' THEOLOGIES

In Dionysius, *theologia* must be understood, as in Proclus, as a mythical discourse, that is, finally, as the Word of God reported in the Bible, without involving a rational elaboration. *Theologia* therefore refers above all to divine revelation: 'And here also let us set before our minds the scriptural rule that in speaking about God we should declare the Truth, not with enticing words of man's wisdom, but in demonstration of the power which the Spirit stirred up in the Sacred writers (*theologoi*)'.[5] To interpret inspired words about God, we must seek the truth, relying not on the capacities of human reason, but on the power inspired by the Spirit in the statements of the Holy Scriptures: 'theologians' (*theologoi*) are, as in Proclus, 'spokesmen of God', the inspired authors of this scripture. They have benefited from a contact with the divine, which makes their discourse superior to what we can achieve by reason. It is therefore from the sacred texts that the deciphering of myths with their contradictions, the analysis of images according to their similarities, and rational speculation on the attributes of God are constructed.

The principle of all knowledge of God defines at the same time its limit: man cannot speak of God while ignoring what has been divinely revealed in the scriptures.[6] These form a 'theophany', a manifestation of God adapted to the reader's mind[7]. Dionysius even claims not to affirm

---

[4] Proclus, *Theologia Platonica* I, 4, 17, 18–23; 19, 23–20, 5; I, 2 (9, 20–10, 7); *In Parmenidem* I, 646. Cf. Jean Pépin, 'Les modes de l'enseignement théologique dans la *Théologie Platonicienne*', in *Proclus et la théologie platonicienne*, ed. Alain-Philippe Segonds and Carlos Steel (Leuven, Paris: Leuven University Press, 2000), 1–14.

[5] Denys l'Aréopagite [Dionysius the Areopagite], *De divinis nominibus. Les Noms divins*, ed. and trans. Ysabel de Andia (Paris: le Cerf, 2016), I, 1 (PG 3, 585 B; SC 578, 312); Dionysius Areopagita, *On the Divine Names and the Mystical Theology*, trans. Clarence Edwin (London, New York: Macmillan, 1920), 51.

[6] Denys [Dionysius], *De divinis nominibus*, I, 2 (PG 3, 588 C; SC 578, 320).

[7] Ibid, I, 2 (PG 3, 589 A; SC 578, 322).

anything that he does not get from scripture.[8] But this does not imply that divine names are limited to the names given in scripture. On the contrary, the exegesis of the Bible must unfold its full depth to overcome the inappropriateness of the narratives. And Dionysius does not hesitate to use concepts that are not of biblical origin to attribute them to God.[9] Scripture therefore does not exclude rational speculation, but it directs it towards a unified understanding of God.

Dionysius himself analyses the method to be followed in this knowledge: 'The spokesmen of God (*theologoi*) deliver their knowledge in a double way: unspeakable and hidden on the one hand; obvious on the other hand, and more easily known. The first mode is symbolic and implies an initiation; the second is philosophical and takes place by way of demonstration. Let us add that the inexpressible intertwines with the expressible.'[10] Dionysius thus distinguishes two ways of access to God: the initiatory way of the symbol revealed by scripture, and the philosophical way of demonstration. Does that define two strictly separate areas? In fact, when he evokes the discovery of God from visible nature, Dionysius relies on both 'true reason' and Saint Paul. So, the two paths to the knowledge of God are revealed to us by *theologoi*. Philosophical knowledge must not be opposed to symbolic and religious initiation: it is at the very heart of revelation that reason must be placed.

Now the human intellect possesses a double power, that of thinking the intelligible by contemplating it, and that of uniting with the One who is beyond all intellect by exceeding all knowledge: intellection and union.[11] This double power in turn draws two forms of theology: *mystical theology* reaches union with God, but is beyond all knowledge, in an exit from oneself (*extasis*); what we now call *speculative theology* starts from our experience of being, and, following the images of creatures, goes back to their divine model.[12] It then reaches God as negation, transcendence, and cause of all: thus, 'God is known through knowledge and through unknowing':[13] knowledge uses names, but in order to name Him who is

---

[8] Ibid, I, 1 (PG 3, 585 B; SC 578, 312). [9] Ibid, IV, 11 (PG 3, 708 B; SC 578, 466).

[10] Denys [Dionysius], *Epistula*, IX (PG 3, 1105 D).

[11] Denys [Dionysius], *De divinis nominibus*, VII, 1 (PG 3, 865 C; SC 579, 52–54). Cf. Plotin [Plotinus], *Traité 38*, trans. Pierre Hadot (Paris: Les Éditions du Cerf, 1988), 173–4 (*Enneads* VI, 7, 35, 19–23).

[12] Denys [Dionysius], VII, 3 (PG 3, 872 A; SC 579, 64); these three expressions are the indirect origin of the three 'ways' of the knowledge of God (affirmation, negation, and eminence).

[13] Ibid, VII, 3 (PG 3, 872 A; SC 579, 64), Dionysius, *On the Divine Names*, 152.

ineffable; and unknowledge consists in union with God, but beyond the intellect.

Symbolic Theology

The extant works of Dionysius refer to three kinds of 'theology', that is, three ways of speaking of the divine based on scripture. The first degree of knowledge of God is provided by 'symbolic theology', by the word of God expressed in sensitive symbols. It consists of the inappropriate anthropomorphisms of Scripture, which present themselves as 'metonymies of the sensitive to the divine'.[14] This word of God presents sensate images such as 'the eyes, ears, hair, hands' of God.[15] But any reading articulates an interpretation. It is therefore necessary to explain the metaphorical images applied to the transcendent God: 'what the divine forms are; what the divine shapes, parts, and organs are . . . what the rages are; what the griefs and ravings are' in God.[16] All these images must be overcome, for God is absolutely different from all things; he is simple, and nothing is similar to him. This is also why we must prefer the most dissimilar symbols: they elevate us more effectively; by a radical short-circuit, they immediately lead us to overcome them.[17] The dissimilar symbol brings us back to the Principle more than the similar image, because we do not risk adhering to vile or monstrous images.[18]

The Divine Names

Just as, in the sensitive field, the similar symbol must be opposed to the dissimilar symbol, in the intelligible field, the negative word of God (*theologia*) must be opposed to the affirmative word. But both belong to

---

[14] Denys l'Aréopagite [Dionysius the Areopagite], *De mystica theologia. La théologie mystique*, ed. and trans. Ysabel de Andia (Paris: le Cerf, 2016), III (PG 3, 1033 B; SC 579, 308).

[15] Denys [Dionysius], *De divinis nominibus*, I, 8 (PG 3, 597 B; SC 578, 354).

[16] Denys [Dionysius], *De mystica theologia*, III (PG 3, 1033 B; SC 579, 308), translated in Michael L. Harrington, *A Thirteenth-Century Textbook of Mystical Theology at the University of Paris. The Mystical Theology of Dionysius the Areopagite in Eriugena's Latin Translation with the Scholia Translated by Anastasius the Librarian and Excerpts from Eriugena's Periphyseon* (Paris, Leuven, Dudley, MA: Peeters, 2004), 87.

[17] Denys [Dionysius], *De coelesti hierarchia. La Hiérarchie Céleste*, ed. Gunther Heil, trans. Maurice de Gandillac (Paris: le Cerf, 1970), II, 2 (PG 3, 137 C; SC 58bis, 75).

[18] Cf. Olivier Boulnois, *Au-delà de l'image. Une archéologie du visuel au Moyen Age, Ve–XVIe siècle* (Paris: Seuil, 2008), 161–71.

the treatise *On the Divine Names*. Through affirmation, the intellect applies to God the intelligible names of the creature's perfections: Good, Life, Wisdom, and so on, because God is by eminency the Cause. This is why it must be said that affirmative theology follows the order of the 'procession', that is, the descending dialectic of Neoplatonism.[19] First we will affirm the noblest names, then the whole series of intelligible names. This treatise establishes all the attributes common to God in his transcendent nature: goodness, being, life, wisdom, the 'intelligible names of God'.[20]

However, the *Treatise on the Divine Names* also includes a negative aspect. God being absolutely transcendent, he is nothing of what can be said of him: he is not Good, nor being, nor life. That is why, at the same time as all the names of intelligible perfections are affirmed about God, they must be denied, because they are inadequate.[21] As dissimilar symbolism corrects similar symbolism, negative speech is the reverse of affirmative speech. Having affirmed everything, we must deny everything, to name God correctly. We then follow an ascending dialectic, and go from the less noble attributes to the higher ones.[22]

But negation is not the last word either. For, says Dionysius, this suppression (*aphairesis*) must not be taken in a private sense, but in a sense of eminence, of excess.[23] What we deny are our representations as they are finite. But God is infinitely beyond affirmation and negation. We must therefore understand the knowledge of God as a transcendence, a simultaneous overcoming of affirmation and negation: it escapes any finite category, any experience, and any thought.

Dionysius speaks of 'affirmative theology', but he does not speak of 'negative theology'. He speaks only of *aphairesis*, that is, divine 'subtraction',[24] which refers to the idea of separation of the divine. (The concept of *aphairesis* refers to the Plotinian image of the sculptor: by removing all the superfluous, he reveals the true shape of the statue, hidden in the marble block: 'the suppression alone manifests the beauty

[19] Cf. Ysabel de Andia, 'Introduction', in Denys [Dionysius], *De theologia mystica. La théologie mystique*, SC 579, 265–79.

[20] Denys [Dionysius], *De mystica theologia*, III (PG 3, 1033 A; SC 579, 308).

[21] Denys [Dionysius], *De divinis nominibus*, I, 6 (PG 3, 596 AC; SC 578, 346–8).

[22] Denys [Dionysius], *De mystica theologia*, III (PG 3, 1033 C; SC 579, 310).

[23] *Hyperokhè: De divinis nominibus*, VII, 2 (PG 3, 869 A; SC 579, 58); VII, 3 (872 A; SC 579, 64). *Hyperokhikôs: Epistula ad Gaium*, I (PG 3, 1065 A).

[24] Denys [Dionysius], *De theologia mystica*, 3 (PG 3, 1033 C; SC 579, 310).

that was hidden there'.)[25] It is an anonymous copyist who has inserted the concept of 'negative theology', in order to give a symmetrical title to the third chapter: 'What the affirmative and the negative theologies are'.[26] There is therefore no negative theology articulated to affirmative theology in Dionysius, and one can even less summarize his theology of divine names only as 'negative theology'. Like the expression 'divine position', which refers to the act of placing the divine as separate, the expression 'divine subtraction' indicates a movement, the act of rising beyond the intelligible. 'Affirmative theology' and 'divine subtraction' are therefore not two sciences, they do not delineate two domains; they describe two paths towards the transcendence of God.

Theological Hypotyposes

Dionysius also refers to his '*Theological Hypotyposes*'. 'Hypotyposes' are descriptions that represent reality through images, but without resorting to stylistic figures;[27] they are 'theological' because, based on statements in the sacred text, they reveal God's attributes. This (lost or fictional) treatise dealt with *affirmations*; based on grammatically positive expressions, it indicated 'the main points of affirmative theology', that is, the meaning of the main affirmations of the Christian faith: unity and trinity in God, incarnation of Jesus.[28] The theological hypotyposes aim at the differentiation within God's nature, beyond being. They aim higher than the sensuous world we describe in symbolic theology, even higher than the intelligible structure that lies beneath and beyond this world and enables us to speak of God through divine names.

Mystical Theology

Finally, our knowledge and language leads us to union with God, the object of mystical theology, beyond all intellect. God is only reached in himself, without veil, without image and without words, by uniting

---

[25] Ibid, 2 (PG 3, 1025 B; SC 579, 304); see Plotin [Plotinus], *Ennéades*, ed. E. Bréhier (Paris: Les Belles Lettres, 1976), I, 6, [1] 9, 7–15.

[26] The addition is found in all manuscripts, but the critical edition of A. M. Ritter (1991), 146 (critical apparatus) puts the *Capitula* among the rejected variants. I believe that this is doctrinally justified.

[27] Cf. Yves Le Bouzec, 'L'*hypotypose*: un essai de définition formelle', *L'information grammaticale* 92 (2002), 3–7.

[28] Denys [Dionysius], *De mystica theologia*, III (PG 3, 1032 D; SC 579, 306).

oneself with him. It deals with inverting all human activity into passivity: 'to undergo the divine' (*paskhein ta theia*).[29] The subject alienates himself, to become the possession of the one he loves, which is the definition of ecstasy, or leaving oneself (*extasis*).[30]

Since 'symbolic theology' starts from the colourful multiplicity of the sensitive, it is necessarily very profuse; the *Theological Sketches* and *Divine Names*, which explain affirmative statements about God, are necessarily shorter; and at its very end, if it could achieve its goal, beyond all thought and name, mystical theology should be totally silent: 'When the whole ascent is passed, [our language] will be totally dumb, being at last totally united with Him Whom words cannot describe.'[31] But by nature, mystical theology fails to be absolutely silent. It is therefore caught in a living contradiction: 'through the loss of sight and knowledge', mystical theology wishes 'to know that which is beyond all perception and understanding (for this emptying or our faculties is true sight and knowledge)'.[32] It is a knowledge in unknowledge. Mystical theology is nevertheless the end and achievement of all theologies. Beyond the symbolic order of the sensitive, beyond the intelligible order of divine names, the mystical requirement leads man to perfect unity in divinization.[33] It allows to reach in its nakedness the divine Principle that the procession in the world has veiled.

One can also say that mystical theology covers the whole revelation of God through created realities:

We will discover that mystical theologians (*mystikous theologous*) use [these images], not only in a holy way, to manifest celestial dispositions, but sometimes also for revelations concerning thearchy. Sometimes they celebrate it from precious phenomena, such as the 'Sun of Justice' . . . but sometimes, from intermediate images, such as the one of fire that does not burn. I would add that the most unworthy image of all, the one that seems most unreasonable, is the one used by the sublime messengers of the divine tradition, when they were not afraid to shape thearchy in the form of an earthworm.[34]

Bible-inspired authors (*theologoi*) are mystical, because their discourse on the gods reveals what is hidden.

---

[29] Denys [Dionysius], *De divinis nominibus*, II, 9 (PG 3, 648 B; SC 578, 396).

[30] Ibid, IV, 13 (PG 3, 712 A; SC 578, 474).

[31] Denys [Dionysius], *De mystica theologia*, III (PG 3, 1033 C; SC 579, 310); trans. *The Mystical Theology*, 198.

[32] Ibid, II (PG 3, 1025 A; SC 579, 304); trans. *The Mystical Theology*, 194.

[33] Denys [Dionysius], *De divinis nominibus*, IV, 11 (PG 3, 708 D; SC 578, 468).

[34] Dionysius, *De coelesti hierarchia*, II, 5 (PG 3, 144 C–145 A; SC 58bis, 82–4).

These three 'theologies' are not in opposition. They describe different paths to God, based on its manifestations revealed by Scripture. Thomas Aquinas explains:

Since there are three ways of naming God, we deal with the first, which is the nomination by suppression (remotio), in mystical theology; the second, which is the nomination by intelligible processions, in this book [*On the Divine Names*]; the third, which is the nomination by sensitive similarities, in the book *On Symbolic Theology*.[35]

Thomas therefore takes over the tripartite articulation of Dionysian theology. But if we take inspiration from the titles inserted by the copyists, we must divide the theology of divine names, and distinguish affirmative theology from negative theology, which leads, no longer to three 'theologies', but to four.[36]

THE LATIN THEOLOGIA

When Latin scholastics developed the concept of *theologia* as a rigorous knowledge of God, from what source did they draw? They knew the Proclian concept transmitted by Dionysius (translated into Latin by Hilduin and John Scotus Eriugena). But the Latin world was also familiar with another *theologia* concept: the Stoic concept. It is mentioned by Augustine, even if he does not adopt it. (He mentions the Varronian division of the three theologies, and recalls the distinction between the three corresponding kinds of God: the mythical gods, developed by the art of poets; the gods of cities, which the different peoples have adopted by law; the gods of physics, thought by philosophers, taught and considered by the philosophers.)[37] It was also necessary to know a concept of theology as a science.

In a nutshell, in order to build a scholastic and dogmatic theology, it was necessary to bring together both halves of Augustine's discourse: Christian doctrine and philosophical theology. This required a triple movement: (1) The repetition of the Stoic concept of *theologia*, or 'reason

---

[35] Thomas Aquinas, *In librum beati Dionysii De divinis nominibus expositio*, ed. Ceslas Pera (Rome, Turin: Marietti, 1950), §104, 32.

[36] It is this quadripartite structure, influenced by the spurious capitulation, that we find in René Roques, 'Les "théologies" dionysiennes: notions, fonctions et implications', in *Structures théologiques. De la gnose à Richard de Saint-Victor* (Paris: Presses Universitaires de France, 1962), 135–63.

[37] Augustine, *De civitate Dei. Œuvres de saint Augustin, La cité de Dieu*, Livres VI–X (Paris: Desclée de Brouwer, 1959), VI, 5–10, 64–98.

on the gods', in its third part, physical theology. To do this, it was necessary to reverse the value judgement of Tertullian and Augustine. (2) The transmission of the metaphysical project of 'theological science'. Here, the key role was played by Boethius. (3) The revival of the Greek concept of a science of mythological discourse. Here, it is necessary to go through the Latin translation of Dionysius and the analyses of Eriugena.

Augustine: The Stoics' Discourse on the Gods

Augustine is careful when using *theologia*. Almost all the uses of the term are found in the *City of God*, in a way that clearly designates *theologia* in the Stoic sense, and in particular the three theologies according to Varro. But he once uses the term in an epistle: 'For the superstition of the Gentiles or the philosophers diverted them, by the principalities and powers, when they preached *what they call this theology* according to the elements of this world.'[38] Paul's purpose, according to Augustine, is to warn the inhabitants of Colossae, lest they be diverted from the truth of things by misleading speeches that are only shadows. Theology here is nothing more than the discourse claimed by some pagan philosophers, locked in their 'superstition'. Augustine therefore distances himself from this discipline. Theology is the discourse according to the elements of the world, a submission to evil powers, which diverts the first Christians from the true faith.

But it is in Cassiodorus, that the expression *theologia* applies to Christianity: 'We know, among the first bishops and writers, noble and eloquent men who use, in the theology of the Father and the Son, that is, in the divine reasoning (*divina ratiocinatio*), the word consubstantial.'[39] Here, theology clearly refers to a learned discourse on the relationship between the Father and the Son within the divinity. Hence the identification of theology with 'divine reasoning', that is, reasoning on the divine. Are we close to the Augustinian meaning? In Augustine, we already had an equivalence between *theologia* and the 'reason that is unfolded about the gods' (*ratio quae de diis explicatur*).[40] But here, it is clearly a discourse that can be taken up by Christians on their own. And according to Cassiodorus, it is not reduced to sacred scripture, since the very issue of

---

[38] Augustine, *Epistolae*, Patrologia Latina 33, ed. Jacques-Paul Migne (Paris, 1863), 149, 1, 25 (PL 33, 541); Augustine comments *Colossians* 2, 8–9.

[39] Cassiodorus, *Epiphani historia ecclesiastica tripartite*, ed. Walter Jakob and Rudolph Hanslik (Vienna: Holder-Pichler-Tempski, 1952), 101, 1.63 (II, 11, 9).

[40] Augustine, *De civitate Dei*, VI, 5, 1 (BA 34, 64).

the debate is for him to know how a non-biblical term (such as 'consubstantial') can be introduced in the Christian faith. We will find the same movement in Boethius.

Boethius: A Second Meaning for Theological Science

The concept of theological science was transmitted to the Latin world by Boethius, who distinguished, following Aristotle's *Metaphysics* E, three main theoretical sciences: physical [science] (*naturalis*), mathematical [science] (*mathematica*), and theological [science]. To be precise, Boethius calls it 'theologics' (*theologica*), and almost never theology (*theologia*). It is of course the Latin transcription of the supreme science of the divine evoked by Aristotle (*theologikè epistémè*), which he distinguishes perfectly from the mythical narratives of the *theologia*.

But now, Aristotelian theory of science serves to elucidate the divine nature. Without ceasing to be the highest science known to philosophy, theology puts itself at the service of Christian dogmatics: it is a question of establishing 'how the Trinity is a single God and not three gods' (exact title of Boethius' *De Trinitate*):

> Speculative Science may be divided into three kinds: Physics, Mathematics, and Theologics (*theologica*). Physics deals with with motion and is not abstract (i.e. ἀνυπεξαίρετος); for it is concerned with the forms of bodies together with their constituent matter, which forms cannot be separated in reality from their bodies. These bodies are in motion ... Mathematics does not deal with motion and is not abstract, for it investigates forms of bodies apart from matter, and therefore abstract from motion ... Theologics (*theologica*) does not deal with motion and is abstract and separable, for the Divine Substance is without either matter or motion.[41]

To define the object of the 'theological' science is to deduce its method: it will be necessary to investigate pure, separate forms, thus proceeding intellectually without being dispersed by images.[42]

John Scotus Eriugena, Reader of Dionysius: A Third Meaning of Theologia

In perfect fidelity to the Greek lexicon, Dionysius' translators transcribed the word *theologia* into Latin to designate the biblical texts; and, until

---

[41] Boethius, *Quomodo Trinitas unus Deus ac non tres dii*, II, 9 (slightly corrected). Cf. Aristotle, *Metaphysics* E, 1, 1026a13–16.

[42] Boethius, *Quomodo Trinitas unus Deus ac non tres dii*, II, 8–10.

Peter Damien at least, a *theologus* was an author of Holy Scripture. But it was above all Eriugena's commentaries that played an essential role.

For Eriugena, theology 'is the first and highest part of wisdom; and rightly so':

for it is concerned wholly or for the most part with speculation about the Divine Nature. And it is divided into two parts, I mean into affirmation and negation, which are called in Greek *apophatikè* and *kataphatikè*. . . . in the first book . . . we denied that the ten categories and all the genera and species and individuals . . . can be literally predicated of God; and again in the present book . . . we said that God Himself understands that in His Essence (there is) none of the things which are and are not, because He surpasses all essence.[43]

Eriugena places theology at the top of the science system. It is the summit of philosophy, because it is a theoretical activity (*speculatio*) that concerns the highest nature, that of God. But, relying on the title of chapter 3 of *Mystical Theology*, he immediately divides it into two parts, affirmative ('cataphatic') and negative ('apophatic') theology. The two symmetrical theologies no longer refer only to the grammatical form (positive or negative) of Scripture expressions, but to two kinds of speculation, that is, two theoretical attitudes. Indeed, God is so transcendent that he is nothing of what is (negation of being), nor anything of what is not (negation of negation). Both forms of theology are ways of seeking to reach his transcendence.

But Eriugena is one of the leading figures of the Carolingian renaissance. For him, the study of sacred scripture presupposes training in the liberal arts. Exegesis is submitted to logico-grammatical methods: we must question the validity of our predicates when we apply them to God. This is the role of 'dialectic' (another name for logic), which analyses reality, starting with the most general categories. But precisely, this new problem affects the concept of theology: 'as the holy father Augustine says in his books *On the Trinity*, when we come to *theology*, that is, *to the study of the Divine Essence,* the relevance of the categories is wholly extinguished (*extinguitur*)'.[44] Theology is no longer simply the Word of God, it has become a conceptual enquiry (*inuestigatio*) of God, his nature

---

[43] Johannes Scottus seu Eriugena, *Periphyseon* II, ed. Edouard Jeauneau (Turnhout: Brepols, 1997), 599 BC (CCCM 162, 101); John Scotus Eriugena, *Periphyseon (Division of Nature)*, trans. J. O'Meara (Montreal, Washington: Bellarmin, Dumbarton Oaks, 1987), 208.

[44] Johannes Scottus seu Eriugena, *Periphyseon* I, ed. Edouard Jeauneau (Turnhout: Brepols, 1996), 463 B (CCCM 161, 33 Eriugena, *Periphyseon (Division of Nature)*, 51. Italics are mine.

and attributes. Eriugena questions the validity (*virtus*) of the categories of
ordinary language applied to God. Even if the answer remains the same
(the finite categories do not apply to God), the question is raised in a new
manner. An Augustinian vocabulary appears: God is characterized as an
'essence'; the human approach is conceived as an 'investigation'.[45] And
Augustine devotes part of *De Trinitate* to showing the impossibility of
applying our categories to God. But Eriugena makes a new synthesis, in
which the concept of theology goes beyond the two approaches (the
'negative' theology attributed to Dionysius, and the investigation to
know the divine nature proper to Augustine), by integrating them into
a new problematics.

Eriugena interprets scripture from a logical and grammatical point of
view, inspired by Aristotle's *Organon*, that of the categories: can we attribute
to God the categories drawn from our finite experience? Are they transposed
in a metaphorical way? Can all of them be said literally, or only some of
them? 'You had inquired whether [all] the Categories are [properly] to be
predicated of God, or [only] some of them'.[46] These questions are still
answered on the basis of Dionysius' analyses. If we want to attribute relevant
predicates to God, we must combine the approaches, and use the two main
theological paths (affirmative and negative):

> The one, that is *apophatikè*, denies that the Divine Essence or Substance *is* any one
> of the things that are, that is, of the things which can be discussed or understood;
> but the other, *kataphatikè*, predicates of it all the things that are, and for that
> reason it is called affirmative – not that it affirms that it is any of the things that are,
> but (because) it teaches that all things which take their being from it can be
> predicated of it. For that which is the cause can reasonably be expressed in terms
> of the things that are caused. . . . And not only does it draw its lessons about it from
> those things which accord with nature, but from the things which are contrary to
> nature, since it describes it as being drunken [and] foolish [and] mad. . . . Enough is
> said about such things by St. Dionysius the Areopagite in his 'Symbolic
> Theology'.[47]

Four conclusions can be drawn from this text:

First, in this question concerning predication, it is clearly Eriugena who
   opposes affirmative theology and negative theology (following the
   chapter title added by the scribes), while Dionysius spoke on the one

---

[45] Augustine, *De Trinitate* IX, 4, 5 (BA 16, 82–4).
[46] Eriugena, *Periphyseon* I, 458 C (CCCM 161, 26–7); Eriugena, *Periphyseon (Division of
   Nature)*, 45.
[47] Ibid, 458 B (CCCM 161, 26); Eriugena, *Periphyseon (Division of Nature)*, 45.

hand of *theologoi*, that is, sacred authors, and on the other hand of positive or subtractive statements.

Second, negative theology states that because of its transcendence, the divine essence is nothing of what is and can be predicted. If God is God, he is unique and unequalled. That is, he is beyond any finite attribute. To speak of God rigorously, we must deny everything we preach about the creature.

Third, affirmative theology symmetrically aims at the same transcendence of God. Through its statements, it does not reduce God to worldly beings, but attributes everything that comes from him to him. Thus, affirmative theology does not claim that God is everything, but that he is the cause of everything. Thus, starting from finite realities, we do not identify them with God, but we mean that he is their cause. Affirmative theology follows the path of causality. It goes back to God as a principle.

Fourth, if we attribute everything to God, we must attribute to him both the noble and the ignoble, the beautiful and the ugly, the similar image and the dissimilar image. However, the study of dissimilar symbols belongs to symbolic theology, the third type of theology mentioned by Eriugena. We then move on to a discipline other than the theology of divine names: symbolic theology.

This shift comes from the fact that we can understand the articulation of these disciplines in two manners: either they make two parts, and if negative theology denies everything, affirmative theology predicates everything, including similar and dissimilar images (hence symbolic theology); or they make three parts, and negative theology must be opposed to affirmative theology (which deals with intelligible names and similar forms), and then symbolic theology (which deals with dissimilar names and concepts). The first reading is inspired by the interpolated title of chapter 3 of the *Mystical Theology*, while the second is more faithful to the actual content of Dionysian theologies. And if we add a mystical theology, we move towards a new quadripartite division of theology: (1) symbolic theology (which presents God through dissimilarities); (2) affirmative theology (which presents God through similarities); (3) negative theology (which reaches God by denying dissimilarities); (4) mystical theology (which leads to union with God).

The bipartite interpretation of theology (of divine names) is present in the preface to Dionysius' translation by Eriugena:

This book is subdivided into the two largest parts of the logical discipline: cataphatic theology and apophatic theology, that is, being and non-being. It uses the rules of analysis, and it warns us very clearly that, in order to be able to reach the Truth, which is the cause of all that has been created from him and by him, in him and for him, we must practise the elimination (*privatio*) of all that can be said or thought, through the eminence of its essence.[48]

Incidentally, Eriugena *does not see any difference between logic and theology*. To state the rational structure of reality is to describe by eminency the transcendence of God.

He adds: 'Not in vain, I think, was the trouble we have been willing to take over the two branches of theology.'[49] Thus, there is a common rational approach, which guides both affirmative and negative theology. Certainly, this one remains oriented towards the transcendence of God, that is, the negation of divine attributes prevails over affirmation. There is a rule of conceptual analysis common to both forms of theology: the need to be critical of categorical terms when they are attributed to God. We can therefore allow ourselves to speak in general of a single *theologia*, affirmation and negation being only parts of it.

Eriugena even argues that affirmative terms can be considered negative theology:

You have very subtly observed *behind the outward expression (pronuntatio)* of the affirmative branch *the concept (intellectum)* of the negative. . . . [And] these names which are predicated of God by the addition of the particles *super-* or *more-than-*, such as *superessential, more-than-truth, more-than-wisdom*, and the like, comprehend within themselves the two previously mentioned branches of theology.[50]

The theologian seeks to identify a concept under statements, that is, to bring the discourse back to its logical scope. Even if the eminence of God turns affirmative theology and negative theology against each other by overcoming their unilaterality, eminence is above all a form of negation. For Eriugena, theology is *fundamentally negative*: the expression of the eminence, despite its apparently affirmative grammatical form, is secretly but fundamentally negative.[51]

---

[48] Johannes Scotus [Eriugena], *Preface to his Versio Dionysii* (PL 122, 1035 A–1036 A).

[49] Eriugena, *Periphyseon* I, 463 C (CCCM 161, 33); Eriugena, *Periphyseon (Division of Nature)*, 52.

[50] Eriugena, *Periphyseon* I, 462 C (CCCM 161, 32); Eriugena, *Periphyseon (Division of Nature)*, slightly modified, 50. Italics are mine. Cf. Veronika Limberger, *Eriugenas Hypertheologie* (Berlin, Boston: De Gruyter, 2015), 161–9.

[51] Harrington, *A Thirteenth-Century Textbook*, 28: 'Eriugena here weakens affirmative theology considerably, by restricting its literal application to God's causality and denying that it can speak of God himself.'

Thus, in Eriugena, the term *theologia* merges the 'Word of God' in the sense of Dionysius with the Augustinian meaning: 'reason that is unfolded about the gods' (or that of Chalcidius). But it does so in the name of a more rigorous concept of *logos*: it brings out, through analysis, a concept underlying ordinary language, and methodically questions the relevance of the application of our categories to God (in the name of an Aristotelian theory of predication). Theology refers to a more speculative content than simply adhering to the text of Scripture: an investigation into the essence of God and a logico-grammatical question about how we apply attributes to it. Theology has become a method.

However, this does not mean that it is a science of God (in the sense of a science that man could have of God). Valid predication is limited to the recognition of the existence of God, since it fails to reach him in his essence:

Does not this very *theology* that you have just mentioned, ... hold – plainly enough for those who can see the truth – that from what has been created by itself one can deduce merely that this Nature subsists (*subsistere*) as an essence, but not what that essence is (*quid sit*)? For, as we have often said, it exceeds not only the endeavours of human reasoning, but even the most perfectly pure intellections of the celestial essences.[52]

Therefore, *theologia* is not a science: neither for us, because of the weakness of our intellect, nor in itself, because no intellect, not even that of the separate angels, can have the intelligence of what it is. We can only know that God exists, or rather that he 'essentially subsists', beyond all things. But what this essence is remains radically unknown to us.

Ultimately, *theologia* is God himself. Indeed, God is identical to the science he has of himself: '*Theologia*, that is, the reason of God (*Dei ratio*), who is also God, since it is [his] wisdom.'[53] Theology is the 'reason of God' in the dual sense of the objective genitive (the reason one can have of God), and the subjective genitive (the reason God possesses). This also explains why it remains inaccessible to us. Theology is the science of God, but this science of God is accessible only to him.

However, this divine theology (of which God is the subject) is then spread in creatures through divine revelation, and this is how we recover its Dionysian meaning (Word of God): 'The very wise theology is either

---

[52] Eriugena, *Periphyseon* I, 455 B (CCCM 161, 22); Eriugena, *Periphyseon (Division of Nature)*, 42 (corrected by me).

[53] Iohannes Scoti [Eriugena], *Expositiones in ierarchiam coelestem*, ed. Jeanne Barbet (Turnhout: Brepols, 1975), 6 (CCCM 31, 89).

a cognitive power naturally innate to angelic and human spirits, or the divinity itself. Indeed, because divinity is the principle of hierarchy, it is the source and illumination of all cognitive power within and through the hierarchy. That is why it is rational to call it theology.'[54] *Theologia* is both the main and supreme part of philosophy, which culminates in the natural knowledge of God's existence, and a participation in divine science, through the illumination of the Word of God.

Thus, the loop is closed: since this revelation is given in the Bible under the guise of contradictory narratives, symbolic theology is necessary: the symbolic is an oxymoronic manifestation, made under the species of the opposite. But where Dionysus claimed that the Bible expresses itself 'without art' (*atechnôs*),[55] Eriugena translated on the contrary *valde artificialiter*, 'with much art'.[56] For Dionysius, biblical symbols have no value of their own, they betray an uncultivated form, remain below art and form. But Eriugena reads Dionysius with Augustine's glasses, for whom God acts 'thanks to an art that is much more perfect'[57] than human art, but which remains the model of our art of knowing. For him, Holy Scripture provides a clever encryption, which requires the reader to decrypt it accordingly.

Theology becomes precisely the art of encrypting thought into symbols and symmetrically deciphering them:

It is indeed with much art (*multum artificiose*) that theology, that is, that power which is naturally inherent to human minds, to seek, examine, contemplate and love divine reasons, has used forged images (*factitiis*), that is, holy and feigned images (*fictis*), to mean divine intellects, which lack any circumscribed and sensitive figure and form.[58]

Theology has become a natural power of the human intellect: a form of natural reason. It seeks to reach the 'divine reasons', the relevant concepts meant to describe God. Therefore, it strives to match the concepts accepted by the authors of Scripture, who use forged images to do so. It is possible, through reason, to decode the narratives and metaphors of Scripture, to reach the divine reasons underlying the literal formulas. Nevertheless, the divine realities are non-representable, so we must remember that any image is fictitious and inadequate.

---

[54] Ibid, 4 (CCCM 31, 76).
[55] Denys [Dionysius], *De coelesti hierarchia*, II, 1 (PG 3, 137 A; SC 58bis, 74).
[56] Eriugena, *Expositiones*, II, 124–8 (CCCM 31, 23).
[57] Augustine, *83 Questions diverses*, q. 78 (BA 10, 340–2).
[58] Eriugena, *Expositiones*, II, 129–34 (CCCM 31, 23–4).

Contrary to what Dionysius claimed, all Scripture can be deciphered by reason, in the opposite direction of its encryption by a very learned 'art'. Reason produced scripture in the first place. It is therefore necessary that it be the reason that deciphers it: 'All natural arts converge to signify Christ in figure, and the totality of divine Scripture is included within their limits. *For there is no sacred Scripture that is exempt from the rules of the liberal arts.*' Scripture itself is subject to the rules of the liberal arts, grammar and logic, and leads to a philosophical knowledge of God (what Varro called a 'natural theology').

Theology is a kind of natural knowledge of God (a 'natural power'). Originally, intelligence participated in the science that God has of all things. But as a result of the fall, it lost this knowledge of God, and must return to him indirectly, through two ways: abstraction from the sensible, and the images of scripture. Now, people have lost their capacity for contemplation: in principle they could access the intelligible from nature, but in fact scripture helps them to do so. The authority of scripture is therefore a help, an initiation, for the natural functioning of reason. That is why reason prevails over authority. People are not made for scripture, but scripture is made for people. It is a help, in order to compensate for the defects of our intelligence after the fall. It presents itself as a substitute for nature: it reveals in fact truths that are intelligible in principle.

It is the science that the authors of scripture possessed to encrypt the text. This is indeed an art or a science:

For the human spirit was not created for the divine Scripture, nor would it have needed it if it had not sinned; but it is for the human spirit that sacred scripture was woven with various *symbols* and teachings, so that, by its initiation, our rational nature – which has, by its deviation, fallen from the contemplation of truth – might be brought to the summit of the pure contemplation it originally enjoyed.[59]

Therefore, the liberal arts make it possible to achieve intelligible contemplation of God, but in the present state we must pass through sacred scripture: 'All types of the visible and invisible creation and all allegories, whether in acts or in words, through the entire holy scripture of both testaments, are the veils of the paternal ray.'[60] Scripture is everywhere intelligible, and it means God, but so does the world. The world is therefore the symbol of the intelligible. In this way, Eriugena sets up two

---

[59] Ibid, II, 151–8 (CCCM 31, 24).
[60] Eriugena, *Expositiones*, I, 420–3 (CCCM 31, 12); Paul Rorem, *Eriugena's Commentary on the Dionysian Celestial Hierarchy* (Toronto: Pontifical Institute of Mediaeval Studies, 2005), 190.

equivalences: between the metaphor and the allegory, between the textual metaphor and the sensitive image. That is, between allegory *in things* and allegory *in words*, between historical interpretation and literary interpretation.[61]

And where we need scripture, it is submitted to reason, which holds the keys to its interpretation. In scripture, the very things are meaningful: the mountain means contemplation, the tree of life is the image of the cross, and so on. However, in nature, according to Eriugena, the same is true:

> Just as poetic art, through forged myths and *allegorical* similarities, develops moral or physical teaching to exercise human minds – for this is the hallmark of heroic poets, who figuratively celebrate the actions and conduct of heroes – so theology, as a kind of poetics (*veluti quaedam poetria*), uses fabricated images to conform Sacred Scripture to the capacities of our mind, to lead it from the physical and external senses to the perfect knowledge of intelligible realities, as well as from imperfect childhood to a certain maturity of the inner man.[62]

The Book and the world lead both to God:

> The eternal light manifests itself to the world in two ways: through scripture and through creatures. For divine knowledge can only be restored in us through the letters of Scripture and the forms of creatures. Learn the words of scripture, and in your mind conceive the meaning (*intellectum*) of them: you will recognize in them a Word. Through your bodily senses, observe the forms and beauties of sensitive things: in them, your intelligence will recognize the Word of God. And in all this, the Truth will show you nothing but the One who has done all things; apart from him you will have nothing to contemplate, for he himself is all things.[63]

In Hugh of St Victor, because of the reciprocal meaning of words and things, the world itself will be interpreted as a book, and hermeneutics will unfold itself within *two books*: the book of the world and the book of scripture.

Eriugena thus establishes a correspondence between *poetic theology* (the 'mythical theology' of the Stoics) and *rational theology* (their 'natural theology'). It adapts and conforms the intelligible truth to the capacities of

---

[61] The allegory in words (*in verbis*) is a prolonged metaphor: 'one says one thing, and one wants another to be understood' (Quintilian, *Institutio oratorio* IX, 2, 92). The allegory in things (*in rebus*) refers to events that themselves refer to another reality; 'one thing happens, and another is figured' (Ambrosius, *De Abraham* I, 4, 28). This second meaning is properly Christian: the holy story carries a message that opens onto another reality, the Old Testament refers to the New (Paul, Galatians 4:24).

[62] Scoti [Eriugena], *Expositiones*, II, 142–151 (CCCM 31, 24).

[63] Jean Scot [Eriugena], *Homélie sur le Prologue de Jean*, ed. Edouard Jeauneau (Paris: le Cerf, 1969), 289 C (SC 151, 254).

our mind. Exegesis and speculation are the two sides of theology. But exegesis follows the opposite path of decryption.

With Eriugena, *theologia* retains its Dionysian sense of God's word; but it deals with the categorical problem, according to Aristotle's *Organon*, it becomes a rational investigation, with Augustine's *De Trinitate*, and a poetic art, which is also an art of decryption. It has become at the same time a hermeneutic, a logical procedure, and an investigation into God, his attributes, and nature.[64]

FROM ERIUGENA TO ABELARD

It is only from Abelard on that theology will claim its name, and that it can be said to be the heir to Aristotle's 'theological science'. It took a long journey for the Middle Ages to achieve the elision of the 'c', that is, for it to pass from *theologica* to the *theologia*, and for God's speculative science, the most abstract of all, to be confused with the reading of sacred scripture. Theology as a science is *the future of an elision*. Boethius himself practised this elision once: in his Second Commentary on the *Isagoge* of Porphyry, he places at the top of theoretical philosophy the contemplation of the intelligible (*noeta, intelligibilia*) – the immutable essences, the divine realities, which only the intellect can reach. He adds: 'This part of science, the Greeks call it *theologia*'.[65] The scholastic concept of *theologia* was coined by Abelard. For him, *theologia* is not yet the name of a science, but it is the title of his work: a rational discourse on the divinity, its unity and trinity, its properties and attributes. (1) Abelard knew the Eriugenian interpretation of Dionysius' theologies: the concept of theology as rational interpretation of the predicates given in *theologia* as *sacred scripture*. (2) He read Boethius closely; he used it in his own *Gloses* upon the *Isagogè*. Thus, at a time when Aristotle's *Metaphysics* was not yet available in Latin, Boethius gave an overview of the theological science developed by Aristotle, but interpreted it in a Neoplatonist spirit as the science of 'intellectibles'. The concept of theology as a science took on a precise metaphysical colour. (3) Abelard was also the heir of Augustine's analysis

---

[64] Cf. Wayne J. Hankey, '*Ad intellectum ratiocinatio*: Three Procline logics, *The Divine Names* of Pseudo-Dionysius, Eriugena's *Periphyseon* and Boethius' *Consolatio Philosophiae*', *Studia Patristica* 29 (1997), 244–51 at p. 250: 'John the Scot unites the Boethius of the *Consolation* with the logic by which Aquinas connects the *Theological Tractates*.'

[65] Boethius, *In Isagogen Porphyrii Commenta, ed. Secunda*, ed. Samuel Brandt (Vienna, Leipzig: Tempsky, 1906), 8, 3–9.

of natural theology (the philosophical science of the gods among the stoics). But Abelard makes a new synthesis of it.

Bibliography

Aquinas, Thomas. *In librum beati Dionysii De divinis nominibus expositio.* Edited by Ceslas Pera. Rome, Turin: Marietti, 1950.

Aristotle. *Metaphysica.* Edited by Werner Jaeger. Oxford: Clarendon Press, 1980 (1957).

Augustinus. *De civitate Dei. Œuvres de saint Augustin, La cité de Dieu,* Livres VI–X. Paris: Desclée de Brouwer, 1959.

    De Trinitate. Œuvres de saint Augustin, La Trinité, Livres I–VII. Paris: Desclée de Brouwer, 1959.

    Epistolae, Patrologia Latina 33. Edited by Jacques-Paul Migne. Paris, 1863.

Boethius. *In Isagogen Porphyrii Commenta, ed. Secunda.* Edited by Samuel Brandt. Vienna, Leipzig: Tempsky, 1906.

    The Theological Tractates: The Consolation of Philosophy. Edited and translated by Hugh Fraser Stewart, Edward Kennard Rand, and S. Jim Tester. Cambridge, Mass., and London: Heinemann, 1978.

Boulnois, Olivier. *Au-delà de l'image. Une archéologie du visuel au Moyen Age, Ve–XVIe siècle.* Paris: Seuil, 2008.

Cassiodorus. *Epiphani historia ecclesiastica tripartite.* Edited by Walter Jakob and Rudolph Hanslik. Vienna: Holder-Pichler-Tempski, 1952.

Denys l'Aréopagite [Dionysius the Areopagite]. *De coelesti hierarchia. La Hiérarchie Céleste.* Edited by Gunther Heil and translated by Maurice de Gandillac. Paris: le Cerf, 1970.

    De divinis nominibus, Les Noms divins. Edited and translated by Ysabel de Andia. Paris: le Cerf, 2016.

    De mystica theologia. La théologie mystique. Edited and translated by Ysabel de Andia. Paris: le Cerf, 2016.

Dionysius Areopagita. *Corpus Dionysiacum* I. Edited by Beate Regina Suchla. Berlin, New York: De Gruyter, 1990.

    Corpus Dionysiacum II. Edited by Gunther Heil and Adolf Martin Ritter. Berlin, New York: De Gruyter, 1991.

    On the Divine Names and the Mystical Theology. Translated by Clarence Edwin. London, New York: Macmillan, 1920.

    Opera Omnia, Patrologia Graeca 3. Edited by Jacques-Paul Migne. Paris, 1857.

Hankey, Wayne J. 'Ad intellectum ratiocinatio: Three Procline logics, *The Divine Names* of Pseudo-Dionysius, Eriugena's *Periphyseon* and Boethius' *Consolatio Philosophiae*'. *Studia Patristica* 29 (1997): 244–51.

Harrington, Michael L., ed. and trans. *A Thirteenth-Century Textbook of Mystical Theology at the University of Paris. The Mystical Theology of Dionysius the Areopagite in Eriugena's Latin Translation with the Scholia Translated by Anastasius the Librarian and Excerpts from Eriugena's Periphyseon.* Paris-Leuven-Dudley, MA: Peeters, 2004.

Jean Scot [John Scotus Eriugena]. *Homélie sur le Prologue de Jean*. Edited by Edouard Jeauneau. Paris: le Cerf, 1969.

Iohannes Scoti [John Scotus Eriugena]. *Expositiones in ierarchiam coelestem*. Edited by Jeanne Barbet. Turnhout: Brepols, 1975.

Johannes Scottus seu Eriugena [John Scotus Eriugena]. *Periphyseon* I. Edited by Edouard Jeauneau. Turnhout: Brepols, 1996.

Periphyseon II. Edited by Edouard Jeauneau. Turnhout: Brepols, 1997.

Periphyseon (Division of Nature). Translated by J. O'Meara. Montreal, Washington: Bellarmin, Dumbarton Oaks, 1987.

Le Bouzec, Yves. 'L'*hypotypose*: un essai de définition formelle'. *L'information grammaticale* 92 (2002): 3–7.

Limberger, Veronika. *Eriugenas Hypertheologie*. Berlin, Boston: De Gruyter, 2015.

Pépin, Jean. 'Les modes de l'enseignement théologique dans la *Théologie Platonicienne*'. In *Proclus et la théologie platonicienne*, edited by Alain-Philippe Segonds and Carlos Steel, 1–14. Leuven, Paris: Leuven University Press, 2000.

Plotin, *Ennéades*. Edited by E. Bréhier. Paris: Les Belles Lettres, 1976.

Traité 38. Translated by Pierre Hadot. Paris: Les Éditions du Cerf, 1988.

Proclus. *Théologie Platonicienne*. Edited by Henri-Dominique Saffrey and Leender Westerink Gerrit. Paris: les Belles Lettres, 2017 (1968).

Roques, René. 'Les "théologies" dionysiennes: notions, fonctions et implications'. In *Structures théologiques. De la gnose à Richard de Saint-Victor*, 135–63. Paris: Presses Universitaires de France, 1962.

Rorem, Paul. *Eriugena's Commentary on the Dionysian Celestial Hierarchy*. Toronto: Pontifical Institute of Mediaeval Studies, 2005.

Saffrey, Henri-Dominique. 'Theology as Science (3rd–6th centuries'). *Studia Patristica* 29 (1997): 321–39.

I.6

Participation: Aquinas and His Neoplatonic Sources

Rudi A. te Velde

INTRODUCTION: PARTICIPATION AS A KEY WORD
OF CHRISTIAN PLATONISM

The notion of participation (in Greek *methexis*) is commonly associated with the philosophy of Plato. For Plato, it is a word signifying transcendence, insofar as it signifies the relationship between the changeable reality of the senses and the transcendent reality of the Forms. Participation connects the world of Becoming with the world of true Being: what comes to be is explained by reference to an eternal paradigm, which is the truth behind the changing reality of our experience. Participation entails the presence of the higher in the lower, of the universal Form in the particular instance of that Form. It explains why a particular thing is subject of a universal predicate. "When something is found to be beautiful, then it is beautiful because it participates in the absolute beauty," Socrates says in the *Phaedo*.[1]

In handbooks on the history of philosophy, one is likely to read that Aristotle, Plato's famous pupil, rejected participation together with the doctrine of ideas. In the first book of the *Metaphysics*, Aristotle criticized the supposed existence of ideas for being unable to explain the generation of things: "other things [the generated individuals] are not in any accepted sense derived from the Forms. To say that the Forms are patterns (*paradeigmata*), and that other things participate in them, is to use empty phrases and poetical metaphors."[2] For Aristotle, the problem of participation is not only that it does not succeed in explaining the generation of things; the

---

[1] *Phaedo*, 100c.   [2] *Metaphysics* I, 9, 991a20. (trans. H. Tredennick).

main objection against participation seems to be that it threatens to dissolve the essential unity of the individual substance.[3]

Aristotle's negative verdict, however, did not mean the definitive end of participation as a philosophical concept.[4] In later Neoplatonism, the term was widely used, mostly in a specific causal sense according to which a hypostatic principle impresses its formal character upon a manifold of instances derived from it, which all "participate" in that formal character. One might say, for instance, that good things are good by participation in the Good Itself, or that living beings are alive by participation in the form of Life Itself.

If we look at the Christian version of Platonism in the period of the Fathers (Dionysius, Augustine, Boethius), participation is used in connection with creation and the causal relationship between God and the world of creatures. Especially where God, in a Platonic fashion, was conceived of in terms of Goodness Itself, the creative source of all existence, the term participation was likely to be used in a causal sense of derivation and dependency. But one has to wait for the scholastic age, for the theologian Thomas Aquinas, to encounter a full-blown metaphysical account of creation, based on the concept of participation of being. For Aquinas, the causality of creation is a participative causality according to which the effect – the creature – is said to participate in being (*esse*) received from God, who is thought of as the fullness of Being Itself (*ipsum esse subsistens*). In this way participation is granted a central place in the philosophical account of the Christian notion of creation. Within a basically Aristotelian framework of philosophy, thus accepting to a certain extent Aristotle's criticism of Plato's doctrine of Forms, Aquinas developed a profound and original view of creation as participation, the main elements of which were derived from his Neoplatonic sources, in particular Dionysius and the *Liber de causis*. This is in short what I intend to present in my contribution to this volume on Christian Platonism.

Until recently the formative presence of the notion of participation in Aquinas has hardly received any attention in the tradition of Thomistic thought. It is only since the important studies of Fabro and Geiger that the significance of participation in Aquinas, and in general of the Platonic

---

[3] Cf. *Metaphysics* VII, 4, 1030a11–14. What a thing essentially is, its specific identity, is it not by participation nor in the way of an accident. Here we see Aristotle associating the mode of predication according to participation with the predication of an accident.

[4] For a useful survey of the history of the notion of participation, see Cornelio Fabro's lemma on participation in the *New Catholic Encyclopedia* (www.encyclopedia.com/religion/encyclope dias-almanacs-transcripts-and-maps/participation).

dimension of his thought, has been more and more acknowledged by Thomistic scholars.[5] If Aquinas must be regarded primarily as an Aristotelian qua philosophical orientation, then only as incorporating much of the Neoplatonic tradition of philosophy, in particular with respect to the theory of the transcendent causes of being as being.[6]

As said, Aquinas conceives the causality of creation in terms of participation. The mode of being of a creature is "being by participation" (ens per participationem). With regard to the theme of Christian Platonism, one will presumably be particularly interested in knowing whether the participation model of creation leads to a genuinely Christian view of the relationship between God and his creation. In other words: are there good reasons to defend Aquinas' decision to use the Platonic model of participation in his account of the causality of creation?[7] I will propose four conditions of the Christian idea of creation, which in this article will be used as criteria to determine whether the participation theory of creation is arguably consonant with Christian faith.

First, the ex nihilo condition of creation. Christian teaching about the creation of the world out of nothing is a cardinal doctrine. It views all things, without any exception, with reference to God as their absolute beginning and end. "Ex nihilo" means, among other things, that there is nothing in the creature which is exempt from God's power and influence. The question is whether and how participation enables one to think this radical dependency of the creature with respect to God along with the acknowledgment that the creature, once created, has a being of its own.

---

[5] C. Fabro, La nozione metafisica di partecipazione secondo S. Tomaso d'Aquino, 3rd ed. Turin, 1963 (French edition: Participation et causalité selon saint Thomas d'Aquin, Louvain, 1961); L.-B. Geiger, La Participation dans la philosophie de S. Thomas d'Aquin, Montreal, 1952 (2nd ed., Paris, 1953). See also the essay by John Wippel, "Thomas Aquinas and Participation," in Studies in Medieval Philosophy, ed. J. Wippel (Washington, D.C.: The Catholic University of America Press, 1987), pp. 117–58; Rudi A. te Velde, Participation and Substantiality in Thomas Aquinas (Leiden: E. J. Brill, 1995).

[6] This is what I argued for in my article "Aquinas's Aristotelian Science of Metaphysics and its Revised Platonism," Nova et Vetera 13, no. 3 (2015), pp. 743–64.

[7] According to Schindler, the notion of participation seems to be contrary to a Christian view of the world in at least two respects. First, the notion seems to tend toward pantheism, and second, the notion of participation seems to deprive the physical world any reality of its own. See David C. Schindler, "What's the Difference? On the Metaphysics of Participation in a Christian Context," The Saint Anselm Journal 3, no. 1 (2005), pp. 1–27 at pp. 2–3.

The second condition is that the created world itself is nondivine, and as such really distinct from God. Only God is God. The creature is not an extension of God, something of a semi-divine status. In this respect one sometimes speaks of the "Christian Distinction."[8] Participation, however, suggests a very close and intimate presence of God in his creatures. Does participation sufficiently respect the radical distinction between God and the realm of creatures?

Third, creation is the work of a free God, not a necessary emanation from a divine source. The world exists because God wanted it to exist, not because it is a necessary consequence of his nature. The Christian view of creation essentially differs from emanation accounts as found in various strands of Neoplatonism (e.g. Avicenna). How is the freedom of God in his act of creation accounted for by Aquinas? What is left of this freedom if Aquinas says, following the logic of participation, that God, like any natural reality, "tends to communicate a likeness of his goodness to others as much as possible"?[9] Does God have a choice to create or not?

The fourth condition to be mentioned is that, from the Christian perspective on creation, the plurality and diversity in the world must be positively valued. That creation results in a manifold of diverse and unequal creatures is not a matter of an "ontological fall" from the simple perfection of God, but it marks finite reality in its own order as intended by God. This raises the question whether the fact of plurality in creation as intended by God can be reconciled with the participation model with its implication of diminishment of perfection in the effect.

In what follows, I will first examine Aquinas' view on participation as developed by him in dialogue with his main Neoplatonic sources, namely Boethius' *De hebdomadibus*, Dionysius' *De divinis nominibus*, and the *Liber de causis*. These sources have all contributed significantly to the formation of the notion of participatory causality. Then, in the next section, I will pay attention to the principal argument for creation, as found in the *Summa theologiae* I, q.44, a.1. Most of the essential aspects of participation as conceived by Aquinas are present in this text. Finally, I will conclude with an evaluative section about participation and Aquinas' version of Christian Platonism.

---

[8] The expression is introduced by Robert Sokolowski; see his *The God of Faith and Reason: Foundations of Christian Theology* (Notre Dame, IN: University of Notre Dame Press, 1982).

[9] See especially *Summa Theologiae* (*S.Th.*) I, q.19, a.2, about whether God wills other things; this text is remarkably full of reminiscences of Plotinus.

BOETHIUS' DE HEBDOMADIBUS: THE PROBLEM
OF PARTICIPATION

For Aquinas, an important text which caused him to reflect on the conceptual structure of participation and the questions raised by it is a relatively small work by Boethius (*c.* 480–524), commonly known as the *De hebdomadibus.*[10] The relevance of this text for us is due to the fact that Aquinas wrote a commentary on it, which is of great importance for understanding the early development of his view on participation.[11] In what follows we will treat some aspects of the text of Boethius together with Aquinas' commentary, as the question discussed by Boethius prompted Thomas to reflect on the relationship between being and goodness and the conceptual possibilities of participation in this regard.

The treatise of Boethius is devoted to a question put to him by a friend, John the Deacon, about the status of the goodness of things. It was a common assumption in Neoplatonic circles that the first principle, God, is the very essence of goodness, and that all things are good by participation in the divine Goodness; in other words, they have their goodness as received from God. According to Neoplatonism, the Good must be regarded as the primary reason and cause of all existence, a view expressed nicely in the statement of St. Augustine: "because God is good, we exist; and insofar we exist, we are good."[12] For the Christian Fathers, one of the attractive aspects of Neoplatonism is undoubtedly this view of God as "Goodness Itself," as the reason of creation and its good order.

In his question John the Deacon assumes that all created substances are good insofar as they exist; what he particularly wanted to know is "how substances are good in virtue of their existence without being substantial goods." What makes this question so difficult, Aquinas remarks in his commentary, is the apparent contradiction between, on the one hand, the assumption that created substances are good insofar as they exist and the denial that they are "substantially" good on the other. To be substantially

---

[10] The text is published under the title "Quomodo substantiae": Boethius, *The Theological Tractates with an English Translation by Stewart, Rand, and Tester*, Loeb Classical Library (Cambridge, MA and London: Harvard University Press, 1973).

[11] *In librum Boetii De hebdomadibus expositio.* This commentary is written during the first Parisian regency of 1256–1259. In my book *Participation and Substantiality in Thomas Aquinas* (Leiden: Brill, 1995), I argued that Boethius' treatise provided for Aquinas the starting point of his explicit reflection on participation in relation to the structure of finite being.

[12] Augustine, *De doctrina christiana*, L.1, c.32. "Quia enim bonus est, sumus; et in quantum sumus, boni sumus."

good is something that belongs exclusively to the divine good. But the claim that things are good insofar as they exist, seems to imply that they are substantial goods, and so the distinction with respect to the divine good tends to disappear. It is clear that the ontological vocabulary of "substance" and "substantially," central to Aristotle's philosophy, creates a problem when used in formulating the Neoplatonic assumption that things are good by reason of their very existence.

The problem stems from a tension between respectively the Platonic and the Aristotelian scheme of predication. This is clear from the way Boethius reformulates the question: "We must, however, inquire how they are good – by participation or by substance."[13] "Participation" refers to a transcendent principle, "substance" stands for what a thing is in itself. Both possibilities are then examined, and after examination rejected. Boethius is, apparently, too much an Aristotelian to accept the solution of participation in explaining the goodness of created things. His argument goes as follows: he starts from the premise that the things which exist are also good. The reason for this is that all things desire the good. This fundamental desire for the good could not be explained if things were not already good in themselves, since a thing necessarily seeks its like. Now, when we suppose that things are good by participation, then it would follow that they are not good in themselves (*per se ipsa*); for what is white by participation, for instance, is not white in itself but receives the whiteness from without. But what is not good in itself, cannot seek the good either; but this was assumed.

The alternative proves to be impossible as well. Good things are not good by substance, for in that case they would be identical with the divine goodness. Thus neither the predication *per participationem* nor that of *substantialiter* provides a satisfactory answer to the question of how things are good. Boethius is confronted here with an aporia with no way out. Considering the fact that Boethius explicitly rejects participation, it may come as a surprise when we see Aquinas, in his *Summa theologiae*, attributing to him the view that creatures are good by participation.[14] This is a telling detail. When writing his *Summa*, Aquinas apparently retrospectively associates his own position concerning the goodness of

---

[13] Boethius, *Quomodo substantia* (ed. Rand, p. 43).

[14] See *S.Th.* I, q.6, a.3: "Sed contra est quod dicit Boethius, in libro De hebdom., quod alia omnia a Deo sunt bona per participationem. Non igitur per essentiam." Boethius' term "substantialiter" is replaced by "per essentiam," which means that a predicate is said of a thing as part of its essence.

things with the problem of *De hebdomadibus*, which he himself had solved by deepening his understanding of participation in such a way that it no longer has the connotation of "extra-essentially."

Boethius himself seeks to solve the problem concerning the goodness of created things in terms of their relation to the First Good (God). Since the being of things has "flowed" (*defluxit*) from the First Good, he says, the being itself of created things can be said to be good. Thus, things are good insofar as they exist, because their (essential) being has its origin in the Good. This solution implies that created things are only good by extrinsic denomination. For Aquinas, this is not an acceptable solution. He agrees with Boethius that creatures cannot be said to be good by reason of their essence, thus *substantialiter*. On the other hand, some form of goodness must be attributed to things in the very heart of their being, and not merely in an accidental sense. And although this form of goodness, received from the divine goodness, cannot be part of the essence of things, it nevertheless must be something inherent to their very being. This is only possible if one assumes a nonidentity between the essence of a thing and its being (*esse*). Thus, only in the light of the real distinction in creatures between essence and *esse*, can the thesis be upheld that created things are good by participation while at the same time good by reason of their being, since that very being is participated. Thus, things are good by participation, because and insofar as they are beings by participation.[15]

Boethius' *De hebdomadibus* in the first place formulates a problem. Although it did not offer an acceptable solution to the problem, it certainly suggested to Aquinas how to articulate an inner difference in created being together with a new and unprecedented use of participation. It can be defended that his Commentary on *De hebdomadibus* marks the beginning of an explicit reflection on participation as pertaining to the being of things.

DIONYSIUS' DE DIVINIS NOMINIBUS: PARTICIPATION AND THE TRANSCENDENTALS

For Aquinas, another important source of Platonically inspired thought on God and creation is Dionysius' *On Divine Names*. Dionysius – or rather the

---

[15] Cf. *De veritate* q.21, a.2: "Ipsum igitur esse habet rationem boni. Unde sicut impossibile est quod sit aliquod ens quod non habeat esse, it necesse est quod omne ens sit bonum ex hoc ipso quod esse habet." See also a.5, ad 6: "unde, sicut habet esse per participationem, ita et bona est per participationem."

unknown Christian and Neoplatonic author of the late fifth century who hides behind the name and authority of Dionysius, the pupil of St. Paul himself, is held in high esteem by Aquinas. The treatise *On Divines Names* is one of the main sources of his metaphysical doctrine of God, in particular of his view of how the one and simple God can be named by many names derived from the perfections, such as "being," "life," "wisdom," which creatures participate in derivation from God. Dionysius is a Christian author, a theologian of great reputation, and as such, to Aquinas, an authoritative source of what the faith teaches. If there is, for Aquinas, a source of Christian Platonism, then Dionysius certainly is.

In the preface of his Commentary on *De divinis nominibus*, Aquinas sets out to introduce the writings of Dionysius to his readers and to clarify his philosophical allegiance. One of the difficulties one will experience in reading the books of Dionysius, he says, is caused by the fact that he frequently uses a Platonic style and way of speaking which is no longer customary in our times (*apud modernos*). Dionysius' philosophical language is unmistakably Platonic in character. But apparently, that does not make him a full-blooded Platonic thinker who subscribes to the basic positions of Platonic philosophy. In a subtle manner, Aquinas argues that Dionysius distances himself from those aspects of Platonism, in particular the doctrine of the ideal Forms, which are contrary to the Christian faith and to (rational) truth. The Platonism of Dionysius is a revised Platonism, which does not fall under Aristotle's critique of the doctrine of the Forms; a revised Platonism which is compatible with the Christian faith.

Characteristic of the *Platonici*, Aquinas explains, is that they hypostatize the forms and species of things. They hold that the species of things exist separately through themselves. Thus, they say, for instance, that this human individual is not essentially a human being, but is human by participation in "separate man." Now, this way of abstraction is not only applied to the species of natural things, but also to the most common predicates such as "good," "one," and "being." Aquinas distinguishes between the categorial order of species and genera and the so-called *maxime communia* which extend to all things. These *communia* are also called "*transcendentia*," transcendental properties of being.[16] With the help of this distinction Aquinas is able to grant a relative truth to the position of the Platonists:

---

[16] For the medieval doctrine of transcendentals, see Jan Aertsen, *Medieval Philosophy and the Transcendentals. The Case of Thomas Aquinas* (Leiden: Brill, 1996).

The Platonists not only considered abstraction of this kind regarding the ultimate species of natural things, but also concerning the most common features, which are good, one, and being. . . . This reasoning of the Platonists concords neither with faith nor with the truth in so far as it concerns the separateness of natural species, but regarding what they say concerning the first principle of things, their opinion is most true and consonant with the Christian faith.[17]

With respect to the transcendentals the Platonic abstraction does have an acceptable and legitimate sense, Thomas says: the Platonists posit a first principle, which is the "essence of goodness," "the essence of unity," and the "essence of being," and this we call "God"; all things are said to be good, or one, or being, by way of derivation from that primary principle. This is, in a nutshell, the Platonic doctrine of the first principle and its participative causality as present in the theology of Dionysius, and which is judged by Aquinas to be most true and consonant with the Christian faith.

An essential element of this Christian Platonism is the identity of "being" and "good" in the realm of the divine. "Being" must be the primary name of the divine cause. The reason of this is that the supreme Good of Plato must be more than an ideal principle; it must be an Aristotelian *agens*, a real principle with an effective power. For Aquinas, God can only be an efficient agent by reason of his being. The divine attribute of being is particularly associated with God's efficient causality, just as the attribute of good is associated with the final causality in God, the motivating cause of his creative action. God creates because he wants to communicate his goodness as much as possible to others, according to the Platonic principle *bonum est diffusivum sui*; but he can create by reason of the infinite power of being he incorporates. For God, to create means to let others share in the being he himself has in fullness.[18]

The central place granted to being in the transcendent realm is an important modification with respect to the Platonic priority of the Good. The Good is not any longer "above being," as Plato has said.[19] For Aquinas, the good is coextensive with being (*ens et bonum convertuntur*),

---

[17] Thomas Aquinas, *In librum De divinis nominibus*, prooemium.

[18] In reading Dionysius, Aquinas is careful to avoid pantheism. When creatures are said to participate being, that being is distinguished from the being of God himself; they participate in the *ipsum esse commune*, which is a 'likeness' of God's being. Participation is a three-term relationship between a subject which participates a likeness received from the cause, which remains in its essence transcendent (unparticipated).

[19] Plato, *Republic* VI, 509b; in the series of divines names, treated in the *De divinis nominibus*, the name of the Good comes first (ch. 4), then the name of Being (ch. 5). Being is said the oldest effect of the Good; and see the *Liber de causis*, prop. 4, where it is said that "being is the first of all created things."

and thus is the "absolute good" (*ipsum per se bonum*) identical with absolute being, and because of its identity with being, the absolute good may be called "God." The assumption is that the name God stands for a real (effective) principle. Thus, only as identical with being can the absolute good be identified with God in the sense of an effective principle which grants being to creatures, and together with being, a basic form of goodness. Thus, things are good by participation because and insofar as they are beings by participation. Here we see an important shift from the Neoplatonic primacy of the Good to the primacy of Being in Aquinas.

THE LIBER DE CAUSIS: IN SEARCH OF A UNIVERSAL CAUSALITY

One of the most influential and appreciated Neoplatonic sources of Aquinas is the *Liber de causis*. The identity of the author of *Liber de causis* remains a debated issue. When the work began to be circulated at the Latin universities during the thirteenth century under the title *Liber de Expositione Bonitatis Purae* (*Book of the Exposition of Pure Goodness*), it was attributed to Aristotle himself and it was commonly understood to be the completion of his science of metaphysics.[20] Even Aquinas considered Aristotle to be its author for a long time, at least until Proclus' *Elements of Theology* became available to him in the translation of his fellow Dominican William of Moerbeke. Then he discovered, as he explains in the preface to his Commentary, that the *Liber de causis* is the work of an unknown Arabic author who had excerpted it from Proclus' *Elements of Theology*.[21] Aquinas no longer thinks, thus, that the work is Aristotle's own theology. Nevertheless, it seems to me that he continues to regard the *Liber de causis* as a kind of supplement of the Aristotelian science of metaphysics. Together with Dionysius, the *Liber de causis* was the main source from which Aquinas took the necessary

---

[20] See the remark of Saffrey in the introduction of his edition of Aquinas' Commentary on the *Liber de causis*, p. xix: "On voit que dès cette époque, dans l'université, le Liber est rattaché à la Métaphysique d'Aristote." (H. D. Saffrey, ed., Sancti Thomae de Aquino, Super librum De causis expositio (Fribourg: Societé Philosophique, 1954)).

[21] Commentary on the *Book of Causes*, preface: "And in Greek we find a book handed down by the Platonist Proclus, which contains 211 propositions and is entitled The Elements of Theology. And in Arabic we find the present book which is called *On causes among Latin readers*, known to have been translated from Arabic and not known to be extant at all in Greek. Thus, it seems that one of the Arab philosophers excerpted it from this book by Proclus, especially since everything in it is contained much more fully and more diffusely in that of Proclus."

elements for constructing a metaphysical account of the First Cause (God), free from the problematic aspects of Neoplatonism, its polytheistic implications in particular, and compatible with the project of metaphysics as defined in an exemplary fashion by Aristotle. As Hankey writes, "Thomas found that the doctrine of the *De divinis nominibus* was a monotheistically modified Platonism like that of the *Liber de causis*."[22]

There is no room here to give a full overview of the *Liber de causis* as read by Aquinas. I will focus on his exposition of the third proposition of the *Liber*. Here he first offers a presentation of the Neoplatonic hierarchy of divine Forms and then he goes on to explain that both Dionysius and the author of the *Liber* correct this position of pagan Platonism with respect to the plurality of divine Forms.

In order to present the complex system of Proclean metaphysics, Aquinas begins with the basic position of Platonism. Plato posited universal forms that were separate and subsistent. Because such universal forms exercise a certain causality over particular things that participate in them, one can call such forms "gods." Furthermore, among these forms he assumed a certain order according to the principle that the more universal a form is, the more simple and prior a cause it is, for it is participated by later forms. In this order of ideal Forms the first is the separate One and Good itself, which he calls "the highest god" and the "first cause of all things." In Proclus these divine Forms are called *henad*s, the order of intelligible forms prior to the lower hypostatical orders of intellects, souls, and bodies.

Now, Aquinas continues, Dionysius corrected this view of the plurality of ideal Forms. They must all be one and identical with the first cause of all things. This Dionysian "modification" results in what is the very essence of Aquinas' conception of God: God is being itself, and the very essence of goodness, and thus whatever belongs to the perfection of being belongs essentially to him, so that he is the essence of life, wisdom, power, and the rest. God himself contains all the formal perfections in simple unity, so that he possesses the universality of causality with respect to the lower reality.

The author of the *Liber* follows Dionysius in this monotheistic correction of pagan Platonism. He does not speak of a multitude of Gods either, but rather establishes unity in God (*unitatem in Deo constituit*). So the Muslim author of the *Liber* agrees with the Christian theologian on the point of unity in the divine realm.

---

[22] W. Hankey, "Aquinas and the Platonists," in The Platonic Tradition in the Middle Ages: A Doxographic Approach, ed. Stephen Gersh and Maarten Hoenen (Berlin: de Gruyter, 2002), pp. 279–324 at p. 311.

However, a difficulty remains in the text of the *Liber*. Its author uses a phrase which suggests a mediated process of creation: "the first cause created the being of the soul with the mediation of an intelligence" (prop. 3). It cannot be the case, Aquinas emphasizes, that the created soul receives her essential being from the first cause (Being), while she subsequently receives life and intelligence from other lower principles, "the first Life" and "the first Intelligence." Although this is an interpretative possibility of the text, Aquinas makes it clear that the position of a mediated creation must be rejected as contrary to "the truth as well as to the opinion of Aristotle." A plurality of divine causes with respect to the ontological constitution of material reality would result in individual substances being no longer essentially one:

If the [created] soul had being from one thing and an intellectual nature from something else, it would follow that it would not be absolutely one. Therefore, one has to say that the soul not only has essence but also has intellectuality from the first cause.[23]

Both Dionysius and the author of the *Liber* grant to God the universality of causality in the sense that only God is the creator, since he is responsible for the being all things have in common and also for the essential difference of each thing's proper being. Only in this way, through conceiving the first cause as the fullness of perfection, and thus as including in itself the principle of difference, can the substantial unity of created things be accounted for. In deviating from pagan Platonism, the author of the *Liber* is found to be in agreement with Dionysius (and with the position of Aristotle) with respect to the unity in the realm of the divine. An important corollary of this monotheistic position is the Aristotelian accent on the "substantiality" of finite reality. Each thing has its own being by reason of its intrinsic form, and this form, according to which a thing participates in being, is responsible for all the essential determinations of that being (e.g. life, intelligence). The typical Thomistic doctrine of the unity of substantial form is thus the reverse side of the view of the unity of the transcendental causality of being.[24] In this way, Platonic

---

[23] *Commentary on the Book of Causes*, prop. 3 (trans. Guagliardo, Hess, Taylor, p. 25).

[24] Schindler emphasizes the importance of a principle of difference in God to account for the reality of the many particular things in the world. "Creation is ultimately *good*, and we encounter that goodness not merely in looking *past* things to their source, but also in looking *at* them, in celebrating their intrinsic solidity and their irreducible uniqueness. If the Neoplatonic tradition is correct to say that the form is, as it were, infinitely higher than any particular instance of that form, because that instance will always express a partial reflection of the whole idea, Kierkegaard is also right to affirm that the individual is

participation is reconciled with the Aristotelian accent on the substantial reality of things.

SUMMA THEOLOGIAE: CREATION AS PARTICIPATION

The basic text on participation in Aquinas' writings can be found in the treatise on creation of his *Summa theologiae* (I, q.44, a.1). The term participation as applied to creation is part of a distinctive Neoplatonic vocabulary of metaphysical causality which includes expressions as *emanatio, communicatio, influxus*, and the like. In the *Summa*, creation is defined as the "emanation of the whole of being from the universal cause."[25] God is said to be a universal cause, responsible for the whole of a thing's being, including its matter. Creation is thus *ex nihilo*, in the sense that nothing is presupposed to this universal mode of becoming. In this context, Aquinas uses the term "emanation" in the sense that the effect proceeds immediately, according to the whole of its being, from the universal cause which is God. There is no preexisting substrate, nothing which is presupposed to God's causal "influence."

The denial of a preexisting substrate is but one aspect of how the *ex nihilo* is usually conceived. Another aspect of the *ex nihilo* is that the creature is not a natural extension of the divine, flowing from the divine as a sort of emanation of it. Note that we use here the term emanation in the sense of a necessary creation. In the Christian view of creation, however, the world is constituted by a free act of God as a nondivine reality, really distinct from and totally dependent on God. This raises the question how the Platonic vocabulary of participation (and the implicated "flowing out of God") can be reconciled with the Christian accent on the nondivine character of the world as radically distinct from God and freely willed by him. In other words: does participation not imply some form of pantheism?[26]

---

infinitely higher than the universal, because the individual alone exhibits the ineluctable seriousness of existence. From a Christian perspective, an adequate notion of participation must somehow have room for both of these affirmations." ("What's the Difference?," p. 3).

[25] *S.Th.* I, q.45, a.1: "emanationem totius entis a causa universali, quae est Deus; et hanc quidem emanationem designamus nomine *creationis*."

[26] Because of its possible pantheistic association one should avoid, I think, formulations as "participation in God." Cf. the recent book by Andrew Davison, *Participation in God* (Cambridge: Cambridge University Press, 2019). Thomas himself is always aware of an essential difference: God himself is not participated in by something else but a likeness of God. God himself is said to be *imparticipabilis*. One must say that, in creation, God does not communicate himself *as himself*, in its proper divinity, but as distinguished from God

The argument of creation as developed in the *Summa* article (I, 44, 1) intends to show that nothing can exist which is not caused by God.[27] In this argument, a distinctive Platonic logic is at work which makes Aquinas resort to the notion of participation. The starting point lies in the concept of God as *Subsistent Being Itself*. As the first cause of everything, God is being in identity with himself. Now, Aquinas argues, what is such that it is subsistent being itself, can only be one. In the Platonic sense, any form taken in itself or in identity with itself, must be one and singular. Although there are many things which are white, there is but one form of whiteness. From this it follows that all things other than God are not their own being but, as Aquinas formulates, "participate in being." A being which is not God is only conceivable insofar as the identity which defines God's mode of being is negated in it: thus any reality other than God can only exist in such a way that it is *not* its being but has being. It includes a difference with respect to its being, that means, it is being in a differentiated way, by having being in a particular way. But what has being in a particular way cannot explain its own being but must have received it from a cause which has being by reason of its essence (*essentialiter*). Therefore, Aquinas concludes, "it must be that all things which are diversified by a diverse participation of being, so as to be more or less perfect, are caused by one First Being, who possesses being most perfectly."[28]

The reasoning is extremely succinct. At least it is clear that the idea of participation is at the center of the argument. One can distinguish three aspects in the meaning of participation as used in this context. First, participation has to do with the difference internal to the created being: everything which is not God can only be understood as a being (*ens*) when it differs with respect to its *esse*. An important corollary of this is that the whole of created reality is formally defined as nondivine. Participation does not in any sense blur the fundamental distinction between what is God and what is not God (but dependent on him), only one must keep in

---

himself, thus in such a way that, in each creature, the identity of essence and being, that defines God, is negated in a determined manner.

[27] Cf. the opening of *S.Th.* I, q.44, a.1: "necesse est dicere omne quod quocumque modo est, a Deo esse" ("it is necessary to affirm that anything that exists in whatever way is from God"). The argument in this article is treated more fully in my *Aquinas on God* (Aldershot: Ashgate, 2006).

[28] Ibid: "necesse est igitur omnia quae diversificantur secundum diversam participationem essendi, ut sint perfectius vel minus perfecte, causari ab uno primo ente, quod perfectissime est."

mind that the distinction of the effect with respect to the cause goes together with a positive relationship, the *likeness* the effect has received from the cause. It is thus a distinction as implied in the relationship of the creature to its creator. Second, from the internal difference in each thing with respect to its being follows that things differ from each other according to a diverse participation of being; creatures differ in degree so as being more or less perfect, as a result of the fact that each of them has a different "share" of being. This means that even the principle of difference among things – and thus the diversity and plurality of creatures – must be reduced to God. Third and last, that being (*esse*) which is found differentiated in many and diverse beings is received from God who is the fullness of being. "Whatever is found in anything by participation must be caused in it by that to which it belongs essentially." Thus participation implies: having received a perfection in a diminished way from a cause or source which is that perfection essentially and maximally.

Participation, we can conclude, is primarily applied to the being of things, and it explains the derivation of being as found differentiated in all things from a first being by way of creation. How must the mode of being of a creature be understood according to this model of participation? A creature is not its being, it shares being with others in a common world, each according to its own nature or essence. A creature is internally related to its being, and through its being also related to God as the universal cause of its being.

EVALUATION: PARTICIPATION AND CHRISTIAN PLATONISM

It is not self-evident to build a philosophical explanation of the Christian idea of creation on the concept of participation. Some will suspect the unavoidable influences of pagan Platonism, for instance a compromising of the radical distinction between God and creation; or one might point out the unbiblical dualism between the perfect and eternal being of God versus the temporal and changeable being of creatures which have but a diminished likeness of the divine perfection. One also might worry about the association of participation with a necessary emanation. There are serious questions to raise about whether the Platonic causality of participation can be reconciled with free creation. By way of evaluation I will conclude with a brief discussion of some points of possible conflict between participation and the Christian view of creation: first, the issue of creation *ex nihilo*, second, free creation.

First, *ex nihilo* to Aquinas simply is part of what creation means. The term creation designates the emanation of the whole of a thing's being, *totius esse rei*, without a presupposed substrate. Without substrate, this means that the whole substance of a thing must come into existence "at once," immediately, without going through a process of change (*mutatio*). The character of *ex nihilo* is, for Aquinas, conveniently expressed in terms of a universal causality which acts through an *influx* of being. The Neoplatonic notion of *influx* conveys three aspects, to wit, immediacy (without change), totality (without presupposition), and continuousness (not temporal).

The notion of *influx* (compared to the illumination of air from a source of light) emphasizes the fact that the creature remains totally dependent on the creative act of God. A creature does not receive being in such a way that, after a first moment of creation, it can sustain itself in existence from then on. Just like the air is illuminated as long as the sun illuminates it, so the creature exists as long as it receives the *influx* of being from God. When the *influx* stops, the creature falls back into nothingness.[29] At the same time, the *influx* of being is mediated in the thing itself by the immanent principle of form.[30] The creature receives being *according to a form*, which accounts for the specific determination of its received being. Here we see the synthesis in the notion of participation between transcendence and immanence. The *influx* (total dependency) from the cause results in a proper and substantial reality of the creature. Thanks to the permanent *influx*, the creature has become an actual being in its own right, with an own nature and an own natural operation.

The second point that demands some discussion concerns the freedom of God in his creation. God is not in any way necessitated to create the world, Aquinas says; the idea of a necessary emanation is explicitly

---

[29] Cf. *S.Th.* I, q.104, a.1: "Sic autem se habet omnis creatura ad Deum, sicut aer ad solem illuminantem."

[30] Ibid, ad 1: "esse per se consequitur formam creaturae, supposito tamen influx Dei." The form is the principle of ontological integrity and stability. One cannot say that, for Aquinas, the creature has an inherent tendency for nothingness. I am, therefore, not happy with the way Milbank, in his critical discussion of my interpretation of participation, accentuates in an almost "Eckhartian" fashion the inherent nothingness of creatures in Aquinas. In a certain sense, he says, creatures are, indeed, "dependent manifestations," precisely because of the idea that apart from God's creative act and presence, there is only "nothing." But the creative presence of God means precisely this that out of nothing there arises a new being, a creature with a proper nature, and which is thus no longer "nothing." See John Milbank, *Beyond Secular Order: The Representation of Being and the Representation of the People* (Chichester: Wiley-Blackwell, 2014), p. 100, n. 196.

rejected. But the question is whether free creation can be integrated in the participation model of creation; or is freedom just a matter of a prior and arbitrary decision from the part of God to start his work of creation?

Aquinas' thoughts on God's freedom in his creation are subtle and complex. There is no room here for more than a rough indication of how divine freedom is conceived of as an essential aspect of the way creatures proceed from God. In Aquinas' view, one must say that God by reason of its natural perfection tends to communicate a likeness of his goodness to others. This is not a matter of choice, this is what God is. Out of love for his goodness God wants to create, to share his goodness with others. The reason why there exists a world is thus God's goodness; the world is an expression (or likeness, *similitudo*) of God's goodness, and as such good, something that can be affirmed by God in relation to his own goodness. Now, Aquinas argues, a freely willable expression of God's goodness in a finite effect is only conceivable if it concerns a goodness of an ordered whole of many diverse creatures. Any possible finite good, compared to God's infinite goodness itself, does not contain in itself sufficient reason to be willed by God, since it is not in any way implicated in God's willing its own perfect goodness. The only reason is love of his goodness, and that love seeks a form of expression which is a likeness-in-otherness, thus not a semidivine likeness but a likeness which consists in ordered manifold of diverse creatures (*ordo universi*), intended as such by God. Since only by representing God's goodness by many and diverse creatures can the world, as expression of God's goodness, be willed by God, not necessarily, but as something that is worthy to exist from God's point of view, otherwise it would not be created.

In this way we have shown that the criteria of the Christian idea of creation are all met by the model of participation. There is no reason, I think, to suppose that the idea of participation led Aquinas astray from the path of Christian thinking.

Bibliography

Aertsen, Jan. *Medieval Philosophy and the Transcendentals. The Case of Thomas Aquinas*. Leiden: Brill, 1996.

Aristotle. *Metaphysics, Books I–IX*, translated by Hugh Tredennick. Loeb Classical Library. Cambridge, MA: Harvard University Press, 1996, 1933.

Davison, Andrew. *Participation in God: A Study in Christian Doctrine and Metaphysics*. Cambridge: Cambridge University Press, 2019.

Fabro, Cornelio. *La nozione metafisica di partecipazione secondo S. Tommaso d'Aquino*. 3rd ed. Turin: Società ed. Internazionale, 1963.

"Participation." www.encyclopedia.com/religion/encyclopedias-almanacs-tran
scripts-and-maps/participation.

Geiger, L.-B. *La participation dans la philosophie de Saint Thomas d'Aquin.*
Montréal: Institut d'Etudes Médiévales, 1952.

Hankey, W. "Aquinas and the Platonists," in *The Platonic Tradition in the Middle
Ages: A Doxographic Approach*, ed. Stephen Gersh and Maarten Hoenen.
Berlin: De Gruyter, 2002.

Milbank, John. *Beyond Secular Order: The Representation of Being and the
Representation of the People.* Chichester: Wiley-Blackwell, 2014.

Saffrey, H. D., ed. *Sancti Thomae de Aquino, Super librum De causis exposition.*
Fribourg: Societé Philosophique, 1954.

Schindler, David C. "What's the Difference? On the Metaphysics of Participation
in a Christian Context," *The Saint Anselm Journal* 3, no. 1 (2005): 1–27.

Sokolowski, Robert. *The God of Faith and Reason: Foundations of Christian
Theology.* Notre Dame, IN: University of Notre Dame Press, 1982.

St. Thomas Aquinas. *An Exposition of the "On the Hebdomads" of Boethius*,
introduction and translation by Janice L. Schultz and Edward A. Synan.
Washington D.C.: The Catholic University of America Press, 2001.

Te Velde, Rudi A. *Aquinas on God.* Aldershot: Ashgate, 2006.

"Aquinas's Aristotelian Science of Metaphysics and its Revised Platonism,"
Nova et Vetera 13, no. 3 (2015): 743–64.

Participation and Substantiality in Thomas Aquinas. Leiden: E. J. Brill, 1995.

Thomas Aquinas: Commentary on the Book of Causes, translated by Vincent
A. Guagliardo, O.P., Charles R. Hess, O.P., and Richard C. Taylor.
Washington, D.C.: The Catholic University of America Press, 1996.

Wippel, John F. "Thomas Aquinas and Participation," in *Studies in Medieval
Philosophy*, ed. J. Wippel. Washington, D.C.: The Catholic University of
America Press, 1987: 117–58.

II

HISTORY

The Bible and Early Christian Platonism

Mark Edwards

The subject on which I am asked to write, affords material either for a very short chapter or for a very long one. No one accepts the fanciful itineraries that apologists once constructed to make it possible for Plato to read the Septuagint in Egypt. On a charitable reading this was never more than persiflage in the style of the day, a sophistical rejoinder to the equally baseless charges of Christian theft from the schools of Greece. An inquiry into this pagan accusation would throw up a few coincidences on thought and phrasing, some of them remarkable; nevertheless, one cannot build a theory of intellectual filiation on the fact that both Christ and Socrates speak of orphaning their disciples by their deaths[1] or on the Christological ring of the words *monogenês* and *eikôn* in the last sentence of the *Timaeus*.[2] But if we enlarge the units of comparison, we may find warrant for a longer investigation into the evolution of two competing systems, a philosophic religion and a devoutly religious philosophy, both of which ascribe the origin of the world to a benign deity who orders all things for good, though often through intermediate beings, and confers on its rational denizens the power of attaining his likeness, but also the choice of living contrary to his laws, with concomitant honours or punishments in the afterlife. Those who admit the symmetry have traced it sometimes to cultural diffusion (in one direction or both),[3] sometimes to the aboriginal

---

[1] For examples see M. J. Edwards, 'Socrates and the Early Church', in M. Trapp (ed.), *Socrates from Antiquity to the Enlightenment* (London: Routledge, 2007), 127–42.

[2] W. Temple, *Readings in St John's Gospel* (London: Macmillan, 1947), quoting *Timaeus* 92c.

[3] See further M. Hengel, *Jews, Greeks and Barbarians* (Philadelphia: Fortress Press, 1980).

unity of Hebraism and Hellenism; others (few of whom are distinguished Hebraists or Hellenists) continue to hold that the Jew and the Greek are as incommensurable as the prophet and the philosopher.[4] Early Christians were certainly inclined to look upon Plato as an ally, and in the first part of this chapter, I shall ask how far Eusebius and other apologists succeeded in making out the opposite case, that the Bible and Plato proclaim the same God. In the second, I shall propose that the Johannine concept of the Logos was at once more foreign to Plato and more palatable to certain of his followers than Augustine supposed it to be. I shall conclude by examining two indictments of the hermeneutic method of the Fathers – first, that they co-opted the Platonic device of allegoresis to overwrite the plain sense of the scriptures, and secondly that under Platonic influence they surrendered faith to philosophy in their mystical readings of the Song of Songs.

A MEETING OF ANTIPODES?

It has long been fashionable for theologians to deplore the surrender of the Christian church to a pagan idiom, which removes God to a great distance from the world, and to an even greater distance from the joys and sorrows, actions and desires of human beings in the world, by superimposing a vocabulary of abstractions and negations on the vivid and concrete imagery of the scriptures.[5] The Israelite grew up loving and fearing a God who was joined to his people by the indissoluble bonds of fatherhood and matrimony, ready indeed to castigate Israel like a disappointed father and to vilify her like a jealous lover, but also ready at hand (after four hundred years) to bring her dryshod through the Red Sea, to settle her in Canaan, to declare 'you only have I known of all nations' (Amos 3.2) and to indemnify this love with a promise of universal sovereignty, which, though delayed, was underwritten by the Word that could not return to him void (Isaiah 55.11). By this Word, which had brought forth light from darkness at the beginning, he continues to speak in the hearts of those who are truly his children, and uttering immortal verse through the mouths of his prophets without once finding occasion to proclaim his immutability,

---

[4] For a sceptical commentary see J. Barr, *Biblical Words for Time* (Chicago: Allenson, 1962).

[5] Theologians (but not students of any discipline which puts a high value on scholarship) will be familiar with C. Gunton, *The One, the Three and the Many* (Cambridge: Cambridge University Press, 1993).

his incorporeality, his eternity or that most inhuman of traits his impassibility. This is the God whose Word, by the church's own confession, has taken on our vulnerable flesh so that he may lead us into his kingdom on the far side of the Cross where he died alone. But how could the church which proclaimed this have fallen at the same time into the Platonic fallacy of imagining God to be exempt from change, incapable of becoming an object to any other agent, and hence (as must surely follow) a stranger alike to pain and love?[6]

The first response of a Platonist would have been that he was wholly unconscious of the alienation which has been visited upon him by his Christian sympathisers. The sense of a God within did not die with Socrates, and nothing is more common in Platonic literature than the assertion that the wise man is neighbour to the divine. Nor was it ever denied that the gods communicate by oracles with those who have yet to liberate the intellect from the senses, and the practice of theurgy in late antiquity enabled its adepts to meet the divine on a plane that was tempered to their own capacities. To complain that the deities whom they encountered were not the highest God would have been as petulant as to demand that every repair to an aqueduct should be authorised by the Emperor; nor was it unconditionally true that the highest God was free of anthropomorphic properties, for the demiurge of the *Timaeus* not only resolves to create a world because he is God but takes delight in his creation.[7] In other Platonic texts it is possible even for Zeus to feel pity, while the lesser deities of the *Timaeus* ensure that the operation of divine justice are not limited to the heavens but reward each soul according to its deserts.[8]

Some human traits, then, are thinkable even in a Platonic deity. On the other hand, we cannot assume that when thoughtful Jews and Christians of the same period divested the biblical God of his caprice, his irascibility, his shoulders, limbs and loins and his propensity to walk in the cool of the day, they were merely following an intellectual vogue set by the philosophers. Most Christians today instinctively set aside the literal construction of such images, and we cannot be certain that they were

---

[6] On misunderstandings of divine impassibility, see P. Gavrilyuk, *The Suffering of the Impassible God* (Oxford: Oxford University Press, 2004), 5–14 and 171–3; R. D. Williams, *Christ the Heart of Creation* (London: Bloomsbury, 2018), 90–1.

[7] *Timaeus* 37c; cf 34b, and, on later attempts to purge the dialogue of its anthropomorphism, S. C. O'Brien, *The Demiurge in Ancient Thought* (Cambridge: Cambridge University Press, 2015), esp. 18–27.

[8] *Symposium* 191b5; *Timaeus* 90a–92b.

more than metaphors to those who first conceived them. We can be certain that no Greek would have embraced the Jewish or the apostolic proclamation of a God who was still conceived in such demotic terms – not only because the philosophers did not wish to be children again, but because no adult who was hearing of God for the first time would have accepted any promise in his name, or any claim on his part to the role of king or father, if no argument for believing it were advanced apart from 'this is the faith of Israel'. To commend this faith to the nations, it was necessary to demonstrate first that a God must have certain properties, and then that these properties were more fully instantiated in Yahweh than in the object of any pagan cult. Hence both Jewish and Christian apologists set out to prove that God can be everywhere present to us (as the Bible teaches) because he is necessarily incorporeal, that his Word can be trusted because he is immutable, that he sees the end of all his own acts because he is eternal, and that his victory is assured because, being impassible, he cannot be acted upon by another being against his will.

Nevertheless, it is now increasingly common to maintain that any notion of transcendence is an alien graft upon the Hebraic concept of a God who is always near and tutelary. This departure from a long tradition of Christian thought was promoted in part by a *faux-naïf* misunderstanding of transcendence as spatial remoteness rather than ontological primacy. Those better schooled in metaphysics, however, can point to the venerable, and surely valid argument, that if the Deity is to be omnipresent and universally active, he cannot occupy any particular space or be subject to any external restraint. Immanence, in short, entails transcendence: indeed, if it has its proper sense which would imply that God inhabits the world as the soul inhabits the body, immanence is the more questionable of the two attributes. While many Platonists did indeed find it hard to reconcile the contemplation of the eternal forms with knowledge of either present or future contingents, no early Christian permitted this scruple to outweigh the clear attestations of special providence in the scriptures and in the history of the church. In this as in every instance of conflict between the Word and philosophy, the Word prevails; and as Lactantius argues, once the Word has revealed the love of God, philosophy has no choice but to entertain the notion of his wrath.[9]

---

[9] See *De la Colère de Dieu*, ed. C. Ingremeau (Paris: Cerf, 1982), esp. chapter 21.8–10 (pp. 196–8) on the imperturbability of divine wrath.

LOGOS AND CREATOR

It was this fact of being known by revelation rather than by metaphysical reasoning that seemed to early Christians to raise their God above any principle that the schools had been able to excogitate. The Demiurge and the Form of the Good are both necessary postulates in the light of Plato's teleological premises; hence they must remain prisoners of the logic that reduced them, and cannot be other than that logic has shown them to be. By contrast, the Christian God is above our thoughts, and therefore, while he meets every philosophical criterion of divinity, he gives all the more evidence of his unlimited potency, as Origen and Tertullian urge, in the arbitrary creation of the cosmos or in that seeming contradiction of his own nature which we call the incarnation.[10] In a more irenic vein than either, Eusebius recruits Plato and Plutarch as witnesses to that freedom to be what he will which is expressed (as he believes) in God's disclosure of his name as I AM at Exodus 3.14, but his God too is able to exercise tutelage over all that he has created, because he acts not through the lesser gods but through his own Logos, or Word.[11]

Platonism is frequently alleged to have been the source of the title Logos, or at least of many Christian elaborations of that title which purport to be exegeses of the Fourth Gospel. Indeed it is often surmised that the Evangelist himself was indebted to the same philosophy: once the study of texts is allowed to take the place of loose allegation, however, we find that no intermediary between the highest God and the world receives the name Logos from any recognised Platonist save Philo of Alexandria. And Philo, while his writings account for more than four-fifths of what is now styled Middle Platonism, is also a Jew who, like the Fourth Evangelist, has a perfect recollection of every biblical testimony to creation by the Word.[12] Even the very notion of an intermediary who transcends creation – in contrast to the immanent Logos of Plutarch[13] – is not clearly attested in sources earlier than Philo: the Demiurge in the *Timaeus* does not mediate between the eternal paradigm and matter because the paradigm is not characterised as a God. The relation between

---

[10] Tertullian, *On the Flesh of Christ* 3–5; Origen, *First Principles* 3.5.1.
[11] Eusebius, *Praeparatio Evangelica* II, ed. K. Mras (Berlin: Akademie Verlag, 1983), 24.3 (= *Preparation* 11.9.1).
[12] See above all Genesis 1.3 and Psalm 33.6.
[13] Plutarch, *Convivial Questions* 720b and *On Isis and Osiris* 373a–b; see further J. M. Dillon, *The Middle Platonists* (London: Duckworth, 1977), 200–2; J. G. Griffiths *Plutarch's De Iside et Osiride* (Cardiff: University of Wales Press, 1970), 236 and 557.

the Form of the Good and the thoughts in the mind of God in the Republic remains elusive, as does the relation of God to the world. In the system of Numenius, who surely wrote too late to have any influence on the Gospels, a first God or first intellect corresponds roughly to the Form of the Good, a second to the Demiurge;[14] the appellation 'second God', however, is rare in Christian authors before the Nicene era. Origen uses it only in reply to Celsus, for whom it was a familiar locution;[15] and even catholics after Arius were content that the Father should always be the first and Christ the second person of the Trinity. As Gregory of Nyssa says, his being second in order of invocation need not entail that he is the lesser being, any more than the second Adam was a lesser being than the first.[16]

By Gregory's time the locution 'second God' was proscribed, not so much because it suggested inequality between persons (to Cyril of Alexandria, in fact, it suggests the opposite)[17] but because it appeared to countenance polytheism. Eusebius of Caesarea therefore eschews it in controversial works addressed to other Christians, though he admits it in his apologetic writings.[18] In the *Preparation for the Gospel,* his search for homologies between Platonic and Christian thought ensures that the adjective 'second' will connote subordination, and it is evident on other grounds that he does indeed hold a view of the status of Christ which would have savoured of Arianism in the age of Athanasius and the Cappadocian Fathers. The appeal to Platonism therefore vindicates not only the antiquity and universality of the Christian dogma but the rationality of his own reading of it, which was not inconsistent with the creed to which he had subscribed at the Nicene Council. It is certainly the intention of Eusebius to show that competent Platonists had acknowledged the Logos not only by implication but under that name. At the same time, he is looking only for allies, not precursors, and the pagan who holds the most perspicuous doctrine of the Logos is Amelius, student or colleague of Plotinus and an enthusiast for Numenius, whose works he had almost by heart.[19] In this quotation, however, he is commenting without disguise on the prologue to the Fourth Gospel:

---

[14] Numenius, Fr. 16 in the edition of E. Des Places (Paris: Belles Lettres, 1973), derived from Eusebius, *Preparation* 11.22.3–5.

[15] Origen, *Against Celsus* 5.39. 6.61.

[16] *Against Eunomius* 1.197–204 = *Gregorii Nysseni Opera* I, ed. W. Jaeger (Leiden: Brill, 1960), 84–5.

[17] Cyril of Alexandria, *Against Julian*, in *Patrologia Graeca* 76, 316a.

[18] See M. J. Edwards, 'Nicene Theology and the Second God', *Studia Patristica* 40 (2006), 191–5.

[19] Porphyry, *Life of Plotinus* 3.

And this indeed was the everlasting word through which the things that come to be came to be, as Heraclitus would seem to opine, and which the barbarian does opine, by Zeus, to be next in place to God in the rank and dignity of the beginning, and to be what God is; to be that through which all things came to be without exception, in which that which came to be was by nature alive and life and being, and which descended to bodies, put on flesh, assumed human guise and therewith displayed the grandeur of his nature, and withal, after dissolution, was made god again and god as he had bene before his translation to body, flesh and [existence as] a man. (Eusebius, *Preparation for the Gospel* 11.19.1, p. 45 Mras)

Little else is known of Amelius, and we cannot assume that his exposition implies an endorsement, or even a high estimation, of Johannine teaching. There is at least no trace of the satire that colours the observations of his junior colleague Porphyry on the same passage. Knowing perhaps that some Christians had distinguished logos as thought from logos as utterance, ascribing to the second person first a latent existence as the *logos endiathetos* of the Father and then a procession as the *logos prophorikos* which created the world, Porphyry retorts that if there are not to be two Christs he must be one or the other, either *endiathetos* or *prophorikos*. If he is the latter, he does not belong to the Godhead; if he is the former, he remains within God and did not become incarnate.[20] Porphyry is evidently not the man who, according to Simplicianus of Milan in conversation with Augustine, declared that the Johannine prologue should be inscribed in letters of gold.[21] If, as some guess, this author was Amelius, we must either conclude that Augustine failed to read him carefully or that he had some other Platonist in mind when he drew his famous contrast between pagan and the Christian appropriations of the Gospel:

I read there [in 'certain Platonic books', 13.9.13] that God the Word was born not of flesh, nor of blood, nor of the will of man nor of the will of the flesh, but of God (John 1.13). But that the Word was made flesh and lived among us (John 1.14) I did not read there. (*Confessions* 13.9.14)

Augustine's aim is not to convey historical information to modern scholars, but to expose the pride that detains the Greeks – or rather, every half-believing Christian like his old self – on this side of the gulf between reason and revelation. We may safely take *Platonici* to mean 'everyone who clings to his seclusion in Cassiciacum for fear of an encounter in Milan'.

---

[20] The evidence is complex: see M. J. Edwards, 'Why did Constantine Label Arius a Porphyrian?', *L'Antiquité Classique* 82 (2013), 239–47.

[21] *City of God* 10.29.

The biblical text that occupies the last three books of Augustine's
Confessions is the opening chapter of Genesis, which proclaims the irreducible contingency of our mundane existence by ascribing it to no other
cause than the Creator's will and by assigning it to a measurable distance
from us in time. Where Plato's world is a copy of the paradigm in a mobile
substrate, Augustine agrees with Origen in interpreting creation in the
beginning as creation in the Word. Christians held fast to the scriptural
doctrine of a temporal creation in the teeth of both philosophical and
theological arguments for the eternity of both matter and the cosmos.
Since the second century, most Christians had concurred in regarding
matter as a creation of God himself and thus coeval with the cosmos; to
the Aristotelian cavil that no time would be more apposite for the origin of
the world than any other they simply turned a deaf ear until Philoponus
undertook to prove that a temporal universe was more consistent than an
eternal one with the principles of Aristotle's own philosophy.[22] Augustine
escapes the question, 'What was God doing before the first day?' by
denying that time could be spoken of before the world was created as
a theatre of change and motion.[23] If instead we ask why the world is so old
and not any older, the Christian answer is that God makes his own
reasons. Just as there is no pre-existing paradigm and no pre-existent
matter, the church does not assert with Plato that God's largesse is
dictated by his nature. Both the Demiurge and the Mosaic deity rejoice
in their handiwork, but whereas the former creates because he is good, the
latter pronounced that to be good which he creates.[24]

The theological difficulty might seem to be more intractable: if the
proper function of the Logos is to create, and the world that he creates
is temporal, can the Logos share the eternity of the Father? We have
already noted that before Porphyry a common expedient was to posit
two phases in the existence of the Logos, first as immanent ('endiathetic')
thought and then as 'prophoric' utterance. Origen had already pre-empted
Porphyry's objection by maintaining that the Logos is eternally prophoric
and by assigning to him an intellectual realm as the object of his eternal
governance; at the same time he affirmed the temporality of the present
material world, although he is willing to postulate at least one temporal
world before us.[25] The Athanasian argument that the true function of the
Logos is to be the eternal object of the Father's love[26] had not yet been

---

[22] John Philoponus, *De Aeternitate Mundi*, ed. H. Rabe (Leipzig: Teubner, 1899).
[23] *Confessions* 11.12.14–17.   [24] *Timaeus* 29d–e; Genesis 1.31 etc.
[25] *First Principles* 1.2.2–3 and 2.9.4; 1.4.5; 3.5.1–3.   [26] *Against the Arians* 1.20–22.

formulated when Eusebius composed his *Demonstration* and *Preparation*. In keeping with his own view that we should not innovate on the scriptures, he refrains from either asserting or denying the eternity of the Logos, while maintaining that he existed as a distinct hypostasis before the ages. The temporal creation of the world, on the other hand, he affirms with confidence, and all the more so because he has to hand not only the *Timaeus*, which he reads as literally as all other Christians,[27] but the vigorous defence of this literal reading by the pagan philosopher Atticus and the picturesque speculations of Numenius, which clearly imply that the world is a sudden and contingent product of a perturbation in the second mind. Again it is Philoponus who presents the strongest arguments for taking Plato into alliance against the Peripatetics, mingling extracts from other dialogues which had escaped his fellow-Christians with the annotations of Porphyry, Atticus and Calvisius Taurus.[28] For him as for other Christians, the Bible must prevail when it cannot be reconciled with the philosophers; in contrast, however, to others for whom authority suffices against all argument, he thinks his case unproved until philosophy conspires in its own defeat.

ALLEGORY

Some modern authorities tell us that the virus of Platonism enters Christian exegesis on the first day of creation, when the light which shine forth from darkness at God's command is understood by Augustine to represent either the angels or the intellectual heaven that they inhabit.[29] Thus, says Colin Gunton,[30] the creation came to be seen in Christian teaching as a mere afterthought to the world which is our true home, where all narratives are suspended and the body with all its passions counts for nothing. It is hard to believe that either Augustine or Plato had the power to hide the meaning of the scriptures from so many generations of close readers, and it is far from certain that either Paul or Jesus wished their disciples to live so thoroughly for the present world as we now do with the sanction of both the church and the academy. Paul and Jesus both understood the faithful reading of scripture to imply a studious reverence for its every jot and tittle which is alien to the modern sensibility,

---

[27] *Preparation* 11.9.4, citing *Timaeus* 27d–28a; 11.9.7, citing 37e–38b: see pp. 28029 Mras.
[28] See especially, *De Aeternitate Mundi* 125.7–168.2 Rabe.
[29] *Confessions* 12.15; *City of God* 11.7; *On Genesis according to the Letter* 1.32–3.
[30] Gunton, *The One, the Three and the Many*, 2.

yet equally characteristic in late antiquity of philosophers and of bishops. Augustine held the same principle, and his postulation of an intelligible universe resolves the contradiction between the creation of light on the first day and the absence of luminous bodies before the fourth. His modern detractors, having relegated the opening chapter of Genesis to the category of myth, do not admit any obligation to explain how there can be light without the sun. They are offended by Augustine, not because he makes light of scripture, but because he takes it more seriously than they do. The term of abuse that they throw at him, and at every ancient Christian who will not give up the letter for the spirit, is 'allegory', although more careful scholars distinguish allegory, as a mode of composition, from allegoresis, which is the reading of a text as an allegory.

What then is allegoresis? It is frequently contrasted with literal exposition of a text, but this cannot be a sufficient definition. The literal is also contested with the metaphorical, and a reader who perceives a metaphor as a figure of speech is not said to be reading allegorically, but simply to be demonstrating competence as a user of the language. Hence it would seem more accurate to contrast the allegoretic reading with the natural one, or as Protestants commonly put it, the 'plain and natural' one, where this is understood to make all due allowance for metaphor, hyperbole, litotes and other tropes which are recognised by any practised speaker. It is by declining to make such allowances when interpreting prophecy that early Christians were able to prove that Christ was the only subject to which they applied in every particular: the identification of Christ with the suffering servant of Isaiah 53 is unnatural in that it takes no account of the poetical character of the text or of the author's circumstances and the expectations of those to whom he addressed it; it is not, for all that, an example of allegoresis but of officious literalism.

Is it enough to say then that an allegoretic reading is one which is neither literal nor natural? If it is to define a certain school of exegesis, we must attach the further condition that the text to which it is applied must be one that could also have been adequately interpreted, according to its natural if not its literal meaning, if the common linguistic conventions had been observed. A Platonic myth is patently allegorical, and to recognise it as such is therefore not to interpret it allegoretically.[31] Again, one is merely showing linguistic competence by seeking more in a parable, a riddle or a proverb than its plain and natural meaning. And irony is

---

[31] See J. A. Stewart, *The Myths of Plato* (London: Macmillan, 1905); R. Rutherford, *The Art of Plato* (London: Duckworth, 1995), 171–8.

another case in which, although it is certain that one thing is said and another intended (to quote an ancient definition of allegoresis), the divination of this hidden intent would be an act of discernment rather than allegoresis, since it does not involve the substitution of any other sense for the words themselves than the one established by convention. According to its etymology, allegoresis is the discovery of 'another' meaning – another, that is, than the literal one, the natural one, the one explicitly demanded by the text, or the one suggested by our knowledge of the speaker's character and circumstances.

Even etymology, as the ancients practised it, is not allegoresis, because it makes no use of any information outside the text.[32] Personification is not so much allegoresis as synecdoche: Bunyan's Christian is simply a representative Christian, Langland's Gluttony is the most egregious of gluttons. The exhibition of a historical figure as a universal type of vice or virtue, as in Dante, is a variant of the same trope. The true definition of allegoresis is illustrated in the introduction to the *Homeric Allegories* of Heraclitus, where the exemplar of allegory (that is, of poetry which should be read allegoretically although formally it admits of being read otherwise) is a poem by Alcaeus in which a vessel toiling in violent waves is an emblem of his city.[33] Here we observe a substitution of new terms for only for properties and actions of the ostensible subject but for the subject itself: the poet has not metaphorically invested the ship with the attributes of a city but has hidden the city under a grand conceit in which every detail could have been literally predicated of a ship. On the same premise Augustine could produce an *ad litteram* commentary on the first three chapters of Genesis which denies that the days of creation are days and that the first created light was a visible beam. So long as the specious subject, God's creation of the world, is agreed to be the proper subject, the text is not being read as allegory, as it is when his earlier *Commentary against the Manichaeans* equates the Garden of Eden with the soul and its rivers with the four cardinal virtues. It will now be apparent that much that we call allegory would not meet the strictest definition of this term in late antiquity; we may add that certain tropes which were allegoretic to Origen and Clement would now fall into the province of metaphor. We do

---

[32] G. W. Most, 'Allegoresis and Etymology', in A. Grafton and G. W. Most (eds.), *Canonical Texts and Scholarly Practices* (Cambridge: Cambridge University Press, 2014), 52–74.

[33] Heraclitus, *Homeric Problems*, ed. D. A. Russell and D. Konstan (Atlanta: Society of Biblical Literature, 2005), 9 (chapter 5).

not need to be told that God has neither a leg but an arm of flesh, that his shoulders and bowels represent his power and his compassion, and his utterance takes the form of syllabic speech only in his prophets. The Christians of Alexandria, like Philo before them, assumed that every pagan was an idolater, and set out to correct him in disquisitions that seem to us fruitlessly verbose.

Origen is frequently said to be practising allegoresis when he is merely purging a historical narrative of its anthropomorphic diction. When he denies that God planted a garden in Eden or that he came down to overthrow Babel, he is not denying the historicity either of the Garden or of the tower, but pointing out that verbs which commonly connote the use of physical organs cannot be applied without qualification to an incorporeal Agent who creates and destroys by fiat.[34] He is not advancing any alternative to the historical story but removing a vulgar impediment to belief in its historicity. He performs a similar act of elucidation when he argues that the dimensions of the ark have been stated not in Hebrew but in Egyptian cubits, so that in length, breadth and height it was far more commodious than detractors of the biblical text imagine.[35] Having thus proved that the ark had room enough for every species of beast, he goes on to propound an allegorical reading in which the storeys of the ark represent two levels of intellection, while the clean and unclean animals correspond to our virtuous and vicious passions. Allegoresis differs from typology in that the latter presupposes, while the former is indifferent to, the veracity of the text as history. Nevertheless, it is not the intention of Origen that allegoresis should supplant the literal or historic reading, except where this is patently illogical, absurd or inconsistent with the moral character of God. Typology incorporates, while allegoresis supplements, the facts which are chronicled in the narrative portions of the Old Testament.

It will be useful to compare the methods of Origen with those of Porphyry, the only Platonist who has left us an extended specimen of allegoresis. Porphyry is of course aware that Plato had denounced allegoresis as an arbitrary device to mask the obscenity and absurdity of myth;[36] knowing that Plutarch had taunted the Stoics for the violent application of this palliative to Homer, he ridiculed Origen's handling of the Old

---

[34] *First Principles* 4.3.1 (Eden); *Against Celsus* 4.5 (Babel).
[35] *Homilies on Genesis* 2.2, pp. 28–9 in the edition of W. Baehrens (Leipzig: Hinrichs, 1920).
[36] *Phaedrus* 229c–230a.

Testament as an incongruous transference of Stoic principles to a barbarous subject.[37] He also hints that Origen had betrayed his Platonic schooling; yet this was not so much an intimation that sound philosophy excludes allegoresis as a rebuttal of Origen's claim, in his work *Against Celsus*, that the blemishes of Greek poetry are irreparable, whereas those of the Hebrew scriptures disappear when we learn to read on a higher mode.[38] The *Cave of the Nymphs* is his demonstration that Homer will yield to strategies that cannot be emulated by the wilfully illiterate partisans of the one religion which admits no other path to the divine.

His text is the poet's description of the cave which is the first landmark that Odysseus encounters on his return to Ithaca.[39] It is clearly something more than a natural feature, for it is adorned with carvings dedicated to nymphs and other deities, while one of its mouths is reserved for mortals and the other for gods. Porphyry does not profess to know whether it was a real structure or a literary figment: the question matters little for him, since ancient masons seldom failed to endow their works with meaning, while the imagination of an inspired poet does not change its images at random.[40] The key to interpretation is the cave of ignorance in *Republic* 7, together with the myth of Er in Republic 10, where souls are said to enter and leave the cosmos by the gates of Cancer and Capricorn.[41] Thus the cave is the world, the two doors are the tropics, and the mariner's egress from it is the ascent of the soul to that plane in which, as Plato says in his allegory of the cave,[42] it looks directly on the forms which it glimpsed only as shadows in the material realm.

The olive-tree which Odysseus sees as he quits the cave is sacred to Athene, and hence an emblem of the *skopos* or true intent of the poem which the reader is seeking. He acknowledges a precursor in Numenius, who is cited with approval by Origen as a commentator on the deeds of Christ and Moses, though Origen shows no interest in his metaphysics. Numenius declared that it was necessary for lovers of truth to look beyond Plato to those from whom he learned,[43] and Plato himself had co-opted the language of the mysteries to describe the initiation of the soul into higher orders of understanding. Porphyry, more eclectic than either, culls

[37] Eusebius, *Church History* 6.19.8.   [38] *Against Celsus* 4.38–45.
[39] *Odyssey* 13.101–12, cited by Porphyry, *Cave of the Nymphs*, chapter 1, p. 55 in A. Nauck (ed.), *Porphyrii Opuscula* (Leipzig: Teubner, 1886).
[40] *Cave* 4, 5.2–18 Nauck.
[41] *Cave* 9, 62.1–8 Nauck; *Cave* 22, 71.17–19 Nauck, citing *Republic* 615d–e.
[42] *Republic* 509c and 516b–d.   [43] Fr. 1 Des Places (Eusebius, *Preparation* 9.7.1).

his parallels almost indiscriminately from Greek and barbarian, tumbling Eleusis and Egypt on to the philosophic interpretations of Mithraic icons, which he evidently believes to be more authentic than the apocryphon ascribed by Christian Gnostics to Zoroaster.[44] Just as in another work he illustrates the parity of Greek and Egyptian cult by his decipherment of the statues of both peoples, so he argues here that Homer is only the Greek redactor of the mysteries known to all nations. And as the treatise *On Statues* ridicules the 'unlettered' Christians who mistake every sacred icon for an idol, so the *Cave of the Nymphs* declines to seek elucidation from this sect which has preserved no ancestral faith.[45]

Origen's allegoresis has much in common with that of Porphyry – more, perhaps, than with that of the Stoics to whom the latter has insidiously compared him. He agrees with him, for example, in his readiness to affirm both the historic and the figurative sense of canonical narratives; the charge that he was interested only in anecdotal history, taking no account of the linear evolution of a narrative, is easily refuted by a perusal of his *Commentary on the Song of Songs*, where the loftier exegesis of each section is always prefaced by an exposition of its dramatic tenor. It is thus not true to say that this is a book which has for him no literal sense, although he certainly maintains that the literal sense is too prurient to be edifying. Again he concurs with Porphyry in seeking a clue in the text itself to the presence of allegory. As the olive-tree betokens wisdom for Porphyry, so a well dug by a patriarch is for Origen a clear signal that we must look beneath the surface of a text.[46] Other indices of profundity are, in his words, the stumbling-blocks which the Holy Spirit has planted to remind us of the inadequacy of the literal sense.[47]

An analogue can be found in the contention of Iamblichus that obscenity in the mysteries is designed to prevent our taking them for adequate representations of that which cannot be manifested to the senses.[48] Nevertheless, it is not the custom of Origen – and here he differs from Clement as well as Porphyry – to borrow symbols of ineffability from any cultivated practice. It is possible that in his proem to the *Commentary on the Song of Songs*, the contemplative vision of God which supersedes ethical and physical instruction is characterised as an

---

[44] *Life of Plotinus* 16; *Cave* 17–18, 68.16–698.22 Nauck and 24, 72.15–73.11 Nauck.

[45] G. Miles, 'Stones, Wood and Woven Papyrus: Porphyry's *On Statues*', *Journal of Hellenic Studies* 135 (2015),78–94.

[46] *Homilies on Genesis* 13.2–3, pp. 115–16 Baehrens.   [47] *First Principles* 4.2.9.

[48] *On the Mysteries* 11. See M. Masterson, 'Authoritative Obscenity in Iamblichus and Arnobius', *Journal of Early Christian Studies* 22 (2014), 373–98.

epopteia;[49] it is even possible, as I surmised some years ago, to equate ethics with the *drômenon* and physics with the *legomenon* which preceded the sacred vision;[50] yet Origen himself correlates the three levels of insight not with the stages of initiation but with the three Hebrew books of Solomon and the three branches of Gentile philosophy. Nor have we any reason to think that Origen was acquainted with any distinction between the physical and the theological modes of allegoresis or between the civic, poetic and philosophic allophones of myth.[51] Clement compares the cryptic sayings of scripture to the *akousmata*, or cryptic aphorisms, handed down by the Pythagoreans,[52] but for Origen the rule of interpreting scripture from scripture is as inviolable as the old Alexandrian rule of interpreting Homer from Homer. As his Hebrew teacher informed him, the scripture is a hall of many doors, and the keys to every door lie in the hall, although not every key is beside its own room.[53]

MYSTICISM

Plato is agreed to be the foster-father of Christian mysticism, whether this be said in his honour or in dispraise of that tradition. Its cradle, however, must be sought elsewhere, for the goal of the Christian ascent is not the One or the good but God, not the extinction of desire but the perpetual intensification of love – a love that waxes all the more when it consummates the nuptial union with its Bridegroom, thus invariably casting the seeker into the role of Bride. In the *Symposium* Socrates speaks with disdain of those who marry only to father mortal offspring (208 c–209a), and whether he is celebrating the pupil's desire for the wisdom of his teacher or the sublimated attraction of the teacher to the beauty of his pupil, the conjugal elements are not the feminine and the masculine, but body and intellect or youth and age. By contrast the

---

[49] Prologue 3.1. V. Limone and C. Moreschini (eds.), *Origene e Gregroio di Nissa, Sul Cantico dei Cantici* (Milan: Bompiani, 2016), 180.2 read 'epoptic' rather than 'enoptic': see further P. Tzamalikos, *Origen: Philosophy of History and Eschatology* (Leiden: Brill, 2007), 259.

[50] M. J. Edwards, *Origen against Plato* (Farnham, Surrey: Ashgate, 2002), 130.

[51] Cf. Eusebius, *Preparation* 4.4.1, 6.5.1 etc.

[52] See C. Riedweg, *Mysterienterminologie bei Platon, Philon und Klemens* (Berlin: De Gruyter, 1987), 145–7. For Clement on *epopteia* see *Stromateis* 7.68.3, 7.106.1, as cited by Riedweg.

[53] *Philokalia* 2.4 = J. A. Robinson, *The Philokalia of Origen* (Cambridge: Cambridge University Press, 1893), 39.

motherlode of the Christian quest is the prophetic symbolism of the oft-betrayed yet indissoluble marriage of Yahweh and Israel, which acquires a new force in the gospels through its application to Christ; in the Book of Revelation Jewish and Christian images meet when the New Jerusalem descends from God like a bride adorned for her husband. As Protestants have rightly observed, however, this symbolism may serve Paul as an archetype of matrimony between man and woman (Ephesians 5.32), but nowhere does it furnish a scriptural charter for the individual's aspiration to union with God.[54] In Plato the possibility of such union is grounded in the natural divinity of the soul, and the realisation of 'likeness to god according to one's capacity' will mean for the best of us nothing less than being a God oneself, as we read in the oracle near the end of the *Life of Plotinus*.[55] How could Christianity, which repeatedly proclaims the gulf between Creator and creature to be unbridgeable, permit itself to be influenced by a philosophy for which that gulf is merely an illusion caused by the soul's estrangement from its proper home?

It will not suffice to adduce the canonical status of the Song of Songs, for it owes this to the presence of motifs which suggested to Jewish readers that Israel rather than any member of Solomon's populous harem is the object of his eulogies. Once the prospective Bride is understood as a type of Israel, Solomon in his turn becomes a type of God himself; there is, however, no reason for construing her nocturnal perambulation through Jerusalem – even if this were yet the new Jerusalem – as the itinerary of a bewildered soul. There is indeed one versatile Platonist, Apuleius of Madaura, who makes Psyche or Soul the heroine in a tale of darkness, separation and wandering,[56] but we do not hear of any ancient writer, Christian or Platonist, who discovered the key to this heteroerotic fantasy. When Origen decided that the male protagonist of the Song of Songs was Christ he was following the usual Christian rule of substituting the church for Israel; when he adds, however, that in relation to the soul Solomon is the logos, is he not justly charged with superimposing eros on agape and concocting a theory of spiritual senses to throw a veil upon his own fusion of Platonic egocentricity with the ecclesiastical ideal of wedlock?

---

[54] See further A. Nygren, *Agape and Eros*, trans. P. S. Watson (London: SPCK, 1953).

[55] Plato, *Theaetetus* 176a.

[56] Apuleius, *Metamorphoses* 4.28 to 6.24; see C. Moreschini, *Apuleius and the Metamorphoses of Platonism* (Turnhout: Brepols, 2014), chapter 3.

Origen, as we have noted, labours to show that the three branches of Greek philosophy are prefigured in the ordering of the three Solomonic texts of the Hebrew canon. He himself says that he might have included logic, and he ought to have confessed that its usual place in the Greek taxonomies was the one that he has awarded to enoptics or epoptics. In fact, as Philoponus tells us, there was some agreement as to the divisions of philosophy but none as to the ranking of these divisions:[57] a Platonist, whatever scheme he followed, would not set aside epoptics as a separate branch of study but might use the term *epopteia* to characterise the goal to which all his studies tended. For a Plotinus ritual was an analogue to, but not an element in, the emancipation of the soul. A Christian might regard the material sacrament as an instrument of union or communion with the divine, but it is not clear that Origen was such a Christian. It is possible that he was more prepared to borrow a trope from the mysteries because he saw it coupled in philosophic discourse with conceits that, in his eyes at least, were of scriptural origin. The Son in the discourse of the church was an image of his Father, as Philo's Logos was both the image and the firstborn Son of God. In Plato's *Timaeus*, by contrast, it is the world that is both an image and *monogenês* of the Demiurge. How then to explain the repeated use in the *Enneads* of the term eikon or image to characterise the relation of nous to the One? And was a Christian provenance not all the more likely if, as many alleged, Plotinus was the modern amanuensis of Numenius, who not only described the second God as a *mimêma* or likeness of the first but reinforced his own doctrines by allegorical readings of the acts of Christ?[58]

A uniform obliteration of God-sent *agape* by man-made Eros will not explain how Proclus, alone of his school, could speak of an Eros descending from the higher to the lower, from one who needs nothing to the one in need. The reciprocal traffic between the church and pagan Athens enabled each to profit from the other without betraying its parentage; as the first part of this essay indicates – and as Origen says on behalf of the church in his exhortation to spoil the Egyptians – each could argue that it was merely taking back its own. Complete assimilation was impossible so long as Platonism and Christianity were

---

[57] *Commentary on the Categories*, ed. A. Busse (Berlin: Reimer, 1898), 5.15–34.
[58] See Fr 20 Des Places (Eusebeius, *Preparation* 11.22.9–10); Frs 1b and 1c (Origen, *Against Celsus* 1.15 and 4.51).

rival institutions. No catholic of that era, not even the indefatigable
Eusebius, anticipates Ralph Cudworth's voluminous efforts to prove
that the Trinity is homologous with the Plotinian triad of One, Nous
and Soul; we may add that even Cudworth shrinks from the polytheism implied by the term 'second god'.[59] No churchman of antiquity
could maintain, as Leo Hebraeus was to maintain in the fifteenth
century, that Aristophanes' fable in the *Symposium* has the same
moral as the story of Adam and Eve.[60] Both, says Leo, describe the
first humans as androgynous beings in whom reason is the masculine
and sensation the feminine element. In the biblical narrative man and
woman become distinct when Eve is drawn forth from the side of
Adam – an intimation that sense must be dissociable from reason if
each is to pursue its proper end. The Platonic myth, in which Zeus
bisects our ancestors to prevent them from storming heaven, tells us
that, without the body to tame it, reason is too overweening even to
bear the yoke of its Creator; the attempted reunion of sense and
intellect becomes possible only when Zeus sews them together face
to face – that is, each learns that it must seek not only its own but the
other's good.

Leo is improvising both on Plato (who does not conceive all the
original humans as androgynes) and on Philo, who equates Adam with
reason and Eve with sensuality in his commentary on the Fall.[61] He
may have been familiar with Augustine's position that the true cause
of the fall was not the seduction of reason by sense but the liability of
reason itself; it is not so likely that he had perceived the pity of God in
Athanasius as an echo of Plato's innovative ascription of pity to
Zeus.[62] In any case, it is clear that he too innovates, in order to
reach conclusions that would not have been applauded by a patron
of either school in the Roman era. Nevertheless it is from the Roman
era that he draws his inspiration, and the wall that he takes down is
one that could hardly have stood for ever once the Academy itself had
become extinct.

---

[59] R. Cudworth, *True Intellectual System of the Universe*, ed. T. Birch (London: Priestly, 1820), 39–41.
[60] Leone Ebreo, *The Philosophy of Love*, trans. F. Friedeberg-Seeley and J. H. Barnes (London: Soncino, 1937), 243–64. For the Aristophanic myth (in which, in fact, only a fraction of the first humans are androgynous) see Plato, *Symposium* 189c–193e; for Adam and Eve see Genesis 2.4–24.
[61] Philo of Alexandria, *On the Origin of the World* 149–51.
[62] Athanasius, *On the Incarnation* 8, citing *Symposium* 191b5.

Bibliography

Barr, J. *Biblical Words for Time*. Chicago: Allenson, 1962.

Cudworth, R. *True Intellectual System of the Universe*. Edited by T. Birch. London: Priestly, 1820.

Dillon, J. M. *The Middle Platonists*. London: Duckworth, 1977.

Edwards, M. J. 'Nicene Theology and the Second God'. *Studia Patristica* 40 (2006): 191–5.

   Origen against Plato. Farnham, Surrey: Ashgate, 2002.

   'Socrates and the Early Church'. In *Socrates from Antiquity to the Enlightenment*, ed. M. Trapp, 127–42. London: Routledge, 2007.

   'Why did Constantine Label Arius a Porphyrian?' *L'Antiquité Classique* 82 (2013): 239–47.

Gavrilyuk, P. *The Suffering of the Impassible God*. Oxford: Oxford University Press, 2004.

Gunton, C. *The One, the Three and the Many*. Cambridge: Cambridge University Press, 1993.

Hengel, M. *Jews, Greeks and Barbarians*. Philadelphia: Fortress Press. 1980.

Leone Ebreo, *The Philosophy of Love*. Translated by F. Friedeberg-Seeley and J. H. Barnes. London: Soncino, 1937.

Masterson, M. 'Authoritative Obscenity in Iamblichus and Arnobius'. *Journal of Early Christian Studies* 22 (2014): 373–98.

Miles, G. 'Stones, Wood and Woven Papyrus: Porphyry's *On Statues*'. *Journal of Hellenic Studies* 135 (2015), 78–94.

Moreschini, C. *Apuleius and the Metamorphoses of Platonism*. Turnhout: Brepols, 2014.

Most, G. W. 'Allegoresis and Etymology'. In *Canonical Texts and Scholarly Practices*, ed. A. Grafton and G. W. Most, 52–74. Cambridge: Cambridge University Press, 2014.

Nygren, A. *Agape and Eros*. Translated by P. S. Watson. London: SPCK, 1953.

O'Brien, S. C. *The Demiurge in Ancient Thought*. Cambridge: Cambridge University Press, 2015.

Riedweg, C. *Mysterienterminologie bei Platon, Philon und Klemens*. Berlin: De Gruyter, 1987.

Rutherford, R. *The Art of Plato*. London: Duckworth, 1995.

Stewart, J. A. *The Myths of Plato*. London: Macmillan, 1905.

Temple, W. *Readings in St John's Gospel*. London: Macmillan, 1947.

Tzamalikos, P. *Origen: Philosophy of History and Eschatology*. Leiden: Brill, 2007.

Williams, R. D. *Christ the Heart of Creation*. London: Bloomsbury 2018.

2.2

Platonism and Christianity in Late Antiquity

John Peter Kenney

The relation of early Christianity to ancient Platonism has been a conflicted issue in historical scholarship, bringing to the fore latent questions about the nature of philosophy and shape of Christian theology.[1] While such concerns may still linger, recent scholarship has come to a more nuanced understanding of the complexity of that relationship in late antiquity. That is due to the efforts by historians to survey the full scope of early Christianity in all its variety, based in part on a renewed recognition of richness of Hellenistic Judaism.[2] So too has Platonism itself come to be understood in reference to the broad sweep of its ancient development and its disparate schools.[3] Moreover the role that Greco-Roman philosophy played in the process of Christian self-definition has come to be appreciated, and no longer deprecated – after the fashion of dehellenizing theology.[4] And as scholars have become more cognizant of the genealogies and limitations of terms like "religion," "philosophy," and "theology," there has emerged a new diffidence superseding earlier

---

[1] Some portions of this chapter were initially published in the online open source internet journal *Religions* 2016, 7 (9), 114; doi:10.3390/rel17090114 in a special isssue entitled: "Plato and Christ: Platonism and Early Christianity," ed. W. Smith. The article is "'None come closer to us than these:' Augustine and the Platonists."

[2] On Hellenistic Judaism: Martin Hengel, *Jews, Greeks and Barbarians* (Philadelphia: Fortress Press, 1980). On Early Christianity: Helmut Koester, *History, Culture, and Religion of the Hellenistic Age. Introduction to the New Testament*; 2nd ed. (Berlin: Walter de Gruyter, 1995), 1: 41–45.

[3] Lloyd Gerson (ed.), *The Cambridge History of Philosophy in Late Antiquity* (Cambridge: Cambridge University Press, 2010).

[4] Esp. Adolf Harnack, *History of Dogma*, trans. Neil Buchanan; 7 vols.; 3rd German edition (London: Williams and Norgate, 1897) esp. 1: 46–47.

categories of interpretation.[5] All these developments offer the promise of a revised assessment of that tangled intellectual skein that has come to be known as "Christian Platonism." This chapter is intended to build upon these advances and perhaps to disentangle some long-standing interpretive issues.

PLATONISM

We now possess a detailed map describing the intellectual terrain of late ancient philosophy and a foundation for sketching the variations among the Platonist schools. It is thus no longer possible to make generic doctrinal comparisons between Christianity and Platonism, considered as a whole, since separate Platonist schools – while sharing a basic family resemblance in their views – held significantly different positions.[6] We can also now understand much better the essential continuity of the Platonic tradition behind its separate schools, including shared intellectual styles, a textual canon, forms of discourse, modes of personal formation, and, in some cases, types of religious praxis. Indeed the very force of that continuity has led recent scholarship to restore the use of the term "Platonism" to denote the whole historical sweep of this tradition and to reject the modern neologism "Neoplatonism," based as it is on a critical ascription of rupture and revisionism to the fourth-century Roman school of Plotinus.[7] For the study of early Christianity, these advances in understanding the full scope of Platonism mean that judgments can no longer be made about Platonism based primarily on the dialogues of Plato, but must bear in mind Platonism's historical development around that initial, canonical core.

This historical recovery of ancient Platonism has laid the groundwork for several important interpretive advances in understanding this tradition, developments that bear directly on any assessment of its relation to Christianity, and these require our consideration. First, there is the matter of locating Platonism within our interpretive categories. In recent years, religious studies scholarship has helped to promote salutary circumspection in regard to notions like "religion," "philosophy," and "theology," terms that been previously used as natural categories with clear edges.

[5] Thomas A. Lewis, *Why Philosophy Matters for the Study of Religion & Vice Versa* (Oxford: Oxford University Press, 2015), ch. 5.
[6] This scholastic diversity and continuity is evident throughout Gerson, *Cambridge History.*
[7] Gerson, *Cambridge History,* 3.

This new hermeneutical awareness has subtly shifted and enlarged our perspective on ancient philosophy and its cultural valences in antiquity. In an earlier time, Platonism was straightforwardly seen as a philosophy and as a product of the exercise of reason – understood in a broadly rationalist fashion. It was thus represented as something quite distinct from Christian theology, rooted in revelation, and also from Greco-Roman religion, understood as being a diverse set of cults, rituals, and archaic stories about the gods. Philosophy was understood to stand apart from ancient myths and cultic practices and was usually seen as critically rejecting or abstaining from them. In the case of Platonism, this historiographical model faced tensions in its narrative because of the undeniable but awkward fact that Platonism in late antiquity experienced a "failure of nerve," becoming increasingly open to the oracular and prophetic aspects of paganism, such as the *Chaldaean Oracles*, and even explicitly supportive of cultic practice, in particular theurgy.[8]

But if we shuffle our categories, Platonism begins to look quite different. For starters, scholarly discussion of traditional religion in Greco-Roman antiquity was usually confined to cultic practice and mythic discourse. And that religion had no name, at least until late antiquity, when some Platonists started to call themselves "Hellenes," and Christians began to call them "pagans." It was therefore easy to segregate religion – when so narrowly defined – from philosophy, making the former seem inchoate and the later an emancipating voice of reason. Yet this older scholarly model missed several important features of the cultural dynamic of antiquity. "Paganism" might best be understood as an umbrella term, encompassing a cluster of ancient accounts of the gods and a wide range of cults and ritual traditions. But crucially Greco-Roman culture also each developed philosophical schools that engaged with these mythic and cultic elements, providing divergent readings of those texts and practices. These schools helped to elaborate, criticize, and revise these mythic and cultic elements. When so viewed, for example, Plato's Socrates emerges not as a rationalist critic of the pieties of paganism, but as its reformer. Indeed, that spirit of revisionism might be seen to be characteristic of Platonism throughout much of its history. More importantly, Platonism and other philosophical schools gave theological and ethical voice to paganism, articulating what had been mute in archaic times and

---

[8] Cf. John Dillon, *The Middle Platonists* (Ithaca, NY: Cornell University Press, 1977), ch. 8. Gregory Shaw, *Theurgy and the Soul: The Neoplatonism of Iamblichus* (University Park, PA: Pennsylvania State University Press, 1995).

redirecting the tradition itself. In that sense the philosophers were the systematicians of paganism. When thus represented, Platonism can be seen as playing an integral and enriching role with the wider religious culture of paganism, rather standing critically aloof from it. Its deployment in late antiquity as the rallying point of that tradition in the face of Christianity was a natural extension of its antecedent role and not a sudden flight from reason.

Moreover, Platonism throughout antiquity was seldom just a philosophy in the modern sense, that is, a problem-solving set of conceptual techniques and a type of discourse centered on theoretical analysis. While it was certainly that, it was also – in Hadot's now famous phrase – a "way of life." This point follows from the broader representation of philosophy just iterated.[9] What Hadot grasped was the extent to which philosophy played the central role of ethical articulation and, most importantly, moral formation in antiquity. To be a philosopher meant, in some significant measure, to adopt a specific way of life associated with moral principles set down by one's school and grounded in its metaphysics. Those ethical principles and practices radiated out beyond the schools themselves in the wider pagan culture. But their epicenter was in the philosophical schools themselves. Thus to become a philosopher was sometimes akin to a conversion experience, as can be seen in Porphyry's description of Plotinus' adoption of philosophy at the age of twenty-eight in his *Life of Plotinus*.[10] Admittedly, not all ancient philosophers were austerely observant; some were just professional instructors of doctrine, as the young Plotinus' disappointed search for a committed philosopher among the pedantic lecturers of Alexandria indicates.[11] But the point remains that philosophy was culturally understood in antiquity to include a transformation of the self in accordance with a specific form of life.

This insight from Hadot is dispositive for our consideration of Platonism and early Christianity. Philosophical doctrines remained essential to the Platonist schools, as did dialectic and textual exegesis. But these were not stand-alone activities. Nor were they ends in themselves. They nested in a culturally sanctioned praxis that gave further meaning to these ideas, adding, if you will, a real-life valence to those abstractions. Most significantly, the goal of philosophy was the cultivation of the person, not systematic theory formation.

---

[9] Pierre Hadot, *Philosophy As a Way of Life* (Malden, MA: Blackwell, 1995).
[10] Porphyry, *Life of Plotinus*, 3.   [11] Ibid.

To speak of Platonism in antiquity is, first and foremost, to refer to this full composite of theory and practice. But when we refer in contemporary scholarship, for example, to the "Platonism of Augustine," we usually call attention only to a limited subset of what constituted ancient Platonism, perhaps some aspects of its doctrine or contemplative practices acquired by Augustine second-hand. But that is a reductive use of the term "Platonist." It bears mention that we have evidence of only a few ancient Christians who studied formally as members of a Platonist school – Origen, a student in the Alexandrian school of Ammonius, the teacher of Plotinus, being the best-known exception. Thus, Christians were never really Platonists in antiquity when we understand more fully what being a Platonist actually meant. Their "Platonism" was informal and fragmentary and borrowed. And, most importantly, they did not remain under the direction of a Platonist scholarch once they became Christians. For they followed a different way and belonged to what came to be seen as a different and distinctive school, even if they were, in some important ways, fellow travelers with the Platonists.

An additional point requires reflection, one that follows from those just made. Early Christian thinkers were indeed influenced by the Platonists to varying degrees. But we need to be very wary of what this means when we make that assertion. It is easy enough to find concepts or theories whose original provenance was Platonist, but it is tricky to determine what such concepts actually meant in their new contexts. As already noted, since meaning is closely associated with use, the patterns of practice in which these notions were originally embedded were critical to their actual significance. Their new Christian contexts can thus subtly shift their semantics, losing earlier fields of association and acquiring new ones. We need only consider the challenge of tracking the meaning of *ousia* or *substantia* from philosophy into Christianity.[12] This caveat we should keep in mind as we turn to a final but crucial aspect of the philosophical association between Platonism and Christianity, one whose significance necessitates careful parsing. That is the development of a type of monotheism within the pagan tradition.

"Pagan monotheism" seems like a category mistake of some sort, challenging the received narrative that monotheism is exclusively a product of the Jewish tradition. But a careful reading of ancient pagan theology makes it difficult to ignore its growing, indigenous effort to systematize the layered strata of gods and powers that had constituted

---

[12] Christopher Stead, *Divine Substance* (Oxford: Clarendon Press, 1977).

the ancient pantheon. Moreover, that drive toward greater unity and coherence seems to have been conjoined to a desire for an account of divine justice beyond the anthropomorphic stories of the classical gods. This dynamic generated theological discussion within the philosophical schools, for it was in those philosophical schools that ancient pagan culture did its thinking about the nature of divinity. That discussion is evident during the classical period in Plato's Academy, which generated a spectrum of philosophical theologies including those of Plato, Speusippus, Xenocrates, and Aristotle. Despite a limited period of neglect during the New Academy, the Platonist tradition remained committed to that theological project throughout antiquity, intensifying this concentration during the Roman period. It was within the Platonic schools that efforts were made to develop an account of a single divine principle that was responsible for the existence of all reality outside itself.

The theistic turn of paganism was, needless to say, a convoluted process, finally coming to fruition in the Roman school of Plotinus around AD 250.[13] This Platonic theism was distinctive in its logic, starting as it did by acceptance of multiple gods and then pressing toward a deeper divine unity behind the manifest image of plurality. Its logic was therefore different from that of Jewish or Christian monotheism and its modes of articulating the nature of the ultimate One were consequently separate in character. Great emphasis was placed on the hierarchy of divine powers, stretching out to the remote divine unity beyond the surface of divine manifestations in this world. The gods thus appeared as individuated aspects of the One, each with its own spiritual value, each an expression of divinity itself and a path to the One. This embrace of the power of multiple gods is captured by the famous expression of Symmachus: "not by one path alone to so great a mystery."[14] That sentiment points beyond the many to the One, and for that reason pagan monotheism relied on a logic of ultimacy in which the surface powers of the One were seen to point toward that initial divine source from which they had emerged. At the same time, pagan monotheism traded on this notion of hierarchical depth so that specific characteristics found in the individual gods, for example, personality or emotion, were understood to be grounded in the vast richness of the One itself.

---

[13] J. P. Kenney, *Mystical Monotheism: A Study in Ancient Platonic Theology* (Hanover and London: Brown University Press, 1991).

[14] *Memorial of Symmachus, Prefect of the City*, 10.

Platonism was in the vanguard of these developments. Its special contribution was the articulation of metaphysical theology that served to elaborate this pagan understanding of the divine. Several conceptual advances emerged within the Platonic schools that became essential to pagan monotheism. First, the traditional hierarchical aspect of pagan thinking about the Gods was supported by an ontology of degrees of reality. The notion of spatio-temporal transcendence also emerged, postulating a level of stability and perfection deeper than the world of change. That was the true level of reality, "being itself," a world that was truly divine. And deep beyond the level of true being was the ultimate source of divinity and perfection, the One or Good itself. Central to this theology was an emphasis on the One's position at a level exceeding all forms of finitude and the limitations of anthropomorphic description. Apophatic theology was the conceptual instrument for articulating this metaphysical depth, becoming the signature of Platonic monotheism after Plotinus. Platonic theology was thus committed to a higher world beyond the manifest image of the physical cosmos. It was, therefore, responsible for developing the critical notion of divine transcendence and the consequent understanding of the divine as being beyond space and time, and also as eternal. Moreover, Plotinus ascribed the positive notion of infinity to the One, revolutionizing the very notion of the divine. Henceforth the ultimate first principle would come to be understood as the infinite source of all finite reality. And, because it utterly transcended all finite beings, it could then be understood to be present to them in a non-spatial fashion. It was omnipresent because it was the ontological sustaining cause of all finite reality, spatially removed from all things, but most intimately present to them by their very existence. Beyond being, the One was the eternal root of all beings. Finally, this innovative understanding of the One was allied with another innovation, the rejection of *hyle* or matter as a fundamental principle of reality. Again, it was Plotinus who struggled to dissolve the ancient commitment to a material principle, a substrate that served to underlie and resist the rational power of order. That thinking was characteristic of the cosmologies of Plato and Aristotle, and it remained a staple of Greco-Roman theology until Plotinus. But in Plotinian Platonism, the infinity of the One left, as it were, no conceptual room for an independent principle of matter upon which the ordering powers of the divine were applied. Everything emerged from the One, even matter, and, while it may have a role to play at the base of the process of emanation from the One, it was not an independent power over against the Good.[15]

---

[15] *Ennead* I. 8 [51] 7; II. 3 [52] 17; III. 4 [15] 1.

One additional aspect of the notion of transcendence bears special mention. Because the One was not a supreme being within space and time, it was not a being that could be reached, or contacted, at a distance. It was infinite and so, one might say, it was beyond spatial relationality entirely. Therefore, the spiritual vector began to shift among some Platonists, focusing no longer on a distant and remote supreme deity to whom propitiation and sacrifice might be offered. Instead the path to the transcendent One was to be found within the self. By going down into the self through the practice of dialectic and meditation, the soul could unite with its omnipresent spiritual source directly. Here Hadot's insight mentioned above is especially apposite, for the practice of philosophy came to be seen among Platonists as the practice of transcendence, a disciplined way of life by which the soul could rediscover its roots in the infinite One beyond time, space, and the material cosmos. While Platonists in the period after Plotinus would come to believe that most souls were unable to unite with the One completely during their current reincarnations, and so required divine assistance in their journey through the practice of theurgy, they nonetheless maintained the contemplative path as the ultimate ideal.

It seems reasonable, in light of this powerful trajectory of philosophical theology, to describe the Platonists of late antiquity as harbingers of monotheism, even if the shape of their theology was different from that of the Jewish tradition. Indeed, their thinking became the foundation for philosophical theology among some Hellenistic Jews and early Christians, and thereafter into the medieval period for Muslims, Jews, and Christians alike. But Platonic theism was, nonetheless, a distinctive tradition, emerging from pagan thought and part of its ambient religious culture. It nested within that culture and gave voice to it. Integral to that developing monotheism was the recognition of intelligible transcendence. For this reason, Platonism was the principal catalyst of what might be called the developing transcendentalism that transformed the spiritual culture of late antiquity.

PLATONISM AND ANTE-NICENE CHRISTIANITY

The story of Christianity's relation to Platonism begins with Hellenistic Judaism, out of which it emerged and whose philosophical resources informed the ambient ideas of the culture in which this new movement took shape. Philo of Alexandria, a contemporary of Jesus and St. Paul, is the most innovative example of the effort to reframe the exegesis of the

Hebrew scriptures in terms of the Platonism and to offer a philosophical account of the God of ancient Israel.[16] The earliest Christian writings evince that Hellenistic Jewish theological context, for example, Paul's letters or the prologue to the Gospel of John, even if their exact sources are difficult to determine with certainty. But, by the mid-second century, the Christian philosopher Justin Martyr offers a detailed, if somewhat stylized, account of his intellectual biography. Born around 100 in the Roman city of Flavia Neapolis in Samaritan Palestine, Justin recounts how he had encountered philosophers from many different schools: Stoic, Aristotelian, Pythagorean, and finally Platonist. It is the last of these that captured his imagination. In his description of his discovery of Platonism Justin reports that a grasp of immateriality suddenly took hold of him and he expected to contemplate God, which is the goal of Platonism.[17] Divine transcendence was the conversionary insight that drew him to the Platonist school, although a vision of God did not ensue. This conviction of transcendent existence together with the failure of the philosophical contemplation would subsequently become an apologetical trope among Christians, exhibited most prominently in Augustine's *Confessions* VII. Justin goes on in his *Dialogue with Trypho* to recount how he met an old man by the sea, a Christian, and listened to his account of the power of the Holy Spirit working through the prophets. From him Justin learned that the scriptures of the Christians contain those prophecies, which are now being manifested through the incarnation of Jesus Christ, the Son of God. The prophecies of the Old Testament and the memoirs of the disciples of Christ are the foundation for the true philosophy. Scripture does not contain conceptual demonstration, as do the books of the pagan philosophers, but rather the accounts of the prophets who were witnesses to what they saw and heard through the Holy Spirit. True wisdom must be secured, then, through the reading of scripture and through prayer, for only by the power of God and his Christ is that wisdom imparted.

Here we can see the initial constitution of "Christian Platonism" – a merging of Platonic elements into Christianity. Justin turns to Christianity and its distinctive account of the living God of the prophets whose purposes are manifest in salvation history and were fulfilled in the

---

[16] Dillon, *The Middle Platonists*, 139–83; Adam Kamesar (ed.), *The Cambridge Companion to Philo* (Cambridge: Cambridge University Press, 2009), part 2. For the Christian reception of Philo: David T. Runia, *Philo in Early Christian Literature: A Survey* (Assen: Van Gorcum, 1993).

[17] *Dialogue with Trypho*, 2.6.

life and death of Jesus Christ. But that account was itself transposed into a metaphysical key by Justin's recognition of the Platonic conception of transcendence. His God is God the Father, whose nature is articulated in Platonic terms. God is "that which always is the same and in like manner and is the cause of the being of all else."[18] God is, in consequence, unbegotten, unchangeable, and incorruptible. This fusion of the Platonic conception of being itself with the God of Exodus 3:14, who identified himself as the one who is, will henceforth become the linchpin of Christian metaphysics. In the manner of the Platonists of his age, Justin adopted a hierarchical understanding of reality and with it the assumption that the transcendent God required various means of mediation to cross the line of ontological separation from his creatures. That God, both unknowable and unnameable by creatures, has revealed himself through scripture and by the incarnation of his Logos. The unbegotten Father of all generated a divine secondary power who exercised creative and redemptive roles within the created world of the cosmos. But the exact nature of the Logos in reference to the Father is unclear. While it is evident that the Logos is the first product of the transcendent God, his status as a creature is undefined, and cosmological role in reference to matter is murky. What is evident is Justin's use of themes derived from the dominant reading of the *Timaeus* among contemporary Platonists, especially the temporal origins of the universe and the consequent claim that the world continues to exist according to the will of God.[19] Despite his embrace of philosophy, Justin was martyred for his Christianity during the reign of the Stoic Emperor Marcus Aurelius.

Justin established a fundamental template for the relationship between Christianity and Platonism throughout antiquity by rejecting Platonism as a spiritual path, while simultaneous embracing Platonic transcendentalism as the basis for reading the Christian scriptures. In doing so he also helped to initiate the development of Christian monotheism, committed to a God beyond the frame of space and time, a God whose metaphysical status could explain his unique creative function. That same pattern emerged in a more systematic form among the "Christian Platonists of Alexandria," including Clement of Alexandria and especially Origen.[20]

---

[18] Ibid, 3.4

[19] Denis Minns, "Justin Martyr," in *The Cambridge History of Philosophy in Late Antiquity*, ed. Lloyd Gerson (Cambridge: Cambridge University Press, 2010), 1:261–67.

[20] To use the title of C. Bigg's 1886 Bampton lectures, *The Christian Platonists of Alexandria* (Oxford, 1913, 2nd ed.) which brought the term "Christian Platonism" into the English scholarly lexicon.

Clement was born in midcentury and migrated to Alexandria, studying with a Christian philosopher there named Pantaenus. Clement is said to have succeeded him as a catechetical teacher, but seems to have left the city around 211, dying before 216. Clement regarded Platonic philosophy as a necessary propaedeutic for mature Christian faith, giving Christians the intellectual foundations for their faith and offering a sophisticated grasp of transcendent reality. From his affirmation of the integral nature of faith and reason emerged the charter of subsequent orthodox Christian theology, at once rooted in the scriptures but also informed by a nonmaterialist or spiritual hermeneutic. What Clement sought was a higher Christian *gnosis*, a knowledge of spiritual reality revealed in scripture, whose deeper meaning is disclosed through reason. For this reason, Christianity was for him a path to wisdom and salvation open both to the uneducated, whose only access is through scripture, and to the philosophically trained. Two features of his thought are particularly noteworthy. Clement's Christian philosophy was clearly in debt to Philo of Alexandria, the early first-century Jewish philosopher who began the process of grafting Platonic transcendentalism onto the Hebrew Bible through the use of allegorical or spiritual exegesis. Moreover, he took from Philo a strong emphasis on the unknowability of God.[21] This negative theology, which was central to the articulation of transcendence in pagan monotheism, was now employed in the context of Christian exegesis of scripture. The transcendent Father was for Clement beyond human knowledge and exceeded the mind's capacity for comprehension. God was only discovered through his Logos or Son, the ontological revelation of the Father. Through him the world was made and by him the Father's hidden nature is made manifest. God is, therefore, definitively made known as a beneficent Father, whose Son was incarnate in Jesus the Christ. As in the Platonic theism of the period, the key to this hierarchical theology is divine transcendence. But at the same time, that sense of hierarchy did not serve to underscore the remoteness of the Father, whose sense of personal presence remained vivid to the human soul. In that respect Clement exhibits the selective adoption of Platonic philosophical ideas by Christians.

These early versions of Christian philosophy were eclipsed by Origen of Alexandria (*c.* 185–*c.* 254). In Origen we find the most comprehensive

---

[21] H. F. Hägg, *Clement of Alexandria and the Beginnings of Christian Apophaticism* (Oxford: Oxford University Press, 2006); S. Lilla, *Clement of Alexandria: A Study in Christian Platonism* (Oxford: Oxford University Press, 1971).

integration of the Christian scriptures with Platonic transcendentalism.[22] Origen was born into a Christian family and his father was martyred when Origen was seventeen. He was a prodigy as a student of the Bible but studied as well with Ammonius, the Alexandrian Platonist and teacher of Plotinus. His knowledge of the varieties of contemporary Platonism is evident throughout his works, and his approach to philosophy is based on his confident recognition of its supplemental usefulness in the exposition of Christian truth. Following in the tradition of Philo and Clement, his central project was scriptural exegesis pursued with the aid of Platonic metaphysics. While Origen relies on the same Platonic account of the degrees of reality and divinity, culminating in the One God, he did not articulate its transcendence by means of negative theology. His emphasis is on the self-diffusion of God, the divine Father, who generates the Word, its finite image. The Word is the locus of the Platonic intelligibles, and thus the Word is the archetype through whom all lower levels of reality are created. The Word is, therefore, transcendent of the material cosmos, since it is an intelligible being. Its status is as an ontological and cosmo-gonic intermediary between the One God and creation. Unlike Clement, Origen is clearer about the production of matter from God. In this respect he followed the growing tendency among some Platonists to read the *Timaeus* in a less literal manner and to regard the Receptacle as a product of the divine Demiurge rather than as an independent and primordial realty. In doing so they were more consistently articulating their pagan monotheism, removing the notion of a material substrate upon which God fashioned the cosmos.

Origen's thought accords central importance to the freedom exercised by rational creatures, including humans.[23] Human souls were created with a level of free choice that was at once moral and ontological. They had, as it were, a cursive character – to use computer jargon – that allowed them to choose the level of reality on which they wished to dwell. Initially created in the presence of God, humans had chosen to turn their attention away from God and to seek another level of reality. Through this collect-ive choice, humans lost the perfection of their initial creation and sank

---

[22] Henry Chadwick, "Origen," in *Cambridge History of Later Greek and Early Medieval Philosophy*, ed. A. H. Armstrong (London: Cambridge University Press, 1967), 182–92; M. J. Edwards, *Origen Against Plato* (Aldershot: Ashgate, 2002); Peter W. Martens, *Origen and Scripture: The Contours of the Exegetical Life* (Oxford: Oxford University Press, 2012), 72–77; 119–26.

[23] Benjamin P. Blosser, *Become Like the Angels: Origen's Doctrine of the Soul* (Washington, D.C.: Catholic University of America Press, 2012), 145–219.

down into a lesser reality, becoming through this psychic precipitation diminished versions of themselves. Origen conceived this fall on a vast scale, with varying levels of reality corresponding to the different degrees of the declension of souls. The evil that seems a brute fact within our world, and an affront to the creative goodness of a God of love, is, in fact, the dark by-product of our own choice to abandon the perfection of our initial creation.[24] Death and suffering what humans chose in their decision to abandon God, although these evils serve an educative function, since Origen conceived of the human soul as having a post-mortem existence at other levels of reality consistent with the moral progress made in the present life. Ultimately this vast, cosmic process of reeducation would eventuate in the return of all souls to the perfection of their prelapsarian condition, that "God may be all in all" (1 Cor. 15:28).

The figures discussed thus far fall into the proto-orthodox trajectory, even if, like Origen, aspects of their thought would later be rejected in the process of orthodox Christian self-definition. But that dimension of early Christianity leaves out of account the many heterodox or "Gnostic" sects, many of which were conspicuous in their adoption of Platonic elements.[25] Both Clement and Origen were concerned to push back against these theologies, and their adoption of the Greek tradition of philosophical rationality was partly meant to buttress their interpretation of Christianity. But gnostic groups like the Valentinians and the Sethians made appeal as well to the transcendental ontology of Platonism. In this respect they are similar to pagan oracular literature, such as the *Poemandres* tractate in the *Corpus Hermeticum* or the *Chaldaean Oracles*, which also draw upon Platonic transcendentalism. Hierarchical theology, beginning with a totally transcendent first God, is a common theme throughout all this literature. Negative theology is particularly conspicuous in the architecture of the Valentinian and Sethian Gnosticism, emphasizing the remoteness of the first God.[26] But the grammar of pagan monotheism is employed in these forms of Gnosticism to

---

[24] Mark S. M. Scott, *Journey Back to God: Origen on the Problem of Evil* (New York and Oxford: Oxford University Press, 2012).

[25] Karen L. King, *What is Gnosticism?* (Cambridge, MA: Harvard University Press, 2003).

[26] Karen L. King, *The Secret Revelation of John* (Cambridge, MA: Harvard University Press, 2006), ch. 7; J. P. Kenney, "The Platonism of the Tripartite Tractate," in *Neoplatonism and Gnosticism*, eds. R. T. Wallis and J. Bregman (Albany: State University of New York Press, 1992), 187–206; J. P. Kenney, "Ancient Apophatic Theology," in *Gnosticism and Later Platonism: Themes, Figures, and Texts*, eds. John D. Turner and Ruth Majercik (Atlanta: SBL Symposium Series 12, 2000), 259–275.

distance that God and his initial creation, the *pleroma*, from the subsequent emergence of evil. Unlike in Platonism, the natural world is seen as saturated with evil, even if within it there are souls who contain within themselves a residual spirit or spark of the highest God – knowledge of which is salvific. It bears mention that both proto-orthodox Christians like Clement and Origen, as well as Platonists, such as Plotinus, Amelius, and Porphyry made common cause in their opposition to Gnostic Christianity in this regard.

AFTER NICAEA

The most important innovations in the development of philosophical monotheism in late antiquity were those initiated by Plotinus (205–270), who studied under Ammonius in Alexandria before coming to teach in Rome in 244. Around him gathered a school that included fellow philosophers like Amelius and Porphyry, as well a variety of students, among whom were Sethian Gnostics.[27] The treatises that circulated among these Sethians were the targets of the polemical efforts of Plotinus and other members of his school.

The chief innovations of Plotinus include: a positive understanding of divine infinity, the omnipresence of the infinite One to all subsequent reality, a philosophical account of the divine levels as deeply interconnected hypostases, the rejection of matter as a primordial substrate, and the nonbeing of evil. All of these conceptual advances would resonate in later Christian thought.

Thus far this essay has emphasized the hermeneutic role of Platonic transcendentalism among proto-orthodox Christians such as Justin, Clement, and Origen. This approach was fundamental to Christian exegesis and contemplative practice in late antiquity, for it was the interpretative key by which the archaic scriptures of ancient Israel could be unlocked and their "spiritual" meaning disclosed. This Christian exegetical use of Platonism drew the ire of pagans such as Porphyry. According to Eusebius, writing in his *Ecclesiastical History* around 303, Porphyry argued this point against Origen and the Christians who followed him.[28] That underscores the importance of this transcendentalist hermeneutic for Christian philosophy and helps supply a contemporaneous sense of what "Christian Platonism" might substantively mean as an interpretive

---

[27] Porphyry, *Vita Plotini*, ch. 16.
[28] *Ecclesiastical History*, 6. 19 in reference to Porphyry's *Against the Christians*.

category. After its legitimation in 313, those forms of Christianity that regarded themselves as in communion with the worldwide *ecclesia* were able to begin defining their beliefs. The creedal sketch that emerged was itself reliant on philosophical terminology, for example, *ousia* and *homoousion*, whose theological significance was open to further exploration. That larger theological articulation was the project of the great Nicene thinkers of the late fourth century, especially the Cappadocian bishops in the Greek East – Basil of Caesarea, Gregory Nazianzen, and Gregory of Nyssa – as well as the bishops of the Latin West – especially Ambrose of Milan and Augustine of Hippo. All are indebted to the earlier Platonizing tradition in earlier Christianity. Gregory of Nyssa is particularly innovative, revising the theology of Origen in reference to Nicene orthodoxy and informed by the Platonism of Plotinus. In the wake of the rejection of the Arian description of the divine Word as a creature, the concept of creation became the central boundary between God and all other beings.

In the theology of Gregory of Nyssa, this uncreated/created distinction is developed more fully, and the notion of transcendence deepened. Gregory's thought moves beyond the initial conception of divine transcendence understood as God's existence beyond the material cosmos and thus beyond the limits of space and time. Gregory expands that insight by recognizing that God must therefore be beyond finitude entirely.[29] As infinite, God is outside the domain of finite reference, and is unknowable. Human efforts to grasp the inner life of the One God must be exceed the logic of finite analysis. While negative theology in Philo and Clement helped to establish the idea of transcendence, in Gregory it is conjoined to the notion of infinity and applied in a novel way to God and to the three divine hypostases. That shift into an infinite mode of theological reflection allowed Gregory to quash the hierarchism that was endemic to earlier Platonic theology, for example, Origen, and also to reconceive the divine hypostases. In *Against Eunomius*, Gregory maintains that the infinity of God precludes the logic of finite separation of hypostases, so that infinite deity can be seen to saturate the three divine persons entirely.[30] Uncreated and infinite, God is the unlimited source of all created beings. For humans,

---

[29] Andrew Radde-Gallwitz, *Basil of Caesarea, Gregory of Nyssa, and the Transformation of Divine Simplicity* (Oxford: Oxford University Press, 2009) and Gregory of Nyssa's Doctrinal Works: A Literary Study (Oxford: Oxford University Press, 2018); Andrew Meredith, "Gregory of Nyssa," in Cambridge History of Philosophy in Late Antiquity, ed. Lloyd Gerson (Cambridge: Cambridge University Press, 2010), 471–81.

[30] *Against Eunomius*, Book I.

that means the journey of the soul will itself be without limit. As the soul ascends into the divine darkness beyond finite understanding, it stretches itself out toward the infinity of God. That concept of stretching out, *epektasis*, resonates with the "stretching forward to what lies ahead" at Philippians 3:13, now understood in a metaphysical key. This conception of eternal contemplation is the culminating theme of Gregory's *Life of Moses*, where the infinity of the Good, the Beautiful, and Being itself are seen face to face, but without satiety. For a true glimpse of divine infinity engenders in the soul a desire to look upon the depths of God without ceasing.[31] In this respect Gregory has taken up the transcendentalism of Plotinus, with its novel logic of divine infinity, and used it to refine the triune monotheism of Nicaea. In doing so Gregory has moved beyond earlier Christian Platonists in his recognition that the uncreated God – including all three hypostases – is beyond the first order transcendence of spiritual but finite creatures, such as angels. In that sense his theology of divine infinity articulates a double transcendence theory, one that is sourced from post-Plotinian Platonism but employed in the elaboration of Christian orthodoxy.

In the Latin West, Augustine of Hippo (354–430) offers the most articulate account of the value and limitations of Platonism from the standpoint of Catholic Christianity. In doing so he presents an understanding of pagan Platonism that is continuous with the tradition that reached back through Origen to Justin Martyr. In book five of his *Confessions* he recounts that, throughout his North African youth as a Catholic catechumen and his early adulthood as a Manichaean, he had never encountered the idea of non-material or "spiritual" reality.[32] The antidote to that materialism was Platonism. He says that he encountered "some books of the Platonists" at the behest of Catholics in the circle of Ambrose, the bishop of Milan, whose spiritual readings of the Bible he had encountered. Augustine regarded the discovery of Platonism to be providential, suggesting that he might have been seduced away from the scriptures by the force of Platonism.[33] But instead he read the Platonic texts first and they opened for him the novel metaphysical vista of transcendence. But just as in Justin, transcendence became the dispositive insight that directed him to a spiritual reading of the Christian scriptures. His earliest, contemporaneous texts, written from before his baptism, record this moment of the discovery of Platonism. He tells us in both *On the Happy Life* and *Against the Academics* 2. 2. 5 that his encounter

---

[31] *Life of Moses*, II.219-55.   [32] *Confessions*, V. 14. 25.   [33] *Confessions*, VII. 20. 26.

with Platonism led him to read the letters of St. Paul closely and intently.[34] What Platonism had given him was the transcendentalist hermeneutic necessary to get beyond the literal meaning of the scripture. Moreover, the ascension narratives of *Confessions* VII attest to the fact that contemplation succeeded in drawing his soul into unmediated knowledge of eternal being.[35] But those moments of transcendental insight were not enough to sustain his soul's association with "eternal truth, true love and beloved eternity," that is, with God. His soul is still freighted down with its moral condition. Augustine regards that as a universal aspect of the human condition. Upon it he develops the sustained critique of Platonism that concludes *Confessions* VII.[36] But notwithstanding the transformative value of Platonic transcendentalism for his own life and thought, he insists that the Platonists of the school of Plotinus harbor an unrealistic, indeed hubristic, representation of human nature. By claiming that the soul was not fully descended into the material world and could thereby contemplate the One through its own spiritual power, Platonists were culpably overestimating both the cognitive and moral capacity of human beings. For we are not gods and there is no recessive divinity within us. This leads him to his defining image of Platonists, as catching but a glimpse of the "homeland of peace" from a wooded hilltop, but unable to find the way there. On Augustine's account, it is Christ who can supply the path and the power for that transcendent journey.[37]

This same understanding of the value and limitations of Platonism can be found in Augustine later work, *City of God*. Platonism has as its goal the imitation, knowledge, and love of God, and in this respect "none come closer to us than these."[38] They are the philosophical proponents of antimaterialism and a spiritual conception of God.[39]

Moreover, they are philosophical monotheists since all Platonists understand God as "the supreme and true being, the author of created things, the light of knowledge, the good of all actions, the source is our being, the beginning of nature, the truth of doctrine, and the happiness of life."[40]

Notwithstanding their philosophical monotheism, the paradox of Platonism is its continued countenancing of polytheistic worship.[41]

---

[34] *On the Happy Life*, 1.4; *Against the Academics*, 2. 2. 5.
[35] *Confessions*, VII. 10. 16 and VII. 17. 23.   [36] *Confessions*, VII. 20. 26–21. 27.
[37] J. P. Kenney, *The Mysticism of Saint Augustine: Rereading the Confessions* (London: Routledge, 2005) and *Contemplation and Classical Christianity* (Oxford: Oxford University Press, 2013).
[38] *City of God*, 8. 5.   [39] *City of God*, 8. 6.   [40] *City of God*, 8. 9.
[41] *City of God*, 10. 1.

As in the *Confessions*, Augustine expands his account of the inadequacy of Platonism. Here he concedes that Porphyry may have seen the need for a divine mediator to purify the soul, but he failed to recognize Christ in that role: Augustine notes that even Porphyry recognized that the faults and ignorance of the soul can only be purified by a mediator.[42] Again the dominant image of Platonism is knowledge at a distance. The Platonists have an intuitive grasp of much that Augustine's Nicene Christianity teaches, but they overestimate their own epistemic and soteriological capacities.[43]

Platonism is, therefore, notionally the soundest philosophy, one that offered him the conversionary insight of transcendence and with it the hermeneutic foundation necessary to uncover the deeper truths of the scriptures, obscured by his former literalism and materialism. While Platonism offers an obscured vision of the truth, only Christianity can complete the soul's journey to the One God.

CHRISTIANITY AND LATER PLATONISM

This review of the Nicene theology indicates the subtlety with which Christian thinkers, such as Gregory of Nyssa and Augustine, appropriated and redefined aspects of Platonic monotheism, rethinking elements useful for their exegetical and creedal traditions while constructing novel ideas that better suited the creedal commitments of orthodox Christianity. That process of adoption and reinvention continued into the fifth and sixth centuries, even as the character of pagan Platonism was being transformed as well. The Platonic schools in the Greek East looked in particular to the successors of Plotinus, especially Iamblichus of Chalcis, whose central project was to use Platonism as a foundation for reinterpretation of pagan rituals and practice in light of the advance of Christianity. Later pagan Platonism tended to attenuate the levels of reality that emerge from the One, and to press the logic of apophatic theology, even postulating an absolutely ineffable One, beyond the One of Plotinus. Doing so placed further emphasis on the myriad ranks of gods and powers who are the intermediaries between divine infinity and material cosmos. They form the bases for the continuing pagan cultic practices, known as *theurgy*. In this respect Platonism was the systematic theology of paganism, joining its polytheistic practices to a philosophical monotheism.

It is this context that serves as the interpretive key to the thought of the most important Greek Christian Platonist of late antiquity, who wrote

---

[42] *City of God*, 10. 28   [43] *City of God*, 10. 29

under the pseudonym Dionysius the Areopagite, taken from the name of St. Paul's philosophical convert in Acts of the Apostles 17. Written before 528, when the corpus emerged, these texts are a sustained exposition of the "unknown god" enigmatically mentioned by St. Paul in his speech at the Areopagus in Athens.[44] Dionysius emphasizes the unknowability of God, articulating the deep, double transcendence theory with greater systematic force than Gregory of Nyssa.[45] It is when the soul grasps the inadequacy of human knowledge and the deep hiddenness of the infinite God that it can discover a unity that transcends the duality of knowing.[46] But Dionysius is alert as well to the inadequacy of that negative discourse, for it is necessary to negate that negative discourse in order to appreciate the richness and beauty of the reality that has emerged from the One.[47] Christian theology is thus equipoised in the paradoxical space between negative and positive theology as it attempts to convey the mystery of God. It is in this respect that scripture has a central role in the theology, revealing the divine names and the central aspects of God that can be captured, however inadequately, through the sacred discourse of Biblical revelation. God is thus beyond both being and nonbeing, so ontologically unique that both predication and negation are inadequate. But by ascending through the ecclesial path of the scriptures and the sacraments, and then through a disciplined use of negative theology, the soul can discover its immediate presence in God.[48] Although dependent upon the highly ramified hierarchies of late antique Platonism, the thought of Dionysius presents those levels in a fashion that underscores the presence of God throughout all reality, rather than attenuating divine distance. Once again, as in earlier Christian thinkers, the logic of transcendence is employed to articulate the central themes of orthodox Christianity.

CONCLUSION

Late Antiquity was the age of monotheism, a momentous peripety in Western culture, as belief in one God emerged and became pervasive. Behind the surface of that apparently sudden shift was the idea of

---

[44] Andrew Louth, *Denys the Areopagite* (London: Continuum, 1993); Eric Perl, *Theophany: The Neoplatonic Philosophy of Dionysius the Areopagite* (Albany, NY: State University of New York Press, 2008); Paul Rorem, *Pseudo-Dionysius. A Commentary on the Texts and an Introduction to Their Influence* (Oxford: Oxford University Press, 1993).

[45] *The Mystical Theology*, esp. chs. 2 and 3.   [46] *The Divine Names*, ch. 1.

[47] *The Mystical Theology*, ch. 5.   [48] *The Ecclesiastical Hierarch*, ch. 2.

transcendence, of a level of reality more real than that seen in the manifest image of the physical world of space, time, and materiality. While Platonism was the philosophical initiator of this arresting idea, it was not its sole bearer. For it was Christianity that became the most persuasive exponent of that arresting account of reality, albeit in its own distinctive version. By the end of the fourth century, Catholic Christianity had become the dominant form of monotheism in the late Roman Empire, and the principal proponent of belief in a spiritual world accessible to the soul through interior contemplation. To speak of "Christian Platonism" is to call attention to that transcendentalist foundation of orthodox Christian theology, essential to its biblical exegesis, its theological doctrines, and its sacramental practices. But to regard Platonism as a philosophical addition to Christianity is to misconceive the larger intellectual and religious changes that gripped the world of late antiquity. For Western society had become – by the end of antiquity – a culture fixed upon the presence of the spiritual world and upon a transcendent God made manifest in Christ. In this sense "Christian Platonism" is an apt term to call attention to the underlying transcendentalism of Nicene Christianity and to its principal philosophical source.

Bibliography

Bigg, Charles. *The Christian Platonists of Alexandria*. Oxford: Oxford University Press, 1913.

Blosser, Benjamin P. *Become Like the Angels: Origen's Doctrine of the Soul*. Washington, D.C.: Catholic University of America Press, 2012.

Chadwick, Henry. "Origen." In *Cambridge History of Later Greek and Early Medieval Philosophy*, edited by A. H. Armstrong, 182–192. Cambridge: Cambridge University Press, 1967.

Dillon, John. *The Middle Platonists*. Ithaca, NY: Cornell University Press, 1977.

Edwards, M. J. *Origen against Plato*. Aldershot: Ashgate, 2002.

Gerson, Lloyd, ed. *The Cambridge History of Philosophy in Late Antiquity*. Cambridge: Cambridge University Press, 2010.

Hadot, Pierre. *Philosophy as a Way of Life*. Malden, MA: Blackwell, 1995.

Hägg, H. F. *Clement of Alexandria and the Beginnings of Christian Apophaticism*. Oxford: Oxford University Press, 2006.

Harnack, Adolf. *History of Dogma*. Translated by Neil Buchanan. London: Williams and Norgate, 1897.

Hengel, Martin. *Jews, Greeks and Barbarians*. Philadelphia: Fortress Press, 1980.

Kamesar, Adam, ed. *The Cambridge Companion to Philo*. Cambridge: Cambridge University Press, 2009.

Kenney, J. P. "Ancient Apophatic Theology," In *Gnosticism and Later Platonism. Themes, Figures, and Texts*, edited by John D. Turner and Ruth Majercik, 259–275. Atlanta: SBL Symposium Series 12, 2000.

Contemplation and Classical Christianity. Oxford: Oxford University Press, 2013.

Mystical Monotheism: A Study in Ancient Platonic Theology. Hanover and London: Brown University Press, 1991.

The Mysticism of Saint Augustine: Rereading the Confessions. London: Routledge, 2005.

"The Platonism of the Tripartite Tractate." In *Neoplatonism and Gnosticism*, edited by R. T. Wallis and J. Bregman, 187–206. Albany: State University of New York Press, 1992.

King, Karen L. *The Secret Revelation of John*. Cambridge, MA: Harvard University Press, 2006.

What is Gnosticism? Cambridge, MA: Harvard University Press, 2009.

Koester, Helmut. *History, Culture, and Religion of the Hellenistic Age. Introduction to the New Testament*. Berlin: Walter de Gruyter, 1995.

Lewis, Thomas A. *Why Philosophy Matters for the Study of Religion & Vice Versa*. New York and Oxford: Oxford University Press, 2015.

Lilla, S. *Clement of Alexandria: A Study in Christian Platonism*. Oxford: Oxford University Press, 1971.

Louth, Andrew. *Denys the Areopagite*. London: Continuum, 1993.

Martens, Peter W. *Origen and Scripture: The Contours of the Exegetical Life*. Oxford: Oxford University Press, 2012.

Meredith, Andrew. "Gregory of Nyssa." In *The Cambridge History of Philosophy in Late Antiquity*, edited by Lloyd Gerson, vol. I, 471–481. Cambridge: Cambridge University Press, 2010.

Minns, Denis. "Justin Martyr." In *The Cambridge History of Philosophy in Late Antiquity*, edited by Lloyd Gerson, 261–267. Cambridge: Cambridge University Press, 2010.

Perl, Eric. *Theophany: The Neoplatonic Philosophy of Dionysius the Areopagite*. Albany, NY: State University of New York Press, 2008.

Radde-Gallwitz, Andrew. *Basil of Caesarea, Gregory of Nyssa, and the Transformation of Divine Simplicity*. Oxford: Oxford University Press, 2009.

Gregory of Nyssa's Doctrinal Works: A Literary Study. Oxford: Oxford University Press, 2018.

Rorem, Paul. *Pseudo-Dionysius. A Commentary on the Texts and an Introduction to Their Influence*. Oxford: Oxford University Press, 1993.

Runia, David T. *Philo in Early Christian Literature: A Survey*. Assen: Van Gorcum, 1993.

Scott, Mark S. M. *Journey Back to God: Origen on the Problem of Evil*. New York and Oxford: Oxford University Press, 2012.

Shaw, Gregory. *Theurgy and the Soul: The Neoplatonism of Iamblichus*. University Park, PA: Pennsylvania State University Press, 1995.

Stead, Christopher. *Divine Substance*. Oxford: Oxford University Press, 1977.

2.3

Christian Platonism in the Medieval West

Lydia Schumacher

The history of Christian Platonism in the Middle Ages has been written many times before, from a number of different perspectives. In the past, it has tended to focus on the medieval reception of figures like Augustine and Dionysius, who represent its main channels of influence in this period.[1] As is well known, there was very little direct access in the Middle Ages to Plato's own works. For the most part, only his *Meno*, *Phaedo*, and *Timaeus* were available. Thus, the reception of Platonism has been bound inextricably to those Christian thinkers of late antiquity who were primarily responsible for the transmission of Platonic themes to the medieval west.

In addition to Augustine and Dionysius, numerous other works played a role in this process. Among them, the writings of Boethius were quite significant. His objective, short-changed by his untimely death, had been to translate the entire Greek philosophical corpus into Latin and to demonstrate the harmony of Plato and Aristotle. In addition, there was Calcidius' translation and commentary on Plato's *Timaeus*, completed around 321; Martianus Capella's (fl. 410–20) Platonic account of the seven liberal arts; and the writings of Macrobius, who flourished in the early fifth century.[2]

---

[1] Gerard O'Daly, *Platonism Pagan and Christian: Studies in Plotinus and Augustine* (Aldershot: Ashgate, 2001). John M. Rist, *Augustine: Ancient Thought Baptized* (Cambridge: Cambridge University Press, 1994). Stephen Gersh, *From Iamblichus to Eriugena: An Investigation of the Prehistory and Evolution of the Pseudo-Dionysian Tradition* (Leiden: Brill, 1978).

[2] On these authors and others, see Stephen Gersh, *Middle Platonism and Neoplatonism*, vol. 2: *The Latin Tradition* (Notre Dame: University of Notre Dame Press, 1994). See also Gersh, 'The First Principles of Latin Neoplatonism: Augustine, Macrobius, Boethius', *Vivarium* 50:2 (2012), 113–38.

Alongside Augustine, such texts formed the core of Platonic sources that were available to medieval Christian thinkers until the introduction of Dionysius in the ninth century – 862 to be exact – which is when John Scotus Eriugena translated his complete works from Greek into Latin, improving on a version produced by Hilduin only a generation earlier.[3] Dionysius worked in the late fifth or early sixth century to transform the pagan Neoplatonism of Plotinus and Proclus into a distinctly Christian form thereof. In the Middle Ages, he was ascribed virtually apostolic authority, given the widespread belief that he was a disciple of Saint Paul.

The standard tale of Christian Platonism in the Middle Ages has tended to start precisely with Eriugena's reception of Dionysius alongside Augustine.[4] In most cases, it moves on to treat the so-called School of Chartres of the twelfth century, which underwent a revival of interest in Platonic works to the extent they were available.[5] From this point, the story generally makes reference to the starkly divergent ways in which Platonism was incorporated by Franciscans and Dominicans – chiefly Bonaventure and Aquinas – in the high scholastic period of the mid-to-late thirteenth century, with Aquinas ultimately subjecting Platonic to Aristotelian interests.

Finally, reference is often made to Meister Eckhart (1260–1328), who represents the last major stop in the history of Platonic thought before the translation of Plato's works in the Renaissance.[6] Although interesting and important, this is not the story of Platonism that I want to tell in this context. A great deal of ink has already been spilt on the thinkers and schools mentioned immediately above. What I want to do, instead, is to describe another indirect channel of Platonic influence in the Middle Ages and in the high scholastic period specifically which has been almost completely uninvestigated hitherto.

---

[3] The form in which the Dionysian corpus was available is indicated by Henri F. Dondaine, *Le corpus Dionysien de l'Université de Paris au XIII siècle* (Rome: Edizioni di Storia e letteratura, 1953), 124. J. J. O'Meara, *Eriugena* (Oxford: Clarendon Press, 1988).

[4] Willemien Otten, 'Christianity's Content: (Neo)Platonism in the Middle Ages, Its Theoretical and Theological Appeal', *Numen* 63:2–3 (2016), 245–70.

[5] See a number of relevant entries in Peter Dronke (ed.), *A History of Twelfth-Century Philosophy* (Cambridge: Cambridge University Press, 1988). Richard Southern, *Platonism, Scholastic Method and the School of Chartres* (Reading: Reading University Press, 1979).

[6] An excellent example of the trajectory described above, from Augustine, through Dionysius, to Eckhart, is Denys Turner's *The Darkness of God: Negativity and Christian Mysticism* (Cambridge: Cambridge University Press, 1995). See also Thomas Finan and Vincent Twomey (eds.), *The Relationship Between Neoplatonism and Christianity* (Dublin: Four Courts Press, 1992).

This concerns the influence of Islamic readings of the Greek philosophical tradition on those who worked in the generation before
Bonaventure and Aquinas, during the very first years of the University
of Paris, which was the centre for theological study at the time. In this
connection, I will focus on figures who worked in the early Franciscan
school of thought, precisely because members of this school have been
widely regarded as the more 'Augustinian' and thus 'Platonic' of the two
schools – Franciscan and Dominican – that dominated high medieval
thought. Another reason for focusing on scholastics and indeed the
Franciscan school – as opposed to the forms of Christian Platonism
that were proffered by earlier figures based at Chartres, for instance –
is that this school had a lasting influence on the understanding of key
theological and philosophical topics that were debated in the Middle
Ages, and thereby, on the understanding of what Platonism in its various
forms – Augustinian, Dionysian, or otherwise – is all about.

This can not necessarily be said of earlier schools of Christian
Platonic thought in the medieval period. The works of Eriugena, for
one, were condemned in 1225 on grounds of pantheism and fell into
disrepute afterwards. Following the translation of the major works by
Aristotle and his Islamic counterparts in the late twelfth century,
moreover, Chartrian thought could not help but seem somewhat
elementary.

By examining the early Franciscan school specifically, consequently,
I aim not only to highlight how Islamic readings of Platonic sources
impacted the scholastic understanding of Platonism but also, potentially,
to propose a pathway for investigating how that understanding of
Platonism came to be passed on to subsequent generations.
Paradoxically, however, the place to look for the Latin conception of
Plato and by default Augustine, concerns the Latin conception of
Aristotle. In the period under consideration, this conception was directly
informed by Islamic interpretations of Aristotle.

That in turn was guided overwhelmingly by the belief that Plato and
Aristotle were in fundamental agreement. The result in the Arabic-
speaking and so by implication the Latin tradition was a deeply theological and thus Platonic reading of Aristotle which must be regarded as
a prime source for grasping the contours of Christian – not to mention
Islamic – Platonism in this period. Thus, we must turn to investigate the
means by which this Platonic account of Aristotle was transmitted to the
West via Islamic philosophy, before considering how the Islamic conception of Platonism infiltrated the Latin West in the early scholastic period.

THE TRANSMISSION OF GREEK PHILOSOPHY
TO THE ARAB WORLD

The tradition of commenting on Aristotle was instigated in the late third century by the great student of the Neoplatonist Plotinus, namely, Porphyry, who inherited the task of editing his teacher's *Enneads*. The goal of writing such a commentary as Porphyry's *Isagogue* was primarily to demonstrate the harmony of Aristotle with his own teacher Plato, at least as Plotinus understood him.[7] Porphyry was the one who included Aristotle's works in the Neoplatonic curriculum for the first time, setting a precedent whereby the Stagirite was studied as preparation for reading Plato.[8]

From that point forward, the trend in interpreting Aristotle was set, and Neoplatonists, especially in Alexandria, proceeded to articulate deeply Platonic positions through the genre of Aristotelian commentary. They did this, among other ways, by interpreting ambiguous aspects of Aristotle's thought in a distinctly Platonic way, or by foregrounding Platonic themes while jettisoning others. Among the more influential of these commentators in the Arabic world was John Philoponus. Philoponus was known by al-Kindi, who is rightly credited with establishing the Islamic tradition of philosophy or *falsafa* in the ninth century. This tradition turned primarily on appropriating the Greek philosophical tradition to the end of developing a rational theology, which did not derive specifically from the Koran but supposedly coincided perfectly with it.[9]

Like their Latin counterparts, however, Arab thinkers at this stage did not have much recourse to the works of Plato and Aristotle themselves.[10]

---

[7] George E. Karamanolis, *Plato and Aristotle in Agreement? Platonists on Aristotle from Antiochus to Porphyry* (Oxford: Oxford University Press, 2001).

[8] Cristina D'Ancona, 'Greek into Arabic: Neoplatonism in Translation', in *The Cambridge Companion to Arabic Philosophy*, ed. Peter Adamson and Richard Taylor (Cambridge: Cambridge University Press, 2006), 10–31 at p. 14.

[9] Emma Gannagé, 'The Rise of *Falsafa*: Al-Kindi (d. 873), On First Philosophy', in *The Oxford Handbook of Islamic Philosophy*, ed. Sabine Schmidtke and Khaled El-Rouayheb (Oxford: Oxford University Press, 2017), 30–62. See also Cristina D'Ancona, 'The Origins of Islamic Philosophy', in *The Cambridge History of Philosophy in Late Antiquity*, vol. 2, ed. Lloyd P. Gerson (Cambridge: Cambridge University Press, 2010), 869–93 at pp. 871–2.

[10] Gerard Endress, 'Building the Library of Arabic Philosophy: Platonism and Aristotelianism in the Sources of Al-Kindi', in *The Libraries of the Neoplatonists*, ed. Cristina D'Ancona (Leiden: Brill, 2007), 319–50. See also Franz Rosenthal, 'The Knowledge of Plato's Philosophy in the Islamic World', *Islamic Culture* 13:4 (1940), 387–422, see especially 393–5 where it is noted that they had excerpts of *Meno*, *Phaedo*, and *Timaeus*.

In the absence of other resources, Arabic knowledge of the Greek tradition was mediated primarily through Neoplatonic authors like Plotinus, whose *Enneads* were translated into Arabic in the circle of Kindi. Although Kindi himself did not know Greek, he served as the corrector for this work, which he took considerable liberties to interpret in a way that would render it intelligible to the Arabic-speaking world.[11] The result was the so-called *Theology of Aristotle,* in which Kindi construed Plotinus' doctrines particularly in books IV–VI of the *Enneads,* 'as the exposition genuinely made by Aristotle himself of the pinnacle of the *Metaphysics,* a work whose translation into Arabic was [also] commissioned by al-Kindi'.[12]

This attribution of an otherwise spurious work was justified insofar as Plotinus and to some extent Proclus came to Kindi under the name of Aristotle. The main teachings of these Neoplatonists had long been confused with the so-called 'unwritten doctrines' of the late Plato, which Aristotle had supposedly learned first-hand from his teacher. According to legend, Aristotle had decided in his old age to articulate and endorse these doctrines. That, at least, is how any discrepancies between Pseudo-Aristotle and Aristotle himself were explained away, paving the way for a Plotinian reading of Aristotle.

As the theological culmination of the Aristotelian corpus, the *Theology of Aristotle* laid the foundation for the more refined *Liber de causis,* which draws on the *Enneads* as well as the *Elements of Theology* by Proclus, which were also translated within the circle of Kindi.[13] While such compilations were the product of his team's editorial endeavours, Kindi nonetheless considered them emblematic of the philosopher's mature theological thought, on account of the allegedly Aristotelian texts on which they were based. Thus, they quickly became so closely associated with the Aristotelian tradition that later thinkers like al-Farabi (d. 951) and Avicenna (980–1037) apparently did not question their authenticity.[14]

---

[11] Peter Adamson, *Al-Kindi* (Oxford: Oxford University Press, 2006), 25.

[12] Cristina D'Ancona, 'The Theology Attributed to Aristotle: Sources, Structure, Influence', in *The Oxford Handbook of Islamic Philosophy,* ed. Sabine Schmidtke and Khaled El-Rouayheb (Oxford: Oxford University Press, 2017), 8–29.

[13] Cristina D'Ancona, 'The *Liber de causis*', in *Interpreting Proclus: From Antiquity to the Renaissance,* ed. Stephen Gersh (Cambridge: Cambridge University Press, 2014), 137–62.

[14] Robert Wiznovsky, 'Avicenna and the Avicennian Tradition', in *The Cambridge Companion to Arabic Philosophy,* ed. Peter Adamson (Cambridge: Cambridge University Press, 2004), 92–136 at pp. 97–8.

THE TRANSMISSION OF ARAB THOUGHT TO THE LATIN
WORLD

The reference to Avicenna brings us to the question of the means by which Arab *falsafa* was transmitted to the Latin world, for it was primarily through him that this occurred. Avicenna was without a doubt the greatest philosopher and scientist the Islamic tradition had produced to date. Although his works bore the same titles as Aristotle's, they were not mere commentaries and far surpassed anything Aristotle or any other thinker to that time had offered in terms of their philosophical sophistication and scientific resources.

Following the prior Arabic tradition, Avicenna harmonized his treatment of Aristotelian themes with certain Neoplatonic commitments, which he nonetheless parsed in what were ultimately unique and innovative ideas on metaphysics, psychology, and theology.

Despite the significance of Avicenna, standard accounts of Western intellectual history generally link the emergence of scholasticism in the early universities to the recovery of Aristotle's major works through the translation movement that spanned the latter half of the twelfth century and continued well into the thirteenth. During this period, and at least through the 1240s, however, access to Aristotle was limited and mitigated by various factors, and scholars had a somewhat confused idea of his thought.[15] This was partly due to reservations about the quality of the Greco-Latin translations; and partly to the wide circulation of spurious Aristotelian works like the *Liber de causis*. The Proclean sources of this work were not recognized until Aquinas read William of Morebeke's translation of the *Elements of Theology*, which was produced in 1268. Until this time, consequently, the *Liber* circulated under Aristotle's name and was regarded as the theological culmination of his *Metaphysics*.[16]

By many accounts, Aquinas also commissioned William in the 1250s and 60s to produce new and superior translations of Aristotle's entire corpus for his own benefit. By this point, the works of Averroes were also starting to be studied in earnest. As a genuine commentator on Aristotle, Averroes facilitated efforts which were now gaining momentum to

---

[15] Richard C. Dales, 'The Understanding of Aristotle's Natural Philosophy by the Early Scholastics', in *The Intellectual Climate of the Early University: Essays in Honor of Otto Gründler*, ed. Nancy van Deusen (Kalamazoo: Medieval Institute Publications, Western Michigan University, 1997), 141–50.

[16] Pasquale Porro, 'The University of Paris in the Thirteenth Century: Proclus and the *Liber de causis*,' in *Interpreting Proclus*, ed. Stephen Gersh, 264–98 at p. 276.

understand Aristotle on his own terms. Although his commentaries were introduced to Latin speakers around 1230, they were neglected for some time, perhaps because Latin thinkers did not quite know what to make of them, short of a clearer understanding of Aristotle himself.[17] Prior to the full-scale incorporation of Averroes and Aristotle from the 1250s, consequently, scholastics relied on Avicenna to interpret Aristotle and often described both interchangeably as 'the philosopher'.[18]

At the time, this was unexceptional, given that Avicenna's major works on the main topics of interest – such as metaphysics and psychology – had been translated in entirety into Latin before Aristotle's, between 1152 and 1166, and were more popular and attractive to Latin thinkers precisely because of the ways they advanced beyond Aristotle.[19] These factors fostered a habitual dependence upon Avicenna that proved difficult to discard, even after Aristotle's entire oeuvre became available in the first quarter of the thirteenth century. The ongoing proclivity for Avicenna was largely due to the Neoplatonic leanings of Latin thinkers themselves, which were passed down through the likes of Augustine and Dionysius, who had nonetheless not left behind treatises of comparable philosophical rigour to those of the Persian philosopher. In this context, Avicenna seemed to provide the optimal source for interpreting Christian Neoplatonic texts at the level of sophistication that was increasingly in demand. This is the very approach to reading traditional Western authorities, above all, Augustine, that was championed more than anywhere in the early Franciscan school.

For a long time, scholarship has operated on the assumption that early Franciscan scholasticism is little but an attempt to systematize the work of Augustine in an unoriginal way. The reason Franciscans took up this task, scholars like Étienne Gilson have surmised, was to give Augustine's legacy a chance of withstanding the competition posed by Aristotle, whose growing popularity in the early thirteenth century ultimately secured his

---

[17] Sander de Boer, The Science of the Soul: The Commentary Tradition on Aristotle's De anima c. 1260–1360 (Leuven: Leuven University Press, 2013), 17.

[18] Amos Bertolacci, 'On the Latin Reception of Avicenna's Metaphysics before Albertus Magnus: An Attempt at Periodization', in *The Arabic, Hebrew and Latin Reception of Avicenna's Metaphysics*, ed. Dag Nikolaus Hasse and Amos Bertolacci (Berlin: De Gruyter, 2012), 197–223. D. A. Callus, 'Introduction of Aristotelian Learning to Oxford', *Proceedings of the British Academy* 29 (1943), 229–81, 264–5.

[19] Dag. N. Hasse, *Avicenna's De Anima in the Latin West* (London: The Warburg Institute, 2000). See also Amos Bertolacci, 'A Community of Translators: The Latin Medieval Versions of Avicenna's Book of the Cure', in *Communities of Learning: Networks and the Shaping of Intellectual Identity in Europe 1100–1500*, ed. Constant J. Mews and John N. Crossley (Turnhout: Brepols, 2011), 37–54.

primacy in the generation of Aquinas and beyond.[20] According to Gilson, the appropriation of Avicenna was key to the Franciscans' efforts in this regard. In his view, Avicenna provided Franciscans with the philosophical resources to articulate what Augustine did not yet have the tools or impetus to say, yet which ultimately represented the mature statement of his thought.

Although it has remained popular, this view comes into doubt when we consider that Avicenna worked in a very different time period and religious context than Augustine, with objectives that had nothing to do with the systematization of Augustine.[21] While both Augustine and Avicenna were admittedly Platonists of a sort, it stands to reason that there are as many kinds of Platonism as there are Platonists. What might be described as traditionally Platonic themes can be extrapolated in such a great variety of ways, some utterly unrelated to or even incompatible with one another, that the meaning of the term ultimately breaks down. Paradoxically, the diversity amongst interpretations is fostered by the writings of Plato and Augustine themselves, which leave scope for very different readings, depending on which texts and topics are emphasized and how terms and arguments are elaborated. The upshot is that it is not legitimate to conflate Avicenna and Augustine on the basis of the fact that both were Platonists of some variety.

This does not seem to have mattered to early Franciscans, who justified their Avicennian renderings of Augustine on the basis of spurious works that were attributed to Augustine at the time, chiefly, the *De spiritu et anima*.[22] This text was actually written by a twelfth-century Cistercian and represents a compilation of wide-ranging schemata and sources that 'encouraged the conviction that virtually anything could in some way be connected with aspects of the doctor's theory of the soul',[23] including the ideas of Avicenna. As Bernard McGinn elaborates, 'the popularity of *The Spirit and the Soul* is at least partially explained by its association with currents of thought introduced by Arabic works'.[24] Although Philip the Chancellor and Albert the Great had already raised doubts about the

---

[20] Étienne Gilson, 'Les sources greco-arabes de l'augustinisme avicennisant', *Archives d'histoire doctrinale et littéraire du moyen age* 4 (1929), 5–107.

[21] The 'Avicennized Augustinianism' of Gilson is addressed and partly refuted by Dag. N. Hasse, *Avicenna's De Anima*, 224–34.

[22] Bernard McGinn (ed.), *Three Treatises on Man* (Kalamazoo: Cistercian Publications, 1977), 71.

[23] Bernard McGinn (ed.), *Three Treatises on Man*, 69.

[24] Bernard McGinn (ed.), *Three Treatises on Man*, 25.

work's authenticity, early Franciscans persisted in employing it to interpret Augustine, precisely on account of its amenability to an Avicennian
interpretation.[25]

By reading Augustine in an Avicennian way, they situated themselves at
the cutting edge of contemporary research, engaging with the most challenging and exciting new material. At the time, this show of academic
prowess was highly pertinent, given tensions that had arisen between the
Franciscans and other scholars in the university who felt that the religious
orders were usurping their authority and robbing them of their students
and thus their income. The full-scale incorporation of Avicennian philosophy proved they had both the intellectual resources and thus the right
to operate and indeed dominate in the university context.

In addition to this rather pragmatic reason for engaging with Avicenna,
early Franciscans had principled reasons as well. For there appears to have
been a sort of happy coincidence between the Avicennian materials that
were available and popular at the time and what was well-suited to
articulating a distinctly Franciscan form of thought, namely, one which
resonated with the charism of the order's founder, Francis of Assisi. As is
well documented, his memory was still fresh in the minds of many friars
who had known him before his death in 1226.[26] These same friars were
outspoken in their opposition to the high-level intellectual pursuits of
some of their academic confreres, which they regarded as illegitimate for
members of an order that was founded on the principles of poverty and
service to the poor. To articulate a system that exhibited at least some
correlation to the Franciscan ethos was therefore to alleviate to some
extent the concerns of these conservative friars.[27]

With these considerations in view, it is no wonder that, of all the
thinkers and schools of thought that interacted with Avicenna before the
1250s, the Franciscans did so most enthusiastically and in the most
concerted and comprehensive way. The main Dominican counterpart of
the Franciscans, Albert the Great, and even the early Aquinas, also naturally regarded Avicenna as a prime interlocutor. Yet they engaged with him
in a more critical and revisionist way that already edged towards a more
faithful incorporation of Aristotle. By contrast, the case studies below will

---

[25] Gabriel Théry, 'L'authenticité du *De spiritu et anima* dans Saint Thomas et Albert le
Grand', *Revue des sciences philosophiques et théologiques* 10 (1921), 373–7.
[26] Neslihan Senocak, *The Poor and the Perfect: The Rise of Learning in the Franciscan
Order 1209–1310* (Ithaca: Cornell University Press, 2012).
[27] Neslihan Senocak, *The Poor and the Perfect*, 143.

illustrate that early Franciscan readings of Aristotle, like those of Augustine, were thoroughly Avicennian in nature.

The tendency to read both of these sources through the same lens illustrates effectively the extent to which the founders of Franciscan thought had fully embraced the attitude they inherited through their own Western tradition, not least through Boethius, and more directly, through Avicenna himself, regarding the internal agreement of Platonism and Aristotelianism. Although the scholastics did not have access to the *Theology of Aristotle*, which was only translated into Latin in 1519, the full-scale absorption of its themes into the mindset of Avicenna could not help but influence them indirectly.[28] These Franciscans, chiefly, Alexander of Hales and John of La Rochelle, were happy to accept that Aristotle would have endorsed the highly idiosyncratic rendering of Platonic principles that Avicenna had to offer and that was so well fitted to the formulation of their own budding intellectual tradition.

This is laid down for the first time in the so-called *Summa Halensis*, which was a collaborative work on the part of the founders of the Franciscan school at Paris, above all John and Alexander.[29] The project of composing this Summa was initiated by Alexander himself on his entrance to the order in 1236, after a long career as one of the most distinguished and celebrated theologians at the University of Paris, which had only been founded officially around twenty years earlier. As a leading figure in this context, Alexander played the instrumental role in establishing the academic practices that would continue to define university education in theology into early modernity. For instance, he instigated the practice of lecturing not only on the Bible but also on the theological themes treated in Lombard's *Sentences*, thereby establishing in effect the university discipline of systematic theology.[30] He also was among the first to write a commentary on the *Sentences*. Although this activity was controversial at first, he soon established it as the precursor to obtaining what was effectively the doctoral degree in the medieval university.[31]

[28] Cristina D'Ancona, 'The Textual Tradition of the Graeco-Arabic Plotinus', in *The Letter Before the Spirit: The Importance of Text Traditions for the Study of the Reception of Aristotle*, ed. Aafke M. I. van Oppenraaii (Leiden: Brill, 2012), 37–71 at p. 46.
[29] Lydia Schumacher, *Early Franciscan Theology: Between Authority and Innovation* (Cambridge: Cambridge University Press, 2019).
[30] Philipp W. Rosemann, *The Story of a Great Medieval Book: Peter Lombard's Sentences* (Toronto: University of Toronto Press, 2007).
[31] Nancy Spatz, 'Approaches and Attitudes to a New Theology Textbook: The Sentences of Peter Lombard', in *The Intellectual Climate of the Early University* (Kalamazoo: Medieval Institute Publications, 1997), 27–52.

For a long time, the Summa that bears Alexander's name has been neglected on the basis of the aforementioned assumption that it is simply a rehearsal of Augustine, albeit with the help of Avicenna, and because of the difficulties in determining the precise author of each section. As the research of the Summa's editors has shown, however, John of La Rochelle likely completed volumes 1 and 3, and a student of Alexander composed volumes 2.1 and 2.2 on the basis of works by John and Alexander.[32] Together, these authors produced precisely what the Summa was intended from the start to be, namely, an internally consistent and doctrinally exhaustive account of the 'collective mind' of the early Franciscan school. This monumental text was received as such a coherent whole at the time of John and Alexander's deaths in 1245, upon which only the fourth volume on the sacraments remained to be completed, in 1255–6.[33]

In many respects, this Summa was the first great instalment in a genre that would quickly become a defining feature of scholasticism; it was completed twenty years before Thomas Aquinas even set his hand to the task of writing his magisterial *Summa Theologiae* and represents a structural and conceptual prototype for that work. A major reason why the size of the *Summa Halensis* mushroomed far beyond that of the few Summae that pre-date it is that it incorporated a comprehensive set of philosophical questions – mainly under the inspiration of Avicenna – into the scope of theological inquiry for the first time in intellectual history. Thus, the Summa was ultimately comprised of 3,408 questions where its most significant predecessor – the *Summa aurea* of William of Auxerre – includes only 808.[34]

The inclusion of so many philosophical questions is precisely the respect in which the *Summa Halensis* would set the agenda for much of subsequent scholastic debate. Later thinkers like Aquinas would be compelled to address many of those questions, even if they gave starkly different answers to them. Of course, Christian Platonic authorities like Augustine and Dionysius also feature in the work of Aquinas, whose

---

[32] Victorin Doucet, 'Prolegomena in librum III necnon in libros I et II *Summa Fratris Alexandri*', in *Alexandri de Hales Summa Theologica* (Quaracchi: Collegio S Bonaventurae, 1948); see also Doucet's 'The History of the Problem of the Summa', *Franciscan Studies* 7 (1947), 26–41, 274–312.

[33] The coherence of the work has been emphasized by Elisabeth Gössmann in *Metaphysik und Heilsgeschichte: Eine theologische Untersuchung der Summa Halensis (Alexander von Hales)* (Munich: Max Hueber, 1964).

[34] Ayelet Even Ezra, 'The *Summa Halensis*: A Text in Context', in *The Summa Halensis: Sources and Doctrines*, ed. Lydia Schumacher (Berlin: De Gruyter, 2020).

legacy, for better or worse, is often associated more closely with the genuine recovery of Aristotelian thought. However, the distinctive reception in his thought has been treated extensively already in other contexts.[35] As noted already, my aim here is to tell a story that has not yet been told about the development of Christian Platonism in the medieval school that has come to be most closely associated with it, that of the early Franciscans.

CHRISTIAN PLATONISM IN EARLY FRANCISCAN THOUGHT

The story of Platonism in the early Franciscan school normally begins with Bonaventure, who is widely regarded as its chief representative and the foremost 'Augustinian' and even 'Dionysian' of the period. As I have already hinted above, however, the generation that separates Bonaventure's teachers from Bonaventure himself and indeed from Aquinas made all the difference in terms of the constellation of sources and assumptions that prevailed. By the mid-thirteenth century, the work of Aristotle was coming to be understood in its own right, and that required Bonaventure to distance himself from the Stagirite where Alexander and John had invoked him, or rather the Avicennian reading of him, the deeply Neoplatonic flavour of which allowed for interpreting Christian Platonic sources like Augustine along Avicennian lines as well.

As Aristotle came to be regarded as a distinct thinker from Augustine and Avicenna, the Franciscans of the next generation came into the light as the more Platonizing thinkers that they always were. This, however, did not alter the basic features of the intellectual tradition that had already been founded in the *Summa Halensis* above all. This was a tradition in which ideas about what it means to be a Christian Platonist were forged in the course of the Avicennian reception that was undertaken in the first-generation school. Admittedly, Bonaventure does not often cite Avicenna by name, a practice which had fallen out of fashion by this time. However,

---

[35] Fran O'Rourke, *Pseudo-Dionysius and the Metaphysics of Aquinas* (South Bend: University of Notre Dame Press, 2006); Michael Dauphinias et al. (eds.), *Aquinas the Augustinian* (Washington, D.C.: The Catholic University of America Press, 2007). Wayne J. Hankey, 'Aquinas, Plato and Neoplatonism', in *The Oxford Handbook of Aquinas*, ed. Brian Davies (Oxford: Oxford University Press, 2012), 55–64. Patrick Quinn, *Aquinas, Platonism and the Knowledge of God* (Aldershot: Ashgate, 1996). David Burrell and Isabelle Moulin, 'Albert, Aquinas and Dionysius', *Modern Theology* 24:4 (2008), 633–49.

Avicenna's legacy lived on in the way that he and members of his school continued to interpret Christian Platonic sources and thereby elaborate the themes that had been initially laid out by their Franciscan forebears. In what follows, I would like to offer some examples of key ways that Franciscans before Bonaventure – and the authors of the *Summa Halensis* specifically – read Avicenna, Augustine, and Aristotle in more or less convertible terms. The first example is taken from what is often regarded as one of the hallmarks of Platonism, namely, body–soul dualism.

Body–Soul Dualism

This is a topic that Augustine had famously left unresolved, affirming in some places that the soul is intimately connected with the body, while suggesting elsewhere that it can be separated from it.[36] As McGinn claims, Augustine ultimately never managed to explain the relationship between the two and seems to have regarded it as something of a mystery.[37] As a result, this was one area where philosophical clarity was desperately needed, which Avicenna's philosophy assisted to provide. Famously, Avicenna regarded the body and the soul as two separate substances, the second of which goes on existing after the death of the body.[38] On his understanding, consequently, the relationship between the body and soul is purely accidental – it holds only temporarily, during this present life.

Although the soul itself is entirely simple, the body is comprised of its own kind of 'form of corporeity', printed on prime matter, which is what renders it a substance in its own right. By this account, therefore, the soul is not what makes the body a body but only what makes it actually living. The body is responsible for its own form.[39] In the Middle Ages,

---

[36] Bernard McGinn, 'Introduction', in *Three Treatises on Man*, 8; citing Augustine on the connection with the body, *De ordine* II.11.31, *De quantitatae animae* I.25.47, *De civitate dei* IV.13, and on the separation from the body: Augustine, *De quantitatae animae* I.13, 22; *De moribus ecclesiasticae catholicae* I.4.6 and I.27.52; *In Iohannes Evangelium* 19.5.15; *De civitate Dei* IX.9–10, X.6.

[37] Bernard McGinn, 'Introduction,' in *Three Treatises on Man*, 8.

[38] Bernardo Carlos Bazán, 'The Human Soul: Form and Substance? Thomas Aquinas' Critique of Eclectic Aristotelianism', *Archives d'histoire doctrinale et littéraire du Moyen Age* 64 (1997), 95–126 at p. 104. See also his article entitled, 'Pluralisme de formes ou dualisme de substances? La pensée pré-thomiste touchant la nature de l'âme,' *Revue philosophique de Louvain* 67 (1969), 30–73.

[39] *Avicenna Latinus: Liber de Anima seu Sextus de Naturalibus I–III*, ed. Simone Van Riet (Leiden: Brill, 1972), I.4.

Franciscans found this idea attractive because it allowed them to affirm
that the dead body of Christ was still his body. It also guaranteed the
resurrection of a person's self-same body at the end of time. The Halensian
Summist, following John of La Rochelle in his earlier *Summa de anima*,
enthusiastically adopted this position as an interpretation of Augustine.[40]

Since Augustine's own texts were so ambivalent on the matter, the
Summists turned instead to the pseudo-Augustinian texts which were
very clear in positing a substantial distinction between the soul and the
body. This is true not only of the *De spiritu et anima* but also of the
popular *De ecclesiasticis dogmatibus,* written by Gennadius Massiliensis
(d. 496), both of which are quoted in the early Franciscan context.[41] As
Magdalena Bieniak has shown, however, these scholars did not leave
Avicenna's doctrine entirely unamended. Rather, they supplemented it
with an idea from their Dominican contemporary Hugh of St Cher, who
argued that the body is in fact intrinsic to the substance of the soul, which
exhibits the quality of *unibilitas substantialis* or a substantial unitability to
the body.[42] This idea was crucial for affirming not only the resurrection of
the body but also the value of the human body as part of God's creation.
Although some scholastics before Hugh entertained a more purely
Avicennian idea of the body–soul relationship, they quickly realized that
this was out of step with their own Christian commitments.[43]

The account of this issue takes an interesting turn when the Halensian
Summists, following John, proceed to attribute an Avicennian account of
the body–soul relationship not only to Augustine but also to Aristotle.
This is particularly remarkable given that Aristotle seems to have
defended exactly the opposite position to Avicenna. On his account, the
soul is the form of the body, which implies both that the soul cannot exist
without a body – having a body is part of what it means to be human – and
that the soul ceases to exist at the death of the body. This is generally taken
to be the upshot of Aristotle's famous definition of the soul in *De anima*

---

[40] John of La Rochelle, *Summa de anima,* ed. Jacques Guy Bougerol (Paris: Vrin, 1995).

[41] Alexander of Hales, *Doctoris irrefragabilis Alexandri de Hales Ordinis minorum Summa
theologica,* 4 vols. (Quaracchi: Collegii S. Bonaventurae, 1924–48) = *SH* 2.1 In4, Tr1, S1,
Q3, Ti2, C1, Ar1, Contra a, b, 418. Richard C. Dales, *The Problem of the Rational Soul
in the Thirteenth Century* (Leiden: Brill, 1995), 4–5.

[42] Magdalena Bieniak, *The Soul-Body Problem at Paris* (Leuven: Leuven University Press,
2010), 26 on William of Auvergne, 33. Magdalena Bieniak, 'Una questione disputata di
Ugo di St Cher sull'anima edizione e studio dottrinale', *Studia Antyczne I Mediewistyczne*
37 (2004), 127–84 at p. 169.

[43] John of La Rochelle, *Summa de anima,* 52.

II.1, 412a18–19, which describes the soul as the 'form of the natural organic body having the potential for life'.[44]

In this period, scholars had available to them not only the translation of Aristotle from Greek but also the translation from Arabic. There was a slight discrepancy between the two translations in that the latter substituted the term 'perfection' for the term 'form' which was in the Greco-Latin original. This eased the way for early scholastics and indeed Franciscans to read Aristotle in line with Avicenna, who had used the term 'perfection' to explain his particular understanding of the soul's relationship with the body.[45] The discrepancy was by and large not lost on early scholastics, most of whom saw the tension between the two terms, namely, form and perfection. However, John of La Rochelle and the Summists following him found clever ways effectively to explain the problem away.

In his *Summa de anima,* John in one breath calls the soul both the form and the perfection of the body.[46] He justifies his use of technically contradictory terms by explaining that there are three different ways to understand a form.[47] The first kind of form, found for example in inanimate bodies like rocks, is totally supported by matter and does not rule or sustain it but is sustained by it. The second kind of form depends upon matter and rules it but can only operate through it, as in the case of plants and animals. According to John, however, the situation is entirely different for the human soul, interpreted as the form of the body. For although the soul rules its matter, which in turn depends upon it, its principal operation is not in matter but in itself, that is, in the work of the rational soul, the proper function of which is to abstract from matter.

For this reason, it is not contradictory to say that in this particular case, the form of the body is also a perfection which is by definition separable from the body. A variation on this same argument is subsequently presented in the *Summa Halensis* to justify the conflation of the terms 'form' and 'perfection'.[48] The example of the body–soul union nicely illustrates therefore how early Franciscans drew on Avicenna not only to interpret Augustine, or at least Pseudo-Augustine, but also to interpret Aristotle. In this example, we

---

[44] *Summa de anima,* 53, citing *De spiritu et anima* 6.
[45] Magdalena Bieniak, *The Soul-Body Problem at Paris,* 14.
[46] John of La Rochelle, *Summa de anima,* 126.
[47] John of La Rochelle, *Summa de anima,* 124–5.
[48] *SH* 2.1 In4, Tr1, S1, Q2, Ti1, C3, Ar1, Solution, 394.

have seen, Aristotle is pressed into affirming a quintessentially Neoplatonic idea of the body and soul as separate substances, which he himself did not affirm. As a result, he is rendered in agreement with Augustine, interpreted in line with Avicenna.

Divine Illumination

Another doctrine traditionally associated with Augustine and indeed the Franciscan tradition is that of the theory of knowledge by divine illumination.[49] On this topic, the Summa draws on the *De spiritu et anima* to explain how the mind acquires the resources from above to know things that are 'below', 'next to', and 'above' the self, namely, natural things, angels, and God, which are the objects of ratio, intellectus, and intelligentia, respectively. While an illumination from angels and God respectively is needed to know angels and God, which exceed the capacities of the mind, another kind of illumination is given by God, which allows the mind independently to cognize natural objects and even itself. The illumination in question takes the form of several innate transcendental concepts – first and foremost, being – and its properties, unity, truth, and goodness, which give the mind the resources to obtain accurate knowledge of beings.

This doctrine of transcendentals, mediated by Philip the Chancellor, derived first and foremost from Avicenna, whose famous expression, 'being is the first object of the intellect',[50] is explicitly quoted by the Summa.[51] Although Augustine himself did not articulate or affirm the idea of innate transcendental concepts, the Summa claims that he does on the ground of his argument that the image of God consists in an orientation to the 'first truth', or an interior 'intelligible light' that makes knowledge possible.[52] On this score, the Summa emphasizes that the concepts do not represent the content or objects of human knowledge as such, but

---

[49] Lydia Schumacher, Divine Illumination: The History and Future of Augustine's Theory of Knowledge (Oxford: Wiley-Blackwell, 2011).

[50] SH P1, In1, Tr3, Q1, M1, C1, Respondeo II, 113: 'Dicendum quod cum sit ens primum intelligibile eius intentio apud intellectum est nota' (Avicenna, Metaphysics I.6); 'primae ergo determinations entis sunt primae impressions apud intellectum eae sunt unum, verum, bonum'.

[51] Jan A. Aertsen, Medieval Philosophy as Transcendental Thought: From Philip the Chancellor to Francisco Suárez (Leiden: Brill, 2012), 112.

[52] See especially SH P1, In1, Tr3, Q1, C2, 113–15, quotations to Augustine's *83 Questions* 18, De Trinitate 6.10.12, De civitate Dei 11.28, De vera religione 3; cf. SH Tr Int, M II, C 4, Respondeo, p. 28.

rather the means by which the human mind is able accurately to grasp any ordinary being in terms of its identity, or what makes it one thing as distinct from others (one); intelligible as such (true); and thus, fit for a certain purpose (good). In these respects, the concepts allow the mind not only to know beings as God knows them, but also, through them, to catch a finite glimpse of the nature of God.

Although all knowledge is made possible by the illuminated concepts, the Summist recognizes that there is more to say about the mechanisms of obtaining such knowledge. To this end, the account of cognition in the Summa builds on John of La Rochelle's extensive treatment of this topic in the *Summa de anima*. In that text, John had lifted almost verbatim the theories of Avicenna on the human cognitive powers, especially internal sensation or imagination, and the work of the intellect itself. Dag Hasse has explained why John exhibited such a strong tendency to adopt Avicenna's theories on these matters: they were by far the most philosophically complex to date and had no rival in the Christian tradition.[53]

As regards internal sensation, which lays the groundwork for cognition, Avicenna holds that the common sense is that which receives forms imprinted by the five external senses and provides a unified picture of their different aspects.[54] The imagination retains those forms after they are no longer directly accessible by experience. The excogitative sense is able to compose and divide the different accidents attached to a given form. Estimation registers what is beneficial or harmful in the forms perceived, while the fifth internal sense of the memory apprehends and retains the product of estimation, that is, the intentions of sensible things, the images of things with their connotational attributes or positive or negative connotations. The *Summa Halensis* basically repeats this account of the internal senses.[55]

After detailing the work of each of these faculties, the Summa seeks to justify its interest in Avicenna in relation to Pseudo-Augustine as well as John of Damascus, the eighth-century Greek Church Father, who was increasingly regarded as a theological authority following the translation of his *De fide orthodoxa* in the mid-twelfth century. According to the Damascene, who is generally regarded as more Aristotelian than

---

[53] Dag Nikolaus Hasse, *Avicenna's De anima in the Latin West* (London: Warburg, 2001), 189–91.

[54] *Avicenna Latinus: Liber de Anima seu Sextus de Naturalibus IV–V*, ed. Simone Van Riet (Leiden: Brill, 1968), IV.1.

[55] *SH* 2.1, In4, Tr1, S2, Q1, C4, Ar1, I, 438.

Neoplatonist in his leanings, the Summa notes that there are three facets of
the sensitive soul, namely, imagination, excogitation, and memory.[56] The
imagination is located in the front of the brain and captures images of
sense objects apart from matter; the memory is in the back of the brain and
retains those images; the excogitative power is in the middle and composes
and divides different features of imaged objects.[57]

On this basis, the Summist concludes that the Damascene's three
powers basically perform the functions described by Avicenna in delineating his five internal senses. While his imagination performs an appre-
hending function, his excogitative faculty seemingly performs the
functions that could be attributed to the imaginative faculty and estimation, and his memory completes the work that is assigned to the phantasia and the sense memory.[58] This conclusion leads to a more general
question whether Avicenna's five-fold and Damascus' three-fold account
of the internal senses can both be contained under Pseudo-Augustine's
category of imagination.[59] Since this faculty deals broadly with sensible
forms absent matter, and the various faculties mentioned by John and
Avicenna do the same in different ways, supplementing Augustine with
Avicenna's complex theory in particular is perceived by the Summists as
entirely unproblematic.[60]

This account of the imagination leads naturally to a discussion of the
work of the intellect. In his *Summa de anima,* John of La Rochelle once
again unabashedly articulated a straightforwardly Avicennian theory on
this score, invoking Avicenna's signature doctrine of the four stages of
potential for knowing in the intellect.[61] The first so-called material intellect has the possibility of knowing all things. The second *intellect in effectu*
possesses the disposition to know which consists in the innate first principles of knowledge, or the transcendental concepts already mentioned.
The third is the *intellectus in habitu,* which has drawn conclusions from
those principles about actual realities, but is not considering them at the
moment. The fourth is *the intellectus adeptus,* which considers conclusions in fact.

---

[56] *Saint John Damascene, De fide orthodoxa: Versions of Burgundio and Cerbanus,* ed.
Eligius M. Buytaert (St Bonaventure: Franciscan Institute, 1955), II, 17, 19, 20.

[57] *SH* 2.1, In4, Tr1, S2, Q2, Ti1, M2, C1, b, 434, citing Avicenna's *De anima* IV.1 and IV.2.

[58] *SH* 2.1, In4, Tr1, S2, Q2, Ti1, M2, C4, A2, Solutio, 439.

[59] Bernard McGinn (ed.), *Three Treatises on Man,* 185.

[60] *SH* 2.1, In4, Tr1, S2, Q2, Ti1, M1, C2, Contra 1, 435.

[61] *SH* 2.1, In4, Tr1, S2, Q3, Ti1, M2, C4, Ar3, Ad objecta 3, 459. See also Avicenna, *De
anima* V.6.

Although Avicenna believed that the so-called active or agent intellect, which makes the work of the *intellectus adeptus* possible, was actually God, we have seen already that the Halensian Summists, following John, considered the human mind sufficient for obtaining natural knowledge on the basis of the transcendentals. For them, God is only agent intellect when the object of knowledge is God himself.[62] Whereas John simply laid out Avicenna's doctrine of the intellect in detail alongside the theories of the Damascene and Augustine, as if that alone was self-explanatory in terms of reconciling them, the Summa highlights all the conceivable points of contact between the three theories with the ultimate goal of showing that the pseudo-Augustinian notion of ratio provides a broad umbrella under which the schemes of Damascus and Avicenna can be incorporated to explain the knowledge of things below and including the self.

The Summa deals first with John of Damascus' four-fold scheme of intelligence, intention, excogitation, and phronesis. According to its interpretation, intelligence is the act of the intellectual power of grasping something; intention is intelligence about or understanding of something, excogitation is the preliminary movement of reason to gain understanding, and phronesis is the consequent movement of reason to draw a conclusion about what is to be understood.[63] The Summa basically disregards the meaning that the Damascene himself attributed to these terms in order to argue that they represent precisely the four acts performed by Avicenna's four intellects.[64]

Thus, the Summa redefines the meaning of intelligence so that it corresponds to the material intellect; intention to intellect in effect; excogitation to intellect in habit; and phronesis to *intellectus adeptus*.[65] Aristotle also finds a home in this picture, which represents a new development from John of La Rochelle, who does not mention the Stagirite. The ten or fifteen years between the time John wrote the *Summa de anima* and the early 1240s when the section in question of the *Summa Halensis* was probably written accounts for this difference, in that pressure was increasing by this time to engage with Aristotle, even though resources remained thin on the ground for doing so. In fact, the intellectual schema that the Summa attributes to Aristotle does not come from Aristotle at all.

[62] *Summa de anima*, 277–9. *SH* 2.1, In4, Tr1, S2, Q3, Ti1, M2, C1, Solutio III, 450. See also Lydia Schumacher, *Early Franciscan Theology*, 80–9.

[63] *SH* 2.1, In4, Tr1, S2, Q3, Ti1, M2, C4, Ar3, Ad objecta 2, 459.

[64] *SH* 2.1, In4, Tr1, S2, Q3, Ti1, M2, C4, Ar3, 458.

[65] *SH* 2.1, In4, Tr1, S2, Q3, Ti1, M2, C4, Ar3, Ad objecta 3, 459.

This scheme includes the material intellect, which in this context turns out to be another term for the imagination, or the power which procures that on the basis of which abstraction is performed, that is, an image of a sense object; the possible intellect, or the power that undertakes the process abstracting an image from all material conditions; and the agent intellect, which comprehends abstract forms or universals.[66] The source of this three-fold schema has been the focus of much debate of the past century, with some insisting it comes from a superficial reading of Averroes, whose works were introduced between 1225 and 1230.[67] However, that attribution is called into question by the fact that John of La Rochelle associated this scheme with Avicenna, who also did not adhere to it exactly. According to Bazán, the scheme of material-possible-agent intellect is in fact the unique product of early Latin scholastic attempts to synthesize the new natural philosophy.[68]

In this regard, it was not uncommon for scholastics like John to attribute to 'the philosopher' practically any view they found compelling. For them, the philosopher was more or less a construct whose presumed thought contained many authentic and accurate aspects of Avicenna's thought but was not entirely reducible to it and included insights from other thinkers as well. According to the Summa, the philosopher in question, presumably Aristotle, pursues with his three-fold scheme the intelligible forms of natural things that Pseudo-Augustine's faculty of ratio beholds. Within the pseudo-Augustinian framework, consequently, there is room not only for John of Damascus to be invoked as a means of smuggling Avicenna's doctrine of the four possible intellects into the picture, but also for an Aristotelian theory of the intellect which did not really belong to Aristotle at all. Ultimately, therefore, the Summa author manages to harmonize all of his sources and make them agree with or at least supplement on some level the work of the Pseudo-Augustine.

---

[66] *SH* 2.1, In4, Tr1, S2, Q3, Ti1, M1, C1, Solutio, 448:

[67] Dominique H. Salman, OP, 'Jean de La Rochelle et les débuts de l'Averroisme Latin', *Archives d'histoire doctrinale et littéraire du Moyen Age* (1947–8), 133–44 at p. 143; G. Théry, OP, *Autour du décret de 1210* (Paris: Bibliothèque thomiste, 1932), 81. Daniel A. Callus, 'The Powers of the Soul: An Early Unpublished Text', *Recherches de Théologie ancienne et médiévale* 19 (1952), 131–70 at p. 145.

[68] Bernardo Carlos Bazán, 'Was There Ever a First Averroism?' in *Geistesleben im 13. Jahrhundert*, ed. Jan A. Aertsen and Andreas Speer (Berlin: Walter de Gruyter, 2000), 31–53 at p. 36.

CONCLUSION

The early Franciscan examples of body–soul union and human psychology – two quintessentially Christian Platonic topics of inquiry – have highlighted the extent to which Avicenna informed readings of both Augustinian and Aristotelian sources, which were all perceived as compatible. Though no scholastic text can be reduced to the sum or function of its sources, I have been trying to suggest that understanding Avicenna's role in the development of early Franciscan readings of those sources is crucial to understanding not only the friars' true scholarly allegiances but also to appreciating how they departed from their tradition precisely in quoting its leading authorities.

For a fact, the examples given above call into question the longstanding notion that early Franciscans simply systematized or rehearsed ideas from Augustine and highlight instead how they employed Avicenna and Arabic philosophy to forge a completely new understanding of the bishop's thought. Although this version of Augustinianism was initially passed off as a reading of the Aristotelian tradition as well, it became disassociated with Aristotle as the next generation came to a more authentic understanding of the Greek philosopher's thought. By contrast, the Augustinianism invented by early Franciscans continued to be widely promulgated and defended for generations and thus impacted conceptions of Christian Platonism that remain influential to this day.

Bibliography

Adamson, Peter. *Al-Kindi*. Oxford: Oxford University Press, 2006.

Aertsen, Jan A. *Medieval Philosophy as Transcendental Thought: From Philip the Chancellor to Francisco Suárez*. Leiden: Brill, 2012.

Alexander of Hales. *Doctoris irrefragabilis Alexandri de Hales Ordinis minorum Summa theologica*, 4 vols. Quaracchi: Collegii S. Bonaventurae, 1924–48.

Avicenna Latinus: Liber de Anima seu Sextus de Naturalibus I–III, ed. Simone Van Riet. Leiden: Brill, 1972.

Avicenna Latinus: Liber de Anima seu Sextus de Naturalibus IV–V, ed. Simone Van Riet. Leiden: Brill, 1968.

Bazán, Bernardo Carlos. 'The Human Soul: Form and Substance? Thomas Aquinas' Critique of Eclectic Aristotelianism'. *Archives d'histoire doctrinale et littéraire du Moyen Age* 64 (1997): 95–126.

'Pluralism de formes ou dualism de substances? La pensée pré-thomiste touchant la nature de l'âme'. *Revue philosophique de Louvain* 67 (1969): 30–73.

'Was There Ever a First Averroism?' In *Geistesleben im 13. Jahrhundert*, ed. Jan A. Aertsen and Andreas Speer. Berlin: Walter de Gruyter, 2000.

Bertolacci, Amos. 'A Community of Translators: The Latin Medieval Versions of Avicenna's Book of the Cure'. In *Communities of Learning: Networks and the Shaping of Intellectual Identity in Europe 1100–1500*, ed. Constant J. Mews and John N. Crossley, 37–54. Turnhout: Brepols, 2011.

'On the Latin Reception of Avicenna's Metaphysics before Albertus Magnus: An Attempt at Periodization'. In *The Arabic, Hebrew and Latin Reception of Avicenna's Metaphysics*, ed. Dag Nikolaus Hasse and Amos Bertolacci, 197–223. Berlin: De Gruyter, 2012.

Bieniak, Magdalena. *The Soul-Body Problem at Paris*. Leuven: Leuven University Press, 2010.

'Una questione disputata di Ugo di St Cher sull'anima edizione e studio dottrinale'. *Studia Antyczne I Mediewistyczne* 37 (2004): 127–84.

Burrell, David and Isabelle Moulin. 'Albert, Aquinas and Dionysius'. *Modern Theology* 24, no. 4 (2008): 633–49.

Callus, Daniel A. 'Introduction of Aristotelian Learning to Oxford'. *Proceedings of the British Academy* 29 (1943): 229–81, 264–5.

'The Powers of the Soul: An Early Unpublished Text'. *Recherches de Théologie ancienne et médiévale* 19 (1952): 131–70.

Dales, Richard C. *The Problem of the Rational Soul in the Thirteenth Century*. Leiden: Brill, 1995.

'The Understanding of Aristotle's Natural Philosophy by the Early Scholastics'. In *The Intellectual Climate of the Early University: Essays in Honor of Otto Gründler*, ed. Nancy van Deusen, 141–50. Kalamazoo: Medieval Institute Publications, Western Michigan University, 1997.

D'Ancona, Cristina, 'Greek into Arabic: Neoplatonism in Translation'. In *The Cambridge Companion to Arabic Philosophy*, ed. Peter Adamson and Richard Taylor, 10–31. Cambridge: Cambridge University Press, 2006.

'The Liber de causis'. In *Interpreting Proclus: From Antiquity to the Renaissance*, ed. Stephen Gersh, 137–62. Cambridge: Cambridge University Press, 2014.

'The Origins of Islamic Philosophy'. In *The Cambridge History of Philosophy in Late Antiquity*, vol. 2, ed. Lloyd P. Gerson, 869–93. Cambridge: Cambridge University Press, 2010.

'The Textual Tradition of the Graeco-Arabic Plotinus'. In *The Letter Before the Spirit: The Importance of Text Traditions for the Study of the Reception of Aristotle*, ed. Aafke M. I. van Oppenraaii, 37–71. Leiden: Brill, 2012.

'The Theology Attributed to Aristotle: Sources, Structure, Influence'. In *The Oxford Handbook of Islamic Philosophy*, ed. Sabine Schmidtke and Khaled El-Rouayheb, 8–29. Oxford: Oxford University Press, 2017.

Dauphinias, Michael et al., eds. *Aquinas the Augustinian*. Washington, D.C.: The Catholic University of America Press, 2007.

de Boer, Sander. *The Science of the Soul: The Commentary Tradition on Aristotle's De anima c. 1260–1360*. Leuven: Leuven University Press, 2013.

Dondaine, Henri F. *Le corpus Dionysien de l'Université de Paris au XIII siècle*. Rome: Edizioni di Storia e letteratura, 1953.

Doucet, Victorin. 'The History of the Problem of the Summa'. *Franciscan Studies* 7 (1947): 26–41, 274–312.

'Prolegomena in librum III necnon in libros I et II *Summa Fratris Alexandri*'. In *Alexandri de Hales Summa Theologica*. Quaracchi: Collegio S Bonaventurae, 1948.

Dronke, Peter, ed. *A History of Twelfth-Century Philosophy*. Cambridge: Cambridge University Press, 1988.

Endress, Gerard. 'Building the Library of Arabic Philosophy: Platonism and Aristotelianism in the Sources of Al-Kindi'. In *The Libraries of the Neoplatonists*, ed. Cristina D'Ancona, 319–50. Leiden: Brill, 2007.

Even-Ezra, Ayelet. 'The *Summa Halensis*: A Text in Context'. In *The Summa Halensis: Sources and Doctrines*, ed. Lydia Schumacher. Berlin: De Gruyter, 2020.

Finan, Thomas and Vincent Twomey, eds. *The Relationship Between Neoplatonism and Christianity*. Dublin: Four Courts Press, 1992.

Gannagé, Emma. 'The Rise of *Falsafa*: Al-Kindi (d. 873), On First Philosophy'. In *The Oxford Handbook of Islamic Philosophy*, ed. Sabine Schmidtke and Khaled El-Rouayheb, 30–62. Oxford: Oxford University Press, 2017.

Gersh, Stephen. 'The First Principles of Latin Neoplatonism: Augustine, Macrobius, Boethius'. *Vivarium* 50, no. 2 (2012): 113–38.

From Iamblichus to Eriugena: An Investigation of the Prehistory and Evolution of the Pseudo-Dionysian Tradition. Leiden: Brill, 1978.

Middle Platonism and Neoplatonism, vol. 2: *The Latin Tradition*. Notre Dame: University of Notre Dame Press, 1994.

Gilson, Étienne. 'Les sources Greco-arabes de l'augustinisme avicennisant'. *Archives d'histoire doctrinale et littéraire du moyen age* 4 (1929): 5–107.

Gössmann, Elisabeth. *Metaphysik und Heilsgeschichte: Eine theologische Untersuchung der Summa Halensis (Alexander von Hales)*. Munich: Max Hueber, 1964.

Hankey, Wayne J. 'Aquinas, Plato and Neoplatonism'. In *The Oxford Handbook of Aquinas*, ed. Brian Davies, 55–64. Oxford: Oxford University Press, 2012.

Hasse, Dag. N. *Avicenna's De Anima in the Latin West*. London: The Warburg Institute, 2000.

John of La Rochelle. *Summa de anima*. Ed. Jacques Guy Bougerol. Paris: Vrin, 1995.

Karamanolis, George E. *Plato and Aristotle in Agreement? Platonists on Aristotle from Antiochus to Porphyry*. Oxford: Oxford University Press, 2001.

McGinn, Bernard, ed. *Three Treatises on Man*. Kalamazoo: Cistercian Publications, 1977.

O'Daly, Gerard. *Platonism Pagan and Christian: Studies in Plotinus and Augustine*. Aldershot: Ashgate, 2001.

O'Meara, J. J. *Eriugena*. Oxford: Clarendon Press, 1988.

O'Rourke, Fran. *Pseudo-Dionysius and the Metaphysics of Aquinas*. South Bend: University of Notre Dame Press, 2006.

Otten, Willemien. 'Christianity's Content: (Neo)Platonism in the Middle Ages, Its Theoretical and Theological Appeal'. *Numen* 63, nos. 2–3 (2016): 245–70.

Porro, Pasquale. 'The University of Paris in the Thirteenth Century: Proclus and the *Liber de causis*'. In *Interpreting Proclus: From Antiquity to the*

Renaissance, ed. Stephen Gersh, 264–98. Cambridge: Cambridge University Press, 2014.

Rist, John M. *Augustine: Ancient Thought Baptized*. Cambridge: Cambridge University Press, 1994.

Rosemann, Philipp W. *The Story of a Great Medieval Book: Peter Lombard's Sentences*. Toronto: University of Toronto Press, 2007.

Rosenthal, Franz. 'The Knowledge of Plato's Philosophy in the Islamic World'. *Islamic Culture* 13, no. 4 (1940): 387–422.

Saint John Damascene, De fide orthodoxa: Versions of Burgundio and Cerbanus. Ed. Eligius M. Buytaert. St Bonaventure: Franciscan Institute, 1955.

Salman, O.P., Dominique H., 'Jean de La Rochelle et les débuts de l'Averroisme Latin'. *Archives d'histoire doctrinale et littéraire du Moyen Age* (1947–8): 133–44.

Schumacher, Lydia. *Divine Illumination: The History and Future of Augustine's Theory of Knowledge*. Oxford: Wiley-Blackwell, 2011.

  Early Franciscan Theology: Between Authority and Innovation. Cambridge: Cambridge University Press, 2019.

Senocak, Neslihan. *The Poor and the Perfect: The Rise of Learning in the Franciscan Order 1209–1310*. Ithaca: Cornell University Press, 2012.

Spatz, Nancy. 'Approaches and Attitudes to a New Theology Textbook: The Sentences of Peter Lombard'. In *The Intellectual Climate of the Early University*, 27–52. Kalamazoo: Medieval Institute Publications, 1997.

Quinn, Patrick. *Aquinas, Platonism and the Knowledge of God*. Aldershot: Ashgate, 1996.

Southern, Richard. *Platonism, Scholastic Method and the School of Chartres*. Reading: Reading University Press, 1979.

Théry, Gabriel. *Autour du décret de 1210* (Paris: Bibliothèque Thomiste, 1932).

  'L'authenticité du *De spiritu et anima* dans Saint Thomas et Albert le Grand'. *Revue des sciences philosophiques et théologiques* 10 (1921): 373–7.

Turner, Denys. *The Darkness of God: Negativity and Christian Mysticism*. Cambridge: Cambridge University Press, 1995.

Wiznovsky, Robert. 'Avicenna and the Avicennian Tradition'. In *The Cambridge Companion to Arabic Philosophy*, ed. Peter Adamson, 92–136. Cambridge: Cambridge University Press, 2004.

Christian Platonism in Byzantium

Torstein Theodor Tollefsen

INTRODUCTION

Platonism in Byzantine Christianity is a complex topic. It must have been rather diverse traditions of Platonism that had an impact on Byzantine theologians. If we consider the three thinkers that are our main focus in this chapter, Dionysius the Areopagite, St Maximus the Confessor, and St Gregory Palamas, we may say that their writings seem to betray some knowledge of some of Plato's dialogues, some knowledge of what one calls Middle Platonism (*in casu* Philo), some knowledge of Neoplatonism (maybe Plotinus, definitely Proclus), and some knowledge of some of the commentators on Aristotle. Since the theologians seldom quote or mention any pagan thinkers by name, it is probably easier to identify influential Platonic ideas and doctrines than their exact sources, even though ideas do not live lives of their own but are found in human minds and committed to writing. Maybe we can say with Andrew Louth that Byzantine theologians witness to a 'diffused Platonism' to be distinguished from a 'formal Platonism'.[1] The 'diffused Platonism' is the Platonism of Christian thinkers who were not conscious of being Platonists, and who rather criticized 'the Greeks' for their false doctrines even if it is obvious that they had several notions in common with these 'Greeks'. Louth understands 'diffused Platonism' as 'the kind of Platonic notions that became part of the intellectual equipment of virtually any thinking Greek Christian'. Of such doctrines we could mention the idea of the radical transcendence of God,

---

[1] Andrew Louth, 'Platonism from Maximos the Confessor to the Palaiologian Period', in *The Cambridge Intellectual History of Byzantium*, ed. Anthony Kaldellis and Niketas Siniossoglou (Cambridge: Cambridge University Press, 2017), 325–40 at p. 325.

doctrines of providence, the doctrine of Forms – in late antiquity transformed into creative *logoi* in the mind of the Creator, the Plotinian doctrine of double activity,[2] the late antique doctrine of procession and conversion, notions of the human intellect and recollection. There are a lot of other, minor Platonic features that might be identified. One basic feature adopted by the Christians is the distinction between intelligible and sensible reality. St Gregory of Nyssa, for example, distinguishes between τὸ νοητόν (*to noêton*) and τὸ αἰσθητόν (*to aisthêton*) and describes how the higher world of intelligible reality is woven together with the lower world of sensible things into a harmonious cosmos.[3] He also distinguishes more specifically between divine knowledge of what might be created and the power and will that actually brought all beings into being.[4] Such a distinction combines a Platonic as well as a Christian motif into a unified philosophical vision, viz. (i) that God *knows* in His mind all Forms that are patterns of what is going to be created, but (ii) these Forms are not realized in a created realm before God actually *wills* them to be. Notions like these seem to be established as parts of a general outlook of Byzantine Christian thought. In addition to this 'diffused Platonism' there is a more defined notion of Platonism, a 'formal Platonism': 'those who adhered to this would call themselves "Platonists"'.[5] Our concern here is 'diffused Platonism', the Christian Platonism of a few important Byzantine thinkers, theologians, and philosophers, who would not have called themselves Platonists.[6] In addition to the three mentioned above, I shall also have a few things to say about John Philoponus and John of Damascus.

DIONYSIUS THE AREOPAGITE (EARLY SIXTH CENTURY)

In the beginning of the sixth century an unknown author published four treatises and ten letters under the pseudonym of 'Dionysius the Areopagite'.

---

[2] For double activity, see Eyjolfur K. Emilsson, *Plotinus* (London: Routledge, 2017), 48–57 and Torstein T. Tollefsen, *Activity and Participation in Late Antique and Early Christian Thought* (Oxford: Oxford University Press, 2012), 21–2, 47–8, 69–70.

[3] Gregory of Nyssa, *Oratio catechetica*, GNO iii.iv, 21–2.

[4] Gregory of Nyssa, *In hexaemeron*, GNO iv.i, 14–15.

[5] Louth, 'Platonism', 325 and 327.

[6] Maybe Eric D. Perl, *Theophany: The Neoplatonic Philosophy of Dionysius the Areopagite* (Albany: State University of New York Press, 2007), would disagree that Dionysius represent 'diffused Platonism'. He interprets Dionysius' thought within the framework of Platonic and especially Neoplatonic philosophy. Even if I am not convinced about all aspects of his interpretation I find his approach highly stimulating.

The four treatises are *The Divine Names, The Mystical Theology, The Celestial Hierarchies,* and *The Ecclesiastical Hierarchies.* The pseudonym is taken from St Paul's convert from Athens, according to Acts (17:34): 'However, some men joined him and believed, among them Dionysius the Areopagite, a woman named Damaris, and others with them.' For centuries it was held that this historical Dionysius was the author of the writings. When it was established that the author could not be a figure of the Apostolic age scholars added a 'pseudo' to his name and he became Pseudo-Dionysius. Early in the twentieth century scholars tried to figure out who was the real author behind what many now considered a forgery. Later research moved away from this and tried to approach the writings from another angle: to look at the Dionysian corpus as a forgery would only lead to a dead end and one should rather ask why the unknown author chose to write under this particular pseudonym. I believe this approach is the right one and the best key to evaluate the writings.

How should we then understand the pseudonym? 'Dionysius the Areopagite' most probably links this person to Athens and Athens means, as Louth says, philosophy or ancient wisdom, especially Plato.[7] There is more to this. Acts (17:22–3) tells the following story:

Paul then stood up in the meeting of the Areopagus and said: 'Men of Athens! I see that in every way you are very religious. For as I walked around and looked carefully at your objects of worship, I even found an altar with this inscription: to an unknown God. Now what you worship as something unknown I am going to proclaim to you.'

One reasonable implication of this Pauline background is that our anonymous author, in imitation of St Paul, is willing to proclaim his Christian doctrine within the context of genuine philosophical lore of old. Dionysius has therefore applied certain Pauline linguistic usages as vehicles to bring in both terminological and structural devices from Neoplatonist philosophy in order to expand his Christian world-view. The Pauline usages I refer to are *prepositional constructions* that in early Christian thought developed into a 'metaphysics of prepositions'.[8] The following Pauline texts are relevant in this connection:

For from him (ἐξ αὐτοῦ, *ex autou*) and through him (δι᾽ αὐτοῦ, *di autou*) and to him (εἰς αὐτὸν, *eis auton*) are all things. To him be glory for ever! Amen. (Rom. 11:36)

---

[7] Andrew Louth, *Denys the Areopagite* (Wilton: Morehouse-Barlow, 1989), 10.
[8] I borrow this term from Dillon (who borrowed it from Theiler). See John Dillon, *The Middle Platonists* (London: Duckworth, 1977), 138.

Yet for us there is but one God, the Father, from whom (ἐξ οὗ, *ex hou*) all things came and for whom (εἰς αὐτόν, *eis auton*) we live; and there is one Lord, Jesus Christ, through whom (δι᾽ οὗ, *di hou*) all things came and through whom (δι᾽ αὐτοῦ, *di autou*) we live. (1 Cor. 8:6)

He is the image of the invisible God, the firstborn over all creation. For by him (ἐν αὐτῷ, *en autô*) all things were crated: things in heaven and on earth, visible and invisible, whether thrones or powers or rulers or authorities; all things were created by him (δι᾽ αὐτοῦ, *di autou*) and for him (εἰς αὐτόν, *eis auton*). He is before all things, and in him (ἐν αὐτῷ, *en autô*) all things hold together. (Col. 1:15–17)

Dionysius' *The Divine Names* abounds in the application of such prepositional phrases that obviously have a Pauline background.[9] These phrases are not just an insignificant detail of his vocabulary. They rather serve as tools to expand a rudimentary Pauline theological cosmology into a Byzantine Christian cosmology using Neoplatonist terms and conceptual devices. We return to this below.

Dionysius' philosophical inspiration should be sought in fifth-century CE Athens. In the nineteenth century scholars like Koch and Stiglmayr showed that Dionysius is to some degree influenced by the Neoplatonist Proclus.[10] In the twentieth century this verdict has been further documented. The Neoplatonist school of Athens had since the middle of the fifth century been increasingly dominated by the towering figure of Proclus who had joined the school around 450 as Syrianus' pupil. We may gather from several sources that by the end of the fifth century an intellectual clash took place between Christianity and Neoplatonism. Proclus died in 485. At that time his pupil Ammonius had already returned to his native Alexandria. Between 485 and 487 Zacharias of Gaza, later the bishop of Mytilene, stayed in Alexandria and became Ammonius' pupil. Zacharias' dialogue *Ammonius*, in which the philosopher, the teacher of Philoponus and Simplicius, plays a part, shows what the tension and conflict between Christianity and Neoplatonism concerning cosmology was about.[11] Proclus had taught that the cosmos is

---

[9] Cf. *DN* 1.5; 2.1; 4.4; 4.10; 5.5; 9.8–9; 9.10; 11.5; 13.3; see Pseudo-Dionysius Areopagita, *De divinis nominibus*, ed. Beate R. Suchla (Berlin: Walter de Gruyter, 1990), respectively: 117, 124, 148, 154–5, 184, 212–13, 214, 221, 228. (There may even be more.)

[10] Hugo Koch, 'Proclus als Quelle des Dionysius Areopagita in der Lehre vow Bösen', *Philologus* 54 (1895): 438–54; Joseph Stiglmayr, "Der Neuplatoniker Proclus als Vorlage des sogenannten Dionysius Areopagita in der Lehre vom Übel', *Historisches Jahrbuch* 16 (1895): 253–73 and 721–48.

[11] Cf. Aeneas of Gaza: *Theophrastus* with Zacharias of Mytilene: *Ammonius*, translated by Sebastian Gertz, John Dillon, and Donald Russell (London: Bloomsbury, 2012); Michael

everlastingly created and has no temporal beginning a definite number of time-units ago. Zacharias, however, following mainstream Christian doctrine of fourth-century theologians like St Basil, argues that the cosmos definitely has a temporal beginning. Given this intellectual situation it is remarkable to find in Dionysius a Christian thinker who shows his willingness to develop his Christian outlook in Proclean terminology and to be vague indeed in the presentation he gives of creation. One has to wonder what on earth was his agenda.[12]

The Divine Names gives the impression that the world has no temporal beginning and is everlasting since it results from the being of the Creator and not from any particular act of divine choice:

> For even as our sun without calculating or choosing but by its very being (αὐτῷ τῷ εἶναι, *autô tô einai*) enlightens all things that in accordance with their logos are able to participate of its light, so too the Good, which as archetype transcends the obscure image of the sun, by its existence alone (αὐτῇ τῇ ὑπάρξει, *autê tê hyparxei*), sends to all beings proportionally the rays of its whole Goodness.[13]

The point is, in short, that God, being eternally good, has, eternally, contemplated the making of the cosmos in His own mind. Therefore, what is eternally contemplated is eternally (or, better, everlastingly) executed. This is very similar to what Proclus says about the Creator. In his commentary on Plato's *Parmenides* he says that God 'creates by his very being (αὐτῷ γὰρ τῷ εἶναι δημιουργεῖ, *autô gar tô einai dêmiourgei*)'.[14] Creating in that way, the product, i.e. the cosmos, exists everlastingly.

According to Dionysius creatures exist by *participation* in God, that is, figuratively speaking, in the 'rays' of God's goodness, not in the transcendent divinity as such. Once again he applies Proclean concepts when he distinguishes between the unparticipated cause, the participations, and the participants (ὁ ἀμέθεκτος αἴτιος, αἱ μετοχαί, τὰ μετέχοντα, *ho amethektos*

W. Champion, *Explaining the Cosmos* (Oxford: Oxford University Press, 2014); PG 85: 1012–1144.

[12] Christian Schäefer, *The Philosophy of Dionysius the Areopagite* (Leiden and Boston: Brill, 2006) says: 'For the inner structure of *DN* displays the entire ontological development around which the philosophy of the Areopagite revolves' (p. 23). I agree with Schäefer and therefore the following exposition is mainly built on *DN*.

[13] *DN* 4.1, Dionysius, *De divinis nominibus*, ed. Suchla, 144. For a fuller argument for this interpretation, cf. Torstein T. Tollefsen, 'The Doctrine of Creation according to Dionysius the Areopagite', in *Grapta poikila II. Saints and Heroes* (Helsinki: Papers and Monographs of the Finnish Institute at Athens, vol. 14, 2008), 75–89.

[14] Proclus, *In Platonis Parmeniden commentaria*, ed. Carlos Steel (Oxford: Oxford University Press, 2007), vol. 1, 762; cf. 786 (αὐτῷ τῷ εἶναι ποιεῖ τὸ ποιοῦν, *autô tô einai poiei to poioún*); 791 (αὐτῷ τῷ εἶναι, *autô tô einai*).

aitios, hai metochai, ta metechonta).[15] God as the unparticipated cause transcends all properties we may understand but even so manifests Himself 'externally' in the so-called 'rays'. There is no participation in God as such but only in what God manifests out of Himself.[16] The participants partake of these 'rays' as participations, 'what is shared' of God.

The sun sends out its rays of light and figuratively speaking God also manifests His 'rays', viz. *processions* (πρόοδοι, *proodoi*) like goodness and beauty, being, life, and wisdom.[17] Goodness is the basic procession and permeates (διήκει, *diêkei*) to all creatures from the highest to the lowest.[18] According to Dionysius all processions seem to be contained in goodness and may therefore be conceived as specifications of it.[19] Goodness extends to beings and non-beings, being extends to all beings, life to all living things, and wisdom to intellectual and rational beings, i.e. angels and humans. At this point we should note what seems to be a difference between Proclus' and Dionysius' thought. This difference is probably due to Dionysius' Christian presuppositions. According to Proclus it is *creatures* that eternally remain, proceed, and convert in relation to their causes.[20] An entity *remains* in its cause in the sense that its properties pre-exist in a more perfect condition there. It *proceeds* in order to be separated in relation to its cause, and it *converts* in order to be constituted as a complete entity on the level immediately below its cause. According to Dionysius the processions are not stages in the emergence of creatures as such but are powerful manifestations (δυνάμεις, *dynameis*) of the transcendent God. These manifestations are deifying, being-making, life-giving, wisdom-giving, and so on.[21] Proclean processions culminate in the establishment of divine entities in a hierarchical system. Dionysius, however, denies that processions like goodness, being, life, and wisdom are to be understood as separate hypostases or divinities in such a system.[22] He even considers it stupid and a sign of lack of knowledge to hold the divine processions, like being itself, life itself, and wisdom itself (τὸ αὐτοεῖναι, ἡ

---

[15] DN 12.4, Dionysius, *De divinis nominibus*, ed. Suchla, 225; cf. Proclus, *The Elements of Theology*, translation, introduction, and commentary by Eric R. Dodds (Oxford: Clarendon Press, 1963, reprinted 2004), Proposition 23.

[16] For an interesting interpretation of the similar doctrine in Proclus, cf. Perl, *Theophany*, 22–4.

[17] Cf. DN 5.6, and 7, Dionysius, *De divinis nominibus*, ed. Suchla, 184–5.

[18] DN 4.4, Dionysius, *De divinis nominibus*, ed. Suchla, 147.

[19] DN 5.1, Dionysius, *De divinis nominibus*, ed. Suchla, 180.

[20] Proclus, *The Elements of Theology*, Proposition 35 in Proclus, ed. Dodds.

[21] DN 5.1, Dionysius, *De divinis nominibus*, ed. Suchla, 180; 2.7, ibid, 131.

[22] DN 5.2, Dionysius, *De divinis nominibus*, ed. Suchla, 181.

αὐτοζωή, ἡ αὐτοσοφία, *to autoeinai, hê autozôê, autosophia*), to be divinities engaged in the making of the cosmos.[23] Of course, terminology like this, strongly reminiscent of the Platonic tradition, needs to be explained or made precise if one wants to avoid misunderstandings. It seems clear, however, that for Dionysius being itself, life itself, and so on are not to be understood as some kind of substantial entities or Platonic Forms, but rather as God's powers, activities, or processions. It seems probable that Dionysius' critical remarks springs from his Christian convictions and are directed against certain aspects of Proclus' Neoplatonic system that are not acceptable from a Christian point of view.

We have seen that Dionysius often applies the terminology of procession. As a matter of fact the Neoplatonist and Proclean triad of remaining, procession, and conversion is basic to his thinking even if adapted to his own specific ends.[24] As I remarked above, for the Christian Dionysius there is a Pauline background that facilitates the importation of this Neoplatonic triad to the system, viz. St Paul's prepositional constructions. Dionysius amplifies the 'from which' into the concept of procession and the 'to which' into conversion.[25] He develops the 'in which' into the idea of remaining. The Pauline phrase ἐν ᾧ τὰ πάντα συνέστηκεν (*en hô ta panta sunestêken*, 'in which all things hold together') is interesting.[26] The verb συνίστημι (*synistêmi*) means preserve, keep together. It seems reasonable to think that Dionysius expresses the same idea when he says God 'is all things as the cause of all things, and holding together and pre-possessing (συνέχων καὶ προέχων, *synechôn kai proechôn*) in Himself all principles, all limits of all beings'.[27] With this idea of *remaining* in God we find an ancient Platonic doctrine, viz. the doctrine of Forms: God keeps together all the principles that *constitute* created being before the making of the cosmos, and at the same time He *delimits* them in their relatedness to one another.[28]

Dionysius designates these principles as paradigms and pre-existing logoi that are unified in God.[29] These paradigms or logoi are also called

---

[23] *DN* 11.6, Dionysius, *De divinis nominibus*, ed. Suchla, 221–3.

[24] For the elaboration of this triad, cf. *DN* 4.7, Dionysius, *De divinis nominibus*, ed. Suchla, 150–3.

[25] *DN* 4.4, Dionysius, *De divinis nominibus*, ed. Suchla, 147–8. As documented in note 9 above, 'Dionysius' alludes to this Pauline usage in several places.

[26] Cf. Col. 1:17.

[27] *DN* 5.8, Dionysius, *De divinis nominibus*, ed. Suchla, 187. Cf. Maximus, *Ambiguum* 7, PG 91: 1081a.

[28] Cf. *DN* 9.8–9, Dionysius, *De divinis nominibus*, ed. Suchla, 212–13.

[29] *DN* 5.8, Dionysius, *De divinis nominibus*, ed. Suchla, 188. Cf. Maximus, *Ambiguum* 7, PG 91: 1080a and 1085a.

predeterminations (προορισμοί, *proorismoi*) and divine and good wills (θεῖα καὶ ἀγαθὰ θελήματα, *theia kai agatha thelêmata*) that are being-making or essence-making: 'in accordance with these the supra-essential [i.e. God] predefined and produced all things'. How shall we understand the relation between God's activities or processions of goodness, being, and so on, and these paradigms or predeterminations? One possible interpretation is that the latter are the delimiting principles in accordance with which God creates beings and hence is participated in as manifested goodness, being, life, wisdom, and so on. In that case, the paradigms or predeterminations predetermine the *degree* in which the divine is present in creatures. Founded on these paradigms God makes an ordered and hierarchical cosmos of intellects, souls, irrational souls, growing and moving things, and soulless substances, or, in other terms: angels, human beings, animals, plants, and lifeless things.[30]

We find in Dionysius an author who expands his Christian convictions into a philosophical system in the Platonic tradition. The Platonic doctrines he makes room for are terminologically and conceptually mainly inherited from Athenian Neoplatonism.[31]

FROM DIONYSIUS TO ST MAXIMUS

If we judge from authors like Aeneas of Gaza, Zacharias of Mytilene, and Procopius, there were rising tensions between Christians and pagans in the Middle East and Egypt over cosmological matters in the last decades of the fifth and the first decades of the sixth century.[32] One of the main issues was the temporal beginning of the world. For this reason it is somewhat strange that Dionysius expresses himself so vaguely on the doctrine of creation, and that he leaves the impression that there is no temporal beginning of the cosmos. The case of John Philoponus (*c.* 490–*c.* 575) is, maybe, even stranger. The literary remains suggest that there were two phases in his intellectual life: a first phase in which he acted mainly as an Aristotelian commentator in accordance with the outlook of his teacher Ammonius, Proclus' pupil from Athens, and a second phase in which he came out defending Christian cosmology and acted as a theological

---

[30] *DN* 4.2 and 8.4–5, Dionysius, *De divinis nominibus*, ed. Suchla, 145–6, 201–2.

[31] The main argument for a Proclean 'influence' on Dionysius in Koch and Stiglmayr was his obvious dependence on Proclus for his doctrine of evil in *DN* 4.18–34. See the introduction in Proclus, *On the Existence of Evils*, translated by Jan Opsomer and Carlos Steel (London: Bloomsbury, 2013).

[32] For these three authors, see Champion, *Explaining the Cosmos*.

writer.[33] I shall not try to speculate over the personal reasons for the change but only mention that despite the difference between the doctrines put forward in these two phases, there are some Platonic elements that linger on from the first to the second period.

In his first period Philoponus expressed the view that the cosmos is everlasting due to the eternal activity of God: fire has the power to heat and has not the power not to heat, likewise snow cools and has not the power not to cool, and God has the power to make good things and has not the power not to make.[34] The sun is the natural image of the first cause: the sun transcends all things enlightened by it and the first cause transcends all things that participate in its good-making activity in proportion to measure.[35] This last recalls my interpretation of Dionysius' saying about proportionate reception above. The cosmos is made on the foundation of Platonic Forms that exist in the mind of the Maker as logoi.[36] In the sixth century Philoponus turned to defending Christianity against the cosmology of Neoplatonism. He published two books against Proclean and Aristotelian cosmology: *Against Proclus On the Eternity of the World* (528) and *Against Aristotle On the Eternity of the World* (the 530s).[37] In these works he attacked the doctrine of an everlasting world, argued for a temporal beginning and the corruptible character of the cosmos. He retained the doctrine that God is a creator from eternity and that the world was made from pre-existing logoi in the divine mind. However, that God is a Creator from eternity does not mean that He creates eternally. Philoponus holds that there is a distinction between the logoi as what God knows and the same logoi as God's principles of making. The transition from the first to the second is not a movement or change in God, but takes place instantaneously.[38]

---

[33] Cf. Koenraad Verrycken, 'John Philoponus', in *The Cambridge History of Philosophy in Late Antiquity*, vol. 2, ed. Lloyd P. Gerson (Cambridge: Cambridge University Press), 733–55 and Theresia Hainthaler, 'John Philoponus, Philosopher and Theologian in Alexandria', in *Christ in Christian Tradition*, vol. 2, part 4, ed. Aloys Grillmeier with Theresia Hainthaler (London: Mowbray, 1996).

[34] Philoponus, *In Aristotelis categorias commentaria*, CAG XIII, ed. Adolfus Busse (Berlin: Georg Reimer, 1898), 145.

[35] Philoponus, *In Aristotelis physicorum libros tres priores commentaria*, CAG XVI, ed. Hieronymus Vitelli (Berlin: Georg Reimer, 1887), 163.

[36] Philoponus, *In Aristotelis de anima libros commentaria*, CAG XV, ed. Michael Hayduck (Berlin: Georg Reimer, 1897), 37.

[37] Both are translated in the Ancient Commentators on Aristotle series.

[38] Cf. Philoponus, *De aeternitate mundi contra Proclum*, ed. Hugo Rabe (Hildesheim: Georg Olms Verlagsbuchhandlung, 1963), 61–3.

Did Philoponus change his mind and decide to become explicit on cosmological matters due to local controversy? At any rate some time before 529 he sets his philosophical resources to defending his Christian convictions. It is rather striking that at the beginning of the sixth century Dionysius is vague and Philoponus seems non-committed but later he becomes very committed on this issue. However that may be, Dionysius' influence in general, though not his doctrine of creation, stretches to major Byzantine theologians like St Maximus the Confessor and St Gregory Palamas. Now we turn to Maximus.

ST MAXIMUS THE CONFESSOR (580–662)

Dionysius is at least one source of Maximus' Platonism. Other influences are Platonic features in writings from earlier Christian tradition, from the time of Origen onwards. There are also some features of Middle Platonic and Neoplatonic doctrines including the tradition of the Aristotelian commentators, but in general it is difficult to identify exactly from which sources they stem and whether Maximus in fact knew such material first hand. We know for certain, however, that Maximus read and utilized Nemesius of Emesa's *De natura hominis*. Nemesius was a Christian bishop who lived between the end of the fourth century and the early fifth century. *De natura hominis* shows that he knew philosophical traditions, especially Platonism, well.

Maximus' divinity, like the divinity of Dionysius, overflows – to put it metaphorically – with creative power or activity. Creatures participate in this activity in accordance with the receptive capacity defined by logoi. We return to Maximus' doctrine of the logoi below. He distinguishes between participable beings (τὰ ὄντα μεθεκτά, *ta onta methekta*) and participating beings (τὰ ὄντα μετέχοντα, *ta onta metechonta*).[39] The participable beings are also called 'works that He [i.e. God] did not begin to create' and participating beings are 'works He began to create'. This terminology of beginningless ἔργα θεοῦ (*erga theou*) and beginningless ὄντα (*onta*) is surprising and daring. We would immediately think of them as creatures, but they cannot be this since Maximus says they are not created. Further, he obviously does not speak of certain entities that exist in an ideal realm 'between' God and creatures, but rather of something that God 'gives off', like the processions in Dionysius. God, Maximus says, transcends these 'works of God' and 'beings':[40] 'God is infinitely many removes from all beings, both participating and participated.'

---

[39] *Th.oec.* 1.48, PG 90: 1100c.   [40] Ibid, 1.49, PG 90: 1101a.

These distinctions recall the distinctions made by Dionysius and Proclus between the unparticipated cause, the participations, and the participants. Maximus presents several lists of such participations.[41] Important items in these lists are being, goodness, life, wisdom, virtue, and holiness. Being and goodness seem to be the basic features of God's manifestations. In some places these items are called God's ἰδιώματα (*idiômata*, properties).[42] As 'properties' they are attributes and not *essential* features of God Himself. God, as we saw, transcends all the so-called participations.

Maximus' Christian philosophy is developed as a vision of the whole cosmos as centred in Christ, the Logos of God, the second hypostasis of the Holy Trinity. I have therefore (in an earlier publication) described his world-view as a Christocentric cosmology.[43] Maximus worked a detailed doctrine of divine Ideas or Forms into this Christocentric cosmology, calling them logoi. One might even say that this doctrine of his is the most detailed doctrine of such Forms in the whole of mainstream late antique Christian thought. The doctrine of logoi is the most perspicuous Platonic element of his thinking and it is a thorough Christianized version of the doctrine of transcendent Forms. Among other Platonic features of Maximus' thinking are his doctrine of providence and certain elements of his anthropology, especially his doctrine of the human intellect (νοῦς, *nous*) that is defined in the context of an already established Christian tradition on the subject.

One could claim that Maximus' conception of reality is basically in the Platonic tradition except for the fact that he teaches the 'recent' creation of the cosmos,[44] has a clear teaching on God's will to create for the sake of His creatures, and a doctrine of divine intervention in the world through a threefold Incarnation. We return to this below. The cosmos owes its being to one, transcendent source and is because of the logoi a unified totality in its relation to this source. This unification is secured both metaphysically and historically. The late antique Platonic doctrine of Forms in the mind of God is transformed into a doctrine of the one Logos who multiplies Himself into many logoi at the making of the world, i.e. in its procession (πρόοδος, *proodos*) from God, and who

---

[41] Ibid, 1.48, PG 90: 1100c; 1.49.50, PG 90: 1101a–b; *Car.* 1.100, PG 90: 981d–984a; *Car.* 3.25, cf. 3.27, PG 90: 1024b-c and 1025a; *Car.* 2.52, PG 90: 1001b.

[42] *Car.* 3.25, cf. 3.27, PG 90: 1024b-c and 1025a; *Car.* 2.52, PG 90: 1001b.

[43] Cf. Torstein T. Tollefsen, *The Christocentric Cosmology of St Maximus the Confessor* (Oxford: Oxford University Press, 2008).

[44] *Car.* 4.5, PG 90: 1048d.

again draws the multiplicity of logoi into the unity of the one Logos in the conversion (ἐπιστροφή, *epistrophê*) to God.[45] The one becomes many and the many becomes one in the two cosmic 'movements' that surrounds the whole cosmic drama. Just as the Logos somehow incarnates Himself in the universals and particulars of the created realm, He also incarnates Himself in the words of Holy Scripture, obviously in the more or less hidden *meanings* of the Scriptures, and eventually He incarnates Himself historically as Jesus Christ.[46] Both cosmological and historical features and events are unified in the one Logos in this world-view. Cosmos or nature and history are linked together in the Logos as the principle of one providential, divine plan.

How should these logoi be understood more precisely? What exactly are they and how do they function cosmologically both in procession and conversion? In *Chapters on Love* Maximus says that 'when the Demiurge willed, He manifested that knowledge of created beings which eternally pre-existed in Him'.[47] This eternal knowledge of beings is the sum of logoi. There are logoi of universals and particulars, logoi, that is, of all particulars, species, and genera of natural kinds of substances.[48] As in Philoponus, these logoi have two aspects: they are on the one hand what God the Logos eternally knows, i.e. principles of knowing, and on the other hand they are acts of divine will when God decides to create the different entities, i.e. principles of making.[49] The point of this distinction is to clarify that even if God knows eternally the essential nature of substances, it does not follow that these substances exist eternally: the creative process is not similar to the sun's heating or the snow's production of cold as if there was some kind of immediate ontological and eternal relationship between condition and conditioned.

As principles of making the logoi are denoted in accordance with what Dionysius says in *The Divine Names*:[50] 'St Dionysius the Areopagite teaches us that Scripture calls these logoi "predeterminations" and "divine wills".' Dionysian philosophy lacks a context for adding any real significance to these wills as intended and focussed divine *decisions*, while Maximus, on the other hand, stresses the importance of the divine decision.

---

[45] *Ambiguum* 7, PG 91: 1081b–c.
[46] Ibid, 7, PG 91: 1084c–d; *Ambiguum* 33, PG 91: 1285c–1288a.
[47] *Car.* 4.4, PG 90: 1048d. Cf. *Ambiguum* 7, PG 91: 1081a.
[48] Cf. the whole of *Ambiguum* 41, PG 91, especially 1312d–1313b.
[49] *Ambiguum* 7, PG 91: 1081a–b.   [50] Ibid, 7, PG 91: 1085a.

The logoi, therefore, function as that on the basis of which God with purpose directs His creative power to the instantaneous making of the cosmos. However, the logoi have a couple of additional functions to play: they are not just constitutive of essences, they also prescribe the natural movement or behaviour of entities. Finally they even define a possible development of natural beings so that these may transcend their naturally defined limits into the transfigured way of being called deification. Maximus therefore distinguishes a triadic structure in each logos: the logos of being, the logos of well-being, and the logos of eternal well-being.[51]

It was said above that there are logoi of particulars as well as of universals. As a matter of fact, even universals are created beings.[52] The logoi prescribe (predefine) not only the essence of particulars but the essential natures of the total cosmic order. In this order particulars are gathered into species and species into genera until everything is circumscribed in the highest or most basic genus of created being.[53] I call this cosmic arrangement *holomerism* from the Greek words for whole (ὅλος, *holos*) and part (μέρος, *meros*). This well-ordered world mirrors the world-order as conceived in God's eternal mind. All creatures are fitted together into an original harmonious whole of natural movement and development.

What ontological status do created universals have? How do they exist? There is obviously a kind of ontological realism here. On the one end of the scale one has the divine plan of the eternal logoi that defines what exactly it means to be this particular entity and this particular *kind* of entity. God defines the kinds and God keeps the whole together in its natural arrangement. On the other end of the scale, in the realm of created beings, particular creatures are, ontologically speaking, constituted in such a way that they are internally related: a particular human is, qua human being, ontologically related all other humans. The particular human is further a 'mammal', an 'animal', and so on. These universals really exist in the structure of particulars.

The All, the universe, therefore, is a unified whole in its logoi as well as in its actual whole-part arrangement. Such a unified arrangement follows from the Platonic as well as the Christian principles on which Maximus builds. The 'prepositional metaphysics' from St Paul, mentioned above, plays an important role in the development of Maximian philosophy as

<hr />

[51] Ibid, 7, PG 91: 1084a–d.   [52] Ibid, 7, PG 91: 1080a.   [53] Ibid, 10, PG 91: 1177b–d.

well. That the cosmos is not particularly harmonious or peaceful is due to the fall of Adam and Eve. The human fall has disturbed the natural order of beings and because of it corruption and death are introduced in the world. The original metaphysical arrangement of the cosmos has, however, built into it an internal medium of healing: human nature.[54]

Human nature is made as a kind of centre of created being. In its ontological structure the human being is a microcosm since its own essence relates it to all levels of the created cosmos, to intellectual beings like the angels, to sentient animals, vegetative plants, and the minerals. There is something of everything in every human being. For this reason God the Logos becomes incarnate in human nature. The incarnate Logos is an interesting phenomenon: humanely speaking He is ontologically related to all creatures and divinely speaking He is the one who contains the whole cosmic plan eternally in Himself (the one Logos is many logoi). Christ is, therefore, the perfect microcosm and mediator.

It is interesting to see that, according to Maximus, the whole world is kept together in its order by one unifying principle: the Logos. The Logos interconnects all things metaphysically or cosmologically and historically, in creation as well as in redemption. There is, consequently, one bond that unites all: God.

ST GREGORY PALAMAS (1296–1359)

The Platonism of Dionysius and Maximus left its traces on the further development of Byzantine theology. Meyendorff calls Maximus the real founder of Byzantine theology, since it is through his system that 'valid traditions from the past found their legitimate place'.[55] Maximus' writings, however, were found hard to understand. Anna Comnena, for instance, says they are highly contemplative and theoretical.[56] Even so Maximus' had a definite impact on Palamas' theology if not in all then at least in some aspects of the latter's thought.

With Gregory Palamas we encounter a prominent representative of Byzantine mysticism. He may in a way be seen as the culmination of a long spiritual tradition of 'hesychasm' in Byzantium that has received much attention in the twentieth century. The main issue of the hesychast

---

[54] Cf. *Ambiguum* 41, PG 91.

[55] John Meyendorff, *Christ in Eastern Christian Thought* (New York: St Vladimir's Seminary Press, 1975), 131–2.

[56] Anna Comnène, *Alexiade* (Paris: Société d'édition "Les Belles lettres", 1967), book 5.9.3.

controversy in the early fourteenth century was the possibility of seeing the light of the divinity itself. According to Palamas, this light is a divine activity or operation (ἐνέργεια, *energeia*). Divine activities are certain powers (δυνάμεις, *dynameis*) that are deifying, essence-making, life-making, and giving wisdom (ἐκθεωτικὰς ἢ οὐσιοποιοὺς ἢ ζωογόνους ἢ σοφοδώρους, *ektheôtikas ê ousiopoious ê zôogonous ê sophodôrous*).[57]

Even if Palamas utilizes both Dionysius and Maximus in the defence of his position on the spiritual life, there are not many traces of Maximus' detailed cosmology to be found. As with Dionysius and Maximus, God is radically transcendent: 'For if God is nature, other things are not nature, but if each of the other things is nature, He is not nature: just as He is not a being, if others are beings; and if He is a being, the others are not beings.'[58] Even so beings exist by *participation* in God, not in His nature, but in His *activity*.[59] These activities are processions.[60] As such they are μετοχαί (*metochai*), participations, something shared, something partaken. Here we have a word with the same conceptual sense as Maximus' ὄντα μεθεκτά (*onta methekta*), 'partcipated beings'. However, Palamas does not seem to distinguish between these participations on the one hand and logoi on the other. The participations are said to be paradigms of beings pre-existing in a transcendent unity in God. (This reflects Maximus' idea that the one Logos is many logoi in the act of creation, and the many are one in the conversion.) He follows Dionysius (and Maximus) in referring to these paradigms as logoi, predeterminations, and acts of will. However, Palamas shows little interest in developing these notions further into something similar to a detailed Dionysian or Maximian cosmology.

What has made Palamas renowned is his spiritual or mystical theology, and in this we find features that may be said to be a flowering of a Christian Platonic tradition.[61] Palamas' *Triads in Defence of the Holy Hesychasts* was written in connection with the so-called hesychast controversy. We shall not go into any details on the controversy as such. In the *Triads* two approaches to the knowledge of God are put in opposition to one another, the one is 'scientific' ('the outside wisdom') while the other is

---

[57] Gregory Palamas, *Triads*, 3.2.11; critical text in Grégoire Palamas, *Défence des saints hésychastes I–II*, ed. Jean Meyendorff (Louvain: Spicilegium Sacrum Lovaniense, 1959).

[58] Palamas, *Capita 150*. 78; critical text in Gregory Palamas, *The One Hundred and Fifty Chapters*, critical edition, translation, and study by Robert E. Sinkewicz (Toronto: Pontificial Institute of Mediaeval Studies, 1988).

[59] Palamas, *Capita 150*.78.   [60] Palamas, *Capita 150*.87.

[61] See Louth, Origins *of the Christian Mystical Tradition* (Oxford: Clarendon Press, 1981).

experiential. He repudiates the first and defends the last that is the hesy-chast approach.[62] The opponents of hesychasm are said to teach that the logoi of created beings are contained in God as creative Nous. The human soul contains images (εἰκόνες, *eikónes*) of these logoi that we should try to understand by the use of philosophical methods. We have already met a similar Platonizing doctrine of creative logoi in God in Dionysius, Philoponus, and Maximus. The notion of images of such logoi in the soul looks very Platonic indeed and reminds one of Plato's theory of recollection (ἀνάμνησις, *anámnêsis*). One should expect Palamas to reject such a teaching outright but in effect he accepts it: there are images of the logoi in the human soul. How should we understand this?

In Plato's *Meno*, Socrates puts forward the theory of learning as recol-lection in order to solve a dilemma: how can we learn what we do not know?[63] The answer is that we have in fact some kind of knowledge since the soul exists forever and has seen all things but when incarnated in a particular body it seems to forget what it knew. The remedy for this is the Socratic elenchus that dialectically helps to uncover what has been buried in forgetfulness.

Of course, Palamas does not endorse any doctrines of pre-existence or everlastingness of the soul, nor of transmigration. His notion seems to be that God has left some images in the soul of the principles behind the created cosmos. This is probably because the human being is made an intellectual being in the image of God. Contemplation of these images contributes to the path towards deification. At this point it might be relevant to mention that according to St Maximus, natural contemplation is one of the stages on the way to regeneration and deification. Maximus' natural contemplation is a contemplation that is free from passionate relationship to created things. One so to say 'sees' the cosmos in the light of the divine plan of the logoi. This is maybe what Palamas has in mind as well: only the purified soul can contemplate these images of the logoi in the mind. The key to gaining access to these logoi is therefore not secular learning, but *prayer*. Interestingly enough, this idea echoes a Platonic motif: the soul needs to be purified in order to contemplate truth in the eternal Forms.

---

[62] 'The outside wisdom' is also called 'Greek learning' and is presented as some kind of secular learning. See Grégoire Palamas, *Défence des saints hésychastes I–II*, ed. Jean Meyendorff (Louvain: Spicilegium Sacrum Lovaniense, 1959), 4–7, translation in Saint Gregory Palamas, *The Triads: Book One*, trans. Robin Amis (Wellington, Somerset: Praxis Institute Press, 2002), 31–2.

[63] *Meno*, 80d–81e.

As in Platonic recollection, the purpose of Palamite recollection is to rid the soul of 'the shadows of ignorance'.[64] Both Plato as well as Palamas think that evil is (at least partly) due to ignorance. Palamas makes a distinction between the hesychast exhortation 'be attentive to yourself' and the admonition of secular philosophy 'know yourself'.[65] The context seems to be a critique of Proclus since Palamas brands the false doctrine of transmigration and those who say that knowledge of one's true self can only be obtained through the evil spirit. What is hidden behind this epithet is probably one of the demoniac entities in the Proclean cosmic building that could support the soul in its search for its true self. According to Palamas, knowledge of one's true self is obtained in what he calls the *circular* movement of the mind.[66] In this movement the mind comes back to itself from its observation of external things, becomes aware of itself, and transcends itself in ecstasy.[67] However, the ecstasy is not yet union with God, since this is fulfilled when the Holy Spirit illuminates the mind form above. In this illumination one is ravished in the contemplation of divine light. Palamas has a most daring description of this deified condition:[68] 'Those who attain it become uncreated, unoriginate and uncircumscribed, although in their own nature they derive from nothingness.'

How should this last saying be understood? Within the context of Palamas' thought it cannot mean that the human essence is transformed into the divine essence in such a way that human hypostases become additional hypostases of the Trinity. Its sense must be sought in Palamas' idea that creatures are transformed or glorified by participating in the natural *activity* that is manifested out of God's being.[69] Since God's activity is uncreated, unoriginate, and uncircumscribed, beings that become fit to receive this activity participate in these same characteristics.

What we touch upon in these last paragraphs is the Byzantine doctrine of deification. It is well known that Plato lets Socrates say in the *Theaetetus* that evils cannot be done away with. He continues:[70] 'Therefore we ought to try to escape from earth to the dwelling of the gods as quickly as we can; and to escape is to become like God (ὁμοίωσις θεῷ, *homoíôsis theó*), so far as this is possible; and to become like God is to become righteous and holy and wise.' In the Byzantine Christian

[64] *Triads* 1.1.4.   [65] Ibid, 1.1.10.   [66] Ibid, 1.2.5.   [67] Ibid, 2.3.35.   [68] Ibid, 3.1.31.
[69] On this topic, cf. Torstein T. Tollefsen, *Activity and Participation*.
[70] *Theaetetus*, 176a–b.

tradition, however, the notion of deification is developed on the basis of scriptural sources into a common doctrine among the Church Fathers.[71] Dionysius says:[72] 'Deification (θέωσις, *théôsis*) is the attaining of likeness to God and union with Him so far as is possible.' The history of the idea of deification culminates in the spiritual theology of St Gregory Palamas: deified human beings do not participate in the essence of God but in His manifested, powerful activities.

CONCLUSION

Louth says in a recent article on Platonism in Byzantium that 'Platonism in the Byzantine intellectual world is omnipresent',[73] I believe this is correct. One finds not only a 'Christian Platonism' but also sporadically a more philosophical or humanist interest in Platonic tradition. However, the latter has not been the topic of the present chapter. Culturally speaking, Platonism had a great impact on late antique and Byzantine culture. Theologically speaking, one may detect Platonist features in a lot of late antique and Byzantine theological thinkers but the three main figures treated in this chapter left the most influential and lasting traces in the theological traditions of the East.

Bibliography

Aeneas of Gaza: Theophrastus with Zacharias of Mytilene: Ammonius. Translated by Sebastian Gertz, John Dillon, and Donald Russell. Ancient Commentators on Aristotle. London: Bloomsbury, 2012.

Anna Comnène. *Alexiade.* Paris: Les Belles Lettres, 1967.

Champion, Michael W. *Explaining the Cosmos.* Oxford: Oxford University Press, 2014.

Dillon, John. *The Middle Platonists.* London: Duckworth, 1977.

Emilsson, Eyjolfur K. *Plotinus.* London: Routledge, 2017.

Gregory Palamas. *Défence des saints hésychastes I–II.* Introduction, critical text, translation, and notes by Jean Meyendorff. Louvain: Spicilegium Sacrum Lovaniense, 1959.

---

[71] There is an excellent study of this tradition, viz. Norman Russell, *The Doctrine of Deification in the Greek Patristic Tradition* (Oxford: Oxford University Press, 2009).

[72] *De ecclesiastica hierarchia* 1.3, cf. Pseudo-Dionysius Areopagita, *De coelesti hierarchia, De ecclesiastica hierarchia, De mystica theologia, Epistulae,* Corpus Dionysiacum II, ed. Günter Heil und Adolf Martin Ritter (Berlin: Walter de Gruyter, 1991), 66.

[73] Louth, 'Platonism', 325.

The One Hundred and Fifty Chapters. Critical edition, translation, and study by Robert E. Sinkewicz. Toronto: Pontifical Institute of Mediaeval Studies, 1988.

The Triads: Book One. Translated by Robin Amis. Wellington, Somerset: Praxis Institute Press, 2002.

The Triads. Translated with an introduction by John Meyendorff. Classics of Western Spirituality. London: Paulist Press, 1983.

Gregory of Nyssa. *In hexaemeron*. Gregorii Nysseni Opera (GNO) iv.i. Leiden: Brill, 2009.

Oratio catechetica. Gregorii Nysseni Opera (GNO) iii.iv. Leiden: Brill, 1996.

Hainthaler, T. 'John Philoponus, Philosopher and Theologian in Alexandria'. In *Christ in Christian Tradition*, ed. Aloys Grillmeier with Theresia Hainthaler vol. 2, part 4. London: Mowbray, 1996.

Koch, Hugo. 'Proclus als Quelle des Dionysius Areopagita in der Lehre vow Bösen', *Philologus* 54 (1895): 438–54.

Louth, Andrew. *Denys the Areopagite*. Wilton: Morehouse-Barlow, 1989.

The Origins of the Christian Mystical Tradition. Oxford: Clarendon Press, 1981.

'Platonism from Maximos the Confessor to the Palaiologian Period'. In *The Cambridge Intellectual History of Byzantium*, ed. A. Kaldellis and N. Siniossoglou, 325–40. Cambridge: Cambridge University Press, 2017.

Maximus the Confessor. *On Difficulties in the Church Fathers: The Ambigua*. Edited and translated by Nicholas Constas. Cambridge, MA and London: Dumbarton Oaks Medieval Library, 2014.

Selected Writings. Translation and notes by George C. Berthold. New York: Paulist Press, 1985.

Meyendorff, John. *Christ in Eastern Christian Thought*. New York: St Vladimir's Seminary Press, 1975.

Patrologiae cursus completus, series graeca, Maximus the Confessor vols. 90–1. Ed. J. P. Migne. Paris: 1860; republished Turnhout: Brepols, 1983.

A Study of Gregory Palamas. New York: St Vladimir's Seminary Press, 1964.

Perl, Eric D. *Theophany. The Neoplatonic Philosophy of Dionysius the Areopagite*. Albany: State University of New York Press, 2007.

Philoponus. *De aeternitate mundi contra Proclum*. Edited by Hugo Rabe. Bibliotheca Teubneriana. Hildesheim: Georg Olms Verlagsbuchhandlung, 1963.

In Aristotelis categorias commentaria. Edited by Adolfus Busse. Commentaria in Aristotelem Graeca XIII. Berlin: Berolini, 1898.

In Aristotelis de anima libros commentaria. Edited by Michael Hayduck. Commentaria in Aristoteles Graeca XV. Berlin: Berolini, 1897.

In Aristotelis physicorum libros tres priores commentaria. Edited by Hieronymus Vitelli Commentaria in Aristotelem Graeca XVI. Berlin: Berolini, 1887.

Procli In Platonis Parmenidem commentaria I–III. Edited by Carlos Steel. Oxford: Oxford University Press, 2007–9.

Proclus. *The Elements of Theology*. Translation, introduction, and commentary by Eric R. Dodds. Oxford: Clarendon Press, 1963, reprinted 2004.

On the Existence of Evils. Translated by Jan Opsomer and Carlos Steel. London: Bloomsbury, 2013.

Pseudo-Dionysius Areopagita. *De coelesti hierarchia, De ecclesiastica hierarchia, De mystica theologia, Epistulae.* Ed. Günter Heil und Adolf Martin Ritter. Corpus Dionysiacum II. Berlin: Walter de Gruyter, 1991.

De divinis nominibus. Edited by Beate R. Suchla. Corpus Dionysiacum I. Berlin: Walter de Gruyter, 1990.

Russell, Norman. *The Doctrine of Deification in the Greek Patristic Tradition*. Oxford: Oxford University Press, 2009.

Schäfer, Christian. *The Philosophy of Dionysius the Areopagite*. Leiden and Boston: Brill, 2006.

Stiglmayr, Joseph, 'Der Neuplatoniker Proclus als Vorlage des sogenannten Dionysius Areopagita in der Lehre vom Übel'. *Historisches Jahrbuch* 16 (1895): 253–73, 721–48.

Tollefsen, Torstein Theodor. *Activity and Participation in Late Antique and Early Christian Thought*. Oxford: Oxford University Press, 2012.

The Christocentric Cosmology of St Maximus the Confessor. Oxford: Oxford University Press, 2008.

'The Doctrine of Creation according to Dionysius the Areopagite'. In *Grapta poikila II, Saints and Heroes*. Papers and Monographs of the Finnish Institute at Athens, vol. XIV Helsinki: Foundation of the Finnish Institute at Athens, 2008, 75–89.

Verrycken, Koenraad. 'John Philoponus'. In *The Cambridge History of Philosophy in Late Antiquity*, vol. 2, ed. Lloyd P. Gerson, 733–755. Cambridge: Cambridge University Press, 2010.

2.5

Renaissance Christian Platonism and Ficino

Stephen Gersh

Marsilio Ficino (1433–1499) is undoubtedly the paradigm of a "Renaissance Platonist." As the first translator of the complete works of Plato and Plotinus and individual works by Porphyry, Iamblichus, Proclus, and other late ancient Platonists into a western language (i.e. Latin), Ficino has a unique status in the philological and humanistic studies of his era. As the author of extensive *argumenta* ("analyses") and commentaries on Plato, Plotinus, and Dionysius the Areopagite, he holds an equally important position as the initiator of a variety of Christian Platonism that flourished alongside the institutional Aristotelianism of the universities and survived at least in northern Europe well into the seventeenth century. Ficino's Christian Platonism, which is the subject of this chapter, is characterized by two overriding features. First, it is expressed in works that are elaborated along traditional medieval lines in the form of commentaries either standing alone or incorporated into writings in other genres. Second, the configuration of this Platonism is inseparable from the history of Platonism as a tradition embodying both a continuous progress towards the light and a rhythmic alternation of revelation and concealment.[1]

In the proem to his *Platonic Theology: On the Immortality of the Soul,*[2] Ficino explains why he is writing a "theology," why this theology is

---

[1] James Hankins, *Plato in the Italian Renaissance.* 2 vols. (Leiden: Brill, 1990) includes the best general survey of Ficino's work as a "Renaissance Platonist." See especially his discussions of Ficino's Platonic canon (306–311); his methods of translating Plato (311–318); his styles of commentary on Plato (318–341).

[2] Ficino, *Platonic Theology* I, pr. 2–3 (eds. Allen and Hankins).

"Platonic," and why it is subtitled "On the immortality of the soul." He answers these questions by noting that the ancient Greek philosopher Plato was accustomed to turning every subject including ethics, dialectic, mathematics, and physics into theology. Moreover, St. Augustine chose Plato to be his object of imitation on the grounds that with just a few changes the Platonists would be Christians. Therefore, relying on this Latin father's authority he, Ficino, is writing the present book to express "an image of Plato" (*Platonis simulacrum*) that is very close to "the truth of Christianity" (*christiana veritas*), the image–truth relation here having an obvious metaphysical connotation. In addition, the ancient Greek writer was well known for the special emphasis that he placed upon one doctrine: namely, that of the divinity and immortality of the soul. Ficino further notes that divine providence has arranged that many philosophers and especially those who divorce the study of philosophy from sacred religion[3] who are unwilling to yield to the divine authority of scripture will accept the arguments that the Platonists supply in the greatest abundance. Finally, he underlines the close connection between theology and psychology by noting that it is in the mirror in the middle of things represented by the rational soul that we will be able not only to observe the works of the creator but also contemplate and worship the mind of the creator himself.

The incredibly close relation between Platonic and Christian doctrine is explicitly stated in many other passages of Ficino's writings. In the proem to his translation of Plato's writings,[4] he argues that in order to make religion accessible to the more advanced as well as relative beginners, divine providence decided not only to arm it with prophets, sibyls, and holy teachers, but also to embellish it with a certain pathway of eloquent philosophy. Therefore, at the appointed time it sent down the divine soul of Plato to shed the light of religion through the nations. In the proem to his translation and commentary on Plotinus,[5] he argues that those who are intelligent and philosophical cannot be enticed to perfect religion by any other bait than a philosophical one and that, when these people have received a rational argument, they will accept religion in a generic sense – i.e. philosophical religion – and will then be more easily transferred to the better species of religion comprehended in the genus – i.e. Christian

---

[3] It is generally assumed that Ficino is here referring to the "Averroists" who represented the dominant intellectual tendency in the Italian universities of his time.

[4] Ficino, *Prooemium in Platonem, Opera Omnia*, 1128.

[5] Ficino, *Prooemium in Plotinum*, 2 (ed. Gersh).

religion. For this reason, divine providence ordained that the ancient theological tradition would be brought to perfection by Plato in Athens, interpreted definitively by Plotinus, and then revealed to Latin Christendom by Marsilio Ficino's translations. Finally, in a letter to his friend Braccio Martelli entitled "The Harmony of Moses and Plato" (*Concordia Mosis et Platonis*),[6] Ficino explains that the philosopher Numenius, who was ranked highest among the Pythagoreans by Origen, had read the works of both Moses and Plato, and had said that he recognized Moses in Plato, and indeed that Plato was a second Moses speaking the Athenian language.[7]

As we have seen, the idea of a rapprochement between Plato and Christianity was justified by Ficino on the authority of Augustine, and this should by no means be thought an exaggeration on the Florentine's part, at least if one ignores the more circumspect attitude towards the pagan thinker revealed in the church father's later *Retractationes*.[8] In *Contra Academicos*[9] Augustine clearly states that the doctrine of the Platonists is not in opposition to holy scripture. In *De Beata Vita*,[10] he reports that he had read very few books of Plato, compared them with the authority of those who had given to Christians the tradition of the divine mysteries, and was inflamed by the Platonic writings. In *Confessions*,[11] Augustine recalls how God came to his aid by obtaining for him certain books of the Platonists translated from Greek into Latin, and how he was admonished by the Platonists' books to search for incorporeal Truth.[12] In *De Doctrina Christiana*[13] he contends that, if the so-called philosophers and especially the Platonists have said things that are true and well accommodated to the Christian faith, their doctrines should not be feared. In *De Civitate Dei*[14] Augustine argues that no school of philosophy has come closer to Christianity than that of the Platonists. Finally, in *De Vera Religione*[15] he suggests that, if the ancient Platonists could live their lives again, they would see by whose authority measures are best taken for men's salvation and, with the change of a few words or sentiments, would

[6] Ficino, *Epistula ad Braccium Martellum, Opera Omnia*, 866–867.

[7] Eusebius, *Praeparatio Evangelica*, XI.10.14; Clement of Alexandria, *Stromata* I. 22. 150. Cf. Ficino, *Plat. Theol.*, XVII.4.6.

[8] Ficino here follows a well-established medieval Platonic style of reading Augustine (by the "School of Chartres," Berthold of Moosburg, Nicholas of Cusa, etc.).

[9] Augustine, *Contra Academicos*, III.20.43.   [10] Augustine, *De Beata Vita*, 4.

[11] Augustine, *Confessions*, VII.9.   [12] Ibid, VII.20.

[13] Augustine: *De Doctrina Christiana*, II.40.61.   [14] Augustine, *De Civitate Dei*, VIII.5.

[15] Augustine, *De Vera Religione*, 4.7.

become Christian, as many Platonists of recent times have done. Ficino was of course familiar with all these texts, although the last passage was perhaps Ficino's favorite, for he explicitly cites it at strategically important points in both his *Platonic Theology*[16] and *Vita Platonis*.[17]

Now, in order to make Ficino's interpretation of the world-historical significance of Plato's philosophy clear, it will perhaps be most useful to consider first, Plato's thought as the bringing to perfection of a rather enigmatic theological doctrine that had been evolved by earlier thinkers; and second, the later Platonists' interpretation of Plato's writings in terms of a distinction between what might be called its "literal" and its "non-literal" components.

THE PRE-PLATONIC THEOLOGICAL TRADITION
AND ITS STRATEGY OF CONCEALMENT

Ficino speaks on many occasions of a more ancient theological tradition leading up to Plato himself.[18] A passage in the *Platonic Theology*[19] states that there was a chronological succession of six "supreme theologians" (*summi theologi*) who were in accord with one another: first, Zoroaster; second, Mercurius Trismegistus; third, Orpheus; fourth, Aglaophemus; fifth, Pythagoras; and sixth, Plato who embraced, enhanced, and illuminated in his writings the universal wisdom of all the earlier theologians.[20] Later in the same work,[21] Ficino clarifies Plato's literary relation to this earlier tradition and emphasizes the Pythagorean component. He notes that Plato learned about the Pythagorean wisdom

---

[16] Ficino, *Plat. Theol.*, I, pr. 2.

[17] Ficino, *Vita Platonis*, pr., *Opera Omnia*, 769. In the same work, Ficino also cites the discussion in Augustine, *Confessions*, VII.9 noted above together with Augustine's report in *De Civitate Dei*, II. 14 – via Cornelius Labeo – that Plato was ranked among the demigods by the pagans.

[18] The classic study of this topic is Daniel P. Walker, *The Ancient Theology. Studies in Christian Platonism from the Fifteenth to the Eighteenth Century* (Ithaca, NY: Cornell University Press 1972). For Ficino's foundational contribution see also Michael J. B. Allen, *Synoptic Art. Marsilio Ficino on the History of Platonic Interpretation* (Florence: Olschki, 1998), 1–49.

[19] Ficino, *Plat. Theol.*, XVII.1.2.

[20] Ficino's list of ancient theologians varies from one work to another although the principle of derivation and the six-fold numerology is constant. For instance, in the *argumentum* ("analysis") prefixed to his translation of the *Pimander* (i.e. the *Corpus Hermeticum*) the list omits Zoroaster, begins with Mercurius Trismegistus, and introduces Philolaus as the fifth theologian (*Opera Omnia*, 1836). See also Ficino, *In Plotinum*, pr. 2 (ed. Gersh).

[21] Ficino, *Plat. Theol.*, XVII.4.4.

that was ultimately derived from Zoroaster through his more immediate predecessors Archytas, Eurytus, and Philolaus. In fact, Plato had traveled the world and examined all the doctrines of philosophers, concluded that the Pythagorean school had come closest to truth, and decided that he would illuminate this in his writings. He therefore introduced as debaters in his dialogues such Pythagoreans as Timaeus, Parmenides, and Zeno from whom Socrates learned everything that he repeats to others.[22]

Ficino further notes that it was the custom of the ancient theologians – and this was continued by Plato – to veil the divine mysteries both with mathematical numbers and figures and with poetic fictions in case they might be rashly shared with all and sundry.[23] In the *Platonic Theology*,[24] he goes on to explain that this led to a variety of interpretations of the ancient theology on the part of later thinkers that can be associated with six "academies" following one another in sequence of which the first three were Greek and the second three foreign.[25] These schools were the "old" academy headed by Xenocrates, the "middle" one under the headship of Arcesilas, the "new" one headed by Carneades, the "Egyptian" academy headed by Ammonius,[26] the "Roman" one under the headship of Plotinus, and the "Lycian" one headed by Proclus. In the proem to the *Commentary on Plotinus*,[27] Ficino goes on to explain that Plotinus was the first and only thinker who by stripping away the mathematical and poetic coverings produced the definitive interpretation of the ancient theology.

THE LITERAL, MYTHICAL, AND PROPHETIC ASPECTS OF PLATO'S WRITING

Ficino lays the groundwork of his own interpretation of Plato – and by implication of the tradition leading up to Plato – by rating these different

---

[22] One aspect of Ficino's Platonic-Christian synthesis that will not be studied in this essay is the role of Socrates. See especially Ficino's *Epist. ad Paulum Ferobantum ("Confirmatio Christianorum per Socratica"), Opera Omnia*, 868 where the Platonic hero is defended against the ridicule of Lucian. Ficino argues that Socrates is a "forerunner" (*adumbratio ... praesignare*) of Christ and sets the two lives in parallel by drawing especially on Plato's *Apology* and the Gospels.

[23] Ficino, *In Plotinum*, pr. 2.   [24] Ficino, *Plat. Theol.*, XVII.1.2.

[25] The symmetry with the set of six ancient theologians is obvious and deliberate on Ficino's part. For him, the entire history of philosophy is governed by divine providence which proceeds in an orderly – and hence, numerical – manner. On Ficino's history of the six academies see Hankins, *Plato in the Italian Renaissance* I, 283, nn. 41–42 and Allen, *Synoptic Art*, 56–79.

[26] i.e. Ammonius Saccas.   [27] Ficino, *In Plotinum*, pr. 2.

academies according to the manner in which they differentiated between doctrines that could be interpreted on the one hand as either true or probable and on the other in a literal or nonliteral manner.[28] He argues that the first four Academies agreed that the writings of Plato cannot be understood as simply teaching a true doctrine, although they disagreed in that according to Carneades' academy all the teachings are doubtful, according to Arcesilas' all the teachings are probable, whereas according to Xenocrates' and Ammonius' academies some teachings are probable and others true. With reference especially to the doctrine of transmigration of souls, he further argues that the first four academies interpreted whatever Plato said here in a nonliteral manner, whereas the last two observed the literal sense of this Platonic doctrine. Ficino's preference is to follow the academies of Xenocrates and Ammonius with respect to their general distinction between what is true and what is probable in Plato's writings and to follow the first four academies with respect to the non-literal understanding of the doctrine of transmigration.

In practice, the distinction between the true and the probable teachings roughly coincides with that between the literal and the nonliteral ones in Ficino's reading of Plato in *Platonic Theology* XVII. Of course, it is obvious that there are conceptual distinctions between true and literal on the one hand and between probable and nonliteral on the other. But Ficino clearly decides to ignore these in order to further his exegetical strategy with respect to the history of the ancient theologians and the later academies. This is presumably because Ficino was aware of the association suggested by Augustine in *Contra Academicos* between the probabilism of the New Academy and the latter's strategy of concealment.[29]

Ficino's understanding of the contrast between these different types of teaching can be further clarified from the continuation of his discussion of the six schools of Platonists and from his citation of certain passages in Plato's own *Letters*. In connection with the Platonic schools, Ficino states his approval of the opinions of Xenocrates and Ammonius that Plato had enunciated a few literal truths: namely, those concerning the providence of

---

[28] Ficino, *Plat. Theol.*, XVII.4.1. Ficino here calls the nonliteral reading "poetic" (*poetica*).

[29] See Augustine, *Contra Acad.*, II.7.16, II.10.24, III.7.14, III.17.38. The assimilation between probable and nonliteral – which is ultimately a distinction between a logical term associated with proof and a hermeneutic term associated with concealment/disclosure – is easier when expressed in Latin where "probable" is often expressed by the phrase *veri simile* ("truth-like"). In the passages just cited, Augustine dwells on this verbal peculiarity.

God and the immortality of souls, and his own conclusion from this that in Plato's writings certain statements are to be understood as true whereas others are to be understood in a nonliteral manner.[30] In the next paragraph he goes into more detail by stating that among the doctrines that can be admitted as literally true are those concerning the *genera* of things,[31] the musical composition of the soul, and the four species of souls,[32] together with the notions that the soul can during a single embodiment be equally intent on the divine and the lower[33] and that the rational soul is pregnant with every form of life compatible with its human status, whereas among the doctrines that must be understood in a nonliteral manner is especially that of transmigration.[34] A few paragraphs later, Ficino cites the enigmatic statements in Plato's *Letters II* and *VII* to the effect that no written work of his has existed or ever will exist on divine matters and therefore that nobody has existed or will exist who will understand his views on such questions,[35] and responds to this interpretative conundrum by converting Plato's denial into a restriction. According to Ficino, the great Athenian can be understood as affirming as literally true regarding divine matters only what is stated in those of his writings where he speaks in his own person, whereas the statements regarding similar topics contained in his other dialogues where he is reporting the views of the ancients should be understood in a nonliteral manner.[36] In order to exemplify the true assertions, Ficino argues that Plato can himself be found as declaring in the *Laws* and *Letters* that God cares for human affairs, that the rational soul is immortal, and that rewards and punishments await it in the afterlife.[37] Ficino now adds an interesting example of an ambivalence between possible literal and nonliteral readings of a doctrine when he refers to Plato's account of the divine craftsman's fashioning of the world. If the *Timaeus* is to be understood as positing the world's existence "from the beginning of an appointed time" (*ab initio*

---

[30] Ficino, *Plat. Theol.*, XVII.4.1.

[31] The reference is to the "greatest kinds" (*megista genē*) mentioned in Plato's *Sophist* and applied to the soul's composition in the *Timaeus*.

[32] i.e. the divine, daemonic, human, and animal.

[33] That the soul *cannot* do these things equally during a single embodiment was one of the arguments mustered in favor of transmigration.

[34] A further argument in favor of transmigration was that the soul precontained forms of human *and nonhuman life.*

[35] Ibid, XVII.4.5. The references are to Plato: *Letter* II.314c and *Letter* VII.341c. For Ficino's further discussion of these passages see his *Argumentum in Epistulam II, Opera Omnia,* 1530–1532 and *Argumentum in Epistulam VII, Opera Omnia,* 1534–1535.

[36] *Plat. Theol.*, XVII.4.6, XVII.4.14.   [37] Ibid, XVII.4.6.

temporis ordinati)[38] – i.e. taking the account as literally true –, this would fit best with Plato's doctrine. But if the dialogue is to be understood as positing the world's eternity[39] – i.e. understanding the doctrine in a nonliteral manner –, then this will not be Plato's own view but rather that of the dialogue's Pythagorean speaker.

As already noted, a doctrine of Plato's that should be understood strictly in a nonliteral manner is that of the soul's transmigration between different bodies and especially between human and nonhuman ones, the reason being that the aim of demonstrating Plato's agreement with the orthodox Christian doctrine that souls are created daily, i.e. do not temporally precede their assigned bodies, can only be achieved with such an interpretation.[40] Ficino's first argument for a nonliteral interpretation of transmigration is based on the historical provenance of the doctrine, for he suggests that Plato in speaking of transmigration was merely reporting the views of earlier thinkers such as the Egyptian priests who invented it as a figurative expression of the notion of psychic purgation, the poets Orpheus, Empedocles, and Heraclitus who subsequently intoned it in their verses, and Pythagoras who introduced it into his habitual conversations and symbols.[41] His second argument involves the mustering of three general pieces of evidence from within Plato's own writings to show that he himself in no way endorsed "those *Pythagorean* notions" (*Pythagorica illa*). First, Plato introduces characters who had formerly endorsed those views as now debating them; second, he depicts Socrates as being in doubt about what he had heard from others; and third, the elderly Plato did not confirm what he had written as his

---

[38] Ficino notes that this is the view of Moses and Hermes Trismegistus.

[39] Ficino attributes this view to Porphyry, Iamblichus, and Proclus.

[40] The Christian teaching is summarized by Ficino at *Plat. Theol.*, XVIII.3.1ff. The literal interpretation of the doctrine of transmigration agrees more easily with the heretical Christian teaching of Origen which is mentioned at ibid, XVII.4.6. For an explanation of the historical context of Ficino's account of transmigration and a summary of his arguments against it see James Hankins, "Marsilio Ficino on *Reminiscentia* and the Transmigration of Souls," *Rinascimento* 2, no. 45 (2005), 3–17 and Stephen Gersh, "The *Timaeus* as Intertext in Marsilio Ficino's Commentary on the '*Third Ennead*' of Plotinus," in *Lectures Médiévales et Renaissantes du* Timée *de Platon*, ed. Béatrice Bakhouche and Alain Galonnier, preface by Pierre Caye (Leuven and Paris: Peeters 2016), 242–244. The thesis of Brian Ogren, "Circularity, the Soul-Vehicle, and the Renaissance Rebirth of Reincarnation. Marsilio Ficino and Isaac Abarbanel on the Possibility of Transmigration," *Accademia* 6 (2004), 63–94, that Ficino accepted transmigration in a limited sense from human to human is based on the misreading of a key text.

[41] Ibid, XVII.4.1.

younger self.[42] Ficino also discusses numerous passages in specific
Platonic dialogues in order to show that transmigration amounts to the
crossing over of souls not into various species but into different habits.[43]
For example, in the *Republic*, Plato introduces a monster composed of
many beasts being thrashed by a man,[44] and in the *Phaedrus* a charioteer
attempting to drive a chariot with a good and a bad horse,[45] these being
in both cases figures of the soul's inner composition and conflict. When
Plato in his *Laws* seems to indicate that souls are prior to bodies, he
probably does so on the understanding that this priority is according to
their natural dignity rather than according to time.[46] Ficino's final
argument for a nonliteral interpretation of transmigration is an appeal
to the authority of other representative thinkers, for among the ancient
theologians before Plato the nonliteral reading of transmigration in the
manner described above was advocated by Mercurius Trismegistus,[47]
Zoroaster,[48] Orpheus,[49] and Pythagoras,[50] while among the members of
the various later academies Porphyry,[51] Iamblichus,[52] Syrianus,[53]
Hermias,[54] and Proclus[55] all sought at least to qualify the literal doctrine
in various ways.[56]

Now, the solution of the interpretative conundrum presented by
Plato's denial of writing about the divine by restricting the range of
true theological statements to those uttered in that writer's own person
is not the only one.[57] Another solution canvassed by Ficino takes a more
metaphysical turn and is based on a combination of assumptions regarding the ineffability of God, the revelatory and prospective character of

---

[42] Ibid, XVII.4.5.   [43] Ibid, XVII.4.7–10.

[44] Ibid, XVII.4.8 referring to Plato, *Republic* IX, 588e–589a. At *Plat. Theol.*, XVII.4.10
Ficino also cites the similar image at Plato, *Phaedrus* 230a.

[45] *Plat. Theol.*, XVII.4.10 referring to Plato, *Phaedrus* 246a–256e.

[46] *Plat. Theol.*, XVII.4.6 referring to Plato, *Laws* X, 892a–c, 896b–c.

[47] *Plat. Theol.*, XVII.4.11.   [48] Ibid.

[49] Ibid, XVII.4.10 – with explicit reference to the *Hymni*.

[50] Ibid – with explicit reference is to the *Aurea Carmina*. The agreement of the Pythagorean
Timaeus of Locri is also cited.

[51] Ibid, XVII.4.3.   [52] Ibid.   [53] Ibid, XVII.4.4.   [54] Ibid.   [55] Ibid.

[56] It is notable that Ficino passes over Plotinus in discreet silence in these paragraphs. Ficino
attacks this thinker's literal interpretation of transmigration in several passages of his
commentary on the *Enneads* – see especially *In Plotini Enneadem* III.3.16 and III.4.9–15
(ed. Gersh) –, this being one of the few instances in which the Florentine criticizes a writer
whom for the most part he treats as the supreme practitioner of Platonic interpretation.
Ficino was undoubtedly correct in holding that Plotinus believed in transmigration quite
literally, the latter's authentic view being carefully explained by Audrey N. M. Rich,
"Reincarnation in Plotinus," *Mnemosyne* 10 (1957), 232–238.

[57] See p. 000 above.

any affirmative statements, and our immediate reliance upon negative theology. This argument is fully elaborated in the *argumentum* to his translation of Plato's *Second Letter*[58] where the starting point is the notion of the absence of any proportionality between the infinite Good and finite goods. Ficino notes how it is shown in the *Parmenides* that there is no name, definition, or knowledge of God because he is beyond the limits of our understanding: a point that is also made in the period before Plato by Mercurius[59] and in the period after him by Dionysius the Areopagite. In fact, one can attain to the divine substance not by any intelligent *action* but only with a well-intentioned *passivity*,[60] and the divine cannot be discovered by us but must be revealed from above, this revelation taking place "eventually" (*quondam*).[61] It is for these reasons that Plato writes nothing about the divine substance although, by using negative, metaphorical, instructional, and exhortatory language, he writes a great deal that will bring us to our divine goal. With a combination of references to 2 Corinthians 12:2 and the Platonic *Letter,* the argument continues by noting that what is finally attained by us in our approach to God is according to St. Paul something that it is unlawful to utter and according to Plato something that it is more unlawful to write, "lest the sacred be given to dogs" (*ne detur sanctum canibus*). However, Ficino concludes with the qualifying observation that, although such truths should neither be uttered nor written, the oral transmission of doctrine from teacher to a select disciple as practiced by the Hebrews[62] and Pythagoreans is at least the safer of the two options.

---

[58] Ficino, *Argum. In Epist. II, Opera Omnia*, 1530–1532.

[59] i.e. Mercurius Trismegistus.

[60] For this notion of passivity see Dionysius, *De Divinis Nominibus* 2.9, 648B. The whole passage makes intertextual use not only of Dionysius but also of Proclus and of these authors' shared notions of approaching God with faith and through the soul's unity.

[61] At *De Christiana Religione,* 22.73–79 (ed. Bartolucci) Ficino describes Plato as "prophesying" (*vaticinari*) in the *Second Latter* and also identifies an exact point in history corresponding to the *quondam* mentioned in his *argumentum*. This was the time of Philo and Numenius where "the mind of the ancient theologians in Plato's writings first began to be understood" (*primum coepit mens priscorum theologorum in platonicis cartis intelligi*). In this time immediately subsequent to the teachings of the apostles and their disciples, "the Platonists used the divine light of the Christians to interpret the divine Plato" (*divino Christianorum lumine usi sunt Platonici ad divinum Platonem interpretandum*). On the prophetic aspects of Plato's writing see also Ficino, *In Epistulas Divi Pauli,* 3, *Opera Omnia*, 431 which states that when Plato was asked how long his teachings would endure, he replied that they would last until the birth of someone holier who would reveal the truth to all mankind and would be followed by all.

[62] i.e. the Kabbalists.

THE IMPACT OF THE CHRISTIAN REVELATION

It is worth noting that Ficino's account of the six academies in the *Platonic Theology* rather curiously passes over an important feature of the Florentine's own view of the history of philosophy that can fortunately be supplied from his other writings: namely, his idea that the ability of later Platonists – by which he means those in the academies under Ammonius, Plotinus, and Proclus respectively – correctly to understand the mysteries of Plato was actually the result of their partial exposure to certain Christian teachings, and especially to those of St. John the Evangelist and Dionysius the Areopagite. Two passages in his early work *De Christiana Religione* provide decisive evidence here. In the first,[63] Ficino reports his discovery that the principal mysteries of Numenius, Philo,[64] Plotinus, Iamblichus, and Proclus were certainly received from John, Paul, Hierotheus,[65] and Dionysius the Areopagite; in the second,[66] he notes Amelius' declaration that St. John the Evangelist had concisely expressed the Platonic and Heraclitean doctrine of the divine Logos and Simplicianus' statement that a certain Platonist had urged the inscription of the prologue to St. John's Gospel in gold letters in all the temples.[67]

Ficino expresses enormous admiration for Dionysius the Areopagite in particular, whom he describes as both the pinnacle of Platonic doctrine and the pillar of Christian theology.[68] In one of his *Letters*[69] he declares that no form of knowledge is more pleasing to him than the Platonic, that this form is nowhere more venerable than in Dionysius, and that he loves Plato in Iamblichus, admires him in Plotinus, and venerates him in Dionysius. Although Ficino still believes that the Dionysian corpus is a product of the apostolic period and that its author was a correspondent of St. John the Evangelist[70] – the eventual reassignment of these works to the milieu of fifth-century Neoplatonism only beginning to take hold around the middle of the fifteenth century –, he does detect the

---

[63] Ficino, *De Christ. Relig.*, 22.73–86.   [64] For Philo and Numenius see n. 61.

[65] "Hierotheos" was the (probably fictitious) teacher quoted by Dionysius.

[66] Ibid, 35.14–19.

[67] Cf. Ficino, *In Dionysii De Divinis Nominibus*, 15.9 (ed. Allen), *Argumentum in Rempublicam VI, Opera Omnia*, 1408. Ficino took this information from Eusebius, *Praep. Evang.*, XI.18.25.

[68] Ficino, *In Dionysii De Mystica Theologia*, 3.1 (ed. Allen). Cf. Ficino, *Epistula ad Pierleonum, Opera Omnia*, 920–921.

[69] *Epist. ad Pierleon., Opera Omnia*, 925.

[70] Ficino, *In Epist. Divi Pauli*, 15, *Opera Omnia*, 451.

problem of explaining why such allegedly apostolic works are not cited by any of the early Christian writers. In the continuation of the letter cited above he notes his suspicion that Platonists who preceded Plotinus such as Ammonius and Numenius had read the works of Dionysius before they were hidden away as a result of some unknown calamity to the Church. Nevertheless, from these writings certain Platonic sparks were transferred to Plotinus and Iamblichus from which in turn a great conflagration has arisen.

In order to consider Ficino's view of the impact of the Christian revelation on the later Platonists' reading of Plato and his consequent attribution of a kind of *prophetic* doctrine to Plato himself, it will be useful to consider his presentation of the various later responses to that nexus of questions surrounding the Trinity, the Logos, and the Ideas in which a symbiotic relationship between Platonism and Christianity is most apparent.[71] This symbiosis hinges on the problem of reconciling a theory positing a set of three terms considered as separate substances and arranged in a metaphysical hierarchy with a dogma that assumes a set of three terms considered to be consubstantial with one another and without metaphysical subordination: i.e. the view of non-Christian Platonists or Christian Platonists who are Arian and the doctrine declared official by the Catholic Church respectively.

PLATO AND THE PLATONISTS ON THE TRINITY, LOGOS, AND IDEAS

According to Ficino, some of the later Platonists explicitly bear witness to the doctrine of the Trinity as a result of their partial exposure to the Christian revelation, at the same time uncovering this same teaching in the enigmatic and prophetic utterances of the ancient theologians and Plato. Among the later Platonists whom the Florentine has in mind was Iamblichus first and foremost. In a passage of his commentary on Dionysius' *De Divinis Nominibus*,[72] Ficino notes that Iamblichus refers

---

[71] Michael J. B. Allen, "Marsilio Ficino on Plato, the Neoplatonists and the Christian Doctrine of the Trinity," *Renaissance Quarterly* 37 (1984), 555–84 provides a good analysis of some of the texts discussed in the remainder of the present chapter. Basing his approach primarily on Ficino's *Epistula ad Iacobum Rondonum, Opera Omnia*, 956, he perhaps errs on the side of caution regarding the extent to which Plato can be seen as anticipating the Christian Trinitarianism, and also argues for a gradual evolution in Ficino's view of the doctrinal relation between Plato and Christianity on this point.

[72] Ficino, *In Dion. De Div. Nom.*, 15.7.

to the Egyptian mysteries where they introduce God as "radiating forth" (*emicare*) from himself and – in positing in the First the one nature of the generator and the generated – name this God as "Father and Son of himself" (*sui ipsius pater filiusque*).[73] For Ficino, therefore, the most important aspect of Iamblichus' account of the Trinity seems to be that it avoids the Arian tendencies that infect the various intimations of the Trinity in other writings of the Platonists.[74] This point is underlined in his *argumentum* to the sixth book of the *Republic* where he explains that some Platonists – especially Julian in his book *De Sole* – make a distinction "of substance" (*per substantiam*) in the Arian manner between the God who is the Son of God and the God who is his Father, although Iamblichus – Julian's teacher – brings up the mysteries of the Egyptians where there seems to be the "same substance" (*eadem substantia*) of Father and Son albeit "a difference of relation" (*diversa ratio*).[75]

The consubstantial second person of the Trinity as understood or intimated in this Platonic literature is, according to Ficino, the *Logos/Ratio* that contains the transcendent Ideas or Forms of created things or more precisely the "reason-principles" (*logoi/rationes*) governing the unfolding of those Ideas or Forms. In the *argumentum* to *Republic* VI,[76] Ficino cites as the earliest witness to this doctrine Philo[77] who urges us in his book *De Causis*[78] to rise up to being itself – of which it is said "I am who am" – or at least to its "image and most sacred Reason-principle: the first-born Word" (*imago sacratissimaque ratio verbumque primogenitum*). There immediately follows a citation of Amelius[79] who reinforces the view of Heraclitus and Plato that all things are made through this Reason-principle and Word with the testimony of St. John the Evangelist. Finally, Ficino turns to the "Egyptian" doctrine of Iamblichus summarized in the Dionysius commentary, now adding to that statement that the God who is the Father is the "model" (*exemplar*) of the God who is the Son because the former is the unitary "source of the Ideas" (*fons idearum*) from which the self-sufficient God has "unfolded himself" (*seipsum explicavit*) into the light.[80]

---

[73] Iamblichus, *De Mysteriis*, VIII.2 (ed. des Places, 195–196).

[74] Including the writings of Plotinus, as we will see below, 242–44.

[75] Ficino, *Argum. In Remp. VI, Opera Omnia*, 1408.   [76] Ibid.

[77] The "Platonist" (*platonicus*).

[78] Ficino seems here to be citing Philo's *De Opificio Mundi*, 24–36. The use of the inexact title "On Causes" may indicate that he is citing him from memory, through the intermediary of Eusebius, *Praep. Evang.*, XI.24.1–12, or both.

[79] The "Platonist" (*platonicus*).

[80] Ficino goes on to note that Iamblichus' God is therefore the Father of himself who is "above all essential being and [is] the causal principle of essential being" (*super essentiam*

Of course, since Iamblichus and the other Platonists are viewed as unraveling the enigmatic thoughts of Plato himself, it is not surprising to find Ficino attributing a trinitarian doctrine in germinal form to the latter. This teaching is frequently mentioned in Ficino's works including *De Amore* and the *Platonic Theology*,[81] although it is in the *argumenta* to two of the Platonic *Letters* that we find the best illustrations of all.[82]

In his *argumentum* to the *Sixth Letter*,[83] Ficino calls attention to the way in which Plato urges the three addressees of his letter to invoke God in the bond of their triplicity because God himself delights in the number three. He continues by noting that in this letter Plato introduces the three "causal-principles of things" (*rerum principia*) touched upon in the first letter: namely, 1. almighty God, the Good itself, by using the words "father and lord" (*pater ... dominus*); 2. a divine mind which is a mediate principle – since the aforementioned lord is said to be both "of the leader" (*ducis*)[84] and "of the cause" (*causae*);"[85] and 3. the world-soul, by using the words "leader of all things present and future" (*omnium dux praesentium atque futurarum*) – since a temporal process implies motion which in turn implies soul.[86] Having further noted that in Plato's writings generally, the word "king" (*rex*) refers to the Good itself, the word "cause" (*causa*) to mind, and the word "leader" (*dux*) to soul, Ficino explores various possible interpretations of this brief and cryptic passage. Thus, because cause is here related to mind, the Platonists argue that principle 2 – which is also called the Son of the Good[87] – corresponds to the intellect that is the proximate craftsman of the world mentioned in the *Timaeus*, Ficino himself arguing that principle 2 also corresponds to the "the most divine Reason-Principle and Word" (*ratio divinissima verbum*) that is the fashioner of the visible world mentioned in the *Epinomis*.[88] He further notes that the entire interpretation summarized

---

omnem principiumque essentiae). This entire paragraph about Iamblichus' theology is a summary of the relevant passage in Ficino's translation-paraphrase of Iamblichus' *De Mysteriis*. See Ficino, *Versio Iamblichi De Mysteriis, Opera Omnia*, 1903.
[81] On these citations see below, ooo.
[82] Ficino is of course aware of discussions of Plato's metaphysical "trinity" in such texts as Plotinus, *Enn.* V.1[10] 8 and Proclus, *Theologia Platonica*, II.8–9 (ed. Saffrey and Westerink, 51–61).
[83] Ficino, *Argum. In Epist. VI, Opera Omnia*, 1533. [84] i.e. 1 referring to principle 3.
[85] i.e. 1 referring to principle 2.
[86] Ficino's translation here reads: *testando deum rerum omnium ducem praesentium et futurarum, ac ducis et causae patrem dominum.*
[87] This addition is justified by Ficino's argument below.
[88] [Plato], *Epinomis* 986c. On the importance of the *Epinomis* which Ficino sees as a genuine text by Plato and in fact the climax of the Athenian's thought (since it is as

above whereby the Good is said to be father of mind and lord of soul – i.e. specifying the relations between principles 1 and 2 and between principles 1 and 3 respectively – is probably how the majority of Platonists and a Christian Platonist who was an Arian would understand Plato's text. He continues by suggesting that there is also the possibility of understanding the mind mentioned in the passage as the "Son" (*filius*) – because the reference to a father also implies a reference to a son – and that of understanding the "leader" mentioned there as the "Holy Spirit" (*sanctus spiritus*). Finally, he comments that the notion of assigning a single "substance" (*essentia*) to the three causal-principles mentioned in the passage – and thereby intimating a Trinitarian consubstantiality – would seem to oppose the view of many Platonists although it is clearly not inconsistent with their position.[89]

Ficino's association of "the most divine Reason-Principle and Word" mentioned in the Platonic *Epinomis* with the second of the causal-principles is expanded in his *argumentum* to the *Second Letter* into a full discussion of the relation between the Christian *Logos* and the Platonic Ideas.[90] In explaining what he terms the third of four "mysteries" presented by this letter,[91] the commentator first summarizes Plato's teaching here that there are three orders of things that can be referred back to three primary sources: namely, 1. the "Ideas" (*ideae*) to the Good itself, these Ideas descending into a mind from the Good; 2. the "reason-principles" (*rationes*) to the angelic mind, these reason-principles being received by the world-soul from the Ideas in the mind; and 3. the "forms" (*formae*) to the world-soul, these forms being produced in matter through the reason-principles in the world-soul. Ficino now turns to Plato's actual

---

though the "last book" of the *Laws*) see Michael J. B. Allen, "*Ratio omnium divinissima.* Plato's *Epinomis*, Prophecy and Marsilio Ficino," in *Epinomide. Studi sull'opera e la sua ricezione*, ed. Francesca Alesse and Franco Ferrari with Maria Cristina Dalfino (Naples: Bibliopolis, 2012), 469–490. The passage cited above is discussed by Allen on 483–490.

[89] Ficino comments on the Arian tendency of most of the Platonists' accounts of their trinity of first principles at *Commentarius In Parmenidem*, 55.2 and 94.1 (ed. Vanhaelen, II, 34 and 238).

[90] Ficino, *Argum. In Epist. II*, *Opera Omnia*, 1531. For a good account of Ficino's interpretation of the *Second Letter* see Allen, "Marsilio Ficino on Plato, the Neoplatonists and the Christian Doctrine of the Trinity," 571–577.

[91] See also Michael J. B. Allen, "Sending Archedemus. Ficino, Plato's Second Letter, and Its Four Epistolary Mysteries," in *Sol et Homo. Mensch und Natur in der Renaissance. Festschrift E. Kessler*, ed. Sabrina Ebbersmeyer, Helga Pirner-Pareschi, and Thomas Ricklin (Munich: Fink, 2008), 413–428. Although Allen here concentrates on the last mystery and its broader epistemological significance, he adds to his earlier treatment of the third mystery on pp. 419–421.

text by noting that in the phrase "around the king of all things" (*circa omnium regem*), the same word *circa* ("around") applies 1 to the Ideas, 2 to the reason-principles, and 3 to the forms, and also that with respect to principle 1 the word *circa* signifies that this principle is an exemplary cause, the phrase "on its account" (*eius gratia*) that it is a final cause, and the phrase "cause of all beautiful things" (*causa pulchrorum omnium*) that it is an efficient cause.[92] Finally, Ficino reports the Platonists' conclusion that Plato has here named "each of those three rulers" (*quodlibet illorum trium principium*) because he uses similar but not equivalent names when speaking of 1. God "through himself" (*per se*) as the One or the Good; of 2. the highest mind a. "existing through God" (*per Deum … esse*) as something unitary and good, and b. existing through itself as mind; of 3. the world-soul a. being "produced by the primal God" (*a primo Deo … producta*) as something unitary and good, b. produced "by the mind itself" (*ab ipsa mente*) as a mind, and c. produced by itself as mobile.

Now, Ficino's view was not only that the later Platonists were unraveling the enigmatic thoughts of Plato but also that Plato was doing the same thing with respect to the even more ancient theologians.[93] So when quoting Plato's trinitarian doctrine in *De Amore*[94] and in the *Platonic Theology*,[95] he adds a parallel reference to Zoroaster's or the Magi's[96] teaching concerning the three princes of the world: Ormuzd, Mithras, and Ahriman.[97]

According to Ficino, another witness to the Christian doctrine of the Trinity among the later Platonists was Plotinus. In the immediate continuation of the passage already cited in connection with Iamblichus' consubstantial trinity,[98] Ficino notes that Plotinus, when speaking about divine love, the One and the Good, and the freedom of the First,[99] maintains that there is a certain inner generation in the divine in which something

---

[92] In his *In Epist. Divi Pauli*, 7, *Opera Omnia*, 437, Ficino elaborates a more overtly Christian interpretation of this passage by identifying the efficient, exemplary, and final causality of principle 1 with the power, wisdom, and goodness of God respectively.

[93] As already noted, Iamblichus' doctrine of the consubstantial trinity was "Egyptian" i.e. derived from Hermes Trismegistus, a cofounder of the ancient theological tradition.

[94] Ficino, *De Amore*, II.4 (ed. Laurens, p. 33).   [95] Ficino, *Plat. Theol.*, IV.1.25

[96] The connection between Zoroaster and the Magi was established by Plethon. See the next note.

[97] The testimony is derived from Plutarch, *De Isid. et Osir.*, 369d–e via Gemistus Plethon, *Commentary on the Chaldaean Oracles*, oracle 34.1–22 (ed. Tambrun-Krasker, p. 19). Cf. also Plutarch, *De Anim. Procr. In Tim.*, 1026b.

[98] Ficino, *In Dion. De Div. Nom.*, 15.7.   [99] Plotinus, *Enn.* VI.8 [39]14.40–15.37.

existent is generated and also that God proceeds from himself. The introduction of the terminology associated with "generation" (*generatio*) and "procession" (*prodire*) that was the shared heritage of pagan and Christian Platonists corroborates a certain historical analysis. Here,[100] from the facts that Plotinus was a pupil of the lifelong Christian Ammonius, was said to have always been united in friendship with the most Christian Origen, and had promised together with Origen and Herennius never to depart from Ammonius' teaching, Ficino concludes that the doctrine of Plotinus was "not altogether foreign to the law of Christianity" (*non a Christiana lege penitus aliena*).[101]

There are several passages in Ficino's *Commentary on Plotinus' Enneads* that explore the close relation between Plotinus' teaching and Christian Trinitarianism in more detail.[102] In one of these, Ficino declares that Plotinus, Origen,[103] and Ammonius held – and he stresses that this is his own belief – that the divine intellect and the Son related to God who is the Father: that is, the Good itself, as light does to light, and also that the Spirit: that is, the life of the world, relates to the intellect as heat does to light. Indeed, even if these thinkers seem to have introduced "a certain essential difference" (*essentialis quaedam differentia*) between these three principles, he argues, in other respects they confirm there to be in them a unity so great that no unity can be conceived as "more singular" (*singulatior*). Ficino adds that it is thus far that the genius of philosophers was able to advance given the conditions of their era, and then cautions his reader to evaluate any further inferences from the philosophers' doctrine strictly according to the principles laid down by the councils of the saints and of the fathers.[104]

Two further passages investigate the parallels with Christian Trinitarianism in Plotinus' thought, the first being more confident and the second more circumspect. In the *summa* prefixed to his commentary on *Ennead* V. 2, Ficino argues that the Christian Trinity very much confirms the Platonic and Zoroastrian trinity of causal principles, for

---

[100] Ficino, *In Plot. Enn.*, II.9.1 (ed. Gersh).

[101] This information is derived partly from Porphyry's *Vita Plotini* and partly from Eusebius. Ficino's historical narrative concerning the doctrinal relations between these thinkers depends on two assumptions that many modern scholars would find questionable: namely, that Ammonius Saccas was at some point or remained a Christian, and that the Origen mentioned in Porphyry's *Vita* is identical with the great Christian exegete.

[102] Ficino, *In Plot. Enn.*, I.8.12 (ed. Gersh) refers explicitly to Plotinus' interpretation of Plato, *Letter II*, 312c, considers the meaning of the preposition "around" (*circa*), and explains the three orders of Ideas, reason-principles, and forms.

[103] Origen, *De Principiis*, 1.2.4 and 1.2.6–7.   [104] Ficino, *In Plot. Enn.*, I.2.9.

the fecundity of the Father includes the Good itself, the emanation of the Son itself includes the Intellect, and the procession of the Spirit includes the Soul through the modality of its will and quasi-vital motion.[105] However, in the commentary on the second chapter of *Ennead* V. 9, Ficino concludes that although Plotinus often touched upon the mysteries of the Apostles John and Paul in his writings, with respect to mystery of the Christian Trinity in particular, he does not seem so much to have grasped it as to have investigated it and imitated it to the best of his powers.[106]

At the beginning of this chapter, it was suggested that Ficino's Christian Platonism was characterized by the two overriding features that it is expressed in works elaborated in the form of commentary either standing alone or incorporated into writings in other genres, and that the configuration of this Platonism is inseparable from the history of Platonism as a tradition. After exploring this material in detail, it has perhaps become clearer how Ficino's Christian Platonism is at the same time a psychology and a theology grounded in a sort of two-directional hermeneutic. Here, Plato the non-Christian writer is prophetic of his own reading by later non-Christian Platonists who acquired the possibility of this reading on the one hand, through their partial illumination by Christian intermediaries and on the other, through their judicious distinction between the literal truth and nonliteralness of some of the master's most important teachings.

Bibliography

Allen, Michael J. B. "Marsilio Ficino on Plato, the Neoplatonists and the Christian Doctrine of the Trinity." *Renaissance Quarterly* 37 (1984): 555–584. Reprinted in his *Plato's Third Eye*.

   Plato's Third Eye. Studies in Marsilio Ficino's Metaphysics and its Sources. Aldershot: Variorum, 1995.

   "*Ratio omnium divinissima.* Plato's *Epinomis*, Prophecy and Marsilio Ficino." In *Epinomide. Studi sull'opera e la sua ricezione.* Edited by Francesca Alesse and Franco Ferrari with Maria Cristina Dalfino, 469–490. Naples: Bibliopolis, 2012.

---

[105] Ficino, *In Plot. Enn.*, V.2, *Opera Omnia*, 1758.

[106] Ficino, *In Plot. Enn.*, V.9, *Opera Omnia*, 1770. There are, of course, numerous passages in Ficino's commentary on Plotinus which describe triadic structures of various kinds and treat them very loosely as being analogues of the Christian Trinity. For example, see his commentary on *Ennead* I.3 *passim* and the continuation of his *summa* of *Ennead* V.2.

"Sending Archedemus. Ficino, Plato's Second Letter, and Its Four Epistolary Mysteries." In *Sol et Homo. Mensch und Natur in der Renaissance. Festschrift E. Kessler.* Edited by Sabrina Ebbersmeyer, Helga Pirner-Pareschi, and Thomas Ricklin, 413–428. Munich: Fink, 2008.

Synoptic Art. Marsilio Ficino on the History of Platonic Interpretation. Florence: Olschki, 1998.

Ficino, Marsilio. *Commentaire sur* le Banquet *de Platon, De l'Amour.* Edited and translated by Pierre Laurens. Paris: Les Belles Lettres, 2002.

Commentaries on Plato: Parmenides. 2 vols. Edited and translated by Maude Vanhaelen. Cambridge, MA: Harvard University Press, 2012.

Commentary on Plotinus. 2 vols. (to date). Edited and translated by Stephen Gersh. Cambridge, MA: Harvard University Press, 2017.

De Christiana Religione. Edited by Guido Bartolucci. Pisa: Istituto Nazionale di Studi sul Rinascimento, 2019.

On Dionysius the Areopagite. 2 vols. Edited and translated by Michael J. B. Allen. Cambridge, MA: Harvard University Press, 2015.

Opera et quae hactenus extitere et quae in lucem nunc primum prodiere omnia. 2 vols. Basel: Heinrich Petri, 1576 [= *Opera Omnia*]. Photographic reprint Turin: Bottega d'Erasmo, 1959; and later and Lucca: Société Marsile Ficin, n.d.

Platonic Theology. 6 vols. Edited by James Hankins and translated by Michael J. B. Allen. Cambridge, MA: Harvard University Press, 2001–2006.

Gersh, Stephen. "The *Timaeus* as Intertext in Marsilio Ficino's Commentary on the '*Third Ennead*' of Plotinus." In *Lectures Médiévales et Renaissantes du Timée de Platon.* Edited by Béatrice Bakhouche and Alain Galonnier, preface by Pierre Caye, 229–250. Leuven and Paris: Peeters, 2016.

Hankins, James. *Plato in the Italian Renaissance.* 2 vols. Leiden: Brill, 1990.

"Marsilio Ficino on *Reminiscentia* and the Transmigration of Souls." *Rinascimento* 2, no. 45 (2005): 3–17.

Ogren, Brian. "Circularity, the Soul-Vehicle, and the Renaissance Rebirth of Reincarnation. Marsilio Ficino and Isaac Abarbanel on the Possibility of Transmigration." *Accademia* 6 (2004): 63–94.

Plethon, Georgios Gemistos. *Magika Logia tōn apo Zōroastrou magōn ... Oracles chaldaïques, recension de Georges Gémiste Pléthon.* Edited by Brigitte Tambrun-Krasker. Athens: Academy of Athens, 1995.

Rich, Audrey N. M. "Reincarnation in Plotinus." *Mnemosyne* 10 (1957). 232–38.

Walker, Daniel P. *The Ancient Theology. Studies in Christian Platonism from the Fifteenth to the Eighteenth Century.* Ithaca, NY: Cornell University Press, 1972.

2.6

Northern Renaissance Platonism from Nicholas of Cusa to Jacob Böhme

Cecilia Muratori and Mario Meliadò

The present chapter explores how Christian Platonic ideas have been received and transformed in northern Europe from the fifteenth to the mid-seventeenth centuries, as a result of textual transmission and philosophical rewritings of the past, and as a reaction to critique.[1] It was in the seventeenth century, and particularly in the German milieu, that a strong historiographical awareness of Christian Platonism as a coherent tradition first arose. The idea of a Platonic Christianity became the subject of heated debates, in which the legacy of Plato was connected with a northern European tradition supposedly characterised by mystical (or, in the eyes of the critics, heretical) tendencies. Affinities were highlighted between authors like Johannes Tauler and Meister Eckhart, Nicholas of Cusa, Paracelsus, Valentin Weigel, and Jacob Böhme.[2] The following pages analyse what it meant to combine Platonism and Christianity against a changing cultural and historical background from the time of Nicholas of Cusa to that of Jacob Böhme, explaining how those 'affinities' emerged and shaped the

---

[1] Mario Meliadò wrote the sections on the fifteenth century, and Cecilia Muratori those on the sixteenth and seventeenth; the whole chapter is nevertheless the result of exchange between the two authors. All translations are our own unless otherwise stated. We warmly thank James Vigus for proofreading our text.

[2] On the construction of such a tradition see Wilhelm Schmidt-Biggemann, *Philosophia perennis: Historical Outlines of Western Spirituality in Ancient, Medieval and Early Modern Thought* (Dordrecht: Springer, 2004); Sicco Lehmann-Brauns, *Weisheit in der Weltgeschichte. Philosophiegeschichte zwischen Barock und Aufklärung* (Tübingen: Niemeyer, 2004). See further on this, 261–3 below.

sense of philosophical continuity. Yet, the moment when the label of 'Platonic Christians' started to be used in (critical) historiographical accounts to define these thinkers was only the latest development in the construction (or self-construction) of this tradition, rather than its beginning.

The chapter proceeds in two steps to explore the contours of northern Christian Platonism. The first part uncovers the crucial role played by the circulation of Platonic sources and ideas, outside of the well-known context of Renaissance Italy. It shows how academic debates, especially on issues such as the theory of knowledge and of knowledge of the Divine in particular, operated with Platonic and Aristotelian tenets within the Christian heritage and exercised their influence beyond the sphere of the university. Nicholas of Cusa, John Wenck, and Heymeric of Campo are the main case studies, considered within the twin contexts of Albertism and the reception of Platonic works on the other. The second part of the essay brings to light the sixteenth- and seventeenth-century developments of a theory of knowledge based on Platonic tenets. It shows how the interest of authors like Paracelsus, Valentin Weigel, and Jacob Böhme in natural philosophy is rooted in the conviction that to know nature is to know the Divine. As Platonic views became embedded in natural investigation, references to earlier sources – from the *Corpus hermeticum* to Eckhart and Nicholas of Cusa – were often employed to give shape to a tradition that sought to provide a comprehensive theory of knowledge, according to the motto 'all in all'. The role of the opposites in acquiring knowledge is crucial in this respect, and is immediately linked to the problem of how to think the Divine as transcendent and immanent: this is a common thread linking the authors discussed in both parts of this essay.

As a whole, the essay highlights theoretical trajectories of Christian Platonism that become visible by considering a broad canon of texts, and by following the circulation of sources – sometimes unacknowledged by the authors – through various cultural pathways, including both university and religious environments and autodidactic scholarship. What transpires is not a homogenous tradition or a linear reception from the fifteenth to the mid seventeenth century. Rather, Christian Platonism emerges as an 'eclectic' phenomenon, which remained open to other philosophical impulses even as it crystallised as a tradition in this period.

NICHOLAS OF CUSA AND THE PATHS OF PLATONISM
IN FIFTEENTH-CENTURY NORTHERN EUROPEAN
UNIVERSITIES

The inclusion of Nicholas of Cusa in the tradition of Christian Platonism is not merely the result of subsequent historiography.[3] This is an idea already largely attested among his fifteenth-century contemporaries and particularly in the Italian Renaissance milieu that witnessed a unique revival of Platonic thinking in the Latin world. Thus the famous portrait of Nicholas, sketched in the preface to the first edition of Apuleius' works (1469) by the humanist Giovanni Andrea de' Bussi, foregrounded Nicholas's eager commitment to Platonic studies.[4] Similarly, in a well-known letter (1489) to Martin Prenninger intended to introduce its recipient to the knowledge of the 'Platonic books', Marsilio Ficino mentioned the name of Nicholas at the end of a catalogue of eminent Platonic authors whose writings were available 'among the Latins' ('apud latinos').[5] This early recognition is also indicative of an historical link between 'Cusanian Platonism' and Italian humanistic culture, to which modern scholarship has paid special attention in the wake of Ernst Cassirer's work.[6] Indeed, Nicholas read most of Plato's dialogues thanks to translations prepared in Renaissance Italy. His private library included, among others, Leonardo Bruni's version of the *Apology*, the *Phaedo*, the *Crito*, and part of the *Phaedrus* (cod. Cusanus 177), Pier Candido Decembrio's translation of the *Republic* (cod. Cus. 178) as well as the *Laws* (cod. Harleianus 3261)

---

[3] The work of Werner Beierwaltes has played a decisive role in establishing an interpretation of Nicholas of Cusa's philosophy as a paradigmatic mediation and 'symbiosis' of Platonism and Christian thought in the footsteps of Dionysius Areopagite. See exemplarily Werner Beierwaltes, *Platonismus im Christentum* (Frankfurt am Main: Klostermann, 1998), esp. 130–71. For a recent and well-documented account of Nicholas's Platonism (with further bibliographical references) see Claudia D'Amico, 'Plato and Platonic Tradition in the Philosophy of Nicholas of Cusa', in *Brill's Companion to German Platonism*, ed. Alan Kim (Leiden and Boston: Brill, 2019), 15–42.

[4] Giovanni Andrea Bussi, *Prefazioni alle edizioni di Sweynheym e Pannartz prototipografi romani*, ed. Massimo Miglio (Milan: Il Profilo, 1978), 11–19, in particular 17. See also Martin Honecker, *Nikolaus von Cues und die griechische Sprache* (Heidelberg: Winter's Universitätsbuchhandlung, 1938), 66–76.

[5] See Raymond Klibansky, *The Continuity of the Platonic Tradition during the Middle Ages* (3rd ed., Munich: Kraus-Thomson, 1981), 42–46.

[6] Ernst Cassirer, *Individuum und Kosmos in der Philosophie der Renaissance* (Leipzig: Teubner, 1927). On Nicholas of Cusa and Italian culture see the essay collection, *Nicolaus Cusanus zwischen Deutschland und Italien*, ed. Martin Thurner (Berlin: Akademie Verlag, 2002).

and the *Parmenides* (cod. Volaterranus 6201) translated into Latin by George of Trebizond.[7] The Latin transmission of Proclus' *Theology of Plato* offers another good example of the network of personal and intellectual relationships through which Nicholas became acquainted with newly available Platonic sources. Having brought back from his journey to Constantinople as a papal delegate a Greek manuscript of the work (1438), Nicholas solicited a Latin version from Ambrogio Traversari, the celebrated translator of Dionysius the Areopagite and Diogenes Laertius. Traversari, however, died in 1439 without accomplishing the task. It was not until 1462 that Nicholas obtained a complete translation of Proclus' treatise (cod. Cus. 185) by Pietro Balbi of Pisa, an associate of Cardinal Bessarion. Nicholas cast Balbi as an interlocutor in his later dialogue *De non aliud* [*On the Not-Other*], which was written in the same period and reflects attentive reading of the *Theology of Plato*.[8] Here Nicholas connects the Neoplatonic conception of the One with the notion of 'the coincidence of opposites', which had constituted the cornerstone of his philosophical researches from the earlier writings. Further, he asserts a fundamental harmony between Plato, Proclus, and the Christian theology of Dionysius the Areopagite.[9]

It has been argued that Nicholas's discussion of Platonic doctrines emerged more explicitly in his mature works (1450–1464) in step with his reception of new translations from Italy and also as a reaction to the dispute over the primacy of Plato or Aristotle which arose at the time of the Council of Ferrara-Florence after the composition of George Gemistos

---

[7] On Nicholas of Cusa's Platonic library and on his knowledge of the Platonic dialogues cf. Johannes Hirschberger, 'Das Platon-Bild bei Nikolaus von Kues', in *Nicolò Cusano agli inizi del mondo moderno* (Florence: Sansoni, 1970), 113–35; and Giovanni Santinello, 'Glosse di mano del Cusano alla *Repubblica* di Platone', *Rinascimento* 9 (1969), 117–45.

[8] The marginal glosses preserved in Nicholas of Cusa's personal copy of the work provide ample evidence of this reading and its theoretical focus: see Hans Gerhard Senger (ed.), *Cusanus-Texte, III. Marginalien, 2. Proclus Latinus: Die Exzerpte und Randnoten des Nikolaus von Kues zu den lateinischen Übersetzungen der Proclus-Schriften, 2.1 Theologia Platonis. Elementatio theologica* (Heidelberg: Winter Universitätsverlag, 1986). Earlier (fragmentary) knowledge of the *Theology of Plato* seems to be attested by some Latin extracts copied by Nicholas in the manuscript Strasbourg cod. lat. 84. See Rudolf Haubst, 'Die Thomas- und Proklos-Exzerpte des "Nicolaus Treverensis" in Codicillus Strassburg 84', *Mitteilungen und Forschungsbeiträge der Cusanus-Gesellschaft* 1 (1961), 17–51. Haubst supposes that Nicholas's extracts relied on the partial and unfinished translation of Traversari.

[9] See Werner Beierwaltes, '"Centrum tocius vite." Zur Bedeutung von Proklos' "Theologia Platonis" im Denken des Cusanus', in *Proclus et la Théologie platonicienne*, ed. Alain-Philippe Segonds and Carlos Steel (Leuven: Leuven University Press, 2000), 629–51.

Plethon's *De differentiis Platonicae et Aristotelicae philosophiae* [*On the Differences between Platonic and Aristotelian Philosophy*] (1439).[10] At the same time, commentators have also observed that the development of Nicholas's thought resisted its direct assimilation to the Italian approach to Platonism.[11] As Stephen Gersh has pointed out,[12] Nicholas early established certain core philosophical theses that did not alter substantially during his later career. These depended on a set of Platonic or Platonising sources still belonging to what can be labelled the 'medieval' legacy of Christian Platonism: chiefly the work of Dionysius the Areopagite and its commentary tradition, Boethius, the *Liber de causis* [*Book of Causes*], the texts of the school of Chartres, and, not least, those of German Dominican theologians such as Albert the Great and Meister Eckhart. Therefore, in order to address the genesis of these early teachings, it is necessary to take into account the context of Nicholas's intellectual formation, in which the knowledge of these sources has been conveyed. This points to a different story of fifteenth-century Platonism, which precedes or at least is not dependent on the rediscovery of Plato in Renaissance Italy. Such an approach will also shed light on the mutual influence and opposition between Nicholas and the north European university culture and on the forms of Platonism (or anti-Platonism) within the academic practice of fifteenth-century philosophy founded on the exegesis of Aristotle.

The School of 'Learned Ignorance' and the 'Aristotelian Sect'

The most eloquent document of Nicholas's confrontation with academic thinking is his *Apologia doctae ignorantiae* [*Apology of Learned Ignorance*] (1449), composed as a response to a violent attack from John Wenck of Herrenberg, a theologian of the University of Heidelberg. In a pamphlet entitled *De ignota litteratura* [*On Unknown Learning*] (1442), Wenck had sharply criticised Nicholas's early work *De docta ignorantia* [*On Learned Ignorance*] (1440), dismissing its content as

---

[10] Hans Gerhard Senger, 'Aristotelismus vs. Platonismus. Zur Konkurrenz von zwei Archetypen der Philosophie im Spätmittelalter', in *Aristotelisches Erbe im arabisch-lateinischen Mittelalter*, ed. Albert Zimmermann (Berlin and New York: De Gruyter, 1986), 53–80.

[11] Especially Eugenio Garin, 'Cusano e i platonici italiani del Quattrocento', in *Nicolò da Cusa. Relazioni tenute al convegno interuniversitario di Bressanone nel 1960* (Florence: Sansoni, 1962), 75–100.

[12] Stephen Gersh, 'Nicholas of Cusa', in *Interpreting Proclus. From Antiquity to the Renaissance*, ed. Stephen Gersh (Cambridge: Cambridge University Press, 2014), 318–49, esp. 318.

dangerous both for Christian faith and science.[13] The main target of Wenck's censure was the doctrine of the coincidence of opposites, in which Nicholas argued that the infinity of God, not admitting any limitation, cannot be conceived of as opposed to anything but rather as enfolding all things and attributes in a unity superior to all determination. This idea, Wenck contended, not only abolished any substantial difference between God and the world and made it impossible to conceive the personal distinctions in the divine nature. It also openly violated the fundamental principle of human knowledge, as established by Aristotle's law of non-contradiction, since it implied for each predication about God the validity of its negation, too.[14] In Wenck's opinion, Nicholas thus undermined the legitimacy of affirmative theology and, with his ambiguous profession of non-knowing, presumed to elevate the intellect beyond its natural limit toward the apprehension of the incomprehensible.

Wenck's criticism highlights two key doctrinal aspects that are helpful for approaching the question of Nicholas's Platonism: first, the conditions of human understanding of the Divine and the status of the law of non-contradiction in this respect; and second, the metaphysical categories used to describe the relationship between God and the world. Indeed, it is primarily with regard to these points that Nicholas's defence against Wenck posited an explicit antagonism between the Aristotelian school dominating the university and the followers of the 'learned ignorance', the latter representing a tradition rooted in the teaching of Plato. As the title of his reply already suggests, Nicholas presented himself in the guise of a Platonic Socrates denouncing the presumption and inadequacy of academic science. 'The Aristotelian sect now prevails', Nicholas complained at the beginning of the *Apology*. 'This sect regards as heresy the coincidence of opposites, whose admission is the beginning of the ascent to mystical theology.'[15] For Nicholas, the law of non-contradiction and the dictates of

---

[13] For an analysis of the dispute see Kurt Flasch, 'Wissen oder Wissen des Nicht-Wissens. Nikolaus von Kues gegen Johannes Wenck', in *Kampfplätze der Philosophie. Große Kontroversen von Augustin bis Voltaire* (Frankfurt am Main: Klostermann, 2008), 227–42; and K. Meredith Ziebart, *Nicolaus Cusanus on Faith and the Intellect. A Case Study in 15th-Century Fides-Ratio Controversy* (Leiden: Brill, 2014), 53–136.

[14] Cf. Johannes Wenck, *De ignota litteratura*, ed. Jasper Hopkins in *Nicholas of Cusa's Debate with John Wenck. A Translation and an Appraisal of 'De ignota litteratura' and 'Apologia doctae ignorantiae'* (Minneapolis: Banning Press, 1981), 97–118, here 98–9.

[15] Nicolaus de Cusa, *Apologia doctae ignorantiae*, ed. Raymond Klibansky, 2nd ed. (Hamburg: Meiner, 2007), n. 7, 6. For the English translation see Hopkins, *Nicholas of Cusa's Debate*, 463 (slightly modified).

Aristotelian logic apply to the investigation of the finite being, which is the domain of discursive reasoning, but do not extend to the non-discursive, intellectual domain of theological research. They fail to grasp the simultaneous transcendence and immanence of God. Against Wenck, Nicholas sought to clarify that the divine nature does not distinguish itself from the created things in the way the created things differ from and oppose each other. On the contrary, the separation of the Divine from the creation paradoxically results from its indistinction ('indisticta distinctio').[16] In fact, according to Nicholas, it is not only necessary to say that God is *not* this or that creature, transcending all things and names. Since nothing can be excluded from the divine infinity, the intellect should remove these negations, too, in order to see, with the eye of the mind, that God is in everything and that everything is enfolded in the simple and ineffable unity of God.

It is noteworthy how Nicholas consciously constructed the philosophical lineage in which he embedded his own conception. He anchored the dialectic between the eminence of the cause and its constitutive presence in the effects primarily in the theological authority of Dionysius the Areopagite. Further, he traced back the origins of the way (*via*) for uncovering such a dialectic to Plato's *Parmenides*, adding even that 'Dionysius imitated Plato to such an extent that he is quite frequently found to have repeated the words of Plato verbatim'.[17] At that time, Nicholas knew (a portion of) the *Parmenides* thanks to the Latin translation of Proclus' commentary made by the Dominican William of Moerbeke in the second half of the thirteenth century.[18] It was by subscribing to Proclus' interpretation of the *Parmenides* that Nicholas recognised in Plato the initiator of negative theology. Plato showed that apophatic practice was the way to elevate the human mind to the intellectual vision of the divine principle.[19]

---

[16] Nicolaus de Cusa, *Apologia doctae ignorantiae* n. 12-13, 9-10.

[17] Ibid., n. 13, 10 (English translation in Hopkins, *Nicholas of Cusa's Debate*, 466, modified).

[18] Later, Nicholas of Cusa read Plato's *Parmenides* in the already mentioned translation by George of Trebizond (1459), which he himself commissioned. Cf. Ilario Ruocco, *Il Platone latino. Il* Parmenide: *Giorgio di Trebisonda e il cardinale Cusano* (Florence: Leo S. Olschki, 2003).

[19] A similar idea, this time with an explicit reference to Proclus' commentary, appears in Nicolaus de Cusa, *De beryllo*, ed. Hans Gerhard Senger and Karl Bormann (Hamburg: Meiner, 1988), n. 12, 15: 'Recte igitur, ut Proculus recitat in commentariis Parmenidis, Plato omnia de ipso principio negat. Sic et Dionysius noster negativam praefert theologiam affirmativae.' Nicholas's engagement with Proclus' exposition of the *Parmenides* is also testified by the copious marginalia in his manuscript of the work (cod. Cus. 186): see Karl Bormann (ed.), *Cusanus-Texte, III. Marginalien, 2. Proclus latinus: Die Exzerpte*

Thus, in contrast to the academic theology that Nicholas considered overly conditioned by its veneration of Aristotle, the *Apology of Learned Ignorance* is committed to justifying the existence of an alternative intellectual tradition in the footsteps of Dionysius and Plato.[20] This included, in Nicholas's view, Latin commentators on the *corpus areopagiticum* such as John Scotus Eriugena and Hugh of Saint Victor as well as more controversial medieval figures like Meister Eckhart and the commentator on Proclus' *Elements of Theology*, the German Dominican Berthold of Moosburg. Nicholas's representation of a frontal opposition between the Aristotelian sect and the 'school of learned ignorance' has often been uncritically adopted in modern historiography.[21] Yet, this opposition tends to conceal at least two crucial aspects of the paths of Platonism in the fifteenth century: first, the diffusion of Platonising thought within the Peripatetic schools of north European universities; and second, the impact these schools had on Nicholas's own philosophy, in contributing to shape the orientation of his Platonism. As we will now show, the dispute attested in the *Apology* is more accurately viewed as the later result of an earlier intellectual proximity rather than as the clash of two antithetical worlds.

The Albertist School: The Neoplatonic Legacy of a Peripatetic Sect

Academic philosophy of the fifteenth century was characterised by an almost obsessive effort to develop various models for assimilating the heritage of a tradition that had been rendered extremely complex and diversified after two centuries of academic discussion on the *corpus aristotelicum*. The attempt to reorganise this tradition was often accompanied

---

und Randnoten des Nikolaus von Kues zu den lateinischen Übersetzungen der Proclus-Schriften, 2.2 Expositio in Parmenidem Platonis (Heidelberg: Winter Universitätsverlag, 1986).

[20] Nicholas's allegiance to the Platonic tradition did not prevent him from explicitly refuting certain Platonic or Neoplatonic theories, such as the doctrine of the separation of universal forms and numbers or the idea that the divine intellect produces the cosmos out of necessity dictated by its own nature (e.g. in *De beryllo*).

[21] Nicholas developed further the contraposition between academic culture and Platonic-Socratic ignorance shortly after in the *Idiota* trilogy (1450). Incidentally, the expression 'school of learned ignorance' stems from the title of Wenck's response *De facie scholae doctae ignorantiae*, today lost. Cf. Rudolf Haubst, *Studien zu Nikolaus von Kues und Johannes Wenck. Aus Handschriften der Vatikanischen Bibliothek* (Münster: Aschendorff, 1955), 113.

by rigid divisions among schools of thought.[22] Each school maintained its own understanding of academic knowledge, and specifically of Aristotelian science, relying upon one of the great scholastic authorities of the thirteenth or fourteenth centuries.

In the early fifteenth century, a group of masters of the Parisian Faculty of Arts, first and foremost John of Nova Domo, defended an interpretation of Aristotle in the light of the teaching of Albert the Great and advocated an ideal of 'Peripatetic wisdom' that rested on a philosophical theology of Neoplatonic inspiration.[23] The Albertist school spread quickly to some academic centres in northern Europe, as Parisian masters and students migrated to German universities. It was as a major exponent of this intellectual movement that John Wenck taught in Paris before moving to the Faculty of Theology of Heidelberg in 1426. Similarly, John of Nova Domo's most celebrated pupil, Heymeric of Campo, contributed to establishing Albertism as an influential and institutionally recognised movement in Cologne. Nicholas of Cusa, who enrolled at the University of Cologne in 1425, probably attended Heymeric's courses, inaugurating a longstanding intellectual exchange and friendship with the Albertist master.

The Albertist school took an unconventional view of the Aristotelian tradition by proposing a significant revision of the textual canon upon which the philosophical disciplines and their teaching were founded. In particular, Albertists regarded two treatises as forming the theological completion of Aristotle's *Metaphysics* and thus the crown of philosophical wisdom: Boethius' *De hebdomadibus* [*On Hebdomads*] and the pseudo-Aristotelian *Liber de causis*, the latter being an epitome of Proclus' *Elements of Theology* composed in Arabic and translated into Latin by Gerald of Cremona in the twelfth century.[24] Both treatises drew

---

[22] On this subject, see Maarten J. F. M. Hoenen, 'Thomismus, Skotismus und Albertismus. Das Entstehen und die Bedeutung von philosophischen Schulen im späten Mittelalter', *Bochumer Philosophisches Jahrbuch für Antike und Mittelalter* 2 (1997), 81–103; and Hoenen, '*Via antiqua* and *via moderna* in the Fifteenth Century: Doctrinal, Institutional, and Church Political Factors in the *Wegestreit*', in *The Medieval Heritage in Early Modern Metaphysics and Modal Theory, 1400–1700*, ed. Russell L. Friedman and Lauge O. Nielsen (Dordrecht: Kluwer Academic Publishers, 2003), 9–36.

[23] On John of Nova Domo and the Parisian milieu at the beginning of the fifteenth century see Zénon Kaluza, *Les querelles doctrinales à Paris. Nominalistes et réalistes aux confins du XIVe et du XVe siècle* (Bergamo: Lubrina, 1988). The view of the history of Albertism outlined in this paragraph follows Mario Meliadò, *Sapienza peripatetica. Eimerico di Campo e i percorsi del tardo albertismo* (Münster: Aschendorff, 2018), in particular chs. 4–5 and 7.

[24] Unlike the *Liber de causis*, mentioned in the Parisian statutes from 1255, *De hebdomadibus* was not on the curriculum of the university. Only one commentary, by Aquinas,

from the intellectual legacy of the Neoplatonic school of late antiquity and transmitted to the Middle Ages a theory of the emanation of reality from the highest Good which was adapted to the doctrinal premises of monotheistic religion.[25] As master of the faculty of arts, Wenck provided commentaries to both works.[26] Heymeric's first philosophical treatise, the *Compendium divinorum* [*Compendium of Divine Things*] (1420–1422), was demonstrably indebted to this strand of the Proclean tradition. He used a rigorous axiomatical method in the first introductory part, and employed a triadic structure for the subsequent exposition, which is divided into three sections, respectively on the first cause, on the emanation of multiplicity, and on the return of the creatures to the Principle.[27]

The Albertist masters developed a hierarchical conception of the cosmos in compliance with the Neoplatonic scheme of four universal principles, which they borrowed from the *Liber de causis* and re-expounded in line with Albert the Great's commentaries on the *Liber de causis* and on Dionysius' *De divinis nominibus* [*On the Divine Names*]. The first cause endows all things with being through creation (*per creationem*); the intelligence shapes the creative efflux by unfolding the intellectual forms; the noble soul and nature, considered as third and fourth primary cause, determine the intellectual being in the spheres of celestial and of sublunary bodies respectively. In this framework, the being (*esse*) of the whole cosmos is conceived as the universal and enduring emanation from God's mind and the original effect of his creative act. The existence of

was written during the thirteenth and fourteenth centuries, as far as is known. On the joint reception of the two treatises in the Albertist school see also Mario Meliadò, 'Axiomatic Wisdom: Boethius' *De hebdomadibus* and the *Liber de causis* in Late-Medieval Albertism', in *Bulletin de philosophie médiévale* 55 (2013), 71–131.

[25] On the *Liber de causis* see the seminal studies collected in Cristina D'Ancona, *Recherches sur le Liber de Causis* (Paris: Vrin, 1995). On the Latin reception, see among others Dragos Calma, 'Du néoplatonisme au réalisme et retour, parcours latins du *Liber de causis* aux XIIIe–XVIe siècles', in *Bulletin de philosophie médiévale* 54 (2012), 217–76. Concerning the Proclian inspiration of Boethius' *De hebdomadibus*, see Jean-Luc Solère, 'Bien, cercles et hebdomades: forms et raisonnement chez Boèce et Proclus', in *Boèce ou la chaîne des savoirs. Actes du colloque international de la fondation Singer-Polignac*, ed. Alain Galonnier (Louvain and Paris: Peeters, 2003), 55–110.

[26] On Wenck's still unedited commentaries on *Liber de causis* and *De hebdomadibus*, see Klaus D. Kuhnekath, *Die Philosophie des Johannes Wenck im Vergleich zu den Lehren des Nikolaus von Kues* (diss., Cologne, 1975), and Meliadò, *Sapienza peripatetica*, 109–48.

[27] Cf. Henryk Anzulewicz, 'Zum Einfluss des Albertus Magnus auf Heymericus de Campo im *Compendium divinorum*', in *Heymericus de Campo. Philosophie und Theologie im 15. Jahrhundert*, ed. Klaus Reinhardt (Regensburg: Roderer, 2009), 83–112.

each particular reality is guaranteed by the participation in the intellectual ray streaming from the divine light.

Against this metaphysical background, the Albertist school took up its position in the major academic controversies of the period, such as the debate on universals and on the distinction between essence and being. Yet this stance did not admit any explicit profession of Platonism. On the contrary, John of Nova Domo rejected the Platonic doctrine of ideas as heretical, to the extent to which it seems to postulate, as it were, a quaternity in the divine nature ('quaternitas in divinis'), namely the existence of the universals as separated entities co-eternal to God's Trinity.[28] John of Nova Domo claimed that the 'sentence of the Peripatetics' ('sententia peripateticorum'), as re-expounded by the Albertist masters, was not only scientifically sounder but also more compatible with Christian revelation than the teachings of other philosophical schools.[29]

From the Albertist perspective, the ideal structure of human science, too, is rooted in the emanative pattern of the universe. In the wake of a genuine Proclean ideal, the order of axioms and philosophical demonstrations is regarded as an image of the hierarchy of causes that generates and governs reality. Reflecting the gradual procession of multiplicity from the One, metaphysical knowledge derives from a first proposition, which has a superior degree of evidence and simplicity than all others, and from which the complex totality of conclusions derives. Significantly, the Albertists identify this axiom with Aristotle's law of non-contradiction. In his commentary on Boethius' *De hebdomadibus*, Wenck developed a detailed reflection on the nature and the function of axioms, affirming that they all derive from the intellect's original apprehension, which is being.[30] As being is the perfection in which everything first participates through creation, so being is the most simple and universal concept impressed originally in the human intellect. It is the constitutive concept of all operations of the intellect, without which there can be no knowledge. In similar terms to his attack on Nicholas in *De ignota litteratura*, Wenck

---

[28] Johannes de Nova Domo, *Capitulum de universali reali*, ed. Henryk Wels, in *Aristotelisches Wissen und Glauben im 15. Jahrhundert* (Amsterdam: Grüner Publishing Company, 2004), xciii–xciv.

[29] Johannes de Nova Domo, *De esse et essentia*, ed. Gilles Meersseman, in *Geschichte des Albertismus*, vol. 1: *Die Pariser Anfänge des Kölner Albertismus* (Paris: R. Haloua, 1933), praef., 91–2.

[30] Cf. Johannes Wenck, *Quaestiones super Hebdomades*, Mainz, Wissenschaftliche Stadtbibliothek, Hs. I 610, q. 2, f. 49v–52v.

affirmed that the foundational impression of being in the mind determines the primary rule inherent in each and every act of cognition, which depends upon the opposition between being and its negation. The law of non-contradiction is considered here not merely as a norm of scientific discourse but also as the source from which every metaphysical doctrine derives. The knowledge of this principle – Wenck emphasises – is situated in the divine part of the intellect, which is shaped by the light of the divine mind. Wenck describes then the unfolding of theorems and their relations in terms of emanation ('profluxus conceptionum ab una et prima conceptione'). Human wisdom develops as the extension, or the ultimate degree, of a noetic cosmos flowing from the first cause and informing, through the mediation of the separated intelligences, the animated and natural world.

In two short treatises composed in Cologne towards the end of the 1420s, the *Theoremata totius universi fundamentaliter doctrinalia* [*Theorems on the Fundamental Doctrine of the Whole Universe*] and the *Ars demonstrativa* [*Demonstrative Art*], Heymeric argues for and exemplifies this epistemological model not least through the formal style of his philosophical writing. These works are founded on a hierarchy of syllogisms that are scrupulously deduced from the law of non-contradiction. The ambition of Heymeric was to re-interpret Aristotelian logic in a strongly realist sense as the key to expounding the order of the universe and to revealing the common rational foundation of theological, cosmological, and anthropological investigation. These works are preserved in Nicholas of Cusa's library (cod. Cus. 106) and bear traces of their owner's attentive reading.[31]

Heymeric of Campo and Nicholas of Cusa, or the Entangled History of Fifteenth-Century Platonism(s)

The intellectual exchange between Heymeric and Nicholas of Cusa begun in Cologne and intensified during their joint stay at the Council of Basel.

---

[31] As regards the *Ars demonstrativa* see the following paragraph. On the *Theoremata*, published together with the glosses of Nicholas of Cusa, cf. Cecilia Rusconi and Klaus Reinhardt, 'Die dem Cusanus zugeschriebenen Glossen zu den *Theoremata totius universi fundamentaliter doctrinalia* des Heymericus de Campo', in *Heymericus de Campo. Philosophie und Theologie*, 58–74. It should be noted that Heymeric developed more extensively a similar approach in another work composed in Basel a few years later and dedicated to Nicholas, the *Colliget principiorum*, cf. Dragos Calma and Ruedi Imbach, 'Heymeric de Campo, auteur d'un traité de métaphysique. Étude et édition partielle du *Colliget principiorum*', in *Archives d'histoire doctrinale et littéraire du Moyen Âge 80* (2013),277–423.

Nourished over the years by a shared interest in Raimund Llull's doctrine and in geometric theology, it gave rise to reciprocal influences.[32] In Heymeric's works, Nicholas found a sustained reflection about the limits and conditions of human knowledge, which came to have a profound impact on the original claims of Nicholas's first philosophical treatises, the *De docta ignorantia* (1440) and the *De coniecturis* [*On Conjectures*] (1440–1445).[33]

The case of the *Ars demonstrativa* is particularly illuminating. Heymeric seeks here to derive an argumentative procedure from the law of non-contradiction ('ars demonstrativa … ex illo principio elicita') that is applicable to all fields of knowledge, from metaphysics to theology. His aim is to elaborate a universal method capable of tracing back the conclusions of every scientific inquiry to the paradigm of evidence typical of the law of non-contradiction. According to Heymeric, however, the indubitable certainty of the first axiom is purely negative as it limits itself to affirming that truth must necessarily exclude its opposite. The 'negative' nature of the principle is founded upon a precise anthropological and theological basis.[34] Just as humankind was created from nothing, Heymeric explains, so the 'shadow of negation' ('umbra negationis') precludes the pure affirmation of truth by the created intellect. Human reason cannot attain truth unless by penetrating the shadow of negation, that is by excluding any falsehood that opposes the truth. Thus, the law of non-contradiction expresses not only the inescapable rule that governs rational discourse but even the very essence of humankind's epistemic constitution. From this premise Heymeric deduces the rules of his art, which identifies the so-called *demonstratio ad impossibile* as the main principle of scientific inquiry. This argumentative technique does not aim at a direct demonstration of truth, but at the confutation of falsehood,

[32] See Florian Hamann, *Das Siegel der Ewigkeit. Universalwissenschaft und Konziliarismus bei Heymericus de Campo* (Münster: Aschendorff, 2006), 230–62; and the seminal study by Eusebio Colomer, *Nikolaus von Kues und Raimund Llull. Aus Handschriften der Kueser Bibliothek* (Berlin: De Gruyter, 1961).

[33] On this point see Ruedi Imbach, '*Primum principium*. Anmerkungen zum Wandel in der Auslegung der Bedeutung und Funktion des Satzes vom zu vermeidenden Widerspruch bei Thomas von Aquin, Nikolaus von Autrécourt, Heymericus de Campo und Nikolaus von Kues', in *Die Logik des Transzendentalen*, ed. Martin Pickavé (Berlin and New York: De Gruyter, 2003), 600–16, here esp. 613 and 615 (with further bibliographical references).

[34] Heymericus de Campo, *Ars demonstrativa*, ed. Jean-Daniel Cavigioli, in Heymericus de Campo, *Opera selecta*, ed. Ruedi Imbach and Pascal Ladner (Fribourg: Universitätsverlag, 2001), 139.

thereby investigating 'what something is not' ('quid non') rather than the 'what it is' ('quid').[35] This epistemological construct is explicitly placed under the aegis of Dionysian authority. In Heymeric's view, the method of the *ars* is not only in perfect conformity with the negative theology of Dionysius the Areopagite, but constitutes precisely the application of its principles to the whole edifice of human knowledge. Therefore, negative theology is for Heymeric both the origin and ultimate realisation of this art. It is meant to indicate that divine truth is fundamentally different from the created intellect, and it transcends everything that can be named or expressed conceptually.

Yet a different aspect of the Dionysian heritage in Heymeric's thought emerges in the assertion that the first cause reveals itself in the shadowy image of the creature, just as a seal's imprint makes visible the nature of its model. The metaphor of the seal, taken from Dionysius' *De divinis nominibus* (II, 5), supports Heymeric's attempt to investigate invisible reality through a symbol that represents in a geometrical way the original imprint left by divine wisdom on human intellect. In a work written in Basel and preserved in Nicholas's library, too, the *De sigillo aeternitatis* [*On the Seal of Eternity*], Heymeric delineates this image as a circumference in which is inscribed an equilateral triangle and from whose vertices three convergent rays extend to the centre.[36] According to Heymeric, the circle represents God's infinite and actual being as well as the convertibility of his attributes (unity, truth, and goodness); the triangle illustrates the intra-trinitarian life of the Principle and the inward generation of the divine persons; the three rays exemplify the creative, outward, emanation and God's threefold causality (efficient, formal, and final).[37] When examined in its particular aspects, the figure of the seal orients the positive discussion of the divine perfections; when considered from a synoptic perspective, it represents the endpoint of the intellectual contemplation of the first cause, and as such it is the image before which discursive language comes to a halt.

The idiosyncrasies in Heymeric's thought shed light on the intellectual context in which Nicholas developed the doctrine of coincidence (at least in its early version). Nevertheless, Nicholas's reception of the works of Heymeric was accompanied by a conscious shift of perspective. Nicholas

[35] Ibid.

[36] Cf. Heymericus de Campo, *De sigillo eternitatis*, ed. Ruedi Imbach and Pascal Ladner in Heymericus de Campo, *Opera selecta*, 100. For a detailed discussion of this symbology in the context of Heymeric's conception of universal science see Hamann, *Das Siegel der Ewigkeit*, 65–99; and Meliadò, *Sapienza peripatetica*, 217–31.

[37] Heymericus de Campo, *De sigillo eternitatis*, 101.

accepted the idea that the law of non-contradiction constitutes reason's
mark of finitude and that it defines the 'negative' status of human knowledge. With this in mind, however, Nicholas postulated the inadequacy of
the law of non-contradiction in the realm of the infinite, which is to say that
God must be thought of as infinitely beyond the disjunction of the opposites. Turning Heymeric's characteristic method on its head, Nicholas writes
in *De docta ignorantia* that all theology 'is elicited from this very great
principle' ('ex hoc tanto principio elicitur')[38] and is thus concerned with the
task of combining contradictory sentences about the divine.

Similarly, Nicholas draws on Heymeric's use of geometric figures as
a guide for contemplating God, even though he ultimately proceeds in the
opposite direction. Nicholas conceives the symbol not as the endpoint of
vision, in which God's perfections are represented together, but as a point
of departure for an ascent beyond the visual image. He applies the proportions between the different finite figures to the infinite in order to show
how the mind is constrained to admit that the line, the triangle and the
circle coincide, collapse into a single figure. Inasmuch as this infinite figure
eludes any representation, it guides the intellect towards the incomprehensible vision of the simple infinite, which is altogether independent of
every figure ('transsumere ad infinitum simplex absolutissimum etiam ab
omni figura').[39]

Finally, the clash between Heymeric's and Nicholas's positions allows
us to reassess the polemical opposition between Aristotelianism and the
Platonic tradition depicted by Nicholas in the *Apologia* in terms of
a competition between two distinct models of reception of Dionysian
Platonism (at least as far as the view of Aristotelianism elaborated within
Albertist school is concerned).[40] The first, put forward by Heymeric, tried
to reconcile Dionysius and Aristotle and assumed the universal validity of
the law of non-contradiction as a consequence resulting from the adoption
of Dionysius' ideal of negative theology; the second, elaborated by
Nicholas, challenged this conciliation and drew on Dionysius' authority
to elevate theology towards the darkness of the coincidence. Nicholas was
perfectly aware of the originality of his interpretation with regard to the

---

[38] Nicolaus de Cusa, *De docta ignorantia*, ed. Ernst Hoffmann and Raymond Klibansky
   (Leipzig: Meiner, 1932), I, ch. 16, 30, l. 24.

[39] Ibid, I, ch. 12, 24, ll. 22–3.

[40] In the years when Nicholas wrote the *Apologia*, Wenck conceived the project of writing
   an exposition of all works of Dionysius in the context of his teaching at the University of
   Heidelberg – an idea inspired by Albert but not at all conventional in the contemporary
   panorama of academic theology.

tradition that preceded him. An eloquent testimony to this can be found in a later marginal note to Albert the Great's commentary on Dionysius' *De divinis nominibus* (cod. Cus. 96, f. 105rb): 'Albert and almost everyone else [among the interpreters of Dionysius]', Nicholas remarks, 'seem to fail in one respect, namely in that they are afraid to penetrate the darkness ("intrare caliginem"), which consists in admitting contradictories. Indeed, reason shuns it and is afraid to enter, and because of this evasion of the darkness it fails to attain at the vision of the invisible.'[41]

'PLATONIC CHRISTIANITY' IN THE SIXTEENTH AND SEVENTEENTH CENTURIES

If the Cambridge Platonist Henry More played a key role in establishing the conception of 'Christian Platonism',[42] his contemporary Ehregott Daniel Colberg (1659–1698), a Lutheran theologian, was possibly the first who tried to demonstrate a coherent Christian Platonic tradition linking Antiquity to present-day Germany.[43] Colberg viewed the flourishing of the ancient pagan theology of Plato in his own era as dangerous, threatening orthodox Christian doctrine. In his lengthy denunciation of Christian Platonism, *Das Platonisch-Hermetische Christentum* [*Platonic-Hermetic Christianity*, 1690–1691] Colberg proposes a series of characteristics common to Platonic 'fanatics', from Plato to early modern thinkers like Paracelsus, Weigel, and Böhme. Drawing ideas from the 'springing fountain

---

[41] Ludwig Baur (ed.), *Cusanus-Texte, III. Marginalien, 1. Nicolaus Cusanus und Ps. Dionysius im Lichte der Zitate und Randbemerkungen des Cusanus* (Heidelberg: Winter's Universitätsbuchhandlung, 1941), n. 269, 102. On Nicholas of Cusa as reader of Albert the Great, cf. Rudolf Haubst, 'Albert, wie Cusanus ihn sah', in *Albertus Magnus Doctor universalis (1280–1980)*, ed. Gerbert Meyer and Albert Zimmermann (Mainz: Matthias-Grünewald-Verlag, 1980), 167–94. On Nicholas's study of Dionysius see Hans Gerhard Senger, 'Die Präferenz für Ps.-Dionysius bei Nikolaus Cusanus und seinem italienischen Umfeld', in *Die Dionysius-Rezeption im Mittelalter*, ed. Tzotcho Boiadjiev, Georgi Kapriev, and Andreas Speer (Turnhout: Brepols, 2000), 505–39.

[42] Paul Richard Blum, 'Platonismus', in *Historisches Wörterbuch der Philosophie*, ed. Joachim Ritter, Karlfried Gründer, and Gottfried Gabriel (Darmstadt: Wissenschaftliche Buchgesellschaft, 1971–2007), vol. 7, 977–84.

[43] On the innovation of Colberg's approach see Lehmann-Brauns, *Weisheit in der Weltgeschichte*, 116–86. On the context of Colberg's polemical attack see Kristine Hannak, 'Theologie als Theosophie, oder: Hermes Trismegistos und die Wiedergeburt des radikalen Pietismus um 1700', in *Pietismus und Neuzeit* 34 (2008), 135–66. On the legacy and success of Colberg's work see Friedrich Vollhardt, 'Pythagorische Lehrsätze', in *Offenbarung und Episteme: Die Wirkung Jakob Böhmes im 17. und 18. Jahrhundert*, ed. Wilhelm Kühlmann and Friedrich Vollhardt (Berlin: De Gruyter, 2012), 363–83, especially 365.

of Plato', the new Platonic Christians mixed philosophy and theology to concoct their heresies.[44] Colberg underlines the vitality of the Platonic 'fanaticism' of the sixteenth and sixteenth centuries, especially in northern Europe. With a broad brush, Colberg includes under the heading of fanatical Platonism three main groups: Paracelsians (followers of Theophrastus Bombastus von Hohenheim, 1493–1541), Weigelians (followers of Valentin Weigel, 1533–1588), and Böhmians (followers of Jacob Böhme, 1575–1624). Taken together, they form what he calls the 'swarm society' ('Schwarm Gesellschaft'), a diffuse phenomenon, confused and changing like the swarming of bees (*schwärmen*) from which the German term *Schwärmer* (fanatic) derives its name.[45]

Platonic-Hermetic Christianity reveals much about what Christian Platonism was perceived to be in the seventeenth century. Despite his polemical hostility, Colberg's work is useful in framing questions such as these: where can direct links to Platonic and Neoplatonic sources be identified? How is Platonism integrated within Christianity for the authors in question? The concept of a homogenous Christian Platonism emerges in Colberg's work from a mixture of aspects, including the contrast between ancient paganism and Christianity, especially after the Reformation.[46] Colberg stands at the beginning of a historiographical debate regarding the status of these thinkers, their philosophical allegiances with the schools of Antiquity, their innovations, and their relationship with the troubled religious panorama of the time.[47]

---

[44] Ehregott Daniel Colberg, *Das Platonisch-Hermetische Christentum* (Leipzig: Gleditsch, 1710), 2 vols., here vol. 1,)( )(1r.

[45] Colberg, *Das Platonisch-Hermetische Christentum*, vol. 1, 105. Lehmann-Brauns, *Weisheit in der Weltgeschichte*, 122 points out that the terms fanatic, *Schwärmer*, and enthusiast were still used as synonyms.

[46] See Colberg, *Das Platonisch-Hermetische Christentum*, vol. 1, 4 on fanaticism as emerging from pagan philosophy, Kabbalah, and Christianity. At the same time, the Platonic Christians tended to emancipate themselves from the Church: Rosemarie Zeller, 'Böhme-Rezeption am Hof von Christian August von Pflaz-Sulzbach', in *Offenbarung und Episteme*, 125–41, here 131.

[47] For this reason, they have been variously named in modern critical literature: Alexandre Koyré, *Mystiques, spirituels, alchimistes du XVIe siècle allemand. Schwenckfeld, Franck, Weigel, Paracelse* (Paris: Colin, 1955). R. Emmet McLaughlin, 'The Radical Reformation', in *The Cambridge History of Christianity*, ed. R. Po-Chia Hsia (Cambridge: Cambridge University Press, 2008), 37–55. See the critique of the use of 'theosophy' in Siegfried Wollgast, *Philosophie in Deutschland zwischen Reformation und Aufklärung 1550–1650* (Berlin: Akademie Verlag, 1993), 102–3. Richard Henry Popkin, *The Third Force in Seventeenth-Century Thought* (Leiden: Brill, 1992). See also Heinold Fast (ed.), *Der linke Flügel der Reformation. Glaubenszeugnisse der Täufer, Spiritualisten, Schwärmer und Antitrinitarier* (Bremen: Schünemann Verlag,

Colberg claims that the new, sixteenth- and seventeenth-century Platonists display a mystical tendency, preferring private, extraordinary experiences to reason: in order to learn about the Divine, they look inside themselves (*Einkehrung*) rather than in books.[48] Colberg also identifies several specific 'doctrinal points' (*Lehrsätze*), supposedly common to all fanatical Christian Platonists. The following sections focus on two main ones: the presence of God in nature and the idea of a hidden God. In retracing how these two notions are discussed by Paracelsus, Weigel, and Böhme specifically, the emphasis will be laid on these thinkers' own understanding of the philosophical tradition that stood behind them. Whereas specific references to Neoplatonic and mystical works appear in Weigel (from Dionysius to Tauler/Eckhart, Nicholas of Cusa, and the *Theologia deutsch*), Böhme is elusive regarding sources.[49] The presence (or significant absence) of such references allows us to see the trajectory that leads from the fifteenth to the seventeenth century, shaping the contours of northern Christian Platonism.

God in Nature: The Legacy of Paracelsus

One of the main errors of Christian Platonism, according to Colberg, is that it confuses God with nature, sliding into what John Toland would later label 'pantheism', and which Colberg calls the belief in the 'general spirit of the world [allgemeiner Welt=Geist], or *spiritus mundi*'.[50] The ancestor of this view is Plato's conception of a world soul, or *anima mundi*, present everywhere in the material world, so that everything shares in it.[51] In its most extreme interpretation that soul is the Divine

1962); and John Roth and James M. Stayer (eds.), *A Companion to Anabaptism and Spiritualism 1521–1700* (Leiden: Brill, 2006), especially R. Emmet McLaughlin, 'Spiritualism: Schwenckfeld and Franck and their Early Modern Resonances', 119–61.

[48] Colberg, *Das Platonisch-Hermetische Christentum*, vol. 1, 4. Colberg contrasts Platonism and Aristotelianism on this point: ibid, vol. 1) (7r–7v).

[49] Böhme mentions Weigel in Letter 12: Jacob Böhme, *Theosophische Send-Briefe*, in *Theosophia revelata*, ed. Johann Wilhelm Ueberfeld (s. l. [The Netherlands], 1730), vol. 21, Letter 12.59-60 (pp. 55–6). See on this Kristine Hannak, *Geist=reiche Critik. Hermetik und Mystik und das Werden der Aufklärung in spiritualistischer Literatur der Frühen Neuzeit* (Berlin: De Gruyter, 2013), 315. See also Gabriele Bosch, *Reformatorisches Denken und frühneuzeitliches Philosophieren: Eine vergleichende Studie zu Martin Luther und Valentin Weigel* (Marburg: Tectum, 2000), 296.

[50] Colberg, *Das Platonisch-Hermetische Christentum*, vol. 1, 105.

[51] On the concept of *anima mundi* see Miklós Vassányi, *Anima Mundi: The Rise of the World Soul Theory in Modern German Philosophy* (Dordrecht: Springer, 2011), 'Introduction'. Richard D. Mohr, *The Platonic Cosmology* (Leiden: Brill, 1995), 171–7.

itself, which is co-extensive with the creation. In place of the orthodox Trinity, one would therefore find a Divine embodied in nature, not clearly divided into Persons, but rather diffused in and (at least for Colberg) confused with the creation. This notion of God's immanence in nature is the reason why several of Colberg's Christian Platonists maintain a complex philosophy of nature: to study nature is ultimately to study God himself.

Approaches to sources of knowledge of the natural world – from books to practical engagement with nature – vary greatly in early modern thinkers like Paracelsus, Weigel, and Böhme.[52] While both Weigel and Böhme were influenced by Paracelsus, they did not develop as comprehensive a natural philosophy as Paracelsus's own, which took issue with Galenic medicine and Aristotelian science to develop a new methodology (for this, Paracelsus was even called 'the new Hermes').[53] Differences emerge also with regard to specific ways of combining theology and natural science. For instance, Jacob Böhme claimed that heliocentrism is both theologically and scientifically sound, because the sun (*Sonne*) has to be the centre of light in the universe, just as the Son of God (*Sohn*) is the pulsing heart of the Trinity.[54] Weigel, on the other hand, followed a geocentric, Ptolemaic model.[55] Yet, the common ground between these authors consists in the fact that they see a convergence between knowing God, knowing oneself, and knowing the world. This may be understood as the epistemological application of the mystical idea that 'all is in all', which constitutes a main tenet in the Platonic lineage connecting

---

[52] Wilhelm Kühlmann, 'Paracelsismus und Haeresie. Zwei Briefe der Söhne Valentin Weigels aus dem Jahre 1596', *Wolfenbütteler Barock-Nachrichten* 18 (1991), 24–60, here 24: Paracelsus, Weigel, and Böhme appear as examples of 'theosophical natural speculation', based on impulses from Platonic anthropology.

[53] Wilhelm Kühlmann, 'Das haeretische Potential des Paracelsismus, gesehen im Licht seiner Gegner', in *Heterodoxie in der Frühen Neuzeit*, ed. Hartmut Laufhütte and Michael Titzmann (Tübingen: Niemeyer, 2006), 217–242, here 219.

[54] Andrew Weeks, *Boehme: An Intellectual Biography of the Seventeenth-Century Philosopher and Mystic* (Albany: State University of New York Press, 1991), especially 54 and 69. I discuss key passages by Böhme on this subject in the entries 'Cosmos', 'Darkness', and 'Light', in *Light in Darkness: The Mystical Philosophy of Jacob Böhme*, ed. Claudia Brink, Lucinda Martin, and Cecilia Muratori (Dresden: Sandstein, 2019), 71–83 and 90–5.

[55] Hannak, *Geist=reiche Critik*, 198. Andrew Weeks, *Valentin Weigel (1533–1588): German Religious Dissenter, Speculative Theorist, and Advocate of Tolerance* (Albany: State University of New York Press, 2000), 10 and 108 ('Weigel adheres to the geocentric cosmology, but his vision of the visible world as a vanishing point over against the background of infinity echoes Cusanus').

Proclus with Eckhart and Nicholas of Cusa, through to the seventeenth century, appearing crucially in the *Theologia Deutsch* edited by Luther in 1516 and 1518.[56] If God is everything and in everything – 'God is all in all' (1 Cor. 15:28) – then attending to a detail of creation can forge a path to the knowledge of the whole world.[57] Natural philosophy, therefore, appears intrinsic to (Platonic) theology.

In *De vita beata* [*On the Blessed Life*], Weigel takes up Nicholas of Cusa's idea that the One is everything and all things are in the One.[58] Again he echoes Nicholas when, in *Der güldene Griff* [*The Golden Grasp*], he writes that 'all difference is in its unity', as darkness is in the light – a metaphor with a long tradition.[59] Weigel expands on this theory epistemologically, explaining that 'just as we see outer things instantaneously with the eye, so also the inward eye sees invisible, spiritual things in an instant'. With the 'eye of the intellect or of the mind' ('oculus intellectus oder mentis') we can see things that must remain invisible to the 'eye of the senses, made of flesh'. But in both cases it is the act of seeing that yields the knowledge of the outer and of the inner, spiritual, worlds. Weigel writes that 'everything comes out from inside, from the invisible into the visible'. He uses a very simple image to elucidate this principle of the integration of inward and outward, of human and divine: 'one has and carries in himself that from which he came, the pear comes from the tree, the pip from the pear, therefore a tree can again come from the pip, together with more pears'.[60] Applied to the relationship between the human being and the world, this principle implies viewing the former as a small world (*microcosm*), in which the entirety of the universe (*macrocosm*) is contained. Weigel explains that God created Adam only on the sixth day because the

---

[56] *The Book of the Perfect Life: Theologia Deutsch – Theologia Germanica*, ed. David Blamires (Walnut Creek: Altamira Press, 2003), ch. 46, 86: 'If, then, anyone wishes to or must love God, he loves all in the one as in the one, and all and one in all things as all in one. ... in truth all is one and one is all in God.' See Wollgast, *Philosophie in Deutschland*, 631. On 'all in all' and the Platonic concept of the soul of the world see Hannak, *Geits=reiche Critik*, 230.

[57] On the connection between the idea of 'all in all' and the debate on the restitution of all things: Schmidt-Biggemann, *Philosophia perennis*, 343, 367.

[58] Weigel quotes from *De ludo globi*: Valentin Weigel, *De vita beata*, in *Sämtliche Schriften*, ed. Horst Pfefferl (Stuttgart-Bad Cannstatt: Frommann-Holzboog, 1996–), vol. 2, 93: 'Nihil maius aut minus esse potest eo, quod est in omnibus, et in quo sunt omnia.' See Stephan Meier-Oeser, *Die Präsenz des Vergessenen. Zur Rezeption der Philosophie des Nicolaus Cusanus vom 15. bis zum 18. Jahrhundert* (Aschendorff: Münster, 1989), 96.

[59] This image is repeatedly discussed in *Lux in tenebris: The Visual and the Symbolic in Western Esotericisms*, ed. Peter Forshaw (Leiden: Brill, 2017).

[60] Valentin Weigel, *Der güldene Griff*, in *Sämtliche Schriften*, vol. 8, 11.

human being was to contain everything in the creation: 'the whole world is in the human being', and indeed 'the human being *is* the world'.[61] For Weigel the human is 'vinculum mundi', the bond which connects all creatures in the world: 'he carries in himself the world and all creatures, and the world carries him'.[62] Therefore the motto used as the title of one of Weigel's principal works, *Gnothi seauton* ('nosce te ipsum', 'know yourself'), is to be understood programmatically: to know oneself is to know the whole universe.[63] In turn, to the Divine the world itself is nothing but a microcosm that can be contained in a fist.[64]

This vertiginous change of perspective, between zooming into the smallest detail in the creation and imagining the dimensions of God's hand, is clearly inspired by Paracelsus, who in *Opus paramirum* [*Work Beyond Wonder*] claims that the whole world is contained in a single drop of water.[65] For Paracelsus, the correspondence between microcosm and macrocosm had medical as well as theological implications. The diagnosis of a patient is based on analysis of the analogies between the body (microcosm) and nature (macrocosm).[66] The fundamental conviction is that 'nature is full of wisdom': cures and diseases, organs and natural elements, are interrelated by a net of correspondences that the philosopher can learn to see.[67] In so doing, he follows nature rather than the 'bookish' knowledge of the learned *doctores*.

The idea that nature can be read like a book, even revealing the Divine, already had a tradition in the Renaissance. It also formed the basis for proposing an alternative to the established Aristotelian philosophy of nature.[68] The new book of nature, for Renaissance philosophers, thus

---

[61] Valentin Weigel, *Gnothi seauton*, in *Sämtliche Schriften*, vol. 3, 61 and 60. Italics added.

[62] Valentin Weigel, *Viererlei Auslegung von der Schöpfung*, in *Sämtliche Schriften*, vol. 11, 385. See also Weigel, *Gnothi seauton*, 60, where Weigel calls the human being 'ein Khurzer begriff deß ganzen geschöpfs' ('a summing-up of the whole creation'). On the human being as 'vinculum mundi' see Jill Kraye, 'Moral Philosophy', in *Cambridge History of Renaissance Philosophy*, ed. C. B. Schmitt, Quentin Skinner, Eckhard Kessler, and Jill Kraye (Cambridge: Cambridge University Press, 1988), 303–86, here 311–12.

[63] Weigel, *Gnothi seauton*, 49.   [64] Ibid, 59.

[65] Paracelsus, *Opus Paramirum*, in *Essential Theoretical Writings*, ed. Andrew Weeks (Leiden: Brill, 2008), 446. See also the echo of Paracelsus's *Astronomia magna* in Weigel, *Gnothi seauton*, 59. On micro-/macrocosm see Andrew Weeks, *Paracelsus: Speculative Theory and the Crisis of the Early Reformation* (Albany: State University of New York Press, 1997), introduction (p. 49), on Paracelsus's conceptions of micro-/macrocosm in relation to Nicholas of Cusa.

[66] 'Diseases are viewed as microcosmic counterparts of processes in nature', as Andrew Weeks aptly puts it (Paracelsus, *Essential Theoretical Writings*, 112).

[67] Paracelsus, *Opus Paragranum*, in *Essential Theoretical Writings*, 148.

[68] Germana Ernst, *Tommaso Campanella: The Book and the Body of Nature* (Dordrecht: Springer, 2010), 1.

supported a new science (especially with regard to theories of perception) as well as a new theology. Intertwining these two levels, Weigel encourages his readers to go beyond the letter (*Buchstabe*), beyond any written word, even the Bible. He claims that letters are to the Spirit what an object is to the eye: it is the eye that actively perceives the object, which otherwise would remain completely invisible, unperceived.[69] Therefore the role of books (including Weigel's own) is merely to warn or remind readers, the true source of knowledge being not the written page, but the Spirit, or indeed nature.[70]

Böhme – a shoemaker by profession and not a pastor like Weigel – similarly complains about the vain knowledge conveyed at 'distinguished schools' ('hohe Schulen') and even expressed the (impractical) wish that everything he explained in his books could be ultimately compacted into just one. The multiplicity of books was a sign of the imperfection of human knowledge.[71] His book – declares Böhme – has only three pages, and these are the 'principles of eternity'.[72] As Weigel states, too, 'we would need neither books nor writings if we always lived inwardly in spirit'.[73] Böhme even claims that 'you won't find any book in which you could better discover and investigate the divine wisdom than when you walk on a green and blooming meadow'.[74]

For Paracelsus, the meadow turns into a space not just of theological but also medical knowledge: he claims that 'nature is the physician',[75] and yet there is a master that is above any other, and that is God himself, the 'all in all', everything that there is.[76] Therefore it is not contradictory, in Paracelsus's view, to state both that God is the highest physician, the 'teacher of medicine', and that 'God is the book'.[77] Reflecting this understanding of God's diffused presence, Paracelsus famously declared his preference for a church of the spirit over the *Mauerkirche* (the church of bricks and mortar), the actual institutional church, enclosed in its doctrinal walls.[78]

---

[69] Weigel, *Der güldene Griff*, 38–9 and 154–6.   [70] Ibid, 159–62, and 172.

[71] Böhme, *Theosophische Send-Briefe*, Letter 10.46 (p. 40).

[72] Ibid, Letter 12.15 (p. 46).   [73] Weigel, *Gnothi seauton*, 161–2.

[74] Jacob Böhme, *Beschreibung der Drey Principien Göttliches Wesens*, in *Theosophia revelata*, vol. 2, ch. 8.12 (pp. 76–7).

[75] Paracelsus, *Opus Paragranum*, 148.

[76] Paracelsus, *De mineralibus liber*, in *Sämtliche Werke*, ed. Karl Sudhoff (Munich and Berlin: Oldenburg, 1922–33), vol. 3, 34. See also Paracelsus, *Essential Theoretical Writings*, 210.

[77] Paracelsus, *Opus Paragranum*, in *Essential Theoretical Writings*, 266.

[78] See Carlos Gilly, '"*Theophrastia sancta*" – Paracelsianism as a Religion in conflict with the Established Churches', in *Paracelsus: The Man and His Reputation, His Ideas and Their Transformation*, ed. Ole Peter Grell (Leiden: Brill, 1998), 151–85, here 152.

The conviction of the belief in the pervasive presence of God in nature, coupled with the idea that nature itself is a master to follow, and with a certain disdain for academic presentation, readily attracted accusations of pantheism. If John Calvin spoke of a 'sensus divinitatis', a kind of universal, natural instinct that tells each human of God's existence, these thinkers go further: God can be directly perceived in nature.[79] But while the idea that 'all is in all' has a clear Platonic heritage, when it comes to specifying how exactly God reveals himself in nature, and what God is beyond nature, the Platonic lineage becomes more eclectic.

Beyond Nature and Beyond God: The Hidden God from Weigel to Böhme

In the only book by Böhme published during the author's lifetime, *Der Weg zu Christo* [*The Way to God*], God's presence in nature as 'all in all' is linked to the question of how to think of the Divine as separate from its creation. Böhme writes that God has made his eternal Word 'visible', and he fills all creatures by acting through everything, yet he remains 'hidden'.[80] How to think of the Divine as both in nature and separate from it is a central theme in Böhme's philosophy. Despite his reluctance to quote sources, his terminology betrays the influence of the mystical tradition of the 'Deus absconditus': all words must fail in trying to grasp God's essence.

The ineffability of the One is a typical theme in (Neo)Platonic philosophy, as previously discussed in relation to Nicholas of Cusa. Tracing a tradition from Platonism to Christianity, Colberg writes that the 'Good' of Plato is the equivalent of the 'hidden God' of the mystical tradition.[81] Weigel is a case in point for Colberg.[82] For instance, in *De vita beata* Weigel contrasts God, as the 'highest good' ('summum bonum'), to evil, because whereas God is powerful, evil lacks strength: it

---

[79] On Calvin's 'sensus divinitatis' see Paul Helm, *John Calvin's Ideas* (Oxford: Oxford University Press, 2004), ch. 8: 'Natural Theology and the Sensus Divinitatis'.

[80] Jacob Böhme, 'Vom heiligen Gebet', in *Der Weg zu Christo*, in *Theosophia revalata*, vol. 9, 116.

[81] Ehregott Daniel Colberg, *De origine et progressu haeresium et errorum in ecclesia specimen historicum* (Schneeberg: Weidner, 1694), 6: 'Ignotus DEUS Simoni est Bonum Platonis.'

[82] On Weigel's mediating role, with special regard to Platonic ideas, see Douglas H. Shantz, 'Valentin Weigel', in *Protestants and Mysticism in Reformation Europe*, ed. Ronald K. Rittgers and Vincent Evener (Leiden: Brill, 2019), 243–64.

is feeble and incapable of any action.[83] In Neoplatonic fashion, Weigel declares that evil is nothingness.[84]

Echoing Plotinus' statement that no name suits the Divine as Unity, Weigel states that 'God is one in himself, he has no name, he is called good, and no one else is called good apart from God'.[85] Yet Weigel also follows in the Platonic tradition of using metaphors to describe what is beyond all words. As Werner Beierwaltes noted, words like 'fountain, seed, root' come into play when Platonists try to describe what the Divine would be without, or before creating nature.[86] In *De luce et caligine divina* [*On Divine Light and Darkness*], Weigel claims that no creature can grasp the uncreated God. Referring to Dionysius the Areopagite, Weigel explains that apparent contradictions are inevitable when talking about this hidden God. For instance, we might say that God is light, and yet not comparable to the light we know in the world: he is 'an inaccessible light'.[87] Furthermore, God is also 'light in darkness', shining through the obscurity of creation, since everything that is created is tinged by shade, and thus the gaze of the creature onto God must also be veiled by darkness. Paradoxically, however, Weigel states that God himself can be called 'darkness'. Indeed, where there is no creature to 'see' God, he is equally light and darkness, and beyond both. To say it with Dionysius the Areopagite, no 'words come up to the inexpressible Good, this One, this Source of all unity, this supra-existent Being'.[88] Weigel's insistence on the role of the creature also echoes Eckhart's distinction between God the creator (*Gott*) and the Godhead (*Gottheit*) as distinct from creation. Thus, for Eckhart, everything that can be said of 'God' is always relational to the creation, while the Godhead remains beyond thoughts and words: 'God "becomes" God when all creatures speak God forth: there "God" is born'.[89] Weigel

---

[83] Cf. Plotinus, *Enneads*, ed. Lloyd P. Gerson (Cambridge: Cambridge University Press, 2018), 6.9: 'On the Good or the One.'

[84] Weigel, *De vita beata*, 74: 'Malum enim nihil est.'

[85] Plotinus, *Enneads*, 6.9.5 (p. 889). Valentin Weigel, *Seligmachende Erkenntnis Gottes*, in *Sämtliche Schriften*, vol. 9, 3.

[86] Werner Beierwaltes, *Denken des Einen. Studien zur neuplatonischen Philosophie und ihrer Wirkungsgeschichte* (Frankfurt: Klostermann, 1995), 50 and 66–7. On the 'Divine Names' see Schmidt-Biggemann, *Philosophia perennis*, 59–128.

[87] Valentin Weigel, *De luce et caligine divina*, in *Sämtliche Schriften*, vol. 2, 112.

[88] Dionysius the Areopagite, *The Divine Names*, in *The Complete Works*, trans. Colm Luibheid (New York: Paulist Press, 1987), ch. 1 (pp. 49–50).

[89] Meister Eckhart, *Selected Writings*, ed. Oliver Davies (London: Penguin, 1994), 234 (Sermon 27).

expresses this same conception when he distinguishes between God understood in absolute terms (*absolute*), or in relation to the creatures (*respective*).[90]

Linguistic virtuosity is part of this tradition of thinking the unthinkable. Böhme is a case in point. From the earlier to the later writings, he kept working on vocabulary for the hidden God. In *Clavis* [*Key*], he writes that in composing his own explanation of Divine revelation, he 'tested' some words of 'foreign masters ... which [he] found to be good'. The masters are 'sage pagans and Jews'– a reference to the Kabbalah.[91] Colberg quoted this very passage in order to convey the sense of a homogenous tradition. Yet, Böhme's eclectic approach to the explanation of creation, and especially his discussion of the interplay of good and evil, light and darkness, marks him as an original figure in the panorama of Platonic Christianity.

In his later work, Böhme introduced a new term to define the Divine regarded as immobile, separate from its creation: *Ungrund*, or Unground, that which has no foundation, or *Grund*, on which to support itself.[92] Böhme argues that logically prior to any movement of creation, there is absolute stillness (and the challenge is to avoid thinking of 'before' in a temporal sense). The *Ungrund* is thus permanently still, untouched by motion and change. Following Weigel, who had defined God as separate from creation, 'without person, without time, without place, without action [wirckloβ], without will, without yearning [affectloβ]',[93] Böhme writes that 'one cannot say of God that he is this or that, evil or good, that he has distinction within himself. ... He is in himself the Un-ground ... as a permanent nothingness [ein ewig Nichts].'[94] Despite the clear affinity with the line of tradition just sketched, it is significant that Böhme insists that the Un-ground is beyond both good and evil. Rather than calling the hidden God the supreme Good, Böhme is adamant that any distinction, even between good and evil, must cease with the Un-ground.

---

[90] Weigel, *Seligmachende Erkenntnis Gottes*, 7.

[91] Jacob Böhme, *Clavis*, in *Theosophia revelata*, vol. 9, 77 (cf. Colberg, *Das Platonisch-Hermetische Christentum*, vol. 1, 315).

[92] The adjective *ungründlich* was in use well before Böhme's coinage of the noun *Ungrund*: see Jacob and Wilhelm Grimm, *Deutsches Wörterbuch*, 16 vols. in 32 (Leipzig: Hirzel, 1854–1961), s. v. *Ungrund* (vol. 24, cols. 1030–1033), and *ungründlich* (vol. 24, cols 1033–1034).

[93] Weigel, *Seligmachende Erkenntnis Gottes*, 3.

[94] Jacob Böhme, *Von der Gnadenwahl*, in *Theosophia revelata*, vol. 15, cap. 1 (p. 4).

Böhme frequently discussed how to conceive the Un-ground as becoming God the creator. In *Von sechs theosophischen Puncten* [*On Six Theosophical Points*], he uses a metaphor, comparing the Un-ground to a mirror that reflects only itself. Its surface must be free from all images in order to reflect anything. In the moment of creation, the 'mirror goes within itself', and in so doing 'makes a ground in itself': it gives itself a foundation, pulling itself together from nothingness into something that can be grasped, including verbally.[95] Through this action of pulling, the Un-ground makes itself pregnant and becomes a thick and full darkness. For the image of light radiating from God as its source, Böhme substitutes the idea of a contraction that produces darkness.

The most radical expression of Böhme's eclectic approach is perhaps his doubling of God's creative act – *fiat*. Whereas Weigel had laid emphasis on the moment in which God, as uncreated light, created light ('fiat lux', 'let there be light'), Böhme speaks not of one fiat, or act of creation, but of two: to the fiat of light, he opposes a fiat of death, or hellish fiat.[96] The former produces the 'world of light', the latter the 'world of darkness'. This is indicative of how Böhme reflects on the role of evil, or of darkness: these are not merely inactive opposites of good and light, defined purely by absence. Rather than being nothingness (as Weigel had claimed, following Platonic tradition), negativity is for Böhme an active force, essential to the process of creation.

Böhme conceives of the opposites as equally engaged in the process of creating life. Indeed, according to Böhme all life is the result of an internal struggle between two contrasting impulses, an idea clearly represented in the so-called 'Philosophical Sphere' that Böhme describes in *Vierzig Fragen von der Seelen* [*Forty Questions of the Soul*].

In the centre is the beating heart, which connects and divides the two halves. The light on the right is the realm of the Son and of Love, while the darkness on the left acquires more than one meaning: it is the darkness before the beginning of life, or the Father before the birth of the Son, but it also stands for the polar opposite of God's Son, namely the Devil. Indeed, in his first book, *Aurora*, Böhme underlines the proximity between God and his archenemy, claiming that Lucifer was closer to God than a child to

[95] Jacob Böhme, *Von sechs theosophischen Puncten*, in *Theosophia revelata*, vol. 6, ch. 1.8 (p. 4), and 1.12 (p. 5).
[96] Weigel, *De luce et caligine divina*, 115. Böhme, *Von sechs theosophischen Puncten*, ch. 3.6 (p. 29).

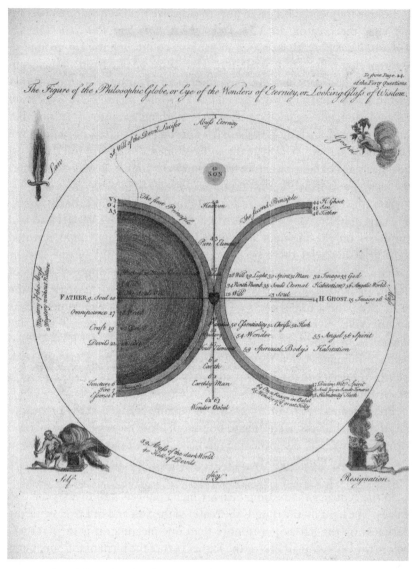

11.6.1 'The Philosophical Sphere', in *The Works of Jacob Behmen*, ed. George Ward and Thomas Langcake, London 1764–1781. Copperplate engraving, handcoloured. © Embassy of the Free Mind, Collection Bibliotheca Philosophica Hermetica. Reproduced by kind permission of the Director of the Ritman Library Collection, Esther Ritman.

its parents.[97] 'Everything has its separation [*Separation*] in itself', he writes in a letter – and that includes God.[98] Therefore the transition from Unground to the revealed God, father to the creation, is not an emanation of light, but a dramatic process of contraction and explosion, that creates opposites: their friction is the spark of life, in all creatures, and also in the Divine, as he faces the Devil as part of himself, as his own child.[99] 'Fiat', therefore, is another word for the separation between light and darkness that occurred through the actions of pulling and of kindling, and even the positive act of creation must have a specular opposite, a 'fiat of death'.

Alexandre Koyré noted that Böhme substituted the metaphysics of light with the metaphysics of fire.[100] Unlike light, fire is ambiguous and potentially dangerous: the flame that provides warmth can also burn, and the flames of Hell are the counterpart to the pure light of Paradise. With his rich imagery and terminological inventions, Böhme introduces the same ambiguity into the tradition of Platonic Christianity, creating new frames of reference for concepts with an established lineage. Thus, he presents the hidden God of the tradition that connected Dionysius the Areopagite with Nicholas of Cusa and Weigel as the stillness that precedes a violent clash between equally active opposites. The pole of negativity, embodied by evil, darkness, and the world itself, becomes the fertile soil in which life germinates – the very opposite of nothingness. Böhme thus leans on a certain traditional framework (always without specific references), while at the same time transforming it from within: he appropriates the Platonic idea of the convergence of the opposites, but breaks with tradition in investing negativity with the role of motor in the action of divine revelation. He is thus a good example of the way in which a living philosophical lineage was developed and challenged at the same time, as interest in certain key ideas about the nature of the Divine, and on human knowledge of it, persisted yet without giving rise to a perfectly uniform tradition – unless in the eyes of its critics.

---

[97] Jacob Böhme, *Morgenröte im Aufgang*, in *Theosophia revelata*, vol. 1, ch. 14.87. English translation: *Aurora (Morgen Röte im auffgang, 1612) and Fundamental Report (Gründlicher Bericht, Mysterium Pansophicum, 1620)*, ed. Andrew Weeks, Günther Bonheim, and Michael Spang (Leiden: Brill, 2013).

[98] Böhme, *Theosophische Send-Briefe*, Letter 47.5 (p. 185).

[99] Jacob Böhme, *Mysterium magnum*, in *Theosophia revelata*, vol. 8, ch. 26.55 (p. 209). Wilhelm Schmidt-Biggemann, 'Das Geheimnis des Anfangs: Einige spekulative Betrachtungen im Hinblick auf Jakob Böhme', in *Gott, Natur, Mensch in der Sicht Jakob Böhmes und seiner Rezeption*, ed. Jan Garewicz and Alois M. Haas (Wiesbaden: Harrassowitz, 1995), 113–27, here 119 on the idea of the 'other' as evil in Plotinus.

[100] Alexandre Koyré, *La philosophie de Jacob Boehme* (Paris: Vrin, 1929), 284.

Bibliography

Anon. *The Book of the Perfect Life: Theologia Deutsch – Theologia Germanica.* Edited by David Blamires. Walnut Creek: Altamira Press, 2003.

Anzulewicz, Henryk. 'Zum Einfluss des Albertus Magnus auf Heymericus de Campo im *Compendium divinorum*'. In *Heymericus de Campo. Philosophie und Theologie im 15. Jahrhundert*, edited by Klaus Reinhardt, 83–112. Regensburg: Roderer, 2009.

Baur, Ludwig. *Cusanus-Texte, III. Marginalien. 1. Nicolaus Cusanus und Ps. Dionysius im Lichte der Zitate und Randbemerkungen des Cusanus.* Heidelberg: Winter's Universitätsbuchhandlung, 1941.

Beierwaltes, Werner. '"Centrum tocius vite." Zur Bedeutung von Proklos' "Theologia Platonis" im Denken des Cusanus'. In *Proclus et la Théologie platonicienne*, edited by Alain-Philippe Segonds and Carlos Steel, 629–51. Leuven: Leuven University Press, 2000.

——— *Denken des Einen. Studien zur neuplatonischen Philosophie und ihrer Wirkungsgeschichte.* Frankfurt: Klostermann, 1995.

——— *Platonismus im Christentum.* Frankfurt am Main: Klostermann, 1998.

Böhme, Jacob. *Aurora (Morgen Röte im auffgang, 1612) and Fundamental Report (Gründlicher Bericht, Mysterium Pansophicum, 1620).* Edited by Andrew Weeks, Günther Bonheim, and Michael Spang. Leiden: Brill, 2013.

——— *Theosophia revelata.* Edited by Johann Wilhelm Ueberfeld. S. l. [The Netherlands], 1730.

Bormann, Karl, ed. *Cusanus-Texte, III. Marginalien, 2. Proclus latinus: Die Exzerpte und Randnoten des Nikolaus von Kues zu den lateinischen Übersetzungen der Proclus-Schriften, 2.2 Expositio in Parmenidem Platonis.* Heidelberg: Winter Universitätsverlag, 1986.

Bosch, Gabriele. *Reformatorisches Denken und frühneuzeitliches Philosophieren: Eine vergleichende Studie zu Martin Luther und Valentin Weigel.* Marburg: Tectum, 2000.

Brink, Claudia, Lucinda Martin, and Cecilia Muratori, eds. *Light in Darkness: The Mystical Philosophy of Jacob Böhme.* Dresden: Sandstein, 2019.

Bussi, Giovanni Andrea. *Prefazioni alle edizioni di Sweynheym e Pannartz prototipografi romani*, edited by Massimo Miglio. Milan: Il Profilo, 1978.

Calma, Dragos. 'Du néoplatonisme au réalisme et retour, parcours latins du *Liber de causis* aux XIIIe–XVIe siècles'. *Bulletin de philosophie médiévale* 54 (2012): 217–76.

Calma, Dragos and Ruedi Imbach. 'Heymeric de Campo, auteur d'un traité de métaphysique. Étude et édition partielle du *Colliget principiorum*'. *Archives d'histoire doctrinale et littéraire du Moyen Âge* 80 (2013): 277–423.

Cassirer, Ernst. *Individuum und Kosmos in der Philosophie der Renaissance.* Leipzig: Teubner, 1927.

Colberg, Ehregott Daniel. *Das Platonisch-Hermetische Christentum.* Leipzig: Gleditsch, 1710. 2 vols.

——— *De origine et progressu haeresium et errorum in ecclesia specimen historicum.* Schneeberg: Weidner, 1694.

Colomer, Eusebio. *Nikolaus von Kues und Raimund Llull. Aus Handschriften der Kueser Bibliothek*. Berlin: De Gruyter, 1961.

D'Amico , Claudia. 'Plato and Platonic Tradition in the Philosophy of Nicholas of Cusa'. In *Brill's Companion to German Platonism*, edited by Alan Kim, 15–42. Leiden and Boston: Brill, 2019.

D'Ancona, Cristina. *Recherches sur le Liber de Causis*. Paris: Vrin, 1995.

Dionysius the Areopagite. *The Divine Names*. In *The Complete Works*, translated by Colm Luibheid. New York: Paulist Press, 1987.

Ernst, Germana. *Tommaso Campanella: The Book and the Body of Nature*. Dordrecht: Springer, 2010.

Fast, Heinold, ed. *Der linke Flügel der Reformation. Glaubenszeugnisse der Täufer, Spiritualisten, Schwärmer und Antitrinitarier*. Bremen: Schünemann Verlag, 1962.

Flasch, Kurt. 'Wissen oder Wissen des Nicht-Wissens. Nikolaus von Kues gegen Johannes Wenck'. In *Kampfplätze der Philosophie. Große Kontroversen von Augustin bis Voltaire*, 227–42. Frankfurt am Main: Klostermann, 2008.

Forshaw, Peter, ed. *Lux in tenebris: The Visual and the Symbolic in Western Esotericisms*. Leiden: Brill, 2017.

Garin, Eugenio. 'Cusano e i platonici italiani del Quattrocento'. In *Nicolò da Cusa. Relazioni tenute al convegno interuniversitario di Bressanone nel 1960*, 75–100. Florence: Sansoni, 1962.

Gersh, Stephen. 'Nicholas of Cusa'. In *Interpreting Proclus. From Antiquity to the Renaissance*, edited by Stephen Gersh, 318–49. Cambridge: Cambridge University Press, 2014.

Gilly, Carlos. '"*Theophrastia sancta*" – Paracelsianism as a Religion in Conflict with the Established Churches'. In *Paracelsus: The Man and His Reputation, His Ideas and Their Transformation*, edited by Ole Peter Grell, 151–85. Leiden: Brill, 1998.

Grimm, Jacob and Wilhelm. *Deutsches Wörterbuch*, 16 vols. in 32. Leipzig: Hirzel, 1854–1961.

Hamann, Florian. *Das Siegel der Ewigkeit. Universalwissenschaft und Konziliarismus bei Heymericus de Campo*. Münster: Aschendorff, 2006.

Hannak, Kristine. *Geist=reiche Critik. Hermetik und Mystik und das Werden der Aufklärung in spiritualistischer Literatur der Frühen Neuzeit*. Berlin: De Gruyter, 2013.

'Theologie als Theosophie, oder: Hermes Trismegistos und die Wiedergeburt des radikalen Pietismus um 1700'. *Pietismus und Neuzeit* 34 (2008): 135–6.

Haubst, Rudolf. 'Albert, wie Cusanus ihn sah'. In *Albertus Magnus Doctor universalis (1280–1980)*, edited by Gerbert Meyer and Albert Zimmermann, 167–94. Mainz: Matthias-Grünewald-Verlag, 1980.

'Die Thomas- und Proklos-Exzerpte des "Nicolaus Treverensis" in Codicillus Strassburg 84'. *Mitteilungen und Forschungsbeiträge der Cusanus-Gesellschaft* 1 (1961): 17–51.

Studien zu Nikolaus von Kues und Johannes Wenck. Aus Handschriften der Vatikanischen Bibliothek. Münster: Aschendorff, 1955.

Helm, Paul. *John Calvin's Ideas*. Oxford: Oxford University Press, 2004.

Heymericus de Campo. *Ars demonstrativa*. Edited by Jean-Daniel Cavigioli. In *Heymericus de Campo: Opera selecta*, edited by Ruedi Imbach and Pascal Ladner. Fribourg: Universitätsverlag, 2001.

De sigillo eternitatis. Edited by Ruedi Imbach and Pascal Ladner. In *Heymericus de Campo. Opera selecta*, edited by Ruedi Imbach and Pascal Ladner. Fribourg: Universitätsverlag, 2001.

Hirschberger, Johannes. 'Das Platon-Bild bei Nikolaus von Kues'. In *Nicolò Cusano agli inizi del mondo moderno*, 113–35. Florence: Sansoni, 1970.

Hoenen, Maarten J. F. M. 'Thomismus, Skotismus und Albertismus. Das Entstehen und die Bedeutung von philosophischen Schulen im späten Mittelalter'. *Bochumer Philosophisches Jahrbuch für Antike und Mittelalter* 2 (1997): 81–103.

'*Via antiqua* and *via moderna* in the Fifteenth Century: Doctrinal, Institutional, and Church Political Factors in the *Wegestreit*'. In *The Medieval Heritage in Early Modern Metaphysics and Modal Theory, 1400–1700*, edited by Russell L. Friedman and Lauge O. Nielsen, 9–36. Dordrecht: Kluwer Academic Publishers, 2003.

Honecker, Martin. *Nikolaus von Cues und die griechische Sprache*. Heidelberg: Winter's Universitätsbuchhandlung, 1938.

Imbach, Ruedi. '*Primum principium*. Anmerkungen zum Wandel in der Auslegung der Bedeutung und Funktion des Satzes vom zu vermeidenden Widerspruch bei Thomas von Aquin, Nikolaus von Autrécourt, Heymericus de Campo und Nikolaus von Kues'. In *Die Logik des Transzendentalen*, edited by Martin Pickavé, 600–16. Berlin and New York: De Gruyter, 2003.

Johannes de Nova Domo. *Capitulum de universali reali*, edited by Henryk Wels. In *Aristotelisches Wissen und Glauben im 15. Jahrhundert*. Amsterdam: Grüner Publishing Company, 2004.

De esse et essentia, edited by Gilles Meersseman. In *Geschichte des Albertismus*, vol. 1: *Die Pariser Anfänge des Kölner Albertismus*. Paris: R. Haloua, 1933.

Johannes Wenck. *De ignota litteratura*, edited by Jasper Hopkins. In *Nicholas of Cusa's Debate with John Wenck. A Translation and an Appraisal of 'De ignota litteratura' and 'Apologia doctae ignorantiae'*. Minneapolis: Banning Press, 1981.

Quaestiones super Hebdomades. In Mainz, Wissenschaftliche Stadtbibliothek, Hs. I 610, ff. 46r–71r.

Kaluza, Zénon. *Les querelles doctrinales à Paris. Nominalistes et réalistes aux confins du XIVe et du XVe siècle*. Bergamo: Lubrina, 1988.

Klibansky, Raymond. *The Continuity of the Platonic Tradition during the Middle Ages*. 3rd ed. Munich: Kraus-Thomson, 1983.

Koyré, Alexandre. *La philosophie de Jacob Boehme*. Paris: Vrin, 1929.

Mystiques, spirituels, alchimistes du XVIe siècle allemand. Schwenckfeld, Franck, Weigel, Paracelse. Paris: Colin, 1955.

Kraye, Jill. 'Moral Philosophy'. In *Cambridge History of Renaissance Philosophy*, edited by Charles B. Schmitt, Quentin Skinner, Eckhard Kessler, and Jill Kraye, 303–86. Cambridge: Cambridge University Press, 1988.

Kühlmann, Wilhelm. 'Das haeretische Potential des Paracelsismus, gesehen im Licht seiner Gegner'. In *Heterodoxie in der Frühen Neuzeit*, edited by

Hartmut Laufhütte and Michael Titzmann, 217–42. Tübingen: Niemeyer, 2006.

'Paracelsismus und Haeresie. Zwei Briefe der Söhne Valentin Weigels aus dem Jahre 1596'. *Wolfenbütteler Barock-Nachrichten* 18 (1991): 24–60.

Kuhnekath, Klaus D. *Die Philosophie des Johannes Wenck im Vergleich zu den Lehren des Nikolaus von Kues*, diss. Cologne: 1975.

Lehmann-Brauns, Sicco. *Weisheit in der Weltgeschichte. Philosophiegeschichte zwischen Barock und Aufklärung.* Tübingen: Niemeyer, 2004.

McLaughlin, R. Emmet. 'The Radical Reformation'. In *The Cambridge History of Christianity*, edited by R. Po-Chia Hsia, 37–55. Cambridge: Cambridge University Press, 2008.

'Spiritualism: Schwenckfeld and Franck and their Early Modern Resonances'. In *A Companion to Anabaptism and Spiritualism 1521–1700*, edited by John Roth and James M. Stayer, 119–61. Leiden: Brill, 2006.

Meier-Oeser, Stephan. *Die Präsenz des Vergessenen. Zur Rezeption der Philosophie des Nicolaus Cusanus vom 15. bis zum 18. Jahrhundert.* Aschendorff: Münster, 1989.

Meister Eckhart. *Selected Writings.* Edited by Oliver Davies. London: Penguin, 1994.

Meliadò, Mario. 'Axiomatic Wisdom: Boethius' *De hebdomadibus* and the *Liber de causis* in Late-Medieval Albertism'. *Bulletin de philosophie médiévale* 55 (2013): 71–131.

Sapienza peripatetica. Eimerico di Campo e i percorsi del tardo albertismo. Münster: Aschendorff, 2018.

Mohr, Richard D. *The Platonic Cosmology.* Leiden: Brill, 1995.

Nicolaus de Cusa. *Apologia doctae ignorantiae.* Edited by Raymond Klibansky. Hamburg: Meiner, 2007.

De beryllo. Edited by Hans Gerhard Senger and Karl Bormann. Hamburg: Meiner, 1988.

De docta ignorantia. Edited by Ernst Hoffmann and Raymond Klibansky. Leipzig: Meiner, 1932.

Paracelsus (Theophrastus Bombastus von Hohenheim). *De mineralibus liber.* In *Sämtliche Werke*, edited by Karl Sudhoff. Munich and Berlin: Oldenburg, 1922–33, vol. 3.

Essential Theoretical Writings. Edited by Andrew Weeks. Leiden: Brill, 2008.

Plotinus. *Enneads.* Edited by Lloyd P. Gerson. Cambridge: Cambridge University Press, 2018.

Popkin, Richard Henry. *The Third Force in Seventeenth-Century Thought.* Leiden: Brill, 1992.

Ruocco, Ilario. *Il Platone latino. Il Parmenide: Giorgio di Trebisonda e il cardinale Cusano.* Florence: Leo S. Olschki, 2003.

Rusconi, Cecilia and Reinhardt, Klaus. 'Die dem Cusanus zugeschriebenen Glossen zu den *Theoremata totius universi fundamentaliter doctrinalia* des Heymericus de Campo', in *Heymericus de Campo. Philosophie und Theologie im 15. Jahrhundert*, edited by Klaus Reinhardt, 58–74. Regensburg: Roderer, 2009.

Santinello, Giovanni. 'Glosse di mano del Cusano alla *Repubblica* di Platone'. *Rinascimento* 9 (1969): 117–145.

Schmidt-Biggemann, Wilhelm. 'Das Geheimnis des Anfangs: Einige spekulative Betrachtungen im Hinblick auf Jakob Böhme'. In *Gott, Natur, Mensch in der Sicht Jakob Böhmes und seiner Rezeption*, edited by Jan Garewicz and Alois M. Haas, 113–27. Wiesbaden: Harrassowitz, 1995.

Philosophia perennis: Historical Outlines of Western Spirituality in Ancient, Medieval and Early Modern Thought. Dordrecht: Springer, 2004.

Senger, Hans Gerhard. 'Aristotelismus vs. Platonismus. Zur Konkurrenz von zwei Archetypen der Philosophie im Spätmittelalter'. In *Aristotelisches Erbe im arabisch-lateinischen Mittelalter*, edited by Albert Zimmermann, 53–80. Berlin and New York: De Gruyter, 1986.

'Die Präferenz für Ps.-Dionysius bei Nikolaus Cusanus und seinem italienischen Umfeld'. In *Die Dionysius-Rezeption im Mittelalter*, edited by Tzotcho Boiadjiev, Georgi Kapriev, and Andreas Speer, 505–39. Turnhout: Brepols, 2000.

Senger, Hans Gerhard, ed. *Cusanus-Texte, III. Marginalien, 2. Proclus Latinus: Die Exzerpte und Randnoten des Nikolaus von Kues zu den lateinischen Übersetzungen der Proclus-Schriften, 2.1 Theologia Platonis. Elementatio theologica*. Heidelberg: Winter Universitätsverlag, 1986.

Shantz, Douglas H. 'Valentin Weigel'. In *Protestants and Mysticism in Reformation Europe*, edited by Ronald K. Rittgers and Vincent Evener, 243–64. Leiden: Brill, 2019.

Solère, Jean-Luc. 'Bien, cercles et hebdomades: forms et raisonnement chez Boèce et Proclus'. In *Boèce ou la chaîne des savoirs. Actes du colloque internationale de la fondation Singer-Polignac*, edited by Alain Galonnier, 55–110. Louvain and Paris: Peeters, 2003.

Thurner, Martin, ed. *Nicolaus Cusanus zwischen Deutschland und Italien*. Berlin: Akademie Verlag, 2002.

Vassányi, Miklós. *Anima Mundi: The Rise of the World Soul Theory in Modern German Philosophy*. Dordrecht: Springer, 2011.

Vollhardt, Friedrich. 'Pythagorische Lehrsätze'. In *Offenbarung und Episteme: Die Wirkung Jakob Böhmes im 17. und 18. Jahrhundert*, edited by Wilhelm Kühlmann and Friedrich Vollhardt, 363–83. Berlin: De Gruyter, 2012.

Weeks, Andrew. *Boehme: An Intellectual Biography of the Seventeenth-Century Philosopher and Mystic*. Albany: State University of New York Press, 1991.

Paracelsus: Speculative Theory and the Crisis of the Early Reformation. Albany: State University of New York Press, 1997.

Valentin Weigel (1533–1588): German Religious Dissenter, Speculative Theorist, and Advocate of Tolerance. Albany: State University of New York Press, 2000.

Weigel, Valentin. *Sämtliche Schriften*, edited by Horst Pfefferl. Stuttgart and Bad Cannstatt: Frommann-Holzboog, 1996–, in particular vol. 2, *De luce et caligine divina; De vita beata*; vol. 3, *Gnothi seauton*; vol. 8, *Der güldene Griff*; vol. 9, *Seligmachende Erkenntnis Gottes*; vol. 11, *Viererlei Auslegung von der Schöpfung*.

Wollgast, Siegfried. *Philosophie in Deutschland zwischen Reformation und Aufklärung 1550–1650*. Berlin: Akademie Verlag, 1993.

Zeller, Rosemarie. 'Böhme-Rezeption am Hof von Christian August von Pflaz-Sulzbach'. In *Offenbarung und Episteme. Die Wirkung Jakob Böhmes im 17. und 18. Jahrhundert*, edited by Wilhelm Kühlmann and Friedrich Vollhardt, 125–41. Berlin: De Gruyter, 2012.

Ziebart, Meredith K. *Nicolaus Cusanus on Faith and the Intellect. A Case Study in 15th-Century Fides-Ratio Controversy*. Leiden: Brill, 2014.

Christian Platonism in Early Modernity

Derek A. Michaud

There seems to be a battle like that of the gods and the giants going on among them, because of their disagreement about existence. ... Some of them drag down everything from heaven and the invisible to earth, ... and maintain stoutly that that alone exists which can be touched and handled; for they define existence and body, or matter, as identical.[1]

The desire to understand and control nature gives practical incentive to follow the lead of the giants while the demands of Christian orthodoxy suggest the necessity of following Plato's gods in contemplating what is above nature. Yet, by revisioning the human heart as a mechanism it has become possible to repair it. But if mechanism is all there is, the truths of religion fall away.

Christian Platonists in early modernity sought to mediate between the new science and the metaphysics of Christianity including above all the immateriality and immortality of the soul and God. A creative tension in early modern philosophy and theology between mechanism and spirit led to dualisms, monisms, and positions in between. The variety of resolutions explored here are only a sampling of the new forms of philosophy and theology sparked by the collapse of the "Aristotelian Amalgam" of Scholasticism.[2] Whereas the earlier "Augustinian Synthesis" had been a Christianized version of Platonic theism, and thus held together organically as a unified body of doctrine, Scholasticism called for a more

---

[1] Plato, *Sophist*, trans. Harold N. Fowler (Cambridge, MA: Harvard University Press, 1921), 246a–b.

[2] Stephen Gaukroger, *The Emergence of a Scientific Culture: Science and the Shaping of Modernity, 1210–1685* (Oxford: Oxford University Press, 2006), 77–86.

delicate balance between Aristotelian philosophy and "Neoplatonically formulated Christianity."[3]

New forms of natural philosophy developed in the same milieu that gave rise to the rebirth of Christian Platonism championed by Ficino. Recognizing the explanatory limits of Scholastic approaches natural philosophers were drawn to corpuscles and efficient causation as the keys to understanding nature. Christian Platonists in early modernity too were often taken by this new science but became unnerved by the conjunction of what we would call materialism, naturalism, mechanism, and empiricism. As Wilson and LoLordo have shown this conjunction was understood as, and in some cases was, a revival of the ancient school of Epicureanism.[4] These early modern "Epicureans" were nearly universally identified as tantamount to atheists.[5]

Continuing a process begun in the Renaissance by figures like Nicholas of Cusa and Ficino many turned to Platonism for a systematic approach to natural philosophy and Christian theology. Yet how to retain the insights of the new mechanical science, which after all *worked*, while not abandoning the central doctrines of Christianity, including not just God as creator, sustainer, and redeemer but the immortality of the soul and divine providence too, was a major challenge. Some embraced forms of substance dualism. Others tried to mediate between body and soul in various ways. While still others were led to forms of idealism and solved the problems of substance dualism by way of a monism of spirit. All drew in various ways from the rich resources of Christian Platonism.

This chapter offers a selective interpretation of the nature of Christian Platonism in early modernity highlighting its place in some canonical philosophers and figures less well known than they should be today.[6] The aim is twofold. First, to offer a point of access for an appreciation of the significance of Christian Platonism in the period. Second, to draw into sharp relief the internal diversity of the tradition.

---

[3] Gaukroger, *Emergence*, 77.

[4] See Antonia LoLordo, "Epicureanism and Early Modern Naturalism," *British Journal for the History of Philosophy* 19, no. 4 (2011), 647–664; and Catherine Wilson, *Epicureanism at the Origins of Modernity* (New York: Oxford University Press, 2008).

[5] Thomas M. Lennon, *The Battle of the Gods and Giants: The Legacies of Descartes and Gassendi, 1655–1715* (Princeton, NJ: Princeton University Press, 1993), 6.

[6] For a more extensive introduction with similar scope see the essays in Douglas Hedley and Sarah Hutton, eds., *Platonism at the Origins of Modernity: Studies on Platonism and Early Modern Philosophy* (Dordrecht: Springer, 2008).

DESCARTES, SMITH, AND MALEBRANCHE

Perhaps the easiest way to accept the innovations of the new mechanical and mathematical physics while protecting traditional Christian beliefs about the spiritual nature of the soul and God is to simply posit two non-overlapping realms. Serendipitously the Platonic tradition has elements seemingly tailor made for just such a purpose in its tendency to distinguish sharply between mind and body. Plato himself famously "sets up a strong anti-thesis between mind and body" in the *Phaedo*, *Phaedrus*, and *Timaeus*.[7] The later Platonic tradition continued to assume the separability of mind and body.[8] The rest of this section calls attention to the Christian Platonism of René Descartes (1596–1650) and relates it to the Alexandrian Christian Plotinianism of John Smith (1618–1652) and the explicitly Augustinian philosophy of Nicolas Malebranche (1638–1715).

Augustine of Hippo famously sought to know two things, the soul and God.[9] Throughout his mature writings he followed a common Platonic pattern of averting attention from the empirical world around us into the soul, and from the soul as image to God as original transcendent source. As Stephen Menn has argued, Descartes "took from Augustine ... a hope and a discipline of drawing the mind away from the senses, through a special kind of contemplation of itself, to a special kind of contemplation of God."[10] This is most clearly seen in the contemplative itinerary of Descartes's *Meditations on First Philosophy* (1641).[11]

The first day of meditation begins the process of aversion from the external world of sense via hyperbolic doubt.[12] Descartes is calling here for his reader to turn within themselves and away from the senses and the

---

[7] John Dillon, "Plotinus, the First Cartesian?" *Hermathena* 149 (1990), 19–31 at p. 20.

[8] Dillon, "Plotinus," 21. See also Anna Marmodoro and Sophie Cartwright, eds., *A History of Mind and Body in Late Antiquity* (Cambridge: Cambridge University Press, 2018).

[9] Augustine, *Soliloquia*, 1.2.7.

[10] Stephen Menn, *Descartes and Augustine* (New York: Cambridge University Press, 1998), x. See also Zbigniew Janowski, *Augustinian-Cartesian Index: Texts and Commentary* (South Bend, IN: St. Augustine Press, 2004). For the suggestion of Teresa of Ávila as the vector for this influence see Christia Mercer, "Descartes' Debt to Teresa of Ávila, or Why we Should Work on Women in the History of Philosophy," *Philosophical Studies* 174 (2017), 2539–2555.

[11] René Descartes, *Meditations on First Philosophy*, in *The Philosophical Writings of Descartes* [CSM], trans. John Cottingham, Robert Stoothoff, and Dugald Murdoch (New York: Cambridge University Press, 1984), II: 3–62; and *Oeuvres de Descartes* [AT], ed. Charles Adam and Paul Tannery (Paris: Librairie Philosophique J. Vrin, 1964–1974), VII: 1–90.

[12] Descartes, *Meditations*, 1 (CSM II: 15/AT VII: 22).

external world. Why would an early modern scientist want to turn away
from the realm of scientific inquiry? Because he is trying, just as Augustine
and Plotinus before him, to break free from the constraints of a sense-
bound ideology, Stoicism and Epicureanism for Plotinus and Augustine,
Scholasticism for Descartes. All three "believe that they can attain wisdom
only through an intellectual intuition purified of sensory traces."[13]

After the first day of meditating Descartes has turned his attention so
entirely from the realm of sense that it is doubtful that he has a body.[14]
Yet, this does not mean that his existence is doubtful. For even when we
doubt, we are present to ourselves as doubters; "cogito, ergo sum."[15]
Augustine too refuted skepticism by appealing to the necessity of our
existence by contemplating our ability to be in error. If I err, I am
alive.[16] Both take these considerations as evidence that they are what
Descartes calls *res cogitans*, a "thinking thing."

Descartes and Augustine both conceptualize body in terms of spatial
extension in three dimensions allowing for movement in space and time
while portraying soul as movable only in time.[17] Descartes then lays out
his famous substance dualism as a consequence of his Augustinian
Christian Platonist spiritual exercise of aversion. He goes on to specify
more clearly the implications of this dualism in later Meditations, and
most fully in his natural philosophy, but the metaphysical basis is set for
a physics of bodily extension and a rational psychology rooted in immaterial spirit. The new science can have, therefore, no adverse effects upon
our understanding of the soul or vice versa.

Like Augustine, Descartes is not satisfied with the rudiments of rational
psychology and pushes on to the contemplation of God as well. On the
third day Descartes' aversion into himself as *res cogitans* leads him to
reflect upon God via his "trademark argument." Descartes argues that
only an infinite mind could be the source of the idea of God he finds within
himself.[18] On the fourth day Descartes sures up his cardinal epistemic

---

[13] Menn, *Descartes and Augustine*, 394.
[14] Descartes, *Meditations*, 1 (CSM II: 15/AT VII: 22–23).
[15] Descartes, *Principia Philosophiae*, 1.7 (CSM I: 194–195/AT VIIIA: 7). Cf. Descartes,
    Meditations, 2 (CSM II: 17/AT VII: 25).
[16] Augustine, *de Trinitate*, 10.10.14.
[17] Descartes, *Meditations*, 2 (CSM II: 16–23/AT VII: 24–34) and Augustine, *Epistulae*,
    166.4. See also Bruno Niederbacher, "The Human Soul: Augustine's Case for Soul-
    Body Dualism," in *The Cambridge Companion to Augustine*, 2nd ed., ed.
    Eleonore Stump and Norman Kretzmann (New York: Cambridge University Press,
    2014), 125–141 at p. 125.
[18] Descartes, *Meditations*, 3 (CSM II: 31–35/AT VII: 45–52).

principle of "clear and distinct ideas" by arguing that God would not allow us to be systematically misled because the idea of God is of a perfect being including moral perfection.[19] On the fifth day Descartes offers a version of the "ontological argument" in order to demonstrate that the supremely perfect Deity he conceives of necessarily exists as existence is part of God's essence.[20] Thus, when we judge carefully about those natural things he reintroduces on the sixth day we can rest assured that we are not in error.[21]

"Descartes conceived his physics – and therefore science more generally – as resting on the metaphysical foundations developed in the *Meditations* and recast in the early sections of *The Principles of Philosophy*."[22] Yet it is by adopting the Augustinian path of aversion that Descartes established these foundations. The whole superstructure then, including the metaphysical dualism so contested then as now, rests upon a form of Christian Platonism.[23] It is little wonder then that many of Descartes's first readers thought him unoriginal, a major insult to Descartes, and specifically pointed out how his major arguments had been anticipated by Augustine. For example, Marin Mersenne called his attention to the Augustinian argument that if I am mistaken I necessarily exist in 1637 as did Andreas Colvius in 1640.[24] Among the first readers of Descartes in England the Cambridge Platonist John Smith (1618–1652) saw in Descartes the latest in a long line of Christian Platonists.

Smith, intruded fellow of Queens' College Cambridge from 1644 till his untimely death, is best known today as a particularly eloquent member of the Cambridge Platonists. His Christian Platonism is clear throughout the posthumously published *Select Discourses* where he often explains scripture and Christian doctrine by way of Plotinus.[25] Smith's "True Way or Method of Attaining to Divine Knowledge" for example identifies the proper approach to theological understanding with the Christian Platonic path of aversion from the realm of sense, into the soul as image of God,

---

[19] Ibid, 4 (CSM II: 37–43/AT VII: 53–62).   [20] Ibid, 5 (CSM II: 45–47/AT VII: 65–69).

[21] Ibid, 6 (CSM II: 50–62/AT VII: 71–90).

[22] Margaret J. Osler, "Eternal Truths and the Laws of Nature: The Theological Foundations of Descartes' Philosophy of Nature," *Journal of the History of Ideas* 46, no. 3 (1985), 349–362 at p. 349.

[23] Menn, *Descartes and Augustine*, 394–395.

[24] See Descartes's letters to Mersenne 25 May 1637 (AT I: 376) and 15 November 1638 (AT II: 435) and his letter to Colvius 14 November 1640 (AT III: 247–248). Cf. Augustine, *De civitate Dei*, XI.26.

[25] John Smith, *Select Discourses* (London: J. Fisher, 1660).

culminating in contemplation of God.[26] For Smith as for Origen, Augustine, and to a limited extent Descartes, "we must shut the Eyes of Sense, and open that brighter Eye of our Understanding."[27] "This," Smith tells us, "is the way to see clearly" for when we avert our attention from the senses "the light of the Divine Word will then begin to fall upon us."[28] Smith's purposes are apologetic and catechetical rather than scientific but he agrees in terms of basic method with Descartes and, as we will see, he embraced a form of illuminationism like Malebranche on this basis.

In Smith's hands this illumination is always a matter of moral purification too:

Divinity indeed is a true Efflux from the Eternal light, which, like Sun-beams does not only enlighten, but heat and enliven; and therefore our Saviour hath in his *Beatitudes* connext Purity of heart with the Beatifical vision. And as the Eye cannot behold the Sun ... unless it be *Sun-like*, and hath the form and resemblance of the Sun drawn into it, so neither can the Soul of man behold God ... unless it be *Godlike*, hath God formed it, and be made partaker of the Divine Nature. And the Apostle S. Paul when he would lay open the right way of attaining to Divine Truth, he saith that *knowledge puffeth up*, but it is *Love that edifieth*.[29]

Smith agrees with Descartes that we must have "an antecedent Converse with our own Souls" in order to understand the true nature thereof.[30] While Descartes does not live up to the promise to demonstrate the immortality of the soul in his *Meditations* Smith makes explicit use of the immateriality of the soul to that purpose.[31]

Smith argues for two basic substances, body and soul. Drawing on both Plotinus and his reading of Descartes he says body is divisible, material, and extended in three dimensions and soul (including mind) is incorporeal, immaterial, dimensionless, and therefore incapable of division.[32] Smith's fourth formal argument for the immortality of the soul is a prime example of his Platonism and how he viewed Descartes in that light. Each of Smith's arguments for immortality follow Proclus' degrees of knowledge.[33] In the fourth, he finally arrives at the level of the "naked

---

[26] John Smith, "True Way or Method of Attaining to Divine Knowledge," in *Select Discourses*, 17–21.

[27] Ibid, 16. [28] Ibid, 16. [29] Ibid, 3.

[30] Smith, "Discourse of the Immortality of the Soul," in *Select Discourses*, 65.

[31] See Descartes, *Meditations*, Dedicatory Letter to the Sorbonne (CSM II: 3/AT VII: 1–2).

[32] Smith, "Immortality," 68. See also Descartes, *Principles*, I.53 (CSM I: 210–211/AT VIIIA: 25).

[33] Proclus, *In Platonis Timaeum Commentarii*, ed. E. Diehl (Leipzig: Teubner, 1903–1906), I.243.26–252.10.

intuition of Eternal Truth," including the archetypes of justice, wisdom, goodness, truth, eternity, and other first principles of moral, physical, and metaphysical sciences.[34] Our ability to intuit these intelligible and immaterial principles means for Smith that the rational soul cannot be material.[35] To these considerations he immediately adds another drawn from Descartes.

Smith argues that "whensoever we take notice of those *Immediate motions* of our own *Minds* whereby they make themselves known to us, we find no such thing in them as Extension or Divisibility."[36] While Smith is not a Cartesian *per se* he clearly understood Descartes as standing within the broad Platonic tradition and therefore as conducive for his own apologetic Christian Platonism.[37] His admiration for Descartes went so far as to accept the interaction of spiritual and bodily substances in the pineal gland as proposed in *The Passions of the Soul*.[38] Whereas Smith attempts to resolve the apparent paradox of body and soul interaction by way of Plotinus, Cartesians were busy coming up with their own solutions. Among them was Nicolas Malebranche (1638–1715) dubbed the "premier philosopher of our age" by Pierre Bayle.[39]

Malebranche read Descartes's *Traite de l'Homme* in 1664 and found in it "the true philosophy, firmly based on clear and distinct ideas, and providing demonstrative arguments with all the rigour of mathematical proofs."[40] The following decade saw Malebranche adapt Cartesian natural philosophy to the needs of Christian theology as he understood them. His mature fusion of Cartesianism and Augustinianism appeared in *Recherche de la Verité* (1674). Relying heavily on the Cartesian notion of clear and distinct ideas it is here that Malebranche set forth the two doctrines most often associated with his name: occasionalism and vision in God.

---

[34] Smith, "Immortality," 97.

[35] Smith is implicitly drawing upon the "affinity argument" from Plato's *Phaedo*, 78b4–84b4 and Plotinus, *Enneads*, IV.7.8.1–7, IV.7.9.26–27, IV.7.10.1–6, IV.7.3.1–4.

[36] Smith, "Immortality," 98. Cf. Descartes, *Meditations* 2 (AT II: 23–34; CSM II:16–23).

[37] Derek A. Michaud, *Reason Turned into Sense: John Smith on Spiritual Sensation* (Leuven: Peeters, 2017), 161–189.

[38] Smith, "Immortality," 113–117; Descartes, *The Passions of the Soul*, 30–36 (CSM I: 339–342/AT XI: 351–357).

[39] Tad Schmaltz, "Nicolas Malebranche," in *The Stanford Encyclopedia of Philosophy*, ed. Edward N. Zalta, https://plato.stanford.edu/archives/win2017/entries/malebranche/, accessed 31 January 2020.

[40] Andrew Pyle, *Malebranche* (London and New York: Routledge, 2003), 2.

While Descartes might not strictly speaking have been a "Cartesian dualist" Malebranche clearly was.[41] Unlike Smith who seems not to have appreciated the issue, Malebranche is clear that interaction between unlike substances is unintelligible.[42] Malebranche's solution was to embrace occasionalism. Malebranche's position is based on Augustine's belief that all things rest on the creative and sustaining act of God. God has seen to it that regular patterns obtain between states of the body and states of the mind, yet they do not actually interact at all.[43]

In epistemology Malebranche's debt to Augustine is most pronounced and profound. For "as the eye needs light to see, so the mind requires ideas in order to know."[44] If sensation itself is a mode of immaterial mind as it is for Malebranche it is not clear how we can have basic sensory experience of material things. Malebranche's answer is that we perceive things around us *in* God. All knowledge therefore is revealed knowledge for Malebranche because any human knowing relies on our having access to the ideas by which God continuously creates the cosmos.

All Malebranche's central doctrines, occasionalism, vision in God, his denial of theological voluntarism, and so on, served a single purpose; that of unifying the new science and his ancient faith in a single "system." But Malebranche was not the only seventeenth-century philosophical theologian seeking to make new again the harmonious system of Christian Platonism. In England two colleagues of Smith were also attempting to synthesize a truly rational theology or "intellectual system."

CUDWORTH, MORE, AND CONWAY

Ralph Cudworth (1617–1688) was perhaps the most prominent of the Cambridge Platonists.[45] With Henry More (1614–1687) and others he

---

[41] Pyle, *Malebranche*, 6. On the unity of mind and body in Descartes see Jean-Luc Marion, *On Descartes' Passive Thought: The Myth of Cartesian Dualism*, trans. Christina M. Gschwandtner (Chicago and London: University of Chicago Press, 2018).

[42] Nicholas Malebranche, *The Search after Truth*, trans. Thomas M. Lennon and Paul J. Olscamp (Cambridge: Cambridge University Press, 1997), 101–109 (bk 1, pt. 2, ch. 5).

[43] Malebranche, *Search*, 101–102. Occasionalism is not an *ad hoc* solution to the mind–body problem, however. See Schmaltz, "Malebranche," §4.

[44] Pyle, *Malebranche*, 7. Lydia Schumacher, *Divine Illumination: The History and Future of Augustine's Theory of Knowledge* (Oxford: Wiley-Blackwell, 2011) is the best account of the theme in Augustine.

[45] David Leech, "Defining 'Cambridge Platonism'," in *The Cambridge Platonism Sourcebook*, ed. Douglas Hedley, David Leech et al., www.cambridge-platonism.divinity.cam.ac.uk/about-the-cambridge-platonists/defining-cambridge-platonism, accessed 31 January 2020.

exercised considerable influence upon Latitudinarianism, Romanticism, and Idealism both in Germany and Britain.[46] Cudworth's fame rests primarily on the massive, yet incomplete, *True Intellectual System of the Universe* (1678), a Christian Platonist rebuttal of various forms of "atheism." Above all Cudworth opposed as detrimental to good morals and Christian truth those philosophies which banish spirit from the material world. Explicitly citing Plato's conflict between the gods and giants he sought to reanimate what the Cartesians and others had made lifeless.[47] "They make a kid of Dead and Wooden World, as it were a Carved Statue, that hath nothing *Vital* nor *Magical* at all in it."[48] In contrast, those who give the matter proper consideration will clearly see that "there is a Mixture of Life or Plastic Nature together with Mechanism, which runs through the whole Corporeal Universe."[49] In so claiming Cudworth is calling upon the resources of the ancient theology he and other Renaissance Platonists identified with the tradition from Pythagoras through Plato, the late ancient commentators, Plotinus, Proclus, and so on, and the Christian Fathers of Alexandria Clement and Origen. In calling upon the Christian Platonist tradition to answer competing philosophies Cudworth followed a then long-established pattern in Anglicanism that came to flower in Cambridge, and to a lesser extent also at Oxford in the seventeenth century.[50]

First, like Descartes and others in this chapter Cudworth sought to resist the encroachment of the giants of "Epicureanism" upon faith and morality. Where Descartes painted himself into a dualistic corner, and Malebranche leaned heavily on a micromanaging Deity to bridge that gap, Cudworth endeavored to enliven atomism by uniting it with an active principle. This "Plastic Nature" plays a mediating role therefore between matter and mind like the World Soul of Plato's *Timaeus* and Plotinus' Soul. Cudworth insisted that while corporeal things are composed of atoms this cannot be the result of unguided happenstance as the Epicureans would have it because matter is essentially passive. Something beyond the atoms themselves must be the

---

[46] Douglas Hedley, "Gods and Giants: Cudworth's Platonic Metaphysics and his Ancient Theology," *British Journal for the History of Philosophy* 25, no. 5 (2017), 946–951. My discussion of Cudworth is much indebted to Hedley's synopsizing work.

[47] Ralph Cudworth, *The True Intellectual System of the Universe* (London: Richard Royston, 1678), 18.

[48] Cudworth, *System*, 148.   [49] Ibid.

[50] See for example Paul Anthony Dominiak, *Richard Hooker: The Architecture of Participation* (London and New York: Bloomsbury, 2019) and James Bryson, *The Christian Platonism of Thomas Jackson* (Leuven: Peeters, 2016).

stimulus for their motion. They cannot simply move each other for that would reach an endless regress of secondary causes.[51]

To avoid the inanimate world of Descartes Cudworth picks up on and develops a notion of Henry More's that accounts for physics via the "Spirit of Nature."[52] For both Cambridge Platonists this active yet incorporeal principle actuates corporeal processes in the visible world composed of atoms. Cudworth sought to gain the physical insights of atomism without accepting the metaphysical consequences; to tame the giants to the service of the gods. Conceptually he accomplishes this by appealing to the long-held Christian Platonist notion that the entirety of the cosmos "be nothing else by *Deum Explicatum, God Expanded or Unfolded.*"[53] That is, Cudworth "wishes to sustain the vision of a universe originating in its transcendent Cause and suffused with the energy of that First Cause into the lower levels of Being as 'radii Deiatis'."[54] To this end Cudworth stressed "four tenets of 'emanative power to create'."[55]

Emanation involves a procession from the greater to the lesser.[56] Created things arise by a "*Gradual Descent into Greater Multiplicity*" from Divine Unity such that "*That which is Generated or Emaneth, immediately from the First and Highest Being, is not the very same thing with it.*" Indeed, "it must needs be *Gradually subordinate* and *Inferiour* to it."[57]

Nature reflects its transcendent source while remaining distinct from it. The visible realm is an ectype reflecting and participating in the archetypes in the mind of God.[58] Cudworth compares these archetypes and ectypes to the "*Verbum Mentis*" and verbal speech or "*Articulate Sound.*" The former is original and known by the mind that conceives it while the latter is informed by the former while remaining itself unknowing.[59]

The reflection of the cause is present in the effect just as an image in a mirror. As Cudworth says, "the *Plastic life of Nature* is but the *Umbrage* of *Intellectuality*, a faint and shadowy *Imitation* of *Mind* and *Understanding*; upon which it doth as Essentially depend, as the shadow doth upon the Body, the Image in the Glass upon the Face, or the Echo upon the Original Voice."[60]

---

[51] Sarah Hutton, "The Cambridge Platonists," in *The Stanford Encyclopedia of Philosophy*, ed. Edward N. Zalta, https://plato.stanford.edu/archives/win2013/entries/cambridge-platonists/, accessed 31 January 2020.

[52] John Henry, "Henry More," in *The Stanford Encyclopedia of Philosophy*, ed. Edward N. Zalta, https://plato.stanford.edu/archives/win2016/entries/henry-more/, accessed 31 January 2020, §3.

[53] Cudworth, *System*, 308. [54] Hedley, "God and Giants," 941. [55] Ibid.

[56] Cudworth, *System*, 581. [57] Ibid. [58] Ibid, 155. [59] Ibid. [60] Ibid, 172.

Finally, the Divine Source is not reduced by emanation. God, for Cudworth, is like a fountain continuously pouring out the world yet never running dry.[61] All of this is consistent with Neoplatonism but Cudworth is a *Christian* Neoplatonist. His emanationism made it easy to identify the ancient Platonic hypostases as partial glimpses of the Christian Trinity, but Cudworth was clear that it is only as revealed in Christ and interpreted by the Christian Fathers that this theology comes to completion.[62]

By 1642 Henry More was a committed Christian Platonist emphasizing matter and spirit dualism and the immortality of the soul in his first publication the *Psychodia Platonica* (*Platonic Song of the Soul*). Like Cudworth and Smith, More came to an early rejection of Calvinist predestination too. In its place More embraces the Alexandrian Patristic tradition of Clement and Origen with its emphasis on free will. More's dualism and interest in natural philosophy led him to Descartes's *Principia Philosophiae* in 1646 and he soon began teaching Cartesian mechanical philosophy at Cambridge. The very word "Cartesianism" in English is his coinage. More however was never an uncritical Cartesian. Over time he became more publicly critical of Cartesian philosophy as it became clear, especially after Descartes's death in 1650, that they did not agree on the limits of material mechanism in physics.[63]

An early example of the argument that led More away from Cartesian philosophy as insufficient can be found in a letter from Descartes to More where the Frenchman portrayed animals as mechanical automata that move without thinking.[64] Ever concerned to guard against creeping atheism More saw this banishment of soul as an opening for denying the immaterial, and immortal, soul of human beings. The Scholastic consensus had it that nonhuman animals have vegetative and animal soul but that these are material things composed of fluids and material spirits. Descartes rejected this and simply assigned the functions of these lower souls to material mechanism. More too rejected the scholastic view but

---

[61] Ralph Cudworth, *A Sermon Preached before the Honourable House of Commons at Westminster, March 31, 1647* (Cambridge: Roger Daniel, 1647), A1r, 33, 34; Cudworth, *System*, 43, 45, 595, 598, 600.

[62] Ibid, 406–408, 546–632.

[63] Henry, "More," §2. See also David Leech, The Hammer of the Cartesians: Henry More's Philosophy of Spirit and the Origins of Modern Atheism (Leuven: Peeters, 2013).

[64] René Descartes, letter to Henry More, 5 February 1649, in *The Philosophical Writings of Descartes, Vol. III: The Correspondence*, ed. John Cottingham, Robert Stoothoff, Dugald Murdoch, and Anthony Kenny (Cambridge: Cambridge University Press, 1991), 366 (AT V: 277–278).

also the Cartesian. For him only immaterial animal souls can animate material bodies. The central assumption for More is that matter is passive and only immaterial substances are active, a view he initially thought was accepted by Descartes as well.[65] With Smith, and all Christian Platonists, More saw the doctrine of soul as an essential stepping stone for the doctrine of God. As he eloquently put it, "*No Spirit, no God.*"[66]

More's written work is voluminous and touches on the soul, natural philosophy, the Spirit of Nature, atheism, enthusiasm, Christian piety, and more. The guiding principles of his thought however are all clearly drawn from Christian Platonism; a qualified dualism of body and spirit, the incorporeality and immortality of the soul, the rejection of voluntarist theology, spiritual extension, and his affinity for the "ancient theology" and Platonized Kabbalah. In this he stands definitively with the other Cambridge Platonists against Hobbesian materialism, Spinozism, and Cartesianism. Involved in many notable polemics in his day More's lasting influence has been minor outside a committed group of followers and critics. Among the most interesting of these is Viscountess Anne Conway (1631–1679).

Conway came to be mentored by More via letter through her brother who was his student at Christ's College, Cambridge. Their extent philosophical correspondence concerns Cartesianism primarily. Through the Flemish philosopher and physician Francis Mercury van Helmont she was introduced to Lurianic Kabbalah and Quakerism. She is remembered primarily today for a single posthumously published treatise, anonymously published in 1690 in Latin translation and then retranslated back into English as *The Principles of the Most Ancient and Modern Philosophy* in 1692.

As would be expected from More's "heroine pupil" Conway's book is a work of Platonic metaphysics and theology as well as a riposte to Descartes, Hobbes, Spinoza, and in some respects, More himself.[67] Her philosophy is composed of a three-part hierarchy of "species." The highest species is God as eternal creator and source of all being. The lowest species is "creature" or created substance which even though contingent remains wholly spiritual.[68] Conway in fact denies the existence of material

---

[65] Henry, "More," §2.

[66] Henry More, An Antidote Against Atheisme, Or an Appeal to the Natural Faculties of Man, whether there be not a God (London: Roger Daniel, 1653), 164.

[67] Richard Ward, *The Life of Henry More*, ed. Sarah Hutton, Cecil Courtney, Michelle Courtney, Robert Crocker, and A. Rupert Hall (Dordrecht: Springer, 2000), 177.

[68] Sarah Hutton, "Lady Anne Conway," in *The Stanford Encyclopedia of Philosophy*, ed. Edward N. Zalta, https://plato.stanford.edu/archives/fall2015/entries/conway/, accessed 31 January 2020, §2.

bodies on the grounds that such lifeless bulk contradicts the nature of the Divine as life itself. While spiritual like God, creature consists of particles called "monads" whereas God is purely simple.[69] Moreover, creature differs from God in being mutable. Creaturely substance is animate and perceptual too. There is no purely passive substance in this vitalist ontology. While distinct from each other as principle and principled, creator to creature, Divine substance and created substance nevertheless share a likeness in that creature participates in God's life, goodness, and justice. This continuum between creator and creature is mediated by "middle nature" or Christ.[70] The middle nature of Christ participates simultaneously in God and creature creating a bridge between the extremes of Conway's spiritual monism.[71]

Thus, Conway's whole metaphysics is based on the existence and attributes of God with which she opens her treatise.[72] God is wholly spiritual, omniscient, omnibenevolent, omnipotent, omnipresent, timeless, and creator of all things.[73] In God "there is an idea which is his image or the word existing within himself, which in substance or essence is one and the same with him through which he knows himself as well as other things and, indeed, all creatures were made or created according to this very idea or word."[74] Moreover, "there is spirit or will in God, which comes from him and which is in terms of substance or essence nevertheless one with him, through which creatures receive their essence and activity."[75]

In addition to the metaphysical and theological core of her positive vision Conway's treatise contains chapters devoted to pointing out the flaws of Cartesian and Morean dualism.[76] Like Malebranche, and in differing ways Leibniz and Berkeley, Conway answers the dualism of mind and body with a continuum of single substance (spirit) differing only in mode (at once more gross and corporeal, elsewise more spiritual and incorporeal). Conway too dismisses the materialism of Hobbes and Spinoza.[77] Thus, Conway was an apologist for the Christian Platonist tradition, heavily influenced by Renaissance

---

[69] Hutton, "Conway," §2 and Anne Conway, *The Principles of the Most Ancient and Modern Philosophy*, ed. Allison P. Coudert and Taylor Corse (Cambridge: Cambridge University Press, 1996), 20 (ch. III, §10).

[70] Hutton, "Conway," §2 and Conway, *Principles*, 24 (ch. V, §2).

[71] Conway, *Principles*, 26 (ch. V, §5).   [72] Ibid, 9–11 (ch. I).   [73] Ibid, 9 (ch. I, §§ 1–5).

[74] Ibid, 10 (ch. I, §6).   [75] Ibid, 10 (ch. I, §7).

[76] Ibid, 41–61 (chs. VII–VIII) and 63–64 (ch. IX, §§2–3).

[77] Ibid, 63–70 (ch. IX, §§2–9).

Kabbalah, against "Epicureanism" who tried to advance a positive account of the system of the world without the problems of strict dualism.

Through the mediation of Christ and purgative suffering creatures can become more like God, more spiritual and morally better. Evil in this approach is the result of a kind of falling away from divine perfection. Following Origen, she argues that our fallen condition cannot result in an eternal damnation. Rather, our mutability allows us to seek perfection. Conway's metaphysics is therefore also a theodicy. This dual nature of her thought has long invited comparisons to Leibniz. However, while he was gifted a copy of Conway's treatise by van Helmont, a friend of both, their common use of the term "monad" likely has more to do with common Platonic sources from antiquity than each other.[78] Still, Leibniz was undoubtably correct when he observed in a letter to Thomas Burnett in 1697 that "My philosophical views approach somewhat closely those of the late Countess Conway, and hold a middle position between Plato and Democritus, because I hold that all things take place mechanically as Democritus and Descartes contend against the views of Henry More and his followers, and hold too, nevertheless, that everything takes place according to a living principle and according to final causes – all things are full of life and consciousness, contrary to the views of the atomists."[79]

LEIBNIZ, BERKELEY, AND COLONIAL AMERICA

Gottfried Wilhelm Leibniz (1646–1716) has been called the "last great Christian Platonist."[80] The remaining chapters of the present volume speak to the dubious claim to be the last, but it is beyond doubt that Leibniz was a Christian Platonist. Leibniz framed his differences with Locke in terms of ancient philosophy, saying "His is closer to Aristotle and mine to Plato."[81] Far from a mere epistemic family resemblance though Leibniz is here signally that the true heart of his system lies in a Platonism ever in the service of Christian orthodoxy. Best remembered today for his discovery of calculus and the notion that despite all appearances this is the best of all possible worlds, Leibniz came by his Platonism

---

[78] Hutton, "Conway," §2.   [79] Quoted in Conway, *Principles*, xxx.

[80] Jack Davidson, "Leibniz: The Last Great Christian Platonist," in *Brill's Companion to German Platonism*, ed. Alan Kim (Leiden and Boston: Brill, 2019), 43–75.

[81] Gottfried Wilhelm Leibniz, *New Essays on Human Knowledge*, trans. and ed. Peter Remnant and Jonathan Bennett (Cambridge: Cambridge University Press, 1996), 47.

easily from his teachers. For, the "two most prominent professors at Leipzig in the middle of the seventeenth century, Johann Adam Scherzer [1628–1683] and Jakob Thomasius [1622–1684]" were both committed to Christian Platonism of an eclectic kind.[82]

Among the Platonic themes that have been identified in Leibniz's philosophy include the rational soul as paradigm of substance, our immediate first-person access to our own souls, the relative unreality of the material world, and the ultimate reality of the immaterial ideal world, among many others.[83] Providing key support for three of Leibniz's most characteristic doctrines however is the classic concept of emanative creation.

Leibniz speaks often of the relation between God and creatures as one of emanation. The *Discourse on Metaphysics* offers a telling example.

For one sees clearly that all other substances depend on God, in the same way as thoughts emanate from our substance, that God is all in all, and that he is intimately united with all creatures, in proportion to their perfection, that it is he alone who determines them from the outside by his influence, and, if to act is to determine immediately, it can be said in this sense, in the language of metaphysics, that God alone operates on me.[84]

Leibniz thus is clearly an emanationist and this emanative creativity is not just an act in the beginning. Rather, for him, God continuously emanates creation. As Leibniz puts it in the *Monadology*, "God alone is the primitive unity or the first [*originaire*] simple substance; all created or derivative monads are products, and are generated, so to speak, by continual fulgurations of the divinity from moment to moment."[85]

In Leibniz's mature formulation simple substances or monads are "the true atoms of nature."[86] As non-composite monads cannot come to be by natural processes nor can they pass away by them. Monads only come to be by emanative creation.[87] Each monad expresses the Divine in a different way thus there are an infinite number of monads which form

---

[82] Christia Mercer, *Leibniz's Metaphysics: Its Origin and Development* (Cambridge: Cambridge University Press, 2002), 200. Leibniz was also influenced by Erhard Weigel (1625–1699) and, of course, his own wide-ranging reading in the history of philosophy and theology.

[83] Davidson, "Leibniz," 53.

[84] G. W. Leibniz, *Discourse on Metaphysics*, in *Philosophical Essays*, ed. and trans. Roger Ariew and Daniel Garber, 35–68 (Indianapolis, IN: Hackett Publishing Company, 1989), §32.

[85] G. W. Leibniz, *Monadology*, in *Philosophical Essays*, 213–225, §47. Bracketed text in translation.

[86] Leibniz, *Monadology*, §3.   [87] Ibid, §6.

the composites we identify as the elements of the phenomenal world.[88] Monads are mind-like in that they have perceptions, representations of the multitude within their unity, yet they "have no windows through which something can enter or leave."[89] Created substances therefore do not interact with each other but are instead created by God with the internal principles necessary to respond in perfect harmony with each other. As Mercer summarizes, "Each monad acts eternally according to its own complete concept, but it does so in a way that is perfectly parallel with every other substance."[90] Thus, by emanative creation God creates a preestablished harmony across the universe of monads.

Emanative creation accounts for Leibniz's idiosyncratic theodicy as well. Like all Christian Platonists Leibniz places the archetypes of created substances in the mind of God. Within God's ideas "there is an infinity of possible universes."[91] From among the possibilities God selects the universe that is most fit, i.e., having "the highest degree of perfection" in it.[92] God produces a harmonious cosmos of monads, each containing a perspective on all the others such that each is a kind of living mirror of the whole. The resultant universe of universes results in as much variety as possible, in the greatest order possible, leading to the greatest perfection possible.[93] Thus conceived, the universe "could not be otherwise."[94] Our world then is the best possible in addition to being a plenitude devoid of empty space and even undividable atoms, a true plenum where "each body is affected, not only by those in contact with it ... but also, through them, it feels the effects of those in contact with bodies with which it is itself immediately in contact."[95] Leibniz's cosmos then is a preestablished harmony of monads some of which form composite bodies that exist in sympathy with each other all to bring about the greatest possible perfection.

Given the impossibility of interaction between monads and the way emanative creation deposits complete conceptions of monads within them from the start it is no wonder that Leibniz accepts innate knowledge. In fact, it is difficult to see how knowledge could be anything but innate in the

---

[88] Ibid, §19.   [89] Ibid, §7.

[90] Christia Mercer, "The Platonism at the Core of Leibniz's Philosophy," in *Platonism at the Origins of Modernity: Studies on Platonism and Early Modern Philosophy*, ed. Douglas Hedley and Sarah Hutton (Dordrecht: Springer, 2008), 225–238 at p. 230.

[91] Leibniz, *Monadology*, §53.

[92] Ibid, §54. Also G. W. Leibniz, *Theodicy*, trans. E. M. Huggard, ed. Austin Farrar (Chicago: Open Court, 1990), §§ 8, 78, 80, 119, 204, 206, and 208.

[93] Leibniz, *Monadology*, §§56, 57, and 58.   [94] Ibid, §60.   [95] Ibid, §61.

sense that it must arise within the rational soul and cannot be transmitted from the outside as it were.[96] As Mercer has shown for Leibniz any knowledge includes knowledge of all potentially. Thus, "in order to glimpse God, all we have to do is escape 'the shadow world' and have a momentary insight in any area of knowledge."[97] With his metaphysics of "mind-like simple substances endowed with perceptions and appetite" Leibniz reduces "bodies, motion, and everything else" to composites of these monads.[98]

Leibniz though was not the lone advocate of substance monism and idealism in early modernity. Famously the empiricist George Berkeley (1685–1753) too arrived at this position. Leibniz reports that "There is much," in Berkeley's *Treatise Concerning the Principles of Human Knowledge*, "that is correct and close to my own view." Unsurprisingly Leibniz is particularly pleased to see that Berkeley understands "True substances" to be "perceivers" (i.e., monads).[99]

Berkeley is best known today as the middle figure in the triad of British Empiricists with Locke and Hume. A close second is the fact that he advanced a form of idealism ("immaterialism") that not only prioritizes the mental but denies the existence of the material. Berkeley argued for the thesis that the objects of knowledge are either sense impressions, operations of the mind, or ideas formed via memory and imagination.[100] These objects of knowledge are known or perceived by what Berkeley calls "mind" or "spirit."[101] He argues that the opinion that objects of sense exist as distinct from being perceived is contradictory.[102] Thus, for Berkeley, to exist is to be perceived or to perceive (*esse est percipi aut percipere*). Like Leibniz then there is only one kind of substance for Berkeley, mind or spirit, including finite minds like our own and infinite mind of God. The physical world exists as immaterial mind-dependent ideas caused by God.

Since Berkeley's arguments are empiricist and he explicitly argued against abstract ideas he has been typically seen as opposed to Platonism.[103]

---

[96] On Leibniz's innatism see, Brandon C. Look, "Gottfried Wilhelm Leibniz," in *The Stanford Encyclopedia of Philosophy*, ed. Edward N. Zalta https://plato.stanford.edu/archives/sum2017/entries/leibniz/, accessed 31 January 2020, §6.3.

[97] Mercer, "Core," 237–238.   [98] Look, "Leibniz," §5.1.

[99] Leibniz, *Remarks on Berkeley's Principles* (Winter 1714–1715), in *Philosophical Essays*, 307.

[100] George Berkeley, *Of the Principles of Human Knowledge: Part 1*, in *The Works of George Berkeley, Bishop of Cloyne*, ed. A. A. Luce and T. E. Jessop, 2:41–113 (London: Thomas Nelson and Sons, 1948–1957), §1.

[101] Ibid, §2.   [102] Ibid, §4.

[103] On Berkeley's antiabstractionism see *Principles*, Introduction, §§6–24.

However, Berkeley's last work *Siris* is full of positive references to Platonism. This text, often dismissed by philosophers intent on reading Berkeley as a stepping stone from Locke to Hume, proclaims that the "Pythagoreans and Platonists had a notion of the true System of the World," specifically with their insistence that "mind, soul, or spirit truly and really exists" and "that bodies only [exist] in a secondary and dependent sense."[104] References to Christian and pagan Platonists abound including discussion of Plotinian intimations of the Trinity reminiscent of Cudworth.[105] While the relationship between the early Berkeley and the *Siris* is far from settled, some more recent studies have argued that the latter should not be understood as a radical departure from the former. Of especial interest here is the role of archetypes in Berkeley's philosophy.[106]

For Berkeley, God sustains the universe by continually thinking and willing it.[107] It is by means then of God's mental activity that the world is born, and my sensory ideas of the physical world are the same as God's ideas thereof because it is by God's having them that they arise in me. God's archetypal ideas of the physical world are my ectypal ideas thereof, not in addition to my creation as a mind, but as part of the continuous creation of myself qua perceiver. For there can be no mind without ideas nor ideas without mind.[108] While Berkeley does not embrace the language of emanation to describe God's creative activity, perhaps owing to his discomfort at the occasionalism of Malebranche, he arguable embraces the spirit thereof nonetheless.

While the lasting influence of Berkeley has been limited, during his lifetime he earned a significant following in British Colonial America where idealism of a Christian Platonist flavor remained a powerful intellectual force well into the twentieth century. Samuel Johnson (1696–1772), first president of King's College (now Columbia University), was an enthusiastic adopter of Berkeley's philosophy. Intriguingly he pushed Berkeley to elaborate and further develop his

---

[104] George Berkeley, *Siris*, in *Works* 5:25–164, §266.   [105] Berkeley, *Siris*, §§341–363.

[106] For example, Peter S. Wenz, "Berkeley's Christian Neo-Platonism," *Journal of the History of Ideas* 37, no. 3 (1976): 537–546; Robert McKim, "Wenz on Abstract Ideas and Christian Neo-Platonism in Berkeley," *Journal of the History of Ideas* 43, no. 4 (1982), 665–671; and Stephen H. Daniel, "Berkeley's Christian Neoplatonism, Archetypes, and Divine Ideas," *Journal of the History of Philosophy* 39, no. 2 (2001), 239–258.

[107] Berkeley, *Principles*, §§45-46, 62, 94, 151. Also, Berkeley, *Three Dialogues between Hylas and Philonous*, in *Works* 2:250-256 and Letter to Johnson, 25 November 1729, in *Works* 2:280–281.

[108] Berkeley, *Principles*, §7.

notion of archetypes.[109] As we have seen this was at the heart of the increasingly Platonic work produced by Berkeley later in life culminating with the *Siris*. Johnson too would go on from his productive friendship with Berkeley to develop his own account of Platonic archetypes in his *Elementa Philosophica* published by Benjamin Franklin in 1752.[110] Jonathan Edwards (1703–1758) widely viewed as the first great philosophical mind in British America developed a form of immaterialism that may well have both historical and conceptual debts to Berkeley as well.[111] Edwards, with many in America, was also well acquainted with the Christian Platonism of the Cambridge Platonists.[112] By the middle of the eighteenth century the geographic range if not popularity of Christian Platonism was one the rise. But it was about to face a new challenge from one equally opposed to the naturalism of the giants for whom the old Platonic path was no longer credible.

CONCLUSION

Despite his early flirtation with Platonism by 1781 Immanuel Kant (1724–1804) famously denied any access by the understanding to positive noumenal reality.[113] While he presented devastating critiques of traditional arguments for the existence of God it is the critique of rational psychology that struck most fully at the heart of the Christian Platonist tradition.[114] For if we do not have access to the immaterial and immortal

---

[109] Michael Jonik, "Mind and Matter in Early America: The Berkeley–Johnson Correspondence," *The Pluralist* 11, no. 1 (2016), 39–48 at p. 44.

[110] Ibid, 46.

[111] Scott Fennema, "George Berkeley and Jonathan Edwards on Idealism: Considering an Old Question in Light of New Evidence," *Intellectual History Review* 29, no. 2 (2019), 265–290.

[112] Michael J. McClymond and Gerald R. McDermott, *The Theology of Jonathan Edwards* (New York: Oxford University Press, 2012), 43, 413–414, 534, 582–583, 596 n. 41.

[113] Immanuel Kant, "On the Form and Principles of the Sensible and the Intelligible World," in *Theoretical Philosophy, 1755–1770*, ed. David Walford and Ralf Meerbote (New York: Cambridge University Press, 1992), 375–416. Immanuel Kant, *Critique of Pure Reason*, ed. P. Guyer and A. Wood (Cambridge: Cambridge University Press, 1998), A250/B307.

[114] Ibid, A567–642/B595–670 (on rational theology) and A341–405/B399–432 (on rational psychology). See also Beatrice Longuenesse, "Kant's 'I Think' versus Descartes' 'I am a Thing that Thinks'," in *Kant and the Early Moderns*, ed. Daniel Garber and Beatrice Longuenesse (Princeton, NJ: Princeton University Press, 2008), 9–31, esp. 20–25, and Garth W. Green, *The Aporia of Inner Sense: The Self-Knowledge of Reason and the Critique of Metaphysics in Kant* (Leiden and Boston: Brill, 2010), 223–289.

soul as *imago Dei* the path to the contemplation of God is blocked. As Henry More might have put it, no rational psychology, no rational theology.

This chapter has just scratched the surface of the influence of the Christian Platonist tradition upon early modern philosophy. This influence appears across denominational affiliations in the work of Protestants (e.g., Cudworth and Conway) as well as Catholics (e.g., Descartes and Malebranche). Empiricists like Berkeley and rationalists like Leibniz both found Christian Platonism congenial to their philosophical system building too. Christian Platonists argued for dualisms, monisms, and systems in between. As Christian Platonists always have, they disagreed on many issues and drew their Platonism from many sources with a wide variety of interpretations. But, in early modernity as in antiquity, they shared a common enemy in the form of "Epicurean" naturalism.[115] With the coming of the Enlightenment period, and in the face of the seemingly decisive blows against Christian Platonism at the hands of Kant, echoes of this dynamic and resilient tradition would persist in Idealism, Romanticism, *Lebensphilosophie*, and Transcendentalism through the nineteenth and into the twentieth centuries.

Bibliography

Berkeley, George. *The Works of George Berkeley, Bishop of Cloyne.* Edited by A. A. Luce and T. E. Jessop. 9 vols. London: Thomas Nelson and Sons, 1948–1957.

Bryson, James. *The Christian Platonism of Thomas Jackson.* Leuven: Peeters, 2016.

Conway, Anne. *The Principles of the Most Ancient and Modern Philosophy.* Edited by Allison P. Coudert and Taylor Corse. Cambridge: Cambridge University Press, 1996.

Cudworth, Ralph. *A Sermon Preached before the Honourable House of Commons at Westminster, March 31, 1647.* Cambridge: Roger Daniel, 1647.

The True Intellectual System of the Universe. London: Richard Royston, 1678.

Daniel, Stephen H. "Berkeley's Christian Neoplatonism, Archetypes, and Divine Ideas." *Journal of the History of Philosophy* 39, no. 2 (2001): 239–258.

Davidson, Jack. "Leibniz: The Last Great Christian Platonist." In *Brill's Companion to German Platonism*, edited by Alan Kim, 43–75. Leiden and Boston: Brill, 2019.

---

[115] See Lloyd Gerson, *Platonism and Naturalism: The Possibility of Philosophy* (Ithaca, NY and London: Cornell University Press, 2020) for the bold thesis that any attempt to reconcile Platonism and naturalism is doomed.

Descartes, René. *Oeuvres de Descartes*. Edited by Charles Adam and Paul Tannery. 13 vols. Paris: Librairie Philosophique J. Vrin, 1964–1974.

The Philosophical Writings of Descartes. Edited by John Cottingham, Robert Stoothoff, Dugald Murdoch. 2 vols. Cambridge: Cambridge University Press, 1984–1985.

The Philosophical Writings of Descartes, Vol. III: The Correspondence. Edited by John Cottingham, Robert Stoothoff, Dugald Murdoch, and Anthony Kenny. Cambridge: Cambridge University Press, 1991.

Dillon, John. "Plotinus: The First Cartesian?" *Hermathena* 149 (1990): 19–31.

Dominiak, Paul Anthony. *Richard Hooker: The Architecture of Participation*. London and New York: Bloomsbury, 2019.

Fennema, Scott. "George Berkeley and Jonathan Edwards on Idealism: Considering an Old Question in Light of New Evidence." *Intellectual History Review* 29, no. 2 (2019): 265–290.

Gaukroger, Stephen. *The Emergence of a Scientific Culture: Science and the Shaping of Modernity, 1210–1685*. Oxford: Oxford University Press, 2006.

Gerson, Lloyd. *Platonism and Naturalism: The Possibility of Philosophy*. Ithaca, NY and London: Cornell University Press, 2020.

Green, Garth W. *The Aporia of Inner Sense: The Self-Knowledge of Reason and the Critique of Metaphysics in Kant*. Leiden and Boston: Brill, 2010.

Hedley, Douglas. "Gods and Giants: Cudworth's Platonic Metaphysics and his Ancient Theology." *British Journal for the History of Philosophy* 25, no. 5 (2017): 932–953.

Hedley, Douglas and Sarah Hutton, eds. *Platonism at the Origins of Modernity: Studies on Platonism and Early Modern Philosophy*. Dordrecht: Springer, 2008.

Henry, John. "Henry More." In *The Stanford Encyclopedia of Philosophy*, edited by Edward N. Zalta, https://plato.stanford.edu/archives/win2016/entries/henry-more/. Accessed 31 January 2020.

Hutton, Sarah. "The Cambridge Platonists." In *The Stanford Encyclopedia of Philosophy*, edited by Edward N. Zalta, https://plato.stanford.edu/archives/win2013/entries/cambridge-platonists/. Accessed 31 January 2020.

"Lady Anne Conway." In *The Stanford Encyclopedia of Philosophy*, edited by Edward N. Zalta, https://plato.stanford.edu/archives/fall2015/entries/conway/. Accessed 31 January 2020.

Janowski, Zbigniew. *Augustinian-Cartesian Index: Texts and Commentary*. South Bend, IN: St. Augustine Press, 2004.

Jonik, Michael. "Mind and Matter in Early America: The Berkeley–Johnson Correspondence." *The Pluralist* 11, no. 1 (2016): 39–48.

Kant, Immanuel. *Critique of Pure Reason*. Edited by P. Guyer and A. Wood. Cambridge: Cambridge University Press, 1998.

"On the Form and Principles of the Sensible and the Intelligible World." In *Theoretical Philosophy, 1755–1770*, edited by David Walford and Ralf Meerbote, 375–416. New York: Cambridge University Press, 1992.

Leech, David. "Defining 'Cambridge Platonism'." In *The Cambridge Platonism Sourcebook*, edited by Douglas Hedley, David Leech, et al., www.cambridge-platonism.divinity.cam.ac.uk/about-the-cambridge-platonists/defining-cambridge-platonism. Accessed 31 January 2020.

The Hammer of the Cartesians: Henry More's Philosophy of Spirit and the Origins of Modern Atheism. Leuven: Peeters, 2013.

Leibniz, Gottfried Wilhelm. *New Essays on Human Knowledge.* Translated and edited by Peter Remnant and Jonathan Bennett. Cambridge: Cambridge University Press, 1996.

Philosophical Essays. Edited and translated by Roger Ariew and Daniel Garber. Indianapolis, IN: Hackett Publishing Company, 1989.

Theodicy. Translated by E. M. Huggard and edited by Austin Farrar. Chicago: Open Court, 1990.

Lennon, Thomas M. *The Battle of the Gods and Giants: The Legacies of Descartes and Gassendi, 1655–1715.* Princeton, NJ: Princeton University Press, 1993.

LoLordo, Antonia. "Epicureanism and Early Modern Naturalism." *British Journal for the History of Philosophy* 19, no. 4 (2011): 647–664.

Longuenesse, Beatrice. "Kant's 'I Think' versus Descartes' 'I am a Thing that Thinks'." In *Kant and the Early Moderns*, edited by Daniel Garber and Beatrice Longuenesse, 32–40. Princeton, NJ: Princeton University Press, 2008.

Look, Brandon C. "Gottfried Wilhelm Leibniz." In *The Stanford Encyclopedia of Philosophy*, edited by Edward N. Zalta, https://plato.stanford.edu/archives/sum2017/entries/leibniz/. Accessed 31 January 2020.

Malebranche, Nicholas. *The Search after Truth.* Translated by Thomas M. Lennon and Paul J. Olscamp. Cambridge: Cambridge University Press, 1997.

Marion, Jean-Luc. *On Descartes' Passive Thought: The Myth of Cartesian Dualism.* Translated by Christina M. Gschwandtner. Chicago and London: University of Chicago Press, 2018.

Marmodoro, Anna and Sophie Cartwright, eds. *A History of Mind and Body in Late Antiquity.* Cambridge: Cambridge University Press, 2018.

McClymond, Michael J. and Gerald R. McDermott. *The Theology of Jonathan Edwards.* New York: Oxford University Press, 2012.

McKim, Robert. "Wenz on Abstract Ideas and Christian Neo-Platonism in Berkeley." *Journal of the History of Ideas* 43, no. 4 (1982): 665–671.

Menn, Stephen. *Descartes and Augustine.* New York: Cambridge University Press, 1998.

Mercer, Christia. "Descartes' Debt to Teresa of Ávila, or Why we Should Work on Women in the History of Philosophy." *Philosophical Studies* 174 (2017): 2539–2555.

Leibniz's Metaphysics: Its Origin and Development. Cambridge: Cambridge University Press, 2002.

"The Platonism at the Core of Leibniz's Philosophy." In *Platonism at the Origins of Modernity: Studies on Platonism and Early Modern Philosophy*, edited by Douglas Hedley and Sarah Hutton, 225–238. Dordrecht: Springer, 2008.

Michaud, Derek A. *Reason Turned into Sense: John Smith on Spiritual Sensation.* Leuven: Peeters, 2017.

More, Henry. *An Antidote Against Atheisme, Or an Appeal to the Natural Faculties of Man, whether there be not a God.* London: Roger Daniel, 1653.

Niederbacher, Bruno. "The Human Soul: Augustine's Case for Soul-Body Dualism." In *The Cambridge Companion to Augustine*, 2nd ed., edited by Eleonore Stump and Norman Kretzmann, 125–141. New York: Cambridge University Press, 2014.

Osler, Margaret J. "Eternal Truths and the Laws of Nature: The Theological Foundations of Descartes' Philosophy of Nature." *Journal of the History of Ideas* 46, no. 3 (1985): 349–362.

Plato. *Sophist.* Greek text with English translation by Harold N. Fowler. Cambridge, MA: Harvard University Press, 1921.

Plotinus. *Enneads.* Greek text with English translation by A. H. Armstrong. 7 vols. Cambridge, MA: Harvard University Press, 1968–1988.

Proclus. *In Platonis Timaeum Commentarii.* Edited by E. Diehl. 3 vols. Leipzig: Teubner, 1903–1906.

Pyle, Andrew. *Malebranche.* London and New York: Routledge, 2003.

Schmaltz, Tad. "Nicolas Malebranche." In *The Stanford Encyclopedia of Philosophy*, edited by Edward N. Zalta, https://plato.stanford.edu/archives/win2017/entries/malebranche/. Accessed 31 January 2020.

Schumacher, Lydia. *Divine Illumination: The History and Future of Augustine's Theory of Knowledge.* Oxford: Wiley-Blackwell, 2011.

Smith, John. *Select Discourses.* London: J. Fisher, 1660.

Ward, Richard. *The Life of Henry More.* Edited by Sarah Hutton, Cecil Courtney, Michelle Courtney, Robert Crocker, and A. Rupert Hall. Dordrecht: Springer, 2000.

Wenz, Peter S. "Berkeley's Christian Neo-Platonism." *Journal of the History of Ideas* 37, no. 3 (1976): 537–546.

Wilson, Catherine. *Epicureanism at the Origins of Modernity.* New York: Oxford University Press, 2008.

2.8

Christian Platonism in the Age of Romanticism

Douglas Hedley

There is a painful yearning to bring forth the infinite in the finite.

F. Creuzer, *Symbolik und Mythologie* (1819), I, 58

INTRODUCTION

'The first great Romantic was Plato'.[1] Any account of Platonism in the Romantic age cannot be clear cut. Yet the deep influence of Platonism is one of the most profound aspects of the Romantic period. For Christianity, it meant a renewed stress upon inwardness and spiritual renewal. For this reason, the links with Pietism and movements otherwise remote from the concerns of the Athenian philosopher cannot be discounted. The influence of Jacob Böhme in the Romantic period is a good instance of the complex intellectual threads. Böhme is not straightforwardly a Platonist, or even a philosopher. Yet the effect of his thought upon this period is indubitable.

SOME CONCEPTUAL ISSUES

The Hellenism of the Romantic period is a fervent and earnest phenomenon. During the Napoleonic sway over Rome, various northern explorers, pundits and connoisseurs were barred from the familiar path of the Grand Tour, and turned their attention to Ottoman Greece. The appropriation of Greek treasures such as the Elgin Marbles and the Aegina

[1] H. J. C. Grierson, *The Background of English Literature and Other Collected Essays & Addresses* (London: Chatto & Windus, 1925), 235.

marbles that came to adorn European capitals, London and Munich amongst others, belong to age of vigorous zeal and devotion to ancient Greek civilization as a mark of cultural prestige and a catalyst of national renewal. At the same time, the uncompromisingly secular spirit of the French revolution, the military might and sweeping reforms of Napoleon Buonaparte throughout Europe threatened the ancient privileges of Christendom. A mood of nostalgia for a lost Christian culture can be seen in the Nazarene painters in Germany or Novalis or Chateaubriand, even in the era of the soi-disant 'Holy Alliance'.

Not since the peril of Ottoman presence at the gates of Vienna and the subsequent victory of Prince Eugene of Savoy, had the Christian Church encountered such a substantial trial. In this context, Platonism could serve as a buttress for the Christian tradition, as it had served apologetic purposes in the Alexandrian tradition, the German mystics or the Cambridge Platonists. On the other hand, it could also serve as an alternative, as it did for Thomas Taylor 'The Pagan' or Percy Bysshe Shelley.

The terms Counter Enlightenment and Romanticism are highly controversial. The term 'Counter Enlightenment' was a construction of the Oxford philosopher Isaiah Berlin, for whom Vico (1668–1744) and Herder (1744–1803) represented advocacy of pluralism and a robust critique of philosophical universalism. Berlin's model of the Counter Enlightenment was reinforced by Michel Foucault's *The Order of Things* and *Discipline and Punish*, in which he developed the perspective of the *Marxisant* Frankfurt School philosophers Adorno and Horkheimer that the Enlightenment had a barely concealed despotic core. Works like MacIntryre's *After Virtue* (1981) and Rorty's *Philosophy and the Mirror of Nature* (1979) continued this critique of an Enlightenment project of universal knowledge and morality. In most of these narratives, the Enlightenment emerges as a primarily philosophical movement out of the Renaissance via Bacon and Descartes, Newton, Locke and Hume, and indeed the French *philosophes* up to Kant. This vision of the Enlightenment is driven by philosophical considerations and envisages it in connection with secular concerns and opposed to religion.

'Romanticism' is itself a vexed and troublesome term. Here were shall take the term to refer a period in the second half of the eighteenth century and first half of the nineteenth century, and myriad cultural reactions to various aspects of the mechanistic science, empiricist philosophy and utilitarian politics of the Enlightenment. Given the broad scope of this essay, we will eschew any minute (and indeed important!) distinctions between Idealism, Classicism and Romanticism. This is a highly problematic vision of the Enlightenment and many historians have abandoned it. Similar problems can be attributed to the term 'Romanticism'.[2] Many intellectual historians regard the Romantic period as beginning in Germany and then spreading to the rest of Europe.[3] Some of the major British Romantics, such as Coleridge, were deeply influenced by German thought. For the purposes of the essay we will take a pragmatic approach to this terminology.

Generally, Plato or Platonism in the narrow sense has rarely been on the curriculum in European universities and was not taught in universities during this period. There is a shift from scholasticism to other school philosophies, such as a form of Locke's thought in Cambridge or the Leibnizian-Wolffian philosophy in Germany. Broadly speaking, while Platonism was not part of the curriculum, it was important for many writers outside academia.[4] Leibniz and Shaftesbury are paradigmatic example of this as two of the most influential 'Platonists' in the eighteenth century, whose ideas were widely disseminated.

Furthermore, in an age of strict censorship, it can difficult to ascertain the sincere attitude to questions of religious dogma. Was Lord Shaftesbury a Christian? Probably not in doctrinal terms and yet he clearly belonged to culture that was profoundly Christian, as were some of his deepest influences, such as Benjamin Whichcote. We will take a pragmatic approach again and treat Shaftesbury as a key background figure, even though he could be viewed as a Deist and indeed in opposition to Christianity. The same applies to figures like Frans Hemsterhuis (1721–90).

THE PLATONIC LEGACY OF LEIBNIZ AND SHAFTESBURY

Shaftesbury is often associated with the British moralists of the eighteenth century, especially Hutcheson, Adam Smith and Hume. His writing on ethics, religion and aesthetics was a powerful organ of Hellenic Platonic

[2] England is a case since many aspects of 'Romanticism' can be found much earlier than German Romanticism. The phenomenon of the 'Gothic', for example, might be taken as an instance of the Romantic movement. Horace Walpole's house known as Strawberry Hill (begun in 1749) is often taken as an example of early Gothic, and he was the author of *The Castle of Otranto*, the first Gothic novel.

[3] John Robertson, *The Enlightenment: A Very Short Introduction* (Oxford: Oxford University Press, 2015).

[4] For a more nuanced view of the absence of Platonism in the curriculum, see Christa Mercer on the curriculum in Jena and Leipzig: Christa Mercer, *Leibniz's Metaphysics: Its Origins and Development* (Cambridge: Cambridge University Press, 2001), 32–9. See also M. R. Antognazza, *Leibniz: An Intellectual Biography* (Cambridge: Cambridge University Press, 2008).

ideas. His influence was particularly strong in Germany, especially upon such luminaries as Lessing and Herder. While not wishing to state that Shaftesbury's *Characteristics of Men, Manners, Opinions, Times* (1711) is a Platonic work, it certainly contains strongly Platonic elements, especially the claim that the idea of beauty is closely interwoven with an innate longing and disposition of the soul. Shaftesbury's earliest work was an edition and preface to Benjamin Whichcote's *Select Sermons* of 1698 which was a critique of the ethical scepticism of Hobbes that reduced virtue to selfish prudence.[5] Even though tutored by Locke, the temper of Shaftesbury was more Platonic than Empiricist. Moreover, Cassirer was correct to see Shaftesbury as transmitting the philosophical legacy of the Cambridge Platonists into the eighteenth century, and brought notions like 'disinterested pleasure' into German philosophical discussion of figures such as Mendelssohn and Kant.

Leibniz was a more original mind than Shaftesbury but he clearly provided an impetus for Platonic thought. Leibniz states that his intent is to address the shortcomings of the metaphysical basis of the mechanical philosophy, and, like the Cambridge Platonists, he thinks that Platonism can be used to make the appropriate adjustments. In his The *New Essays on the Human Understanding* of 1703–5, Leibniz writes of his work:

This system appears to unite Plato with Democritus, Aristotle with Descartes, the Scholastics with the moderns, theology and morality with reason. Apparently, it takes the best from all systems and then advances further than anyone has yet done. ... I now see what Plato had in mind when he talked about matter as an imperfect and transitory being; what Aristotle meant by his 'entelechy' ... How to make sense of those who put life and perception into everything ... I see everything to be regular and rich beyond what anyone has previously conceived ... Well, sir, you will be surprised at all I have to tell you, especially when you grasp how much it elevates our knowledge of the greatness and perfection of God.[6]

Leibniz's Platonism is evident in his view of the relationship between God and world and the nature of mind. God is a self-sufficient unified being and is no way depleted by the causal emanation of the world, and the structure of the world is shaped by the Divine ideas or *rationes*. Moreover, in his late philosophy, the idea of monads as 'fulgurations of the Divinity' (§47) is stridently Platonic.

---

[5] Michael Gill, *The British Moralists and the Cambridge Platonists* (Cambridge: Cambridge University Press, 2009), 77–82.

[6] Gottfried Wilhelm Leibniz, *Nouveaux essais sur l'entendement* (of 1703–5) in *Sämtliche Schriften und Briefe* [Akademie], ed. Deutsche Akademie der Wissenschaften (Berlin: Akademie Verlag, 1923), VI, vi, 71–3.

TOP-DOWN METAPHYSICS

A characteristic feature of Platonism is a top-down mode of explanation. The higher must explain the lower and not vice versa. Book 10 of Plato's laws is the paradigmatic text in this respect. The very order and structure of the world requires a Divine mind as its source and telos. Leibniz gives clear expression to this top-down metaphysics:

Now, in rigorous metaphysical truth, there is no external cause acting on us except God alone, and he alone communicates himself to us immediately in virtue of our continual dependence. From this it follows that there is no other external object that touches our soul and immediately excites our perception. Thus we have ideas of everything in our soul by virtue of God's continual action on us, that is to say, because every effect expresses its cause, and thus the essence of our soul is a certain expression, imitation or image of the divine essence, thought, and will, and of all the ideas comprised in it. It can then be said that God is our immediate external object and that we see all things by him . . . God is the sun and the light of souls, the light that lights every man that comes into this world, and this is not an opinion new to our times. *Discours de métaphysique,* 28

   The Platonic language of illumination is tied up with the characteristic-ally top-down metaphysics in which the finite realm participates in its transcendent source. Leibniz freely concedes that the notion that 'we see all things' by God who is the 'the sun and light of souls' is of ancient (Platonic) provenance. It is perhaps ironic that Spinoza should be the galvanizing point of a renewal of top-down metaphysics in the Romantic period. The major writers of this period wanted to furnish a system of philosophy like that of Spinoza but avoiding the determinism and mechanism of Spinoza's own philosophy. The distinction in Spinoza between *natura naturans* and *natura naturata* become the starting point of absolute Idealism. Schopenhauer rather scornfully dismissed these phil-osophies of the absolute as barely disguised theologies.[7]

CRITIQUE OF MECHANISM

The French Enlightenment seemed to entrench the mechanistic vision of the Newtonian cosmos endorsed by John Locke and given sanction by Voltaire and Diderot. Such a mechanistic vision of the Universe could only be opposed by Platonists. And one of the most potent strands of Christian Platonism gave rise to a re-visioning of the natural realm as a theophany,

---

[7] Chris Ryan, *Schopenhauer's Philosophy of Religion: The Death of God and the Oriental Renaissance* (Leuven: Peeters, 2010).

as the domain of a *natura natura* with the clear impress of a *natura naturans*. This was the movement spawned in the wake of the visionary Silesian cobbler Jacob Böhme. Böhme cannot be designated a Platonist in any straightforward manner and yet he was keenly affected by Platonic strands in Patristic, Lutheran and Kabbalistic thought, and was an inheritor of Paracelsus and the alchemical tradition. He fuses many different strands of thought: alongside Patristic Platonism, the Hermetic tradition, the Kabbalah and Lutheran tenets. The absolute nature of God is the abyss of the 'Father', who is designated the nothing, the primordial depths from which the creative will struggles to emerge as self-consciousness, the love that is in Trinitarian terms the 'Son'. Like Blake later, Böhme was a visionary who draws deeply upon scripture, and his individual religious experience – there are no institutional forms of mediation in his thought. Scripture, the book of Nature and human consciousness are revelations of the Divine. Deeply affected by melancholy, depressed by the suffering in his war ravaged region, in 1600 he has a vision while in a state of reverie, looking at a polished pewter bowl reflecting the rays of the sun, which he interprets spiritually.

The Platonic dimension of his thought was transmitted through Christian spiritualism and Pietism, whether in England by figures such as William Law or in Germany by J. A. Bengel and F. C. Oetinger. The reception of Böhme was initially strongest in England and the Low Countries in the seventeenth century but largely through the transmission of Pietist circles, especially Johann and Johanna Petersen, his influence was renewed, especially in Tieck and Novalis.[8] Whether in Coleridge or Schelling, the presence of Böhme is inescapable when one is considering the Platonic dimension in the Romantic Age.

PLATONISM AND FAITH: HAMANN, JACOBI AND THE MÜNSTER CIRCLE

J. G. Hamann (1730–88) and F. H. Jacobi (1743–1819) were part of an important circle around the Princess Gallitzin, a group that included such luminaries as Hemsterhuis, Johann Friedrich Kleuker, Stolberg and Schlosser. Jacobi is a philosopher who frequently appeals to Plato and he evidently was familiar with the broader Platonic tradition. However, Jacobi's Platonism is perhaps tenuous, even if he quotes Plato with

---

[8] Ernst Benz, *Mystical Sources of German Romantic Philosophy* (Eugene, OR: Pickwick Publications, 1983).

affirmation. Yet along with Hemsterhuis and other figures in the Circle he helped create a fertile ground for a renaissance of Platonism.

Whatever he may have thought, Jacobi was not of the Platonic family, and his thought evokes Pascal more for us than Plato. Therefore, it was only in a very marginal way that he participated in the revival of Plato, of which Tennemann and Hemsterhuis were the best artisans.[9]

Hemsterhuis was an expert scholar of the thought of Plato and has even been described as a Neoplatonic sage: 'Hemsterhuis est un sage, un néo-platonicien dans la tradition des penseurs de Cambridge et de Shaftesbury.'[10] The combined energies and influence of Jacobi and Hemsterhuis formed a vital conduit in this period: 'Par l'intermédiare de Jacobi, l'influence de Hemsterhuis s'étendra à Lessing, Herder, Goethe, Schiller et de là aux jeunes romantiques, en particuler à Novalis.'[11] The battle cry of German Idealism that Jacobi attributes to Lessing, 'Hen kai pan', is derived from the erudite Cambridge Platonist Ralph Cudworth and not from Spinoza. Moreover, 'Ex nihilo nihil fit' is taken by Jacobi to be the core of Spinoza's thought. This principle of Lucretius is discussed at length by Cudworth and his translator Mosheim. Indeed, Herder on 6 February 1784 observes that this is not an adequate description of Spinoza, whose philosophy is better designated through the tag 'quidquid est, illud est', which is 'whatever is, is'.

Hamann was closely linked to the Münster circle and was buried in the town. Like Jacobi, Hamann is an admirer of Plato and doubtlessly has a Platonic dimension to his thought, though it was expressed in terms of an advocacy of Socrates in conjunction with a rather idiosyncratic reading of Hume as a fideist and a mystical interpretation of Luther.

A less familiar but significant figure among this group was Kleuker and his *Magikon oder das geheime System einer Gesellschaft unbekannter Philosophen* (1784). Kleuker is familiar with Neoplatonism and the metaphysics of the Cambridge Platonists. While Kleuker was not an original mind, he is a reminder that the tradition of Renaissance Neoplatonism, mediated by the Cambridge Platonists, was a distinctive and significant presence in eighteenth-century Germany, and this strand can be seen especially in the work of Friedrich Creuzer.

---

[9] Jean-Louis Vieillard-Baron, *Platon et l'idealisme allemand [1770 – 1830]* (Paris: Beauchesne, 1979), 83.
[10] Georges Gusdorf, *Naissance de la Conscience Romantique au Siècle des Lumières* (Paris: Payot, 1976), 280.
[11] Ibid, 28.

PLATONIC POLITICS: DE MAISTRE AND THE TERROR
OF THE NUMINOUS

Plato offered one of the incisive critiques of democracy in the Western canon. Plato Book VI of the *Republic* argues that democracy is inferior to monarchy, aristocracy and oligarchy since it will favour those skilled at appealing to the masses rather than those skilled in ruling. Plato's critique of the anarchical propensity of democracy appeared to assume renewed relevance in the wake of the French Revolution and the terror through the polemics of the Savoyard writer Joseph de Maistre and his chef de pièce, Les Soirées de St Peterburg. A brilliant and original mind, admirer of Plato and critic of Bacon, Locke and Voltaire, Joseph de Maistre (1753–1821) represents an instance of Origenism.[12] Maistre views the necessity of government as a medicine for human wickedness and not because of the rational character of human nature. He is opposed to the rationalism of the French Enlightenment. The English constitution, for example, he describes as 'the most complex unity and the most propitious equilibrium of political powers that the world has ever seen'.[13]

Yet Maistre was far from being reactionary or demonstrating a merely archival interest in the history of thought. Much of his Platonism exhibits parallels with contemporary thought. Maistre was, for example, close to Rousseau in his Romantic reaction to the arid rationalism of the Enlightenment. Like the Swiss writer, Maistre considered feeling and the dictates of the heart to be instruments of truth, he valued the natural bond of loyalty and affection between the individual and the community.

Maistre's long-standing association with Freemasonry is significant in this context. From 1774 up to the French Revolution he was a member of lodges in Chambéry and was familiar with Scottish Rite Masons in Lyon. It would seem that his familiarity with deeply Platonic forms of 'illuminism' and 'Martinism' was linked to his Lyon contacts. Maistre described his own philosophy as 'a mélange of Platonism, Origenism and hermetic philosophy on a Christian base'.[14] Despite the fact that Maistre relinquished his membership of the Masons in 1790, he remained fascinated by the 'illuminist' works that he discovered through Masonry.

---

[12] The question of the Platonism of Origen is a subject of debate. See Mark Edwards, from the point of view of ante-Nicene Christianity and Platonism, with explicit focus on Origen in *Origen Against Plato* (Aldershot: Ashgate Publishing, 2002). For the purposes of the essay, I will assume (like Maistre) that Origen is clearly a Platonist.

[13] Joseph de Maistre, *On God and Society*, 18.

[14] Joseph de Maistre, *Oeuvres, Soirées de Saint-Pétersbourg*, V, 248.

The influence of Maistre upon the seminal German writer Franz von Baader is indisputable. The long-term impact upon Russian literature is also striking. Dostoyevsky read Maistre and much of his literary work circles around the idea of reversibility, i.e. the atoning power of the vicarious suffering of the innocent for the guilty.

THE RECOVERY OF MYTHOLOGY

The much-vaunted rationalism of the Enlightenment was unlikely to be fertile territory for the realm of myth. The role of mythology in the writings of *De l'origine des fables* of 1684, republished in 1724, by Bernard Le Bovier de Fontenelle presents myth as attributable to the ignorance of superstitious peoples. Such an attack on myth was aimed at Christianity as much as any heathen mythology. Descartes, Locke and Kant have little space for the realm of the mythic and Hegel's subordination of 'Vorstellung' to 'Begriff' could be viewed as in this tradition. Reason should be deployed to replace the dark vestiges of myth. Yet both Plato and Plotinus explore myths philosophically. Whereas in the Enlightenment myth tends to be rejected or at least reinterpreted as misunderstood history, the Romantics tend to develop mythology in relation to logos. Herder and Vico might be viewed as instrumental in the rehabilitation of myth among Romantic writers, and those in their wake demanding a new mythology appropriate for the modern age[15]. Much of this was emerging out of a tradition of Philhellenist neohumanism, questions about the status of Christian scripture in the light of higher criticism and issues about the significance of Asia for the West.[16]

The remarkable literary phenomenon of James Macpherson's 'Poems of Ossian', was published in 1760 as *Fragments of Ancient Poetry*. Though Samuel Johnson realised that these were forgeries, the celtic bard of Ossian as the 'Homer of the North' attracted intense interest and admiration.

Jacob Bryant, Winckelmann, Herder, Moritz and Schiller and Friedrich Schlegel were all significant figures in this process. When Schelling describes Christianity as the 'revealed mystery', he is drawing on

---

[15] Marion Heinz, *Herder und die Philosophie des deutschen Idealismus* (Amsterdam: Rodopi, 1997). Giambattista Vico was barely mentioned in Germany during the zenith of German Idealism.

[16] George S. Williamson, *The Longing for Myth in Germany: Religion and Aesthetic Culture from Romanticism to Nietzsche* (Chicago: University of Chicago Press, 2004).

a fascination for ancient myth.[17] Schelling's speculation about mythology, culminating in his philosophy of mythology, Hölderlin's identification in his *Abendmahl* of Christ and Dionysus, Coleridge's the Prometheus of Aeschylus, or Blake's highly idiosyncratic mythological universe might all be seen as part of this revival of mythology, and bound to questions about the relationship between Christianity and mythology, and indeed the relationship between Christianity and other religions.[18]

JENA ROMANTICISM

The circle of writers associated with Jena between 1798 and 1804, especially Friedrich Schlegel, Friedrich Daniel Ernst Schleiermacher and Novalis are deeply significant in terms of the reception of Platonism.[19] Georg Philipp Friedrich Freiherr vom Hardenberg or Novalis was an enthusiastic admirer of Plato and Hemsterhuis. Novalis discovered Plotinus but his knowledge was second hand. Goethe quotes Plotinus enthusiastically.[20]

Schleiermacher (1768–1834) is a pivotal figure, both as a classical philologist and as a theologian. Indeed, he is widely regarded as the first modern Plato interpreter. Friedrich Schleiermacher is viewed as offering the most momentous shift in the reading of Plato since Marsilio Ficino's fifteenth-century translation and commentary. His major early works were written in Berlin while he was the chaplain of the Charite Hospital (1796–1802): his speeches of 1799 and his Soliloquies. The immediate pre-reflective awareness of the Divine is explored in the Speeches. In his major dogmatic work *The Christian Faith* he defines religion as 'the feeling of absolute dependence' (*Der christliche Glaube* §4).

---

[17] 'Das Christenthum dagegen ist das geoffenbarte Mysterium und, wie das wie das Heidenthum seiner Natur nach exoterisch, ebenso seiner Natur nach esoterisch.' Friedrich Wilhelm Joseph von Schelling, *Philosophie und Religion* (Tübingen: J. G. Cotta, 1804), SW I, 6, 66.

[18] E. Shaffer, '*Kubla Khan' and 'The Fall of Jerusalem'. The Mythological School in Biblical Criticism and Secular Literature, 1770–1880* (Cambridge: Cambridge University Press, 1980); Anthony John Harding, *The Reception of Myth in English Romantic Poetry* (Columbia: University of Missouri Press, 1995).

[19] Paola Mayer, *Jena Romanticism and Its Appropriation of Jakob Böhme: Theosophy, Hagiography, Literature* (Montreal: McGill University Press, 1999); Alexander J. B. Hampton, *Romanticism and the Re-Invention of Modern Religion: The Reconciliation of German Idealism and Platonic Realism* (Cambridge: Cambridge University Press, 2019).

[20] Werner Beierwaltes, *Platonismus and Idealismus* (Frankfurt: Verlag Vittorio Kostermann, 2004), 97ff.

THE SOUTHERN GERMAN MILIEU: HEIDELBERG
AND MUNICH

Friedrich Creuzer is one of the most significant Platonists of the period. A native of Marburg, his translation into German of Plotinus Treatise 16 on Beauty and III 8 on Nature was a significant moment in the German reception of Platonism. Creuzer deployed a Platonic approach to myth and developed a philosophical theory of the symbol which he placed at the core of his comprehensive theory of religion, one which linked Greece with the great cultures of antiquity, especially India and Egypt. Ancient Greek religion had its distant roots in a monotheism carried from India and borne by migrant priests, and transmitted in the Eleusinian and Samothracian mysteries, Orphism and Pythagoreanism.

Deeply admired by Hegel and Schelling, Creuzer's romantic critique of the Enlightenment intensified the fascination with Greek culture in Germany. In this context, both Lutherans theologians and Classicists attacked the symbolism of Creuzer. For the strict Lutheran orthodoxy, the work on mythology and symbol of Creuzer and Schelling represented a dangerous quasi-medieval mysticism, a corrupting crypto-Catholicism. For the Hellenists, Schelling and Creuzer were polluting the noble stream of authentic Greek thought and sensibility with degenerate Asiatic abstractions. Schelling was deeply impressed by Creuzer. Indeed, the origins of Schelling's philosophy of Mythology probably lie partly in the work of Creuzer, whose work links the symbol to monotheism and mythology to polytheism. Schelling attempted to respond to Creuzer's critique of mythology as an organ of polytheism. Creuzer saw deep affinities between Schelling's *Naturphilosophie* and the vision of nature contemplated in Plotinus. Furthermore, Schelling's theory of art has a profoundly Neoplatonic aspect.[21] In his philosophical aesthetics, he uses the Platonic-Spinozistic language of *natura naturans* and *natura naturata*. The artist shares in the *natura naturans* and thus able to go beyond mere imitation of nature.

Munich assumed a special importance within Germany as the capital of the newly founded kingdom of Bavaria in 1805, when Maximilian IV Joseph became Maximilian I Joseph. Asserting itself as a force against both the Austrian and Prussian empires, Munich becomes an important

---

[21] Thomas O'Meara, *Romantic Idealism and Roman Catholicism: Schelling and the Theologians* (Paris: University of Notre Dame Press, 1982).

cultural centre and Jacobi becomes President of the Bavarian Academy of Science and Schelling the General Secretary of the Academy of Fine Arts, and both are colleagues of Franz von Baader. Jacobi, who initiates the Pantheism controversy and the origins of German Idealism, becomes the source of another vigorous controversy in southern Germany, sometimes known as the theism controversy. Jacobi accuses Schelling (and by implication those like Baader who hold to a speculative theology) of pantheism and fatalism. Schelling pens an intemperate reply to Jacobi's renewed challenge, his *Denkmal Der Schrift von den göttlichen Dingen* (1812).

Franz von Baader was deeply influenced by the mystical speculations of Meister Eckhart, Saint Martin, and above all those of Böhme. Baader's philosophy is based upon idea of participation in God. Man's consciousness is simultaneous Divine consciousness: hence his reversal of Descartes: *cogitor ergo cogito*. Baader develops a speculative philosophy that is deeply reliant upon the thought of Jacob Böhme, not least the Silesian shoemaker's speculations about the immanent Trinitarian life of the Godhead. Human existence is radically dependent upon its divine source and hence knowledge is always *con-scientia* – knowing with and through the Divine. Baader is intent upon developing a dynamic conception of the Deity rather than as an abstract entity, and the voluntarism of Böhme clearly influenced his philosophical theology with a stress upon the abysmal Divine ground, and the vital essence of the deity. Baader's thought revolves around the idea of coincidence of the spiritual and the natural, finite and infinite, without collapsing into fideism. He could not accept Jacobi's fideism and during the period of Jacobi, Schelling and Baader's membership of the Bavarian Academy of Sciences, there emerged a final phase in the so-called *Pantheismusstreit* or Pantheismus controversy.

BERLIN ROMANTICISM AND IDEALISM

Schleiermacher was a pre-eminent figure at the University of Berlin. Indeed, as Dean of the Theology Faculty and Rector of the University he was a commanding presence. Schleiermacher was detested by Hegel. Hegel was also a Platonist of sorts, as becomes clear when he writes of 'the science of religion'. He writes:

The object of religion, like that of philosophy, is the eternal truth, God and nothing but God and the explication of God. ... Thus religion and philosophy coincide in one. In fact philosophy is itself the service of God, as is religion. .... The linkage between them is nothing new. It already obtained among the more eminent of the church fathers, who had steeped themselves particularly in Neopythagorean, Neoplatonic, and Neoaristotelian philosophy.[22]

For Hegel, the Idea is alone the truly real, and the Begriff as the Platonic *eidos* is identity in difference. Hegel takes up a distinctively Neoplatonic strand in which the philosophy of religion considers the fulfilment of the timeless Idea through its extension into its difference as temporal and historical back to source. This mediation of reality is the self-unfolding of the Absolute itself.[23] Prompted by Franz von Baader, Hegel quotes Meister Eckhart in his Lectures on the Philosophy of Religion: 'The eye with which God see me is the eye with which I see him; my eye and his eye are one and the same.' In a swipe against Schleiermacher, Hegel explicitly commends the stress upon comprehension in the thought of Meister Eckhart rather than the attention given to mere piety by contemporary Protestant theology, i.e. by Schleiermacher.

Moreover, when Hegel claims that The Divine is the centre of all representations of art,[24] one might say that, just as in Schelling, the Neoplatonic tradition – Plotinus, not Plato – finds forceful expression in Hegel's claim that art furnishes a reconciliation of sensual and intelligible worlds.[25]

WORDSWORTH, BLAKE AND COLERIDGE

Wordsworth might be thought of as a Platonic poet par excellence. His magnificent Ode subtitled 'Intimations of Immortality from Recollections of Early Childhood' develops the notion that the human soul exists before conception and birth, an argument to be found in the *Phaedo* (72e–78b) and the *Phaedrus*, 245c, a central tenet in the Platonic tradition, and to be found in Origen and Henry More.[26] If we are to deem Wordsworth

---

[22] Georg Hegel, *Lectures on the Philosophy of Religion, Volume 1*, ed. Peter C. Hodgson (Oxford: Oxford University Press, 2007), 152–3.

[23] Werner Beierwaltes, *Differenz, Negation, Identität: Die reflexive Bewegung der Hegelschen Dialektik, in Identität und Differenz* (Frankfurt: Verlag Vittorio Klostermann, 1980), 241–68.

[24] 'Die Kunst habe vor allem das Göttliche zum Mittelpunkte ihrer Darstellungen zu machen.' *Vorlesungen über die Ästhetik* 1 (Frankfurt am Main: Surhkamp, 1986), p. 175.

[25] Kai Hammermeister, *The German Aesthetic Tradition* (Cambridge: Cambridge University Press, 2002), 95.

[26] On Wordsworth and the Cambridge Platonists, see Graham Davidson, '"A Track Pursuing No Untrod Before": Wordsworth, Plato and the Cambridge Platonists', in

a Platonist, it is on the basis of instinct or propensity rather than book learning. John Stewart once referred to Wordworth as a personal Platonist rather than a traditional Platonist steeped in the arguments and terminology of the school.[27]

Blake's was a highly idiosyncratic vision composed of Platonic and Christian themes. It is quite possible that he learnt his Platonism within Westminster Abbey, where he worked as an apprentice. As a poet and an illustrator, many of his engravings were illustrations of biblical scenes, the great Christian poets – Dante, Spenser, Milton or Bunyan. Some of his sources, like Böhme and Swedenborg, were in the illuminist tradition. The *Marriage of Heaven and Hell* contains a distinctive Böhme dimension. Blake read Plato and the Neoplatonists in the translations of Thomas Taylor. George Mills Harper and Kathleen Raine have stressed this Neoplatonic dimension to his thought.[28] Yet the relation between Blake and Böhme is also deep, and, in some respects, only Platonic in a doubtful sense. Blake was also deeply shaped by the radical, sometimes antinomian, sometimes Gnostic, traditions of the English seventeenth century within which Böhme played a powerful role. His genius was nourished by a range of traditions, but many of them Platonic.

There were other poets of the period deeply shaped by Platonism, but their attitude to Christianity was either hostile or apathetic. This cannot be claimed of Coleridge, who came from a clerical home and could never escape his Christian inheritance.

THE CHRISTIAN PLATONISM OF SAMUEL TAYLOR COLERIDGE

We began this chapter by noting the significance of the rediscovery of inwardness. S. T. Coleridge represents a good instance of this pre-eminence and urgency of the retrieval of the spiritual dimension. When confronted with notion of external proofs of Christian belief, Coleridge writes: '*Evidences* of Christianity! I am weary of the WORD. Make a man

---

Revisioning Cambridge Platonism: Sources and Legacy, ed. D. Hedley and D. Leech (Cham: Springer International Publishing, 2019), 215–40.

[27] J. Stewart, 'Platonism in English Poetry', in *English Literature and the Classics* (Oxford: Oxford University Press, 1912), 25–48. See my *Living Forms of the Imagination* (London: T & T Clark, 2008), 24.

[28] Edward Larissy, *Blake and Platonism*, in Sarah Hutton and Anna Baldwin (eds.), *Platonism and the English Imagination* (New York: Cambridge University Press, 1994), 186–98.

feel the *want* of it; rouse him, if you can, to the self-knowledge of his *need* of it; and you may safely trust it to its own EVIDENCE.'[29] Samuel Taylor Coleridge (1772–1834) was born the son of a learned Church of England clergyman in Ottery St Mary in Devon. A year after the death of his father in 1781 Coleridge was sent to Christ's Hospital, a London school for orphans. Coleridge's friends Charles Lamb in his essay 'Christ's Hospital Thirty-five years ago', wrote the follow words about his precocious and ingenious contemporary at the school:

> Come back into memory, like as thou wert in the day-spring of thy fancies, with hope like a fiery column before thee – the dark pillar not yet turned – Samuel Taylor Coleridge – Logician, Metaphysician, Bard! – How have I seen the casual passer through the Cloisters stand still, intranced with admiration (while he weighed the disproportion between the *speech* and the *garb* of the young Mirandula), to hear thee unfold, in thy deep and sweet intonations, the mysteries of Jamblichus, or Plotinus (for even in those years thou waxedst not pale at such philosophic draughts), or reciting Homer in his Greek, or <u>Pindar</u> – while the walls of the old Grey Friars re-echoed to the accents of the *inspired charity-boy!*[30]

S. T. Coleridge was a 'Grecian', a schoolboy scholar, and enthusiastic Hellenist at Christ's Hospital. In a letter to his friend John Thelwell in 1796, Coleridge wrote that Metaphysics and poetry and 'facts of the mind are my darling studies. Dreamers from Thoth the Egyptian to Taylor the English pagan, are my darling studies.'[31] Coleridge insists in his *Biographia Literaria* that his mind has been decisively shaped by 'The early study of Plato and Plotinus, with the commentaries and the THEOLOGIA PLATONICA of the illustrious Florentines; of Proclus, and Gemistus Pletho.'[32] This is not merely an early obsession: in 1806–7, Coleridge lists various intellectual plans, including 'to hunt for Proclus'.[33] On 26 August 1814 his old friend Charles Lamb wrote to Coleridge,

> "I *will not forget* to *look* for *Proclus*". In the chapter on abstract ideas I might introduce the subject by quoting the eighth Proposition of Proclus' *Elements of Theology*: The whole of religion seems to me to rest on and in the question: The

[29] Samuel Taylor Coleridge, *Aids to Reflection*, ed. J. Beer (Princeton, NJ: Princeton University Press, 1993), 405–6.

[30] Charles Lamb, *The Complete Works in Prose and Verse of Charles Lamb* (London: Chatto & Windus, 1875), 19.

[31] Samuel Taylor Coleridge, *Collected Letters, Volume 1*, ed. Earl Leslie Griggs (Oxford: Oxford University Press, 1956), 260.

[32] Samuel Taylor Coleridge, *Biographia Literaria* (Princeton: Princeton University Press, 1983), 144.

[33] Samuel Taylor Coleridge, *The Notebooks of Samuel Taylor Coleridge, Volume 1: 1794–1804*, ed. Kathleen Coburn (New York: Pantheon Books, 1957).

One and the Good – are these words or realities? I long to read the schoolmen on the subject).[34]

Coleridge is one of the most brilliant Platonists of the period and yet he can also be oddly disparaging about the Neoplatonists, and indeed present Proclus as the embodiment of a propensity to sterile scholasticism in the later school:

Who that had even rested but in the porch of the Alexandrian philosophy, would not rather say, of substantiating powers and attributes into being? What is the whole system from Philo to Plotinus, and thence to Proclus inclusively, but one fanciful process of hypostasizing logical conceptions and generic terms? In Proclus it is Logolatry run mad.[35]

It is quite possible that Coleridge is influenced by Cudworth in this respect. Like Cudworth, Coleridge integrates his (Neo)Platonism into his Christian theology and is given to occasional polemics about the 'pagan' Platonists and their eighteenth-century follower, Thomas Taylor the Pagan. Referring to Thomas Taylor's 1816 edition of Proclus' *Elements of Theology* and *Platonic Theology*, Coleridge rather disdainfully observes that it is so translated 'that difficult Greek is translated into incomprehensible English'.[36]

Yet Coleridge is quite properly seen as an inheritor of the Cambridge Platonists and working within the Alexandrian tradition of Christian Platonism. When Newman says of Coleridge that he 'indulged in a liberty of speculation that no Christian can tolerate', and 'advocated conclusion which were often heathen rather than Christian', he is referring to Coleridge's Alexandrian tendencies, as well as his fascination for German metaphysics.[37]

The Platonizing strand in Coleridge was developed by Julius Hare, F. D. Maurice, and B. F. Westcott in Cambridge. Drawing upon John's prologue and various passages in St Paul in particular, Christ is, for Maurice, the head of humanity and in this role dwells 'in every man'. In this way, Christ as the image of the Father, is a mirror of the true self.

---

[34] Ibid, 1626, 525.

[35] Samuel Taylor Coleridge, *The Notebooks of Samuel Taylor Coleridge, Volume 5: 1827–1834*, ed. Kathleen Coburn (Princeton: Princeton University Press, 2002); William Greenough Thayer Shedd and A. H. Harding (ed.), *The Complete Works of Samuel Taylor Coleridge, Volume V* (Harper & Brothers, 1856), 454–5.

[36] Samuel Taylor Coleridge, *Collected Letters, Volume 3*, ed. Earl Leslie Griggs (Oxford: Oxford University Press, 1956), 279.

[37] J. H. Newman, *Essays Critical and Historical, Volume 1* (London: Longmans, Green and Company, 1872), 268.

CONCLUSION

Christian Platonism has a protean character in the Romantic Age and yet it is a pivotal role in the spirit of the era. If the Enlightenment was frequently shaped by critique of dogma, tradition and superstition, the Romantics were fuelled by a longing for the transcendent, which for Christians was identified with the supernatural and the very possibility of revelation. For many thinkers, Platonism offered a path of renewal, a means a revitalizing a Christianity pilloried by the cultured despisers of religion in the Enlightenment, without simply reverting to sterile orthodoxy. It provided an antidote to the dreary rationalism and soulless mechanism of the Enlightenment; it held out hopes for a union of heart and head: it bespoke the union of finite and infinite.

Bibliography

Antognazza, M. R. *Leibniz: An Intellectual Biography*. Cambridge: Cambridge University Press, 2008.

Baldwin, A., and Hutton, S., eds. Platonism and the English Imagination. Cambridge: Cambridge University Press, 1994.

Beierwaltes, Werner. *Differenz, Negation, Identität: Die reflexive Bewegung der Hegelschen Dialektik, in Identität und Differenz*. Frankfurt: Verlag Vittorio Klostermann, 1980.

Platonismus and Idealismus. Frankfurt: Verlag Vittorio Kostermann, 2004.

Benz, Ernst. *Mystical Sources of German Romanticism*. Eugene, Oregon: Pickwick Publications, 1983.

Coleridge, Samuel Taylor. *Aids to Reflection*. Edited by J. Beer. Princeton, NJ: Princeton University Press, 1993.

Biographia Literaria. Princeton, NJ: Princeton University Press, 1983.

Collected Letters, Volume 1. Edited by Earl Leslie Griggs. Oxford: Oxford University Press, 1956.

Collected Letters, Volume 3. Edited by Earl Leslie Griggs. Oxford: Oxford University Press, 1959.

The Complete Works of Samuel Taylor Coleridge, Volume V. Edited by William Greenough Thayer Shedd and A. H. Harding. New York: Harper & Brothers, 1856.

The Notebooks of Samuel Taylor Coleridge, Volume 1: 1794–1804. Edited by Kathleen Coburn. New York: Pantheon Books, 1957.

The Notebooks of Samuel Taylor Coleridge, Volume 5: 1827–1834. Edited by Kathleen Coburn. Princeton, NJ: Princeton University Press, 2002.

Davidson, Graham. "'A Track Pursuing No Untrod Before'": Wordsworth, Plato and the Cambridge Platonists'. In *Revisioning Cambridge Platonism: Sources and Legacy*, edited by D. Hedley and D. Leech, 215–40. Cham: Springer International Publishing, 2019.

Edwards, Mark. J. *Origen Against Plato*. Aldershot: Ashgate Publishing, 2002.

Foucault, Michel. *The Order of Things*. Paris: Editions Gallimard, 1966.

Discipline and Punish. London: Penguin, 1991.

Gill, Michael. *The British Moralists on Human Nature and the Birth of Secular Ethics*. Cambridge: Cambridge University Press, 2009.

Grierson, H. J. C. *The Background of English Literature and Other Collected Essays & Addresses*. London: Chatto & Windus, 1925.

Gusdorf, Georges. *Naissance de la Conscience Romantique au Siècle des Lumières*. Paris: Payot, 1976.

Hammermeister, Kai. *The German Aesthetic Tradition*. Cambridge: Cambridge University Press, 2002.

Hampton, Alexander J. B. *Romanticism and the Re-Invention of Modern Religion: The Reconciliation of German Idealism and Platonic Realism*. Cambridge: Cambridge University Press, 2019.

Harding, Anthony John. *The Reception of Myth in English Romantic Poetry*. Columbia: University of Missouri Press, 1995.

Hedley, Douglas. *Living Forms of the Imagination*. London: T & T Clark, 2008.

Hegel, Georg. *Lectures on the Philosophy of Religion*. Edited by Peter C. Hodgson. Oxford: Oxford University Press, 2007.

Heinz, Marion. *Herder und die Philosophie des deutschen Idealismus*. Amsterdam: Rodopi, 1997.

Lamb, Charles. *The Complete Works in Prose and Verse of Charles Lamb*. London: Chatto & Windus, 1875.

Larissy, Edward. 'Blake and Platonism'. In *Platonism and the English Imagination*, edited by Sarah Hutton and Anna Baldwin, 186–98. New York: Cambridge University Press, 1994.

Leibniz, Gotfried Wilhelm. *New Essays on the Human Understanding*. London: MacMillan & Co., 1896.

Nouveaux essais sur l'entendement. Berlin: Akademie Verlag, 1923.

Mayer, Paola. *Jena Romanticism and Its Appropriation of Jakob Böhme: Theosophy, Hagiography, Literature*. Montreal: McGill University Press, 1999.

Mercer, Christa. *Leibniz's Metaphysics: Its Origins and Development*. Cambridge: Cambridge University Press, 2001.

Newman, J. H. *Essays Critical and Historical, Volume 1*. London: Longmans, Green and Company, 1872.

O'Meara, Thomas. *Romantic Idealism and Roman Catholicism: Schelling and the Theologians*. Paris: University of Notre Dame Press, 1982.

Robertson, John. *The Case for The Enlightenment*. Cambridge: Cambridge University Press, 2005.

The Enlightenment: A Very Short Introduction. Oxford: Oxford University Press, 2015.

Ryan, Chris. *Schopenhauer's Philosophy of Religion: The Death of God and the Oriental Renaissance*. Leuven: Peeters, 2010.

Schelling, Friedrich Wilhelm Joseph von. *Philosophie und Religion*. Tübingen: J. G. Cotta, 1804.

Shaffer, E. *'Kubla Khan' and 'The Fall of Jerusalem'. The Mythological School in Biblical Criticism and Secular Literature, 1770–1880.* Cambridge: Cambridge University Press, 1980.

Stewart, J. 'Platonism in English Poetry'. In *English Literature and the Classics*, 25–48. Oxford: Oxford University Press, 1912.

Vieillard-Baron, Jean-Louis. *Platon et l'idealisme allemand.* Paris: Beauchesne, 1979.

Whichcote, Benjamin. *Select Sermons of Benjamin Whichcote.* Delmar, NY: Scholars' Facsimiles & Reprints, 1977.

Williamson, George S. *The Longing for Myth in Germany: Religion and Aesthetic Culture from Romanticism to Nietzsche.* Chicago: University of Chicago Press, 2004.

2.9

Christian Platonism and Modernity

Joshua Levi Ian Gentzke

BETWEEN EROS AND THANATOS: THE PLATONISM OF POETS

In *Theatrum Philosophicum*, an essay on the ostensibly anti-Platonic theorist Gilles Deleuze, Michel Foucault contends that Plato is "the excessive and deficient father" of western thought.[1] And certainly, while Platonism has provided a deep well of philosophical, poetic, and religious inspiration from antiquity to the present, it has also been an object of controversy and even derision, momentarily uniting such unlikely bedfellows as early modern Protestant theologians and postmodernist theorists. Never uniform, despite the ideal of unity enshrined at its core, the tradition has been reenvisioned in wildly divergent ways across diverse cultures and histories. To tackle the complex subject of Platonism's relationship with western modernity, this examination will first underscore this term's instability by highlighting one of the deepest rifts that cuts through late modern interpretations of Platonism. To this end, I turn now to two poets whose works helped define the creative occidental culture of the twentieth century: William Butler Yeats (1865–1939) and Allen Ginsberg (1926–1997). Both invoke the notion of Platonism; yet they do so in order to make sense of very different visions of modern selfhood.

In 1928 W. B. Yeats published *The Tower*, a collection of poems whose title references the Thoor Ballylee Castle, a Late Medieval Hiberno-Norman building he had acquired.[2] In the volume's second poem, Yeats

---

[1] "Platon, père excessif et défaillant." Michel Foucault, "Theatrum Philosophicum," Critique, no 282. Novembre 1970, 885; online version: http://1libertaire.free.fr/MFouca ult244.html

[2] James Plethica, *Yeats's Poetry, Drama, and Prose* (New York: Norton, 2000), 491.

wrestles with a host of imagined indignities, catalyzed by his passage into old age.[3] Amidst this struggle he situates Plato and the third-century forefather of Neoplatonism, Plotinus – metonymically invoking the tradition of Platonism *tout court* – in opposition to the fires of visionary *poiesis* and its erotic engines. While an alluring Muse embodies the inspiration that once ignited the flames of youthful poetry, Plato and Plotinus beckon the aged poet to renounce his carnal passions and pursue the chaste insights of philosophical idealism. Yet the irony inherent in the poem becomes apparent as Yeats claims to heed the call of the latter while performing a creative act proper to the former:

> It seems that I must bid the Muse go pack,
> Choose Plato and Plotinus for a friend
> Until imagination, ear and eye,
> Can be content with argument and deal
> In abstract things; or be derided by
> A sort of battered kettle at the heel.[4]

In the poems that follow, Yeats constructs a virtual alternative to mundane existence that compensates for the body's weakening powers; emancipated from the dolorous forces of time and entropy, this ideal world of words shimmers with the noetic light of the intellect rather than the flicker of the body's dark fire. Yeats's imaginal territory is a place wherein poetry and philosophy find common cause. But as the price of this union, the Muse must renounce her loyalty to Apollo and serve a darker god; for Yeats, even in league with the poetic, philosophy remains, as Plato himself seems to claim in the opening discussion of the *Phaedo*, a pious preparation for death.[5] Guided by Yeats's vision, the Platonic realm is mapped as inherently metaphysical – a transcendental territory beyond the transient world of bodies and becoming.

On the other side of the twentieth century and still far from old age, Allen Ginsberg, despite his praise of Yeats's deft musical ear, heard the Platonic chorus sing in a very different key.[6] In the late

---

[3] On Yeats's poetic concern with aging see George Bornstein, "W.B. Yeats' Poetry of Aging," in *Sewanee Review* 120, no. 1 (2012), 46–61; Raymond D. Pruitt, Virginia D. Pruitt, "W.B. Yeats on Old Age, Death, and Immortality," in *Colby Library Quarterly* 24, no. 1 (March 1988), 36–49.

[4] William Butler Yeats, *The Tower* (London, England, New York: Penguin Putnam, 1999), 5.

[5] "The one aim of those who practice philosophy in the proper manner is to practice for dying and death (ἀποθνῄσκειν τε καὶ τεθνάναι)." *Phaedo*, 64a.

[6] "It was rare to find a poet who was writing in rhyme in the twentieth-century that's really got a good ear." https://allenginsberg.org/2018/03/w-m-14/

1940s, Ginsburg found himself subletting an apartment from a theology student at Columbia whose bookshelves housed the works of Plato, Plotinus, and William Blake, as well as the classics of Christian mysticism.[7] During this time, Ginsberg was experimenting with various substances, autoeroticism, and other methods of altering his consciousness. These practices of self-exploration led to an encounter with seminal Platonic texts, including Plotinus' *Enneads*.[8] But the apogee of his engagement with Platonism occurred when the poet was gripped by an intense mystical vision – hymned in the closing lines of the suitably named "Vision 1948":

I

Wake in the deep light
And hear a vast machinery
Descending without sound,
Intolerable to me, too bright,
And shaken in the sight
The eye goes blind before the world goes round.[9]

Immediately following this experience, Ginsberg, in his own words, "rushed to Plato and read some great image in the Phaedrus about horses flying through the sky, and rushed over to Saint John and started reading fragments ... and rushed to the other part of the bookshelf and picked up Plotinus about The Alone [sic]."[10]

Despite his enlightened state, Ginsberg found Plotinus "more difficult to interpret" than the others.[11] But during the narrative process that followed his illumination, Ginsberg gained a deeper appreciation for the Plotinian realms; years later in his celebrated poem "Howl" (1956), he praised "the best minds ... who studied Plotinus Poe St. John of the Cross telepathy and bop kabbalah because the cosmos instinctively

---

[7] David Stephen Calonne, *The Spiritual Imagination of the Beats* (Cambridge: Cambridge University Press, 2017), 85–105, and Michael Schumacher, *Dharma Lion: A Biography of Allen Ginsberg* (New York: St. Martin's, 1992), 94–99; Jeffrey Kripal, "Reality Against Society: William Blake, Antinomianism, and American Counterculture," *Common Knowledge* 13, no. 1 (2007), 102–104.

[8] It is unclear how early in his career Ginsberg encountered Plotinus; from Ginsberg's own recollections, he had encountered Plotinus' writings at least by 1948. He also received a copy of *Enneads* from fellow Beat writer William S. Burroughs (1914–1997).

[9] Allen Ginsberg, "Vision 1948." David Stephen Calonne maintains that this passage echoes Plotinus' Fifth Ennead; it could however be argued that Ginsberg's imagery here is abstract enough to fit with the basic "photocentric" imagery that permeates much of mystical literature. *The Spiritual Imagination of the Beats*, 89.

[10] As quoted in: Michael Schumacher, *Dharma Lion*, 96.   [11] Ibid.

vibrated at their feet in Kansas."[12] These lines playfully couple Platonism with Christian and Jewish mysticism, and ultimately, with the Beat Generation itself, interpreted here as a link in this perennial chain. Plato and Plotinus are invoked as sages of visionary wisdom – luminaries who draw from the same tributary of thought welling up into the current countercultural moment and catalyzing a sense of "immanent transcendence" for those so attuned.[13] While Yeats invoked Platonism as an apotropaic charm against eroticism, under Ginsberg's pen the plains of 1950s Kansas were saturated in cosmic significance; Plato and Plotinus appeared alongside Blake as saints of the poetic-erotic vision. Intentionally or not, Ginsberg amplifies Socrates' evocative line in the *Symposium* that all he knows "is the art of erôs (*ta erôtika*)," rather than foregrounding the Yeatsean correlation of death and philosophy.[14] And whereas Yeats places the tradition firmly in the realm of timeless being, Ginsberg's dynamic Platonism flows with force through the world of becoming.

The discord sounded in these twentieth-century poets' evocations of Plato and Plotinus is indicative of a hermeneutical dissonance endemic to late modern and postmodern western interpretations of Platonism. On the one hand, Platonism is associated with the sober metaphysics of ancient Greek philosophy, in which the roots of either philosophical idealism or ontological realism are to be found; on the other, Platonism is appealed to as a font for the mad and mystical wisdom of the inspired poet.[15] Platonism is alternately placed under the signs of two archetypically antagonistic forces: *Thanatos* and *Eros*. Furthermore, these conflicting portrayals evoke a host of dualities, each of which is paradoxically ascribed to Platonism: vitalism versus world-rejection; mystical eroticism versus intellectual sobriety; esotericism versus ratiocentricism, and so on.

---

[12] Allen Ginsberg, "Howl", originally published in Allen Ginsberg, *Howl and Other Poems*, 1959.

[13] For a brief typology of the term "immanent transcendence," see Lars Sandbeck, "God as Immanent Transcendence in Mark C. Taylor and John D. Caputo," *Studia Theologica* 65 (2011), 18–38 at pp. 19–23.

[14] Plato, *Symposium*, 177d8–9.

[15] The assertion that Platonism is a species of philosophical idealism and the designation of Platonism as a realist stance may seem at first blush confusing; these descriptors point to the fact that Platonism is generally understood to be a form of thought that prioritizes for the existence of abstract objects and entities. So Platonism is idealist in the sense that it hierarchically situates ideality over material reality, but realist insofar as it posits subject-independent meaning, for example, in the case of nature.

CIRCUMSCRIBING CHRISTIAN PLATONISM:
AN UN-PLATONIC APPROACH

How should we then circumscribe the term "Platonism"? As John Sallis and others have argued, Platonism must be understood as a diffuse, dynamic discourse, ever in the process of being reinvented, rather than the hidebound system it is often caricatured as.[16] In the context of the current discussion, the volatility of the notion of "modernity" further complicates matters; whether defined ideologically, chronologically, or sociopolitically, the designation refers broadly to a period wherein Platonism cannot be as clearly tied to official schools, movements, or even self-professed adherents, as is the case in antecedent periods. Moreover, it is not uncommon to encounter contestations that modernity is anti-Platonic by definition – one need think only of Baudelaire's famous formal definition of modernity as "the transient, the fleeting, the contingent" over and against modernity's other, "the eternal and the immovable," which is say: *the Platonic*.[17] Yet, as the works of Friedrich Nietzsche and Martin Heidegger evince, it has also been claimed that the secret root of modernity and its nihilistic tendencies is quintessentially Platonic.[18] In the eyes of its modern interpreters, Platonism appears as Janus-Faced.

If it surfaces at all in contemporary cultural conversations, Platonism either marks out a twilight territory wherein poetic, religious, and philosophical concerns meet and blur – it was after all the poets who did much of the work of carrying the Platonic banner into modernity – or surfaces as a rhetorical trope. Affixing the adjective "Christian" to Platonism muddies the waters further; as noted by the growing body of scholarship on post-secularism, especially in the context of western modernity, religiosity is often markedly diffuse.[19] And although the Weberian model of decline

---

[16] I concur with John Sallis's contention that "in the ever recurrent appropriation, the Platonic legacy is repeatedly reconstituted ... pluralized so thoroughly that there could be little hope of recovering any unity other than the reference back to the Platonic texts; and even the ways in which this reference would be carried out ... would be so various and disparate that one would still be left with a manifold of Platonic legacies." John Sallis, *Platonic Legacies*, 2–3.

[17] Charles Baudelaire, "The Painter of Modern Life," in *The Painter of Modern Life and Other Essays*, trans. and ed. Jonathan Mayne (London, New York: Phaidon, 1970), 1–34 at p. 13.

[18] Stanley Rosen, *The Ancients and the Moderns: Rethinking Modernity* (New Haven: Yale University Press, 1989).

[19] For an attempt to argue for the theosophical validity of post-Christian Platonism see Paul Tyson, "Transcendence and Epistemology: Exploring Truth via Post-Secular Christian Platonism," *Modern Theology* 24, no. 2 (2008), 245–270.

has been found wanting, present-day spirituality has become less amenable to being mapped by reference to overt or official expressions.[20] Likewise, contemporary creative appropriations of Platonism operate within a domain that is often confessionally post-Christian, wherein religious expression is as much informed by globalization, market politics, and personal idiosyncrasies as it is by institutions and dogmas. In short, although it is not impossible to find self-professed Platonists, Christian or otherwise, Platonism exists for the most part as an intellectual or spiritual "tendency" bound up with other threads of thought, at least within the context of Euro-American culture. In this sense, both Yeats and Ginsberg can be seen as heralds of this "diffuse Platonism" that bookend the twentieth century.

In grappling with the relevance of Christian Platonism to contemporary thought, it must also be noted that the (contested) historiographical categories of Platonism, Middle Platonism, and Neoplatonism are not particularly useful. If anything, at least in terms of late modern poetics, theology, and continental philosophy, ideas rooted in what is typically referred to as Neoplatonism take precedence over direct engagement with Plato's corpus.[21] Neoplatonism, a practice of interpreting Platonic concepts that reaches back to Plotinus, largely entered into Christianity and western philosophy by way of Augustine of Hippo in the West, and fourth-century Cappadocian Fathers, such as Basil, Gregory of Nyssa, and Gregory of Nazianzus in the East, as well as the anonymous sixth-century author of the works attributed to Dionysius the Areopagite, whose influence on continental thought is currently undergoing something of a renaissance. In all its diverse expressions, Christian Platonism has deep roots in this lineage.

---

[20] On post-secular religiosity, see Alexander Hampton, *Romanticism and the Re-Invention of Modern Religion: The Reconciliation of German Idealism and Platonic Realism* (Cambridge: Cambridge University Press, 2019), 46–51, *passim*; Egil Asprem, *The Problem of Disenchantment* (Leiden: Brill, 2014); Edward I. Bailey, *Implicit Religion in Contemporary Society* (Leuven: Peeters, 2006); Robert C. Fuller, *Spiritual, but Not Religious* (New York: Oxford University Press, 2001); Christopher H. Partridge, *The Re-Enchantment of the West* (London: T & T Clark, 2004); Boaz Huss, "Spirituality: The Emergence of a New Cultural Category and Its Challenge to the Religious and the Secular," *Journal of Contemporary Religion* 29 (2014), 47–60.

[21] For overviews of the philosophical trajectory of Neoplatonism as it entered modernity, see Stephen Gersh (ed.), *Plotinus' Legacy: The Transformation of Platonism from the Renaissance to the Modern Era* (Cambridge: Cambridge University Press, 2019); John Gregory, *The Neoplatonists: A Reader* (London: Routledge, 1991, 1999); Pauliina Remes, *Neoplatonism* (London: Routledge, 2014).

Thus, I would argue for an approach to Platonism here that is "un-Platonic" by design: I treat Platonism as a historically and culturally contingent mesh of dynamic and diverse ideas, practices, and images, which can nevertheless be heuristically envisioned as a recognizable discourse; in this sense, Christian Platonism continues to unfold as a conversation between an imagined antiquity and the present that forms a living dimension of the western social imaginary. Rather than attempting to answer the question of whether late and postmodern Platonisms are "authentic" manifestations of the tradition – some might be tempted to distinguish Ginsberg's "pop-Platonism" from the scholarly pursuits of Cambridge Platonist Henry More, for instance – I will concern myself with (1) explicating the ways in which the term "Platonism" has been inserted into, defined, and rhetorically mobilized within contemporary philosophical conversations in critical and creative ways; and (2) demarcating key areas where Platonism is playing a revitalized role. In doing so, it will become clear that the received tradition of Platonism is fraught with inner, creative tensions; it is far from the static entity that its adversaries (and some of its proponents) often contend it to be.

After unpacking the critical reception and reconceptualization of Platonism in late modern thought heralded by the work of Friedrich Nietzsche and Martin Heidegger, I will explore a particular point of entanglement between Christianity and Platonism that is receiving renewed attention amidst the contemporary "turn to religion" in continental philosophy: apophatic or *via negativa* mysticism, a tradition with roots in Plotinian henology, seeded in the "aporie of Plato's *Parmenides*."[22] Focusing on the reassessment of apophaticism and foregrounding the interest that prominent "postmodernist" thinkers have shown in it, complicates the notion that anti-Platonism is ubiquitous in

---

[22] On continental thought's "turn to religion," see Hent de Vries *Philosophy and the Turn to Religion* (Baltimore: Johns Hopkins University Press, 1999); Gregg Lambert, *Return Statements: The Return of Religion in Contemporary Philosophy* (Edinburgh: Edinburgh University Press, 2016); Michael Hoelzl and Graham Ward (eds.),*The New Visibility of Religion* (London: Continuum, 2008). On the particular significance that the apophatic tradition currently plays in this "turn," see William Franke, "Apophasis and the Turn of Philosophy to Religion: From Neoplatonic Negative Theology to Postmodern Negation of Theology," *International Journal of Philosophy of Religion* 60, no. 1/3 (2006), 61–76. On the connection between apophasis and Plato in particular, see Franke's remarks on *Parmenides* 137b–144e. On Plotinian henology as a "metaphysics of radical transcendence," see Reiner Schürmann, *Broken Hegemonies*, trans. Reginald Lily (Bloomington: Indiana University Press, 2003), 143–144.

contemporary philosophical and theoretical discourse.[23] But first a few words on the reception history of Platonism in modernity are in order.

THE RECEPTION OF PLATONISM: FROM HUMANISM TO THE HISTORY OF METAPHYSICS

Late modern engagement with Platonism is preceded by the Renaissance work of fifteenth-century humanists, such as Marsilio Ficino and Giovanni Pico della Mirandola, the seventeenth-century Cambridge Platonists Henry More and Ralph Cudworth, and continental metaphysicians such as George Berkeley, Baruch Spinoza, and G. W. F. Hegel.[24] The influence of metaphysically minded poets such as Henry Vaughn, Coleridge, William Blake, in England, and Novalis and R. M. Rilke in Germany, should also not be downplayed in the story of Platonism's entry into modernity. Also of note is the less-celebrated but equally important influence of western esotericism, a tributary of Neoplatonic, hermetic, magical, Kabbalistic, and mystical thought and practice that found expression in the works of Paracelsus (1493–1541), Jacob Böhme (1575–1624), and William Blake (1757–1827). This "platonic-hermetic-Christianity" came under attack in Daniel Colberg's fifteenth-century polemic *Das Platonisch Hermetisches Christenthum*, and later entered the mainstream of western philosophy via the work of the Friedrich Schelling and Martin Heidegger.[25] This lineage subsequently penetrated aspects of popular culture by way of the work of comparative religionists, such as Huston Smith and Mircea Eliade and transpersonal psychologists like Ken Wilber. More recently one can also discern the birth of what might be called a "Pop Platonism" in music, fantasy, and science fiction.[26]

---

[23] On anti-Platonism, Joseph J. Tanke, *Foucault's Philosophy of Art: A Genealogy of Modernity* (London and New York: Continuum, 2009), 121–163.

[24] On the relationship between early modern thought and Platonism, see Douglas Hedley and Sarah Hutton (eds.), *Platonism at the Origins of Modernity: Studies on Platonism and Early Modern Philosophy* (New York: Springer Publishing, 2008).

[25] Wouter J. Hanegraaff has pointed out that Colberg saw that a specific type of "'Platonic-Hermetic Christianity' had come into existence since the 15th century, which would later develop into currents such as Paracelsianism, Rosicrucianism and Boehmian theosophy." Hanegraaff, "Forbidden Knowledge," 242. For a more sustained treatment, see: Hanegraaff, *Esotericism in the Academy: Rejected Knowledge in Western Culture* (Cambridge: Cambridge University Press, 2012), 107–114; cf. Antoine Faivre, *Theosophy, Imagination, Tradition: Studies in Western Esotericism* (Albany: State University of New York Press, 2000), 11–14.

[26] Some work has been done on the Neoplatonic and esoteric influences that entered science-fiction literature in large part through Philip K. Dick; see for example Jeffrey J. Kripal,

In sum, throughout formative periods of western modernity, Platonism was predominantly reimagined as either a humanistic *philosophia perennis*, compatible with the inner truths of Christianity; a font of poetic inspiration and an intellectual weapon in the fight against materialism, the latter often anachronistically glossed as "Aristotelianism"; or part of a larger esoteric tradition that included such "practical" pursuits as magic, astrology, and alchemy. But with the work of Friedrich Nietzsche (1844–1900) a new tradition of interpretation was born – one based on a thoroughgoing skepticism that sought to invert the purported values of Platonism. Here the history of Platonism was reenvisioned as the history of western metaphysics *tout court*, an interpretive move whereby Christianity and Platonism were read ahistorically as twin manifestations of the same cultural slouch toward nihilism. To a large extent, the horizons of Nietzsche's thought continue to implicitly define the contours of the conversation on Platonism and modernity. And at least outside of classicist and philological circles, they often determine how the term is defined across contemporary theoretical discourses. So pervasive was Nietzsche's influence that, by the late twentieth century, Martin Heidegger could make the unequivocal correlation: "Metaphysics is Platonism" (*Die Metaphysik ist Platonismus*).[27] It is toward this quintessentially "postmodern" reimagining of Platonism that I now turn.[28]

Mutants & Mystics: Science Fiction, Superhero Comics, and the Paranormal (Chicago: University of Chicago Press, 2011), 268–290, *passim*. Still in need of research however, are the connections between the heritage of Neoplatonic thought (*sensu lato*) and contemporary avant-garde music, such as the American psyche-folk outfit Six Organs of Admittance, whose creator Ben Chasny has developed an "open system" of musical experimentation that draws upon continental thinkers such as Gaston Bachelard and esoteric luminaries like Raymond Lull and Cornelius Agrippa, and British experimental troubadours Current 93, whose mastermind David Tibet has extended his practice into poetic and scholarly engagements with Christian mysticism, ancient apocalyptic texts, and Coptic Gnosticism. In regard to the former, see Ben Chasny, *The Hexadic System* (Chicago: Drag City Inc., 2015). For the latter, see David Tibet, *Sing Omega: Collected Lyrics and Writings from 2013–1983* (n.p.: The Spheres, 2015).

[27] Martin Heidegger, *Gesamtausgabe 14* (Vittorio Klostermann: Frankfurt am Main, 1992), 71.

[28] For an overview of postmodern readings of the Platonic corpus, see Catherine H. Zuckert, *Postmodern Platos: Nietzsche, Heidegger, Gadamer, Strauss, Derrida* (Chicago: University of Chicago Press, 1996). On the contested relationship between the received tradition of Platonism and European philosophy, see Adriaan Theodoor Peperzak, *Platonic Transformations: With and After Hegel, Heidegger, and Levinas* (Lanham: Rowman & Littlefield, 1997); Drew A. Hyland, *Questioning Platonism: Continental Interpretations of Plato* (Albany: State University of New York Press, 2004).

PLATONISM AS PARASITE: NIETZSCHE, HEIDEGGER, AND THE BIRTH OF ANTI-PLATONISM

A quip Nietzsche penned in 1888 might seem all-too-familiar to anyone who has had the dubious pleasure of teaching philosophy to a less than enthusiastic undergraduate class: "Plato is boring" ("Plato ist langweilig").[29] But Nietzsche's critical engagement with Plato cut much deeper than this glib dismissal suggests. In his eyes, Platonism must be relentlessly opposed, because it is a world-denying ideology; hostile to the body and the physical realm, Platonism devalues life itself. Ironically however, the concept of truth that emerged from its realist ontology became its own undoing: under its unforgiving light the imaginary of Platonism vanished like a shadow. In *Twilight of the Idols*, Nietzsche narrates a descent into nihilism (*Nihilismus*) that begins with Plato and erupts in his own milieu; during this process the very notion of a "true world" is denuded as a hollow idea.[30] Yet since objective truth is but a chimera, nothing is inherently false either. We are set adrift in a phantasmagorical and meaningless world – a fact that one must accept and creatively engage with, if despair and self-deception are to be held at bay. Nietzsche's equation of Platonism with metaphysics, the latter glossed as a general position that affirms and lionizes the reality of abstract principles and the existence of a nonphysical ultimate reality, was meant to underscore his belief that all meta-realms or "backworlds" (*Hinterwelten*) are parasites that feed upon the physical world they purport to give meaning to.[31] Far from unveiling a primordial source of meaning, Nietzsche accuses Platonism of draining color from the here and now; his own philosophy is offered conversely as an exorcism and transposition: "My philosophy an inverted Platonism: the further removed from true being, the purer, the more beautiful, the better it is. Living in appearance as goal" ("Meine Philosophie umgedrehter Platonismus: je weiter ab von wahrhaft Seienden, um so reiner schöner besser ist es. Das Leben in Schein als Zeil").[32]

---

[29] Friedrich Nietzsche, IV.3: 129. All subsequent Nietzsche references are taken from *Nietzsche Werke: Kritische Gesamtausgabe*, edited by Giorgio Colli and Mazzino Montinari (Berlin: Walter de Gruyter & Co., 1968).

[30] An exemplary account of Nietzsche's reading of Platonism can be found in "Wie die 'wahre Welt' endlich zur Fabel wurde: Geschichte eines Irrthums," VI.3: 74–75.

[31] Nietzsche interprets the metaphysical vision as one grounded in psychological delusion: "Leiden war's und Unvermögen – das schuf alle Hinterwelten; und jener kurze Wahnsinn des Glücks, den nur der Leidendste erfährt." V.1: 32.

[32] Nietzsche, III.3: 207. The sentiment here is that Nietzsche wishes to align himself with a dynamic and earthly way of being whereby the radical relativity of all meaning is

What is more, Platonism, by any other name, is not simply a philosophical parasite. Christianity, that ultimate target of Nietzschean derision is merely, "Platonism for the people" ("Christentum ist Platonismus fürs Volk").[33] Plato ideologically antecedes Christ and St. Paul; the seed of moral sickness that blossomed into nineteenth-century nihilism is planted in Platonic discourse but nurtured by Christianity. For Nietzsche, the mantra "God is Dead" ("Gott ist tot") militated against appeal to all transcendental certainties, whether provided by divine revelation or more ambiguous phenomena such as the Platonic "Form of the Good" (ἡ τοῦ ἀγαθοῦ ἰδέα, *he tou agathou idea*) or the Plotinian "One" (τὸ Ἕν, *to hen*). Nietzsche maintains that humanity's hope lies in the rare few who dare invert Platonism/Christianity to embrace a resolutely this-worldly and life-affirming mode of existence: an existential devaluation of all transcendent values that will lead to a new dawn. Heidegger, writing very much under the sway of Nietzsche would echo this call for a new sort of shamanic figure; one who reached not for the light of the Good, but rather, the darkness below the cave, for it "is necessary that there be those who reach into the abyss" ("Dazu ist aber nötig, daß solche sind, die in den Abgrund reichen").[34]

Profoundly shaken by the First World War, Heidegger took Nietzsche's diagnosis of occidental nihilism as one of the central concerns of his thinking.[35] The whole of Heidegger's post-Nietzschean project is naturally too complex to explicate here; but at heart, Heidegger's inquiry into Being (*das Sein*) was an attempt to ask how "meaningful presence" occurs within a fully immanentized vision of existence, which is to say, a world without recourse to any given standards of truth, such as the Platonic teaching of ideas; the Christian notion of revelation; or the Enlightenment's confidence in the transcendental abilities of reason.[36] Heidegger's meta-metaphysical history of philosophy, glossed as the "history of being" (*Seinsgeschichte*), a period during

---

joyfully accepted as a call to creativity over and against the notion of any form of given truth or ontological realism.

[33] For Nietzsche, Plato is just an antecedent Christian, a "higher swindler" (*höherer Schwindel*); Plato simply offers a prefiguration of the world-denying logic of the Christian cross. VI.3: 149–150.

[34] Martin Heidegger, GA 5. 249/270.

[35] William Barrett, *Irrational Man: A Study in Existential Philosophy* (Garden City, NY: Doubleday Anchor, 1962), 205.

[36] For an introduction to the whole of Heidegger's work and its relationship to the history of philosophy, see: Thomas Sheehan, *Making Sense of Heidegger: A Paradigm Shift* (London: Rowman & Littlefield International Ltd, 2015).

which the western world's aptitude for asking fundamental questions regarding existence and meaning had progressively atrophied, resulting in a "forgetting of being" (*Seinsvergessenheit*), was mapped out between the pre-Socratics and the phenomenology of Edmund Husserl, Heidegger's immediate predecessor and former teacher. Emplotted within this narrative, Nietzsche emerges as "the last metaphysician of the West" ("der letzte Metaphysiker des Abendlandes") – a radical thinker who deconstructed Platonism, yet remained within its orbit by virtue of embodying its inversion.[37]

Plato, as might be guessed, also plays a pivotal and not altogether lauded role in Heidegger's *Seinsgeschichte*.[38] Heidegger's Plato makes the decisive move of equating Being (οὐσία) with idea (εἶδος, ἰδέα). Thus, in an echo of Nietzsche's accusations, under the Platonic gaze the phenomenal world (φύσις) fades away under the false lights of ideality; essence is taken to be more real than existence and the intelligible is understood to possess more meaning than the sensible.[39] On Heidegger's view, "[w]hat remains decisive [about Platonism] is not the fact in itself that φύσις was characterized as ἰδέα, but that the ἰδέα comes forth as the sole and definitive interpretation of being."[40] Thus characterized, Platonism catalyzed tendencies that led to the advent of nihilism: it sowed the seeds of an anthropocentric subjectivism by positing essence as the property of intellectual apprehension; it privileged a "metaphysics of presence," which is to say, Being understood as that which exists outside of time, a position that either denies the reality of the ephemeral or sees in it an impoverished mode of being. Under the Platonic gaze, particular beings are seen as deficient instantiations of a universal, generic notion of

---

[37] Martin Heidegger, GA 47: 8.

[38] For an alternate critical reading that seeks to decouple the influence of both Christian Platonism and Nietzsche from Heidegger's understanding of Plato, see Gregory Fried, "Back to the Cave: A Platonic Rejoinder to Heideggerian Postmodernism," in *Heidegger and the Greeks: Interpretive Essays* (Bloomington and Indianapolis: Indiana University Press, 2006), 157–176, and Mark Ralkowski, *Heidegger's Platonism* (London and New York: Continuum, 2009).

[39] Heidegger states: "If we understand the ἰδέα, the intelligible appearance, as [the thing's] presence, then presence shows itself as [a thing's] steadfastness in a double sense. On the one hand, the intelligible appearance entails the standing-forth-from-concealment, the simple ἔστιν ["it is"]. On the other hand, what shows itself in the intelligible appearance is that which looks a certain way, i.e., what stands here, the τί ἔστιν [what-it-is]. Thus the ἰδέα [the whatness or essence of a thing] constitutes the being of the thing." GA 40: 190.14–20 = 202. 1–8. Translation by Thomas Sheehan, *Making Sense of Heidegger*, 43.

[40] Martin Heidegger, GA 40: 191. Translation by Thomas Sheehan, *Making Sense of Heidegger*, 44.

Being.[41] Fostered by Platonism and Christendom, a western worldview arose that interpreted existential concepts such as truth, reality, and Being, in terms of presence, essence, identity, and origin; existence was "overwhelmed" by "essence" ("überwältigt von seinem Wesen").[42] Like Nietzsche, Heidegger turned against the supposedly timeless *kosmos* of Platonism to embrace a modern *chaosmos*, a space wherein "possibility" (*Möglichkeit*) stood higher than "actuality" (*Wirklichkeit*).[43] Yet unlike his predecessor, Heidegger sought to move beyond the logic of inversions. The first beginning of philosophy had obscured Being; Heidegger would seek a new, "second beginning," a place to start again outside of the horizons of metaphysics.[44]

Though Heidegger is often accused of harboring a certain nostalgia for Being that is anathema to postmodernism, his reading of Plato via Nietzsche remains extremely influential and has been echoed by luminaries such as Derrida and Gilles Deleuze, who castigate Platonism for its tendency to hierarchically prioritize ideals of purity, simplicity, and essentiality over the complexities of intersubjective, historical existence.[45] The "deficient" side of Plato's paternal inheritance, noted above by Foucault, comes fiercely to the fore under the gaze of late and postmodern critical thought.

In sum, the twentieth- and twenty-first-century critique of Platonism is (1) *ontological* (Platonism focuses on a supersensible realm, genetically linked to the supernaturalism of Christianity, and thus Being becomes a mere idea and the realm of the intelligible is separated from that of the sensible); (2) *epistemological* (Platonism advocates for a transcendent, static, and hierarchically organized notion of Truth that lies outside of the context of history and culture and fosters a crude realism); and (3) *ethical* (Platonism devalues the earth, the body, is harmful to human flourishing, and places a timeless and abstract ideal of unity over the particular, the aberrant, and the ephemeral). Thus defined, in concert with Christianity, Platonism is

---

[41] "From a rigorous Platonic way of thinking, the essence of a being is impaired by its entanglement with an [individual] actuality, it loses its purity and so in a certain sense its universality." GA 45: 69. Translations, Sheehan, *Making Sense of Heidegger*, 44.

[42] GA 9: 275.

[43] Martin Heidegger, "Höher als die Wirklichkeit steht die Möglichkeit," GA 2: 51–52. "Chaosmos" is a term borrowed from James Joyce's *Finnegans Wake*, ed. Danis Rose and John O'Hanlon (Cornwall: Houyhnhnm, 2010), 1.5.118.

[44] Martin Heidegger, GA 66: 111. Heidegger's "second beginning" signifies "[f]reedom from metaphysics." Thomas Sheehan, *Making Sense of Heidegger*, 255.

[45] For example, see Jacques Derrida, *Limited Inc.* (inc. "Afterword") (Evanston: Northwestern University Press, 1998) and Gilles Deleuze and Rosalind Krauss, "Plato and the Simulacrum," *October* 27 (1983), 45–56.

implicated in multiple modern ills, from ecological devastation to the techno-cratic will to power that erupted into the horrors of mechanized killing.[46]

The Platonism that emerges from the Nietzsche–Heidegger hermeneut-ical tradition, which I will refer to as "Platonism²," formally if not entirely in spirit, recalls Yeats's Platonic poetics. Yet here the existential is trans-posed to the sociocultural: Platonism portrayed as the last refuge of a tired, decadent occident, a philosophical form of thanatophilia. But is this strain of anti-Platonism based on a straw man argument? Should we, along with the eminent Dutch scholar Adriaan T. Peperzak, suspect that this "chorus of antimetaphysical Plato bashers" might be premising their opposition on a "crudely materialistic caricature" of Platonism?[47] This position seems to demand consideration; after all, as Nietzsche himself confessed: "Plato ... becomes in my hands a caricature (*Carikatur*)."[48]

Certainly relevant philological critiques of these aerial interpretations have been made.[49] Yet even if we remain within the discursive parameters of the continental-hermeneutical tradition crucial questions arise. For instance, we might ask: are these critical readings themselves shaped by certain so-to-speak "Platonizing" assumptions? Might it be the case, as William Franke has argued, that "the contemporary philosophical polemic that targets metaphysics as if getting rid of this type of thinking would cure Western culture of its pluri-millenary sickness, is itself another symptom of the tendency to reify and isolate elements by their objective manifestations and to abstract from and forget their deeper roots that reach into the unsayable and unknowable"?[50] Put another way, in order to level these criticisms of Platonism, must not this hermeneutical trad-ition presuppose that Platonism contains a definable and ahistorical essence as well as a static epistemology and ontology? In a seminal lecture on Plato, Heidegger maintains that "a thinker's doctrine is that which is

---

[46] Heidegger's *Die Frage nach der Technik* ("The Question Concerning Technology"), published in 1954, famously – and controversially – argues that physical instances of technology are mere manifestations of a particular stance toward being, which "enframes" the natural world and its inhabitants and subsequently presents them merely in terms of use value. Although many of Heidegger's claims have been met with criticism, this text continues to exert influence on ecocritical discourse.

[47] Adriaan Theodoor Peperzak, *Platonic Transformations: With and After Hegel, Heidegger, and Levinas* (Lanham: Rowman & Littlefield, 1997), 12–17.

[48] Friedrich Nietzsche, VIII.2: 187.

[49] An excellent overview can be found in Hyland, *Questioning Platonism*.

[50] William Franke, *On What Cannot Be Said: Apophatic Discourses in Philosophy, Religion, Literature, and the Arts*, Vol 1 (Notre Dame: University of Notre Dame, 2007), 26.

left unsaid in what he says."[51] Likewise, Nietzsche wrote of uncovering the "concealed history of the philosophers."[52] What then is left "unsaid" or "concealed" in these strong readings of the Platonic corpus? Which dimensions of Platonism are suppressed by this tradition's revelations?

For centuries orthodox readings of Plato's "Allegory of the Cave" have reinforced the idea that Platonism unambiguously privileges the even, clear light of certainty over the chthonic and sensual darkness of the cave – a reading that dovetails with Nietzsche's charge that Platonism valorizes a phantasmal ideal of objective Truth and subsequently betrays the realities of the earth and the body. Yet we must not forget that, when understood as a propaedeutic to initiatory self-transformation, rather than an abstract thought experiment or dogmatic parable, this allegory not only counsels return to the cave, it also underscores the necessary chaos precipitated by liminal moments of existential blindness.[53]

Moreover, even if we temporarily bracket the hypothesis that Plato was an esoteric writer who hid his "authentic" mystical teachings from the uninitiated,[54] it must be recalled that his works evince the influence of the mystery religions,[55] intermittently praise divinely inspired madness

[51] "Die Lehre eines Denkers ist das in seinem Sagen Ungesagte." Martin Heidegger, *GA* 9, 203. As William Richardson helpfully glosses this, "Heidegger is endeavoring to comprehend and express not what another thinker thought/said, but what he did not think/say, and why he could not think/say it." William Richardson, *Heidegger: Through Thought to Phenomenology* (The Hague: Martinus Nijhoff, 1963), 22. If we keep in mind that what the thinker might not *want* to think/say is also a useful hermeneutical stance, I maintain that reading the critiques of Platonism with this in mind may enlighten. On Heidegger's debt to the Neoplatonic tradition, see J. M. Narbonne, *Hénologie, ontologie et Ereignis: Plotin-Proclus-Heidegger*, L'âne d'or (Paris: Les Belles Lettres, 2001).

[52] "Die verborgene Geschichte der Philosophen." Friedrich Nietzsche, VI 3: 257.

[53] Ralkowski maintains that, while Augustine influenced western interpretations of Plato by polemically excluding the possibility that he was "a nondogmatic, transformative philosopher whose philosophy was a *practice* aimed at an ineffable *experiential* truth," it is important "to ask why Plato stressed, and in some cases embraced, non-rational phenomena – for example, myth, madness, religious experience, prophecy, charms, incantations, divine dispensation, mystery religions, and so ... features of the dialogues, which easily connect to the ineffability of Plato's philosophy [and] point much more directly ... to an unsystematic philosophy." Mark Ralkowski, *Heidegger's Platonism*, 20–21.

[54] On the notion that Plato hints at an esoteric core to his thought, specifically in the so-called seventh letter, see Kurt van Fritz, "The Philosophical Passage in the Seventh Platonic Letter and the Problem of Plato's 'Esoteric Philosophy,'" in *Essays in Ancient Greek Philosophy*, ed. John P. Anton and George L. Kustas (Albany: State University of New York Press), 408–447. For an argument against the authenticity of the letter in question, see: Ludwig Edelstein, *Plato's Seventh Letter* (Leiden: E. J. Brill, 1966).

[55] The extent of the influence of the mystery religions on Plato is a subject of some controversy; see D. Dewincklear, "La question de l'initiation dans le mythe de la caverne," in the *Revue de philosophie ancienne* 11, no. 2 (1993), 159–175, and Martin-Velasco, Maria

(μανία, *mania*; ἐνθουσιασμός, *enthusiasmus*),[56] and subvert Platonism's supposed dualist ontology with the "bastard reasoning" (λογισμῷ ... νο ΄θῳ) proper to chora (χώρα).[57] Might there be a shadow discourse, sensed but not explicated by the Nietzsche–Heidegger tradition, "a Platonic thinking anterior to virtually all Platonism," which paradoxically antici-pates the critique of Platonic metaphysics and the advent of nihilism?[58] Whether or not this "dark Neo/Platonism" is rooted in historical antiquity is beyond the present scope of this chapter; yet as the tradition is creatively appropriated by contemporary thinkers and placed once again in conver-sation with Christian mystical thought, there are signs that such a subtradition is already underway.[59]

NEGATIVE POSSIBILITIES: THE CHRISTIAN APOPHATIC TRADITION

As the Nietzsche–Heidegger tradition collapses Platonism and Christianity into a single discourse, it is ironic that, precisely at a node in these intertwining traditions, a discourse emerges, which looks very much like the undoing of Platonism². In modern appropriations of the Neoplatonic-Christian tradition of "apophatic" or *via negativa* mysti-cism, we find an ecstatic Platonism more in line with Ginsberg's eroticized vision than Yeats's thanatological one. This subtradition diverges onto-logically, epistemologically, and ethically in such radical ways from Platonism² that, as the work of John Sallis, William Franke, Drew Hyland, and – if less explicitly – Jean-Luc Marion, suggests, it is possible to see in it (1) a hidden source of the Nietzsche–Heidegger critique; (2) a potential resource for a radical turn in the history of metaphysical thought; and (3) a well of ethical inspiration.

José Blanco, Maria José Garcia (eds.), *Greek Philosophy and Mystery Cults* (Newcastle upon Tyne: Cambridge Scholars Publishing, 2016).

[56] *Phaedrus*, for example, seems to present views of poetry that diverge from those presented in *Republic*, e.g. 244a–245c. The classic text on Greek thought and madness is E. R. Dodds, *Greeks and the Irrational* (Berkeley: University of California Press, 1951). But see also Marke Ahonen, "Plato on Madness and Mental Disorders," in *Mental Disorders in Ancient Philosophy*, 35–67; Paul Vicaire, "Les Grecs et le mystère de l'inspiration poétique," *Bulletin de l'Association Guillaume Budé* 1 (1963), 68–85; Alain Billault, "La folie poétique: remarques sur les conceptions grecques de l'inspira-tion," *Bulletin de l'Association Guillaume Budé* 4 (2002).

[57] *Timaeus*, 52b.   [58] John Sallis, *Platonic Legacies*, 9.

[59] "It is, then, from the limit, from a Platonism at the limit of metaphysics, that this forgotten legacy can, as it were, be restored." Ibid, 93.

From the philosophico-religious dimensions of *Phaedrus, Symposium, Timaeus,* and *Republic,* to Plotinus' *Enneads,* the mystical element in Platonism has deeply influenced Jewish, Christian, and Islamic mysticism and esotericism; it has even been argued that the western tradition of mysticism should be thought of as *definitively* Platonic.[60] The work attributed to Pseudo-Dionysius (*c.* fifth/sixth century CE) marks a pivotal moment in this history.[61] The anonymous author Christianized a tendency found in the work of Plotinus and Damascius to speak of the apogee of reality in aporetic and abyssal terms. In doing so, he ignited the shadowy flame of apophatic or *via negativa* mysticism, laying the groundwork for Meister Eckhart, St. John of the Cross, Marguerite Porete, and Jacob Böhme, among others.[62] Apophatic mysticism eschews the luminous language of positivism to valorise darkness; it speaks paradoxically of the unspeakable nature of its subject matter and brings into play a unique constellation of ontological and epistemological positions.[63] In Pseudo-Dionysius' work, Plato's cave allegory is reimagined as a mystical ascent to God, which mirrors Moses' encounter with Jahweh wrapped in a dark cloud on Mount Sinai (Exod. 19:9); the Platonic notion of "beyond being" (ἐπέκεινα τῆς οὐσίας, *epekeina tes ousias*)[64] is theo-poeticized, not as the light of the Good, but as the darkness of the Divine: the traceless trace of a Godhead beyond all conceptualization, too wild to be caged as an object of the intellect or the senses. Accordingly, the mode of un/knowing proper to Dionysian apophaticism is not luminous certainty, but the gloom of *agnosia* (ἀγνωσία) – an experiential revelation of shadow, rather

---

[60] Arthur Versluis, *Platonic Mysticism: Contemplative Science, Philosophy, Literature, and Art* (Albany: State University of New York Press, 2017), 16.

[61] For a compendium of Pseudo-Dionysius' work in English translation, see Colm Luibheid and Paul Rorem (eds.), *Pseudo-Dionysius: The Complete Works* (Mahwah, NJ: Paulist Press, 1987).

[62] The moniker "apophatic" comes from *apophanai* "to speak off," from *apo* "off, away from" + *phanai* "to speak," thus implying the paradoxical action of speaking of something by speaking its unspeakability. Arguably, one of the earliest roots of this tradition can be found in Plato's *Republic* when he speaks of the good as being "beyond Being" (ἐπέκεινα τῆς οὐσίας, *epekeina tes ousias*). Plato, *Republic*, 509b, 590b. On Neoplatonism and apophaticism, see Raoul Mortley, "Negative Theology and Abstraction in Plotinus," *The American Journal of Philology* 96, no. 4 (1975), 363–377.

[63] On the history of Christian apophaticism, see Denys Turner, *The Darkness of God: Negativity in Christian Mysticism* (Cambridge and New York: Cambridge University Press, 1995); Henny Fiskå Hägg, *Clement of Alexandria and the Beginnings of Christian Apophaticism* (Oxford: Oxford University Press, 2006). On the appropriation of apophaticism in contemporary thought, see William W. Franke, *On What Cannot Be Said*; Nahum J. Brown and Aaron Simmons (eds.), *Contemporary Debates in Negative Theology and Philosophy* (Cham: Palgrave Macmillan, 2017).

[64] *Republic*, 509b; *Phaedrus*, 247c.

than a detached vision of light.[65] The initiate moves from the worlds of sensual and intellectual intelligibility into "the brilliant darkness of a hidden silence."[66] And from this metaphorical metamorphosis emerges not just a metaphysics, but also, an "apophatic anthropology."[67] The apophatic initiate is called to engage in "theurgy" (θεουργία) – literally "god-working" – an experiential knowledge of divinity (Θεός, *theos*), rather than theology, which makes use of reason (λόγος, *logos*) to approach its object of concern.[68]

Due in part to its resonances with deconstructionism, influentially explored by Derrida,[69] apophatic mysticism has garnered renewed attention via the philosophical "return to religion," a loose movement inspired in part by the Platonic ideal of philosophy as a spiritual exercise.[70] Conjoining the heritage of antiquity with the insights of phenomenology and post-Nietzschean existentialism, "alternative" metaphysical positions are probed for their implications vis-à-vis intersubjective, and recently, ecological ethics.[71] The apophatic tradition is plumbed for language capable of answering the "call of this *Other* that [reason] cannot comprehend."[72] Representative of this tendency is Jean-Luc Marion's[73]

---

[65] Pseudo-Dionysius, *Mystical Theology*, chapter 1, 998A–1001A.

[66] Ibid, 998A. Translation in Pseudo-Dionysius, *The Dionysian Mystical Theology*, trans. Paul Rorem (Minneapolis: Augsburg Fortress Publishers, 2015), 9.

[67] See Charles Stang, *Apophasis and Pseudonymity in Dionysius the Areopagite: "No Longer I"* (New York: Oxford University Press, 2012), 153–196.

[68] See Gregory Shaw, "Neoplatonic Theurgy and Dionysius the Areopagite," *Journal of Early Christian Studies* 7, no. 4 (1999), 573–599; Dylan Burns, "Proclus and the Theurgic Liturgy of Pseudo-Dionysius," *Dionysius* 22 (2004), 111–132.

[69] Jacques Derrida, "Sauf le nom," translated as "Sauf le nom (Post-Scriptum)" in *On the Name*, ed. J. Derrida and Thomas Dutoit (Stanford: Stanford University Press, 1995). Derrida wrote rather frequently of apophasis in the last two decades of his life, explicitly treating Pseudo-Dionysius, Eckhart, and Angelus Silesius

[70] Regarding the position that philosophy, in its original sense, is essentially a spiritual exercise, see Pierre Hadot, *Philosophy as a Way of Life: Spiritual Exercises from Socrates to Foucault*, trans. Arnold I. Davidson (Malden, MA: Blackwell, 1995).

[71] Michael Sells has explored the performative dimensions of apophatic approaches to language and their ethical implications in his groundbreaking work on mysticism. See: Sells, *Mystical Languages of Unsaying* (Chicago and London: University of Chicago Press, 1994).

[72] William Franke, "Apophasis and the Turn of Philosophy to Religion," 75.

[73] See Tamsin A. Jones, *Genealogy of Marion's Philosophy of Religion: Apparent Darkness* (Bloomington: Indiana University Press, 2011); Wayne J. Hankey, "Jean-Luc Marion's Dionysian Neoplatonism," *Perspectives sur le néoplatonisme*, in *International Society for Neoplatonic Studies, Actes du colloque de 2006*, ed. Martin Achard, Wayne Hankey, and Jean-Marc Narbonne, Collection Zêtêsis (Québec: Les Presses de l'Université Laval, 2009), 267–280.

insistence that Pseudo-Dionysius' "requirement that 'divine things be understood divinely'" and his radical prohibition on holding "God as an object, or as a supreme being ... escapes the ultimate avatar of the language of an object – the closure of discourse, and the disappearance of the referent."[74] Initially marshaled to evoke the radical transcendence of the Divine, in much post-Derridean speculation, the metaphysics of apophasis are immanentized and transposed into an ethical key.

EROTIC CHOROLOGY & DARK NEOPLATONISM

Via Ginsberg, we have already touched on erôs (ἔρως), one of the unruly forces that haunt the supposedly static, idealized imaginary of Platonism.[75] As presented in the *Symposium*, Platonic erôs is a metaxic and intersubjective phenomenon, a reality rooted neither in the realm of the Forms nor the sensorial world; it is an uncanny visitor whose onto-logical status and epistemological implications dull the sharpness of the Nietzsche–Heidegger critique.[76] This ambiguous quality may account for the fact that, under panoply of disguises, erôs has made a host of appear-ances throughout the Christian speculative tradition, from Hadewijch's "love mysticism" (*Minnemystiek*), to Jacob Böhme's "desire" (*Begierde*), to Jean-Luc Marion's "erotic phenomenon" (*Le phénomène érotique*).[77]

---

[74] Jean-Luc Marion, *The Idol and the Distance*, trans. Thomas A. Carlson (New York: Fordham University Press, 2001), 140.

[75] On erôs and Platonism, see Rachel Barney, "Eros and Necessity in the Ascent from the Cave," *Ancient Philosophy* 28, no. 2 (2008), 357–372; Richard Foley, "The Order Question: Climbing the Ladder of Love in Plato's Symposium," *Ancient Philosophy* 30, no. 1 (2010), 57–72; Jill Gordon, "Eros in Plato's Timaeus," *Epoche: A Journal for the History of Philosophy* 9, no. 2 (2005), 255–278; J. M. E. Moravcsik, "Reason and Eros in the Ascent Passage of the Symposium," in *Essays in Ancient Greek Philosophy, Vol. 1*, eds. John P. Anton and G. L. Kustas (Albany: State University of New York Press, 1971), 285–302; Frisbee C. C. Sheffield, *Plato's Symposium: The Ethics of Desire* (Oxford: Clarendon Press, 2006).

[76] As Hyland states: "We do not ascend to the 'form Eros' because, since Eros has been determined to be 'in the middle' between the divine and the human, and so not a divine entity as a form must be (*Symposium*, 202b–203a), there can be no form of eros." Drew Hyland, *Questioning Platonism*, 43.

[77] Jean-Luc Marion, *The Erotic Phenomenon*, trans. Stephen E. Lewis (Chicago: University of Chicago Press, 2007). On Böhme's notion of "Begierde," see Joshua Levi Ian Gentzke, "Imaginal Renaissance: Desire, Corporeality, and Rebirth in the Work of Jacob Böhme" (diss., Stanford University: 2017), 126–153, *passim*. On Hadewijch's erotic mysticism, see Bernard McGinn, *Meister Eckhart and the Beguine Mystics: Hadewijch of Brabant, Mechthild of Magdeburg, and Marguerite Porete* (New York: Continuum, 1994), 200–222.

Enmeshed with erôs is the notion of chora (χώρα), which stems from a discussion in the *Timaeus* on types of Being and their corresponding modes of knowing. Like erôs, chora is positioned between the mutable sensorial world and the eternal realm of the Forms; it is a "third kind" of reality, an "ever-existing Place, which admits not of destruction, and provides room for all things that have birth"; neither intellectual nor sensual, it can only be apprehensible by a kind of "bastard reasoning," and is seen dimly in dream for it occupies a place "that is neither on earth nor anywhere in the Heaven."[78]

Prior to modern interpretation, the notion of chora was primarily understood to refer to the receptivity of matter (ὕλη, *hyle*), which has been tied back to a (possibly intentional) misreading by Aristotle.[79] A contemporary hermeneutics of "chorology" has developed however, which finds in chora the mysterious trace of an implicitly nondualist impulse at the heart of Platonism: an openness to both a realm of Being and mode of knowing that lies beyond the dichotomies of intelligible/sensible, eternal/temporal.[80] Thus interpreted, chora "decisively interrupts, indeed forces a reformulation of, any sort of 'dualism' of Forms and their instantiations, that is, of that concentration on beings of one sort or another for which we eventually formulate the word 'Platonism.'"[81] As such, it allows for a "poetics of the possibility of the impossible."[82] To employ Heidegger's terms, chora and erôs are read as marks of "the unsaid" in Plato's works – they rend the fabric of the

---

[78] "And a third kind is ever-existing place (χώρας ἀεί), which admits not of destruction, and provides room for all things that have birth, itself apprehensible by a kind of bastard reasoning by the aid of non-sensation (αὐτὸ δὲ μετ᾽ ἀναισθησίας ἁπτὸν λογισμῷ τινὶ νόθῳ), barely an object of belief." Plato, *Timaeus* 52a–b. Trans. R. G. Bury, *Plato*, vol. 7 (Cambridge, MA: Harvard University Press, 1961): 122.

[79] John Sallis contends that Aristotle (intentionally) misreads Plato on Chora in *Physics* in a way that "de-radicalizes" the content of chora. Sallis, *Platonic Legacies*, 31–32.

[80] Drew A. Hyland, "First of All Came Chaos," in *Heidegger and the Greeks*, eds. Drew A. Hyland and John Panteleimon Manoussakis (Bloomington: Indiana University Press, 2006), 18; John Sallis, *Chorology: On Beginning in Plato's Timaeus* (Bloomington: Indiana University Press, 1999); Charles P. Bigger, *Between Chora and the Good: Metaphor's Metaphysical Neighborhood* (New York: Fordham University Press, 2005); Kristeva has also offered a psychoanalytic reading of the significance of chora, see Julia Kristeva, *Revolution in Poetic Language* (New York: Columbia University Press, 1984), 26.

[81] Drew A. Hyland, "First of All Came Chaos," 18.

[82] John Caputo, "Abyssus Abyssum Invocat: a Response to Kearney," in *A Passion for the Impossible: John D. Caputo in Focus*, ed. Mark Dooley (Albany: State University of New York Press, 2003), 123–127 at p. 127.

Platonic *kosmos,* inviting in its shadowy twin, *kháos.* As is appropriate when dealing with the abysmal, the valuation of this injection of chaos has varied greatly among its interpreters: for Derrida, chora is an invitation to think beyond the binary of reason and myth;[83] for John Sallis, it is proof that Platonism thinks beyond its own metaphysics;[84] for Richard Kearney, engaging John Caputo's reading, chora is an existential abyss of meaninglessness;[85] and for Julia Kristeva, it is the symbolization of a prelinguistic stage of psychosexual development.[86]

Ironically, the abysmal thinking that brought this interpretation of chora to the fore of contemporary continental discourse is greatly indebted to Heidegger's search for a "second beginning" in which he creatively appropriated and "existentialized" aspects of the Platonic-Christian apophatic tradition, for example, the thought of the medieval mystic Meister Eckhart and the early modern esoteric dissident, Jacob Böhme, both of whom focused on the dark and abysmal dimensions of Being that resonate with the choric tradition.

One site where Heidegger engaged directly with various aspects of this tradition is Schelling's *Freizeitschrift.*[87] In his 1936 lectures, Heidegger maintained that Schelling's late work hinted at the radical possibility of thought outside the horizons of metaphysics; and in the *Freiheitsschrift* he sensed the "sheet lightning of a new beginning" ("das Wetterleuchten

---

[83] Jacques Derrida, "khôra," in *On the Name,* trans. Thomas Dutoit (Stanford, Calif: Stanford University Press, 1995), 89–91.

[84] John Sallis, *Platonic Legacies,* 4, *passim.*

[85] Richard Kearney, "Khora or God?," in *A Passion for the Impossible: John D. Caputo in Focus,* 107–122 at p. 113.

[86] Julia Kristeva, *Revolution in Poetic Language,* 26.

[87] Schelling was introduced to Böhme's work, most likely as early as 1799 by his friend and sometime mentor, Franz van Baader. Schelling was also deeply influenced by the Böhmean theosopher and Schwabian pietist Christoph Oetinger (1702–1782); see Robert F. Brown, *The Later Philosophy of Schelling: The Influence of Jacob Böhme on the Works of 1809–1815* (Lewisburg: Bucknell University Press, 1977), 114–115; Jean-François Marquet, *Liberté et existence: Étude sur la formation de la philosopie de Schelling* (Paris: Gallimard, 1973), 571–586. An in-depth study of the relationship between the thought of Heidegger and Böhme has yet to be undertaken; however see Hans-Joachim Friedrich, *Der Ungrund der Freiheit im Denken von Böhme, Schelling und Heidegger* (Stuttgart and Bad Canstatt: Frommann-Holzboog, 2009); Robert Paslick, "The Ontological Context of Gadamer's Fusion: Böhme, Heidegger, and Non-Duality," *Man and World* 18 (1985), 405–422 at p. 411; Elliot R. Wolfson, *Alef, Mem, Tau: Kabbalistic Musings on Time, Truth, and Death* (Berkeley: University of California Press, 2006), 34–35. Wolfson, *Language, Eros, Being: Kabbalistic Hermeneutics and Poetic Imagination* (New York: Fordham University Press, 2005), 34–35; John Caputo, *Mystical Elements in Heidegger's Thought* (New York: Fordham University Press, 1986), 98.

eines neuen Anfangs").[88] In Heidegger's interpretation, Schelling thinks outside of the categorical dualism of Platonic metaphysics, for he "does not think in 'concepts' (*Begriffe*); he thinks in forces and thinks from positions of the will (*Willensstellungen*) ... from the struggle of powers that cannot be made to subside by a conceptual technique (*eine Begriffskunst*)," and yet the "whole boldness (*Kühnheit*) of Schelling's thought" is "only the continuation of an attitude of thought (*eine denkerischen Haltung*) that begins with Meister Eckhart and is uniquely developed with Jacob Böhme."[89] Here Heidegger explicitly engages with the conceptual sources for his notions of "abyss" (*Abgrund*) and "the nothing" (*das Nichts*), which, when transposed from a theosophic to an existentialist key, become essential aspects of his overall project.[90]

Likewise, Slavoj Žižek claims that Schelling's later works are animated by a "'regression' from pure philosophical idealism to the pre-modern theosophical problematic *which enabled him to overtake modernity itself.*"[91] Thus interpreted, Schelling is the "last great representative of the pre-modern 'anthropomorphic sexualized vision of the universe'" and yet "only a thin invisible line separates him from openly asserting, in a thoroughly postmodern vein ... a fundamental 'out-of-joint,' a disturbed balance as the positive ontological constituent of the universe."[92] Yet, as with Heidegger, what Žižek interprets as the "postmodern" radicalism of Schelling's later thought is rooted in his engagement with Christian-Platonic theosophy. Although Schelling had focused explicitly on the chora of the *Timaeus* in his early work, it is his later evocation of *Ungrund* that steers him closest to the choric tradition as it is currently articulated.[93]

Ungrund, as Heidegger alludes to, originates in the work of Jacob Böhme (1575–1624).[94] Böhme significantly altered the Neoplatonic-Christian

---

[88] Martin Heidegger, GA 9: 5.   [89] Ibid, 193, 204.

[90] For example, the Eckhartian–Böhmean function of *das Nichts* in "Was Heisst Metaphysik" (1927) and that of *Abgrund* in *Beiträge zur Philosophie* (1936–1938) and *Der Satz vom Grund* (1957).

[91] Slavoj Žižek, *The Indivisible Remainder: On Schelling and Related Matters* (London: Verso, 2007), 10. Italics are mine.

[92] Ibid.

[93] On Schelling's reading of chora see John Sallis, "Secluded Nature: The Point of Schelling's Reinscription of the Timaeus," *Pli: The Warwick Journal of Philosophy* 8 (1999), 71–85; Tyler Tritten, "On Matter: Schelling's Anti-Platonic Reading of the Timaeus," *The Official Journal of the North American Schelling Society*, Vol. 8 (2018), 93–114. On the connection of the *Freiheitsschrift* to Timaeus, see: John Sallis, "Secluded Nature," 74.

[94] For a historical introduction to Böhme's thought, see Andrew Weeks, *Boehme: An Intellectual Biography of the Seventeenth-Century Philosopher and Mystic* (Albany: State University of New York Press, 1991); on *Ungrund*, see Joshua L. I. Gentzke,

tradition of apophaticism: whereas figures such as Pseudo-Dionysius and
Meister Eckhart harnessed the abysmal language of darkness to describe
a divine knowledge that transcended sensual apprehension, Böhme fused this
tradition with nature mysticism and proto-existentialist speculation. In
Böhmean thought, folded into and circumscribing the some-thing-ness of
the world and the perceptible self is *Ungrund*: a primordial ungrounded
openness that enables the paradoxical phenomenon of an "eternal beginning" (*ewigen Anfang*), which never recedes into the distance of the past
tense.[95] Signifying across ontological and epistemological registers, the priv-
ative *un* places this term in an equally antonymic relationship to *Grund* in the
sense of "reason" (*logos*), "foundation," and "cause." *Ungrund* is the
residual, unphenomenalizable groundlessness at the heart of Being/
Nonbeing: the primordial incompleteness, whose mode of non/presence
and a/temporality not only allows for but – to borrow the language of
existentialism – "condemns" all life to the transcendence of longing, and
thus holds open the abyss of freedom. It is "the eternal freedom ... the will
itself" ("die ewige Freyheit ... ist selber der Wille"), "the rarefied freedom
that is nothing" ("der dünne Freiheit, da ist Nichts").[96] In this sense,
Ungrund posits a model of ontology based on the concealment and revelation of a me/ontological continuum, rather than mechanistic creation.
Contextualized within this imaginary, opposites become intimates, ontologically conjoined by nature of their codependence.

Here Böhme's thought veers outside the tradition of western
metaphysics.[97] It is not sequence and causality that weave together the
temporal web of the Böhmean imaginary, but a complex set of

"Imagining the Image of God," 103–129; on Böhme and Schelling see S. J. McGrath, *The
Dark Ground of Spirit: Schelling and the Unconscious* (London and New York:
Routledge, 2012). In regard to Böhme's reception of Platonism, see Chapter 2.6 in this
volume.

[95] "The Ungrund is an eternal nothing. And yet it creates an eternal beginning, which is its
craving – for the nothing is a craving after something" ("Der Ungrund ist ein ewig Nichts
und machete aber einen ewigen Anfang, als seine Sucht; Dann das Nichts ist eine Sucht
nach Etwas"). Jacob Böhme, *Von der Menschwerdung Jesu Christi*, [VII] 3. Teil 5, 5, 10.

[96] Böhme, *Viertzig Fragen*, IV 1: 13, 10, *Von sechs theosophischen Punkten*, VI Punct 1, 1:
38, 10.

[97] That Böhme's thought evinces a rare case of a western religious thinker standing outside
of the tradition designated by Heidegger as "Ontotheologie," is noted by Japanese
philosopher Ryôsuke Ohashi, in his work on Friedrich W. J. Schelling: "der Ungrund
kein Gott nichts in Seiendes ist, somit zu keiner Onto-Theologie bzw. Metaphysik mehr
gehört." Ohashi, "Der Ungrund und das System," in *F. W. J. Schelling: Über das Wesen
der menschlichen Freiheit*, eds. Annemarie Pieper and Otfried Höffe (Berlin: Akademie
Verlag, 1995), 35–252 at p. 248.

interrelations, which, when taken as a whole, give rise to a diffuse ontology that offers a striking parallel to the Buddhist notion of "dependent origination" (*Pratītyasamutpāda*): a vision wherein being arises, not from a single source or cause, but rather, from a complex and ever-shifting field of interrelations.[98] Implicitly, for both Heidegger and Žižek, the potential for the deconstruction of modern metaphysics lies within "Platonism" *sensu lato*. Paradoxically, the postmodern is heralded by the premodern; the space for overcoming Platonic metaphysics opens up between the *Timaeus'* chora and apophaticism's focus on the nonobjectifiable nature of reality or Being. And in this sense, the postmodern desire to move beyond Platonic metaphysics draws deeply upon elements of this very tradition, albeit dimensions that historically stood at its fringes: apophasis, chora, *Ungrund*, and erôs point to the potentiality of a "second beginning" both within and beyond Platonism – a strange, dark Neoplatonism that circulates around an erotic chorology, that posits an ontology that honors the uncanny openness of existence over the fixity of conceptual paradigms; an epistemology that embraces its own limitations; and the potential for an ethics attendant to difference, relativism, and particularity.

CONCLUSION: A NEW WEIRD NEOPLATONISM?

Platonism, whether understood as something to be overcome or creatively appropriated, remains a vital force in a host of critical conversations. Between and beyond the polarities exemplified by the twentieth century poets Yeats and Ginsberg, a thousand Platonic possibilities continue to bloom from a discourse that is hardly dead. In the age of the anthropocene, one of the most decisive conversations wherein Platonism is sure to be engaged, is the speculative realism of second wave, post-Heideggerian eco-criticism.[99] It is not insignificant that Timothy Morton, tireless exponent of the new "dark ecology" and object-orientated ontology (OOO) – someone who could hardly be suspected to harbor nostalgia for the metaphysics that the Nietzsche–Heidegger tradition deride – writes of "[a]esthetic terms mothballed for decades [that] can now make a radical

---

[98] By appending the adjective "diffuse" to ontology, I mean to indicate a theory of being or ontogenesis that understands being as an interdependent and relational phenomenon, rather than one that can be traced back to a discrete cause or origin.

[99] See: S. J. McGrath, *Thinking Nature: Negative Ecology* (Edinburgh: University of Edinburgh Press, 2019).

comeback ... [s]omething that looks like a weird Neoplatonism – aesthetic phenomena beckoning onto a secret beyond – joins forces with a weird Aristotelianism – a nonmaterialist (that is, nonreductionist) realism of substances that are not just vague chunks of matter."[100] Perhaps then this dark Neo/Platonism can both heed Nietzsche's call to be "true to the earth," and yet remain free from the residue of nineteenth-century materialism.[101] A glimpse of this worldly and weird Neoplatonic-Aristotelianism can perhaps be detected in a few lines from the American poet Charles Wright:

> The Soul is in the body as light is in air
> Plotinus thought.
> > Well I wouldn't know about that, but
> *La luna piove*, and shine out in every direction –
> Under it all, disorder, above
> A handful of star on one side, a handful
> > On the other.[102]

Here in the poetic act of apophasis, invocation and unknowing, dream and doubt are spoken together under the silence of the stars, within the chaos of the sublunary realm; the human–nature complex appears, not as a relationship between subject and object, but as a mysterious field of possibility.

Bibliography

Ahonen, Marke. "Plato on Madness and Mental Disorders." In *Mental Disorders in Ancient Philosophy*, 35–67. Cham: Springer, 2014.

Asprem, Egil. *The Problem of Disenchantment*. Leiden: Brill, 2014.

Bailey, Edward I. *Implicit Religion in Contemporary Society*, Leuven: Peeters, 2006.

Barney, Rachel. "Eros and Necessity in the Ascent from the Cave." *Ancient Philosophy* 28, no. 2 (2008): 357–372.

Barrett, William. *Irrational Man: A Study in Existential Philosophy*. Garden City, NY: Doubleday Anchor, 1962.

---

[100] Timothy Morton, "An Object-Oriented Defense of Poetry" in *New Literary History*, Vol. 43, No. 2 (2012), 216. On Morton's notion of "dark ecology," see: Morton, *Dark Ecology: For a Logic of Coexistence* (New York: Columbia University Press, 2018).

[101] "bleibt der Erde treu und glaubt Denen nicht, welche euch von überirdischen Hoffnungen reden!" Friedrich Nietzsche, VI.1:9.

[102] Charles Wright, "The Appalachian Book of the Dead III" in *Poetry*, Vol. 171, no. 1 (1997), 96.

Baudelaire, Charles. "The Painter of Modern Life." In *The Painter of Modern Life and Other Essays*, translated and edited by Jonathan Mayne, 1–34. London and New York: Phaidon, 1970.

Bigger, Charles P. *Between Chora and the Good: Metaphor's Metaphysical Neighborhood*. New York: Fordham University Press, 2005.

Billault, Alain. "La folie poétique: remarques sur les conceptions grecques de l'inspiration." *Bulletin de l'Association Guillaume Budé* 4 (2002): 18–35.

Böhme, Jacob, *Sämtliche Schriften*. Edited by Will-Eric Peuckert. 11 vols. Stuttgart: Günter Holzboog, 1957.

Bornstein, George. "W.B. Yeats' Poetry of Aging." In *Sewanee Review* 120, no. 1 (2012): 46–61.

Brown, Nahum J. and Aaron Simmons, eds. *Contemporary Debates in Negative Theology and Philosophy*. Cham: Palgrave Macmillan, 2017.

Brown, Robert F. *The Later Philosophy of Schelling: The Influence of Jacob Böhme on the works of 1809–1815*. Lewisburg: Bucknell University Press, 1977.

Burns, Dylan. "Proclus and the Theurgic Liturgy of Pseudo-Dionysius." *Dionysius* 22 (2004): 111–132.

Calonne, David Stephen. *The Spiritual Imagination of the Beats*. Cambridge: Cambridge University Press, 2017.

Caputo, John. "Abyssus Abyssum Invocat: a Response to Kearney." In *A Passion for the Impossible: John D. Caputo in Focus*, edited by Mark Dooley, 123–127. Albany: State University of New York Press, 2003.

Mystical Elements in Heidegger's Thought. New York: Fordham University Press, 1986.

Chasny, Ben. *The Hexadic System*. Chicago: Drag City Inc., 2015.

De Vries, Hent. *Philosophy and the Turn to Religion*. Baltimore: Johns Hopkins University Press, 1999.

Deleuze, Gilles, "Plato and the Simulacrum." Translated by Rosalind Krauss. *October* 27 (1983): 45–56.

Derrida, Jacques. *Limited Inc*. Evanston: Northwestern University Press, 1998.

On the Name, edited by Jacques Derrida and Thomas Dutoit. Stanford: Stanford University Press, 1995.

Dewincklear, D. "La question de l'initiation dans le mythe de la caverne." *Revue de philosophie ancienne* 11, no. 2 (1993): 159–175.

Dodds, E. R. *Greeks and the Irrational*. Berkeley: University of California Press, 1951.

Edelstein, Ludwig. *Plato's Seventh Letter*. Leiden: E. J. Brill, 1966.

Faivre, Antoine. *Theosophy, Imagination, Tradition: Studies in Western Esotericism*. Albany: State University of New York Press, 2000.

Foley, Richard. "The Order Question: Climbing the Ladder of Love in Plato's Symposium." *Ancient Philosophy* 30, no. 1 (2010): 57–72.

Foucault, Michel. "Theatrum philosophicum." In *Sur G. Deleuze, Différence et Répétition*, 885–908. Paris: Presses Universitaires de France, 1968.

Franke, William W. "Apophasis and the Turn of Philosophy to Religion: From Neoplatonic Negative Theology to Postmodern Negation of Theology." *International Journal of Philosophy of Religion* 60, no. 1/3 (2006): 61–76.

On What Cannot Be Said: Apophatic Discourses in Philosophy, Religion, Literature, and the Arts, vols. 1 & 2. Notre Dame: University of Notre Dame Press, 2007.

Fried, Gregory. "Back to the Cave: A Platonic Rejoinder to Heideggerian Postmodernism." In *Heidegger and the Greeks: Interpretive Essays*. Bloomington and Indianapolis: Indiana University Press, 2006.

Friedrich, Hans-Joachim. *Der Ungrund der Freiheit im Denken von Böhme, Schelling und Heidegger*. Stuttgart and Bad Canstatt: Frommann-Holzboog, 2009.

Fritz, Kurt van. "The Philosophical Passage in the Seventh Platonic Letter and the Problem of Plato's 'Esoteric Philosophy.'" In *Essays in Ancient Greek Philosophy*, edited by John P. Anton and George L. Kustas, 408–447. Albany: State University of New York Press.

Fuller, Robert C. *Spiritual, but Not Religious*. New York: Oxford University Press, 2001.

Gentzke, Joshua Levi Ian. "Imaginal Renaissance: Desire, Corporeality, and Rebirth in the Work of Jacob Böhme." Ph.D. Dissertation, Stanford University, 2016.

———. "Imagining the Image of God: Corporeal Envisioning in the Theosophy of Jacob Böhme." In *Lux in Tenebris: The Visual and the Symbolic in Western Esotericism*, edited by Peter J. Forshaw, 103–129. Leiden: Brill, 2017.

Gersh, Stephen, ed. *Plotinus' Legacy: The Transformation of Platonism from the Renaissance to the Modern Era*. Cambridge, UK; New York: Cambridge University Press, 2019.

Ginsberg, Allen. *Howl and other Poems*. San Francisco: City Lights Books, 1959.

Gordon, Jill. "Eros in Plato's Timaeus." *Epoche: A Journal for the History of Philosophy* 9, no. 2 (2005): 255–278.

Gregory, John. *The Neoplatonists: A Reader*. London and New York: Routledge, 1999.

Hadot, Pierre. *Exercices spirituels et philosophie antique*. Paris: Editions Albion Michael, 2002.

Hägg, Henny Fiskå. *Clement of Alexandria and the Beginnings of Christian Apophaticism*. Oxford: Oxford University Press, 2006.

Hampton, Alexander. *Romanticism and the Re-Invention of Modern Religion: The Reconciliation of German Idealism and Platonic Realism*. Cambridge: Cambridge University Press, 2019.

Hanegraaff, Wouter J. *Esotericism in the Academy: Rejected Knowledge in Western Culture*. Cambridge: Cambridge University Press, 2012.

———. "Forbidden Knowledge." *Aries: Journal for the Study of Western Esotericism* 5, no. 2 (2005): 225–254.

Hankey, Wayne J. "Jean-Luc Marion's Dionysian Neoplatonism." In *Perspectives sur le néoplatonisme. International Society for Neoplatonic Studies, Actes du colloque de 2006*, ed. Martin Achard, Wayne Hankey, Jean-Marc Narbonne, Collection Zêtêsis, 267–280. Québec: Les Presses de l'Université Laval, 2009.

Hedley, Douglas and Sarah Hutton, eds. *Platonism at the Origins of Modernity: Studies on Platonism and Early Modern Philosophy*. Dordrecht: Springer, 2008.

Heidegger, Martin. *Gesamtausgabe*. Vittorio Klostermann: Frankfurt am Main, 1992.

Hoelzl, Michael and Graham Ward, eds. *The New Visibility of Religion: Studies in Religion and Cultural Hermeneutics*. London: Continuum, 2008.

Huss, Boaz. "Spirituality: The Emergence of a New Cultural Category and Its Challenge to the Religious and the Secular." *Journal of Contemporary Religion* 29 (2014): 47–60.

Hyland, Drew A. "First of All Came Chaos," in *Heidegger and the Greeks*, edited by Drew A. Hyland and John Panteleimon Manoussakis. Bloomington: Indiana University Press, 2006.

   Questioning Platonism: Continental Interpretations of Plato. Albany: State University of New York Press, 2004.

Jackson, Pamela, Jonathan Lethem, and Erik Davis, eds. *The Exegesis of Philip K. Dick*. Boston: Houghton Mifflin Harcourt, 2011.

Jones, Tamsin A. *Genealogy of Marion's Philosophy of Religion: Apparent Darkness*. Bloomington: Indiana University Press, 2011.

Joyce, James. *Finnegans Wake*. Edited by Danis Rose and John O'Hanlon. Cornwall: Houyhnhnm, 2010.

Kearney, Richard. "Khora or God?" In *A Passion for the Impossible: John D. Caputo in Focus*, edited by Mark Dooley, 107–122. Albany: State University of New York Press, 2003.

Kripal, Jeffrey J. *Mutants & Mystics: Science Fiction, Superhero Comics, and the Paranormal*. Chicago: University of Chicago Press, 2011.

   "Reality Against Society: William Blake, Antinomianism, and American Counterculture." *Common Knowledge* 13, no. 1 (2007): 102–104.

Kristeva, Julia. *Revolution in Poetic Language*. New York: Columbia University Press, 1984.

Lambert, Gregg. *Return Statements: The Return of Religion in Contemporary Philosophy*. Edinburgh: Edinburgh University Press, 2016.

Marion, Jean-Luc. *The Erotic Phenomenon*. Translated by Stephen E. Lewis. Chicago: University of Chicago Press, 2007.

   The Idol and the Distance. Translated by Thomas A. Carlson. New York: Fordham University Press, 2001.

Marquet, Jean-François. *Liberté et existence: Étude sur la formation de la philosopie de Schelling*. Paris: Gallimard, 1973.

Martín-Velasco, María José and María José García Blanco, eds. *Greek Philosophy and Mystery Cults*. Newcastle upon Tyne: Cambridge Scholars Publishing, 2016.

McGinn, Bernard. *Meister Eckhart and the Beguine Mystics: Hadewijch of Brabant, Mechthild of Magdeburg, and Marguerite Porete*. New York: Continuum, 1994.

McGrath, S. J. *The Dark Ground of Spirit: Schelling and the Unconscious*. London and New York: Routledge, 2012.

   Thinking Nature: An Essay in Negative Ecology. Edinburgh: University of Edinburgh Press, 2019.

Moravcsik, J. M. E. "Reason and Eros in the Ascent Passage of the Symposium." In *Essays in Ancient Greek Philosophy*, volume I, edited by John P. Anton and G. L. Kustas, 285–302. Albany: State University of New York Press, 1971.

Mortley, Raoul. "Negative Theology and Abstraction in Plotinus." *The American Journal of Philology* 96, no. 4 (1975): 363–377.

Morton, Timothy. *Dark Ecology: For a Logic of Coexistence.* New York: Columbia University Press, 2016.

Narbonne, J. M. *Hénologie, ontologie et Ereignis (Plotin-Proclus-Heidegger).* Paris: Les Belles Lettres, 2001.

Nietzsche, Friedrich. *Nietzsche Werke: Kritische Gesamtausgabe.* Edited by Giorgio Colli and Mazzino Montinari. Berlin: Walter de Gruyter, 1968.

Ohashi, Ryôsuke. "Der Ungrund und das System." In *F. W. J. Schelling: Über das Wesen der menschlichen Freiheit,* edited by Annemarie Pieper and Otfried Höffe, 235–252. Berlin: Akademie Verlag, 1995.

Partridge, Christopher H. *The Re-Enchantment of the West.* London: T & T Clark, 2004.

Paslick, Robert. "The Ontological Context of Gadamer's Fusion: Böhme, Heidegger, and Non-Duality." *Man and World* 18 (1985): 405–422.

Peperzak, Adriaan Theodoor. *Platonic Transformations: With and After Hegel, Heidegger, and Levinas.* Lanham: Rowman & Littlefield, 1997.

Plato. *Plato: Timaeus, Critias, Cleitophon, Menexenus [and] Epistles.* Translated by Robert Gregg Bury. Cambridge, MA: Harvard University Press, 1966.

Plethica, James. *Yeats's Poetry, Drama, and Prose.* New York: Norton, 2000.

Pruitt, Raymond D. and Virginia D. Pruitt, "W.B. Yeats on Old Age, Death, and Immortality." *Colby Library Quarterly* 24, no. 1 (1988): 36–49.

Pseudo-Dionysius. *Pseudo-Dionysius: The Complete Works.* Edited by Colm Luibheid and Paul Rorem. Mahwah, New Jersey: Paulist Press, 1987.

The Dionysian Mystical Theology. Translated by Paul Rorem. Minneapolis: Augsburg Fortress Publishers, 2015.

Ralkowski, Mark. *Heidegger's Platonism.* London and New York: Continuum, 2009.

Remes, Pauliina. *Neoplatonism.* Stocksfield: Acumen, 2008.

Richardson, William. *Heidegger: Through Thought to Phenomenology.* The Hague: Martinus Nijhoff, 1963.

Rosen, Stanley. *The Ancients and the Moderns: Rethinking Modernity.* New Haven: Yale University Press, 1989.

Sallis, John. *Chorology: On Beginning in Plato's Timaeus.* Bloomington: Indiana University Press, 1999.

Platonic Legacies. Albany: State University of New York Press, 2004.

"Secluded Nature: The Point of Schelling's Reinscription of the Timaeus," *Pli: The Warwick Journal of Philosophy* 8 (1999): 71–85.

Sandbeck, Lars. "God as Immanent Transcendence in Mark C. Taylor and John D. Caputo." *Studia Theologica: Nordic Journal of Theology* 65, no. 1 (2011): 18–38.

Schumacher, Michael. *Dharma Lion: A Biography of Allen Ginsberg.* New York: St. Martin's Press, 1992.

Schürmann, Reiner. *Broken Hegemonies.* Translated by Reginald Lilly. Bloomington: Indiana University Press, 2003.

Sells, Michael. *Mystical Languages of Unsaying.* Chicago and London: University of Chicago Press, 1994.

Shaw, Gregory. "Neoplatonic Theurgy and Dionysius the Areopagite." *Journal of Early Christian Studies* 7, no. 4 (1999): 573–599.

Sheehan, Thomas. *Making Sense of Heidegger: A Paradigm Shift.* London: Rowman & Littlefield International Ltd, 2015.

Sheffield, Frisbee C. C. *Plato's Symposium: The Ethics of Desire.* Oxford: Clarendon Press, 2006.

Stang, Charles M. *Apophasis and Pseudonymity in Dionysius the Areopagite: "No Longer I."* New York: Oxford University Press, 2012.

Tanke, Joseph J. *Foucault's Philosophy of Art: A Genealogy of Modernity.* London and New York: Continuum, 2009.

Tibet, David. *Sing Omega: Collected Lyrics and Writings from 2013–1983.* (No location given: The Spheres), 2015.

Tritten, Tyler. "On Matter: Schelling's Anti-Platonic Reading of the Timaeus." *The Official Journal of the North American Schelling Society,* 93–114.

Turner, Denys. *The Darkness of God: Negativity in Christian Mysticism.* Cambridge and New York: Cambridge University Press, 1995.

Tyson, Paul. "Transcendence and Epistemology: Exploring Truth via Post-Secular Christian Platonism." *Modern Theology* 24, no. 2 (2008): 245–270.

Versluis, Arthur. *Platonic Mysticism: Contemplative Science, Philosophy, Literature, and Art.* Albany: State University of New York Press, 2017.

Vicaire, Paul. "Les Grecs et le mystère de l'inspiration poétique." *Bulletin de l'Association Guillaume Budé* 1 (1963): 68–85.

Wolfson, Elliot R. *Alef, Mem, Tau: Kabbalistic Musings on Time, Truth, and Death.* Berkeley: University of California Press, 2006.

Language, Eros, Being: Kabbalistic Hermeneutics and Poetic Imagination. New York: Fordham University Press, 2005.

Wright, Charles. "Appalachian Book of the Dead III." *Poetry* 171, no. 1 (1997): 96.

Yeats, William Butler. *The Tower.* London and New York: Penguin Putnam, 1999.

Zuckert, Catherine H. *Postmodern Platos: Nietzsche, Heidegger, Gadamer, Strauss, Derrida.* Chicago: University of Chicago Press, 1996.

III

ENGAGEMENTS

3.1

Christian Platonism and Natural Science

Andrew Davison and Jacob Holsinger Sherman

One prominent way of narrating the rise of modern science is to see in Platonism precisely what Christianity had to overcome before it could unleash the energies of scientific enquiry that so characterize our epoch. The impetus for such a view in the history and philosophy of science issues especially from a series of articles by the Oxford philosopher Michael Beresford Foster (1903–1959). Foster's narrative presents the Christian doctrine of creation heroically struggling to free itself from the legacy of Platonism, a legacy that burdened it with the enchantments of a pagan nature, on the one hand, and the constraints of a thoroughgoing rationalism, on the other. But, Foster argues, while a certain sort of rationalism is a constitutive component of modern science, the experimental traditions of the seventeenth century and beyond required a particular constellation of ideas, quite different from what he saw in Platonism: the contingency of creation, a voluntarist theology of the Creator, and the concomitant need for empirical science rise together.

The heart of Foster's argument involves drawing a distinction between two different theologies that issue in two different approaches to the pursuit of knowledge of the natural world. On the one hand we have "rationalism in theology," which Foster associates with the legacy of Plato and Aristotle. This is "the doctrine that the activity of God is an activity of reason."[1] The corollary is a similarly high view of human reason: reason is the light of God, the candle of the Lord, and "so far as it is pure, is itself divine." In terms of scientific method, this entails a concomitant quest for

[1] M. B. Foster, "Christian Theology and Modern Science of Nature (II)," *Mind* 45 (1936), 1–27 at p. 1.

the purification of reason and its liberation from sensuality: "the consequence follows that the human reason has only to liberate itself from the impressions of experience in order to think the thoughts of God."[2] According to the rationalists, God made the world through reason and the world accordingly embodies the divine ideas. But because of the intimate connection between human and divine reason, we become capable of seeing the essential shape of creation only by first discovering the divine ideas in our own minds, through the use of our own reason.

Theological voluntarists, by contrast, hold that the divine will may operate in excess of divine reason. Later historiography will associate this with the elevation of the divine *potentia absoluta* (God's power over creation) over the *potentia ordinata* (the ways in which God has actually exercised his power in the creation of the world, the orders of nature, and so forth). Following William of Ockham, the voluntarists held that God's absolute power entailed the ability to do anything short of logical contradiction. Thus, liberated from any rationalistic limitations, God is free to create not after the manner of a demiurge consulting Wisdom, but rather in any manner whatsoever. Insofar as the divine will is inscrutable to our reason alone, we are forced to go beyond the confines of our reason and confront the creation in its own alterity. In order to know the mind of God, we have to look outside ourselves in order to see what God has in fact made. This potent mix of nominalism and voluntarism, while not eschewing rationality entirely, allows Foster and his successors to claim that the advent of early modern science is the story of progressive liberation from the shackles of an intellectualist, spiritualist, or *a prioristic* approach to the study of nature, all associated with Platonism.

There is, of course, some logic to a narrative of this sort but, as with almost all grand genealogical projects, the origins of modern science are more historically overdetermined than this, and the focus on the catalyzing power of nominalism and voluntarism tends to elide alternative, equally illuminating narratives about the advent of our own scientific age. Peter Harrison, for example, has argued forcefully against the voluntarism thesis, suggesting that Augustinian doubts about the cognitive consequences of the Fall provided far more secure and historically consequential reasons to doubt the sufficiency of one's deductions apart from empirical investigation of the world.[3] What is more, a monological

[2] Ibid.
[3] Peter Harrison, "Voluntarism and Early Modern Science," *History of Science* 40, no. 1 (2002), 63–89.

account of the rise of modern science elides the constitutive role played by Christian Platonism in the emergence of the science of nature throughout Christian history.

Popular accounts of the scientific revolution often present it as a contest between anachronistic Aristotelians, simultaneously too cathected to their "organic" vision of universe and too skittish to gaze through Galileo's telescope, and the intellectually adventurous experimentalists of the early modern age wielding the new mathematics and the emerging "mechanical philosophy" to a series of unprecedented successes. But careful historians of science have long since recognized this as a highly sanitized, not to say ideological account. It is now widely accepted that the contest at the beginning of the modern era was not merely staged between a mechanistic and nominalist modern science and its rigid scholastic forebears, for of equal importance were certain Neoplatonic traditions often bound up with renaissance magic, hermeticism, and alchemy.[4] Moreover, even apart from such considerations, the combination of Platonism and Christianity has provided a powerful impetus to scientific inquiry stretching at least from Basil's antique Hexameron through to Leibniz's mathematics, Jonathan Edwards's inquiries, and certain moral intuitions animating contemporary efforts at ecological amelioration.

Suppose, then, that the Foster thesis is incorrect and that voluntarism played an important but hardly exhaustive or sufficient role in the emergence of science. Still, one might object, there is something about the Platonic tradition that just seems opposed to scientific inquiry, at least outside of the purely speculative arena of mathematics and theoretical physics. In this vein, we might consider the voluntarist thesis about the emergence of early modern science as kin to the wider Hellenization thesis that has bedeviled Christian theology since Harnack popularized it in the late nineteenth century. With respect to the Christian doctrine of creation, the argument alleges that Platonism could only hinder the Christian appreciation of the natural world, since the transcendent trajectories of Platonic desire are complicit with a certain *contemptus mundi*, are they not?

Both historically and logically, the answer is unequivocally "No," although Platonists have been subject to this sort of abuse for centuries, first contrasted with the putatively more naturalistic bent of Aristotelians,

---

[4] Brian Easlea, *Witch Hunting, Magic and the New Philosophy: An Introduction to the Debates of the Scientific Revolution, 1450–1750* (Atlantic Highlands: Humanities Press, 1980), 89.

later with the celebration of immanence supposedly vouchsafed by modernity. But close attention to the Platonic texts, to the movements that have coalesced around them, and to the lineaments of Platonic thought calls these commonplaces into question. Indeed, certain passages in the *Phaedo* and other middle-period texts notwithstanding, nothing about Platonism per se entails an axiological depletion of the world. If the fundamental Platonic claim is that sense-perceptible things exist only by receiving their being and identity from a transcendent intelligible source in which they participate, and through which they alone are, then this can lead in two quite differing directions. On the one hand, we might consider that concrete things in their participated modes of existence are axiologically negligible or even impediments to understanding, and so pursue a project of realization through ascetical amputation. But equally, we might see the noncompetitive presence of transcendent realities within the things of this world as bestowing a kind of hyperbolic value upon this world. Only so long as we pay attention to both possible realizations of the Platonic tradition can we account for the historical fact that Platonists have often been at the forefront of both the ascetic abandonment of the world and sacramental, humanistic, and romantic celebrations of art, nature, and society.[5] While some of Plato's successors indulged in a characteristically antique *animus* or hostility towards the world, which even Plato himself never fully escaped, others celebrated a far more sacramental and cosmological *anima mundi* equally rooted in Plato's authentic legacy, a tradition most evident in Iamblichus, Proclus, and Pseudo-Dionysius, in antiquity, but also in twelfth-century rediscovery of nature, the Renaissance Platonism of Nicholas of Cusa or Marsilio Ficino, and the legacy of Cambridge Platonism.

SOME CONCEPTUAL ELEMENTS

Alongside appreciation of the role of Christian Platonism in the development of Western science, Platonic traditions continue to offer resources

---

[5] M.-D. Chenu, *Nature, Man, and Society in the Twelfth Century: Essays on New Theological Perspectives in the Latin West*, trans. Jeremy Taylor and Lester K. Little (Toronto: University of Toronto, Press, 1997), 49–98. Cf. Gregory Shaw, *Theurgy and the Soul: The Neoplatonism of Iamblichus* (University Park: Pennsylvania State University Press, 1995). On the role of Platonism within Romanticism, cf. Frederick C. Beiser, *Romantic Imperative: The Concept of Early German Romanticism* (Cambridge, MA: Harvard University Press, 2003), 56–72, and Alexander J. B. Hampton, *Romanticism and the Re-invention of Modern Religion: The Reconciliation of German Idealism and Platonic Realism* (Cambridge: Cambridge University Press, 2019).

for contemporary theological and philosophical discussions of science. As representative topics, we will consider the relation of the cosmos to its divine origin, the role and preeminence of mathematics in science, and developments in contemporary biology.

Within the Abrahamic traditions, teachings about creation eventually coalesced around the idea of creation *ex nihilo*. This stresses a relation of dependence of creature upon creator, such that nothing about the cosmos is uncreated: *creatio ex nihilo* is *creatio omnia*.[6] As a result, any discussion of temporal beginnings is strictly secondary.[7]

Creation *ex nihilo* may not strike us as a particularly Platonic notion. It departs from the otherwise prevailing perspective in the ancient world that the universe is either coeternal with the divine powers or was fashioned out of chaotic and senseless matter. In contrast, creation *ex nihilo* denies that anything is coeval with the creator, either cosmos or chaos. Writers in the early church went out of their way, however, to stress the proximity of Platonic notions of creation to their own, finding a range of conducive ideas there, including the idea that creation, in its multiplicity, proceeds from a good and unitary source, who created out of generosity not need, according to the pattern of an eternal mind or word.[8]

Kathryn Tanner argues that both the peculiarity and the grandeur of the Abrahamic idea of creation comes from combining two Platonic themes. Seemingly at variance with one another, their conjunction within creation *ex nihilo* allows each to temper the other. Creation *ex nihilo* is, in Tanner's words, a "mixed metaphor":[9] creation is the work of an artisan, on the one hand, and an emanation, on the other. Emanation stresses the complete origin of all things in God, including materiality. That is missing from the artisanal approach, with its preexisting material upon which the demiurge works. Accounts of emanation, however, risk too great a sense of continuity between creature and creator, and may lack a sense of gift or volition. That is headed off by the model of the artisan. Creation *ex nihilo*, then, worked out on the basis of Biblical convictions, is both deeply

---

[6] Andrew Davison, *Participation in God: A Study in Christian Doctrine and Metaphysics* (Cambridge: Cambridge University Press, 2019), 17–18.

[7] Andrew Davison, "Looking Back towards the Origin: Scientific Cosmology as Creation Ex Nihilo Considered 'from the Inside'," in *Creatio Ex Nihilo: Origins and Contemporary Significance*, ed. Markus Bockmuehl and Gary Anderson (Notre Dame, IN: University of Notre Dame Press, 2017), 367–389, at pp. 371–375.

[8] For instance, Justin Martyr, *Second Apology*, 10; Augustine, *City of God*, book 8, chs. 6, 9, 11.

[9] Kathryn Tanner, "Creation Ex Nihilo as Mixed Metaphor," *Modern Theology* 29, no. 2 (2013), 138–55.

Platonic, but also deeply creative, synthetic, and even subversive, as a Platonic exercise.

PARTICIPATION

The depth and vigor of renewed attention to creation *ex nihilo* in recent theology stands parallel to a retrieval of the Platonic notion of 'participation'. This construes creation as a donation from God. It describes a relation of derivation that is abiding and continuous, rather than one-off, or punctiliar: God is the cause of creatures *in esse* (in their continuing to be) rather than simply *in fieri* (in some initial coming-to-be). God is the cause, moreover, both of a creature's *being*, and also a creature's participated *essence* (or *character*): both *that* it exists and the *way* the creature exists issue from the relation of participation.

Although the participatory language of imitation brings in the idea of likeness, it entails an equally important note of unlikeness – and therefore of the distinction of creatures from creator – since an image is not identical with its exemplar. Indeed, within Christian Platonism, God's transcendence is paramount: any likeness that might be proposed between the creature and the creator must be affirmed against the backdrop of a "yet greater unlikeness".[10] However, with that acknowledgement of unlikeness in place – of what would later be called the "infinite qualitative difference" between God and creatures – the reality of the creature's limited similitude to God can be affirmed.

Among the principal benefits that follow from conceiving of the creature–creator relationship in participatory terms is the capacity to weave transcendence and immanence together. Within this Christian Platonic vision, the transcendence of God, beyond and before every creature, is also the basis for immanence, even intimacy.[11] In recent decades, this has been set out in terms of a "non-contrastive" relationship between creatures and creator, the distinction between them being too absolute for creature and creator to be

---

[10] Fourth Lateran Council (Denzinger, *Enchiridion Symbolorum*, 269).

[11] *Confessions* III.6.11; Aquinas, *Summa Theologiae* (hereafter *ST*) I.8.1; Philipp Rosemann, *Omne Agens Agit Sibi Simile: A "Repetition" of Scholastic Metaphysics* (Leuven: Leuven University Press, 1996), for instance 295; Robert Sokolowski, *The God of Faith and Reason* (Washington, D.C. Catholic University of America Press, 1995), 34–37; Kathryn Tanner, *God and Creation in Christian Theology: Tyranny or Empowerment* (Minneapolis, MN: Fortress Press, 2005), especially 28, 42–46; Jacob Holsinger Sherman, *Partakers of the Divine: Contemplation and the Practice of Philosophy* (Minneapolis: Fortress, 2014), 142. Historically, cf. Nicholas of Cusa, *On Learned Ignorance* and *On God as Not-Other*.

contrasting examples within any overarching set (which is part of what it means to speak of God as "beyond being," or to deny that God is "a being"). In the words of Philip Rosemann,

[God's] otherness consists precisely in the fact that he does *not* stand in any relationship of negativity with respect to his creatures. God is *supra omnes* [above all] not although, but precisely *insofar as* he is *in omnibus et intime* [in everything, and most innermostly]. Transcendence is the superlative mode of immanence.[12]

Mapped into a discussion of causation, this noncontrastive rendering of creation proves to be of central importance in addressing the relation of divine and creaturely causation or action: a "problem" which has occupied much theological writing on science over the past fifty years, not always fruitfully.[13] A noncontrastive relationship, founded on divine transcendence and manifest as divine intimacy, translates into noncompetition when it comes to causation and agency, that of the creature not being in competition with that of the creator. This is a "nonzero sum" understanding of the relation of creatures to creator: more of one does not require less of the other. The act of a creature is simultaneously its own and that of God. Aquinas set this out in terms deeply resourced from Platonism:

God is his own power, and ... is in all things not as part of their essence but as upholding them in their being, [and consequently] he acts in every agent immediately, without prejudice to the action of the will and of nature.[14]

A particularly acute formulation is found in the *Book of Causes*, a Neoplatonic work of Islamic authorship, assembled out of sections of Proclus' *Elements of Theology*, in which we read that "it [a higher power] is the power of substantial powers [in a lower thing] because it is the cause of them." From this, Aquinas develops the principle that "the power of the higher cause is the power of the power of the lower cause."[15] The higher cause [God, for Aquinas] is not the *power* of the lower cause but the *power of its power*. In this way, the lower cause has the proper exercise of a power that is its own, while that is also entirely derivative from a higher power. As Aquinas puts it elsewhere, through the participation of the lower in the higher "the dignity of causality is imparted even to creatures."[16] Such discussions of the relation of divine and creaturely caution are the origin of the distinction between "secondary" creaturely

---

[12] Rosemann, *Omne Agens*, 295. See Davison, *Participation in God*, 228–235.
[13] Davison, Participation in God, 217–238.   [14] *De potentia*, III.7, *resp*.
[15] Aquinas, *Commentary on the Book of Causes*, prop. 9, p. 68.   [16] *ST* I.22.3, .

causes operating within the overarching operation of the divine "primary" cause.[17] Serious attention to Aquinas' Neoplatonically motivated distinction between primary and secondary causality suggests that much of the worry in "science and religion" over the past fifty years about how one can possibly account for divine "intervention" is misplaced: the creator is equally too transcendent from creation and too intimate to it for the language of "intervention" to be appropriate.

Contrastive theologies of God and creatures not only trouble discussions of divine action and providence but also many contemporary discussions of creation and cosmology. Consider, for instance, Jürgen Moltmann's contention, in *God in Creation*, that God must "withdraw" in order to "make space" for creation.[18] Framed in terms of a Christological "kenosis" and kabbalistic *tzimsum*, Moltmann's competitive, contrastive approach has been influential within a long reach of theological engagement with science. For those working from the perspective of Christian Platonism, however, the very grammar of Moltmann's formulation is mistaken: creation does not impinge upon God contrastively or competitively; God is not a finite being subject to spatial description and the logic of solid bodies, but the One through whom, in whom, and by whom all things come to be and have their being.[19]

For participatory thinkers, then, there is a derived but real substantiality to creatures, when it comes to being, and a derived but real agency, when it comes to agency, all of which rests on divine generosity. Aquinas brings these two aspects together in the *Summa Contra Gentiles*:

Nor is it superfluous, even if God can by Himself produce all natural effects, for them to be produced by certain other causes. For this is not a result of the inadequacy of divine power, but of the immensity of His goodness, whereby He has willed to communicate His likeness to things, not only so that they might exist, but also that they might be causes for other things.[20]

MATHEMATICS

Within Plato's corpus, mathematics occupies an exalted position on the journey to truest knowledge, a status it inherits from Pythagoras and his followers. Even today, the study of mathematics continues to enjoy an

[17] *De veritate*, 24.1 ad 3.
[18] Jürgen Moltmann, *God in Creation*, trans. M. Kohl (London: SCM Press, 1985).
[19] Davison, *Participation in God*, 136–137.
[20] *Summa Contra Gentiles* III.70. Cf. *ST* I.22.3.

elevated status within pedagogy. Geometry, algebra, and calculus are not taught to schoolchildren, nor to American liberal arts students, only to equip them to solve mundane problems in later life. In the curriculum of the medieval university, mathematics enjoyed a yet more prominent place. That curriculum wound its course first through the *trivium* of grammar, logic, and rhetoric (as the arts of the word), but then through the *quadrivium* of arithmetic, astronomy, music, and geometry, each in its way – including music, as the study of proportions – part of the arts of mathematics.[21]

Although there is clearly already a Platonic air to the way in which mathematics is thought to occupy that improving place in the curriculum, the deeper Platonic question when it comes to science concerns the place of mathematics within the natural world, or in relation to it. That we find mathematics within nature has become so familiar to us that it has lost its power to shock. There is, however, what Eugene Wigner called an "unreasonable effectiveness" to the way in which mathematics is able to chart the course of the universe; there is a fit between them which we ought not to take for granted.[22] Consider, for instance, the capacity for science, through mathematics, to press upon the gyromagnetic ratio, a feature of charged subatomic particles which underlies techniques such as medical magnetic resonance imaging (MRI). Using nescient quantum mechanics, Paul Dirac was able to predict the value of one such ratio to one part in a thousand. Since then, with quantum field theory, this prediction has been improved, for the electron, to one part in a ten billion: an astounding accuracy, equivalent to predicting the distance between San Francisco and Washington, D.C., to the accuracy of the width of a human hair.[23]

Wigner wrote that "the enormous usefulness of mathematics in the natural sciences is something bordering on the mysterious and . . . there is no rational explanation for it."[24] Why, he asks, can we so readily write the laws of nature "in the language of mathematics" (picking up a phase from

---

[21] Platonic influence on the medieval curriculum was especially mediated by Augustine and Boethius in late antiquity and flourished in the twelfth-century schools of Chartres and Saint Victor. Cf. David Albertson, *Mathematical Theologies: Nicholas of Cusa and the Legacy of Thierry of Chartres* (Oxford: Oxford University Press, 2014).

[22] Eugene P. Wigner, "The Unreasonable Effectiveness of Mathematics in the Natural Sciences," *Communications on Pure and Applied Mathematics* 13, no. 1 (1960), 1–14.

[23] Louis Marchildon, *Quantum Mechanics* (Berlin: Springer, 2002), 351; simile from Edward O. Wilson, *Consilience: The Unity of Knowledge* (London: Abacus, 1999), 53.

[24] Wigner, "Unreasonable Effectiveness," 2.

Galileo)?[25] For Wigner, there is a "miracle" in the "appropriateness of the language of mathematics for the formulation of the laws of physics," and "a wonderful gift which we neither understand nor deserve."[26]

The wonder that grasped Pythagoras, and Plato after him, and then other Platonists, at the concord between number and cosmos, geometry and the physical world, rested upon their relatively limited knowledge and the correspondingly circumscribed observations of the ancient world. The science of subsequent centuries has profoundly expanded our knowledge of that concord in both depth and reach. Arguably, our wonder should likewise proportionately expand yet further.

The place of mathematics in the unfolding natural order is a familiar theme, then, for the Platonist. As a related question, we have the status, reality, or "location" of the objects that mathematicians study. One school holds that these "entities" – numbers, sets, shapes, and so on – are just that, "entities": real and existent (with *ens*) in themselves, beyond us or our thought or expression. This realist or objectivist position is routinely described, even as a commonplace, as the "Platonic" position. Mathematical entities would be thought to enjoy a mode of existence equivalent to that accorded them by Plato. Existing timelessly, they would be embodied or reflected in the cosmos after the fashion of his forms. But where do they exist? Since the time of the Middle Platonists, philosophers and theologians have repeatedly spoken of mathematical entities existing within the "mind of God."[27] This theological solution to the location problem has the added explanatory benefit of obviating the very real problem of how abstract – and thus causally effete objects – might influence the concrete world, including the world of our knowledge and its consequences. If mathematics exists in the mind of God then it stands to reason that the world will be susceptible to mathematical description not because of the power of numbers, but because of the power and will of God who creates all things in accord with number, measure, and weight (Wis. 11:20).

Beginning in the nineteenth century, however, this realist or Platonic approach to mathematics began to face severe criticism. In the twentieth century, Ludwig Wittgenstein stands as an example of a "constructivist"

---

[25] Wigner, "Unreasonable Effectiveness," 6. Galileo Galilei, *The Assayer* (1623), in *Discoveries and Opinions of Galileo*, trans. Stillman Drake (Garden City, NY: Doubleday, 1957), 237–238.

[26] Wigner, "Unreasonable Effectiveness," 14.

[27] John M. Dillon, *The Middle Platonists: A Study of Platonism, 80 B.C. to A.D. 200* (London: Duckworth, 1996).

critic of mathematical Platonism, seeing objects of mathematical study as the construction, or fiction, of the mathematician.[28] This aligns with a mathematical "nominalism," so called after the pattern of the realism/nominalism distinction concerning the metaphysics of natures or substantial forms. Indeed, it is even thinner than nominalism, mathematics being on this view nonreferential, or rather self-referential: an elaboration of its own axioms, based on its own syntax. "Arithmetic doesn't talk about numbers," for Wittgenstein, "it works with numbers."[29]

The entire debate here could be said to turn on the two meanings of the word "invent." Wittgenstein used it of mathematics in its contemporary sense, meaning "to originate (a new method of action, kind of instrument, etc.)"[30] For him, "the mathematician is not a discoverer: he is an inventor."[31] A slightly earlier meaning of "invention," however, has the sense of "to come upon, find; to find out, discover," which has the more Platonic meaning.[32] The latter would seem to accord more profoundly with the intuitions of working mathematicians, who tend to believe that they are dealing with something real, which is to say something more-than-fictitious. As the logician and set-theoretician, Yiannis Moschovakis, writes "The main point in favor of the realistic approach to mathematics is the instinctive certainty of almost everybody who has ever tried to solve a problem that he is thinking about 'real objects', whether they are sets, numbers, or whatever."[33]

From its inception, Platonism was understood to have located mathematical entities in the realm belonging to the forms, but it was only with the advent of "Middle Platonism" that a theological solution to the location problem became common.[34] Where are the forms? Where do numbers come from? As we have seen, the elegant Middle Platonist solution held that they exist in the mind of God, a position later widely

---

[28] Ludwig Wittgenstein, *Remarks on the Foundations of Mathematics*, trans. G. H. von Wright, Rush Rhees, and G. E. M. Anscombe (Oxford: Blackwell, 1978), I, §168; II, §38; V, §§5, 9, 11.

[29] Wittgenstein, *Philosophical Remarks*, ed. Rush Rhees, trans. Raymond Hargreaves and Roger White (Oxford: Basil Blackwell, 1975), §109.

[30] *Oxford English Dictionary*, earliest recorded use, 1538.

[31] Wittgenstein, *Remarks on the Foundations of Mathematics* I, §111.

[32] *OED*, earliest recorded use, c. 1475.

[33] Moschovakis, *Descriptive Set Theory* (Amsterdam: Elsevier North Holland, 1980), 605–606. A similar position was defended by Kurt Gödel, "Russell's Mathematical Logic," in *Philosophy of Mathematics: Selected Readings*, ed. Hilary Putnam and Paul Benacerraf (Cambridge: Cambridge University Press, 1984), 447–469.

[34] Cf. Plato, *Phaedo*, 101b9–c7; Aristotle, *Metaphysics*, 987b12.

adopted by Christian Platonists in connection with a doctrine of creation.[35] The question of "location" continues to occupy philosophers today, especially those who want a certain "mathematical Platonism" without theological commitments.[36] Roger Penrose, for instance, argues that reality is constituted by the relationship of the physical world, the mental world, and the Platonic or mathematical world, but these relationships and the existence of these worlds is left unexplained.[37] For the Christian Platonist, the extraordinary susceptibility of the world to mathematical explanation and the "location" of the mathematical entities implied in such analyses is not a mystery that brings thought to a stop, but a properly theological mystery that opens rather to doxology, confession, and the elevation of the mind.

For their part, pagan Platonists, by the time of Plotinus and Proclus, would locate number in the Soul of the Triad. James Bradley cites Augustine, among Christians, as the first theologian to have made the comparable move of locating numbers in the mind of God, in *On the Free Choice of the Will*.[38] This stands in parallel, we might add, to Augustine's identification of the Platonic forms with divine ideas in the forty-sixth of his *Miscellany of Eighty-Three Questions*.

Such an association, even an identification, between mathematical entities and God, as their source, raises questions about the contingency, or necessity of the mathematics we know. Perspectives here run between a form of intellectualist necessitarianism, according to which mathematics was always going to look like it does, since God does not change, and the vehement mathematical voluntarism of Descartes, who wrote that God "was free to make it not true that all the radii of the circle are equal – just as free as he was not to create the world," and could have made "contradictories ... true together," or have made "a mountain without valley, or bring it about that 1 and 2 are not 3."[39] The strongest necessity that Descartes could imagine, when it came to mathematics, would be

---

[35] Cf. Dillon, *Middle Platonists*.

[36] Compare the "placement problem" facing thoroughgoing naturalism: how claims of a more than directly empirical nature, for instance in mathematics or meta-ethics, can find a "place" or justification.

[37] Penrose and Clark, "Discussion of 'Shadows of the Mind'," *Journal of Consciousness Studies* 1, no. 1 (1994), 17–24, at p. 23.

[38] Bradley, "Random Numbers and God's Nature," in *Abraham's Dice: Chance and Providence in the Monotheistic Traditions*, ed. Karl Giberson (Oxford: Oxford University Press, 2016), 59–83 at p. 61.

[39] "To [Mersenne], 27 May 1630," "To [Mesland], 2 May 1644," "For [Arnauld], 29 July 1648," in René Descartes, *The Philosophical Writings of Descartes*, trans.

a form of contingent necessity: that God has accorded these features of reality a certain necessity, as it happens, but it was not necessary for God to do so.[40]

BIOLOGY

The place of mathematics in what scientists study is as significant in biology as in physics, since organisms produce structures along mathematically informed lines. Examples include the logarithmic spiral of the nautilus shell, the fractal spreading of trees and ferns, the hexagonal tiling of the honeycomb, and Fibonacci-like sequences among the rosettes of a cauliflower or house leek. These cases involve invention within biology in the sense of discovery just as much as concoction. Mathematical form underlies each of these structures, which have evolved as beneficial phenotypes, and neither the organism, nor the evolutionary trajectory, had to make that up.[41] These mathematical forms and relations are present in the order of things, there to be discovered, and utilized, by organisms, and by evolution.

This undergirding role of mathematics has been a significant matter of attention in recent evolutionary thought, and is sometimes described as an appreciation of the role of "form."[42] It enjoys a prominent place in discussion of convergence in evolution, where certain evolutionary solutions are so effective that evolution discovers and presses them into service again and again. One example comes from fluid dynamics and its relation to body shape. The laws of aerodynamics have been traced out independently by various evolutionary trajectories producing, for example, the wing of the bird and of the bat.[43] With fish, and mammals such as seals and dolphins, evolution has independently utilized those laws of fluid dynamics to produce convergent body shapes and fins.

Anthony Kenny, John Cottingham, Robert Stoothoff, and Dugald Murdoch, vol. 3 (Cambridge: Cambridge University Press, 1984), 25, 235, 358–359.

[40] "To [Mesland], 2 May 1644," in Descartes, *Philosophical Writings*, vol. 3, 235.

[41] These and other examples are discussed in relation to Christian Platonism in Davison, "'He Fathers-Forth Whose Beauty Is Past Change', but 'Who Knows How?': Evolution and Divine Exemplarity'," *Nova et Vetera* 16, no. 4 (2018), 1067–1102.

[42] Jerry A. Fodor and Massimo Piattelli-Palmarini, *What Darwin Got Wrong* (London: Profile, 2010), 72–92; George R. McGhee, *Convergent Evolution: Limited Forms Most Beautiful* (Cambridge, MA: MIT Press, 2011).

[43] A similar convergence is seen among gliding mammals: the Pteromyini, Petauridae, Cynocephalidae, and Anomaluridae.

The leading scholar in the study of evolutionary convergence is Simon Conway Morris, the recently retired Professor of Evolutionary Palaeobiology at the University of Cambridge, as set out, for instance, in his *Life's Solution*.[44] Written in 2003, it lists nine closely printed columns of evolutionary convergences in its index. We may be struck by the presence of many theologically significant features of life among them, with convergences in perception, intelligence, community, communication, cooperation, altruism, farming, and construction, for instance. Much that the Christian Platonist might stress in their theological metaphysics, as present in the creature as a likeness to God, recurs here: memory, intellect, will, community, communication, poesis. Admittedly, we will for the most part be speaking of qualities or characteristics only analogically alike across diverse creatures and species, but a Christian Platonism will be comfortable with analogy. Indeed, these similarities are already located within the most significant and analogical of all analogies: the similitude of creatures to creator.[45]

Placing this in a broader cosmological setting, discussions of convergence and likeness can inform theological consideration of the possibility of life elsewhere in the universe. If, contrary to a nominalist or nonparticipatory view, one sees personhood or life, for instance, as a universal, one may be more expectant of its multiple instantiation across the universe. Certainly, wings and the shape of fish and dolphins are likely to recur wherever there is life, and air to fly in, or water in which to swim. For the Christian Platonist, that may also be the case for memory, will, intellect, and personhood, as imitations of the divine Trinity.

Whether such life is widespread, or present at all, is an open question. Platonist theologians, however, may have reason for instincts running towards exobiological maximalism. Insofar as they suppose the universe to be a refraction, in creaturely mode, of the plenitude of God, found in the varied, nonidentical repetitions of creaturely finitude, we might suppose that the wider the variety of life, the better the image.[46]

---

[44] Simos Conway Morris, *Life's Solution: Inevitable Humans in a Lonely Universe* (Cambridge: Cambridge University Press, 2008).

[45] See Erich Pryzwara, *Analogia Entis: Metaphysics – Original Structure and Universal Rhythm*, trans. John Behr and David Bentley Hart (Grand Rapids, MI: Eerdmans, 2013).

[46] Andrew Davison, *Astrobiology and Christian Doctrine* (Cambridge: Cambridge University Press, 2021).

PSYCHOLOGY AND THE SOUL

While we now habitually distinguish between biology and psychology, for most Christian Platonists throughout history biological considerations fall properly under the study of the soul, for it is the soul, the *anima*, that animates living bodies. This tradition built upon both Hebrew and Greek roots, and was realized in the early Christian syntheses, especially, of Augustine, Gregory of Nyssa, and Maximus the Confessor. The Hebrew scriptures present a holistic vision not only of human beings, but of all animals, animated by the soul or life (*nephesh*). Likewise, for both Plato and Aristotle, to have a soul (*psyche* or Latin *anima*) does not mean possessing some additional force, but rather describes the state of being-alive. Accordingly, the soul (*nephesh, anima, psyche*) may be seen simply as the principle that accounts for living things being-alive. As a purely grammatical consideration, then, it never occurs to the Christian Platonist to ask whether or not the soul exists, for the soul's existence could no more be denied than life itself. Rather, the salient question is always: what is the soul and how can it be known?

This was a matter of controversy in the early centuries of the Christian church and has continued to be a source of disagreement throughout history. In addition to being universally recognized as the principal of life, the soul was also the principle of whatever sentience, rationality, understanding, and higher modes of intellection a creature possessed. For some traditions, the soul was the mediating link between matter and spirit, justifying the microcosmic centrality of the human being, in whom is united the sublunary world of material and animate creatures alongside the celestial powers of intelligence and understanding. Plato's *Phaedo* considered the soul in its more sublime functions to be immaterial and, therefore, immortal. Plotinus, likewise, took the soul to be eternal and immortal, the third hypostasis proceeding from the One and the Intellect before descending subsequently into its material manifestation. Despite some confusion about Origen's teachings regarding the preexistence of the soul, the church determined that properly speaking human souls were immortal but not eternal, created along with that to which they would be reunited by resurrection in the New Creation.

But even if the Christian tradition tended to focus, in this manner, on questions regarding the eschatological state of human souls, broader reflection on the cosmological aspects of soul itself was not unknown and was especially prominent within Christian Platonism. Consider the ninth-century philosopher and theologian, John Scotus Eriugena. In the course of providing his own hexameral commentary in the third book of his *Periphyseon*, Eriugena asks why the author of Genesis delays mention of "soul" until the Fifth Day (Gen. 1:21). He notes that some claim the elements of the world "are not only without soul [*anima*] but also without any kind of life [*uitae*] at all" (738a).

Immediately, however, Eriugena offers the contrary report of "Plato, the greatest of the philosophers," who held both that the world itself was alive and that all things that live within the world live only by virtue of the soul. According to Eriugena, the scriptures hold that not only animals but also "plants and trees and all things that grow out of the earth are alive." The notion of life, which is to say, ensoulment, is accordingly widened to include not just sentience but all forms of natural, intelligible motion. Drawing on Aristotelian and Neoplatonic categories, Eriugena argues:

> Nor does the nature of things permit it to be otherwise. For if there is no matter which without form produces body, and no form subsists without its proper substance, and no substance can be without the vital motion which contains it and causes its subsistence – for everything which is naturally moved receives the source of its motion from some life – it necessarily follows that every creature is either Life-through-itself or participates in life and is somehow alive, whether the vital motion is clearly apparent in it or is not apparent but the sensible species itself shows that it is hiddenly governed [through] life.[47]

According to Eriugena's Christian Platonism, all creation, indeed being as such, is intelligible. While pure, unformed matter, existing apart from form, may function conceptually as a regulative virtuality, it is not an ontological event: all bodies are informed matter. But, equally, all substances are sustained in their active existence and power by participation in the universal life that is the creative substance from which all genus and species issue. Eriugena's extraordinary conclusion is that Life and Soul are effectively created transcendentals. Nothing that exists within being exists apart from soul. Bodies are constituted by the specification or formation of matter, but species are produced only from soul itself which proceeds from the Verbum. The soul Eriugena has in mind here is not the individual soul per se, but what the Platonists called the World Soul, and what the Jewish and Christian communities called, in a more scriptural idiom, Sophia.

---

[47] Johannis Scotti Eriugenae, *Periphyseon* (*De Diuisione Naturae*) III, trans. John J. O'Meara and I. P. Sheldon-Williams (Dublin: Dublin Institute for Advanced Studies, 2005), 728b.

Now, this universal life is called by the natural philosophers the Universal Soul [*universalissima anima*] which through its species controls the totality which is contained within the orbit of the heavenly sphere, while those who contemplate the Divine Sophia call it the common life, which, while it participates in that one Life which is substantial in itself and the fountain and creator of all life, by its division into things visible and invisible distributes lives in accordance with the Divine ordinance, as this Sun which is known to the sense pours forth its rays on all around.[48]

Unlike the rays of the sun, however, the soul is present always and everywhere, not merely to all things but in all things, at the core of all things, whether sentient or not, which entails the equally biblical and Platonic claim that all things, precisely insofar as they are at all, are intelligible, valuable, and good. Creation is reaffirmed in its goodness: not only in human beings and angels, nor even yet in sentient and animate things alone, but all things to the extent that they are intelligible and thus participate in soul, albeit not necessarily in an individual soul.[49]

The unavoidable question for Christian Platonists was, of course, how to make theological sense of this World Soul. Eriugena himself speculated about associating the World Soul with the Holy Spirit, for like the Spirit the World Soul emanates from the Verbum, hovers over the waters, and is the giver of life. Later, during the twelfth-century renaissance of Christian Platonism and the concomitant "rediscovery of nature," theologians from the School of Chartres such as William of Conches went still further and explicitly equated the World Soul with the third person of the Trinity.[50] Augustine had already warned against such pneumatological conflations, insisting that the world soul, if it exists, is itself a creature.[51] Codifying this Augustinian precedent, the Council of Sens (1140) condemned the direct equation of the World Soul with the Holy Spirit. Neither Augustine nor the Council, however, condemned the doctrine of the World Soul in itself, only its elevation into the Triune divinity. For his part, drawing on aspects of Maximus the Confessor, Eriugena's theological ontology of the World Soul carefully identifies it not with the Holy Spirit *in se*, but rather with the Spirit's operations in the world.

---

[48] 728d–729a.

[49] For Eriugena, all creatures in some manner participate life, but the gifts of life, sense, and rationality are not equally distributed. All things participate in universal soul, but the distinction between living and nonliving things remains (*Periphyseon* III 631c, 733a).

[50] William of Conches, *Philosophia mundi*, 1.15; PL 172:46, 90:1130. Cf. Chenu, *Nature, Man, and Society*, 21–23.

[51] Augustine, *Retractiones*, I.5.3; I.11.4.

Eriugena's arguments in this regard, and the broader traditions of Christian reflection upon the *anima mundi* that he brings to especially sophisticated articulation, are of more than antiquarian interest. The tremendous success of modern science has been purchased largely at the cost of bracketing precisely these sorts of speculations, that is, by treating the natural world as if it were subject to mechanical rather than animate description. However, certain aspects of this modern project seem to be faltering. When it comes to considerations of soul, subjectivity, and the science of consciousness, it is now widely recognized that we find ourselves at an impasse. Jaegwon Kim claims that physicalist approaches to the problem of consciousness were "up against a dead end."[52] As Kim sees it, the central problem of consciousness involved "the problem of delineating the place of mind in a physical world."[53] How is it possible to reconcile an exhaustive understanding of the physical world as governed by natural law, on the one hand, with the conviction that mentality is a "real feature of our world," capable of causal efficacy and thus of making a difference in the events of the world?[54] For Kim, the problem is one of locating mental agency (downward causation) within a causally closed world; others have associated the "hard-problem of consciousness" with the problem of qualia more generally, but in all cases the prospects for a science of consciousness seem vanishingly small.[55] John Searle has declared that the dominant paradigms in philosophy of mind and cognitive science are "obviously false."[56] Others, such as Colin McGinn, so despair of finding solutions that they argue we are simply biologically and cognitively incapable of understanding how the brain generates consciousness.[57] We are so far from a scientific theory of consciousness as such that it seems hard even to imagine what the contours of such a theory might be. Accordingly, Galen Strawson argues that no nonrevolutionary extension of physics or neurophysiology offers any hope of coming to serious terms with the problems of consciousness and experience.[58] Thomas Nagel had already suggested as much: "I believe

---

[52] Jaegwon Kim, *Supervenience and Mind: Selected Philosophical Essays* (Cambridge: Cambridge University Press, 1993).

[53] Ibid, xv.   [54] Ibid.

[55] David John Chalmers, "Facing up to the Problem of Consciousness," *Journal of Consciousness Studies* 2, no. 3 (1995), 200–219.

[56] John R. Searle, *The Rediscovery of the Mind* (Cambridge, MA: MIT Press, 1992), 3.

[57] Colin McGinn, *The Problem of Consciousness: Essays Toward a Resolution* (Oxford: Blackwell, 1991); *Consciousness and Its Objects* (Oxford: Clarendon Press, 2004).

[58] Galen Strawson, *Real Materialism: And Other Essays* (Oxford: Oxford University Press, 2008), 22.

that the methods needed to understand ourselves do not yet exist . . . The world is a strange place, and nothing but radical speculation gives us a hope of coming up with any candidates for the truth."[59]

At present, such radical speculation is increasingly warranted and underway. Prominent philosophers, neuroscientists, and consciousness researchers have begun to entertain riskier ontological revisions as the most parsimonious pathway forward: panexperientialism, hylemorphism, idealism, and other such options are once again being seriously considered. Plato would hardly have been surprised. As Socrates asks in the Phaedrus, "Do you think, then, that it is possible to reach a serious understanding of the nature of the soul without understanding the nature of the world as whole?"[60] Is consciousness the problem, or might it be the case that the real culprit is our received notion of physical reality, the idea of nature as mere mechanism, an idea made possible only by the prior operation of extracting from the world everything redolent of soul? If so, Christian Platonism would suggest that we would find, in earlier conceptions of an ensouled cosmos, some inspiration for contemporary progress on this front.

But still, one might wonder, why turn to Platonism at this point? Is it not Platonism that first taught us to divide body and soul in the peculiarly dualistic way that now appears so aporetic? Here again we might look at Eriugena for a corrective.

Far from leading him to reaffirm some sort of antique dualism, the Platonist tenor of Eriugena's reflections led him instead to a powerfully nondualistic affirmation of the integrality of body and soul. The human soul is the form of the human being, and the human being is substantially constituted by both body and soul. Of course, medieval Christian Platonist that he is, Eriugena holds that the soul is capable of surviving bodily death, but even this extraordinary event does not render the soul any less human, which is to say, any less constituted by its relation to embodiment. As Eriugena writes:

Now man is body and soul; but if he is always man, then he is always soul and body, and although the parts of man may be separated from one another . . . yet by the reason of their nature neither do the parts cease to be always inseparably related to the whole, nor the whole to the parts. For the reason of their relation can never cease to be.[61]

---

[59] Thomas Nagel, *View from Nowhere* (Oxford: Oxford University of Press, 1989).
[60] Plato, *Phaedrus*, 270.   [61] 729d–730a.

Eriugena argues that the soul's more or less subtle relationship to the body is intrinsic to the nature of the soul itself, and persists even through the dissolution we call death. In contrast to dualistic caricatures, what we discover in Eriugena's Christian Platonism is profoundly in accord with the holistic direction of much modern cognitive sciences, especially the emphasis upon embodied, embedded, enactive, and extended cognition – the so-called 4E model – that has become increasingly important.

ECOLOGICAL ETHICS AND CHRISTIAN PLATONISM

Much as Christian Platonism has been critiqued for giving rise to the sorts of body–soul dualisms that, as we have just seen, it equally and perhaps more properly subverts, so too has it been accused of providing the conceptual architecture for the ecologically invidious cultures that have led to so many of our present crises. When it comes to etiologies of our environmental woes, Platonism and Christianity are regularly named. In his seminal work in environmental ethics, for instance, Eugene Hargrove argues that Plato's metaphysics and epistemology conspired to prevent Greek philosophy from thinking ecologically "in any systematic way."[62] By locating the source of both knowledge and reality outside the world of generation, this "Platonic" approach putatively discouraged firsthand observations of the natural world in favor of an appeal to first principles. Besides, Hargrove contends, Platonism would dismiss any understanding of ecological relationships based on observation of the mutable as less than genuine knowledge (i.e. *episteme*).[63] Similarly dismal depictions of Platonism prevail throughout many of the classic works of environmental philosophy. John Passmore views both Platonism and Christianity as leading to "a metaphysic for which man is the sole finite agent and nature a vast system of mechanics for man to use and modify as he pleases."[64] And Val Plumwood argues that Plato originates a "philosophy of death" and the concomitant denial of life that leads to Aristotelian, Christian, and Cartesian rationalisms, alongside the patriarchal devaluation of women, the body, and all nonhuman nature.[65]

---

[62] Eugene Hargrove, *Foundations of Environmental Ethics* (Englewood Cliffs, NJ: Prentice Hall, 1989), 21.

[63] Ibid, 21–22.

[64] John Passmore, *Man's Responsibility for Nature*, 2nd ed (London: Duckworth, 1980), 27.

[65] Val Plumwood, *Feminism and the Mastery of Nature* (London: Routledge, 1993), 69–103.

To be sure, there are elements in the Christian reception of Plato and Platonism that give credibility to the broadly Nietzschean sentiment that Platonism and Christianity conspire to produce a dualistic vision of the world in which what matters most is that one rise above the wilds we find both within and without. And such visions are, indeed, at odds with the moral sources that would motivate environmental consideration. But the important question is whether such elements are either essential to Christian Platonism or exhaust its ecological salience. On both counts, any sober theological, philosophical, and historical consideration would have to answer "No," for the traditions of Christian Platonism are both more varied and more open to a kind of ecological holism than such selective readings allow.

Consider the charge of anthropocentrism that is somehow present in all of the above critiques. Accepting the ecologically desultory consequences of indexing the value of creatures to human utility, J. Baird Callicott argues that "the most important philosophical task for environmental ethics is the development of a non-anthropocentric value theory."[66] Callicott accepts much of the eco-declension narrative of western philosophy, suggesting by contrast that non-western and indigenous traditions provide correctives. But Callicott also notes that Plato and Leibniz do not fit easily into this declension story, and may be regarded as sources in the cultivation of those alternative moral and metaphysical principles "forced upon philosophy by the magnitude and recalcitrance of [environmental] problems."[67] Plato and Leibniz are helpful in this regard because they commend an impersonal, objective Good as axiological source. The objectivity of the Good means that value is not a human projection but attaches to the formal properties of things themselves. Ecologically, such formal properties might include parsimony, harmony, order, biodiversity, and resilience, properties that find operative expression in the "Land ethic" of Aldo Leopold: "A thing is right when it tends to preserve the integrity, stability, and beauty of the biotic community. It is wrong when it tends otherwise."[68]

The objectivity of the Good that Callicott finds in Plato, Leibniz, and Leopold is ubiquitous within the Christian Platonist tradition and calls

---

[66] Callicott, "Non-Anthropocentric Value Theory and Environmental Ethics," *American Philosophical Quarterly* 21, no. 4 (1984), 299–309 at p. 299.

[67] Ibid, 299, 303.

[68] Aldo Leopold, *A Sand County Almanac* (New York: Oxford University Press, 1949), 224. Quoted in Callicott, "Non-Anthropocentric Value Theory," 303.

into question genealogical accounts that simply identify Christianity and Platonism with anthropocentric value theories. Axiologically, has Christian Platonism ever been anthropocentric, or is that charge rooted in anachronistic modern projections onto premodern cosmic geographies? With a few rare exceptions, premodern Christian Platonists accepted Ptolemy's geocentric approach to saving the appearances of cosmic phenomena, but geocentrism hardly implied anthropocentric axiological centrality. The center of Dante's physical cosmology, for instance, is all but scatologically associated with Satan.[69] For Christian Platonists from Chalcidius in the fourth century to Eriugena in the ninth and Dante in the fourteenth, human beings are not cosmographically centralized, but liminal: *homo viatores* in peregrination upon the earth. As C. S. Lewis argues, "For Chalcidius, the geocentric universe is not in the least anthropocentric .... We watch 'the spectacle of the celestial dance' from its outskirts. The Medieval Model is, if we may use the word, anthropo-peripheral. We are creatures from the Margin."[70] Lewis points to Alan of Lille's charming cosmopolitical vision in which the entire universe is imagined to be a great medieval city. The central castle, the place of the Emperor, is the Empyreon, followed by the angelic knighthood. "We, on Earth, are 'outside the city wall'."[71] Far from authorizing an invidious anthropocentrism, then, the human being is cosmologically suburban.

Nor need this decentralization authorize a denigration of the Earth and its creatures. It is the Christian Platonist, Alan of Lille, after all, who put the twelfth-century rediscovery of nature into well-known verse:

> Omnis mundi creatura,
> quasi liber et pictura,
> est in speculum.[72]

Neither anthropocentric nor ecocentric, in Alan's sacramental world nature receives due attention precisely because it is charged with the grandeur and glory of God. As Hugh of Saint Victor put it: "[T]his whole sensible world is a kind of book written by the finger of God, that is, created by divine power, and each creature is a kind of figure, not

---

[69] Dante, *Inferno* xxxiv.

[70] C. S. Lewis, *The Discarded Image* (Cambridge: Cambridge University Press, 1949), 58.

[71] Ibid, citing Alan of Lille, *De Planctu Naturae*, Prosa, III, 108 sq.

[72] "All the world's creatures, as a book and a picture, are to us as a mirror." On the so-called twelfth-century rediscovery of nature, see Chenu, *Nature, Man and Society in the Twelfth Century*.

invented by human determination, but established by the divine will to manifest and in some way signify the invisible wisdom of God."[73]

CONCLUSION

In his seminal articulation of the ecological complaint against Christianity, Lynn White Jr. nonetheless suggested that an alternative possibility for relating to nature existed within the Christian tradition, a possibility that might have led us towards a far more robust vision of ecological and cultural flourishing. White points to the Franciscan tradition as the site of this ecological promise, but closer attention to the sort of sources we have encountered in this chapter suggests that a green future might be found not only in a return to Saint Francis but rather also in a creative retrieval of the traditions of Christian Platonism. Indeed, the argument of this entire chapter has been that far from necessarily motivating a flight in both attention and affection from the world, the Christian Platonist tradition has often been one of the primary motors for the rediscovery of the world in its intelligibility, beauty, and grandeur. Moreover, we have attempted to show that its significance for scientific pursuit is not merely historical, since the resources of the Christian Platonist tradition continue to be theoretically and ethically productive providing means to negotiate many of the central philosophical and theological questions arising from scientific pursuits in our day. The Christian Platonist vision need not abandon the world, but instead is able to read this world doxologically, recognizing in all things not only the trace of the One from whom they come but also the impetus to return through an equally philosophical, scientific, moral, and even mystical ascent.

Bibliography

Albertson, David. *Mathematical Theologies: Nicholas of Cusa and the Legacy of Thierry of Chartres*. Oxford: Oxford University Press, 2014.

Aquinas, Thomas. *Commentary on the Book of Causes*. Trans. Charles R. Hess, Richard C. Taylor, and Vincent A. Guagliardo. Washington, D.C. Catholic University of America Press, 1996.

Disputed Questions on the Power of God [De potentia]. Translated by English Dominican Fathers. Westminster, MD: Newman Press, 1952.

---

[73] Hugh of St Victor, *De tribus diebus*, 4.3, 63–64.

Disputed Questions on Truth [De veritate]. Translated by Robert W. Mulligan, James V. McGlynn, and Robert Schmidt. 3 vols. Chicago: Henry Regnery Company, 1952.

Summa Contra Gentiles. Translated by Anton C. Pegis, James F. Anderson, Vernon J. Bourke, and Charles J. O'Neil. 5 vols. New York: Hanover House, 1955.

Summa Theologiae. Translated by English Dominican Fathers. 2nd ed. 22 vols. London: Burns, Oates & Washbourne, 1912.

Augustine. *The Confessions*. Translated by Maria Boulding. Hyde Park, NY: New City Press, 2012.

Beiser, Frederick C. *The Romantic Imperative: The Concept of Early German Romanticism*. Cambridge, MA: Harvard University Press, 2003.

Bradley, James. "Random Numbers and God's Nature." In *Abraham's Dice: Chance and Providence in the Monotheistic Traditions*, edited by Karl Giberson, 59–83. Oxford: Oxford University Press, 2016.

Callicott, J. Baird. "Non-Anthropocentric Value Theory and Environmental Ethics." *American Philosophical Quarterly*, Vol. 21, no. 4 (Oct., 1984): 299–309.

Chalmers, David John. "Facing up to the Problem of Consciousness." *Journal of Consciousness Studies* 2, no. 3 (1995): 200–219.

Chenu, M.-D. *Nature, Man, and Society in the Twelfth Century: Essays on New Theological Perspectives in the Latin West*. Translated by Jeremy Taylor and Lester K. Little. Toronto: University of Toronto Press, 1997.

Davison, Andrew. *Astrobiology and Christian Doctrine*. Cambridge: Cambridge University Press, 2021.

———. "'He Fathers-Forth Whose Beauty Is Past Change', but 'Who Knows How?': 'Evolution and Divine Exemplarity'." *Nova et Vetera* 16, no. 4 (2018): 1067–1102.

———. "Looking Back towards the Origin: Scientific Cosmology as Creation Ex Nihilo Considered 'from the Inside'." In *Creatio Ex Nihilo: Origins and Contemporary Significance*, edited by Markus Bockmuehl and Gary Anderson, 367–389. Notre Dame, IN: University of Notre Dame Press, 2017.

———. *Participation in God: A Study in Christian Doctrine and Metaphysics*. Cambridge: Cambridge University Press, 2019.

Denzinger, Götz, ed. *Enchiridion Symbolorum*. 43rd ed. San Francisco: Ignatius Press, 2012.

Descartes, René. *The Philosophical Writings of Descartes*. Translated by Anthony Kenny, John Cottingham, Robert Stoothoff, and Dugald Murdoch. 3 vols. Cambridge: Cambridge University Press, 1984.

Dillon, John M. *The Middle Platonists: A Study of Platonism, 80 B.C. to A.D. 220*. Revised edition. London: Duckworth, 1996.

Easlea, Brian. *Witch Hunting, Magic and the New Philosophy: An Introduction to the Debates of the Scientific Revolution, 1450–1750*. Atlantic Highlands, NJ: Humanities Press, 1980.

Fodor, Jerry A., and Massimo Piattelli-Palmarini. *What Darwin Got Wrong*. London: Profile, 2010.

Foster, M. B. "Christian Theology and Modern Science of Nature (II)." *Mind* 45 (1936): 1–27.

Galilei, Galileo. *Discoveries and Opinions of Galileo.* Translated by Stillman Drake. Garden City, NY: Doubleday, 1957.

Gödel, Kurt. "Russell's Mathematical Logic." In *Philosophy of Mathematics: Selected Readings,* edited by Hilary Putnam and Paul Benacerraf. Cambridge: Cambridge University Press, 1984: 447–469.

Hampton, Alexander J. B. *Romanticism and the Re-invention of Modern Religion: The Reconciliation of German Idealism and Platonic Realism.* Cambridge: Cambridge University Press, 2019.

Hargrove, Eugene. *Foundations of Environmental Ethics.* Englewood Cliffs, NJ: Prentice Hall, 1989.

Harrison, Peter. "Voluntarism and Early Modern Science." *History of Science* 40, no. 1 (2002): 63–89.

Hugh of St Victor. *De tribus diebus.* In *Trinity and Creation,* edited by Boyd Taylor Coolman et al. Hyde Park, NY: New City Press, 2011.

Johannis Scotti Eriugenae, *Periphyseon (De Diuisione Naturae) III.* Translated by John J. O'Meara and I. P. Sheldon-Williams. Dublin: Dublin Institute for Advanced Studies, 2005.

Kim, Jaegwon. *Supervenience and Mind: Selected Philosophical Essays.* Cambridge: Cambridge University Press, 1993.

Leopold, Aldo. *A Sand County Almanac.* New York: Oxford University Press, 1949.

Lewis, C. S. *The Discarded Image.* Cambridge: Cambridge University Press, 1964.

Marchildon, Louis. *Quantum Mechanics.* Berlin: Springer, 2002.

McGhee, George R. *Convergent Evolution: Limited Forms Most Beautiful.* Cambridge, MA: MIT Press, 2011.

McGinn, Colin. *Consciousness and Its Objects.* Oxford: Clarendon Press, 2004. *The Problem of Consciousness: Essays Toward a Resolution.* Oxford: Blackwell, 1991.

Moltmann, Jürgen. *God in Creation.* Translated by M. Kohl. London: SCM Press, 1985.

Morris, Simon Conway. *Life's Solution: Inevitable Humans in a Lonely Universe.* Cambridge: Cambridge University Press, 2008.

Moschovakis, Yiannis N. *Descriptive Set Theory.* Amsterdam: Elsevier North Holland, 1980.

Nagel, Thomas. *The View from Nowhere.* Oxford: Oxford University Press, 1989.

Passmore, John. *Man's Responsibility for Nature.* 2nd ed. London: Duckworth, 1980.

Penrose, Roger and J. Clark. "Discussion of 'Shadows of the Mind'." *Journal of Consciousness Studies* 1, no. 1 (1994): 17–24.

Plumwood, Val. *Feminism and the Mastery of Nature.* London: Routledge, 1993.

Pryzwara, Erich. *Analogia Entis: Metaphysics – Original Structure and Universal Rhythm.* Translated by John Behr and David Bentley Hart. Grand Rapids, MI: Eerdmans, 2013.

Rosemann, Philipp. *Omne Agens Agit Sibi Simile: A "Repetition" of Scholastic Metaphysics*. Leuven: Leuven University Press, 1996.

Searle, John R. *The Rediscovery of the Mind*. Cambridge, MA: MIT Press, 1992.

Shaw, Gregory. *Theurgy and the Soul: The Neoplatonism of Iamblichus*. University Park, PA: Pennsylvania State University Press, 1995.

Sherman, Jacob Holsinger. *Partakers of the Divine: Contemplation and the Practice of Philosophy*. Minneapolis, MN: Fortress, 2014.

Sokolowski, Robert. *The God of Faith and Reason*. Washington, D.C.: Catholic University of America Press, 1995.

Strawson, Galen. *Real Materialism: And Other Essays*. Oxford: Oxford University Press, 2008.

Tanner, Kathryn. "Creation Ex Nihilo as Mixed Metaphor." *Modern Theology* 29, no. 2 (2013): 138–155.

   God and Creation in Christian Theology: Tyranny or Empowerment. Minneapolis, MN: Fortress Press, 2005.

Wigner, Eugene P. "The Unreasonable Effectiveness of Mathematics in the Natural Science." *Communications on Pure and Applied Mathematics* 13, no. 1 (1960): 1–14.

Wilson, Edward O. *Consilience: The Unity of Knowledge*. London: Abacus, 1999.

Wittgenstein, Ludwig. *Philosophical Remarks*. Edited by Rush Rhees, translated by Raymond Hargreaves and Roger White. Oxford: Basil Blackwell, 1975.

   Remarks on the Foundations of Mathematics. Translated by G. H. von Wright, Rush Rhees, and G. E. M. Anscombe. Revised edition. Oxford: Blackwell, 1978.

3.2

Christian Platonism, Nature and Environmental Crisis

Alexander J. B. Hampton

This examination makes the case that the tradition of Christian Platonism can constitute a valuable resource for addressing the long-running and increasingly acute environmental crisis that threatens the global ecosystem and all who inhabit it. More than a scientific, technological or political challenge, the crisis requires a fundamental shift in the way humans understand nature and their place within it. Key to implementing this shift is the need to address the problematic anthropocentric conceptualisation of nature characteristic of the contemporary social imaginary that determines a wide range of present-day economic, religious and scientific perspectives. The case made here is that Christian Platonism, and in particular its participatory ontology, can offer a radically non-anthropocentric alternative to the present-day understanding of nature.

First, this examination will contextualise its position in relation to the influential and tendentious argument of the historian Lynn White, the re-evaluation of secularisation in the study of religion, and the notion of the environmental humanities movement more broadly. Together, these establish the important role of religion in determining the social imaginary through which nature is encountered, and the key challenge of addressing the problematic anthropocentric conceptualisation of nature. Next, the examination turns to an explication of how the participatory ontology of Christian Platonism addresses this challenge through three questions: 'What is the meaning of nature?', 'What is the value of nature?', and 'How can we know nature?'. In doing so it will take up key themes in the history of realist metaphysics, such as the nature of divine ideas, their role in shaping the created world and the transcendent nature of art. In answering each question, the thought of seminal key figures in Christian Platonism are taken up to explore the composition of a radically non-anthropocentric conceptualisation of nature.

It is not within the scope of this chapter, nor its intention, to offer an argument for, or historical reconstruction of, a Christian Platonist ecology. Since many of the thinkers taken up here viewed nature (better understood in their eyes by the more expansive term 'creation') through a radically different social imaginary than our own, claiming the existence of a long standing and coherent Christian Platonist ecology would only be anachronistic. Equally, this examination does not aim to offer a declension narrative, where a harmonious human–nature relation adhered under realist metaphysics, which was supplanted by destructive nominalist anthropocentrism leading to ecological crisis. The complex warp and woof of intellectual history warns against monocausal narratives and broad generalisations. Instead, the case made here is for the capacity of Christian Platonism to serve as a resource for addressing environmental crisis in a present-day context. Accordingly, a level of creative appropriation and adaptation is employed in utilising the ideas engaged with in the following examination.

PRESENT-DAY CONTEXT

In 1967 Lynn White published 'The Historical Roots of our Ecological Crisis'.[1] The text, which considered the role of Christianity in the increasingly recognised environmental crisis, was important for a number of reasons. It pointed out the importance of religion in setting the intellectual framework wherein the human–nature relationship is conditioned.[2] White also offered a critical assessment of Western Christianity's role in creating the intellectual conditions that had precipitated the anthropogenic degradation of nature. In particular, it singled out the placing of humans above nature, leading to White's contentious claim that

---

[1] Lynn White Jr., 'The Historical Roots of Our Ecologic Crisis', *Science* 155, no. 3767 (1967), 1203–1207. Originally delivered to the annual meeting of the American Association for the Advancement of Science (26 December 1966). White offered a more detailed consideration in his other works: *Medieval Religion and Technology: Collected Essays* (Berkeley: University of California Press, 1978); *Medieval Technology and Social Change* (Oxford: Oxford University Press, 1962).

[2] White Jr., 'The Historical Roots', 1205–1206.

'Christianity is the most anthropocentric religion the world has ever seen'.[3] Finally, and perhaps most provocatively, White asserted that the solution to the environmental crisis lay neither in science nor technology, but in the philosophical and cultural context in which they are realized, viz. religion. White claimed that humanity would not extract itself 'out of the present ecological crisis until we find a new religion or re-think our old one'.[4] White's identification of religion, and particularly Christianity, with ecological crisis, accelerated an extended consideration of the relationship between religion and the environment, and a debate concerning Christianity's culpability for creating the conditions for environmental degradation.[5]

Two recent developments, the critical consideration of secularisation, and the emergence of the environmental humanities, both re-state and bring into the twenty-first century White's assertions concerning the importance of religion and the challenge of addressing anthropocentrism. In the case of the first, questions concerning 'post-secularity' arose within the study of religion as a result of an increasing reflexive consideration of the assumptions of secularisation.[6] What came to be known as the secularisation thesis had come to constitute an influential intellectual background for a range of disciplines in the social sciences and humanities throughout the twentieth century. The strong version of this thesis postulated an inverse relationship between the practice of religion and the rise of modernity. This correlation became foundational through the thought of prominent thinkers such as Weber, Marx and Durkheim. This version of secularisation mapped the decline of institutional practices and confessional identity onto the advances of scientific naturalism and individual liberty, and understood the presence of

---

[3] Ibid, 1205.   [4] Ibid, 1206.

[5] Elspeth Whitney, 'The Lynn White Thesis: Reception and Legacy', *Environmental Ethics* 35, no.3 (2013), 313–331; Elspeth Whitney, 'Lynn White Jr.'s "The Historical Roots of Our Ecologic Crisis" After 50 Years', *History Compass* 13, no. 8 (2015), 396–410. Michael Nelson, Michael Paul and Thomas J. Sauer, 'The Long Reach of Lynn White Jr.'s "The Historical Roots of Our Ecological Crisis"', *Ecology & Evolution*, updated 13 December 2016, accessed 2 May 2019, https://natureecoevocommunity.nature.com/users/24738-michael-paul-nelson/posts/14041-the-long-reach-of-lynn-white-jr-s-the-historical-roots-of-our-ecologic-crisis/.

[6] Peter L. Berger, *The Desecularization of the World: Resurgent Religion and World Politics* (Grand Rapids, MI: Eerdmans, 1999); Jürgen Habermas, 'Die Dialektik der Säkularisierung', *Blätter für deutsche und internationale Politik* 4 (2008), 33–46; John Milbank, *Beyond Secular Order: The Representation of Being and the Representation of the People* (Chichester: Wiley-Blackwell, 2014).

religion as indicative of an incomplete process of modernisation. Such assumptions have been a matter of contention since at least the mid-twentieth century;[7] however around the turn of the twenty-first century an increasingly critical awareness that the thesis did not reflect the dynamic nature of religion and spiritual change gained momentum. The persistent presence of religious issues on a global scale in contemporary political proceedings, and the ever-growing recognition of the complex hybridised extra-institutional forms present-day religion can take, have complicated any simple understanding of the process of secularisation as one of straightforward religious decline, and destabilised long-held sacred–secular dichotomies.[8] Overall, these developments have had the effect of highlighting the importance of religion in areas previously considered the province of secular political policy, thereby reinforcing White's claim that religion must play a role in addressing environmental crisis.

The second major development is that of the interdisciplinary field of the environmental humanities in the past two decades.[9] It has highlighted the need to seek out alternatives to the problem of environmental crisis that extend beyond the scientific and technical knowledge that is already capable of addressing the problem. Accordingly,

---

[7] Karl Löwith, *Meaning in History: The Theological Implications of the Philosophy of History* (Chicago: University of Chicago Press, 1949); Hans Blumenberg, *Die Legitimität der Neuzeit* (Frankfurt am Main: Suhrkamp, 1966).

[8] Edward I. Bailey, *Implicit Religion in Contemporary Society* (Leuven: Peeters, 2006); Wade Clark Roof, *A Generation of Seekers* (San Francisco: HarperCollins, 1993); Robert C. Fuller, *Spiritual, but Not Religious* (New York: Oxford University Press, 2001); Boaz Huss, 'Spirituality: The Emergence of a New Cultural Category and Its Challenge to the Religious and the Secular', *Journal of Contemporary Religion* 29 (2014), 47–60; Christopher H. Partridge, *The Re-Enchantment of the West* (London: T & T Clark, 2004); Rodney Stark and William Sims Bainbridge, *The Future of Religion* (Berkeley: University of California Press, 1986).

[9] Prominent initial publications in the environmental humanities include: Sherry B. Ortner, 'Is Female to Male as Nature Is to Culture?', *Feminist Studies* 1, no. 2 (1972), 5–31; Bruno Latour, *Nous n'avons jamais été modernes: Essai d'anthropologie symétrique* (Paris: La Découverte, 1991); William Cronon, 'The Trouble with Wilderness: Or, Getting Back to the Wrong Nature', *Environmental History* 1, no. 1 (1996), 7–28; Ramachandra Guha and Joan Martinez-Alier, *Varieties of Environmentalism: Essays North and South* (London: Earthscan Publications, 1997); Lawrence Buell, *The Environmental Imagination: Thoreau, Nature Writing, and the Formation of American Culture* (Cambridge, MA: Belknap Press, 1995); Carolyn Merchant, *The Death of Nature: Women, Ecology and the Scientific Revolution* (San Francisco: HarperCollins, 1990); Donna J. Haraway, *Simians, Cyborgs, and Women: The Reinvention of Nature* (London: Free Association Books, 1991).

a core claim in the literature is the rejection of any characterisation of humanities-based approaches to nature as being of lesser value than those of the natural sciences, as it is the qualitative human context that dictates the direction and employment of that technical knowledge.[10] On this basis, the environmental humanities calls for an exhaustive re-consideration of the conceptual framework wherein we conceive of the concept of nature and the place of humans within it. Central to addressing this challenge, it claims, is the problem of anthropocentrism, which places humans at the centre of meaning-making.[11] This subject-centred thinking, reinforced through an ever-more globalised Western version of the self, has a range of results that minimize the inherent meaning and value in nature, whilst at the same time disembedding humans from nature by placing them outside and above it. From this detached subject-centred standpoint, the external world of nature is rationally ordered by the individual through the culture of science and technology, and adapted in the pursuit of individual happiness. In the anthropocentric context, nature is rendered passive, with meaning and value determined by subject-based narratives of meaning-making. Ultimately, this can lead to an instrumentalist, utilitarian, commodified view of nature, whose basic logic must be reversed if environmental crisis is to be seriously addressed. The development of this perspective within the environmental humanities echoes White's earlier claim that the environmental crisis is one of anthropocentric thinking, which must be addressed within a broad civilisational framework.

With the critical consideration of secularisation and the development of the environmental humanities, White's assertions concerning

---

[10] Robert S. Emmett and David E. Nye, *The Environmental Humanities: A Critical Introduction* (Cambridge, MA: MIT Press, 2017), 7–11, 71–92; Val Plumwood, *Environmental Culture: The Ecological Crisis of Reason* (London: Routledge, 2002), 38–61; Jeremy David Bendik-Keymer and Chris Haufe, 'Anthropogenic Mass Extinction: The Science, the Ethics, and the Civics', in *The Oxford Handbook of Environmental Ethics*, ed. Stephen M. Gardiner and Allen Thompson (Oxford: Oxford University Press, 2016), 427–437.

[11] Val Plumwood, *Environmental Culture*, 52–61, 123–142; Katie McShane, 'Anthropocentrism vs. Nonanthropocentrism: Why Should We Care?', *Environmental Values* 16, no. 2 (2007), 169–185; Ben A. Minteer, 'Anthropocentrism', in *Encyclopedia of Environmental Ethics and Philosophy*, ed. J. Baird Callicott and Robert Frodeman (Farmington Hills, MI: Cengage Learning, 1999), 58–62; Allen Thompson, 'Anthropocentrism: Humanity as Peril and Promise', in *The Oxford Handbook of Environmental Ethics*, ed. Stephen M. Gardiner and Allen Thompson (Oxford: Oxford University Press, 2016), 77–90.

the importance of religion and the problem of anthropocentrism are brought together and sharpened in a twenty-first-century context. The questioning of secularising assumptions, and the re-assertion of the importance of religion, though in increasingly complex forms, reinforces White's claim that religion must play a role in addressing the global anthropogenic crisis after a century of doubting its validity. Additionally, the environmental humanities, with its focus on the problem of anthropocentrism, speaks directly to White's call to reconceptualise the social imaginary wherein nature and our place within it is defined. White's claim that religion must play the central role in addressing environmental crisis is also probably his most provocative. If the environmental challenge must be seen as one which requires us to 'find a new religion or re-think our old one', then a constructive engagement with the metaphysical tradition of Christian Platonism is essential.[12] Having played a dynamic, often controversial, and sometimes determinative role in shaping Christianity, it seems that there is an intellectual obligation to consider the role it could play in either re-thinking the old religion, or indeed finding a new one.

WHAT IS THE MEANING OF NATURE?

The first of the three questions this examination takes up concerns the meaning of nature. From an anthropocentric standpoint it is humans who confer meaning upon nature. The danger of this position is that it allows humans to cultivate an instrumentalist, exploitative, utilitarian relationship to a nature that has no intrinsic meaning in itself. We may look at the tree, and think of all the things it can mean *for* us. It may mean that it falls within our classification of a perennial plant with an elongated woody trunk. It may mean a source of shade, fruit or timber. Or its meaning may lie in its correspondence to our subjective sense of beauty, or its utility to us as a fungible commodity. Christian Platonism provides an alternative model of meaning in nature based upon an understanding of nature informed by the notion of a participatory ontology. In this model, meaning resides in the real ideas that are extramental realities located in the mind of God. Creation constitutes the material instantiation of these divine ideas. Meaning therefore is not human-dependent, but humans, along with all created reality,

---

[12] White Jr., 'The Historical Roots', 1206.

participate in meaning through the divine ideas that make all individuals in nature what they are. To elaborate upon this possibility, it is beneficial to first provide a definition of participation, and a very brief articulation of how it arises in Plato and the Hebrew Bible, before moving on to the thought of Philo and Augustine and the poetry of Thomas Traherne. In examining these thinkers, our aim is not to explore the metaphysical and doctrinal concerns that exercised antique minds, viz. questions of the eternality and order of the cosmos, or the elaboration of creatio ex nihilo. Instead, focusing upon the construction of their non-anthropocentric concept of nature, it is to demonstrate how a view of creation, informed by participation, allows the divine ideas to be directly incorporated into the cosmos, with the result that the meaning in nature has its source in the divine mind, and not the human mind. If creation can be shown to be a realisation of the ideas of the divine mind, nature is rendered radically independent of human-created meaning.

The concept of ontological participation naturally arises within philosophical and theological considerations taking up the basic questions of the relationship between concepts and predicates, the one and the many, ideas and appearances, or universals and particulars.[13] It is therefore a perennial topic, and indeed has been the subject of some recent interest in the philosophy of religion.[14] The fundamental question which the concept seeks to address is the relationship between the fullness and perfection of an idea, and the array of individual instantiations in which it is found. In its initial Greek form, the word participation (μέθεξις/*methexis*) connotes more a sense of sharing in a whole, than it does one of taking part. In the case of Christian Platonism, it is naturally concerned with creation as the mechanism whereby creatures (i.e. individuals in nature) take the form that instantiates the divine idea that constitutes them. Key to participation then is the notion that the

---

[13] It also arises in a secondary matter in terms of the relationship of ideas to one another, which is not considered here (e.g. *Sophist*, 254b–c).

[14] John Milbank, *Theology and Social Theory: Beyond Secular Reason* (Oxford: Blackwell, 1990); Kathryn Tanner, *Christ the Key* (Cambridge: Cambridge University Press, 2010); Hans Boersma, *Heavenly Participation: The Weaving of a Sacramental Tapestry* (Grand Rapids, MI: Eerdmans, 2011); Andrew Davison, *Participation in God: A Study in Christian Doctrine and Metaphysics* (Cambridge: Cambridge University Press, 2019).

individual has its reality, or being, by virtue of something other than itself.

Perhaps the first philosophical articulation of participation may be found in Plato, where an appearance is said to be 'derived' from the idea which is its 'ground' (ἀρχή/*archê*).[15] As such, the idea is the 'prerequisite' (ὑπόθεσις/*hypothesis*) of the appearance, to which our thoughts bend upon philosophical reflection.[16] Participation also implies that the one participating is ontologically distinct by its contingent sharing in the non-contingent form in which it participates.[17] The mythical and metaphorical narratives that contextualise this ontology in Plato's thought describe the abstract intelligible forms as 'beyond being' (ἐπέκεινα τῆς οὐσίας/*epekeina tês ousias*), and residing 'outside of the heaven'.[18] In the cosmogony of the *Timaeus*, Plato explains how the structure of the cosmos is not the result of chance, but the product of the deliberate good intent of God, who through the figure of the craftsman (δημιουργός/*dêmiourgos*), shaped the chaos of existence into as excellent a form as nature permitted by using the changeless ideas as a model.[19] A similar concept of participation emerges, though more implicitly and discontinuously, in the Hebrew Bible. It expresses the presupposition that the world resulted from a divine plan, implying that God created all living beings, according to their kind,[20] that Wisdom arranged or ordered the world when it was established,[21] and that God ordered 'all things by measure, and number, and weight'.[22] These naturally came to influence the Christian biblical authors, as expressed in John's Logos of God, Christ,[23] who is described in Colossians as the creator from whom all things were created, and the being who is 'before all things, and in whom all things hold together'.[24]

The key development carried out in the thought of Christian Platonism is the incorporation of the Platonic doctrine of the ideas with the Hebrew doctrine of creation, such that the Platonic ideas that reside 'outside of the heaven' come to reside in the mind of God as divine

---

[15] *Phaedo*, 101e2–3. For all references to Plato in this chapter, see John M. Cooper and Douglas S. Hutchinson (eds.), *Plato: Complete Works* (Indianapolis: Hackett Publishing, 1997). Plato did not intend the term to be technical and warns against such use in *Phaedo*, 100d. For detailed considerations of participation in Plato, see Helmut Meinhardt, 'Teilhabe bei Platon', *Tijdschrift Voor Filosofie* 31, no. 1 (1968), 150–151; Luc Brisson, 'Participation et prédication chez Platon', *Revue philosophique de la France et de l'étranger* 181, no. 4 (1991), 557–569.

[16] *Phaedo*, 101d–102a; *Republic*, 511b–c.   [17] *Symposium*, 211b.

[18] *Republic*, 509b; *Phaedrus*, 247c.   [19] *Timaeus*, 28a–b, 29e–30b.

[20] Genesis 1:11–12, 21.   [21] Proverbs 8.   [22] Wisdom 11:20.   [23] John 1:1.

[24] Colossians 1:16–17.

ideas.[25] A precursor to this model, often referred to as exemplarism,[26] may be found in the thought of the Middle Platonist Antiochus of Ascalon, who may have been the first to locate the ideas in the mind of God.[27] However, the most important precedent for this is found in Philo's influential *De opificio mundi*, where creation is conceptualised by a two-form process of ideas and matter. God first fully forms 'the intelligible world in order that he might have the use of a pattern wholly god-like and incorporeal in producing the material world'.[28] Philo makes the particular point that ideas have 'no other location than the divine reason [θεῖον λόγον/ *theion logon*]'[29] In support of this, Philo points to 'the creation of man ... molded in the image of God'.[30] This image is the divine idea in the mind of the creator. From this, he reasons that 'if the part is an image of an image, it is manifest that the whole is so too'.[31] Philo elaborates this position through the metaphor of an architect, who, as the master planner of a new city, first devises in his mind all of the parts of the creation that will be made in material form.[32]

Augustine was one of the many, and perhaps the most important, of the early Christian thinkers who followed along the same lines as Philo. In *De diversis quaestionibus octoginta tribus*, he accepts the Platonic notion of ideas as located in the divine mind. Taking up the Platonic ideas, he writes:

The ideas are certain original and principle forms of things, i.e., reasons, fixed and unchangeable, which are not themselves formed and, being thus eternal and existing always in the same state, are contained in the Divine Intelligence [*diuina intellegentia*]. And though they themselves neither come into being nor pass away, nevertheless, everything which can come into being and pass away and everything which does come into being and pass away is said to be formed in accord with these ideas.... It is by participation [*participatione*] in these that whatever is exists in whatever manner it does exist.[33]

---

[25] Torstein Tollefsen, *The Christocentric Cosmology of St Maximus the Confessor* (Oxford: Oxford University Press, 2008), 23–33.

[26] Tollefsen, *The Christocentric Cosmology*, 21–40; Frederick Copleston, *History of Philosophy, Volume 2: Medieval Philosophy* (New York: Doubleday, 1993), 59–73, 258–261, 358–362.

[27] John M. Dillon, *The Middle Platonists, 80 B.C. to A.D. 220* (New York: Cornell University Press, 1977), 82.

[28] Philo, *On the Creation: Allegorical Interpretation of Genesis 2 and 3*, Loeb Classical Library 226, trans. F. H. Colson and G. H. Whitaker (Cambridge, MA: Harvard University Press, 1929), IV.16.

[29] Philo, *On the Creation*, V.20.   [30] Ibid, VI.25; Genesis 1:27.

[31] Philo, *On the Creation*, VI.25.   [32] Ibid.

[33] Augustine, *Eighty-Three Different Questions*, trans. David L. Mosher (Washington, D. C.: Catholic University of America Press, 1981), 46.2; *De Diversis Quaestionibus*

The Platonic ideas inform Augustine's interpretation of the first verse of Genesis, where he describes the establishment of two creaturely realities. According to Augustine's understanding, prior to the creation of days, God creates the heavens and the earth independent of the temporal succession that will follow. At this most nascent state, the earth is pure potential formlessness, whilst heaven is understood to be the 'heaven of heavens'.[34] Augustine conceives of this heaven as 'some kind of intellectual creature', which all of earthly creation approximates.[35] These models are not independent of God, but created; not co-eternal, but sharing in God's eternity. To this end he describes something very much akin to the Platonic realm of ideas:[36] 'The Heaven of Heavens, – that intellectual heaven, where it is the property of the intelligence to know all at once, not in part, not darkly, not through a glass, but in whole, clearly, and face to face not this thing now, and that thing anon; but, as I said, know all at once, without all succession of times.'[37] To experience both creation overall, and ourselves in particular, for Augustine is to experience meaning, through participation, as it is conceived in the divine mind, and not in the human mind.[38]

This position, which has the capacity to transform the constitution of meaning one finds in nature found numerous articulations, even during the early modern period when the prominence of the realist metaphysics of participation has significantly declined. The works of the seventeenth-century writer and priest Thomas Traherne articulate his desire to overcome an anthropocentric conceptualisation of nature by drawing upon the tradition of Christian Platonism.[39] His poems often use childhood and innocence to represent a pre-lapsarian state that serves as a model for the redeemed self. This is contrasted with a fallen self-centred understanding of reality based upon envy, avarice and selfishness. In the poem *Eden*, he

---

Octoginta Tribus, De Octo Dulcitii Quaestionibus, ed. Almut Mutzenbecher, vol. 44A (Turnhout: Brepols, 1975), 46.2.

[34] Augustine, *Confessions, Volume II: Books 9–13*, Loeb Classical Library 27, trans. Carolyn J. B. Hammond (Cambridge, MA: Harvard University Press, 2016), 12.II.

[35] Augustine, *Confessions*, 12.IX.

[36] Rowan Williams, 'Creation', in *Augustine Through the Ages*, ed. Allan D. Fitzgerald (Grand Rapids, MI: William B. Eerdmans Publishing Company, 1999), 251–254.

[37] Augustine, *Confessions*, 12.XIII. See 1 Corinthians 13; *Phaedrus*, 247d–e.

[38] Augustine, *Confessions*, 7.XVII; Augustine, *On the Trinity: Books 8–15*, trans. Stephen McKenna (Cambridge: Cambridge University Press, 2002), 7.12.

[39] Elizabeth S. Dodd, *Boundless Innocence in Thomas Traherne's Poetic Theology: 'Were all Men Wise and Innocent . . . '* (London: Routledge, 2016), 6–10; K. W. Salter, *Thomas Traherne: Mystic and Poet* (London: Edward Arnold Publishers, 1965), 33–37, 74–91.

describes recovering 'A learned and a happy ignorance' that divides him from the vanity, care and sorrow that is 'The Madness and the misery / Of Men.'[40] This allows Treharne to observe nature's own intrinsic meaning beyond that imposed by humans. In his poem *Nature*, he describes how: 'Nature teacheth nothing but the Truth'.[41] It does so by inspiring admiration, which draws one by the senses to the divine ideas: 'His Works He bid me in the World admire. / My Senses were Informers to my Heart, / The Conduits of His Glory, Pow'r, and Art'.[42] Here Traherne emphasises the meaning that adheres 'in the World'. In his poem 'Wonder', Traherne describes how this experience of inherent meaning can be blocked by the imposition of anthropocentric meaning upon nature. In particular, that which designates it as property and determines it as wealth:

> Curs'd, ill-devis'd Proprieties
> With Envy, Avarice,
> And Fraud, (those Fiends that spoil ev'n Paradise)
> Were not the Object of mine Eys;
> Nor Hedges, Ditches, Limits, narrow Bounds:
> I dreamt not ought of those,
> But in surveying all mens Grounds
> I found Repose.[43]

As Traherne describes here, his learned ignorance to the anthropocentric categories that reconstruct nature in human terms alone allows him to see beyond the demarcations that divide nature into property, and the negative feelings that ownership evoke. Instead, 'the Object of mine Eys' become common wealth, wealth which cannot be but held in common, as its meaning is determined by divine participation, and possessed by whomever sees the divine ideas instantiated. This knowledge, that knowing nature's meaning is that it brings 'down the highest Mysteries to sense', as he elsewhere writes, allows him to find tranquility and fulfilment where others experience concern and paucity.[44]

WHAT IS THE VALUE OF NATURE?

The second question this examination considers concerns the value of nature, which is closely related to the question of meaning. Again, from an

---

[40] Thomas Traherne, *The Works of Thomas Traherne VI: Poems from the 'Dobell Folio', Poems of Felicity, The Ceremonial Law, Poems from the 'Early Notebook'*, ed. Jan Ross (Rochester, NY: Boydell & Brewer, 2014), 92, ll. 1, 5–6.

[41] Traherne, *The Works*, 144, l. 3.   [42] Ibid, 144, ll. 6–8.   [43] Ibid, 92, ll. 59–56.

[44] Ibid, 84, l. 5.

anthropocentric standpoint it is humans who confer value, as opposed to nature having its own intrinsic value. Overwhelmingly today the anthropocentric construction of nature is to see it through the eyes of naturalistic materialism, though other narratives are possible. Naturalism largely understands nature as a resource, whose value is determined by humans based on a range of criteria from raw material, to food, to recreation, or even carbon credit.

Thus far the participatory ontology of Christian Platonism has set out an alternative radically non-anthropocentric ontology based upon the divine ideas. However, at this point the exemplarism of participation could seem to point toward a problematic theocentric conclusion where value, while no longer residing with humans, is entirely transferred to God, and not to nature itself. Christian Platonists have pointed out the radical dependency of creation upon God, which is not restricted to the inceptive bestowal of meaning alone, but equally extends to the preservation of creation itself.[45] For example, Gregory of Nyssa recognised this, writing that creatures exist by participation in true being, and that it is because of God's sustaining presence that all things remain in being.[46] Later, Aquinas maintained that it was not possible for creatures to exist separately from God.[47] Rather, 'all things other than God are not their own existence but share in existence'.[48] This preservation of creation is, for Aquinas, a logical extension of the act of creation: 'God does not by one action bring things into existing and by

[45] Torstein Tollefsen, *Activity and Participation in Late Antique and Early Christian Thought* (Oxford: Oxford University Press, 2012), 97–98.

[46] Gregory of Nyssa, *Life of Moses*, trans. Abraham J. Malherbe and Everett Ferguson (Mahwah, NJ: Paulist Press, 1978), 2.24–25.

[47] For considerations of participation in Aquinas, see Cornelio Fabro, *La nozione metafisca di partecipazione secondo S. Thommaso d'Aquino*, 2nd ed. (Segni: Editrice del Verbo Incarnato, 1950); Louis-Bertrand Geiger, *La participation dans la philosophie de s. Thomas d'Aquin* (Paris: J. Vrin, 1942); Arthur Little, *The Platonic Heritage of Thomism* (Dublin: Golden Eagle Books, 1942); W. Norris Clarke, 'The Limitation of Act by Potency in St. Thomas: Aristotelianism or Neoplatonism?,' *New Scholasticism* 26, no. 2 (1952), 167–194; W. Norris Clarke, 'The Meaning of Participation in St. Thomas', *Proceedings of the American Catholic Philosophical Association* 26 (1952), 147–157; John F. Wippel, *The Metaphysical Thought of Thomas Aquinas: From Finite Being to Uncreated Being* (Washington, D.C.: Catholic University of America Press, 2000), 94–131; Rudi te Velde, *Participation and Substantiality in Thomas Aquinas* (Leiden: Brill, 1995). For recent contributions to the debate on the role of participation in Aquinas see te Velde, *Participation and Substantiality*, 95–116; Wippel, *Metaphysical Thought*, 94–131; Gregory T. Doolan, *Aquinas on the Divine Ideas as Exemplar Causes* (Washington, D.C.: Catholic University of America Press, 2008), 194–243.

[48] Thomas Aquinas, *Summa Theologiae*, ed. Thomas Gilby, 61 vols. (Cambridge: Blackfriars, 1964–1976), I.44.1.

another preserve them in existing ... And so God's action intrinsically causing a thing to exist does not differ insofar as it causes the beginning and the continuation of existing'.[49] Accordingly, all creatures have their being from the continuous creation (*creatio continua*) of the higher cause. If God is both the sustaining meaning and being of creation, nature itself may seem to have no intrinsic value. And, if this conclusion is reached, nature may come to be seen merely as a material means to a divine end, and this in turn can lead to a contempt of creation (*contemptus mundi*), a desire to overcome nature that in many ways replicates mutatis mutandis the disembedding of humans from nature that characterises anthropocentrism.[50] It is this contemptuous view of nature, and its secularised descendants, that White has in mind when he characterises Christianity as an anthropocentric religion. To deal with this problem the intrinsic value of nature within the participatory ontology of Christian Platonism must be considered.

The issue of the intrinsic value of nature figures in Aquinas' consideration of how divine goodness relates to the good found in individual things.[51] As already noted, participation figures prominently in Aquinas' thought, yet he explicitly rejects Plato's affirmation of ideas as subsisting in themselves apart from natural things.[52] In this regard he is in agreement with Aristotle, that all things are constituted by substantial forms, but that these do not exist independent of things.[53] Aquinas reconciles the real existence of ideas, and hence participation, and the intrinsic presence of ideas in individuals through the doctrine of the divine ideas, already outlined above, with the assistance of Aristotle's notion of the first mover. According to Aquinas, 'in the divine mind, there are exemplar forms of all creatures, which are called ideas, as there are forms of artifacts in the mind of a craftsman'.[54] These ideas, which

---

[49] Thomas Aquinas, *The Power of God*, trans. Richard J. Regan (New York: Oxford University Press, 2012), 5.1.

[50] Clarence J. Glacken, *Traces on the Rhodian Shore: Nature and Culture in Western Thought from Ancient Times to the End of the Eighteenth Century* (Oakland: University of California Press, 1976), 162–163.

[51] Aquinas, *Summa Theologiae*, I.6.4.; Thomas Aquinas, *The Disputed Questions on Truth*, trans. Robert W. Schmidt (Chicago: Henry Regnery Company, 1954), 21.IV.

[52] Aquinas, *Summa Theologiae*, I.6.4.

[53] Aristotle, *Metaphysics, Volume II: Books 10–14, Oeconomica. Magna Moralia*, Loeb Classical Library 287, trans. Hugh Tredennick and G. Cyril Armstrong (Cambridge, MA: Harvard University Press, 1935), 2.13–15.

[54] Thomas Aquinas, *Quaestiones de quolibet*, ed. Leonine Commission, vol. 25 (Paris: Commissio Leonina, 1996), 1.54: 23–26; Doolan, *Aquinas on the Divine*, 1–43. See also John F. Wippel, *Thomas Aquinas on the Divine Ideas* (Toronto: Pontifical Institute of Mediaeval Studies, 1993); Vivian Boland, *Ideas in God According to Saint Thomas Aquinas* (New York: E. J. Brill, 1996).

include good and being, belong both to Aristotle's first mover and to God:[55] 'there is first something which is essentially being and essentially good, which we call God, and Aristotle agrees with this. Hence from the first being ... everything can be called good and a being, inasmuch as it participates in [the first being]'.[56] In addition to the language of participation, Aquinas also implies the intrinsic presence of the ideas:

> If, therefore, the first goodness is the effective cause of all goods, it must imprint its likeness upon the things produced; and so each thing will be called good by reason of an inherent form because of the likeness of the highest good implanted in it, and also because of the first goodness taken as the exemplar and effective cause of all created goodness. In this respect the opinion of Plato can be held.[57]

That an idea can be both 'inherent' and 'implanted', but more than a vestigial mark by virtue of participation, is based upon the distinction that Aquinas makes between 'created goodness', which he terms 'inherent form' and 'uncreated goodness', which is an 'exemplary form'.[58] In making this distinction Aquinas' aim was not primarily to argue for the goodness in creation which is our concern here. Rather, it was to maintain the distinction between divine goodness and created goodness, and hence the separate identities of God and creation. Indeed, according to Aquinas, participation occurs 'by way of a certain assimilation which is far removed and defective' in relation to the divine ideas.[59]

At first this may seem simply to lead back to the problematic devaluation of nature mentioned above, yet there are two important upshots for developing an alternative to an anthropocentric construction of nature. First, the distinction between created and uncreated forms means that a direct comparison between the idea inherent in nature and the divine ideas is not possible. This means that the ideas in nature cannot be understood merely as lesser facsimiles of a better original. Second, that nature has an intrinsic value through participation. This conveys that

---

[55] Aristotle, *Physics, Volume II: Books 5–8*, Loeb Classical Library 255, trans. P. H. Wicksteed and F. M. Cornford (Cambridge, MA: Harvard University Press, 1934), 8.256a4–256b3; Aristotle, *Metaphysics*, 12(Λ).1071b3–1073a14, 1075a11–15; Stephen Menn, 'Aristotle and Plato on God as Nous and as the Good', *The Review of Metaphysics* 45, no. 3 (1992), 543–573, 547–551.

[56] Aquinas, *Summa Theologiae*, I.6.4.

[57] Thomas Aquinas, *Truth, Vol. 3: Questions XXI–XXIX*, trans. Robert W. Schmidt (Indianapolis: Hackett, 1994), 21.4; see: te Velde, *Participation and Substantiality*, 23–34.

[58] Aquinas, *Truth*, 21.4. [59] Aquinas, *Summa Theologiae*, I.6.4.

there is value in nature that is an alternative to anthropocentrism. That the divine ideas in creation must be inferior to those in the divine mind was long recognised. Philo contended that the feebleness of nature was unable to entertain their abundance 'had not God with appropriate adjustment dealt out to each his due portion'.[60] Similarly Pseudo-Dionysius articulated the necessity that God 'deals out the immeasurable and infinite in limited measure'.[61] What is important here for the question of nature's intrinsic value is the distinction made by Aquinas which distinguishes created and uncreated forms as intrinsically bound in relation to one another, yet equally distinct in kind. The result is that nature is not lacking, but complete in itself, and hence valuable in itself, apart from any anthropocentric valuation.

We find this sentiment expressed in Hildegard von Bingen's *Liber divinorum operum*, where she expresses the relationship of personified Wisdom to creation:

> So too are all her works so fully and comprehensively fortified that no creature is left so incomplete that it lacks whatever it needs for its own nature; rather, each possesses within itself the fullness of total perfection and usefulness. Thus all things that have come forth through Wisdom are like the purest and most elegant beauty within her, gleaming with the radiant brilliance of their being.[62]

We might understand this relationship by the analogy of a composer and a singer. The composer is the originate source and creator of the music, whilst the singer creates the music in performance. The act of composition and the act of performance both have the same object, viz. the music, but each activity is different in kind, and hence not directly comparable. Indeed, the performance is something that is complete in itself, instantiating the music that was in the mind of the composer for the listener, whilst nevertheless being entirely dependent on the composition.

HOW SHOULD WE KNOW NATURE?

That nature is possessed of its own meaning and value independent of humans leads us to the final question taken up in this examination: how can we know nature? More particularly, how is it that we can

---

[60] Philo, *On the Creation*, XXIII.4.
[61] Pseudo-Dionysius, *Pseudo-Dionysius: The Complete Works*, eds. Colm Luibheid and Paul Rorem (Mahwah, NJ: Paulist Press, 1987), 588A.
[62] Hildegard of Bingen, *The Book of Divine Works*, trans. Nathaniel M. Campbell (Washington D.C.: Catholic University of America Press, 2018), 397.

know nature's own meaning and value. From the anthropocentric standpoint, to know nature is to know the symbols, systems and co-ordinates that we impose upon it. For example, some animals are known as symbols for human emotions, plants and animals are known by Latinised binomial nomenclature, and landscapes are known through their translation into mathematical matrices. Each of these imposes an abstract, anthropocentric construction onto a natural object without particular regard for the meaning or value intrinsic to that object. Hence, the *Scaptia beyonceae*, a horsefly native to Australia, is named for the American popular singer Beyoncé. A geographic co-ordinate system enables any location on earth to be specified by an abstract set of letters or numbers. And in poetry, the nightingale becomes a symbol for melancholy. However, as the Romantic poet Samuel Taylor Coleridge observes in his poem 'The Nightingale', 'In nature there is nothing melancholy'.[63] As with questions of meaning and value, the tradition of Christian Platonism can provide an alternative model for how we can know nature. Human beings already exist within the participatory ontology that is at the centre of Christian Platonist thought. However, knowing this involves cultivating a reflexive awareness that breaks out of the epistemology of anthropocentric imposition.

The cultivation of this reflexive awareness played a large part in the Romantic revival of Christian Platonism in late eighteenth- and early nineteenth-century thought. The decline of the participatory ontology of realist metaphysics was a process that occurred over centuries; however the Romantics responded to the confluence of a number of acute changes that highlighted this decline in their own lifetimes. The transition from a transcendent worldview, where the meaning and value of things resided with the supernatural, to an immanent understanding, set over and against the transcendent, where meaning and value resided in the human mind, was sharpened by exponential economic growth, the harnessing of scientific knowledge for mechanistic production and the championing of individual autonomy by Kantian idealism and the Enlightenment philosophes.[64] Arising from these and other developments, the

[63] Samuel Taylor Coleridge, *The Collected Works of Samuel Taylor Coleridge: Poetical Works I: Poems (Reading Text)*, ed. J. C. C. Mays (Princeton, NJ: Princeton University Press, 2001), l. 15.

[64] Alexander J. B. Hampton, *The Romantic Re-Invention of Religion: The Reconciliation of German Idealism and Platonic Realism* (Cambridge: Cambridge University Press, 2019), 1–3, 13–28.

Romantics came to be concerned with the increasing alienation of humans from the meaning and value inherent in nature, and in particular the wonder, as described by Treharne, that was integral to opening our experience to them.

Coleridge, perhaps the English Romantic most engaged with the tradition of Christian Platonism,[65] follows his observation in *The Nightingale* concerning the eponymous bird's supposed melancholy, with advice to the would-be poet:

> he had better far have stretched his limbs
> Beside a brook in mossy forest-dell,
> By sun or moon-light, to the influxes
> Of shapes and sounds and shifting elements
> Surrendering his whole spirit, of his song
> And of his fame forgetful! so his fame
> Should share in Nature's immortality,
> A venerable thing! and so his song
> Should make all Nature lovelier, and itself
> Be loved like Nature![66]

Coleridge advises that instead of echoing the conceits of others that turn nature into a reflection of the self, the poet ought instead to be immersed in nature. This involves the poet momentarily surrendering any pre-conceived song of the self, and opening to a dialogue with nature. The result, to 'share in Nature's immortality', is to know the meaning and value that are present within nature, by their participation in the 'immortal' divine ideas apart from anthropocentric projections of the self. Nature's particulars, like the nightingale, or the albatross in Coleridge's 'Rhyme of the Ancient Mariner' that becomes a mere object of sport for the nature-alienated seaman, ought not to be projections of ourselves. Instead, as objects of veneration, they contain a kind of inexhaustibility through their participation in divine ideas. This, rather than leading to an anthropocentric projection which allows one to turn nature's objects into a reflection of the self, instead requires that one converse with it. To converse with nature, a conception reflected in the full title of Coleridge's poem 'The Nightingale:

---

[65] Douglas Hedley, *Coleridge, Philosophy and Religion: Aids to Reflection and the Mirror of Spirit* (Cambridge: Cambridge University Press, 2000); James Kirwan, 'Coleridge on Beauty: Aesthetic Contemplation as Revelation', in *Coleridge and Contemplation*, ed. Peter Cheyne (Oxford: Oxford University Press, 2017), 47–59; Douglas Hedley, 'S. T. Coleridge's Contemplative Imagination', in *Coleridge and Contemplation*, 221–236.

[66] Coleridge, *The Collected Works*, ll. 25–34.

A Conversation Poem', is to come to nature, to listen to it, and from this dialogue learn about its own intrinsic meaning and value. The poet then represents this process in art.

Coleridge's comment that the poet's 'song / Should make all Nature lovelier, and itself [i.e. the poem] / Be loved like Nature!', suggests that poetry, and more broadly creative art, is a language appropriate to the consideration of nature.[67] The poem is able to make nature 'lovelier' by reflexively expressing how the conversation between the observer and the observed communicates the nightingale's inherent meaning and value. However, even more than this, the poem participates in a second order form of the act of divine creation. Coleridge described the human imagination as 'the living Power and prime Agent of all human Perception, and as a repetition of the finite mind of the eternal act of creation in the infinite I AM'.[68] For Coleridge, each act of perception was a kind of secondary creation, where the divine idea is re-created in the mind of the perceiver. The poem reflexively represents this recapitulated creation to the reader. In this way, for Coleridge, our own participation in creation through the imagination is demonstrated to the reader as an act of perception and cognition which is not merely an anthropocentric process, but one which performs the act of divine creation a second time, instantiating the radically non-anthropocentric meaning and value of divine ideas present in nature in the mind of the perceiver.[69]

Coleridge's Romantic contemporary, Freidrich von Hardenburg, best known by his nom de plume Novalis, was equally concerned with the ever-increasing alienation of modern humans from nature, and the loss of a transcending ground that would unite both. He famously wrote 'we seek everywhere the absolute [*Unbedingte*], and always find only things

---

[67] Ibid, ll. 32–34.

[68] Samuel Taylor Coleridge, *Biographia Literaria, Or, Biographical Sketches of my Literary Life and Opinions*, ed. James Engell and W. Jackson Bate (London: Routledge & Kegan Paul, 1983), I.304.

[69] Coleridge took this further. His language repeats God's self-articulation 'I am what I am' (Exod. 3:14), which he glosses elsewhere as the substantive act of God's being: 'I AM, who *is* by his own *act* – who affirms himself to *be* in that he is; and who *is*, in that he *affirms* himself to be ... In Grammar, this unique Thought or rather Idea is expressed by the appropriate name of Verb Substantive – that which is both Verb and Noun at once & in the *same* relation' (Samuel Taylor Coleridge, *Collected Letters, 1772–1834*, ed. Earl Leslie Griggs (Oxford: Clarendon Press, 1959–1971), 6.817). The repetition of the 'I am' in humans suggests that the perceiving imagination is also the substantive act of human being.

[*Dinge*]'.[70] Rather than finding meaning and value in the objects of nature, Novalis discovered that he and his contemporaries found only things; objects to which they could affix only arbitrary meaning and value which failed to reflect the absolute ideas in which they participated. This would lead Novalis to characterise modern philosophy as really 'a home-sickness – *the drive to be at home everywhere in the world*'.[71] Despite being based in empirical observation, the classification systems of modern natural science were, Novalis argued, a reflection of this alienation and homelessness.[72] They propounded a narrow, instrumental use of language, divorced from the real ideals in which nature participated, and which themselves could be instantiated in our own cognition. The resulting hypostasised language rendered humans deaf to the language nature already spoke. According to Novalis, what we fail to realise in the resulting anthropocentric construction of nature is that, within a participatory ontology, 'It is not man alone that *speaks* – the universe also speaks – everything speaks.'[73]

In his late work *Die Lehrlinge zu Sais*, left incomplete around 1800, Novalis examines the relationship between knowledge of outer nature and inner self, and the role language plays in the connection or estrangement of both. In its first lines, nature is described as a script of ciphers that contains a hidden grammar.[74] Novalis suggests that our exploration of the natural world is equally an exploration of the inner self. Knowledge of the self and knowledge of nature both have the same unified end with the inner and the outer connected by a doctrine of signatures and correspondences that momentarily reveals itself:

Manifold are the ways of man. He who follows and compares them will see wonderful figures arise; figures that seem to belong to that great written cipher that one sees everywhere: on wings, eggshells, in clouds, in the snow, in crystals and rock formations, on freezing waters, in the inside and outside of the mountains, the plants, the animals, the people, in the lights of heaven, on scored disks of

[70] Novalis, *Historische-Kritische Ausgabe – Novalis Schriften*, ed. Richard Samuel, Hans-Joachim Mähl, and Gerhard Schulz, vol. 2 (Stuttgart: Verlag W. Kohlhammer, 1965), 412.

[71] Novalis, *Historische-Kritische Ausgabe – Novalis Schriften*, ed. Richard Samuel, Hans-Joachim Mähl, and Gerhard Schulz, vol. 3 (Stuttgart: Verlag W. Kohlhammer, 1968), 434, no. 857.

[72] Hampton, *Romanticism*, 196–199; Novalis, *Historische-Kritische Ausgabe*, vol. 3, 135–161.

[73] Novalis, *Historische-Kritische Ausgabe*, vol. 3, 267–268, no. 143.

[74] Novalis, *Historische-Kritische Ausgabe – Novalis Schriften*, ed. Richard Samuel, Hans-Joachim Mähl, and Gerhard Schulz, vol. 1 (Stuttgart: Verlag W. Kohlhammer, 1960), 79.

pitch or glass, in iron filings around a magnet, and in the strange conjunctures of chance.[75]

In all of these, according to Novalis, we may glimpse a key to this wondrous script, and yet these intimations of a higher language refuse to accommodate themselves to any fixed form. Only fleetingly does this intimation of a unified language appear before us, and then once again everything dissolves. For Novalis, the endeavour of humans, in all disciplines, and at all times, has been to bring about a correspondence between our language and our world, or our inner ideas and the ideas in nature.

The second part of *Die Lehrlinge*, entitled 'Nature', begins with a comparison of the way language operates in its original ideal form and the way it operates when it falls away from this form: 'It may have taken a long time before people thought to designate the manifold objects of their senses with a common name, and to place themselves in opposition to them.'[76] As this development was furthered, it led to the increasing division of understanding. The 'sickly predisposition' of alienation that characterises later forms of language is due to their inability to bring the manifold ways they understand nature back together in either their original form or to bring about a new unity.[77] Prior to this separation of humans and nature, idealism and realism, explains Novalis, they were one: 'To those earlier people, everything seemed human, familiar, and social, there was freshness and originality in all their perceptions, each one of their utterances was a true natural breath, and their impressions corresponded to the world around them.'[78] The consequence of this development, Novalis explains, can be seen in the loss of the linguistic unity natural to poetry and science:[79] 'Natural scientists and poets have, through speaking one language, always shown themselves to be one people.'[80] In this relationship, scientists gathered and arranged, whilst poets moulded the vastness of nature into smaller pleasing natures.[81] Separated, however, both instrumentalise language to their own ends; they lose contact with the whole and become destructive forces. In the case of the natural scientists: 'Under their hands friendly nature died, leaving behind only dead, quivering remnants.'[82] Alternately, in the case of the artists, the poets indulge their subjective egos, soaring to heaven,

---

[75] Ibid.   [76] Ibid, 82.   [77] Ibid.   [78] Ibid, 83.
[79] Novalis depicts this process in 'Christenheit oder Europa', in *Historische-Kritische Ausgabe*, vol. 3, 507–524.
[80] Novalis, *Historische-Kritische Ausgabe*, vol. 1, 84.   [81] Ibid.   [82] Ibid.

engaging in god-like fancies, and in the process alienate themselves from the everyday, whilst squandering their genius.[83]

For Novalis, the task of the Romantic poet was to overcome this increasing alienation from nature and the languages appropriate to it. This was possible by responding to what his contemporary Friedrich Schlegel called the 'Romantic imperative': 'All nature and all science should become art. Art should become nature and science.'[84] In order to accomplish this, the poet would need to enact a reversal: 'The abstract should be made sense-like, and the sensible abstract – opposite operations'.[85] This is the process Novalis describes as romanticisation:

> The world must be made Romantic. Thus one can find the original meaning again. To romanticise is nothing other than a qualitative exponentiation. In this operation, the lower self is identified with a higher self. Just as we ourselves are as such a qualitative power series. This operation is as yet wholly unknown. By giving the common a higher meaning, the ordinary a mysterious look, the known the dignity of the unknown, the finite the appearance of the infinite, thus I romanticise it – The operation for the higher, unknown, mystical, infinite is reversed – this will through this connection be logarithmised – It takes on a familiar expression. Romantic philosophy. *Lingua romana*. Alternating heightening and lowering.[86]

What Novalis describes is a Plotinian-influenced process of emanation and return,[87] articulated through the mathematical language of exponentialisation and logarithmisation, but transposed from the quantitative to the qualitative. The lower self he describes may be identified with perception, and the higher self with intellection. By moving between perception and intellection, between the objectifying languages of the natural sciences and the subjectifying languages of poetic reflection, both transverse expressions of anthropocentric alienation, it is possible to transcend the limitations of both. As such, romanticisation is not an arbitrary or sentimental act. Rather, it is a creative re-engagement with nature, whereby the meaning and value inherent in nature may be known. Two centuries after Novalis set

---

[83] Ibid.
[84] Friedrich Schlegel, *Kritische Friedrich-Schlegel-Ausgabe*, ed. Ernst Behler et al. (Munich: Schöningh, 1958–2002), vol. 16, no. 586.
[85] Novalis, *Historische-Kritische Ausgabe*, vol. 3, 299, no. 331.
[86] Novalis, *Historische-Kritische Ausgabe*, vol. 2, 545, no. 105.
[87] Plotinus, *Ennead, Volume VI: 6–9*, Loeb Classical Library 468, trans. A. H. Armstrong (Cambridge, MA: Harvard University Press, 1988), VI.7, 7.23–32. See: P. F. Reiff, 'Plotin und die deutsche Romantik', *Euphorion* 19 (1912), 591–612; Max Wundt, 'Plotin und die Romantik', *Neue Jahrbücher für das klassische Altertum, Geschichte und deutsche Litteratur und für Pädagogik* 35 (1915), 648–672; Hans-Joachim Mähl, 'Novalis und Plotin', *Jahrbuch des freien deutschen Hochstifts* (1963), 139–250.

out the task of 'returning sacredness to nature, and infinity to art' the challenge, ever more apposite to the environmental crisis, remains.[88]

RE-THINKING THE OLD OR INVENTING ANEW

Over half a century has passed since White made his argument for a religious solution to environmental crisis. At the centre of this provocative claim was his belief that religion, and the social imaginary it shaped, was responsible for the predicament. Equally however, he maintained that it could only be by finding a new religion, or re-thinking the old, that the crisis could be addressed. This insight was echoed by the poetic observation of Wendell Berry at the turn of the present century:

> There are no unsacred places;
> there are only sacred places
> and desecrated places.[89]

Berry's lines express a contemporary deep concern with the meaning, valuing and knowing of nature. In the present day, the recognition of the continuing importance of religion, and the realisation that the environmental crisis must be addressed on a scale wider than the political and technological, seem to reinforce White's religious imperative over fifty years later.

For much of the latter twentieth, and into the twenty-first century, trends within academic discourse have been aligned against the tradition of Christian Platonism. Many Protestant thinkers influenced by Harnack sought a putatively pure form of biblical Christianity free from the accretions of Platonism. Nietzsche and Heidegger both launched critiques against realist metaphysics, which would subsequently influence the continental tradition of postmodern thought, defined by its incredulity toward metanarratives. The logical positivism of Anglophone philosophy was equally dismissive of metaphysical and especially Platonic thought. Whilst this vast literature offered some legitimate critiques of the application and legacy of key concepts within the Christian Platonic tradition, it has also allowed it to be caricatured and dismissed, often in an a priori manner, by following generations of scholars who accepted wholesale the criticism without turning to examine the object of criticism itself.

What is noteworthy, and what cannot be dismissed with ease, is that these critiques, reflective of the ascendency of a social imaginary

---

[88] Novalis, *Historische-Kritische Ausgabe*, vol. 3, 520.
[89] Wendell Berry, 'How to be a Poet', *Poetry*, January 2001, 20–22.

overwhelmingly characterised by its anti-realist orientation, also coincided with the greatest period of anthropogenic environmental destruction the planet has ever witnessed. Whilst this destruction is also the result of profound industrial and technological shifts, it is the social imaginary which gives rise to and employs them that is determinative. For two millennia the Platonist component within Christianity has functioned as an integral, dynamic and even heterodox element within the religion. If Christianity is to be re-invented, or indeed if a new religion is to be invented to replace it, given the urgency and existential import of the present crisis which faces us, the radically non-anthropocentric understanding of nature found in Christian Platonism is worth our immediate consideration.[90]

Bibliography

Aquinas, Thomas. *The Disputed Questions on Truth*. Translated by Robert W. Schmidt. Chicago: Henry Regnery Company, 1954.

The Power of God. Translated by Richard J. Regan. New York: Oxford University Press, 2012.

Quaestiones de quolibet. Edited by the Leonine Commission, vol. 25. Paris: Commissio Leonina, 1996.

Summa Theologiae. Edited by Thomas Gilby, 61 vols. Cambridge: Blackfriars, 1964–1976.

Truth, Vol. 3: Questions XXI–XXIX. Translated by Robert W. Schmidt. Indianapolis: Hackett, 1994.

Aristotle. *Metaphysics, Volume II: Books 10–14, Oeconomica, Magna Moralia*. Loeb Classical Library 287, translated by Hugh Tredennick and G. Cyril Armstrong. Cambridge, MA: Harvard University Press, 1935.

Physics, Volume II: Books 5–8. Loeb Classical Library 255, translated by P. H. Wicksteed and F. M. Cornford. Cambridge, MA: Harvard University Press, 1934.

Augustine. *Confessions, Volume II: Books 9–13*. Loeb Classical Library 27, translated by Carolyn J. B. Hammond. Cambridge, MA: Harvard University Press, 2016.

De Diversis Quaestionibus Octoginta Tribus, De Octo Dulcitii Quaestionibus. Edited by Almut Mutzenbecher, vol. 44A. Turnholt: Brepols, 1975.

Eighty-Three Different Questions. Translated by David L. Mosher. Washington, D.C.: Catholic University of America Press, 1981.

On the Trinity: Books 8–15. Translated by Stephen McKenna. Cambridge: Cambridge University Press, 2002.

Bailey, Edward I. *Implicit Religion in Contemporary Society*. Leuven: Peeters, 2006.

---

[90] Alexander J.B. Hampton, 'A Post-Secular Nature and the New Nature Writing', *Christianity and Literature*, 67 (2018), pp. 454–471.

Bendik-Keymer, Jeremy David, and Chris Haufe. 'Anthropogenic Mass Extinction: The Science, the Ethics, and the Civics'. In *The Oxford Handbook of Environmental Ethics*, edited by Stephen M. Gardiner and Allen Thompson, 427–437. Oxford: Oxford University Press, 2016.

Berger, Peter L. *The Desecularization of the World: Resurgent Religion and World Politics*. Grand Rapids, MI: Eerdmans, 1999.

Berry, Wendell. 'How to Be a Poet'. *Poetry*, January 2001, 20–22.

Blumenberg, Hans. *Die Legitimität der Neuzeit*. Frankfurt am Main: Suhrkamp, 1966.

Boersma, Hans. *Heavenly Participation: The Weaving of a Sacramental Tapestry*. Grand Rapids, MI: Eerdmans, 2011.

Boland, Vivian. *Ideas in God According to Saint Thomas Aquinas*. New York: E. J. Brill, 1996.

Brisson, Luc. 'Participation et prédication chez Platon'. *Revue philosophique de la France et de l'étranger* 181, no. 4 (1991): 557–569.

Buell, Lawrence. *The Environmental Imagination: Thoreau, Nature Writing, and the Formation of American Culture*. Cambridge, MA: Belknap Press, 1995.

Clarke, W. Norris. 'The Limitation of Act by Potency in St. Thomas: Aristotelianism or Neoplatonism?' *New Scholasticism* 26, no. 2 (1952): 167–194.

'The Meaning of Participation in St. Thomas'. *Proceedings of the American Catholic Philosophical Association* 26 (1952): 147–157.

Coleridge, Samuel Taylor. *Biographia Literaria, Or, Biographical Sketches of my Literary Life and Opinions*. Edited by James Engell and W. Jackson Bate. London: Routledge & Kegan Paul, 1983.

Collected Letters, 1772–1834. Edited by Earl Leslie Griggs. Oxford: Clarendon Press, 1959–1971.

The Collected Works of Samuel Taylor Coleridge: Poetical Works I: Poems (Reading Text). Edited by J. C. C. Mays. Princeton, NJ: Princeton University Press, 2001.

Copleston, Frederick. *History of Philosophy, Volume 2: Medieval Philosophy*. New York: Doubleday, 1993.

Cooper, John M., and Douglas S. Hutchinson, eds. *Plato: Complete Works*. Indianapolis: Hackett Publishing, 1997.

Cronon, William. 'The Trouble with Wilderness: Or, Getting Back to the Wrong Nature'. *Environmental History* 1, no. 1 (1996): 7–28.

Davison, Andrew. *Participation in God: A Study in Christian Doctrine and Metaphysics*. Cambridge: Cambridge University Press, 2019.

Dillon, John M. *The Middle Platonists, 80 B.C. to A.D. 220*. New York: Cornell University Press, 1977.

Dodd, Elizabeth S. *Boundless Innocence in Thomas Traherne's Poetic Theology: 'Were All Men Wise and Innocent...'*. London: Routledge, 2016.

Doolan, Gregory T. *Aquinas on the Divine Ideas as Exemplar Causes*. Washington, D.C.: Catholic University of America Press, 2008.

Emmett, Robert S., and David E. Nye. *The Environmental Humanities: A Critical Introduction*. Cambridge, MA: MIT Press, 2017.

Fabro, Cornelio. *La nozione metafisca di partecipazione secondo S. Thommaso d'Aquino*. 2nd ed. Segni: Editrice del Verbo Incarnato, 1950.

Fuller, Robert C. *Spiritual, but Not Religious*. New York: Oxford University Press, 2001.

Geiger, Louis-Bertrand. *La participation dans la philosophie de s. Thomas d'Aquin*. Paris: J. Vrin, 1942.

Glacken, Clarence J. *Traces on the Rhodian Shore: Nature and Culture in Western Thought from Ancient Times to the End of the Eighteenth Century*. Oakland: University of California Press, 1976.

Gregory of Nyssa. *Life of Moses*. Translated by Abraham J. Malherbe and Everett Ferguson. Mahwah, NJ: Paulist Press, 1978.

Guha, Ramachandra, and Joan Martínez-Alier. *Varieties of Environmentalism: Essays North and South*. London: Earthscan Publications, 1997.

Habermas, Jürgen. 'Die Dialektik der Säkularisierung'. *Blätter für deutsche und internationale Politik* 4 (2008): 33–46.

Hampton, Alexander J. B. 'A Post-Secular Nature and the New Nature Writing'. *Christianity and Literature*, 67 (2018): 454-471.

Hampton, Alexander J. B. *The Romantic Re-Invention of Religion: The Reconciliation of German Idealism and Platonic Realism*. Cambridge: Cambridge University Press, 2019.

Haraway, Donna J. *Simians, Cyborgs, and Women: The Reinvention of Nature*. London: Free Association Books, 1991.

Hedley, Douglas. *Coleridge, Philosophy and Religion: Aids to Reflection and the Mirror of Spirit*. Cambridge: Cambridge University Press, 2000.

'S. T. Coleridge's Contemplative Imagination'. In *Coleridge and Contemplation*, edited by Peter Cheyne, 221–236. Oxford: Oxford University Press, 2017.

Hildegard of Bingen. *The Book of Divine Works*. Translated by Nathaniel M. Campbell. Washington D.C.: Catholic University of America Press, 2018.

Huss, Boaz. 'Spirituality: The Emergence of a New Cultural Category and Its Challenge to the Religious and the Secular'. *Journal of Contemporary Religion* 29 (2014): 47–60.

Kirwan, James. 'Coleridge on Beauty: Aesthetic Contemplation as Revelation'. In *Coleridge and Contemplation*, edited by Peter Cheyne, 47–59. Oxford: Oxford University Press, 2017.

Latour, Bruno. *Nous n'avons jamais été modernes: Essai d'anthropologie symétrique*. Paris: La Découverte, 1991.

Little, Arthur. *The Platonic Heritage of Thomism*. Dublin: Golden Eagle Books, 1942.

Löwith, Karl. *Meaning in History: The Theological Implications of the Philosophy of History*. Chicago: University of Chicago Press, 1949.

Luibheid, Colm, and Paul Rorem, eds. *Pseudo-Dionysius: The Complete Works*. Mahwah, NJ: Paulist Press, 1987.

Mähl, Hans-Joachim. 'Novalis und Plotin'. *Jahrbuch des freien deutschen Hochstifts* (1963): 139–250.

McShane, Katie. 'Anthropocentrism vs. Nonanthropocentrism: Why Should We Care?' *Environmental Values* 16, no. 2 (2007): 169–185.

Meinhardt, Helmut. 'Teilhabe bei Platon'. *Tijdschrift Voor Filosofie* 31, no. 1 (1968): 150–151.

Menn, Stephen. 'Aristotle and Plato on God as Nous and as the Good'. *The Review of Metaphysics* 45, no. 3 (1992): 543–573.

Merchant, Carolyn. *The Death of Nature: Women, Ecology and the Scientific Revolution*. San Francisco: HarperCollins, 1990.

Milbank, John. *Beyond Secular Order: The Representation of Being and the Representation of the People*. Chichester: Wiley-Blackwell, 2014.

——— *Theology and Social Theory: Beyond Secular Reason*. Oxford: Blackwell, 1990.

Minteer, Ben A. 'Anthropocentrism'. In *Encyclopedia of Environmental Ethics and Philosophy*, edited by J. Baird Callicott and Robert Frodeman, 58–62. Farmington Hills, MI: Cengage Learning, 1999.

Nelson, Michael, Michael Paul and Thomas J. Sauer, 'The Long Reach of Lynn White Jr.'s "The Historical Roots of Our Ecological Crisis"', *Ecology & Evolution*, https://natureecoevocommunity.nature.com/users/24738-michae l-paul-nelson/posts/14041-the-long-reach-of-lynn-white-jr-s-the-historical-r oots-of-our-ecologic-crisis/ (updated 13 December 2016, accessed 2 May 2019).

Novalis. *Historische-Kritische Ausgabe - Novalis Schriften*. Edited by Richard Samuel, Hans-Joachim Mähl & Gerhard Schulz. 3 vols. Stuttgart: Verlag W. Kohlhammer, 1965.

Ortner, Sherry B. 'Is Female to Male as Nature Is to Culture?' *Feminist Studies* 1, no. 2 (1972): 5–31.

Partridge, Christopher H. *The Re-Enchantment of the West*. London: T & T Clark, 2004.

Philo. *On the Creation: Allegorical Interpretation of Genesis 2 and 3*. Loeb Classical Library 226, translated by F. H. Colson and G. H. Whitaker. Cambridge, MA: Harvard University Press, 1929.

Plotinus. *Ennead, Volume VI: Books 6–9*. Loeb Classical Library 468, translated by A. H. Armstrong. Cambridge, MA: Harvard University Press, 1988.

Plumwood, Val. *Environmental Culture: The Ecological Crisis of Reason*. London: Routledge, 2002.

Reiff, P. F. 'Plotin und die deutsche Romantik'. *Euphorion* 19 (1912): 591–612.

Roof, Wade Clark. *A Generation of Seekers*. San Francisco: HarperCollins, 1993.

Salter, K. W. *Thomas Traherne: Mystic and Poet*. London: Edward Arnold Publishers, 1965.

Schlegel, Friedrich. *Kritische Friedrich-Schlegel-Ausgabe*. Edited by Ernst Behler et al. Munich: Schöningh, 1958–2002.

Stark, Rodney, and William Sims Bainbridge. *The Future of Religion*. Berkeley: University of California Press, 1986.

Tanner, Kathryn. *Christ the Key*. Cambridge: Cambridge University Press, 2010.

te Velde, Rudi. *Participation and Substantiality in Thomas Aquinas*. Leiden: Brill, 1995.

Thompson, Allen. 'Anthropocentrism: Humanity as Peril and Promise'. In *The Oxford Handbook of Environmental Ethics*, edited by Stephen M. Gardiner and Allen Thompson, 77–90. Oxford: Oxford University Press, 2016.

Tollefsen, Torstein. *Activity and Participation in Late Antique and Early Christian Thought*. Oxford: Oxford University Press, 2012.

The Christocentric Cosmology of St Maximus the Confessor. Oxford: Oxford University Press, 2008.

Traherne, Thomas. *The Works of Thomas Traherne VI: Poems from the 'Dobell Folio', Poems of Felicity, The Ceremonial Law, Poems from the 'Early Notebook'*. Edited by Jan Ross. Rochester, NY: Boydell & Brewer, 2014.

White Jr., Lynn. 'The Historical Roots of Our Ecologic Crisis'. *Science* 155, no. 3767 (1967): 1203–1207.

Medieval Religion and Technology: Collected Essays. Berkeley: University of California Press, 1978.

Medieval Technology and Social Change. Oxford: Oxford University Press, 1962.

Whitney, Elspeth. 'Lynn White Jr.'s "The Historical Roots of Our Ecologic Crisis" After 50 Years'. *History Compass* 13, no. 8 (2015): 396–410.

'The Lynn White Thesis: Reception and Legacy'. *Environmental Ethics* 35, no. 3 (2013): 313–331.

Williams, Rowan. 'Creation'. In *Augustine Through the Ages*, edited by Allan D. Fitzgerald, 251–254. Grand Rapids, MI: William B. Eerdmans Publishing Company, 1999.

Wippel, John F. *The Metaphysical Thought of Thomas Aquinas: From Finite Being to Uncreated Being*. Washington, D.C.: Catholic University of America Press, 2000.

Thomas Aquinas on the Divine Ideas. Toronto: Pontifical Institute of Mediaeval Studies, 1993.

Wundt, Max. 'Plotin und die Romantik'. *Neue Jahrbücher für das klassische Altertum, Geschichte und deutsche Litteratur und für Pädagogik* 35 (1915): 648–672.

3.3

Art and Meaning

Richard Viladesau

CHRISTIAN PLATONISM IN PREMODERN AESTHETICS

For the gilded doors of the church of Saint-Denis, installed as part of the renovations of the abbey in the first half of the twelfth century, the Abbot Suger commissioned reliefs of the passion, resurrection, and ascension of Christ. He also placed on the doors a poetic inscription that addresses the viewer:

> Portarum quisquis attollere
> quaeris honorem,
> Aurum nec sumptus,
> operis mirare laborem.
>
> Nobile claret opus,
> sed opus quod nobile claret,
> Clarificet mentes ut eant
> per lumina vera
> Ad verum lumen,
> ubi Christus janua vera.
>
> Quale sit intus
> in his determinat aurea porta
> Mens hebes ad verum
> per materialia surgit,
> Et demersa prius
> hac visa luce resurgit.[1]

---

[1] Suger of Saint-Denis, "Sugerii Abbatis Sancti Dionysii Liber de Rebus in Administratione Sua Gestis," in Suger, *Œuvres Complètes*, ed. A. Lecoy de la Marche (Paris: Jules Renouard, 1867), 189.

Whoever you are, if you wish to exalt the honor of these doors,
it is not the gold nor the expense that you should marvel at,
but the excellence of the work.

The noble work shines,
But the work that nobly shines
Should clarify minds, so that they proceed
Through true lights
To the true light,
Where Christ is the true door.

How this is inherent
In these [lights] the golden door defines:
The dull mind rises to the truth
Through material things
And, formerly submerged,
Once these things are seen in light rises up again.

The poem abounds in clever analogies, double meanings, plays on words, and classical references.[2] More profoundly, it expounds a Christian-(Neo)Platonic aesthetics based on a metaphysics of light and an ascent of the mind through the hierarchy of being from sense experience to the divine. It is not merely the external splendor that appeals to our senses, but more importantly it is the mental work, the art, that should appeal to the mind. The beauty of worldly things and of artistry is mediated by the mind or soul of the self-conscious perceiver. There is a process of "ascent": we admire first the materials; then the artistry that gives form to material; then the form, the ideas conveyed by the art – in this case, the passion and glorification of Christ. These are events of God's revelation, which is a true light to the mind. But the mind's recognition of both the content and the beauty allows a further progression. From the sight of revelation and its beauty we are raised to contemplating our own minds that receive the revelation, minds illumined by Christ, who is the true light and way to God. And from the experience of Christ's illumination, the mind is raised in prayer to the source of both the illumination and the illuminated soul, Christ himself. The reliefs on the doors portray scenes in the life of Christ; the spectator should go beyond their appearances to meanings, realities: spiritual insight into the means of his or her own rising to glorious life. From their visual beauty, the viewer should proceed to spiritual beauty. As Augustine said: "From

[2] Cf. Ovid, *Metamorphoses*, 2.5.

III.3.1 Interior, Basilica of Saint-Denis, Saint-Denis, France (twelfth–thirteenth centuries). Photo by Bruce Yuanyue Bi/Getty Images.

the beauty of those things that are external we discover the maker, who is internal to us, and who creates beauty in a superior way in the soul, and then, in an inferior way, creates beauty in the body."[3]

The Pseudo-Dionysian theology of light is also embodied in the new Gothic form of architecture, of which Saint-Denis is a prototype, especially in its emphasis on the symbolic beauty of light, which is both the symbol and the physical manifestation of the divinity. New techniques for buttressing allowed expanded spaces for stained glass. Suger removed the rood screen in order to provide increased illumination. He speaks of the expansion of the circuit of the oratory, "through which all the light of the most holy windows should marvelously and continuously illumine the interior with all-pervading beauty."[4] As Pseudo-Dionysius wrote: "Every procession of illuminating light . . . turns us to the oneness of our conducting Father . . . The material lights [are] a likeness of the gift of immaterial enlightenment."[5]

[3] Augustine, *De Diversis Quaestionibus* LXXXIII, q. XLV *Adversus Mathematicos*, n. 1.
[4] Suger, "De Consecratione Ecclesiae Sancti Dionysii," in Suger, *Œuvres Complètes*, 223.
[5] Dionysius Areopagitus, *The Heavenly Hierarchy*, ch. 1; cf. *De Divinis Nominibus*, ch. IV. Cf. Thomas Aquinas, *In librum Beati Dionysii De divinis nominibus expositio*, ed. Ceslai

Medieval sacred art visualizes the synthesis of biblical and Platonic thought found in the church Fathers, especially in Origen, the Cappadocians, Augustine, and Pseudo-Dionysius. The ideal "forms" of Plato are placed in the mind of God, specifically in the Logos of John's gospel, who is Christ, God's word and perfect image.[6] The Pauline idea of the creation of all things in Christ is assimilated to the notion that God creates according to the exemplars that exist in the Logos. Humanity is created in the image of God; the perfect image of God is Christ; hence humanity is created in imitation of its ideal form, Christ.

Artistic examples abound. For example, the archivolt of the center bay of the north portal of Chartres cathedral portrays the six days of the creation of the world. The scene of the sixth day shows the familiar biblical image of God (in the form of Christ) molding Adam like a sculptor. But below this, in the scene of the fifth day, as God creates the birds, there is an image of Adam standing behind Christ, having the same facial features, but beardless: the "ideal" Adam in the mind of God, before his physical forming. Several biblical themes are present: Christ is the perfect image of God; God creates the world through and for Christ (Col. 1:15–19; Heb. 1:1–3; Jn. 1:3, 10); Adam is created in God's image (Gen. 1:26–27); Christ is the new and perfect Adam (1 Cor. 15:45–49). These ideas are synthesized in the Patristic theological notion (ultimately derived from Plato's *Timaeus*, 29–30), that Christ as God's "Word" or Wisdom contains the "ideas" or "archetypes" (Philo's word for the Platonic "ideas") of all creatures, and is himself the exemplar for humanity in particular.

On the façade of Orvieto cathedral we see Adam being "sculpted" by God out of the surrounding clay. While in some representations (e.g. Chartres) God's hand physically molds Adam, here God's act is shown by his pointing finger; his "Word" is represented by the scroll he carries in his left hand. God is represented with the features of Christ, and Adam's face is an exact copy. His posture is reminiscent of classical

---

Pera, O.P. (Turin: Marietti, 1950), cap. IV, lect. 5, 349; *Super 1 Tim.*, 6, 3; *Summa Theologica* I, 67, a.1.

[6] See Augustine, *De Diversis Quaestionibus*, q. 46 ("*De ideis*"), PL 40: 29–31. Cf. *De Civitate Dei* 1, 12 c. 26, PL 41: 375; *Expos. in Ev. Io.* tract 1, PL 35: 1387; *De Genesi ad literam*, 60, 61, PL 34: 243–244.

III.3.2 *Adam in the Mind of God before Creation.* Exterior, north portal, Chartres Cathedral, Chartres, France, early thirteenth century. Photo © Jill K. H. Geoffrion, jillgeoffrion.com, praywithjillatchartres.com.

sculptures that were also used as models for Christ in "deposition" scenes.

In the West, the primary theological rationale for sacred art was its didactic function. But in the Eastern church, the place of images approached that of the scriptures and the sacraments. On the philosophical level, theological writers in the Platonic tradition (sometimes

III.3.3 Lorenzo Maitani, *Creation of Adam in the Image of Christ*. Exterior, Orvieto Cathedral, Orvieto, Italy, early fourteenth century. Drawing by the author.

referring to Pseudo-Dionysius) appeal to a kind of "participation" of images in the "form" of their prototypes. In their thinking, this does not mean simply that the image "looks like" the prototype (although icon makers presumed that the miraculous images represent the true features of Christ and Mary). "Likeness" does not mean mere physical similarity, but "representation" of the "hypostasis" or person.[7] Such representation creates presence in both directions. Christ is present to the worshipper, and our worship is present to Christ through the image. Hence images may be given the same worship as the prototype, who may also act through it.

The new availability of Platonic texts in the Renaissance allowed a previously impossible return to the source. Michelangelo's sculpture,

[7] Origen, *Commentaire sur Saint Jean*. Texte Grec. Edited by Cécile Blanc. *Sources Chrétiennes*, vol. 120 (Paris: Éditions du Cerf, 1966), nos. 104, 105, 107, 108, 243-245, pp. 114–116, 180–182.

painting, and poetry all illustrate the Christian-Platonic aesthetic of Ficino. In one of his most famous poems, he writes:

> Non ha l'ottimo artista alcun concetto
> c'un marmo solo in sé non circonscriva
> col suo superchio, e solo a quello arriva
> la man che ubbidisce all'intelletto.

> The best of artists has no creative idea
> that a single marble block does not contain
> within its surface, and that [idea] is attained only
> by the hand that obeys the mind.

The *concetto* is the idea embodied in the work: its "form," which can be released only by a skillful hand directed by the intellect. Michelangelo "liberated" the ideal figures his mind "found" within the potentiality of the stone, by carving away the excess – as Plotinus had said one must do in life.[8]

Plotinus also refers to the body as a prison or a tomb.[9] Ficino reiterates the metaphor: the soul is imprisoned in the jail of the mortal body.[10] Michelangelo's poetry frequently returns to the idea. To cite only two examples:

> Per ritornar là donde venne fora,
> l'immortal forma al tuo carcer terreno
> venne com'angel di pietà sì pieno,
> che sana ogn'intelletto e 'l mondo onora.

> La carne terra, e qui l'ossa mie, prive
> de' lor begli occhi e del leggiadro aspetto,
> fan fede a quel ch'i' fu' grazia e diletto
> in che carcer quaggiù l'anima vive.

> In order to return there whence it came
> The immortal Form came to your earthly prison
> Like the angel so full of mercy
> That heals every mind and gives value to the world.
>
> (Rime, no. 106)

> My flesh, now earth, and my bones, here deprived
> Of their beautiful eyes and lovely appearance

---

[8] *Ennead*, I.6, 9.   [9] *Ennead*, IV.8.3–4; cf. *Phaedo*, 82–83.

[10] Tammy Smithers, "Michelangelo's Artistic Captivity as Mirrored in His Neoplatonic Captives," in Liana De Girolami Cheney and John Hendrix, eds., *Neoplatonic Aesthetics. Music, Literature, & the Visual Arts* (New York: Peter Lang, 2010), 214.

Bear witness, for him to whom I was grace and joy,
To what a prison the soul lives in here below.

(no. 197)

The Platonic view is two-sided: the body is a prison, but also image and mirror of God, as is affirmed in the widely diffused in the various *specula* of the middle ages:

né Dio, suo grazia, mi si mostra altrove
più che 'n alcun leggiadro e mortal velo;
e quel sol amo perch'in lui si specchia.

God graciously shows himself to me
nowhere more than in some lovely mortal form,
and that I love only because in it he is mirrored.

(no. 106)

The famous sculptures of the *prigioni* or *schiavi* picture the process of release of form from matter, symbolizing the freeing of the soul.

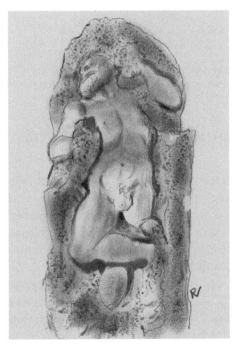

III.3.4 Michelangelo Buonarroti, *I prigioni, schiavo che si ridesta*. Galleria dell'Accademia, Florence, 1525–30. Drawing by the author.

III.3.5 Michelangelo Buonarroti, *I prigioni, schiavo giovane*. Galleria dell'Accademia, Florence, 1525–30. Drawing by the author.

GENERAL CHARACTERISTICS OF CHRISTIAN-PLATONIC AESTHETICS

The Medici Academy provides an example of what an explicitly "Christian-Platonic" aesthetics might be. But even where there is no explicit connection such aesthetics is indirectly relevant to a great deal of Western art. There are a number of characteristics or notions that are associated (although not exclusively) with Christian-Platonic theories and practices of art.

First among these is *mimesis*, "imitation," representation or reference by means of images,[11] in particular visual forms. An artwork may be an "image" in different ways: by portraying some person, thing, or state of affairs; by standing for ideas; by its organizational

---

[11] Cf. Theodor Adorno, *Aesthetics* (Wiley, 2017), loc. 1749–1782.

form; by expressing feelings; by symbolism. Historically the idea of "imaging" has also been applied analogously to other arts – for example by means of "Pythagorean" mathematical proportions in architecture[12] and music,[13] or the musical "rhetoric" of the Baroque period.[14]

Plato in the *Republic* depreciates artistic representations: they are at third remove from reality.[15] But Plotinus "corrected" this attitude: the arts do more than give a re-presentation of vision: "If anyone despises the arts because they produce their works by imitating nature, we must tell him, first, that natural things are imitations too. Then he must know that the arts do not simply imitate what they see, but they run back up to the forming principles from which nature derives; then also that they do a great deal by themselves, and, since they possess beauty, they make up what is defective in things."[16] Renaissance artists interpreted Plato's critique of "imitation" to mean that the artist must not slavishly copy models, but rather use mind and creativity in reproducing them.

Closely related to mimesis, in this context, is *symbolism*. Artistic representation need not simply attempt to show what the eye sees: it can reveal the "form" of things: their meaning or intelligible aspect. In the perspective of Christian Platonism, art is symbolic: visually presented things "stand for" other things and for relations among things: to other things, to ideas and purposes, to the order of the universe, and to being itself.

Symbolism and mimesis are an artistic way of evoking or producing *presence* or *communion*. The representation of a person, scene, or event is meant to bring the viewer (or hearer) into engagement with an absent or invisible reality. In the strongest sense, the presence may go beyond mental recollection to actual encounter – as in the quasi-sacramental view of icons in classical Orthodox theory.

Christian-Platonic aesthetics is grounded in *metaphysical realism*: not in the sense of taking literally the myth of a separate realm of "forms," but

---

[12] Regarding architecture, see John Hendrix, "The Neoplatonic Aesthetics of Leon Battista Alberti," in Liana De Girolami Cheney and John Hendrix, eds., *Neoplatonic Aesthetics. Music, Literature & the Visual Arts* (New York: Peter Lang, 2010).

[13] See for example Férdia J. Stone-Davis, *Musical Beauty. Negotiating the Boundary between Subject and Object* (Eugene, OR: Cascade Books, 2011), 1–10, on Plato and Boethius; John Butt, "Bach's Metaphysics of Music," in John Butt, ed., *The Cambridge Companion to Bach* (Cambridge, UK: Cambridge University Press, 1997), 46–59.

[14] See for example Dietrich Bartel, *Musica Poetica: Musical-Rhetorical Figures in German Baroque Music* (Lincoln: University of Nebraska Press, 1997).

[15] *Republic*, 595a–608b.   [16] *Ennead* V.8.1, 32–38

in the conviction that "the real" is what is known by intelligent judgment.[17] Ideas, concepts, and images convey limited but real knowledge of being: they formulate meanings and values in and of the empirical and interpersonal world, as well as their grounding in the ultimately "Real," God. Reality is fundamentally intelligible; the universe is a "cosmos," an orderly whole, like a work of art.

The cosmos for Christians is created by God. This implies *participation* (Platonic *methexis* [μέθεξις]).[18] Obviously, this term must be taken as an image, with multiple dimensions of meaning. Essentially it signifies that any individual goodness, beauty, truth, does not simply exist in itself, but "takes part" in a community of beings, and, analogously, in being itself. That is: the intelligibility of any finite reality is relational: it is incomplete without reference to others and to its cause, ultimately the absolute. Beings thus have an intrinsic "similarity" to each other and to God.[19] This is the source of the possibility of symbolism and mimesis.

These elements suggest a view of *beauty as a transcendental quality* – a category that, like the true and the good, applies analogously to all beings, in different ways and degrees. Is beauty "objective"? David Hume famously proclaimed the subjectivity of judgments of beauty: "Beauty is no quality in things themselves: It exists merely in the mind which contemplates them; and each mind perceives a different beauty."[20] From a metaphysical point of view, beauty is both objective and subjective. It is possible to think of "beauty" as a "transcendental," ontologically identical with being, truth, goodness. In that case one must regard it as predicated analogously of different beings, at different "levels" and in different ways. If we think of beauty as a transcendental, then we cannot have a proper "concept" of beauty; we can think it only in a dynamic heuristic notion, like truth or goodness. We cannot grasp it in itself, but can name processes that go toward it from many angles and at many levels. On this view – *contra* Hume – beauty is indeed a "quality" of things; but it is a quality of *all* things, and therefore predicated analogously. Hence specific judgments of beauty are subjective in the sense that (like all judgments) they depend on conditions both in the beautiful object and in the perceiving subject.

---

[17] See Bernard Lonergan, *Insight* (New York: Philosophical Library, 1957).

[18] *Phaedo* 102b, *Parmenides* 130e–133d, *Timaeus* 52a.

[19] See Cornelio Fabro, "Participation," in Fabro, *Selected Works of Cornelio Fabro, Volume 1: Selected Articles on Metaphysics and Participation* (IVE Press, 2017). Cf. Adorno, *Aesthetics*, loc. 4091–4098.

[20] David Hume, "Of the Standard of Taste." https://web.csulb.edu/~jvancamp/361r15.html

Such aesthetics is characterized by *humanism* or *personalism*. Although embodied spirit is by its nature close to the bottom of the chain of beings, humans are a microcosm. Created in the image of God, they have the intrinsic capacity to "ascend" to God. While all things "mirror" God, personhood is the most complete reflection of God's self-conscious and free being. In Christianity, through God's condescension in the Incarnation, the image of God takes on a new and essentially higher dimension, and human creativity becomes intimately involved in the "glory" and the "greater glory" of God.

Combined with the sense of presence or encounter, the Renaissance humanist bent gives aesthetics a highly *relational character*, joining it to the Christian moral ideal of love of neighbor. It presents the love of beauty not only as an "ascent," but also as a "horizontal" movement of communion. The light of God not only attracts toward God, but also enlightens the world, so that it becomes visible to us in its reality – including its neediness. This kind of aesthetics can explain and justify communication as an important element in art. Dialogue presupposes not only common language in the narrow sense, but also commitment to reason, truth, value, reciprocity.[21] A corollary to this is a positive stance toward ethical and political engagement as forms of moral beauty – something that is problematic in a consistently relativistic worldview. Art may also be morally didactic, communicating values through narrative, models, and idealized portrayals.

Both the quality of "ascent" toward higher levels of beauty and that of "expansion" toward more inclusive appreciation of other beings, in both their beauty and their neediness, are grounded in the *ekstasis*[22] that is a feature of aesthetic experience: forgetfulness of self and absorption in something other. Nature or the work of art "absorbs" us: it takes us "out of" ourselves, and orients our attention to the thing or work itself. From this we may further attend to what the work indicates or represents, or the feelings it produces. We may stop there, in a kind of communion with the object and feeling of fulness in ourselves; or we may proceed from this to some larger context, a community of being. Iris Murdoch, in dialogue with Plato, explains how such aesthetic experience of transcending the ego in "disinterested" contemplation of art can be the analogy and the basis for moral behavior.[23] A metaphysical view explains why this movement

---

[21] Terry Eagleton, *The Ideology of the Aesthetic* (Oxford: Basil Blackwell, 1990), 405.

[22] See Stone-Davis, *Musical Beauty*, 161, loc. 5211.

[23] Iris Murdoch, *The Fire and the Sun. Why Plato Banned the Artists* (Oxford: Clarendon Press, 1977), 36, 76–86.

beyond the ego is possible, rational, and good. It relates the aesthetic to the moral, the scientific, the philosophical, and the spiritual: from aesthetic absorption to wonder, awe, and worship.

Finally, we should bear in mind that Christian-Platonic aesthetics is not only *about* art, feeling, and beauty: it is itself an artwork, appealing to both intellect and affect – often using images and metaphors like "light" and "ascent." At the same time, it is also a fluid mixture of theory, metaphysics, anthropology, and cosmology.

CONTEMPORARY ISSUES

The modern period, and postmodernity even more, has challenged or rejected all of these grounds of the Christian-Platonic aesthetics of the Middle Ages and the Renaissance. The most obvious challenge to Christian Platonism is the widespread philosophical (and popular?) rejection of a metaphysical worldview, including the notion of God. A critical expression of the rejection of a Christian-Platonic viewpoint finds its epitome in the thought of Friedrich Nietzsche. His writings also explicitly address the question of aesthetics in the light of a de-Platonized worldview. Nietzsche's earlier writings contain many positive references to Plato. But by the end of his life, he expresses virulent hostility to both "Platonism" and Christianity, which he calls "Platonism for the people."[24] Indeed, he can say that the main point of his philosophy – and of every future philosophy – is the overturning of the metaphysical viewpoint he associates with Plato and Christianity.[25] Nietzsche's thought is not coherent; and he is more a cultural critic than a philosopher. But there are philosophical themes that recur in his critique. His crucial point is that for Platonism this world is not real: it consists only of images of the ideal ("real") world. For example: "The great concepts 'good' and 'fair' will be detached from the conditions to which they belong: and as liberated 'ideas' objects of dialectics. One seeks a truth behind them, they are taken as entities or as a sign of entities: to invent a world where they are at

---

[24] "Christentum ist Platonismus fürs 'Volk'." Friedrich Nietzsche, *Jenseits von Gut und Böse,* in *Friedrich Nietzsche: Sämtliche Werke (Kommentiert) mit verlinktem Inhaltsverzeichnis* (2013), loc. 29152.

[25] Nietzsche, *Menschliches, Allzumenschliches. Ein Buch für freie Geister,* in *Sämtliche Werke* (2013), loc. 7557; *Die fröliche Wissenschaft,* in ibid, loc. 23177; *Der Antichrist. Fluch auf das Christentum,* in ibid, loc. 39230. Cf. Gilles Deleuze, *Logique du sens* (Critique) (Minuit, 2014), loc. 5198.

home, where they come from ... In sum, the mischief is at a peak already in Plato."[26]

Hence Platonism, like Christianity, is "nihilistic"[27] in that it devalues and denies earthly life – which is all there is – and the "will to power," which is the basis of higher life. Moreover, Platonism and Christianity proclaim a desire for truth and intelligibility. But for Nietzsche, at least at his most extreme, neither the world nor the self is ultimately intelligible; and neither possesses any intrinsic value beyond our affirming their existence in a sheer act of will. We are faced with meaningless chaos, without and within.[28] Not only metaphysics, but also science is based on the fallacy of intelligibility. Hence we need illusion. That is the purpose of art[29] – as Schopenhauer had already said. "Art makes the sight of life bearable."[30] "We need art all the more because we have seen reality."[31] Art is the means of escape from despair; it gives us a will and power to live every aspect of existence, even the harshest and cruelest.[32] Nietzsche therefore adopts what he calls an "aesthetic" attitude to life. Life can only be "justified" (*gerechtfertigt*) as an "aesthetic phenomenon."[33]

Art and nothing but art! It is the great enabler of life, the great seducer to life, the great stimulant of life.

Art as the only superior counterforce to all will to denial of life, it is the anti-Christian, anti-Buddhist, anti-Nihilistic par excellence.[34]

Because there is no objective standard of truth or goodness, values must be created. "On such a view of truth, truth works not by correspondence or

---

[26] Nietzsche, *Nietzsche's Last Notebooks 1888*. Translated by Daniel Fidel Ferrer. https://philarchive.org/archive/FERNLN, 14 [111], p. 55.

[27] Nietzsche's use of the term "nihilism" is ambivalent. At times it means the rejection of traditional metaphysical values; at times it is used pejoratively for precisely those values. For a survey of the history of the term, see Meidert Evers, *The Aesthetic Revolution in Germany: 1750–1950. From Winckelmann to Nietzsche, from Nietzsche to Beckmann* (Peter Lang, 2017). Kindle edition. 155.

[28] "Die Gesamtcharakter der Welt ist ... in alle Ewigkeit Chaos ... " Nietzsche, *Scherz, List, und Rache*, in *Sämtliche Werke*, loc. 21761; cf. *Also Sprach Zarathustra*, in ibid, loc. 30975.

[29] Nietzsche, *Die Geburt der Tragödie aus dem Geiste der Musik*, in *Sämtliche Werke*, loc. 1566; cf. loc. 1909.

[30] Nietzsche, *Aus der Seele der Künstler*, in *Sämtliche Werke*, loc. 8898.

[31] Nietzsche, *Richard Wagner in Bayreuth*, in *Sämtliche Werke*, loc. 6617.

[32] Nietzsche, *Aus der Seele der Künstler*, in *Sämtliche Werke*, loc. 9444.

[33] Nietzsche, *Die Geburt der Tragödie, Sämtliche Werke*, loc. 379.

[34] Nietzsche, *Nietzsche's Last Notebooks 1888*, 17 [3] p. 188

representation, but by opening nature to language and thought, an event much closer to art on this view than science."[35]

Nietzsche is thus the starting point for much modern and postmodern European philosophical aesthetic thinking, from Heidegger to Deleuze. "Aesthetics" becomes not simply the study of the arts, but the study of human life itself as "art." Nietzsche's philosophy pushes to its ultimate conclusion the Kantian view of the aesthetic as autotelic: "a form of value grounded entirely in itself ... For what the work of art imitates in its very pointlessness ... is nothing less than human existence itself, which ... requires no rationale beyond its own self-delight."[36] For the Nietzschean *Übermensch*, the heroic-aesthetic genius of the new age, art becomes the affirmation of the will to "power" – self-affirming joy in existence – for its own sake. "Art" in the traditional sense may be the means of doing so; or may have little to do with it. (Nietzsche himself was very interested in poetry, drama, and music, especially Wagner's, but seems to have had little concrete knowledge or appreciation of other arts.)

Heidegger could still speak of beauty as the light of truth shining into the artwork: "Beauty is one way in which truth essentially occurs as unconcealment."[37] But in much of postmodern Western aesthetics, the loss of an objective standard of beauty leads to rejection of – or lack of interest in – the notion of "beauty" itself. (Adorno writes, "unless we come directly from the countryside, we would all resist equating the experience of art with the experience of beauty."[38]) In this perspective, insofar as the term "beauty" has any meaning, it is totally subjective and/or ideologically determined. Art and aesthetic theory frequently turn either to decoration or to the "sublime." The purpose of the "sublime" artwork is to reveal being: not as intelligible or good or pleasing, but as the pure (and terrifying) facticity of existence faced with nonexistence.

Contemporary poststructuralist aesthetics also involves the devaluation of art as mimesis or "representation." In part, this is due to developments in art itself, in particular the movements of expression-

---

[35] Stephen Ross, ed., "Introduction," in *Art and Its Significance: An Anthology of Aesthetic Theory* (State University of New York Press, 2010), loc. 302.

[36] Eagleton, *Ideology*, 65.

[37] Martin Heidegger, "The Origin of the Work of Art," in Heidegger, *Basic Writings*, ed. David Farrell Krell (San Francisco: Harper, 1993), 181.

[38] Adorno, *Aesthetics*, loc. 2386.

ism and abstraction.[39] Already in 1925 Fernand Léger spoke of "the error of imitation," and claimed that "the Renaissance ... combined two major errors: the spirit of imitation and the copy of the beautiful subject."[40] Kasimir Malevich, in a 1927 essay, writes that "an objective representation, having objectivity as its aim, is something which, as such, has nothing to do with art ... Art ... wants to have nothing further to do with the object, as such, and believes that it can exist, in and for itself, without 'things.'"[41]

However, absence of physical realism in art does not preclude either mimesis or transcendence. Abstract art, although nonrepresentational, can be mimetic in other ways. Kandinsky's foundational treatise on abstraction, *Concerning the Spiritual in Art*,[42] explained that abstraction was meant to represent emotional states and spiritual realities directly evoked by colors and shapes. Mondrian, like Kandinsky, thought that there were "laws" of the relationship of painted abstract forms to "reality."[43] Many early abstract artists were influenced by Theosophy, which espoused a quasi-Platonic notion of ideas and included Plato in its pantheon of esoteric masters.

In postmodern aesthetics, there is a more philosophical reason alleged for nonrepresentation in art: there is nothing to represent. The artwork is not a "copy" or "image" of anything; it does not re-present another reality or attempt to bring about encounter with a "presence" of anything other than itself. Gilles Deleuze explains that the "Platonic" view of art was based on a world conceived as a series of representations, in which there is a distinction between reality (or essence) and appearance, model and copy. The overturning of Platonism means the subversion of that entire worldview. In this subversive view, the artwork is a "positive power that denies both the original and the copy, both the model and its reproduction."[44] Art as

---

[39] Eric Fernie, *Art History and its Methods: A Critical Anthology* (London: Phaidon Press, 1995), 15–16, quoted in Susan Manghani, Arthur Piper, and John Simons eds., *Images: A Reader* (Los Angeles: Sage Publications, 2010), 83.

[40] Fernand Léger, "The Machine Aesthetic: Geometric Order and Truth," in *Modern Artists on Art: Second Enlarged Edition (Dover Fine Art, History of Art)*, ed. Robert L. Herbert (Dover Publications, 2012), 93–101 at p. 98, loc. 1956.

[41] Kasimir Malevich, "Suprematism," in *Modern Artists*, ed. Robert L. Herbert, 116–124 at p. 117, loc. 2291, 119 loc. 2325.

[42] Wassily Kandinsky, *Concerning the Spiritual in Art*, trans. Michael T. H. Sadler (New York: Dover, 2012).

[43] See Piet Mondrian, "Plastic Art and Pure Plastic Art," in *Modern Artists*, ed. Robert L. Herbert, 151–165 at p. 156, loc. 3055.

[44] Deleuze, *Logique du sens*, loc. 5373–5374.

reproduction, says Deleuze, presumes an ordered, intelligible world. But Nietzsche's myth of the "eternal return" symbolizes a world that is an unintelligible and unconquerable chaos. Art is the positive and joyous affirmation of chaos. "In place of the coherence of representation, the eternal return substitutes something completely different: its own *chao-errance*."[45] The view of art as representation devalues the artwork, because its only meaning is found in imitation, in pointing beyond itself to something else. But the postmodern artwork points to nothing: its value is in itself and in what it does. "Art's old natural tendency to 'point beyond' is variously and ingeniously challenged by artists more conscious of their prophetic role. The object is not 'pictured', it is, just as itself, presented: the kettle, the chair, the Coca-Cola can, the pile of bricks, the revoltingly contingent."[46]

The critique of mimesis is thus also tied to the de-mythologization of the world and the removal of any transcendent reference, "a removal which analyses (deconstructs) the familiar concepts of individual object, individual person, individual meaning."[47] To this extent the postmodern overturning of the Christian-Platonic metaphysical worldview implies a rejection not only of its theism, but also of its humanism and its confidence in knowledge, including scientific knowledge.

It is of course not possible in this space to refute or to criticize the post-Nietzschean view,[48] either as a whole or in its implications for aesthetics; my only purpose here is to offer a coherent alternative vision that calls for more complete justification elsewhere. What kind of aesthetics can a metaphysical philosophy offer to the contemporary world?

THE METAPHYSICAL ALTERNATIVE

In Pasternak's novel *Doctor Zhivago* the protagonist – a physician who is also a poet –writes a note to himself: "he once again verified and noted that art always serves beauty, and beauty is delight in the possession of form, and form is the organic key to life, [since] every living thing must

---

[45] Ibid, loc. 5417–5420. Deleuze's invented word *chao-errance* is a pun on "coherence," but replaces the "coming together" of coherence with the "errance" or dispersion of chaos.

[46] Murdoch, *Metaphysics as a Guide to Morals* (Penguin Publishing Group, 1994), p. 5, loc. 161.

[47] Ibid, p. 5, loc. 154.

[48] See the critique of postmodernism in Paul Crowther, *Phenomenology of the Visual Arts (Even the Frame)* (Stanford, CA: Stanford University Press, 2009).

possess form in order to exist; and in that way art, including tragedy, always recounts the joy of existence."[49]

Contemporary aesthetic theory stresses that art does not always serve beauty; indeed, much postmodern writing tends to avoid the term "beauty" altogether. Moreover, even in traditional understandings it is clear that art can have many expressive and communicative purposes besides the creation of beauty. However, it also seems clear that both nature and art provide experiences that people classify with that word. In Zhivago's (and also Thomas Aquinas')[50] view, what is crucial to such experiences is "delight in form," the ordering principle that is intrinsic to life. We might expand the insight in a "Platonic" way: form is crucial not only to organic life, but also to intellectual life. Hence the essence of the experience of beauty is found in the implicit affirmation of the goodness and joy of existence insofar as it implies an order, an intelligibility, a meaning. In this perspective the work of art necessarily includes a "reference" beyond itself. Contrary to postmodern criticism, this does not devalue the artwork itself. Quite the opposite: it sees in the work a double significance: *both* as an encounter with "being" instanced in itself *and* as an "image" or representation of some aspect of "being" beyond itself.

This kind of experience of the beautiful reveals that the rejoicing in existence (and in the "form" that makes it possible as organized experience or intellection) is tied to an acute awareness of finitude: the gratuitous joy of beauty and its delight in form arise precisely out of contrast with the abyss of nonbeing and nonintelligibility experienced in the fragile, threatened character of human existence, which need not exist at all (this recognition of "absence" of reason-to-be is behind the experience of the "sublime" that postmodern aesthetics emphasizes). The contrast with a radical negation reveals why beauty, as delight in form, is ultimately coextensive with all existence – that is, with all that has "form" and being and is thus over against nothingness. (Nietzsche's defiant aesthetic joy in "chaos" is – as he admits – a creation or projection of "form"; but for him it is an arbitrary and groundless projection). It also explains why the experience of beauty, even if it is characterized as a "recounting" of the

---

[49] Boris Pasternak, Доктор Живаго (Paris: Société d'Édition et d'Impression Mondiale, 1959), pp. 527–528. [English translation: *Doctor Zhivago*, trans. Max Hayward and Manya Harari (New York: New American Library, 1958).] Much of the content of the following section may be found in expanded form in the fourth chapter of my *Theological Aesthetics* (New York: Oxford University Press, 1999).

[50] Aquinas, *Commentarium de Divinis Nominibus*, lect. VI; ST Ia, q. 5, 4, 1m.

joy of existence, as Pasternak says, can have many different emotional shadings (including sadness) and ethical/aesthetic modes (including tragedy).

This observation immediately confronts us with the variety of aesthetic experiences. "Delight" in existence can be simple sensual pleasure. But at least some kinds of aesthetic experience do not remain on a merely sensible level. To speak of "beauty" implies that there is a dimension of aesthetic experience that goes beyond the sort of pleasure that we (apparently) share with the higher animals. Such an experience begins as sensation, but also it involves a spiritual reaction akin to the "wonder" that Aristotle claims is the beginning of philosophy;[51] and it invites the person to an intelligent and free act in which the self recognizes and is "given over" to the joy of existence, or allows itself to be "grasped" by it, in its universal extension.

The view of beauty as a "transcendental" is presumed in much of the Christian-Platonic tradition. But alternatively, one may metaphysically think of beauty as a particular kind of good, present in some things and not in others. Since every finite good is relative and relational, there must be different kinds and degrees of beauty, all of which "refer" to an ultimate absolute Good that is never exhausted by any limited instance. Even if "beauty" is conceived narrowly as a characteristic of certain subjective sensations, such experiences are caused by our finding elements like harmony, order, and form, which are related to unity, intelligibility, and goodness. There can be wide variety in individuals' capacities and sensitivities to such factors, and hence in "taste." Aesthetics is then about taste, about the "health" of our desires, and about the ways these desires correspond (or fail to correspond) to our capacities: physical, psychic, intellectual, and moral. There can be spiritual as well as physical beauty, and they may sometimes be in tension. Something can be aesthetically pleasing on one level, but not on another; something can be aesthetically pleasing in one culture or to one person, and not another. There are some objective limits imposed by our biology and psyche. But even simply at the level of pleasure, there is a common element to experiences of beauty: the

---

[51] "Schönheit – das ist das offen zutage liegende und zu erfahrbarer Realität gewordene Wunder, daß es solch Beglückendes, Hinreißendes oder still Umgebendes überhaupt gibt. Diesem vor Augen liegenden Wunder entspricht auf unserer Seite das Staunen, das sich in den Dank vollendet." Günter Pöltner, "Die Erfahrung des Schönen," in Günter Pöltner and Helmuth Vetter, eds., *Theologie und Ästhetik* (Vienna, Freiburg, Basel: Herder, 1985), 16.

dynamism toward that element of being we anticipate as "value," and that we experience subjectively as being-well.

Because it includes the anticipation of something "more," the delight of the beautiful can at the same time frequently be poignant, perhaps even to the point of bordering on pain: it is accompanied by the realization of finitude, with its threat of annihilation. At the same time, it expresses the spirit's rebellion against non-being and its acute, aching longing to be.[52] Hence the beautiful puts us in contact also with our fear of what transcends our present horizon. Rilke writes in his first Duino elegy:

> Beauty is nothing
> but the beginning of Terror,[53] that we're still just able to bear,
> and we are so in awe of it because it serenely disdains
> to annihilate us.[54]

But even in the face of existential anxiety and suffering, beauty testifies to the more fundamental nature of joy; and joy desires eternity. Nietzsche himself wrote in the famous *Mitternachtslied* in *Also Sprach Zarathustra*:

> O Mensch! Gib acht!
> Was spricht die tiefe Mitternacht?
> "Ich schlief, ich schlief –,
> Aus tiefem Traum bin ich erwacht: –
> Die Welt ist tief,
> Und tiefer als der Tag gedacht.
> Tief ist ihr Weh –,
> Lust – tiefer noch als Herzeleid:
> Weh spricht: Vergeh!
> Doch alle Lust will Ewigkeit –,
> – will tiefe, tiefe Ewigkeit!"

> O Man! Take heed!
> What says the deep midnight?
> "I slept, I slept –
> from a deep dream have I been awakened –
> The world is deep,
> and deeper than day can grasp.
> Deep is its sorrow –

---

[52] See Miguel de Unamuno, *Del Sentimiento Tragico de la Vida* (Madrid: Espasa-Calpe, 1966), 36–49.

[53] Cf. *Phaedrus* 250d and Adorno, *Aesthetics*, loc. 1400, 1572.

[54] "das Schöne ist nichts/ als des Schrecklichen Anfang, den wir noch gerade ertragen,/ und wir bewundern es so, weil es gelassen verschmäht,/ uns zu zerstören." Rainer Maria Rilke, *The Selected Poetry of Rainer Maria Rilke*, ed. and trans. Stephen Mitchell (New York: Vintage Books, 1984), 198–199.

> Joy – deeper still than heartache:
> Sorrow says: Begone!
> but all joy desires eternity –
> – desires deep, deep eternity!"[55]

Where art is seen as centered on beauty and "form," it can be regarded as an expression of appreciation of existence. And the ability to delight in existence – even in its finitude and lacks – points to a fundamental trust in goodness, rationality, and meaning. As Nietzsche's celebration of chaos rests on atheism and on the rejection of both metaphysics and science, so a trust in the goodness and rationality of existence points to God, at least as a question.

However, art can also serve other purposes than the creation, discovery, representation, or celebration of beauty. It may be a means of communication or of self-expression; it may be simply decorative. In its origins modern art was often referential, even though it was nonrepresentational. But much of the "art world" after Kandinsky and Mondrian has renounced for art any goal outside itself. The artwork may make no statement beyond its own existence, leaving it to the viewer to react with joy, or wonder, or puzzlement, or indifference. But the artwork's declaration of its own existence may have metaphysical significance, for it may evoke the experience of "the sublime." Even in the absence of the attraction of beauty, the experience of something "being there" may confront the viewer with his or her contingent "being there," and raise the question of being as opposed to nothingness. The sublime poses the same questions and allows the same process as the beautiful, the true, or the good: from particular existence to my consciousness of it; to my own conscious existence; to wonder; to its source.

Understanding art in the metaphysical context associated with Christianity and with the Platonic tradition seems to have certain intellectual advantages. It allows a very broad understanding of what "art" is. It sees a connection of art with science, knowledge, truth, and morality, because all of these are aspects of the prehension of Being itself. It finds resonances in the art and theory of non-Western cultures (Indian and Chinese aesthetics in particular).

Art may be grounded in beauty, in "sublimity," in expression, or in communication. All of these are in turn grounded in being, seen as ultimately "personal" and hence calling for human intellectual and moral response. Representational or descriptive art seems particularly oriented to the personal. For the artist, it is a way of "appropriating"

---

[55] Nietzsche, *Also Sprach Zarathustra* in *Sämtliche Werke*, loc. 29080.

the object, uniting with it.[56] It can serve that purpose for the viewer or hearer as well. It can also be a form of memory. It permits us not merely to keep and repeat experiences, but also to regard them in another way, through other eyes or at another time. Pictorial or descriptive art teaches us to attend and to see. Even the simple copying or repetition of another's work can be valued as "performance," as in music. As we have remarked earlier, mimesis can exist in many different forms, not merely in physical re-presentation. At the same time, mimesis is not necessary to art. More fundamental is the "sacramentality" of all things: that is, the possibility of things, when viewed by a self-conscious subject, to "refer" to a larger community of things and also to something more ultimate. Far from devaluing the artwork in itself, the metaphysical view gives real (not merely invented or conventional) value to each individual occurrence of being – even if it is a "copy" of something else, but yet more if it is creative. Of course, reference to an absolute relativizes everything that is finite. But precisely because no finite instance of beauty or goodness is Beauty or Goodness itself, there is are infinite ways of being beautiful and good, each having intrinsic value in its concrete being (cf. the Scotists' *haecceitas* and the Buddhist *tathata*) *as well as* in its referentiality: there is no dichotomy. In the Christian metaphysical view, the facticity of the thing reveals the contingency of existence as a reason for awe and joy: being appears as a gift. Creativity – human as well as divine – is an act of love.

Such a metaphysical aesthetics has systematic intellectual value: it allows the world to appear as a cosmos; it proclaims a basic intelligibility that unites art and science; it gives an ultimate sense to both life and art, based on a fundamental trust in existence. I have argued at length elsewhere that its metaphysical justification is implicit in aesthetic experience itself, and can be made critically explicit in transcendental examination of both art and thought.[57] But for many, the rationality of trust in the fundamental beauty of existence can already be known intuitively in the very act of living an ecstatic life.

Bibliography

Adorno, Theodor. *Aesthetics*. Wiley, 2017.
Aquinas, Thomas. *In librum Beati Dionysii De divinis nominibus expositio*. Ed. Ceslai Pera, O.P. Turin: Marietti, 1950.

---

[56] See Adorno, *Aesthetics*, loc. 1782–1789.
[57] See Viladesau, *Theological Aesthetics*, 103–140.

Augustine of Hippo. *De Civitate Dei*. PL 41: 375.
  De Diversis Quaestionibus. PL 40: 29–31.
  De Genesi ad literam. PL 34: 243–244.
  Expositio in Ev. Io. PL 35: 1387
Bartel, Dietrich. *Musica Poetica: Musical-Rhetorical Figures in German Baroque Music*. Lincoln: University of Nebraska Press, 1997.
Belting, Hans. *Likeness and Presence: A History of the Image before the Era of Art*. Translated by Edmund Jephcott. Chicago: University of Chicago Press, 1997.
Buonarroti, Michelangelo (Michelangelo di Lodovico Buonarroti Simoni). *Rime*. Bauer Books, 2018.
Butt, John. "Bach's Metaphysics of Music." In *The Cambridge Companion to Bach*, ed. John Butt, 46–59. Cambridge: Cambridge University Press, 1997.
Crowther, Paul. *Phenomenology of the Visual Arts (Even the Frame)*. Stanford, CA: Stanford University Press, 2009.
Dell'Acqua, Francesca. "The Authority of the Pseudo-Dionysius and Suger of Saint-Denis." *Studi Medievali* 55, no. 1 (January 2014): 189–213.
Deleuze, Gilles. *Logique du sens (Critique)*. Minuit, 2014.
Dionysius Areopagitus. Περὶ Θειῶν Ὀνόματων (*De Divinis Nominibus*). Migne, *Patrologia Graecae*, vol. 3, 586–996.
  Περὶ τῆς Ὀυρανίας Ἱεραρχίας (*De Coelesti Hierarchia*). Migne, *Patrologia Graecae*, vol. 3, 119–369.
Eagleton, Terry. *The Ideology of the Aesthetic*. Oxford: Basil Blackwell, 1990.
Evers, Meidert. *The Aesthetic Revolution in Germany: 1750–1950. From Winckelmann to Nietzsche, from Nietzsche to Beckmann*. Peter Lang, 2017.
Fabro, Cornelio. "Participation." In *Selected Works of Cornelio Fabro, Volume 1: Selected Articles on Metaphysics and Participation*. IVE Press, 2017.
Fernie, Eric. *Art History and its Methods: A Critical Anthology*. London: Phaidon Press, 1995.
Ficino, Marsilio. *Commentarium in Convivium Platonis de Amore*. Edited by Pierre Laurens. Paris: Les Belles Lettres, 2012.
Heidegger, Martin. *Basic Writings*. Edited by David Farrell Krell. San Francisco: Harper, 1993.
Hendrix, John. "The Neoplatonic Aesthetics of Leon Battista Alberti." In *Neoplatonic Aesthetics. Music, Literature & the Visual Arts*, ed. Liana De Girolami Cheney and John Hendrix. New York: Peter Lang, 2010.
Kandinsky, Wassily. *Concerning the Spiritual in Art*. Trans. Michael T. H. Sadler. New York: Dover, 2012.
Léger, Fernand. "The Machine Aesthetic: Geometric Order and Truth." In *Modern Artists on Art: Second Enlarged Edition (Dover Fine Art, History of Art)*, ed. Robert L. Herbert, 93–101. Dover Publications, 2012.
Lonergan, Bernard. *Insight*. New York: Philosophical Library, 1957.
Malevich, Kasimir. "Suprematism." In *Modern Artists on Art: Second Enlarged Edition (Dover Fine Art, History of Art)*, ed. Robert L. Herbert, 116–124. Dover Publications, 2012.
Manghani, Susan, Arthur Piper, and John Simons, eds. *Images: A Reader*. Los Angeles: Sage Publications, 2010.

Mondrian, Piet. "Plastic Art and Pure Plastic Art." In *Modern Artists on Art: Second Enlarged Edition (Dover Fine Art, History of Art)*, ed. Robert L. Herbert, 151–165. Dover Publications, 2012.

Murdoch, Iris. *The Fire and the Sun. Why Plato Banned the Artists.* Oxford: Clarendon Press, 1977.

Metaphysics as a Guide to Morals (Penguin Philosophy). Penguin Publishing Group, 1994. Kindle edition.

Nietzsche, Friedrich. *Nietzsche's Last Notebooks 1888.* Translated by Daniel Fidel Ferrer. https://philarchive.org/archive/FERNLN.

Sämtliche Werke (Kommentiert) mit verlinktem Inhaltsverzeichnis, 2013.

Origen. *Commentaire sur Saint Jean.* Texte Grec, edited by Cécile Blanc. *Sources Chrétiennes*, vol. 120. Paris: Les Éditions du Cerf, 1966.

Pasternak, Boris. *Doctor Zhivago.* Translated by Max Hayward and Manya Harari. New York: New American Library, 1958.

Pöltner, Günter. "Die Erfahrung des Schönen." In *Theologie und Ästhetik*, ed. Günter Pöltner and Helmuth Vetter. Vienna, Freiburg, Basel: Herder, 1985.

Rilke, Rainer Maria. *The Selected Poetry of Rainer Maria Rilke.* Edited and translated by Stephen Mitchell. New York: Vintage Books, 1984.

Ross, Stephen, ed. *Art and Its Significance: An Anthology of Aesthetic Theory.* State University of New York Press, 2010.

Smithers, Tammy. "Michelangelo's Artistic Captivity as Mirrored in His Neoplatonic Captives." In *Neoplatonic Aesthetics. Music, Literature, & the Visual Arts*, ed. Liana De Girolami Cheney and John Hendrix. New York: Peter Lang, 2010.

Suger of Saint-Denis. *Œuvres Complètes.* Edited by A. Lecoy de la Marche. Paris: Jules Renouard, 1867.

Stone-Davis, Férdia J. *Musical Beauty. Negotiating the Boundary between Subject and Object.* Eugene, OR: Cascade Books, 2011.

Theodore the Studite. *On the Holy Icons.* Translated by Catherine P. Roth. Crestwood, NY: St. Vladimir's Seminary Press, 2001.

Unamuno, Miguel de. *Del Sentimiento Tragico de la Vida.* Madrid: Espasa-Calpe, 1966.

Viladesau, Richard. *Theological Aesthetics.* New York, Oxford University Press, 1999.

3.4

Value, Dualism, and Materialism

Charles Taliaferro

Christian Platonism has been contested from the mid-twentieth to the early twenty-first centuries on many fronts. There has been a serious non-Platonic response to the *Euthyphro* dilemma; some philosophers contend that things (persons, events, acts) are good because or when we desire them (or care about them) rather than we should desire those things that are good. There has been a serious movement to establish a radical form of materialism, sometimes called physicalism in a way that undermines the primacy of consciousness.[1] This chapter addresses both of these areas, because of their central importance to Platonic tradition. If values are only a reflection of our desires and if physicalism undermines the reality of consciousness (mind, self, soul), then many of the Platonic tenets about the soul, what matters, love and desire are undermined. A third concern of this chapter is a challenge to Christian Platonism from within: some prominent Christian philosophers have charged that a nonreductive materialist account of human persons is in greater accord with traditional Christian theology than Christian Platonism which advances a dualist or nonmaterialist account of persons. This third concern will be addressed more briefly than the first two. While the focus of this chapter is on these three areas it should be noted that philosophers have contested Platonism on other fronts. And such challenges have been met by some Platonists or allies of Platonism.

---

[1] In this chapter, these terms will be treated synonymously. In the literature, sometimes 'physicalism' is the preferred term as 'materialism' suggests all is matter whereas most philosophers wish to recognize energy, in addition to matter.

Among the other areas where Platonism is challenged, Willard Van Orman Quine and Donald Davidson, among others, have advanced linguistic accounts of truth, and Hilary Putnam has defended the notion that truth is always perspectival, dependent upon conceptual schemes. Such positions seem entirely at odds with our commonsense understanding that truth does not depend on language, perspectives, and concepts. Arguably, there were truths about the cosmos long before the emergence of humans with our languages, and there will be truths about us after we have perished in this cosmos. Some philosophers have proclaimed that the Platonic search for beauty, truth, and goodness is dead (Raymond Geuss) and that we should treat reason along the lines of the Sophists (Richard Rorty) whom Plato and Socrates opposed. Fortunately there have been formidable philosophers who have championed Platonic views of beauty, truth, and goodness (Elaine Scary) and Rorty's "liberal ironism" seems to have few followers today as philosophers now seek to nonironically combat racism, sexism, and economic oppression, and raise awareness of the dangers of climate change. Nominalism in mathematics and metaphysics has had its defenders (Quine, Goodman) and its realist Platonist respondents (Roderick Chisholm). In all, a contemporary Christian Platonist would have much to oppose in contemporary philosophy, taking up all five of the Platonic tenets Lloyd Gerson has identified as key to Platonism: antimaterialism, antimechanism, antinominalism, antirelativism, and antiscepticism.[2]

Rather than attempt to cover such a huge range of issues that the friends and foes of Platonism are engaging (a warfare between the gods and giants as in Plato's *Sophist*), the focus will be on the case for and against a Platonic view of values, a Platonic response to the current case for radical, reductive forms of physicalism, and a Christian Platonic response to Christian materialists.

PLATONIC VALUES

Perhaps the best known thesis in Platonic tradition going back to Plato himself is that the good should be loved because it is good, rather than something (an act or event or thing) becomes good because it is loved (by the gods or God or ourselves). From a Platonic point of view, when you love another person, you love them for the value or worth they have intrinsically (or for their own sake). As Fritz Wenisch (paraphrasing

---

[2] Lloyd Gerson, *From Plato to Platonism* (Ithaca: Cornell University Press, 2013).

Dietrich von Hildebrand) explains, "Love for another human is a response motivated by the other's intrinsic preciousness, by regarding her as what she is in herself rather than viewing her from the perspective of personal gain."[3] In what follows let us consider Harry Frankfurt's contrary position. According to Frankfurt, the source of values is to be found in what persons care about:

It is by caring about things that we infuse the world with importance. This provides us with stable ambitions and concerns; it marks our interests and goals. The importance that our caring creates for us defines the framework of standards and aims in terms of which we endeavour to conduct our lives. A person who cares about something is guided, as his attitudes and his actions are shaped, by his continuing interest in it. Insofar as he does care about certain things, this determines how he thinks it important for him to conduct his life. The totality of the various things that a person cares about – together with his ordering of how important to him they are – effectively specifies his answer to the question of how to live.[4]

Unlike a Platonist who responds to a value that has an independent claim on her affection and allegiance, Frankfurt sees persons as the ones who infuse the world with importance (or at least importance for those of us doing the caring).

Consider two questions at the outset before offering a further investigation into Frankfurt's position. First, to what extent is an appeal to care explanatory? Arguably, Frankfurt's position seems to come close to a tautology. He proposes that our standards, aims, attitudes, actions, and conduct are the results of our caring and what we care about, but in a sense isn't the reference to our standards, and so on, simply a reference to different ways of caring? Imagine this exchange:

JANE: I am looking for a way to get my son to Ireland that meets the highest standards of safety I can afford.
JOHN: Why do you care about spending the most you can afford to get your son to Ireland?
JANE: Because I care about my son.

There might be more reasons that are in the offing. Frankfurt allows that there may be reasons (or causes) for our caring that have a biological, evolutionary background, and Jane may have reasons for pouring more money into her son's transport than into getting him a good haircut. But

---

[3] Fritz Wenisch, Review of *The Nature of Love* by Dietrich von Hildebrand, *Faith and Philosophy*, 29, no. 1 (2012), 118–122 at p. 119.

[4] Harry Frankfurt, *The Reasons of Love* (Princeton: Princeton University Press, 2006), 23.

once care is in place ("I care for my son") and we forego appealing to the value of the son, it seems as though caring itself is basic and not further explained in terms of justification. So, evolutionary biology may partially account for why you love your children, but that does not amount to an account of why your love is *justified* or *warranted* or *good*.

Let us continue to press home the importance of having reasons for caring, but let us put the matter in terms of a related question: casting aside whether Frankfurt's position amounts to an explanatory tautology (we care because we care), let us consider the extent to which Frankfurt's appeal to care matches our prephilosophical (everyday or intuitive) understanding of care and value.

What seems to be missing in Frankfurt's account is concern with what a person *should* care about. In the passage cited above, Frankfurt refers to "his answer to the question of how to live." Evidently, the answer to the question "how should you live?" for any individual will lie in what the individual cares about. If an individual has no cares (consider the central character in Graham Greene's *A Burnt-Out Case*), presumably there is no answer for that individual. In effect, Frankfurt defends this position by contending that an appeal to some kind of independent standard about how to live is problematic.

Frankfurt thinks that appeal to how we should live faces a problem of circularity. This objection is cited at length:

In order to carry out a rational evaluation of some way of living, a person must first know what evaluative criteria to employ and how to employ them. He needs to know what considerations count in favour of choosing to live in one way rather than in another, what considerations count against, and the relative weights of each. For instance, it must be clear to him how to evaluate the fact that a certain way of living leads more than others (or less than others) to personal satisfaction, to pleasure, to power, to glory, to creativity, to spiritual depth, to a harmonious relationship with the precepts of religion, to conformity with the requirements of morality, and so on.

The trouble here is a rather obvious sort of circularity. In order for a person to be able even to conceive and to initiate an inquiry into how to live, he must already have settled upon the judgments at which the inquiry aims. Identifying the question of how one should live – that is, understanding just what question it is and just how to go about answering it – requires that one specify the criteria that are to be employed in evaluating various ways of living. Identifying the question is, indeed, tantamount to specifying those criteria: what the question asks is, precisely, what way of living best satisfies them. But identifying the criteria to be employed in evaluating various ways of living is also tantamount to providing an answer to the question of how to live, for the answer to this question is simply that one should live in the way that best satisfies whatever criteria are to be employed for evaluating lives.[5]

Just as it was suggested earlier that Frankfurt's position seems close to a tautology in the wake of the question "why care?" ("we care because we care"), perhaps those of us who wish to have justificatory reasons as to why we should care about this or that do not have access to the relevant free-standing or independent criteria. After all, what are the differences between "I care about that criteria about how we should live because I care about it" and "I care about that criteria because the criteria seems right to me"? If Frankfurt is correct, then it seems that we would not be able to conceive of such criteria unless we were already working with a prior understanding of what kind of living is satisfying.

To some extent, Frankfurt appears to be correct about one difficulty of appealing to criteria, but I suggest that the use of criteria in assessing ways of living does not involve any vicious circularity. The reply proposed here is similar to the reply that some philosophers make to the problem of the criterion in epistemology. Let us consider the latter and then return to the terrain of values.

In epistemology, it has been charged that one cannot know anything (X) without knowing some criterion in virtue of which X is known. But how do you know that *that* criterion is correct? Perhaps you need an additional criterion by which to know whether the first-order criterion is correct. But then yet another criterion is needed, *ad infinitum*. Roderick Chisholm broke the regress by embracing what he called *particularism*: he held that you could know and grasp certain truths antecedent to possessing a criterion of how you know them. Chisholm's preference for particularism rather than "methodism" (the view that knowledge of particulars is only possible if you know the method you are employing is accurate) was part of his "common sense" approach to philosophical problems. Chisholm was very much of the same mind as Thomas Reid and G. E. Moore; each philosopher claimed to be more certain of such ordinary beliefs as "I have hands" than they were of skeptical arguments that would defeat or undermine such claims.[6]

I suggest that the problem of the criterion in values should not usher in skepticism about the reality and role of values in accounting for why we love this or that any more than the problem of the criterion in

[5] Frankfurt, *The Reasons*, 24–25.

[6] Roderick Chisholm, *The Problem of the Criterion* (Milwaukee: Marquette University Press, 1973).

epistemology should usher in skepticism about the reality and role of epistemic norms in accounting for why we should believe this or that based on evidence. So, I propose that a commonsense, intuitive value that most of us can grasp is that *it is good for parents to care for their children* or, putting the point more poignantly, *parents should care for their children (whether or not they actually care)*. Obviously, all sorts of caveats may need to be introduced to take care of deviant cases, but surely something like such a principle is a decent starting point.

With any invocation of values that are not reducible to statements about "natural facts," naturalists will be most unhappy, but two points may be offered on behalf of Platonists and other moral realists.

First, as a number of philosophers from G. E. M. Anscombe to Derek Parfit have argued, without an appeal to irreducible moral truths or principles, persons who care about doing great harm (e.g. committing genocide) or care about doing what seems utterly bizarre, have reasons for doing the harm and the bizarre. Anscombe introduced the following case in which she claimed that for the agent to reply that they did the act "for no particular reason" is inappropriate. If someone hunted out all the green books in their house and spread them out carefully on the roof, and gave one of these answers ("for no particular reason," "I just felt like doing it") to the question "Why?" their words would be unintelligible unless they are taken as joking or mystification. Arguably, there are cases when reported desires and motives seem so far afield ("I am placing my watch by a tree in case it wants to know the time") when they simply fail to make any sense.

Second, on behalf of accepting irreducible moral principles, it can be argued that this is no worse than accepting irreducible epistemic principles. The attempt to replace epistemic principles (e.g. if it is reasonable to believe that all humans are mortal, it is reasonable to believe that no immortal is human, one should trust appearances unless there is good reason for distrusting them, and so on) with an appeal only to non-normative, causal relations is that we would then be without the resources to identify which causal relations are trustworthy and which are not. It may be that normative epistemic principles are adaptive from an evolutionary point of view, but this is not obvious (belief in the divine may confer enormous adaptive advantage but it is not thereby justified).

Consider another objection to a Platonic realism about values. After advancing his objection about criteria, Frankfurt raises another worry for moral realists like Platonists:

Here is another way to bring out the difficulty. Something is important to a person only in virtue of a difference that it makes. If everything would be exactly the same with that thing as without it, then it makes no sense for anyone to care about it. It cannot really be of any importance. Of course, it cannot be enough for it merely to make *some* difference. After all, everything does make some difference; but not everything is important.[7]

This is a difficult position for someone to assess who is not already committed to moral realism or its denial. I shall press forward the appeal of Platonic moral realism by an appeal to one's ordinary, commonsense understanding of values.

Imagine that the parents of a child possess the economic means to raise the child and live in a society in which they also have the option of placing the child up for adoption by a family with similar economic resources. Imagine that they do not see to it that the child is raised in some other loving family but raise the child themselves with minimal care and without any affective support. They care more for parties with their peers, adult recreation, and playing golf. Imagine the child does not realize that they are neglected, but they grow up living a stunted life, filled with a sense that they are unworthy of love. As a consequence, they take up a high-risk activity and – though they were healthy physically and, under different circumstances, would have lived till ninety – die in their twenties. When the child is dying, they do not care whether they might live. They have never really cared, nor have their parents.

Let's consider this scenario through the lens of a Christian Platonist. Were the parents good parents? No. They failed to live up to their obligations as parents. It does not matter how much the parents cared about golf, nor does it matter whether the child was manipulated into thinking their life had little importance. This judgment seems as reasonable as any that challenge reckless private opinions and commitments. Suppose that someone suspects that every time they disbelieve in fairies, a fairy dies. They think they have killed twenty fairies. Is that person a killer? Maybe in their mind, but really they are no more of a killer than the parents are good parents in the above thought-experiment.

Frankfurt makes one other point that might be interpreted as creating a difficulty for the Platonist: "What is *not* possible is for a person who does not already care at least about *something* to discover reasons for caring about anything. Nobody can pull himself up by his own bootstraps."[8] This may not be a source of deep tension between Platonists and

---

[7] Frankfurt, *The Reasons*, 25.   [8] Ibid, 26.

Frankfurt. Those of us who are Platonists simply hold that it is a rare case when persons do not recognize the intrinsic goodness of at least something that merits, justifies, or calls for our love and care. When we fail to respond to such real goods, we fail to respond to reality itself and instead live a life of fantasy or denial. It may be that, from the standpoint of an external, noncommitted observer, a despondent rogue who is not a good father looks the same to someone quite independent of a commitment to Platonism or Frankfurt's position. But in a Christian Platonist perspective there is, I think, more of a sense that there is something of a failure to live up to what the father should be doing (regardless of what he cares about) than with Frankfurt's alternative, for, given that the person does not care about being a good father, he has no reason to be a good father.

Let us now consider the key point of conflict between Frankfurt and Christian Platonism. It is essential to consider Frankfurt's view at length:

Love is often understood as being, most basically, a response to the perceived worth of the beloved. We are moved to love something, on this account, by an appreciation of what we take to be its exceptional inherent value. The appeal of that value is what captivates us and turns us into lovers. We begin loving the things that we love because we are struck by their value, and we continue to love them for the sake of their value. If we did not find the beloved valuable, we should not love it.

This may well fit certain cases of what would commonly be identified as love. However, the sort of phenomenon that I have in mind when referring here to love is essentially something else. As I am construing it, love is not necessarily a response grounded in awareness of the inherent value of its object. It may sometimes arise like that, but it need not do so. It is not necessarily as a *result* of recognizing their value and of being captivated by it that we love things. Rather, what we love necessarily *acquires* value for us *because* we love it. The lover does invariably and necessarily perceive the beloved as valuable, but the value they see it to possess is a value that derives from and that depends upon his love.

Consider the love of parents for their children. I can declare with unequivocal confidence that I do not love my children because I am aware of some value that inheres in them independent of my love for them. The fact is that I loved them even before they were born – before I had any especially relevant information about their personal characteristics or their particular merits and virtues. Furthermore, I do not believe that the valuable qualities they do happen to possess strictly in their own rights, would really provide me with a very compelling basis for regarding them as having greater worth than many other possible objects of love that in fact I love much less. It is quite clear to me that I do not love them more than other children because I believe they are better.[9]

---

[9] Ibid, 38–39.

Frankfurt offers an extensive further point about the parent–child relationship:

It is not because I have noticed their value, then, that I love my children as I do. Of course I do perceive them to have value; so far as I am concerned, indeed, their value is beyond measure. That, however, is not the basis of my love. It is really the other way around. The particular value that I attribute to my children is not inherent in them but depends upon my love for them. The reason they are so precious to me is simply that I love them so much. As for why it is that human beings do tend generally to love their children, the explanation presumably lies in the evolutionary pressure of natural selection. In any case, it is plainly *on account of* my love for them that they have acquired in my eyes a value that otherwise they would not certainly possess.[10]

I believe this to be a false reading of what it is to love another person, to love one's child in particular, and to be loved by a parent. If Frankfurt is right, then when we love our children and congratulate them (for example) on their volunteer work tutoring students, the reason such work has value is because we love our children and their work. This would mean (philosophically and from our point of view) that our children would lose value when or if we stopped loving them. It also seems to imply that our children's value would fluctuate in line with our degree and depth of care. On one morning, our children's value may be the highest ever because we are fully awake and caring, whereas by the afternoon we may be exhausted with caring and our children's value begins to diminish. This seems profoundly counterintuitive. Frankfurt's view also implies that we would cease having value should our parents, ourselves, and others cease caring about ourselves.

I suggest that Frankfurt is misinterpreting the basic, natural good of the parent–child relationship. He assumes that if he values his children more than strangers and not due to their meriting his love through successful action or superior traits, then *he*, Frankfurt, is the source of value. But this completely puts to one side the apparent *basic good of the parent–child relationship*. The recognition of such a basic good explains why we think that when Frankfurt loves his child he is doing something good and it also explains why we do not think a child's value becomes diminished or fluctuates depending on a parent's love.

[10] Ibid, 40.

Frankfurt does acknowledge that, in our experience, something like the basic account seems right. In a passage cited earlier, Frankfurt claims, "The lover does invariably and necessarily perceive the beloved as valuable, but the value he sees it to possess is a value that derives from and that depends upon his love." I suggest that this conception of value is not possible *if one fully and completely believes that the value is completely derived from the lover.* If one fully accepts Frankfurt's account and has no doubt of its truth, how can one simultaneously perceive one's children as having independent value? Imagine that the *only* reason you value a house is because you think that Brad Pitt spent the night there. And you know that your sense of the worth of the house is *wholly derived* from a visit by that handsome celebrity and not due to the house's intrinsic value. How can you perceive and know this and yet simultaneously perceive the house as possessing intrinsic value? Insofar as perceiving a house or a child as possessing intrinsic value involves believing that they are of intrinsic value, it seems Frankfurt leaves us with a case in which a person must believe his child is intrinsically valuable while believing that the child is not intrinsically valuable.

To sum up, I propose that the Platonic view about love and value has been challenged, but not defeated. There is good reason to believe that love by ourselves (and for gods and God) *is a response to intrinsic goodness* rather than a foundational source of goodness. When we love another person, we love her for the value or worth they have intrinsically or for her own sake, not the other way around. Thus, our love for our partners or for our children is not what gives them value or makes them interesting.

One caveat is worth registering. While it is proposed that the value that you and I have is not based on care or love, there are goods, such as friendship, which can grow (or atrophy) in value depending on care or love. This is why the loss of a friendship that lasted a lifetime is more of a loss than the loss of a friendship of only a weekend. This is partly because the persons in the friendship have intrinsic value.[11]

CONSCIOUSNESS

The biggest assault on Christian Platonism in the intellectual climate since the mid-twentieth century has been the rise of materialism. The spectre of

---

[11] For further reflection on the philosophy of love, see Charles Taliaferro, *The Golden Cord: A Short Book on the Sacred and the Secular* (Notre Dame: The University of Notre Dame Press, 2012).

materialism covers two of the "anti" aspects of Platonism identified by Lloyd Gerson: antimaterialism and antimechanism. In terms of Plato's famous depiction of the warfare between the giants (who are seeking to bring everything down to matter) and the gods (the friends of the forms and the soul) in the *Sophist*, the gods have been dominant.[12] One of the charges on behalf of contemporary materialists is that we possess a much clearer understanding of mind-independent physical objects and their causal properties, than we do of our minds (or Platonists might refer here to the states of our souls). I shall be arguing against this view, maintaining we have a far clearer understanding of mind rather than mind-independent realities. This alone is not enough to establish mind–body dualism, but it is a start (as argued in my *Consciousness and the Mind of God*) and, at the very least, responds to the most aggressive case for materialism.

Let's first consider the merits of the primacy of the physical. Consider two statements in which Daniel Dennett advances the dominant claim about the primacy of our grasp of what is physical. Dennett's position is representative of many contemporary materialists.

There is only one sort of stuff, namely *matter* – the physical stuff of physics, chemistry, and physiology – and the mind is somehow nothing but a physical phenomenon. In short the mind is the brain … We can (in principle!) account for every mental phenomenon using the same physical principles, laws, and materials that suffice to explain radioactivity, continental drift, photosynthesis, reproduction, nutrition, and growth.[13]

Dennett claims that, in contrast with the lucid, monolithic, scientific understanding of a mind-independent world, dualism is hopelessly antiscientific.

Dualism (the view that minds are composed of some nonphysical and utterly mysterious stuff …) [has] been relegated to the trash heap of history, along with alchemy and astrology. Unless you are also prepared to declare that the world is flat and the sun is a fiery chariot pulled by winged horses – unless, in other words, your defiance of modern science is quite complete – you won't find any place to stand and fight for those obsolete ideas.[14]

What to make of these claims? I propose that Dennett's position is self-undermining and confused. It is self-undermining to the extent that Dennett cannot presume to have any clearer concept of nonmental

---

[12] *Sophist*, 245e–249d.
[13] Daniel Dennett, *Consciousness Explained* (New York: Little Brown, 1991), 33.
[14] Daniel Dennett, *Kinds of Minds* (New York: Basic Books, 1996), 24.

physical phenomenon than he has a clear grasp of concepts, reasons, and reasoning, grasping entailment relations, reliance on experience and observations that go into the practice of the sciences or in grasping the kinds of reasoning that goes on at philosophy conferences. When he begins his credo, he writes as though we have a clear idea about physical principles and the physical sciences, when in fact what he is appealing to is our *ideas* (*theories, thoughts, concepts*) of what is physical. To appeal to *physics, chemistry*, and *physiology* is (if it means anything at all) to appeal to what persons as scientists practice with their theories and observations, their conceiving of and intentionally undertaking experiments and making predictions, their recording data and drawing inferences. Nutrition and reproduction as events only come to be understood by us when we engage in understanding, thinking, reasoning, and so on. Stan Klein rightly observes the absurdity of treating the mental or experience as of secondary intelligibility compared to a mind-independent concept of the physical:

According subjectivity, at best, "second class citizenship" in the study of mind is particularly ironic in virtue of the fact that subjectivity is the very thing that makes the scientific pursuit of such knowledge (actually any knowledge) possible. Timing devices, neuroimaging technologies, electroencephalographs, and a host of modern means of obtaining objective knowledge of minds are useless absent an experiencing subject ... To believe otherwise has the absurd consequence of rendering our knowledge of mind (or more generally, of reality) dependent, in its entirety, on the provisions of an experiential conduit stipulated either to be unworthy of study or essentially nonexistent.[15]

I suggest that Dennett's view of selves is far more preposterous than the examples he gives in mordant depiction of dualists (his blustering reference to dualism being on a par with astrology, alchemy, and the belief that the sun is a chariot) because Dennett famously denies that selves are real; we are instead fictive, narrative centers of gravity.[16] I have developed this critique elsewhere and will summarize my proposal:[17] It is Dennett who is profoundly antiscientific because he denies the belief that scientists (as

---

[15] Stan Klein, "A Defense of Experiential Realism: The Need to take Phenomenological Reality in its Own Terms in the Study of the Mind," in *Psychology of Consciousness: Theory, Research and Practice* 2, no. 1 (2015), 41–56 at pp. 43–44.

[16] Daniel Dennett, "The Self as a Center of Narrative Gravity," *Philosophia* 15 (1986), 275–288.

[17] Charles Taliaferro, *Consciousness and the Mind of God* (Cambridge: Cambridge University Press, 1994) and Taliaferro and Jil Evans, *The Image in Mind* (London: Continuum, 2011).

persons who are real and nonfictive) exist. To be intelligible, Dennett must treat as nonfictive (i.e. treat as real) that he and we and scientists truly exist as thinking, feeling, reasoning beings, and yet, in the final analysis, according to Dennett, none of us is fundamentally real. The following observation by S. Gallagher and D. Zahavi may seem so obvious, it is regrettable that it is necessary to put in print, but it is a truth that Dennett's form of materialism drives him to deny or obscure. "Science is performed by somebody; it is a specific theoretical stance toward the world ... scientific objectivity is something we strive for but it rests on the observations of individuals."[18]

Dennett complains about dualists' positing nonphysical stuff. But consider first whether we have a clear idea of *physical stuff?* Does physical stuff have color, taste, and smell? Does it make sounds? These questions take us to the classic, modern problem of conceiving of physical objects that are truly independent of minds. I do not embrace the all-out-subjectivist idealist claim that it is impossible to conceive of something that is ontologically independent of (or not constituted by) minds (though on theistic grounds, I am convinced that no physical object can exist without dependence on the causal power of the divine mind). But we should appreciate that *all our appeals to physical objects are conceptually mediated* (your thinking about any physical object necessarily involves the exercise of your conceptual powers) and as we examine the concepts themselves we face a host of difficulties in terms of identifying the necessary and sufficient conditions for being physical. A commonplace proposal, for example, is that *an object is physical if it is spatio-temporal*, but there are many philosophers from the Cambridge Platonists to G. E. Moore, H. H. Price, and Howard Robinson who recognize sensory images, after-images, and dream-images as spatio-temporal but they are not in the physical space(s) as described in the physical sciences. For reasons outlined above (and so to repeat), identifying the physical in terms of successful or ideal results of the physical sciences does not help us get to a mind-independent notion of the physical because the physical sciences involve the mental.

Stepping back a bit I suggest we are in an epistemic position the very opposite of Dennett's and those like him who contend that we have a clear concept of what is physical but not of what is mental, and this includes

---

[18] Shaun Gallagher and Dan Zahavi, *The Phenomenological Mind* (London: Routledge, 2008), 41.

matters of causation. In Dennett's examples, causation occurs without mental phenomena (radioactivity, continental drift, etc., involves no beliefs, ideas, thoughts, etc.), but we necessarily have a clearer concept of mental causation than we have of mind-independent physical causation. You can form no *understanding* of radioactivity unless you understand *ideas* of particles and what is involved with particles to be emitted from nuclei, *ideas* about many nuclear isotopes and how *those ideas* give rise to *ideas* about different forces. In reasoning about radioactivity, and in fact in reasoning of any sort (deductive, inductive, in abduction or basic perception), we readily grasp the entailments and inferences in which *we believe some things in virtue of (because of, in a causal sense) believing others*. I believe that six is the smallest perfect number because I grasp that it is the smallest number equal to the sum of its divisors including one, but not including itself ($6=1+2+3$). Mathematical reasoning would not make any sense without such mental causation as well as our reasoning about virtually indefinitely many subjects: it is because I believe you are drinking coffee and discussing philosophy that I conclude it is false to deny you are drinking coffee and discussion philosophy, ad infinitum.

In light of the above, let us consider what some philosophers claim is a fatal problem for substance dualism. Philosophers going back to Descartes' lifetime thought it highly problematic to explain how the soul (or mind or person as a nonphysical thing) causally interacts with what is physical. I suggest matters are different. We have a clear grasp of mental causation and in exercising our mental powers we may readily grasp that there is causal interaction between our bodily states and mental lives. We have, however, not a lucid understanding of physical causation, and only a wobbly concept of physical causation; rather, we have a clearer understanding of mental causation and such mental causation is essential for us to even begin to understand what is involved in physical causation. Consider, for example, the extant theories of causation on offer today: Humean association, counterfactuals, the idea that causation is a matter of timeless laws involving states of affairs, and (my preferred account) causation involves concrete, basic powers and liabilities of fundamental objects. None of these are understandable or usable unless we have confidence in mental causation. To understand a thrown baseball breaking a window, you need to be confident or employ (or not deny) first-order logic, grasping basic entailments (if the baseball is smaller than the window, the window is larger than the baseball), and to engage in basic matters of identity and difference. One might object that all kinds of animals can grasp causal relations without such mental apparatus. I believe we can be agnostic about the extensiveness of mental life of nonhuman animals and propose that the primacy of the mental is evident in cases of when persons engage in explicit reflection on what there is; when persons engage in thinking about why things occur and explanations of radioactivity (etc.) and of ourselves (what accounts for our thinking, and so on).

The position advanced here is in the tradition of John Locke and Thomas Reid. Consider this passage from Locke's *Essay on Human Understanding*:

Bodies by our senses do not afford us so clear and distinct an idea of active power as we have from reflection on the operation of minds ... Neither have we from body any idea of the beginning of motion ... The idea of the *beginning* of motion we have only from reflection on that passes in ourselves, where we find by experience, that, barely by willing it, barely by a thought of the mind, we can move the parts of our bodies that were before at rest.[19]

In terms of other historical precedents, the primacy of the mental was robustly defended by Bertrand Russell in *The Analysis of Matter*: "As regards the world in general, both physical and mental, everything that we know of its intrinsic character is derived from the mental."[20]

As noted at the outset, more needs to be done to establish a nonidentity between the mental and physical, but I hope this section at least reverses the aggressive strategy of subordinating in terms of clarity and evidence of the mental versus the mind-independent physical world.[21]

Let's now consider a case of when Christian Platonism has been contested from within. Some Christian philosophers adopt a form of materialism that is less aggressive than Dennett and others (sometimes called eliminativists because they want to eliminate the mental from their ontology). Unlike eliminativists, they accept the reality of selves, consciousness, intrinsic values, and so on. Only they contend that human persons are best seen as material, embodied beings, without an immaterial soul.

---

[19] John Locke, *An Essay Concerning Human Understanding*, ed. Roger Woodhouse (New York: Penguin Books, 2004), chapter 21, sec. 4.

[20] Bertrand Russell, *The Analysis of Matter* (New York: Dover Publications, 1954), 402. For further reflections on rationality and mental causation, see Angus Menuge, *Agents Under Fire* (Lanham, MD: Rowman & Littlefield Publishers, 2004) and Peter Unger, *All the Power in the World* (New York: Oxford University Press, 2006).

[21] See my *Consciousness and the Mind of God* for a further case for dualism.

CHRISTIAN MATERIALISM

In the last thirty years, a range of Christian philosophers have con-
tended that Christian Platonism is out of step with deep Christian
convictions involving the unity of human life and the resurrection.
Some of the more prominent Christian materialists are Peter van
Inwagen, Kevin Corcoran, Lynne Baker, Nancey Murphy, and
Trenton Merricks.[22] Here let us consider reasons against Christian
Platonism that are specifically Christian. That is, if dualism faces
intractable philosophical problems independent of Christianity,
Christian philosophers have good reason to reject dualism and accept
some form of materialism or some other alternative. The question here
is whether there are Christian reasons for rejecting dualism. Consider
two of the advantages of Christian Platonism:

The unity of human life: Christian philosophers have charged that
mind–body dualism creates a bifurcation between the person as the
mind or soul and the body, which amounts to something we inhabit.
Perhaps the most aggressive charge against dualism in this context
comes from Trenton Merricks who contends that if dualism is true then
virtually none of the narratives about Jesus are true. Jesus did not walk
across the water, for example, his body did.[23] Merricks is very much in the
camp of Gilbert Ryle who likened dualism to the belief that there is a ghost
in a machine (in which the soul is likened to a ghost and the body to
a machine).[24] Merricks proposes that dualism generates a preposterous
view of ordinary interaction, concluding that if dualism is true, he has
never kissed his wife as you cannot kiss an immaterial soul.

The Resurrection: Historical forms of Christianity (as opposed to
completely demythologized versions which reject all miracles) affirm the
resurrection of Jesus Christ from the dead. It also affirms that (at the
eschaton or end times) there will be a resurrection of human persons.
Merricks and others argue that if dualism is true, the value of the resurrection is undermined. Why would it matter whether one's body is resurrected if persons are not identical with their bodies? If we are the very same
thing as our bodies, then the resurrection is valued because it involves the
continued personal identify of persons themselves.

---

[22] See the contributions to *Soul, Body, and Survival*, ed. Kevin Corcoran (Ithaca: Cornell
University Press, 2001).

[23] See Trenton Merricks's chapter "How to Live Forever without Saving your Soul:
Physicalism and Immortality," in *Soul, Body, and Survival*, 183–200.

[24] Gilbert Ryle, *The Concept of Mind* (Chicago: University of Chicago Press, 1949).

Replies: The first objection rests on a caricature of mind–body dualism. While Christian Platonists contend that persons (or souls or minds) are not metaphysically identical with their bodies, this is compatible with claiming that under ordinary, healthy conditions the person and body function as a unity. Under normal conditions, to see Jesus of Nazareth walking (on or not on water) is to see the person walking. To kiss your partner's face is to kiss your partner. But conditions can arise where there is a bifurcation. Imagine you see what seems like a person intentionally walking, but they are under hypnosis or sleepwalking or merely stumbling along aimlessly without any intention at all. Or imagine you kiss the person you believe you are married to, but they have gotten divorced, no longer love you, and are plotting your murder. The point is that our interactions with each other are often integrated and holistic, but there can be bifurcations, even at a point where a person might even appear to be like a ghost in a machine.

On the importance of the resurrection, Christian Platonism has some advantage over Christian materialism. Although Christian orthodoxy is not united on this point, many Christians historically and today believe that after death persons are with God prior to a resurrection. If materialism is true, this would not be possible. Materialism also faces the obstacle of accounting for the identity of a resurrected person notwithstanding the at least apparent fact of their bodies being utterly destroyed past any recognition. (Early on, Christians worried about the resurrection of bodies that have been consumed by cannibals and animals.) Christian Platonists can account for the continuity of persons after physical death due to the continuous existence of the person qua nonphysical self.

Christian Platonism has other advantages: if materialism is true, then Jesus of Nazareth is numerically identical with his body. But this seems contrary to a highly important thesis in orthodox Christianity that Jesus is numerically identical with the second person of the Trinity who preexisted not just the body of Jesus but of the cosmos itself.

FURTHER REFLECTION

It would be an exaggeration to propose that the impact of Platonism on Christianity has made Christian theology a series of footnotes on Plato (and one might add, for good measure, Plotinus). And yet, much Christian theology has consisted in critiquing or further developing Christian Platonism. In this chapter we have only considered three points of contention. But, I suggest, just as Christian Platonism has resources to address these, it has further resources to address the points of contention that lie beyond the scope of this chapter.

Bibliography

Chisholm, Roderick. *The Problem of the Criterion*. Milwaukee: Marquette University Press, 1973.

Corcoran, Kevin, ed. *Soul, Body, and Survival*. Ithaca: Cornell University Press, 2001.

Dennett, Daniel. *Consciousness Explained*. New York: Little Brown, 1991.

Kinds of Minds. New York: Basic Books, 1996.

"The Self as a Center of Narrative Gravity." *Philosophia* 15 (1986): 275–288.

Frankfurt, Harry. *The Reasons of Love*. Princeton: Princeton University Press, 2006.

Gallagher, Shaun and Dan Zahavi. *The Phenomenological Mind*. London: Routledge, 2008.

Gerson, Lloyd. *From Plato to Platonism*. Ithaca: Cornell University Press, 2013.

Klein, Stan. "A Defense of Experiential Realism: The Need to take Phenomenological Reality in its Own Terms in the Study of the Mind." *Psychology of Consciousness: Theory, Research, and Practice* 2, no. 1 (2015): 41–56.

Locke, John. *An Essay Concerning Human Understanding*. Edited by Roger Woodhouse. New York: Penguin Books, 2004.

Menuge, Angus. *Agents Under Fire* (Lanham, MD: Rowman & Littlefield Publishers, 2004).

Merricks, Trenton. "How to Live Forever without Saving your soul." In *Soul, Body and Survival*, ed. Kevin Corcoran, 183–200. Grand Rapids, MI: Eerdmans, 1999.

Russell, Bertrand. *An Analysis of Matter*. New York: Dover Publications, 1954.

Ryle, Gilbert. *The Concept of Mind*. Chicago: University of Chicago Press, 1949.

Taliaferro, Charles. *Consciousness and the Mind of God*. Cambridge: Cambridge University Press, 1994.

The Golden Cord: A Short Book on the Sacred and the Secular. Notre Dame: University of Notre Dame Press, 2012.

Taliaferro, Charles and Jil Evans. *The Image in Mind*. London: Continuum, 2011.

Unger, Peter. *All the Power in the World*. New York : Oxford University Press, 2006.

Wenisch, Fritz. Review of *The Nature of Love* by D. von Hildebrand, *Faith and Philosophy* 29, no. 1 (2012): 118–122.

3.5

Christian Love and Platonic Friendship

Catherine Pickstock

There persists a tendency to imagine that Platonism has led Christianity away from its incarnational character, and a biblical acceptance of the realities of this world. It has supposedly encouraged a turn towards the contemplation of the eternal and of eternal verities, to the neglect of the corporeal and the affective. Platonism is held responsible for an over-intellectualising and abstract tendency, distorting Christianity as a religion of love. Yet the following reflections on Plato's negotiation of friendship, and discussions of the same in modern times, will suggest that Plato prepared the way for the gospel insofar as he tended to show that love and knowledge were inseparable, even at the highest level.

Each human individual, one might say, is caught between the imperative to know, on the one hand, and the imperative to socialise, on the other. But is the first imperative, as for René Descartes, an entirely lonely one? And is the second imperative irrelevant to the theoretical quest for truth? Antiquity did not tend to see human life as compartmentalised, but regarded association, transmission and pedagogic formation as essential to philosophical understanding.[1] Conversely, it tended to suppose that serious friendship had to do with a shared engagement in a serious process – a political concern for the city, or a learned concern for the truth. However, the

---

[1] Socrates' examination of the beliefs according to which one should act and live, and his search for the firmest beliefs upon which to act, are, throughout the dialogues, set in the context of testing beliefs against the arguments of others and seeing whether others can bring new insights. This can be seen in his discussions with those who take moral views hostile to his own, such as Callicles in *Gorgias* and Thrasymachus in *Republic*; in the ways he responds to the counter-arguments of Simmias and Kebes in *Phaedo*; and, in the same dialogue, in his insistence that any results are always subject to further argument.

question would seem to arise: if non-trivial friendship is subordinated to the human search for either theoretical or practical wisdom, are not the exigencies of friendship – of chance encounters, obscure affinities and unlikely pairings – themselves trivialised because they are disparaged? Equivalently, is not the serious concern with truth itself trivial if it cannot be related to our existential needs for companionship?

The suggestion that, in the face of this dilemma, Plato provides a mediating route might be greeted with scepticism: surely Plato suppresses the ultimate significance of friendship in pursuit of the good, where Aristotle sees friendship as essential to the good – which is the fully lived life? However, it is just this possibility which I propose to explore.

Does Plato set himself against the ultimate significance of the corporeal specificities of desire and beauty, and does he despise the concrete circumstances of mundane affinity? Does he leave behind such phenomenal mediations, whether human, linguistic, mythical, temporal or bodily? Must we bypass or transcend contingency and everyday distraction? Yet if this is the substantive import of Plato's dialogues, then it clashes with the idiomatic presence of tokens of reported speech and diegetic redundancy within the dialogues. Are these present merely for the sake of ironic contrast with truth, or does this ironic display double back upon itself performatively to suggest affinity after all between final truth and modes of mediation? Does this suggest that far from the true and the good being friendless, friendship is a mode of truth and value?

In this chapter, I will examine Plato's exploration of the aporias of friendship and the broader relationship to the question of the status of finite mediation and participation, as presented in Plato's *Lysis*. One can note at the outset that this wider bearing is indicated by the term *philia* itself, which cannot simply be translated as friendship, since it denotes 'self-belonging', and includes the relations that are conducive to such self-belonging, as well as indicating both befriender and befriended (218d).[2] The stakes of the discourse seem to concern the sustainability of this polyvalent word: is our self-belonging in true goodness compatible with relational affection, and does the self-belonging of the good encompass any exterior concern? Must the double implication of *philia* be prised apart?

---

[2] M. M. Mackenzie, 'Impasse and Explanation: From the *Lysis* to the *Phaedo*', *Archiv für Geschichte der Philosophie* 70 (1988), 15–45, at p. 26; D. K. Glidden, 'The *Lysis* on Loving One's Own', *Classical Quarterly* 31, no. 1 (1981), 39–59, at pp. 40ff.

FRIENDSHIP AND ASYMMETRY

The *Lysis* is generally situated amongst Plato's early but transitional
Socratic dialogues, although it is an open question as to when the dialogue
was actually written.[3] The text is known for its untidy arguments and
collapsed conclusion.[4] How one should read the dialogue is not certain,
but its strange formal twistings seem irreducible and to invite interpretation. The dramatic setting, like several other dialogues,[5] opens with
Socrates *en route* to a particular place, here making straight for the
Lyceum (203a).[6] The main discussion takes place in a new Palaestra just
inside the outer wall, by the Dipylon Gate. Socrates draws two friends,
Lysis and Menexenos, into a discussion about the nature of friendship. At
first, the questions which Socrates poses appear straightforward: which of
you is the older (206b ff)? Which the more beautiful? Which the richer?
The two friends jostle in nervousness and embarrassment; at which point
Socrates suggests that such questions are foolish, for friends are perforce
equal in everything and hold all things in common (207c8 ff). Here one
senses the pall of conceptual perplexity begin to spread: what exactly *do*
friends hold in common? If friendship is not the playground banter of
mutual outdoing, then what is it? What makes friendship take place?
Further questions follow: who becomes the friend of whom, the lover of
a beloved, or the beloved of a lover? And are friends alike to one another?
Is it the case that like seeks like, Socrates asks, alluding to Homer and
Empedocles (214a)?[7] Only those who are good, presumably, are capable
of friendship, and only those who are one with themselves – or 'like'

---

[3] Catherine Osborne, *Eros Unveiled: Plato and the God of Love* (Oxford: Clarendon Press,
   1996), 58; Mackenzie, 'Impasse and Explanation'; David Bolotin, *Plato's Dialogue on
   Friendship* (Ithaca: SUNY Press, 1979).
[4] See, for example, Brian Carr's attempt to distil the dialogue into analytic formulae, in
   'Friendship in Plato's *Lysis*', in *Friendship East and West: Philosophical Perspectives*, ed.
   Oliver Leaman (London: Routledge, 1996), 13–31.
[5] Examples include *Phaedrus* in which Socrates is *en route* to the akademeia and, unusually,
   outside the city walls; *Symposium*, in which he is going to Agathon's celebration party; and
   Republic, in which he has gone down to Peiraieus, but within the Long Walls, and is about
   to return to the city when he is intercepted by Adeimantus and Polemarchus.
[6] See Osborne, *Eros Unveiled*, 86.
[7] Homer, *Odyssey*, xvii.218: 'Yea, ever like and like together God doth draw'. This is an
   allusion to Empedocles, amongst those who 'discuss and write about nature and the
   whole', and invokes one of the two phases of his cosmic cycle: the increasing dominance
   of *eris* (strife) where like joins with like and repels all that is different, in distinction from
   the increasing dominance of *philia*, where all things are intermingled and become an
   indistinguishable whole. So, in a discussion of friendship, an allusion to the dominance
   of strife is particularly significant.

themselves – can be 'like' others (214e3 ff). Friends must surely be alike, otherwise friendship would be compromised by grubby calculations of utility, advantage and lack, which would corrode the communal basis of a relationship (e.g. 218d–e). The bad cannot therefore truly be friends, and thieves are not 'thick' at all.

But does this not promote the opposite argument? If one person is like another, then he has no need of him and is self-sufficient (222b8–10). Surely there will be here no impulse to forge friendships. Socrates cites Hesiod to suggest that envy, jealousy and hatred arise not between unlike people but between like people: 'See potter wroth with potter, bard with bard, beggar with beggar' (215c3 ff).[8] Must not friendship pertain then between unlike persons? Do not the rich attract the poor, the strong the weak, the doctor the infirm, the wise the foolish (215d)? But, taking this line of argument to absurd levels, Socrates notes that, if this is so, then the friend must presumably attract the enemy (216a8–b; 220e ff), and this is surely unsustainable.

He therefore proposes a third logical possibility, which is that a person is drawn to another person who is neither like nor unlike to himself (e.g. 216c–d; 222e); in particular, he who experiences friendship with another person sees in that person a kind of future direction which he might profitably follow. The befriender is drawn beyond his own self-identity, or mundane 'likeness', towards something greater which can disclose a higher selfhood, concealed in the visage of the instructive other. This dynamic of development depends upon asymmetrical or unequal pairings. Most crucially, 'that which is neither good nor evil becomes friends with good' (217b): growth in friendship is an ethical progress.[9]

And yet, amid these asymmetrical slopings and slantings, a certain aspirational symmetry pertains, as we anticipate the real identities into which we will grow, through increased habitual reception of the exterior: 'It cannot be, then, that you have a great notion of yourself if as yet you are notionless' (210d). So we love the guide as already in possession of a good to which we nonetheless aspire reciprocally to recognise alongside him.

---

[8] Hesiod, *Works and Days*, 25.

[9] In *Lysis*, Socrates moves from an example of health to the example of progress from awareness of one's ignorance to a search for knowledge or wisdom. In several other dialogues, the same gap between two types of case is similarly filled in. An analogy between the health of the body and the health of the just soul is drawn at *Gorgias* 444a13–e2, where both are instances of the *kosmos* and the balance that obtains in the world as a whole; at *Republic* 444d–e and 591c–d, an analysis of the virtues, particularly *sophrosune* and justice, is drawn in terms of the healthy balance between the three parts of the soul.

Inversely, the love of guide for follower involves the same complex mixture of hierarchy and balance. This mixture is alien to our post-Kantian sensibilities as it is said by Plato that the friendship of even father and child could not survive were the child not in some fashion useful to the parent (210c). And yet, just this insistence suggests that there is already some substantive symmetrical exchange between parent and child, as between teacher and pupil, which is absent from the pure disinterest of Kantian love for the younger or the aspiring. For in the latter case, the formality of the duty to love and nurture the child or pupil reduces any benefit that the parent or teacher might receive in return to irrelevance. Thus, the apparently shocking instrumentality of Plato's outlook can be taken as challenging the cold indifference of a Kantian outlook to any substantive relational exchange, which is the very thing, within an admitted hierarchy, that already tends to elevate it beyond hierarchy towards mutuality.

For Plato, then, friendship is hierarchical and asymmetrical, and yet incipiently equal and symmetrical. It is the former, as the process of conducting others towards the good (213a), and the latter, insofar as the whole chain already shares in the good and exchanges the good, upwards as well as downwards, since Plato eventually concludes that all mundane friendships are but 'shadows' of our friendship with the *proton philon*, the good which is the first and real object of all loves (219d–220 c).

This higher 'likeness', so alike that it appears as unlikeness, is perhaps something akin to one's 'potential', and it is for this reason that friendship involves a dynamic that is more complex than that driven by a circuit of mere lack or need, for the potential glimpsed in the like-unlikeness of the befriended person or thing is not wholly other from oneself, nor statically the same as oneself; nor can it be attained once and for all. If for Socrates friendship can in any way be understood (and the abrupt closing of the dialogue leaves that open to doubt), it is always as friendship for the *friend* of the good, for those who are neither purely good nor evil, but on their way to a real self-belonging through their belonging together with goodness.

One begins to see just how complicated the relationship of same and different is. Far from the crude mechanical same-sameness of Jacques Derrida's attribution of equivalence in antique exchanges or reciprocations, discussed in Chapter Two, one finds instead an interplay of the one and the many. Moreover, the dialogue seems to hinge on the apparent aporetic truth, with which it concludes, that any attainment of a unity of belonging immediately seems to cancel that reciprocity which is of the essence of friendship or to reduce it to triviality.

The implied neither/nor of Socrates' third position would seem to suggest that, in friendship, one cannot be dear to a person *merely* according to the extent to which he is useful (*chresimos*) to that person. Rather, one must be dear to him in reality (*toi onti*) insofar as the instrumentality of the relationship anticipates a shared goal. For friendship to pertain, there must be a primordial being-dear of the *proton philon* which lies outside the chain of things which are cherished, on account of their usefulness as a means to an end.[10] If friendship depended upon and was exhausted by a calculation of such conditions, it could never be sustained; conditions are always changing, and one's capacity to fulfil those conditions does not remain constant.

This can start to seem like a Kantian distinction between treating people as ends and not as means. Yet Plato, unlike Kant, not only allows people to be treated as means, but also regards all things as possible ends of relating. He envisages friendship with animals and children, and even with things and processes of all kinds.[11]

One can draw the contrast with Kant still further: pure moral regard, according to Kant, must always be one-way and never mutual. He positions the 'sentimental' sharing of affections and good taste as a secondary good, but the highest moral motive is to be exercised in disinterest as to a possible return of affectionate regard.[12] Yet this unilateral direction cannot be extended to our relations with animals and children, since it concerns a regard which is commanded only by the presence of another free, rational, autonomous agent.[13] So for Kant, the moral regard is indifferent as to return, and yet does not fully apply to children and animals who are seen as incapable (animals) or only semi-capable

---

[10] Hans-Georg Gadamer, '*Logos* and *Ergon* in Plato's *Lysis*', in *Dialogue and Dialectic*, ed. P. Christopher Smith (New Haven: Yale University Press, 1980), 1–20 at pp. 13ff.

[11] Stephen R. L. Clark, *The Political Animal: Biology, Ethics and Politics* (London and New York: Routledge, 1999), chapter 9; *Statesman* 263c ff; 310e–311; *Laws* 5.740.

[12] Immanuel Kant, *The Metaphysics of Morals*, trans. Mary Gregor (Cambridge: Cambridge University Press, 1991), 66.

[13] Kant, *The Metaphysics of Morals*, 98–100, 230, 238. Kant nevertheless thought that cruelty to animals was demeaning to human dignity and tended to reduce our moral sensibility. As regards children, they are for Kant *potentially* autonomous subjects and citizens, and for this reason have a right to parental and societal care, which is not, however, as yet the free and equal regard of one adult for another. However, children are already free persons; though it is the case that, for Kant, parents have a right to guide and educate them until the age of 'emancipation' when their free nature can be given its full right of exercise.

(children) of returning to us any moral equivalence. For Plato, by contrast, one discovers an opposite paradox. Here, the purity of non-utilitarian friendship is signalled not by unilateral disinterest, but by reciprocity and mutuality within the horizon of the good;[14] yet for Plato, friendship can be extended to children and animals, despite the relative lack of equal return or symmetry of exchange in these instances. In the case of the Kantian paradox, there is a clear explanation: children and animals do not qualify as fully adequate recipients of the unilateral ethical gift, which requires a full acknowledgement of the free right of the giver, beyond mere gratitude. But in the case of the Platonic paradox, one seems to be presented with a mysterious contradiction. If friendship is a shared gift-exchange, then should not children and animals be excluded from this circle of adult festivity?

But the key here is that, in this unemphatic dialogue, Plato, unlike Kant, does not banish the useful and content-filled altogether from the field of friendship. He does not think in a Kantian version of 'personalist' terms, which involve a sharp post-Cartesian division of subject and object. Rather, Plato is prepared to entertain the idea of a certain community between human beings and everything in the cosmos. But this community is not statically conceived. Even in the case of inter-human relations, one finds a certain 'shaping' of the other, as if she were an object, and a certain benign 'deployment' of the other for the sake of promoting one's own spiritual growth. There is a kind of 'leaning' on the other, in such a way that one passes through moments when contingency and need will shape one's preferences and friendships (e.g. 219e–220a). This circumstance helps to explain why, as Stephen R. L. Clark has noted, Plato draws a far less sharp division between human beings, animals and things than does Aristotle.[15] To some degree, all these cosmic realities are involved in a perpetual exchange of goods. But it is also the case that cosmic hierarchy includes the human political community. This is of a piece with the Stranger's mythic invocation in the *Statesman* of the idea that human beings are 'shepherded' by cosmic guardians. For the higher cosmic powers, we are ourselves but animals, just as for the Athenian of the *Laws*, we are playthings of the gods.[16] Such hierarchic mediation divides

---

[14] *Lysis* 221e–222a; 222b.

[15] Clark, 'Herds of Free Bipeds', *The Political Animal*, chapter 9, especially p. 238.

[16] This hierarchical metaphor is nonetheless complex. As 'playthings' of the gods, the philosopher can come to participate or co-operate in that control by the exercise and proper directing of reason. Moreover, the description at *Statesman* 268b9–c3 of the ruler turns out to be the result of a mistaken division. The myth told by the Eleatic Stranger

the human community itself. In the *Republic,* Socrates speaks of the 'herding' of human beings by the guardian class.[17]

What implications can one draw from this? If things, animals and children are somewhat elevated into the community of exchange, it is inversely the case that human beings remain, for the higher powers, and sometimes for one another, to a degree, playthings, animals and children, and that we perpetually adjust our positions in the economy of use and gratuity. Two reasons for this circumstance can be suggested. First, relatively undeveloped human beings, those deficient in some particular regard, need to be raised, moulded and shaped to develop their potential. Second, the relatively unreflective beauty possessed by one human being may be the occasion for the emergence of a more reflective vision of intellectual beauty on the part of the soul of another. In this benign sense, one human being has been of instrumental assistance to the further raising of an already-elevated (in the sense of more wise and virtuous) other.[18]

This can perhaps help us to understand the contrast between the Kantian and Platonic paradoxes. For Kant, one-way regard cannot extend fully downwards to the non- or semi-rational, because he subscribes to an assumption of merely abstract reciprocity. The unilateral moral gesture paradoxically assumes a formal smooth-surfaced reciprocity of adult free rational beings on an even plane, granting each other mutual rights to negative, unconstrained liberty.[19] But, for Plato, a mutual moral regard

---

assigns this kind of ruler to the age of Cronos, whereas for the age in which we live, the ruler is not a divine shepherd but a human being who weaves together the conflicting tendencies in human souls and the types of character among citizens. Arguably, the picture of the ruler as shepherd in the age of Cronos may be a reference to the philosopher-rulers of the *Republic*. Even at *Republic* 343b, the analogy between rulers and shepherds is used to cast light on some aspects of the character and behaviour of rulers and auxiliaries or guardians. That is, they seek the good of their 'flocks', and, like good sheep-dogs, are gentle towards their fellow citizens, whom they regard as friends, though they are fierce towards enemies.

[17] At *Lysis* 212e–213a, a couplet from Theognis is cited in which the term *philia* arguably applies not just to children but also to horses, hunting dogs and guests. However, the term may here have the sense of 'one's own'.

[18] See especially the relationship between Socrates and Phaedrus in *Phaedrus*.

[19] This mutual or 'dialogical' aspect of the foundation of morality was given yet greater emphasis by Johann Gottlieb Fichte. See J. G. Fichte, *Foundations of Natural Right* (Cambridge: Cambridge University Press, 2000), 29–37. Fichte linked this circumstance of practical reason to the ineluctably non-idealist element in theoretical reason: the final guarantee of the barrier or *Anstoss* of the encountered 'not-self' for the thinking mind is the fact that another, 'philosophical' mind can secondarily reflect upon the problematic relation between mind and what the mind knows. Both the philosopher's problematised

can extend downwards to the non- or semi-rational, since, for him, moral reciprocity seems, by a reverse paradox, to involve a unilateral moment of inexplicable asymmetry which is, at one moment, sustained by use or occasion, but at another, undercut by the same. There is always or usually such a unilateral moment, since individual beings, including human beings, seldom and in all respects obtain to the same level of vision and self-realisation at exactly the same instant. Plato's asymmetrical model therefore accommodates human individual differences within time and space.

From this contrast between Plato and Kant, a further contrast follows: that Plato links one-way regard with (a relative and educative) objectification and instrumentalisation, whereas, for Kant, a purified and unilateral regard is linked with a strict absence of instrumentalisation.[20]

How is one to understand this? Kant has in the background a Lockean-mediated Cartesian absolute contrast of free subject and purely factual extended object drained of inherent meaning. For Plato, by contrast, at least in his mature period, which the *Lysis* arguably intimates (if indeed it is an early dialogue), both subject and object reflect the intelligible realm in differing degrees, and, indeed, can reflect one another, if, by virtue of some affinity, they become associated – thereby problematising our modern dichotomy.[21] Thus, Plato's pairs and contrasts are not as absolute as

---

recognition of the mind of the other, and of the distance between mind and thing known, ensures a 'realist' moment within critical idealism, since without this moment, there would be no philosophy, and no arising of problematic reflection at all. For Fichte, the practically inter-subjective proves the foundation of theoretical understanding, while, inversely, the refusal of either 'metaphysical' realism or idealism in favour of a sceptical critical mutual referring of 'representational' knowledge to the thing as 'represented' is seen as the precondition of a non-metaphysical theory of rights. Significantly, the practical and theoretical perspectives come together in the centrality of education, where the educator as 'philosopher' is theoretically elevating the observed pupil as learning to an eventual practical and political equality of mutual respect. See Luc Ferry, *Political Philosophy I: Rights – the New Quarrel between the Ancients and the Moderns*, trans. Franklin Philip (Chicago: Chicago University Press, 1990), 85–125. In this sense, one can see Fichte as offering an 'immanentised' and non-metaphysical version of Plato's pedagogic fusion of the theoretical with the practical. However, without the metaphysical horizon of recollection of the forms to mediate the role of educator and pupil, the role of the former risks being reduced to an eliciting of freedom already present in the pupil and cannot constitute a 'friendly' offering of an occasion of recollection not otherwise available.

[20] John Milbank, 'Soul of Reciprocity: Part One', *Modern Theology* 17, no. 3 (2001), 335–91.

[21] There are everyday examples of the chain of affiliation bringing unlike things together, such as that deployed at *Hippias Major* 287e ff, and imported at *Phaedo* 73d, 74a. The examples of everyday reminding used at *Phaedo* 84c–88b to prepare for the difficult

are Kant's. In consequence, animals and children 'made use of' through the good affections of a superior individual, in his quest for a greater vision of the good, are themselves thereby elevated to closer proximity to the psychic realm, rather than downgraded from subjectivity, since in receiving the guardian's love, they also catch a glimpse of the vision of Good which that love has helped to trigger (if one might bring the *Phaedrus* to bear upon the matter).

Inversely, it is for this reason, one could venture, that the Kantian objection that returned affection contaminates non-objectifying love does not hold for Plato in the instance of reciprocal friendship. For even such friendship not only can but must have asymmetrical moments if it is to remain a true reciprocity with diverse and essential respective contributions, rather than a levelling out into a bland harmony of coinciding egoisms. In this sense, one could infer, a diverse and mutual hierarchy must remain even at the summit of an equal friendship. For not only are two friends sometimes at different stages in the quest for virtue and wisdom. They both, in the final stage also, irreplaceably exemplify to the other some facet of the reflected good, just as Plato himself in the dialogue points out that hunger and thirst and other desires can survive and be enjoyed, even in the context of their final satisfaction (220d–221a).

For Plato, therefore, there is an implied asymmetry not only on the road to a mutual sharing in the good, but at the heart of this mutuality itself. Therefore he did entertain a respect for the other in their otherness, in a way that Maurice Blanchot and others have thought impossible for Greek antiquity.[22]

The gradient of this asymmetry, for Plato, is often steep. One can think, for example, of the way in which the pupil is beholden to the philosopher who alone can trigger in his soul the discipline and virtuous living required for a recollection of the highest realities, and hence, over time, prompt the release of the pupil's soul from the cycle of metempsychosis.[23] For this to occur, the philosopher's knowledge of the pupil's soul must surely be so intricate and exacting that it cannot be gained by mere swift assessment. But such philosophic love is not necessarily reciprocated, or at least not in equal form or freight. This

---

notion of recollecting what we have not seen and cannot see from what we perceive, are being reminded of a friend by seeing the lyre he plays; being reminded of Kebes by seeing Simmias; being reminded of Simmias by seeing his picture. In each case, there is an association between the reminder and the thing recollected.

[22] Maurice Blanchot, *L'Amitié* (Paris: Gallimard, 1971).

[23] For example, *Phaedrus*, 245d–247c.

might help us to understand why the *Lysis* does not advocate *either* the possibility of the lover's resignation to unreturned love of the lover, or a requited mutual love as paradigmatic of pure friendship. Rather, it seems to point out objections to both cases. One-way love seems to lead to one's loving or being friends with enemies, and enemies thereby becoming friends, which is a contradiction (213b). Yet if love is equal and mutual, of friend for friend, it appears to be an unnecessary fashion-accessory to our self-contained repleteness. Moreover, no virtue appears to accrue to the self in this instance, for one loses the moment of one-way self-giving, or abasement before the beloved, involved in the educative procession of instruction and submission. Does Plato in any way try to resolve this difficulty?

As one ascends towards the final estate of friendship, for Plato, one passes beyond the conditions of need for the useful and desirable, towards what is truly real, both within one-self and in terms of one's own teleological vision: the two being inseparable for a thinker who knows nothing of our modern ethical oscillation between inward deontological integrity, on the one hand, and the pursuit of consequences, on the other. The true realities, when possessed, will, it would seem, surpass any condition of lack or means to an end, since they are replete. But, meanwhile, the trinkets of the finitely useful and desirable form connections in an essential chain of mediation. One cannot simply let go of these, since one cannot jump out of time and dwell in the pure Empyrean. Desire seeks the end of desire; but reaching the end of desire still, at least for now, requires the complexly linked interludes of finite desiring.

This intellectual rhythm is matched by a similar one in the experience of friendship, even if this coincidence of truth with mutual love is later more fully expounded in the Johannine writings of the New Testament. Indeed, one could say that, for Plato, friendship is the necessary exoteric aspect of esoteric understanding and vice versa. If the cognitive ascent to the form of the good (or the One) requires the heterogeneity of friendship, then, inversely, the exterior heterogeneity of friendship can promote the tendency to the inner vision of unity. It follows that friendship, for Plato, is governed by an oscillating rhythm of contrasting pairs – sameness and difference, likeness and unlikeness, unity and multiplicity, giving and receiving, understanding of others and self-understanding. In this way, there is an homology between Plato's account of the philosophical ascent to the forms, on the one hand, and his account of the growth of friendship, on the other. The path of the good involves both, inseparably. Unilateral psychic ascent to the One might be horizontally broken into by the exchange of human love; but this exchange must itself be constituted by the asymmetry of the soul's development.

But how is the relationship of friendship, which is both reciprocal and yet asymmetrical, to be achieved?

Much is made in the *Lysis* of the youthfulness of the friends at hand; and the polemic theatre of the Palaestra is one distinguished by the presence of young people and the disportings of knuckle-bones and other forms of playing (206e). If one thing becomes clear in this unclear dialogue, it is that the mechanical playground one-up-manship of Lysis and Menexenos cannot be taken as true friendship; it depends too much on amounts and calculations of advantage and disadvantage. At the end of the dialogue, when the discussion descends into confusion, Socrates sets out in search of someone 'older' (*presbuteron*) (233a1) with whom to continue the discussion. Must the question of the nature of friendship only be asked of those who have lived longer, just as, for Aristotle, the study of ethics demands that one have reached the age of thirty? Judging by the raucous and vain behaviour of the daemonic, drunkenly other-worldly and barbaric elders who arrive at *Lysis* 223a, Socrates' point is perhaps not that an older person is wiser by dint of age; indeed, Lysis himself shows flickers of solemn wisdom (210d9, 212a), to no lesser degree than the pedagogues who come stumbling drunkenly into the Palaestra show signs of immaturity and vanity (223a). Perhaps Socrates' underlying point is that friendship does not flourish when taken out of context and excavations are conducted to determine its essence. This point might seem obvious enough, that friendship exists best where the question as to its nature is not asked.[24]

Towards the end of the dialogue, Socrates appears to undergo an argumentative collapse: 'If neither the loved nor the loving, nor the like nor the unlike, nor the good nor the belonging ... if none of these is a friend, I am at a loss for anything further to say' (222e1ff). It all seems hopeless: friendship pertains between like and like, unlike and unlike, and neither like nor like, nor unlike and unlike. It is both asymmetrical and symmetrical. It is the former as guiding others to the good, and the latter, as the whole chain already shares in the first good. However, this would suggest that friendship vanishes at the summit of the good. Knowing or being the good, we no longer need friends. But if friendship is not among the forms, it is not fully real and remains aporetic, and this is why it is cancelled; on the other hand, Plato suggests that even when only the

---

[24] Gadamer, '*Logos* and *Ergon* in Plato's *Lysis*', 10.

good is left, we are still friendly with things (221c). Ascending the ladder of guiding friendship only works dialectically through these contradictions. So, the dialogue ends with friendship undefined.

But the final exchange of the dialogue seems to lead us away from this impasse. Friendship in practice remains, though it has been theoretically demolished. The good has been arrived at by the ladder of friendship, and the ladder in theory kicked away, only for it to be restored again in practice: 'To-day, Lysis and Menexenos, we have made ourselves ridiculous – I, an old man, as well as you. For these others will go away and tell how we believe we are friends of one another – for I count myself in with you – but what a "friend" is, we have not yet succeeded in discovering' (223c1 ff).

Is friendship then just incidental or an illusion? Or is it rather that one's most primordial self is immemorially forgotten and unknowable? Like the good, one cannot know the full nature of friendship, yet perhaps as with the good, this is because something essential to our true knowledge and self-identity precedes us somewhat irrecoverably. In order to know at all, we must seek to recollect our constitutive relation to the good. In order to have the desire to recollect, we must already be captivated by the friend we love.

One senses that a link between philosophy and friendship may indeed have been indirectly indicated; that all the time that the interlocutors have engaged in their debate as to the nature of friendship, they have been entering into its estate, even without knowing it. While friendship might not endure its own analysis, it nevertheless arises in the exchanges of discourse. The inconclusiveness of the dialogue might suggest to us that as we edge towards intimations of the link between friendship and the 'way of life' marked out by the philosopher, so also one becomes aware of the zig-zagging haphazardness of real-life friendship, with its argumentative detours and blind alleys. If the condition of friendship has been entered into in the course of the dialogue, then perhaps Socrates' neither/nor has been successfully 'proven'; for the interlocutors have paraded their mechanistic notions, and have been prompted to confront their restricted compass. Meanwhile, they have been drawn outward and beyond those restrictions towards a certain way of life, or a particular future, which, it appears from their concluding exchanges, they might share in friendship with one another.

Is this pragmatic intimation of a resolution of aporia in any way theoretically supported? I have already mentioned that Plato himself suggests at one point (221a–b) that even within eschatological consummation of our desires, we might still enjoy its objects. This suggests that our arrival at true self-belonging in the good will not, after all, cancel affinity or likeness. Friendship remains compatible with knowledge of the good and the route to the good via friendship is eminently caught up into the final goal.

However, just this resolution is apparently questioned at the very end, by Plato himself. He offers us two alternatives: either belonging and likeness are to be differentiated, or they are not (222b–d). If they are different, then true belonging in the good requires no likeness, affinity or friendship. Therefore, friendship will be indifferent to knowledge and merely about affinity: evil will be as friendly to evil as good to good. But it has already been shown that evils are antagonistic towards each other, and therefore that, if friendship is to exist at all, it must have to do with a cleaving to the good. But if, under the supposition of the division of belonging from liking, a cleaving to the good renders friendship irrelevant, then friendship does not really exist at all.

If, however, Plato goes on to say, belonging and likeness are identical, then only the genuine self-belonging of the good to itself can be friendship. But this has, earlier in the dialogue, been shown to be false: the good itself and a state of being good are not in need of friendship. Thus, it seems, *philia* as 'self-belonging' extrudes *philia* as 'being with'. Philosophy has torn this element of inherited language apart.

Or is it the case that Socrates and Plato remain ironically the friends of inherited usage? Could the invoked vision of eschatological fulfilment imply neither division nor total identity of belonging with liking? Could *philia* obtain a validly analogous range? Here it is important to note that the issue posed in the dialogue does not obviously seem to be to do with the true nature of value and identity, *either* as part of a positive build-up to the middle-period theory of forms, or as an exercise in Socratic rather than Platonic scepticism. For a transcendent Good, above the shadows, somewhat like the good of the *Republic*, is simply invoked rather than argued for (219c–d). It is already seen as the final *friend* in the *double* sense of the friend whom we love, like a child, *and* the friend who leads and guides us, like the wise teacher. This suggests a manner in which the good, if it lies beyond friendship, nevertheless incorporates in a simple unity its asymmetrical polarities. As in this way both the final and the first, the *proton philon*, it is the ultimate guiding goal for finite exercises of *philia*, for which it is presented as exemplary. The *relative* self-sufficiency of, for example, one's love for a child does not in any way negate this anticipation of the theory of forms, for nothing in Plato's dialogues at any stage suggests that the separated universals are incompatible with the existence of immanent, relative universal goods and truths of an 'Aristotelian' kind.

Indeed, one can argue that *methexis* and *koinonia* require the existence of just such relatively universal states and processes. And surely, if the seeming topic of friendship in the *Lysis* has wider theoretical bearing, then it already concerns the problematic of participation in the forms, rather than the supposition of the forms themselves as resolving of certain cognitive dilemmas. For, to reiterate, the existence of the good is not assumed: it is not offered either as a solution, nor as in itself a problem. Rather, the problem posed is of our relationship with the good; but not so much of the existence of this relationship or our ability to speak of the good via this relationship; rather – and in a sense, more simply – of the ultimate status of this relationship. Are friendship and desire mere ladders to be kicked away? Do relation and likeness vanish in the face of the good? Or do they permanently share in it? Do they participate? Inversely, is the good so ineffably alien from likeness that desire cannot intimate its nature, save as an obscure blank, on pain of reducing it to the status of just another mediating friend? The third-man problematic is in this way already obscurely in view.

One possible resolution of these problems, and saving of the integrity of *methexis* might involve an invocation of what on many internal and external testimonies appears to have been Plato's final teaching, the date of whose first genesis we cannot know. According to this teaching, ultimate reality is a blend of the hyperforms of the One and the Many, of the determinate Sun of the One-Good and the indeterminate dyad which incorporates all the lesser forms, a 'weaving', as we learn in the *Sophist*, of the same with the different. It is for this reason that even the ultimate level of eternal truth in the realm of the forms might be considered hospitable to the interweaving of friendship which it does not cancel, and this may be why, in the *Phaedrus*, unlike the *Symposium*, the human vehicle of *eros* remains in the transcendent height of its consummation.[25]

---

[25] The question of the unwritten teachings is disputed. Members of the Tübingen School, such as H. J. Krämer and Konrad Gaiser, hold that for most of his writing career, Plato held a set of metaphysical principles which he never expressed in writing, except in the form of allusions. These involve oblique references to a hierarchy of being from the One and Indefinite Dyad downwards. Others hold that Plato may have expressed orally some developments of what he wrote in *Republic* and *Philebus*; for example, in the notorious Lecture on the Good (see Konrad Gaiser, 'Plato's Enigmatic Lecture "on the Good"',

IMPOSSIBLE FRIENDSHIP

Let us now turn, in conclusion, to contemporary debates about friendship, and in particular, Jacques Derrida's aporetic treatment of friendship in *The Politics of Friendship*.[26] For Derrida, the crucial problem is the seeming tension between fraternity and democracy: democracy commands fraternity, and yet renders the privileging of certain people suspicious, even though we can only acquaint ourselves with people one by one.[27] Human rights without fraternity would be abstract and unenacted, yet as soon as they are enacted, they fail to meet the conditions of formal universality and neutrality which constitute these rights as rights.[28] There seems to be an equal imperative to befriend and not to befriend. For Derrida, this concurs in some ways with the view that one can infer from Aristotle that one should only be friends with the dead.[29] This is the only morally unambiguous stance because, for Aristotle, one is to love only the good, but the verdict 'good' properly falls only upon the completely lived life of many swallows and a few summers. Moreover, friendship consists, for Aristotle, more in the act of loving than that of being loved. Yet we cannot really be friends with absent people, since Aristotle insists that friendship is a matter of reciprocity, and the pleasure (which is crucial to it) consists in what comes from the friend as friend, and not from the friend as useful object.[30] Nevertheless, it seems that only a relationship with an absent good is able to rise above the exercise of preference, prejudice and the contaminations of advantage. The aporia of rights and fraternity (whereby each needs the other and yet is destroyed by it) is also the aporia of ideal absence versus enacted presence.

According to Derrida, there is a second aspect to the aporia of enacted friendship in Aristotle. We must have friends who are virtuous, and one should love the virtuous only. That is to say, one should love those who exhibit universal human qualities. And yet Aristotle also indicates that friendship arises as something spontaneous in addition to its preconditions of *habitus*, which include our own established virtue and natural

---

Phronesis 25 (1980), 5–37). Others (notably Harold Cherniss, *The Riddle of the Early Academy* (Berkeley and Los Angeles: University of California Press, 1945) hold that the idea of the unwritten teachings arises from an error or misunderstanding by Aristotle. Others (see especially Kenneth Sayre, *Plato's Late Ontology: A Riddle Resolved* (Princeton NJ: Princeton University Press, 1983)) hold that the reported content of the unwritten teachings can be found in late dialogues, especially *Philebus*.

[26] Jacques Derrida, *The Politics of Friendship*, trans. George Collins (London: Verso, 2005).
[27] Derrida, ibid, 227–70.   [28] Ibid, 75–112.   [29] Ibid, 7, 13.
[30] *Eudemian Ethics*, VII 2 1237 b 1–10

admiration for virtue. Beyond habit for Aristotle, as Derrida points out, there is 'confidence' in friends that is only established by time. That Aristotle has in mind here something supplementary and contingent seems to be indicated by the fact that there can be no primary friendship between human beings and God, the latter being outside the work of time.[31] But such a supplement does not seem to add so much as to transgress: a preference for certain virtuous people appears to contaminate the universal love of virtue. Primary friendship is also not possible between adults and children: even though one can love objects in Aristotle, these cases lack the reciprocity of shared attainment of virtue and so the pleasure of exchanged equality.

A third aspect is also considered. In the case of Plato, we have seen that the *Lysis* insinuates a tension between love merely given and love circulated. Aristotle, by contrast (with his lower positioning of animals, women and children, confined to the *oikos*, in contrast to Plato's *kallipolis*, where the whole polis is 'herded' by the philosopher-guardians), as we have seen, construes friendship more in terms of reciprocity, and confines one-way generosity to the nonetheless supreme virtue of magnanimity, even though he still accords primacy to friendship given over friendship received.[32] The fully virtuous man must be magnanimous and have friends, yet for Derrida, a tension arises here: pure virtue is under our control as magnanimity, but comes by moral luck in the case of friendship. But is it virtuous to offer friendship or not? Plato's question in the *Lysis*, unasked by Aristotle, arises for Derrida in relation to Aristotle: is an offer of friendship coterminous with friendship? If the offer is spurned, how can it count as friendship? There is here a tension between the universal possibility of offering, which is within our power, and the specific instantiation of friendship, which is not. And yet, as moral luck, the latter seems necessary to complete the ethical as absolute obligation to be effective in the particular instance.[33]

Derrida then extends his threefold aporia, somewhat like Socrates, to its extreme consequences: if one were to choose one path of the divided way, one will find that the true friend is the enemy who does not love back, and yet is not our friend because he is our enemy. If we choose instead the other path, we find that we should love the familiar and be true to our

---

[31] *Eudemian Ethics* VII 2 1237 b 10–27; Derrida, op. cit., 17.
[32] For a more detailed account of reciprocity in Aristotle, see Robert Sokolowski, 'Phenomenology of Friendship', *Review of Metaphysics* 55 (March 2002), 451–70.
[33] Derrida, *The Politics of Friendship*, 49–75.

affinities, but since the familiar friend is not yet dead, he remains unknown and we may lose ourselves and our virtue through the mis-prison. And so it is safer to love the enemy, 'my true friend', concludes Derrida, following William Blake.[34]

Despite his discovery of aporias in Aristotle, Derrida still sees Aristotle as more proto-democratic than Plato. He reads Aristotle as saying that there is no Platonic friend, or form of friendship.[35] Even though there are problematic tensions in Aristotle's hovering between the universal and the particular, of the kind just described in its threefold aspect, this points to a post-Kantian tension which democracy cannot avoid, between difference and the universal categorical imperative, according to which, both need and yet refuse the other. What can democracy do but engage in this aporetic shuttle?[36]

FRIENDSHIP WITH THE DIVINE

Can the Platonic zig-zag of friendship and dialectic offer an alternative to this deconstruction of Aristotle? It is arguable that Aristotle is situated midway between Plato and Kant, even though his parity is far greater with the former. For Kant, we cannot be friends with things (or owe categorical respect to them; this is purer than friendship for Kant), nor with less than autonomous human beings. Even though this would be a one-way relationship, it would not be disinterested since it would involve a coalescence between the thing or less-than-subject (since things are objects as the reductive correlative of the representing subject) and myself. For Aristotle, like Kant, we cannot be friends with things in the full sense, though friendly love for them is more significant here than for Kant.[37] We can only enjoy primary friendship with other male, wealthy and so relatively autonomous rational animals. However, unlike Kant, Aristotle maintains that in its ideal form, this relationship involves a substantive reciprocity. One might be tempted to see such mutuality as escaping Kant's formalism, and yet in some ways it does anticipate it: what circulates in this mutuality is predominantly the same general virtue and love of the same good. Moreover, Aristotle emphatically privileges, within the reciprocal circuit, the giving over the receiving of love, and, in this way, tends to conclude to one side of the aporia, in favour of autonomy and

---

[34] Ibid, 26–49.   [35] Ibid, 19.   [36] Ibid, 227–308.
[37] It was noted above that for Plato we can be friends with all that is psychic, even if it does not have full human subjectivity. See *Lysis* 212e ff.

magnanimity (or 'rights', one can say anachronistically), and subordinates the chances of affinity and the event of fraternity (with the same anachronism). This is why he celebrates the disinterested love of the mother who hands her children over to the care of a nurse. Here, as for Plato in the *Lysis*, one-way love is also friendship. But Aristotle's example concerns disinterest rather than Plato's element of 'deploying', in a sense which must be distinguished from mere utilitarian 'use', nor does it echo Plato's notion of 'rising upwards', for nurture has been farmed out.[38]

In order to escape formalism, one has to move beyond Kant's one-way regard of the other and Aristotle's symmetrical reciprocity. Perhaps a balance can be found in Plato for whom there is an ethical one-way,[39] as seen in the dynamic between lover and beloved in the *Phaedrus*, where it is unclear how the beloved could ever adequately reciprocate.[40] The asymmetry of the Platonic model involves a certain action upon the other in his almost-objectivity, which allows Plato to envisage friendship with things, even though there remains an hierarchical scale from unsouled things to the higher mode of souls. This is not, as we have seen, akin to Aristotle's maternal disinterested abandoning, but rather a bonding with the lower thing or person for the sake of its elevation. In Plato, the zig-zag between the mutual and the one-way offering of love is also the zig-zag between seeing the other as subject and seeing the other as object. The latter is not shocking if one is willing to meet their visibility, and if one remembers that, for Plato, there is an ethically right mode of blending with things as well as persons. Moreover, it becomes clear that when the zig-zag of one-way offering and reciprocation has fully unfurled, the binary opposition of subject and object seems no longer sustainable.

This reflection tends to suggest that Derrida is somewhat confined by all-too-modern contrasts of subject and object. These have some very discrete beginnings in Aristotle, perhaps, for whom the ethical sphere of the inter-human is distinguished from that of theoretical knowledge which embraces things. Likewise, Aristotle confines friendship to the immanent realm, whereas Plato speaks directly of friendship with the divine.[41] This does not mean, as Derrida supposes, that Plato is doomed to subordinate particular friendship in time to the universal. Rather, it suggests that Plato avers to a dimension of the not-fully-knowable-outside-desire which we can take as an horizon for the integration of the oscillation between universal and particular, like and unlike, subject and object of love. In

---

[38] *EE* VII 3 1238b 15–1239b; *Nicomachean Ethics*, 1158a31–1159a9.   [39] *Lysis* 212e ff.
[40] See n. 1 above.   [41] *Symposium* 212a; see also 202e. See n. 16 above.

addition, as we have seen, the Platonic notion of friendship with the divine is the counterpart of his notion of friendship with things, and his countenancing of friendship with animals, children and pupils. Curiously, it seems that it is Plato's attention to divine hierarchisation which permits a greater degree of materialism than one finds in Aristotle, and an element also of philosophical *kenosis*, even if his divine realm is still but a mute lure, compared with Aristotle's immanentist etherealisation of *philia*. Since we can elevate things, so the divine realm can elevate us, and friendship takes on the character of a cosmic and ontological bond.[42] In addition, for Plato, there is no sense that for mortals it is superior to be the subject rather than the object in the asymmetrical relation of friendship. Because we are all objects of the divine lure, this means that Plato can exalt our receptive role.[43]

Whereas Aristotle's universal virtue of love tends to fall into a contradictory relation with the contingent, as Derrida discerns, Plato's transcendent good welcomes the particular in its mysterious archexemplarity, and, inversely, the particular in its surprising openness betokens a way to the transcendent.

Derrida is nonetheless aware that one might associate the transcendent with the particular. What he seems less inclined to consider is the way in which the transcendent might speak with a 'middle voice' between the universal and the particular in an analogical zigzag, rather than according to an aporetic shuttle. For Derrida, the association of the transcendent and the particular means 'religion' and the 'theologico-political' which assumes an arbitrary making-divine via a projection of 'this friend', which means exclusively my family, my nation, my race and so forth. And yet he allows no way out of this aporia. It is in consequence Derrida who must accept commitment to an ineluctably racist moment. For Plato, by contrast, preference need not be 'racist'. The specificity of friendship is paradoxically elevated to the divine order. It is in the nature of friendship to enter into the gift of the other as *psyche* which elevates both befriender and befriended in their specificity to union with the transcendent form of the good. Choice, preference and affinity are only

---

[42] A further detail can be found at *Phaedo* 73d–76a where Socrates indicates that 'unlike' things can be likened, or non-identically assimilated to a person with whom they are associated through the mediations of *eros*. See n. 20 above.

[43] At *Laws* 644d, the Athenian describes human beings as puppets and as put together as 'playthings' of the gods. See also 804b4: 'For the most part we are puppets, but with some small share of the truth.' See also 644d–645b and 803b ff.

arbitrary if one does not believe that time is the moving image of eternity.[44]

In the foregoing, we have seen why Plato may be read as anticipatory of St John's understanding of mutual love as persisting in the ultimate, as the content of truth. For this reason, friendship ceases to be an instrumental means towards truth, discard-able as an unnecessary supplement. This conclusion indicates why the Platonic legacy has enabled Christian theology to hold together, with an apocalyptic intensity, a concern with the eternal, and with the seriousness of what occurs within time. Plato implies that the events and particularities of time are and will be ultimately 'caught up' into the heavenly, perhaps in such a way that has not always been noted in interpretations of Platonic philosophy. Because he does not construe the transcendent Forms, and the Form of the Good above all, as in a hostile or competitive relation with the temporal, and construes the participatory relation of the temporal to the transcendent to be an wholly unique and peculiar kind of relation, not permitting of the recursive and receding relationships which finite relations inevitably involve, he is not seeking to displace this world with another one in quite the manner that is often suggested.

There is paradoxically more danger of such a displacement occurring, when an abstract layer or fragment of this world is rendered absolute, this being a danger on some readings of Aristotle. In such cases, specificity, corporeality and motion may be rendered subordinate to a fixed categorial repertoire, and to the universal stability and sway of abstract form. In such cases, there may pertain a risk that friendship in the city will yield to the isolated and rural contemplation of the cosmos, or that friendship may be regarded as the glue of the polity, or as an ingredient of an individually happy life. By contrast, as we have seen, the Platonic emphasis upon the transcendent remoteness of the eternally real, tends to keep finite factors in play: affection and understanding, society and nature, the particular and the general, the substantive and the relational, the temporal and the gestural. The vagueness of the Platonic categorial Forms – the One and the Dyad, and their inter-mixture – ensures that one remain open to complex dialectical plays between identity and difference whose specific combinations are never foreclosed. And truth consisting in this interplay suggests that the deep ontological structure of the real is friendship itself, in various degrees: the wonderment at both affinity and difference, and their live-able resolution, which constitute social possibility. It is Plato, perhaps

---

[44] *Timaeus* 37d.

rather more than Aristotle, at least on one rendering, who construes nature as the social, or the proto-social, and the eternal as something akin to a social realisation or consummation. Christian theology which took this to a further completion, and personalised this vision, understanding its truth as the arrival in time of divinity as friendship.

Bibliography

Blanchot, Maurice. *L'Amitié*. Paris: Gallimard, 1971.

Bolotin, David. *Plato's Dialogue on Friendship*. Ithaca: SUNY Press, 1979.

Carr, Brian. 'Friendship in Plato's *Lysis*'. In *Friendship East and West: Philosophical Perspectives*, edited by Oliver Leaman, 13–31. London: Routledge, 1996.

Cherniss, Harold. *The Riddle of the Early Academy*. Berkeley and Los Angeles: University of California Press, 1945.

Clark, Stephen R. L. *The Political Animal: Biology, Ethics and Politics*. London and New York, Routledge, 1999.

Derrida, Jacques. *The Politics of Friendship*. Translated by George Collins. London: Verso, 2005.

Ferry, Luc. *Political Philosophy I: Rights – the New Quarrel between the Ancients and the Moderns*. Translated by Franklin Philip. Chicago: Chicago University Press, 1990.

Fichte, J. G. *Foundations of Natural Right*. Cambridge: Cambridge University Press, 2000.

Gadamer, Hans-Georg. *Dialogue and Dialectic*. Translated by P. Christopher Smith. New Haven: Yale University Press, 1980.

Gaiser, Konrad. 'Plato's Enigmatic Lecture "on the Good"'. *Phronesis* 25 (1980): 5–37.

Glidden, D. K. 'The *Lysis* on Loving One's Own'. *Classical Quarterly* 31, no. 1 (1981): 39–59.

Kant, Immanuel. *The Metaphysics of Morals*. Translated by Mary Gregor. Cambridge: Cambridge University Press, 1991.

Mackenzie, M. M. 'Impasse and Explanation: From the *Lysis* to the *Phaedo*'. *Archiv für Geschichte der Philosophie* 70 (1988): 15–45.

Milbank, John. 'Soul of Reciprocity: Part One'. *Modern Theology* 17, no. 3 (2001): 335–91.

Osborne, Catherine. *Eros Unveiled: Plato and the God of Love*. Oxford: Clarendon Press, 1996.

Sayre, Kenneth. *Plato's Late Ontology: A Riddle Resolved*. Princeton, NJ: Princeton University Press, 1983.

Sokolowski, Robert. 'Phenomenology of Friendship'. *Review of Metaphysics* 55 (March 2002): 451–70.

3.6

Multiplicity in Earth and Heaven

Stephen R. L. Clark

There is an ethical risk in neglecting the infinite detail and differences of the phenomenal world in favour of a merely 'abstract' understanding, as though only 'the rational' were really significant. But it is also difficult not to believe that there is a 'real world' behind or within the manifold phenomena, and that we can 'get in touch' with the principles from which the phenomenal worlds are made. Egyptian thought (and other traditions worldwide) imagines how those multiple principles emerge from 'Nothing', and together constitute an eternal 'spiritual' reality: Plato's Forms are both the heirs of earlier 'gods' and the parents of later powers, existing in the divine *Nous* (the Spirit) 'before' their reflection in phenomena. Rather than rely on what happens 'always or for the most part' a Christian Platonist may conceive the eternal world as one far surpassing the phenomena, and able to intrude upon or reform what seems to us here-now. Plotinus' Platonism, I suggest, is closer to the Christian version, despite some ambiguities, than most Christian scholars have recognized. Our phenomenal worlds do not now express all that is contained in the divine. He would have agreed, I suggest, with Hopkins: 'All things counter, original, spare, strange ... He fathers-forth whose beauty is past change'.

THE PHENOMENAL AND THE REAL

Lying on the grass beneath a maple tree on a summer afternoon we can see the sparkle of different greens, of shivering lights and shadows. The grass itself is composed of multiple branching shoots, interspersed with daisies, and alive with little beetles, ants and spiders. Hidden away beneath us, the soil from which grass and trees both grow is itself a medley of organic and inorganic matter, ploughed by worms and even smaller creatures, and fizzing with fungi and prokaryotic life. The phenomena are disparate, ever changing, glittering with reflected light. The wind rustles the leaves. Children are playing distantly.

> Glory be to God for dappled things –
> For skies of couple-colour as a brinded cow;
> For rose-moles all in stipple upon trout that swim;
> Fresh-firecoal chestnut-falls; finches' wings.
> Landscape plotted and pieced – fold, fallow, and plough;
> And áll trádes, their gear and tackle and trim.[1]

Each leaf, each grass blade, each small beast is different, and their multiplicity is at once obvious and easily neglected – so that we only (usually) carry away some memory just of trees, grass, insects that cannot be described in detail even as we experience it. The sentiment not quite accurately attributed to Ronald Reagan, that 'if you've seen one redwood tree, you've seen them all' (and so need not be much concerned about the loss of redwoods), may actually represent a common feeling.[2] We cannot take in the multiplicity, the 'blooming, buzzing confusion' of an infant's experience,[3] and we hardly care to bother. What we mostly remember are stock pictures, stereotypes and roughly repeated features. Repeated impressions constitute experience[4] – and such memories necessarily leave out most of the un-repeated detail.

This process, thinning the original whole experience, can be continued as we examine and reflect upon the concepts we have acquired: gradually, it may come to seem to us that our understanding must be abstract. Different classes of things are folded up into genera, and what seems

---

[1] Gerard Manley Hopkins, 'Pied Beauty (1877)', in *Gerard Manley Hopkins: The Major Works*, ed. Catherine Phillips (Oxford: Oxford University Press, 2002), 132–3.

[2] The more accurate quotation seems to be as follows: 'We've got to recognize that where the preservation of a natural resource like the redwoods is concerned, that there is a common sense limit. I mean, if you've looked at a hundred thousand acres or so of trees – you know, a tree is a tree, how many more do you need to look at?' (speaking at the Western Wood Products Association in San Francisco on 12 March 1966): David Mikkelson, 'Ronald Reagan "If You've Seen One Tree ... "', Snopes.com, updated 7 June 2006, www .snopes.com/fact-check/if-youve-seen-one-tree/. The idea that the only reason to preserve the trees must be aesthetic is, obviously, foolish. It is also a rhetorical device, illicitly dependent on the notion of abstract understanding stripped of all merely personal significance that I describe below.

[3] William James, *The Principles of Psychology*, Volume 1 (Cosimo: New York, 2007), 488.

[4] Aetius 4.11.3, in *The Hellenistic Philosophers*, Volume 1, eds. A. A. Long and D. N. Sedley (Cambridge: Cambridge University Press, 1987), 238.

most important will be the widest categories of being. We notice *trees* rather than individual maples, small fluttering brown things rather than individual sparrows (finches, robins or whatever). We may come to notice only *objects* in our way, and think ourselves intelligent because we can – more or less – predict what motions to expect of them. Abstract understanding, sometimes expressed in merely mathematical terms, is granted an authority denied to the immediate, unrepeatable experience. 'Knowledge' can only be of the wide-ranging principles that best describe the etiolated memories. Eventually we may hope to reduce that knowledge to some single formula, the shortest possible description of everything that ever happens: a 'Schrodinger Equation' for all that is.[5] This description is inevitably one stripped of all merely 'personal' significance, emotional affect or aesthetic appreciation. That, said Chesterton, is the 'dreadful dry light' that must at last wither up the moral mysteries as illusions: 'respect for age, respect for property, and the sanctity of life will be a superstition. The men in the street are only organisms, with their organs more or less displayed.'[6]

There is of course a relatively harmless, even an advantageous, reading of this story: it is not that the *real world* consists only of such abstract formulae or even of material objects stripped of their significance, nor even that these are all that we should be concerned about. The advantage of abstract understanding is merely practical: we can achieve a lot by disregarding unnecessary details. The course of a missile is unlikely to be affected by its colour, any more than by whatever pet name it has been given, or whether its target is justly chosen. Even our *moral* conduct may sometimes be improved by recognizing that age, sex, gender, nationality and political associations are of no account when deciding how to treat our neighbours: it is enough that they are human. It may even be enough that they are sentient individuals with their own distinct and unrepeated being – though for that very reason it may also be a mistake to disregard or diminish immediate attachments. Someone who (for example) trusts and cares for their child, their spouse, their parents no more and no less than they would trust and care for any random, unrelated individual may earn a rationalist's approval, but hardly the common herd's! As Aristotle observed, if *all* men are our brothers then none will be treated as we

---

[5] That is, a linear partial differential equation that describes the wave function or state function of a quantum-mechanical system – which might, in principle, be the totality of things.

[6] G. K. Chesterton, *The Poet and the Lunatics* (London: Darwen Finlayson, 1962), 70.

now treat those who are presently reckoned our brothers: the scheme advanced in Plato's *Republic* 'results in each citizen's having a thousand sons, and these do not belong to them as individuals but any child is equally the son of anyone, so that all alike will regard them with indifference'.[7] The rational does not exhaust the real, either in ontology or ethics.

Is this to abandon the long tradition of Platonic (and also Stoic) intellectual theory? Plato, after all, seems to suggest that the rational and the real must be identical: what cannot be described without contradiction must be, in some sense, an illusion, 'rolling around between being and non-being'.[8] We may be forced here-now to rely on our perceptions and our mere unrationalized beliefs, but the truth is only available to intellect, and has no flaws or even any contingencies. Knowledge, it may seem, can only be of necessary truths, and God Himself can know nothing of the merely transient, contingent features of our mortal lives, nor have any reason to be concerned with any merely local experience. The real world has no particular centre (and certainly we ourselves are not central either in being or in value), nor is anything intrinsically 'far away' or 'near', nor yet 'past' or 'future'. Neither is there any preferred *scale* of things, as though our human lives were of more account than an earthworm's or a star's – unless we can persuade ourselves that our mere intuition of the wider, 'real' world itself gives us some reason to think that human life *could* express that knowledge. The World as a whole, we can pretend, can only be for gods and humans, since only gods and humans have any notion of a World that transcends, informs, sustains the little worlds of current, flawed experience to which all other animals (we say) must be confined.

One answer to this ontological and ethical proposal is to insist instead that the real world is the sum of all phenomena: not only what appears to us, but also what appears to birds, ants, fungi, trees and prokaryotes. The world beneath, if it exists at all, is not what anyone or anything experiences. We find this expressed by William James:

We may, if we like, by our reasonings, unwind things back to that black and jointless continuity of space and moving clouds of swarming atoms which science calls the only real world. But all the while the world we feel and live in will be that which our ancestors and we, by slowly cumulating strokes of choice, have extricated out of this, like sculptors, by simply rejecting certain portions of the given stuff. Other sculptors, other statues from the same stone! Other minds, other

---

[7] Aristotle, *Politics* 2, 1262a1–3.   [8] Plato, *Republic* 5, 479d4.

worlds from the same monotonous and inexpressive chaos! My world is but one in a million alike embedded, alike real to those who may abstract them. How different must be the worlds in the consciousness of ant, cuttlefish or crab![9]

On this account it is the phenomenal detail that is real, rather than the abstract similarities and continuities. There are further implications about the nature of past and distant worlds that are only occasionally acknowledged:[10] the past is nothing like what we nowadays experience, and stories about the gradual evolution of our own and cognate species within a merely material, unexperienced somewhat are as mythological as any supposedly primitive narrative about the emergence of Atum from the primordial Nothing. We may further notice, with George Berkeley, that what we shall perceive hereafter need not be 'stinted to ye few objects we at present receive from some dull inlets of perception, but proportionate to wt our faculties shall be wn God has given the finishing stroke to our nature & made us fit inhabitants for heaven, a happiness which we narrow-sighted mortals wretchedly point out to our selves by green meadows, fragrant groves, refreshing shades, crystal streams & wt other pleasant ideas our fancys can glean up in this Vale of misery'.[11] At present we only perceive a little of God's imaginings, and all (perhaps) are dependent only on the single will of God! Creation is the manifestation to finite spirits of what always already exists in the divine imagining.[12]

ARCHAI: PRINCIPLES AND BEGINNINGS

But perhaps we should make a fresh start, exactly from those past myths, if we are to understand what a thorough-going Platonism might contribute. One familiar story of the world's beginning is indeed that everything emerged (or perennially emerges) out of Nothing. That Nothing may itself be characterized, at least in negative terms, as undifferentiated, inconceivable, unlimited and 'Not Many'.[13] Out of that Nothing emerges (for no

---

[9] James, *The Principles of Psychology*, 288–9.

[10] See my 'History of Appearances, or Worlds United', in *Homage to Owen Barfield*, ed. Martin Ovens (forthcoming).

[11] George Berkeley, 'Sermon on Immortality (1708)', in *The Works of George Berkeley, Bishop of Cloyne*, Volume 7, eds. A. A. Luce and T. E. Jessop (Edinburgh: Thomas Nelson, 1967), 12.

[12] George Berkeley, *Principles of Human Knowledge and Three Dialogues*, ed. Howard Robinson (Oxford: Oxford University Press, 1996), 196.

[13] According to Plutarch, *De Ei* 9.388e, the indestructible divinity that undergoes transformations is known as Apollo (that is, *a-polla*, not many) in the Conflagration imagined by Stoic philosophers, and as Dionysus (or cognate identities) when he is rent apart and

particular reason) the First Thing, and from that First distinctly existing being – which is also, in a sense, no thing – all the things there are successively emerge. In Egyptian thought the One (Atum) becomes the Million, which all bear, as it were, the echo or stamp or reflection of that First. In Chinese thought, at the other side of the globe, it is similarly from the Nameless that Heaven and Earth spring, and all their offspring. Even what at first must seem a radically different notion – that 'in the beginning God [Elohim] made heaven and earth' – is difficult to distinguish from the other: what is the difference between an unknowable God and an equally unknowable non-God?[14] Why should it matter whether we call the ultimate, unknowable, uncaused and inexplicable origin and context of all things 'God' or 'Matter'? According to Plotinus the One holds being and beauty before itself like a golden veil (or like a barrier), and Matter – its absolute opposite – is 'bound in golden chains':[15] if neither can be directly seen nor comprehended how do we know they are different? Does it matter whether we say that all things began from an infinite sea of possibility or from an infinite power? Apparently so: the power has purpose. And mere possibility can never be a sufficient explanation for anything.[16]

That there is or was a single beginning to all the myriad things which now constitute the world of our experience may be a necessary tool of thought, a way of expressing or excusing the conviction that there are no really radical divisions: what is true here and now will also, if it is really true, be true in all the world, over however many years and light-years. There is at the same time a certain arbitrariness implicit in the story of what is: everything has emerged from Nothing – a condition without any pre-conditions, limits or definite probabilities. The primeval mound, Atum, just happens. The Lord's command is unconstrained at least by any material conditions. That all things have a single origin may not, of itself, tell us much about their nature, nor help us to identify what exactly will prove 'the same' over all the years and light-years. Newton wrote that:

Without all doubt this world could arise from nothing but the perfectly free will of God. ... From this fountain ... [what] we call the laws of nature have flowed, in which there appear many traces indeed of wise contrivance, but not the least

---

distributed 'into winds, water, earth, stars, plants and animals': Ivan M. Linforth, *The Arts of Orpheus* (Berkeley: University of California Press, 1941), 317–18.

[14] See my 'Who is God', *European Journal for Philosophy of Religion* 8, no. 4 (2016), 1–22.

[15] Compare Plotinus, *Ennead* I.6 [1].9 and I.8 [51].15.

[16] See Aristotle, *Metaphysics* 12, 1071b.

shadow of necessity. These therefore we must not seek from uncertain conjectures, but learn them from observations and experiments. He who is presumptuous enough to think that he can find the true principles of physics and the laws of natural things by the force alone of his own mind, and the internal light of reason, must either suppose that the world exists by necessity, and by the same necessity follows the laws proposed; or if the order of Nature was established by the will of God, that himself, a miserable reptile, can tell what was fittest to be done.[17]

There seems no reason, in modern cosmological theory, for certain pervasive features (the relative power of different distinct forces) to be exactly what they are. Either these features have been dictated, perhaps so as to allow the emergence of life-forms such as ourselves, or this merely happens to be the arrangement that allows for that emergence – and indefinitely many other distinct universes, with utterly different features, somehow exist beyond all possible perception. In postulating such a 'multiverse' cosmologists have moved from the Stoic conception (that only this actual world is possible) to the Epicurean (that all possible worlds are actual). The Platonic conception – that *not* all possibilities are actual – has clear ontological and ethical advantages.[18] That is another story. But at least we may now confirm that there *are* certain definite abiding and universal principles at work, beyond the mere requirement that there be *something*. Or in mythological narrative, 'Atum is the god who "in the beginning was everything," complete in the sense of being an undifferentiated unity and at the same time non-existent, because existence is impossible before his work of creation',[19] and who (on the Heliopolitan story preserved in the Coffin Texts)[20] then sneezes, spits or ejaculates Shu and Tefnut (the dry and the moist). These latter in turn engender Geb and Nut, who are the earth and sky, or else the down below and the up above. The principles and powers that rule the world or worlds might, possibly, have been different, but are now unavoidable. These

---

[17] Isaac Newton as represented by Hooykaas, after Cotes' preface to the second edition of *Principia*: R. Hookyas, *Religion and the Rise of Modern Science* (Edinburgh: Scottish Academic Press, 1972), p. 49.

[18] Plato does suggest in *Timaeus* 30c–d that the phenomenal world must contain reflections of all the living creatures akin to the Maker (that is, present to the divine Intellect), but it does not follow that all possible *events* occur in this one world. As Aristotle observes 'the potential need not necessarily always become actual' (*Metaphysics* 3, 1003a2), or there would be no distinction between the possible and the real.

[19] Erik Hornung, *Conceptions of God in Ancient Egypt: The One and the Many*, trans. John Baines (New York: Cornell University Press, 1982), 67.

[20] See James P. Allen, *Middle Egyptian: An Introduction to the Language and Culture of Hieroglyphs*, 3rd ed. (Cambridge: Cambridge University Press, 2014), 175–8.

principles, it has been suggested by Cornford, lie behind Plato's own account of 'Forms':

The supersensible world is an immutable hierarchy of Ideas, or Types, which throws its image upon the everflowing stream of time. Or, it is a heaven of divine souls, which impart themselves to the groups of transitory things that bear their name. The whole conception is manifestly mythical, but it is of the essence of the theory. The logical interpretation is struggling to get clear of the mythical; the Idea threatens to pass from being an indwelling group-soul to being a mere universal concept, which does not exist at all, and, if it did, could not cause the existence of becoming of particular things. Plato did not realize that he was only making an important discovery in logic; he thought he was discovering the causes – the sole, true causes – of the existence of the world.[21]

Cornford's comment is too patronizing to believe: why not instead acknowledge that Plato's Forms are indeed proposed as causally significant powers, and that they are indeed functionally identical both with Egyptian gods and with Christian angels? According to Jeremy Naydler:

The concept of the First Time is comparable to that of the realm of being in which the Platonic Ideas exist. In Egyptian thought, though, it is not abstract ideas that are to be found here, but living gods and archetypal relationships that obtain among them. The First Time is the realm of metaphysical realities conceived in terms of symbolic images and myths. These are the patterns that are reflected in the mundane world and that need to be participated in if mundane events are to be filled with archetypal power.[22]

This same position is further developed by Raymond Barfield, who writes that 'Proclus took the divine ideas of Plotinus and made them into gods that can not only be known (as in Plotinus) but can also know. Pseudo-Dionysius makes them into angels. Thus it is that the Forms of Plato become the Angels of Christendom.'[23] Barfield's error here lies in supposing that Plotinus – or his predecessors – imagined that the divine ideas were only *objects,* and (being 'abstract') causally inert. Quite otherwise: they could not be thus disentangled from the subjects, the immortal *Nous* that knew them, and they were imagined, exactly, as causes.

In short, the Forms postulated by Platonists are not abstract universals but rather eternal paradigms made manifest both in the phenomena of

[21] F. M. Cornford, *From Religion to Philosophy: A Study in the Origins of Western Speculation* (New York: Harper & Row, 1957), 257–8.
[22] Jeremy Naydler, *Temple of the Cosmos: The Ancient Egyptian Experience of the Sacred* (Rochester, VT: Inner Traditions International, 1996), 93.
[23] Raymond Barfield, *The Ancient Quarrel between Philosophy and Poetry* (Cambridge: Cambridge University Press, 2011), 97.

experience and in the mental calculations of such finite creatures as ourselves. An *arche* is both a ruling principle and a starting point. Even numbers and geometrical figures are more than abstractions or human artefacts – though there is an element of human construction in our employment of them in describing the phenomena. Counting how many 'things' there are in a given volume, or how many temporal intervals have passed during some experience, obviously depends on how we divide up the 'real', fluid phenomena, what 'net' we employ. This is expressed by Allan Watts, who writes, 'The real wiggly world slips like water through our imaginary nets. However much we divide, count, sort, or classify this wiggling into particular things and events, this is no more than a way of thinking about the world: it is never *actually* divided'.[24] Equally it is articulated by the physicist Richard Feynman, first citing an unnamed poet as saying that 'the whole universe is in a glass of wine':

> If our small minds, for some convenience, divide this glass of wine, this universe, into parts – physics, biology, geology, astronomy, psychology and so forth – remember that nature does not know it! So let us put it all back together, remembering ultimately what it is for. Let it give us one more final pleasure: drink it, and forget it all![25]

But the real *archai* are not so wiggly, though they are connected each to each, and manifest in many different ways. So how are we to speak about these Forms, and where (as it were) can they be? The received answer, borrowing perhaps from Aristotle's understanding of the relation of the divine intellect and what it comprehends, was that the Forms, the Intelligibles, existed in union with the divine, eternal Intellect (that is, *Nous* – though the term is better translated as 'Spirit'). Plotinus argued indeed that anything else would make it impossible even for God to be sure that He understood them – there being, on any other hypothesis, a gap between the Forms and God's understanding.[26] This is not to say that the divine Intellect contemplates *propositions*: the objects of Intellect

---

[24] Alan Watts, *The Book on the Taboo Against Knowing Who You Are* (London: Souvenir Press, 2011), 59.

[25] Richard Feynman, *The Feynman Lectures on Physics*, Volume 1 (New York: Basic Books, 2011), 32, cited by Mary Midgley, *Science and Poetry* (London: Routledge, 2001), 64. How seriously Feynman intended this, I am uncertain. Nor do I know whether he was aware of the Neoplatonic background to the metaphor (on which see my *Plotinus: Myth, Metaphor and Philosophical Practice* (Chicago: University of Chicago Press, 2016), 91–104).

[26] See Plotinus *Ennead* V.5 [32]; see my 'A Plotinian Account of Intellect', *American Catholic Philosophical Quarterly* 71 (1997), 421–32.

are not propositions nor formulae but real entities bound together into a complex unity, the very things that *our* propositions are about.[27] Max Tegmark's inference from modern cosmological practice seems to match the older idea:

> According to the Aristotelian paradigm, physical reality is fundamental and mathematical language is merely a useful approximation. According to the Platonic paradigm, the mathematical structure is the true reality and observers perceive it imperfectly.[28]

What flows from that reality are the phenomena of our very various experience – but the real things, as Plotinus writes, are eternal:

> It is already clear that the thought of a horse existed if [God] wanted to make a horse; so that it is not possible for him to think it in order to make it, but the horse which did not come into being must exist before that which was to be afterwards.[29]

Does this constitute a real difference between the Plotinian and the Christian view of God's creative activity? Maybe so – but there are clear parallels in all the Abrahamic faiths. For Jews the Word that is the root of all things is the Torah, or the Wisdom it embodies:

> In human practice, when a mortal king builds a palace, he builds it not with his own skills, but with those of an architect. Moreover, the architect does not build it out of his head, but employs plans and diagrams to know how to arrange the chambers and the wicket doors. Thus God consulted the Torah and created the

---

[27] *Ennead* V.8 [31].5, 2–24: 'One must not then suppose that the gods or "the exceedingly blessed spectators" in the higher world contemplate propositions, but all the Forms we speak about are beautiful images in that world, of the kind which someone imagined to exist in the soul of the wise man, images not painted but real.' It is worth adding that Plotinus' account of what the Egyptian sages intended (IV.3 [27].11; V.8 [31].6) is more accurate than classical scholars have always realized. 'The mixed form of their [the Egyptians'] gods is nothing other than a hieroglyph, a way of "writing" not the name but the nature and function of the deity in question. The Egyptians do not hesitate to call hieroglyphs "gods", and even to equate individual signs in the script with particular gods; it is quite in keeping with their views to see images of the gods as signs in a metalanguage. As is true of every Egyptian hieroglyph, they are more than just ciphers or lifeless symbols; the god can inhabit them, his cult image will normally be in the same form, and his priests may assume his role by wearing animal masks': Hornung, *Conceptions of God*, 124.

[28] Max Tegmark, *Our Mathematical Universe: My Quest for the Ultimate Nature of Reality* (London: Allen Lane, 2014), 49.

[29] *Ennead* VI.7 [38].8, 6–9. What that eternal Horse may be, of course, is not necessarily much like the horses of our current, phenomenal reality (any more than the merely material horse that moderns imagine is 'behind' the manifold phenomena can be much like what *we* perceive). Charles Williams attempted a poetic or literary evocation of such forms, especially in *The Place of the Lion* (London: Faber, 1931).

world, while the Torah declares, 'In the beginning God created' (Genesis 1:1), 'beginning' referring to the Torah, as in the verse, 'The Lord made me as the beginning of His way' (Proverbs 8:22).[30]

Might Wisdom be the first thing that God *made*, before the foundation of the world, and so be everlasting rather than eternal? But the logic of the story must be that it is rather *uncreated*: how, save by Wisdom herself, could He have made Wisdom? The blueprint, or the Will and Reason expressed in the blueprint, always precedes the building or even the drawing of the blueprint. 'How could the predeterminations and the divine volitions that create all existent things be themselves created?'[31] Again: 'how can the Logos, being the Counsel and Will of the Father, come into being Himself by an act of will and purpose?'[32] Muslims (or at least Sunni Muslims) seem to have drawn the same conclusion: the Koran, as the Wisdom of God and the plan for creation, is itself *uncreated*.[33]

Plotinus notes one further implication that Abrahamic tradition has tended to ignore: the Divine Intellect, the *Logos*, contains all Forms as eternal realities: 'it lived not as one soul but as all, and as possessing more power to make all the individual souls, and it was the "complete living being", not having only man in it: for otherwise there would only be man down here'.[34] All real things, all the eternal templates, reside within the single unified Form of all Forms – from which it follows that – if Humanity is to be 'in the image and likeness of God' – it must also be 'a lumpe where all beasts kneaded be'.[35]

---

[30] *Bereisheet Rabbah* [c. AD 500] 1:10: cited by Yakov Z. Meyer, 'Parashat Teruma/The Primordial Torah', *Haaretz*, updated 30 January 2014, www.haaretz.com/jewish/por tion-of-the-week/.premium-the-primordial-torah-1.5317068.

[31] G. E. H. Palmer, P. Sherrard and Kallistos Ware, trans., *The Philokalia: The Complete Text*, Volume 4 (London: Faber & Faber, 1995), 387.

[32] G. L. Prestige, *God in Patristic Thought* (London: SPCK, 1952), 51, after Athanasius, *Against the Arians* 3.64: 'He is external to the things which have come to be by will, but rather is Himself the Living Counsel of the Father, by which all these things have come to be.'

[33] See a brief discussion by Shari L. Lowin and Nevin Reda, 'Scripture and Exegesis: Torah and Qu'ran in Historical Perspective', in *Routledge Handbook of Muslim-Jewish Relations*, ed. Josef W. Meri (London: Routledge, 2016), 57–76 at p. 61. In both Christian and Muslim history the notion that it was 'created' was preferred by rulers, as it suggested both that the Word as it had been previously declared might turn out to be obsolete, and – by analogy – that their own arbitrary commands were valid: see Hugh Kennedy, *The Caliphate* (London: Penguin, 2016), 114–16.

[34] *Ennead* VI.7 [38].8, 29–32; see also VI.6 [34].15, 11–13; VI.7 [38].12.

[35] John Donne, 'To Sir Edward Herbert at Julyers (1651)', in *John Donne: A Critical Edition of the Major Works*, ed. John Carey (Oxford: Oxford University Press, 1990), 200–1.

Hans Urs von Balthasar summarizes the thought of Maximus the Confessor (580–662)[36] on this point as follows: 'in the Logos, all the individual ideas and goals of creatures meet; therefore all of them, if they seek their own reality, must love him, and must encounter each other in his love. That is why Christ is the original idea, the underlying figure of God's plan for the world, why all the individual lines originate themselves concentrically around him.'[37] Which is to repeat Plotinus' metaphor, of the circle's radii meeting in their centre.[38] Maybe there is still room for a distinction between God's eternal *intention* for His creatures and the template He had devised for them, as well as a distinction between those everlasting templates, gods, powers and principalities and their echo or reflection in the common features of phenomena? According to Balthasar,[39] Maximus distinguished the divine ideas, 'the basic outlines, in God, of his plans for the world, the preliminary sketch of the creature within the Spirit of God', from the 'created "universals"' that are the immanent principles of created being. 'The concentration of the ideas of the world in the Creator does not mean the dissolution of the world into God.'[40] The divine essences are, perhaps, not co-eternal with God.[41] But the distinction is hard to maintain: in the one Word all things are implicit, even those things that are not, or not yet, brought out to illuminate or ground phenomena. Our own 'real selves', on a Plotinian account, are eternally resident in the Word, even though our experienced selves are far removed, far fallen, from that beatitude![42]

Might the powers and principalities that govern distinct aspects of the totality themselves be fallen as we are? Plotinus thought the idea at least disrespectful,[43] and denied that such powers could simultaneously 'remember' what should be well enough to help create the worlds and have 'forgotten' so much as to act against what should be.[44] But of course that is exactly our own condition: why may it not apply even to those

---

[36] See *Maximus Confessor: Selected Writings*, trans. George C. Berthold (London: SPCK Publishing, 1985).

[37] Hans Urs von Balthasar, *Cosmic Liturgy: The Universe According to Maximus the Confessor*, trans. Brian E. Daley, S. J. (San Francisco: Ignatius Press, 2003), 133.

[38] *Ennead* VI.8 [39].18, 18; see also Pseudo-Dionysius, *Divine Names*, 644a in *Pseudo-Dionysius: The Complete Works*, trans. Colm Luibheid and Paul Rorem (London: SPCK Publishing, 1987), 62.

[39] Balthasar, *Cosmic Liturgy*, 116–18.   [40] Ibid, 119.   [41] Ibid, 152.

[42] As Dame Julian expressed a similar thought, there is something in each of us that has never consented to sin: Julian of Norwich, *Revelations of Divine Love*, trans. Elizabeth Spearing (London: Penguin, 1998), 93.

[43] *Ennead* II.9 [33].9, 53–64.   [44] *Ennead* II.9 [33].4, 8–18.

agencies that are not embodied in particular times, places and fragile bodies? Abrahamists – and even some 'pagan' Platonists – have found it possible to think that *some* superhuman powers are fallen, if not literally into flesh yet into fleshly attachments, as found in Porphyry:

> They themselves rejoice in everything that is likewise inconsistent and incompatible; slipping on (as it were) the masks of the other gods, they profit from our lack of sense, winning over the masses because they inflame people's appetites with lust and longing for wealth and power and pleasure, and also with empty ambition from which arises civil conflicts and wars and kindred events.[45]

Are they genuinely distinct (though unlocalized) entities, are we to suppose instead that they are merely *images* for distinguishable powers and affections of all souls? There may be no clear answer. The 'fallen' powers are echoes or reminders of their originals. Before Adam fell 'what is now gall in him sparkled like crystal, and bore the taste of good works, and what is now melancholy in man shone in him like the dawn and contained in itself the wisdom and perfection of good works; but when Adam broke the law, the sparkle of innocence was dulled in him, and his eyes, which had formerly beheld heaven, were blinded, and his gall was changed to bitterness, and his melancholy to blackness'.[46] Hildegard was here repeating an ancient theme, about the corruption of what is in origin benign:

> What comes from the stars [that is from the planetary spheres through which the soul descends to earth] will not reach the recipients in the same state in which it left them. If it is fire, for instance, the fire down here is dim, and if it is a loving disposition (*philiake diathesis*) it becomes weak in the recipient and produces a rather unpleasant kind of loving (*ou mala kalen ten philesin*); and manly spirit, when the receiver does not take it in due measure, so as to become brave, produces violent temper or spiritlessness; and that which belongs to honour in love and is concerned with beauty produces desire of what only seems to be beautiful, and the efflux of intellect produces knavery (*panourgia*); for knavery wants to be intellect, only it is unable to attain what it aims at. So all these things become evil in us, though they are not so up in heaven.[47]

---

[45] Porphyry, *On Abstinence from Killing Animals*, trans. Gillian Clark (London: Duckworth, 2000), 72 [2.40, 3].

[46] Raymond Klibansky, Erwin Panofsky and Fritz Saxl, *Saturn and Melancholy: Studies in the History of Natural Philosophy, Religion, and Art* (Edinburgh: Thomas Nelson and Sons, 1964), 80, citing Hildegard of Bingen, *Hildegardis Causae et Curae*, ed. Paulus Kaiser (Leipzig: Lipsiae, 1903), 43.

[47] *Ennead* II.3 [52].11; see my 'Climbing up to Heaven: the Hermetic Option', in *Purgatory: Philosophical Dimensions*, eds. Kristof K. P. Vanhoutte and Benjamin W. McCraw (London: Palgrave Macmillan, 2017), 151–74.

The same, perhaps, is true, on Plotinian terms, of our own selves. We here-now are fallen, separated and confused, but something of us has *not* fallen, and 'our heads are firmly set above in heaven'.[48] Like the powers, we can ourselves contribute, for good or ill, to the constant remaking and reima-gining of this grand image, this *eikon aei eikonizomene*.[49] We are not, as Stoic philosophers would have us, simply cogs within the machine, and neither are the powers above: there are many agencies at work. Indeed, those many agencies are also working within in us – to the point that we cannot reasonably claim yet to be the unitary persons that we would wish to be:

'Know Yourself' is said to those who because of their selves' multiplicity have the business of counting themselves up and learning that they do not know all the numbers and kinds of things they are, or do not know any one of them, nor what their ruling principle is, or by what they are themselves.[50]

Those who seek to follow the Delphic instruction – so St Hesychios was to say – find themselves, as it were, gazing into a mirror and sighting the dark faces of the demons peering over their shoulders.[51] The gods (or demons) are constantly at work in us, as also in the world at large.

Two principles in particular are worth further attention: the Empedoclean duo, Love and Strife. It has been usual to reckon these, respectively, as 'good' and 'evil', but a better version rather acknowledges their equal force and authority. 'Love' brings things together, and 'Strife' separates them – but it is that separation which allows for, and creates, the promise of individual lives, while 'Love', left to itself, brings everything together into an undifferentiated monad.[52] Either principle, power or angel, can lead to disaster. So also many other principles, powers and angels, separated from their origin in *Nous* – or as Plotinus expresses the idea mythologically, in Kronos.[53]

---

[48] *Ennead* IV.3 [27].12; IV.8 [6].8, 1–4.   [49] After *Ennead* II.3 [52].18, 17.

[50] *Ennead* VI.7 [38].41, 22–4.

[51] Palmer, Sherrard and Ware, trans., *The Philokalia: The Complete Text*, Volume 1, 123. See also Plato, *Phaedrus* 229b4–230a6, where Socrates puts aside literal, physicalist interpretations of the creatures of Greek myth, in favour of asking whether he is himself 'a more complex creature and more puffed up with pride than Typhon'.

[52] See Peter Kingsley, *Ancient Philosophy, Mystery, and Magic: Empedocles and Pythagorean Tradition* (Oxford: Clarendon Press, 1995).

[53] *Enneads* V.1. [10].4, 8–10; V.1 [10].7, 33f. See Pierre Hadot, 'Ouranos, Kronos and Zeus in Plotinus's Treatise against the Gnostics', in *Neoplatonism and Early Christian Thought: Essays in Honour of A. H. Armstrong*, eds. H. J. Blumenthal and R. A. Markus (London: Variorum, 1981), 124–52.

THE USUAL, THE ANOMALOUS AND WHAT IS YET
TO COME

The Aristotelian paradigm (which is not entirely or exactly Aristotle's) takes individual entities to be the primary substances, and true science to be the discovery and examination of 'what happens always or for the most part',[54] perhaps in the hope that all such generalities will turn out in the end to be necessities. Such generalities, or 'laws', may be reliable, but they do not really explain anything that happens, but only record it. By Aristotle's own account we may more reasonably look to the *ends* that all such processes may serve: a thing's nature is the path of its growth towards its becoming what its nature requires.[55] The growth of the Whole Thing, the totality of existence, is always already complete, not something to be expected in an apocalyptic future. Platonists may take Aristotle's point more to heart: the nature of anything is rather what it *should* be than what, descriptively, it seems to be at any particular time. The world that embodies the forms, if it should ever come into being, is the real world.[56] And of course, for Platonists, that real world always already exists in the Divine Intellect.

This last point may also be where Abrahamic and ordinarily Hellenic ('pagan') Platonists diverge. For Plotinus the world of our present experience is already as good as such a world could be (granted its existence as a medley of disparate visions and expectations), and the hope of a remade world is at least disrespectful. 'What other fairer image of the intelligible world could there be?'[57] Even a gradual improvement is not something we should care about:[58] if we are always to be aiming to get more or better, 'even the gods will be better off now than they were before, but they will not be perfectly well off; they will never be perfectly well off'.[59] Christians, on the other hand, hoped for a better world, expected 'to judge angels',[60]

---

[54] Aristotle, *Physics* 2.198b36.   [55] Aristotle, *Physics* 2.193b13–15.

[56] C. D. C. Reeve, *Philosopher Kings: The Argument of Plato's Republic* (Indianapolis: Hackett, 2006), 116–17.

[57] *Ennead* II.9 [33].4, 26–7.

[58] Though he does envisage the possibility that 'from adultery or the carrying off of a captive, children may come according to nature and better men, it may happen, and other better cities than those sacked by wicked men': *Ennead* III.2 [47].18, 16–18. And just possibly, in the next performance of the world drama we will play our parts a little better: *Ennead* III.2 [47].17, 45–60.

[59] *Ennead* I.5 [36].2.

[60] Paul, 1 Corinthians 6:1–4. See also 1 John 4:1: 'Beloved, believe not every spirit, but try the spirits whether they are of God.'

and reckoned themselves superior in rank and – hopefully – in eventual virtue even to the highest of created spirits. This – in all the Abrahamic traditions – was the sin of Satan: not to acknowledge Adam (which is to say, Humanity) as God's Chosen. The angels' fall, so tradition tells us, began in Satan's outrage that he could be expected to bow down before an animal![61] 'Pagan' and Abrahamist can agree that there is, in some sense, a 'better world' than this – namely the world eternally envisaged in the Divine Intellect – and can agree that we here-now should model our thoughts and actions, as far as possible on that ideal. We are not to think merely 'mortal thoughts', but rather to 'immortalize' ourselves as much as possible,[62] and remember our celestial identity, as suggested in the *Enneads*:

Even before this coming to be we were there, men (*anthropoi*) who were different, and some of us even gods, pure souls and intellect united with the whole of reality; we were parts of the intelligible, not marked off or cut off but belonging to the whole; and we are not cut off even now.[63]

'Pagan' and Abrahamist, on the other hand, disagreed about the possibility of a real transformation of this whole world, currently groaning like a woman in travail.[64] Some day there will be 'a new heaven and a new earth', and 'the holy city, new Jerusalem will come down out of heaven from God, made ready like a bride adorned for her husband'.[65] That strange possibility, of a radical invasion and disruption, cannot be predicted from within our present system, as one might predict even such catastrophes as global war, disease, volcanic eruption or meteor strike. On any usual pagan aesthetic it is an obvious breach of dramatic protocol, and a reminder (perhaps) that we should attend rather more to the likelihood of exceptions, irruptions, uncovenanted mercies. Rather than looking to see what happens 'always or for the most part' we should instead be alert to anomalies, to the unpredicted, to what does *not* usually happen (or is supposed to happen). This has been articulated by John Wren-Lewis:

---

[61] 'We created you and then formed you and then We said to the Angels, "Prostrate before Adam" and they prostrated except for Iblis [which is the Arabic term for Satan]. He was not among those who prostrated. God said, "What prevented you from prostrating when I commanded you?" He (Iblis) replied, "I am better than him. You created me from fire and You created him from clay." God said, "Descend from heaven. It is not for you to be arrogant in it. So get out! You are one of the abased."' (Koran, Surah 7 (al-A'raf), 11–13). See also *Life of Adam and Eve (Apocalypse of Moses)*, chapters 13–14.
[62] Aristotle, *Nicomachean Ethics* 10, 1177b33.   [63] *Ennead* VI.4 [22].14, 18ff.
[64] Paul, Romans 8:22.   [65] Revelation 21:1–2.

The progress of science is often described by materialists as a continuous process of disillusionment, but the truth is that the main illusion it has shattered is the notion that human beings are limited to the horizons of the ordinary everyday world as normally experienced by average people in most ages of history. By following up the odd extraordinary event that fails to fit into the framework of everyday thought, science has again and again shown that human beings can have far wider horizons and far more dimensions of experience than are dreamed of in the down-to-earth philosophies of people who pride themselves on their common sense.[66]

'Pagan' and Abrahamist can agree at any rate that there are many ways – indefinitely many ways – to be. All things may have a single origin and purpose in what Plotinus calls 'the One', but for that very reason we must also acknowledge the multiplicity of manifested (and unmanifested) intelligible being – 'a sphere all faces, shining with living faces',[67] each of which has its own being and expression. The whole phenomenal world, compounded of all the different phenomenal worlds, is unimaginably various and always open to sudden transformations and intrusions, as expressed by Hopkins: 'Million-fuelèd, nature's bonfire burns on'.[68] After such a transformation and intrusion, we may perhaps look back and see the seeds of what was to come in earlier experience – but it is also possible that the seeds of the new world were held 'aloft' in the eternal, 'the mystery hidden for ages and generations but now revealed to his saints'.[69]

Even Plotinus seems to allow, despite his disapproval of those who think themselves superior to gods, that there *might* after all be a better form of experience than the one or ones implicit in the present phenomena. Zeus (that is, Soul) is the one of Kronos' children who lives outside his Father (*Nous*, or Spirit), for a good purpose (so that there should be 'a beautiful image of beauty and reality'), but bound to be surpassed by those offspring that have stayed 'within', the worlds that have not (yet) had temporal or phenomenal reflections.[70] And perhaps there is a clue to those so-far-unseen realities, exactly, in what is here-now *different*.

---

[66] John Wren-Lewis, 'Resistance to the Study of the Paranormal', *Journal of Humanistic Psychology* 14, no. 2 (1972), 42.

[67] *Ennead* VI.7 [38].15, 25; see my 'The Sphere with Many Faces', *Dionysius* 34 (2016), 8–26.

[68] Gerard Manley Hopkins, 'That Nature is a Heraclitean Fire and of the Comfort of the Resurrection', in *Poems of Gerard Manley Hopkins*, ed. Robert Bridges (London: Humphrey Milford, 1918), 48.

[69] Paul, Colossians 1:26; see also Ephesians 3:4–5.

[70] *Ennead* V.8 [31].12–13. See also Brian P. Copenhaver, *Hermetica: The Greek Corpus Hermeticum and the Latin Asclepius in a New English Translation, with Notes and Introduction* (Cambridge: Cambridge University Press, 1992), 20: 'He is himself the

All things counter, original, spare, strange;
Whatever is fickle, freckled (who knows how?)
With swift, slow; sweet, sour; adazzle, dim;
He fathers-forth whose beauty is past change:
    Praise him.[71]

Bibliography

Allen, James P. *Middle Egyptian: An Introduction to the Language and Culture of Hieroglyphs.* 3rd ed. Cambridge: Cambridge University Press, 2014.

Balthasar, Hans Urs von. *Cosmic Liturgy: The Universe According to Maximus the Confessor.* Translated by Brian E. Daley, S. J. San Francisco: Ignatius Press, 2003.

Barfield, Raymond. *The Ancient Quarrel between Philosophy and Poetry.* Cambridge: Cambridge University Press, 2011.

Berkeley, George. *Principles of Human Knowledge and Three Dialogues.* Edited by Howard Robinson. Oxford: Oxford University Press, 1996.

'Sermon on Immortality (1708)'. In *The Works of George Berkeley, Bishop of Cloyne*, Volume 7, edited by A. A. Luce and T. E. Jessop. Edinburgh: Thomas Nelson, 1967.

Chesterton, G. K. *The Poet and the Lunatics.* London: Darwen Finlayson, 1962.

Clark, Stephen R. L. 'Climbing up to Heaven: The Hermetic Option'. In *Purgatory: Philosophical Dimensions*, edited by Kristof K. P. Vanhoutte and Benjamin W. McCraw, 151–74. London: Palgrave Macmillan, 2017.

'History of Appearances, or Worlds United'. In *Homage to Owen Barfield*, edited by Martin Ovens. Forthcoming.

'A Plotinian Account of Intellect'. *American Catholic Philosophical Quarterly* 71 (1997): 421–32.

Plotinus: Myth, Metaphor and Philosophical Practice. Chicago: University of Chicago Press, 2016.

'The Sphere with Many Faces'. *Dionysius* 34 (2016):8–26.

'Who is God'. *European Journal for Philosophy of Religion* 8, no. 4 (2016): 1–22.

Copenhaver, Brian P. *Hermetica: The Greek Corpus Hermeticum and the Latin Asclepius in a New English Translation, with Notes and Introduction.* Cambridge: Cambridge University Press, 1992.

Cornford, F. M. *From Religion to Philosophy: A Study in the Origins of Western Speculation.* New York: Harper & Row, 1957.

Donne, John. *John Donne: A Critical Edition of the Major Works*, edited by John Carey. Oxford: Oxford University Press, 1990.

things that are and those that are not. Those that are he has made visible; those that are not he holds within him. . . . There is nothing that he is not, for he also is all that is, and this is why he has all names, because they are of one father, and this is why he has no name, because he is father of them all.'

[71] Hopkins, 'Pied Beauty', 133.

Feynman, Richard. *The Feynman Lectures on Physics*, Volume 1. New York: Basic Books, 2011.

Hadot, Pierre. 'Ouranos, Kronos and Zeus in Plotinus's Treatise against the Gnostics'. In *Neoplatonism and Early Christian Thought: Essays in Honour of A. H. Armstrong*, edited by H. J. Blumenthal and R. A. Markus, 124–52. London: Variorum, 1981.

Hildegard of Bingen. *Hildegardis Causae et Curae*. Edited by Paulus Kaiser. Leipzig: Lipsiae, 1903.

Hookyas, R. *Religion and the Rise of Modern Science*. Edinburgh: Scottish Academic Press, 1972.

Hopkins, Gerard Manley. *The Major Works*, edited by Catherine Phillips. Oxford: Oxford University Press, 2002.

Poems of Gerard Manley Hopkins, edited by Robert Bridges. London: Humphrey Milford, 1918.

Hornung, Erik. *Conceptions of God in Ancient Egypt: The One and the Many*. Translated by John Baines. New York: Cornell University Press, 1982.

James, William. *The Principles of Psychology*, Volume 1. Cosimo: New York, 2007.

Julian of Norwich. *Revelations of Divine Love*. Translated by Elizabeth Spearing. London: Penguin, 1998.

Kennedy, Hugh. *The Caliphate*. London: Penguin, 2016.

Kingsley, Peter. *Ancient Philosophy, Mystery, and Magic: Empedocles and Pythagorean Tradition*. Oxford: Clarendon Press, 1995.

Klibansky, Raymond, Erwin Panofsky and Fritz Saxl. *Saturn and Melancholy: Studies in the History of Natural Philosophy, Religion, and Art*. Edinburgh: Thomas Nelson and Sons, 1964.

Linforth, Ivan M. *The Arts of Orpheus*. Berkeley: University of California Press, 1941.

Long, A. A., and D. N. Sedley, eds. *The Hellenistic Philosophers*, Volume 1. Cambridge: Cambridge University Press, 1987.

Lowin, Shari L., and Nevin Reda. 'Scripture and Exegesis: Torah and Qu'ran in Historical Perspective'. In *Routledge Handbook of Muslim-Jewish Relations*, edited by Josef W. Meri, 57–76. London: Routledge, 2016.

Maximus Confessor: Selected Writings. Translated by George C. Berthold. London: SPCK Publishing, 1985.

Meyer, Yakov Z. 'Parashat Teruma/The Primordial Torah'. *Haaretz*, updated 30 January 2014. www.haaretz.com/jewish/portion-of-the-week/.premium-the-primordial-torah-1.5317068.

Midgley, Mary. *Science and Poetry*. London: Routledge, 2001.

Mikkelson, David. "Ronald Reagan 'If You've Seen One Tree ... '." *Snopes.com*, updated 7 June 2006. www.snopes.com/fact-check/if-youve-seen-one-tree/.

Naydler, Jeremy. *Temple of the Cosmos: The Ancient Egyptian Experience of the Sacred*. Rochester, VT: Inner Traditions International, 1996.

Palmer, G. E. H., P. Sherrard and Kallistos Ware, trans. *The Philokalia: The Complete Text*, Volume 1. London: Faber & Faber, 1979.

The Philokalia: The Complete Text, Volume 4. London: Faber & Faber, 1995.

Porphyry. *On Abstinence from Killing Animals*. Translated by Gillian Clark. London: Duckworth, 2000.

Prestige, G. L. *God in Patristic Thought*. London: SPCK, 1952.

Pseudo-Dionysius: The Complete Works. Translated by Colm Luibheid and Paul Rorem. London: SPCK Publishing, 1987.

Reeve, C. D. C. *Philosopher Kings: The Argument of Plato's Republic*. Indianapolis: Hackett, 2006.

Tegmark, Max. *Our Mathematical Universe: My Quest for the Ultimate Nature of Reality*. London: Allen Lane, 2014.

Watts, Alan. *The Book on the Taboo Against Knowing Who You Are*. London: Souvenir Press, 2011.

Williams, Charles. *The Place of the Lion*. London: Faber, 1931.

Wren-Lewis, John. 'Resistance to the Study of the Paranormal'. *Journal of Humanistic Psychology* 14, no. 2 (1974): 42.

Index

Printed in Great Britain
by Amazon

44786280R00290